How to Apply
for Department of Veterans Affairs Benefits

for Veterans and Their Survivors

SENIOR VETERANS SERVICE ALLIANCE 2020 EDITION

Published by the Senior Veterans Service Alliance – January 2020

www.seniorvets.org

2020 All Rights Reserved

ISBN 978-0-9816827-4-7

Printing: DMT Publishing, North Salt Lake, Utah

How to Apply for Department of Veterans Affairs Benefits

for Veterans and Their Survivors

Author: Thomas Day

TABLE OF CONTENTS

Introduction

We are excited about our new 2020 edition of "How to Apply for Department Of Veterans Affairs Benefits for Veterans and Their Survivors." This book represents our ongoing series of how to apply books going back to 2013. This newest version incorporates everything we have learned over the years and specifically over the previous year. We also provide benefit rates for all disability income, survivor and death benefits for the year 2020.

This edition provides detailed instructions on how to file successful claims for Disability Compensation, DIC, and Veterans and Survivor's (Death) Pension with Aid and Attendance. Important new information has been added as VA has been actively upgrading the claim process, adding new forms and incorporating new procedures. One key difference that separates the information in this book from information in other books is the instructions we provide for Fully Developed Claims. The Fully Developed Claim Process was initiated by the Department of Veterans Affairs to provide more timely and more successful decisions. This fast-track process requires much more effort and time in developing the application over the typical slow track claim that most veterans and advocates file with the Department.

If we ignore the 9 million plus enrollees in VA healthcare, the four disability benefits we describe above represent the largest number of claimants for VA income-related benefits. The roughly 5.44 million beneficiaries of these four programs far exceed the total number of veterans receiving the half-dozen other monetary VA benefits that are available. Much of this book focuses on this group of potential claimants for disability income.

The true value of this unique publication is in providing step-by-step instructions for the extremely challenging and difficult applications for Disability Compensation, DIC not granted automatically, Veterans Pension with Aid and Attendance and Survivor's (Death) Pension with Aid and Attendance. The complexity and requirement for supportive documentation for these four benefits make it almost impossible for any non-experienced person to submit a successful application that would be approved in a timely manner. Even many veterans service officers – who are trained and paid to assist veterans and their survivors with applications – are not aware of many of the complications encountered in certain types of disability claims.

There are scores of books available on veterans benefits. We have perused a number of them through purchase and many others through published tables of content and published excerpts and we believe that none of them contain the level of instructions on the complicated claim processes that we provide in this publication. Many of these other books describe how to qualify for the benefits and what the benefits are and then obliquely reference a few forms that can be obtained online. Others do go into more detail on what encompasses a successful claim but they do not provide step-by-step instructions. It is our opinion that none of these books would adequately assist you in filing a successful claim. We believe our book is totally unique in providing you the nuts and bolts, step-by-step instructions and strategies to file successful claims for the four disability income benefits offered by the Department of Veterans Affairs.

In addition to the detailed instructions, we also provide you with a DVD that contains hundreds of forms and medical surveys that at some point could be or are used in the application process. We also include on this DVD thousands of pages of reference material for various types of claims and complete up-to-date version of 38 CFR Part 3 (the adjudication regulations) and 38 CFR Part 4 (the VA Schedule for Rating Disabilities – VASRD). In addition, we provide the 15,000 or so pages from the most current Adjudication Manual M21-1 for those of you who want to know the exact details of the claim process and how VA makes decisions and handles claims. In our claims activities that we provide for others we often go to the adjudication manual to help us understand certain claims.

We continue to follow changes with the structure of the paperless claims process in the Regional Offices. Of course, we have updated all of the pertinent rates for benefits for 2020. We have further refined the forms and procedures that we devised for Compensation and DIC applications. Chapter 6 is a major revision on how to apply for Pension with aid and attendance. On October 18, 2018, VA initiated a major change in pension entitlement rules to include a definition of net estate and a penalty for gifting assets to qualify for Pension. We believe that our treatment of these new rules is the most comprehensive explanation available. We also include new features on our "Claims Support Disc" which is now also available online at www.supportdisc.com and updated regularly. These include important information for accredited representatives and a list of providers of claim support services such as medical records review, PTSD evaluations and licensed health care providers who will write medical opinions and fill out DBQs. We also include case studies on the support disc.

We now have months of experience under the new appeals process due to Title 38 USC under Pub. L. 115–55, §1, Aug. 23, 2017, 131 Stat. 1105 which is called the "Veterans Appeals Improvement and Modernization Act of 2017." These new rules were in effect in February 2019. We also offer a new chapter describing in more depth fully developed claims and their importance in the application process. The new process seems to be working as advertised.

This edition goes into depth on important aid and attendance and housebound income allowances for senior veterans and their survivors. We also include information on Veterans Health Care and State Veterans Benefits and information on other programs that we think are important to veterans, their families and their survivors. This information includes the Loan Guaranty Program, education benefits, Vocational Rehabilitation, CHAMPVA and homeless support. There are of course other programs available to veterans or their survivors and we are only highlighting the ones that we believe are pertinent to the majority of our readers. The VA website at www.VA.gov has been upgraded substantially over the past few years and contains everything anyone would want to know about every VA program available. They just don't tell you how to submit successful applications for benefits.

We do not include step-by-step instructions on how to apply for Veterans Health Care, State Veterans Benefits, the Loan Guaranty Program, education benefits, Vocational Rehabilitation or homeless support. The process for application is fairly straightforward and in most cases there are community advocates, institutions or companies who will help veterans or their survivors with the application process.

We hope you are as pleased as we are with this new publication and we hope you will use it to obtain the benefits that you or your loved ones or the people you are assisting deserve.

About the Author

Thomas Day

I am passionate about helping seniors deal with their elder years and with eldercare issues. This passion also spills over to my helping senior veterans and their survivors plan for their future years. This is because I am a disabled veteran as well. Most importantly, thanks to the VA healthcare system prolonging my life, I am able to help other veterans become aware of their benefits.

After graduating high school in 1962, I pursued a year of study at the University of Utah. The next 2 1/2 years were spent in the European country of Austria for my church where I learned to speak German and serve the Austrian people. I reenrolled at the University of Utah in studies with the Department of Physics in the spring of 1966. I graduated with a BA in physics and math in the winter of 1969. My sweetheart, Susan and I met and married in the spring of 1967.

University of Utah Campus

During my college years, the Vietnam War was in full swing and knowing I would be called up, I decided to enlist in the Air Force ROTC program. In fact, I received a draft notification just a few days after I was sworn into the ROTC program. I subsequently received a commission as a second lieutenant when I graduated college. I left the service with the rank of captain, with an honorable discharge, in the winter of 1973 having completed about 4 1/2 years in active duty service.

The years from 1973 through 1985 were spent in a variety of business pursuits. In 1985, I joined a large insurance company as a registered representative and agent. One aspect or another of financial services has been my profession ever since. In 1997, I struck out on my own as an independent Registered Investment Advisor and fee-based financial planner. Because I no longer had group health insurance for my family, I obtained individual insurance for them and I enrolled in the VA healthcare system. At that time VA was taking Priority Group 8 veterans into the health care system. As it turned out, enrolling in VA health care was one of the more important events in my life because it prolonged my life and allowed me to pursue the goal of helping veterans with their benefits.

During the intervening years I have not only been grateful for veterans health care, but I was able to use the VA loan guaranty for purchasing several homes and the veterans education benefit for completing an MBA at the University of Utah School of Business. And most recently, I was particularly grateful to receive a disability rating for the severe disabling condition that I have experienced for many years. This also ensures my enrollment in the VA healthcare system.

Tom's Educational Background, Credentials and Certifications

Accredited Claims Agent with the Department of Veterans Affairs, 2010
BA in physics and math, University of Utah, 1969
MBA, University of Utah, 1983
Series 6 Exam, 1985 / Series 7 Exam, 1990
CLU, American College, 1992
Series 65 Exam, Registered Investment Advisor, 1996
Author of over 120 web published articles
Author of 6 print published books about eldercare issues and veterans benefits
Author of 6 print published training manuals and marketing booklets
Author - Study Guide and Manual for the VA Accredited Agents Exam
Director of the National Care Planning Council at longtermcarelink.net
Director of the Senior Veterans Service Alliance at seniorvets.org

Founding the National Care Planning Council and the Senior Veterans Service Alliance
I started the precursor to the National Care Planning Council on a part-time basis in 2002 as a result of my working with seniors and helping them plan for long term care challenges in their final years. The Internet was a fairly new phenomenon back then, but I had a good background in computers and decided to provide online resources for the public and design a website for that purpose. Over the years this concept has continued to grow into what is today, The National Care Planning Council. Our focus is to help families support their aging loved ones with the challenges of their final years of life which generally includes assistance with long term care.

The NCPC became involved in helping veterans in 2009 when many of the members of our Council came to us asking how to get benefits for senior veterans. Currently, 47% of all veterans are considered seniors as they are 65 years old or older. Since I am myself a senior veteran, I was interested in adding education on veterans benefits to the resources of the National Care Planning Council.

After a great deal of research, I published a book on veterans Pension benefits for older veterans who had a need for eldercare. This was very popular with attorneys and others who worked with a senior population since at that time roughly 25% of seniors or their surviving spouses could have been eligible for Pension. Of course not all were entitled under the means test. About the same time, I also became an accredited claims agent recognized by the Department of Veterans Affairs and due to the lack of study materials that were available to pass the accredited agents exam, I also put together a study package for individuals who wanted to take the exam.

Creation of the Senior Veterans Service Alliance occurred in 2012 as an effort to provide online resources to senior veterans and their survivors. Currently that website is producing about 39,000 unique visitors a month and it results in 5 to 10 email inquiries a day from individuals who are seeking information about obtaining veterans benefits.

I am passionate about long term care issues. I and my wife, Susan, – she took the brunt of it – went through it with all four of our parents--hers and mine. And at the tender age of 76, I confront daily the reality of long term care for me. Because of our experience, the National Care Planning Council is our attempt to help other caregivers find information and help.

From 1989 to 1992, my mother attended to my father at home. He was flat on his back with Parkinson's Disease. He was as stiff as a board, couldn't move a muscle, could only whisper, had lost his vision and hearing and had dementia. Because his swallowing muscles barely worked, it took us 2 hours to feed him. Due to dementia he called out day and night in a terrified whisper.

My mother chose to care for him at home because she hated nursing homes. She was in excellent health and planned to use their savings on herself when he was gone instead of spending the money on paid care. Besides this was back when Medicare offered forever home care as long as there was a medical need, so she had some help. His need was a catheter. Despite the home care aides, the strain of caring for my father destroyed my mother's physical and emotional health. Against her wishes, I put him in a nursing home where he eventually died. After his death, I had her in and out of a mental institution and hospitals for over a year before she was stable enough to go to an independent living community where she could get supervision and meals. She suffered from some form of dementia or psychosis, which eventually got to a point where the facility couldn't keep her. She moved in with us in September of 1994.

Shortly after arriving, she fell and broke her hip and although she recovered, she made up her mind she couldn't walk. That made it easier to care for her with her abnormal mental state. We also received aides, therapists and nurses from Medicare because she had a bizarre fluctuating blood pressure that had to be monitored every day. She also came home with a pressure sore from her original hip surgery recovery in the hospital. They didn't take very good care of her during the two week stay in the hospital rehab wing. The sore eventually developed into an nasty ulcer that went so deep, it exposed her spine. We also received home health care for that. In the fall of 1997, Medicare changed the rules and cut off home care for chronic patients. We were contemplating a nursing home for Mom but she contracted pneumonia and died at home in December of 1997.

Susan's father suffered a stroke in March of 1998 which deprived him the use of his left arm and leg. He was taking care of Susan's mother at home but Medicare had changed its rules and would no longer provide home care help for chronic conditions, so he went to a nursing home on Medicaid. He died there in January of 2000. We took care of Susan's mother in our home for 2 1/2 years and she died in August of 2001.

Even though we loved our parents, I wouldn't wish this experience on anyone, especially my wife who patiently and without complaint provided most of the care. This book on veterans benefits is my attempt to help create some extra income for senior veterans or their survivors who are suffering from disabilities in their older years. Even though the focus might be on senior veterans, the material in this book applies to all veterans and their survivors.

Chapter 1
Overview of Veterans Benefits and How to Use This Book

IN THIS CHAPTER:

This book will help you understand most of the benefits available from the Department of Veterans Affairs. We believe the information presented in this publication will also assist you in preparing a strong application for disability or survivor benefits that should have a good chance of producing an award and be approved in a timely manner. You should utilize the checklists and forms on the accompanying DVD that comes with this book and which we call the "Claim Support Disc." This support disc also contains an important section we call "Appendix – Additional Information for Accredited Representatives." Providing this appendix information in printed form would have made this already large publication more unwieldy. The Claim Support Disc is also available online and is updated on a regular basis. Go to www.SupportDisc.com

Understanding and Applying for the Right Benefits

The purpose of this chapter is to help you find the right section of this book in order to make application for the benefits to which you believe you are entitled. We also want you to read through this chapter and make sure that you are aware of benefits to which you may be entitled but you currently don't know about.

This introduction is structured to accomplish the twofold task discussed above. If you know which benefit that you wish to apply for, then we provide below a description of each chapter to help you find that section of the book that is pertinent to what you are seeking. This section is entitled "Description of the Chapter Contents and This Book" and is found on the next page.

You may also be entitled to benefits that you are currently not aware of. For example, many claimants, who are receiving DIC, are not aware of an additional $332 that could be available to them if they are receiving the aid and attendance of another person. Or veterans on claim for Compensation or Pension are not aware of housing adaptation grants of up to $6,800. Or yet another benefit for survivors is the possibility of receiving $1,340.14 a month if the veteran suffered a service-connected death and the survivor was not aware at the time that the death was service-connected. We have been able to secure these benefits many years after the veteran died.

DESCRIPTION OF THE CHAPTER CONTENTS IN THIS BOOK

Chapter 1 – Overview of Veterans Benefits and How to Use This Book

This is the chapter that you are currently in. You find in this part of the book, a summary of all of the benefits that are covered in more detail in subsequent chapters. Also covered here is a description of the paperless claim system currently in use for disability and survivor benefits. We also provide a description of the Veterans Benefits Management System (VBMS) and how accredited representatives can sign up for VBMS on their remote computers. Finally, we provide 2020 rate charts for claims and statistical information about the Department of Veterans Affairs and its 2020 proposed budget.

Chapter 2 – Determining Eligibility and Entitlement

Eligibility for benefits pertains to those requirements in the regulations in Title 38 CFR that must be met in order to even consider applying for any benefits. These include, as an example , being considered a veteran, meeting the period of active duty and active duty requirements, having a discharge characterization that allows for the benefit, meeting other requirements such as designation of a war veteran or assignment at a particular time and location that would allow for presumptive service connection. Entitlement is the additional rules pertaining to when benefits can be paid, when benefits start and for means tested programs whether the means testing has been met. Entitlement also pertains to rules that govern benefits for survivors or spouses of living veterans,.

Chapter 3 – Aid and Attendance and Housebound Allowances

There is a great deal of confusion in the community about the terms "aid and attendance" and "housebound." The majority of individuals seeking benefits believe that these terms refer to the Pension benefit with aid and attendance or housebound ratings which is internally referred to by VA as "improved pension." There is no such thing as an "Aid and Attendance Benefit" mentioned in the regulations or that represents a substitute name for the Pension benefit. Aid and Attendance is a misnomer adopted by the media and others to refer to Pension. In actuality, aid and attendance and housebound are additional monetary allowances that are available with Veterans Pension, Survivors Pension, Disability Compensation, Dependency and Indemnity Compensation (DIC) and Special Monthly Compensation (SMC). There are 18 different amounts of allowances available – 4 with Pension and Survivors Pension, 4 with SMC, 2 with DIC, and 8 with Disability Compensation. With the exception of applying for these allowances for Pension, which is covered in Chapter 6, we also provide instructions in Chapter 3 on how to apply for these various allowances for the other benefits mentioned here.

Chapter 4 – Understanding How Claims Are Processed

Chapter 4 discusses the claims model that VA uses for processing applications for Compensation, Pension and DIC. A thorough narrative of a claim for benefits is followed from submission through either paper or online, through the scanning intake center and through the National Work Queue for distribution to the various Regional Offices. The model used in the Regional Office for claims processing is outlined and a thorough analysis of the flaws in the model is discussed. A solution for dealing with the flawed claims process is presented. Finally, Fully Developed Claims are discussed along with a suggested summary of the various necessary pieces of a Fully Developed Claim for Compensation and for Pension.

Chapter 5 – Applying for Disability Compensation

Unfortunately, there is no standard process for applying for Disability Compensation as there is with Pension. Certain forms and evidence are required, but each type of application has its own challenges. Chapter fives includes a generalized process for application that will improve the Regional Office window for decisions and result in award outcomes. All of our claims procedures for Compensation are fully developed. We have identified 17 different types of applications for Compensation that are included in Chapter 5. We have also developed our own specific forms and methods that we believe improve the application and decision process.

Chapter 6 – Applying for Pension and Survivors Pension

Pension and Survivor's Pension applications involve a lot of moving parts due to the amount of evidence, necessary forms, and the general need to establish a medical rating for aid and attendance or housebound. We have developed a standardized process for these applications and will provide you the details of how this process works and checklists to follow. Our method uses the Fully Developed Claim process and results in faster decisions and very few denials.

Chapter 7 – Survivor Benefits and Burial Benefits

Chapter 7 covers the topic of what happens when the claimant dies and the claim is still in process. DIC claims are also covered here as well as how to apply for DIC claims where the death certificate was incomplete or deficient or the veteran died as a result of a presumed service-connected condition, but the surviving spouse was unaware he or she was entitled to a DIC benefit. Other survivor benefits include benefits associated with service-connected deaths. Burial benefits are also included in Chapter 5.

Chapter 8 – Unfavorable Decisions and the New Review Process

Beginning on March 19, 2019, the appeals process was completely revised. Any claims or applications or appeals that were in the system prior to this date are called legacy claims or legacy appeals and are subject to the old rules. As of this date, VA has mostly cleared out these legacy issues and there are few remaining. The new system is colloquially called the AMA meaning the "Appeals Modernization Act," but VA refers to it in the regulations as the "Modernized Review System." Chapter 8 describes the new system and how it works.

Chapter 9 – Loan Guaranty, Housing and Education Benefits

The title is descriptive of what is described in Chapter 9. Loan guaranty programs known as VA loans, housing support in the form of grants for disabled veterans and education benefits for veterans and their survivors are described in detail.

Chapter 10 – Veterans Health Care

Although there are about 19 million living veterans only about 9 million or so are enrolled in VA health care. Some choose not to participate and some are simply not eligible, because there are certain requirements to get into the system. Chapter 10 describes the requirements to get into the VA healthcare system as well as the services that are offered. Since our focus is on senior veterans, a great deal of this chapter is devoted to VA geriatric health care services.

Chapter 11 – State Veterans Benefits

Discussed here are veterans benefits unique to most states that are not offered through the Department Of Veterans Affairs. This might include state veterans homes, state veterans cemeteries, hiring preferences, one-time stipends, property tax abatement and much more.

Chapter 12 – Vocational Rehabilitation and Homeless Veterans Support

Vocational rehabilitation is available to certain veterans to help them find jobs or qualify for better employment. Support for homeless veterans has become a big issue with VA and we cover some VA initiatives to help with this problem

Chapter 13 – Using the Claim Support Disc; Page 543
Here Are the Issues Covered in Chapter 13

(Also online at www.supportdisc.com)
1. Application for Veterans Pension and Survivors Pension (25 different forms and checklists)
2. Application for Compensation and DIC (116 different forms, checklists, DBQs, rate tables and additional instructions)
3. Application for Health Care Benefits (12 different forms)
4. Application for Burial Benefits (8 different forms)
5. Reference Material (thousands of pages)
   - Rate Tables for 2019
   - Most Recent Version of 38 CFR Part 3
   - Most recent version of Adjudication Manual M21-1
   - Department Of Veterans Affairs Reports and Statistics
   - State-By-State VA Utilization Summaries
   - Information on Agent Orange
   - Information on Individual Unemployability
   - Information on PTSD
   - CHAMPVA
   - Homeless Veterans Programs
   - Housing Issues
6. Rules Changes for Pension
7. Sources for Medical Nexus Opinions, Claims File Reviews and Other Claims Support Services
8. Appendix – Additional Information for Accredited Representatives
9. Disability Claims Case Studies

Appendix –Information for Accredited Representatives (On the Claim Support Disc)
- Legally Charging Fees for Assistance with Claims
- Adjudication Manual Rules for DIC, Accrued Benefits and Substitution for Claimant
- Adjudication Manual Marriage Rules
- Adjudication Manual Rules for Evaluating Evidence and Decision-Making
- Adjudication Manual Rules for Determining Service Connection
- Further Discussion of Flaws in the Current Claims Processing Model

Disability Claims Case Studies (On the Claim Support Disc)

A Description of the Paperless Claim System for Disability Benefits

Starting in 2012, VA began migrating its paper-based claim system to a paperless system. By the end of 2015, this process was mostly complete and currently it is considered fully complete. Implementation of the paperless system also required development of a computer database called VBMS – Veterans Benefits Management System. With few exceptions, paper claims folders, sometimes numbering in thousands of pages, are no longer found in Regional Offices. These paper-based folders formally referred to as C files are now called by VA eFolders.

VA encourages all claimants to use an online application process that creates a personal file in VBMS. Many applicants still prefer sending in paper-based claims, because the online application process can be challenging for those who are not computer adept. Paper documents are sent to the Evidence Intake Scanning Center in Janesville, Wisconsin to be converted into PDF documents that are then added through the VA intranet into VBMS for claims processing. To maintain an efficient workload, claims are allocated throughout the 56 State Regional Offices. This process of allocating the workload through any available regional office that has the capacity is called the "National Workload Queue."

In May 2016, VBA completed implementation of the National Work Queue. Previously, a veteran's claim was processed from start to finish by the veteran's local Regional Office of Jurisdiction, and the Regional Office's workload generally depended on how many claims were filed by veterans within its area of jurisdiction. Now, a claim can be processed by multiple regional offices, and claims are distributed based on regional office capacity.

VBA Disability Claims Workload Distribution Before and After the National Work Queue

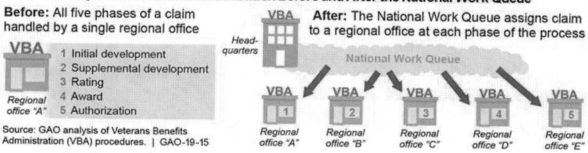

Before: All five phases of a claim handled by a single regional office

VBA
Regional office "A"
1 Initial development
2 Supplemental development
3 Rating
4 Award
5 Authorization

After: The National Work Queue assigns claim to a regional office at each phase of the process

Head-quarters

National Work Queue

VBA 1 — Regional office "A"
VBA 2 — Regional office "B"
VBA 3 — Regional office "C"
VBA 4 — Regional office "D"
VBA 5 — Regional office "E"

Source: GAO analysis of Veterans Benefits Administration (VBA) procedures. | GAO-19-15

The National Work Queue was designed to even out the differences in claims workload across regional offices by having multiple offices complete parts of a claim and allocating claims based on each office's capacity. For example, as shown in the figure on the next page, in fiscal year 2017, about 88 percent of all disability compensation claims were processed by more than one office, and over 75 percent were processed by three or more offices. This distribution method is intended to keep all offices working at their capacity, regardless of the volume of claims filed by veterans in each region. While VBA officials originally stated that they had initially planned to continue to have a majority of claims processed at veterans' local Regional Offices, after implementation of the National Work Queue they determined that the system operates more effectively if veteran location is a lower priority factor for claims distribution. Thus, very few claims are processed entirely at a veteran's local Regional Office, unless the veteran has a documented hardship that may necessitate expediting the claim or face- to-face interaction.

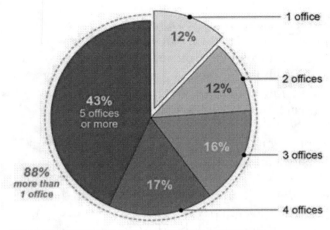

Source: GAO analysis of Veterans Benefits Administration data. | GAO-19-15

Percentage of compensation claims processed by more than one regional office in 2017

The conversion to the new system was not only intended to streamline the claim process for Compensation claims but also to trim away the huge backlog of these applications that was approaching over 900,000 claims that were older than 125 days. New processes built around the new database were also designed to streamline adjudication activities in the Regional Office.

In addition, an online application program was developed which is called eBenefits. More recently, VA is encouraging applications through a portal called vets.gov. Applications through eBenefits or Vets.org feed directly into VBMS through the National Work Queue and avoid the scanning center. Other labor saving procedures were added such as Fully Developed Claims and Decision Ready Claims.

It should be noted that currently claims for Pension, DIC and accrued benefits must be submitted as paper applications through the Janesville Scanning Center. The online process using eBenefits or Vets.org cannot currently be used for these particular claims. Once in the system, however, these claims eventually end up in VBMS. In addition, an effort has been made to keep these particular claims with The 3 Pension Management Centers, in St. Paul, Milwaukee and Philadelphia. We have found that Pension claims are sometimes making their way to other Regional Offices where there is less experience in handling these kinds of applications.

Gaining Access to VBMS for Accredited Claim Representatives

One of the biggest problems facing the Regional Offices claims processors in the past was the cumbersome paper-based claim system where some individual claims files for one veteran could number more than 2,000 pages. Under its paper-based system VA used an assembly-line process with 5 or 6 different decision stations and only one person could access the claims file at any one time. Under this system claims files could easily become lost or end up on someone's desk in a huge pile of other documents and possibly go unnoticed for long periods of time. VA decided to go to a paperless system where all documents are scanned into PDF format and stored in a

6

database that is accessible to all regional office employees on their computers. Now any number of employees can work on the same claim at the same time. Regional Offices even allow employees to work at home accessing VBMS on their home computers.

In order to accommodate the new paperless system, the department decided initially in 2010 to design a one-dimensional database to accommodate all of the PDF documents. This database has now evolved into a relational database management system where the entire claims process can be managed through Internet technology on the cloud and employees can work from home. What was supposed to be a simple database has turned out to cost the government $1.3 billion and growing as new capabilities are being added each year. This database is called the Veterans Benefits Management System or VBMS for short. All accredited agents and accredited attorneys can now apply for and receive access to VBMS on their home or office computers through a vetting and security training program. As of December 2019, VA asserts there are over 500,000 computers tied to VBMS, either in Department offices or from VA employees working at home or in private offices of veterans service representatives.

VA has redesigned all of its forms so that vital information on the form such as names, addresses, Social Security numbers and so forth is scanned directly into the database through optical character recognition. The purpose is to bypass human intervention and by hand input, and feed the vital information directly into the computer system for more efficient handling.

Here is the Veterans Benefits Administration (VBA) Report of Agency Status on VBMS as of November 14, 2017

- By *Centralizing Intake* of claims material, VBA is able to digitize all claims, no matter how received, creating a fully digital operating environment that allows all claims to be processed and delivered electronically.
- Through the *Veterans Benefits Management System (VBMS)*, VBA processes nearly 100% of all compensation claims electronically, allowing us to provide Veterans and their families the benefits they have earned in a more timely manner.
- VBA completed nearly 9 million rating and non-rating claims in VBMS and nearly 7 million rating decisions in VBMS since inception.
- VBA has scanned over 2.9 billion images since we began scanning and uploaded an average of over 100K mail packets per week in FY2017.
- VBA has reduced the average mail processing time for Regional Offices (ROs) to under 4 business days from a peak of 55 business days in early 2015 and reduced the amount of paper mail received by 20%.
- VBA's *National Work Queue* prioritizes and distributes workload across the nation based on the VBA workforce's real-time capacity.
- The average days to complete a Veteran's claim nationally is 113.3 days at the end of FY2017 – a 10.2 day reduction from September 2016.

As of the "Fast Letter" of September 22, 2016, (see next page) all accredited claim representatives including accredited agents and accredited attorneys are eligible to access VBMS on their own computers. The letter describes the process to gain access. As of December 2019, anyone accessing VBMS must have Windows 10 installed on his or her computer.

DEPARTMENT OF VETERANS AFFAIRS
Veterans Benefits Administration
Washington, D.C. 20420

September 22, 2016

VBA Letter 20-16-08

Director (00)
All VBA Regional Offices and Centers

SUBJ: Internal VBA Systems Access for Claimant and Appellant Representatives

Purpose

The purpose of this letter is to provide procedures to grant access to VA information systems to accredited claimant and appellant representatives. Users cannot access internal systems without a Personal Identity Verification (PIV) badge; therefore, in order for accredited claims agents, attorneys, and employees of Veterans Service Organizations (VSOs) to gain access to VBA systems, VA must issue them a PIV badge.

VA has a responsibility to preserve the ability of a claimant's representative to access that claimant's VA claims records while complying with Homeland Safety Presidential Directive 12 (HSPD 12), Federal Information Processing Standards Publication (FIPS PUB 201-2), and applicable laws, rules, and regulations related to access to secure government information systems.

To achieve this balance, VBA follows the policies and procedures of the VA Office of Information Security, specifically in regards to completing identity verification, background investigations, and PIV badge issuance to any individual granted access to VA information systems.

Prerequisites for System Access

Due to the cost involved in establishing system access, VA will only establish access for individuals:

- Accredited by VA's Office of General Counsel (OGC) to represent Veterans as a claims agent, attorney, or employee of a Veterans Service Organization and
- Designated by one or more Veterans to represent him or her in pursuing a claim or appeal for VA benefits.

If a person requesting access does not meet these requirements, VA will not issue a PIV card and establish system access until the need for such access is demonstrated.

VBA System Access Security Requirements

The security requirements for VBA systems access are:

- Fingerprinting (favorable outcome);
- Office of Personnel Management (OPM) background investigation (initiated);
- Completed information security training;
- Completed Optional Form (OF) - 306, Declaration of Federal Employment, and
- Signed Rules of Behavior (ROB).

Upon successful adjudication of the background investigation and issuance of a PIV badge, VA will grant access to the VA network and to the Veterans Benefits Management System (VBMS). An individual granted access to VBMS will have a user role of "POA" and will be associated with the electronic records of Veterans he or she represents.

The VA National Service Desk (NSD) will provide IT support to representatives with remote access to VA systems. The National Service Desk is available to provide assistance 24 hours a day, 7 days a week at 1-855-NSD-HELP or 1-855-673-4357.

Processing VA System Access Requests

To request remote access, accredited representatives should submit a completed OF-306, *Declaration of Federal Employment* and VA Form 20-0344, *Annual Certification of Veterans Status and Veteran-Relatives* to the Change Management Agent (CMA) at the closest regional office. A list of CMAs is available online at:

http://www.benefits.va.gov/COMPENSATION/cma-poc.asp

Upon receipt of a request, the CMA will send the accredited representative an e-mail acknowledging receipt of his or her documents, providing the requestor with the CMA's contact information, and informing the requestor a background investigation will be initiated.

The Information Security Officer (ISO) will verify accreditation or employment with a VSO by searching the Office of General Counsel's (OGC) online Accreditation Database. If the requestor is not accredited, the ISO will refer the case to the VBA's Office of Field Operations (OFO) via email at ofo.vbaco@va.gov. OFO will review the circumstances of the application, communicate with OGC, and if not able to resolve the issue, refer the requestor to OGC to pursue accreditation.

Under exceptional circumstances, OGC may direct VBA to issue a PIV card and grant systems access to an individual who is not an accredited representative. When these situations occur, OFO will contact the regional office directly to provide further instructions.

Regional Office Change Management Agent

The CMA will be the representative's primary point of contact throughout the process. The CMA's role is to ensure timely action is being taken on the representative's request for access and to respond to status inquiries from representatives seeking access. The CMA will also accept documents and forward them to the appropriate office or individual within the RO.

Note: Under no circumstances is the CMA permitted to keep or otherwise maintain application documents containing representative's personally-identifiable information once it has been sent to the appropriate office or individual for action.

Regional Office Human Resource Liaison / Specialist

The Human Resource (HR) Liaison / Specialist is responsible for coordinating PIV card issuance, receiving the completed OF-306 and VA Form 20-0344, and providing security requirements to the requestor. If the attorney fails the background investigation based on HSPD-12 denial guidelines, the HR Liaison / Specialist will deny access and inform both OGC and OFO immediately. HR and Human Resources Centers will follow the same background investigation guidelines used for VSO employees.

Regional Office Training Manager

The RO Training Manager is responsible for establishing a Talent Management System (TMS) account so the requestor can complete required information security training and digitally sign the ROB. Upon the requestor's successful completion of information security training and receipt of a signed ROB document, the regional office may grant access to VBA systems.

Power of Attorney (POA) Code for Accredited Representatives

To gain access to Veteran records, a representative must have a personal login to the VA network and appropriate VA systems **and** be associated with a POA code. For example, an attorney named John Q. Public would receive a login under his name and a POA code in his name as well. In order for this attorney to access client records, a Veteran must have "John Q Public" selected as his or her POA code in the system.

Agents or attorneys can also be associated with multiple POA codes. An example of this would be attorney John Q. Public representing Veterans personally and also on behalf of an organization such as Disabled American Veterans. In this scenario, John Q. Public's account would be associated with both the John Q Public and Disabled American Veterans POA codes.

Note: Association in the OGC accreditation database or a written statement from an additional organization is required prior to associating an account with multiple POA codes.

Some accredited representatives do not have a POA code in the system. For these representatives, the regional office may still guide the representative through the PIV process and establish remote network access, but **may not** grant access to VBMS or any other VA system. When such a representative is found, the regional office will contact the NSD and open a ticket for POA code establishment. NSD personnel will assign this task to the appropriate office within VBA Central Office and notify the regional office of completion.

Questions

Questions regarding accreditation may be directed to the VA Office of General Counsel via e-mail to ogcaccreditationmailbox@va.gov.

Questions regarding other matters may be sent to the Office of Field Operations via e-mail to ofo.vbaco@va.gov.

/s/
Thomas J. Murphy
Principal Deputy Under Secretary for Benefits
Performing the Duties of
Under Secretary for Benefits

Enclosure: Attachment A: Access Process

Attachment A: Access Process

Step 1: To request VA system access, a representative must provide:
OF-306, Declaration of Federal Employment –   (a) Complete OF-306, Declaration of Federal Employment   (b) CMA sends representative acknowledgement e-mail   (c) CMA submits to local Human Resource Liaison/Specialist
Veteran Status and Relative Status –   (a) Complete VA Form 20-0344, Annual Certification of Veteran Status and Veteran-Relatives   (b) CMA submits to local Human Resource Liaison/Specialist

Step 2: The CMA:
Request a background Investigation from their local Human Recourse Liaison/Specialist –   (a) The local Human Resource Liaison/Specialist initiates background investigation and provides the CMA with an e-QIP link. The CMA provides the link information to the representative.   (b) Complete required background investigation including the Special Agreement Check (SAC) for fingerprinting. The SAC is normally completed within 1-3 days of fingerprint submission   (c) If the representative does not pass the background investigation or if the fingerprints are not acceptable, the CMA will notify OFO.
Initiates training requirements -   (a) CMA contacts local Training Manager for creation of the Talent Management System (TMS) account   (b) Training Manager creates TMS account and assigns HIPPA and TMS VA 10176 to representative   (c) The CMA provides the TMS account information to the representative to complete the required training
Requests VA Network Access and User Account –   (a) CMA submits VA Form 20-8824e, *Common Security Services (CSS) User Access Request* to ISO via CSEM

(b) CMA submits VA Form 20-8824f , *Veteran Benefits Administration/Central Office Network Access Request* to their local ISO

(c) ISO reviews and approves 20-8824f and submits to local IT staff for implementation and to create user account

(d) The IT staff sends account creation email and instructions to obtain network access credentials to the CMA

Step 2: After completion of these requirements, the CMA will

Request PIV –

(a) The Human Resource Liaison / Specialist serves as the representative's PIV Sponsor. He or she initiates the PIV card request in PIV enrollment portal.

(b) The CMA will advise the representative of the need to have two forms of ID (acceptable forms of ID listed on FIPS 201-2, section 2.7, and Identity Document Matrix)

(c) The CMA will assist the representative with scheduling an appointment with a badge office

    i.   See the list of PCI Facilities to find the closest one

    ii.   You must bring two forms of ID with you to your appointment

    iii.   Use the new VA PIV Scheduling tool. Click here to determine if your local PCI Facility is utilizing the tool

(d) Activate PIV card.

Provide the representative with VA System Access –
    CMA to provide login instructions to representative

Additional Support for Accredited Claim Representatives

Free membership in the Senior Veterans Service Alliance provides additional support for accredited claim representatives to include the following services:

- Claim representation for initial claims for Pension, DIC, additional aid and attendance and housebound allowances and Disability Compensation
- Claim representation for claims with unfavorable decisions or denials
- National hotline for any questions pertaining to veterans benefits at 800-728-1497 or by email to request.seniorvets.org
- CLE courses for maintaining accreditation for accredited agents and accredited attorneys
- An informative website that includes information on all veterans benefits at www.seniorvets.org

About the Department Of Veterans Affairs

As of 2020 there will be about 18.8 million veterans in the United States, according to population estimates issued by the Department. Rough estimates are that there could be somewhere around 6 million surviving spouses or surviving dependents of veterans as well – putting the total at about 24.8 million individuals who could possibly be eligible for VA benefits. It is interesting even though the population of veterans is declining every year, the amount of benefit payments to those veterans is increasing about 8% a year. More veterans are on claim, they have more disability issues and are getting much more money per capita even taking into account inflation.

Historical and Projected Veterans Population – 2000 to 2030

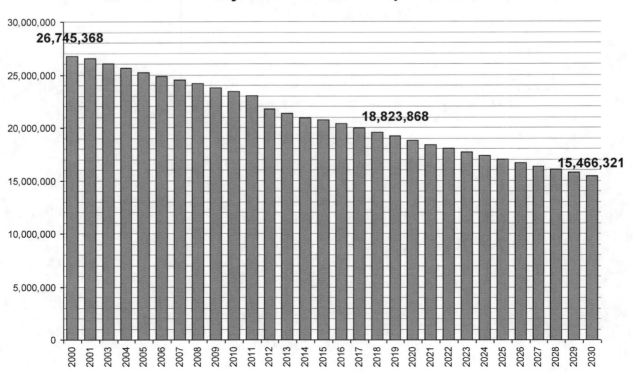

Estimated Population (in Millions) of Living Veterans, Dependents of Living Veterans, Survivors of Veterans Receiving VA Survivor Benefits, and Others U.S. and Puerto Rico, September 30, 2018

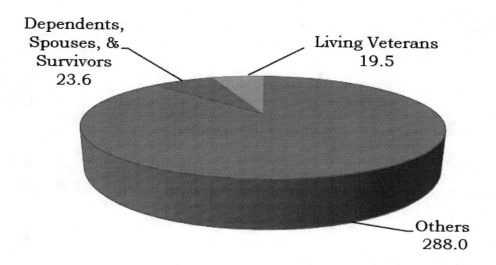

The Department of Veterans Affairs exists to provide the benefits below.

- Health care
- Disability Compensation
- Dependency and Indemnity Compensation (DIC)
- Veterans Pension
- Survivors Pension
- Burial benefits
- Life insurance
- G.I. bill
- Vocational Rehabilitation and employment
- Home loans and other housing allowances, and
- A variety of outreach and support services such as the National Call Center, suicide prevention, counseling specific to veterans and homelessness and a whole lot more.

Not all veterans qualify for the entire list above. As a general rule, all veterans can qualify for life insurance, G.I. bill (depending on their service), home loan guarantys and limited burial benefits. For the rest of this list there are specific eligibility and entitlement requirements.

In this book we cover all of the benefits listed above. However, the specific focus is on service-connected and non-service-connected disability and the survivor benefits associated with these two programs. Currently the Department of Veterans Affairs through one of its three divisions – Veterans Benefits Administration – serves the following number of individuals. (See next page)

Veterans Benefits Administration Number of Beneficiaries

	2018 Actual	2019 Estimate	2020 Estimate
Compensation Beneficiaries including DIC	5,070,505	5,281,013	6,105,364
Pension Beneficiaries including Survivors Pension	462,849	447,805	442,711
Education Program Students	893,656	883,626	876,742
Vocational Rehab & Employment Trainees	97,770	122,500	123,725
New Housing Loans	581,767	556,281	562,178
Insured Persons	5,924,525	5,909,865	5,867,231

Source: DVA 2020 budget proposal

By far, the the most costly portion of the VA budget is the disability benefits payments to veterans and their survivors exceeding $100 billion a year in outlays. VA is the second largest cabinet department in the US government by number of employees and the fifth-largest by budget size. Unlike other departments in the government, VA's budget has grown at 9.44 % on average every year since 2010. All others, with one exception, have seen their allocations shrink or remain static. The one exception is the Department of Defense which is the largest agency by budget and number of employees and has seen continued yearly increases in funding.

The Department of Veterans Affairs structure consists of 3 operational divisions and various other departments that provide general administration, support and other services to also include a robust construction program. The three operational divisions are

1. **Veterans Health Administration** (VHA) which accounts for 37.4% of the budget and 348,389 employees, representing 89% of the workforce. The Veterans Health Administration is America's largest integrated health care system, providing care at 1,243 health care facilities, including 172 medical centers and 1,062 outpatient sites of care of varying complexity (VHA outpatient clinics), and serving 9 million enrolled Veterans.

2. **National Cemetery Administration** (NCA) which accounts for 0.4% of the budget and has 2,008 employees.

3. **Veterans Benefits Administration** (VBA) which accounts for 10.3% of the budget and utilizes 23,899 employees. It is this division of VA that this book is mostly about as all of the benefits covered in this book – with the exception of the chapter on veterans health care – are furnished through the Veterans Benefits Administration or VBA

Department of Veterans Affairs Full-Time Equivalent Employees by Administration and Office

	2018	2019	2020
Veterans Health Administration (VHA)	321,669	335,273	348,389
Veterans Benefits Administration (VBA)	22,961	23,692	23,899
Number of VBA Employees Working in Compensation	*14,181*	*14,713*	*14,662*
Number of VBA Employees Working in Pension and DIC	*1,168*	*1,189*	*1,190*
Percent of VBA Employees in Compensation, Pension, DIC	*66.85%*	*67.12%*	*66.33%*
National Cemetery Administration (NCA)	1,865	1,941	2,008
Office of Information Technology	7,152	7,589	7,575
General Administration	2,520	2,818	3,136
Board of Veterans' Appeals	920	1,125	1,125
Office of the Inspector General	849	975	1,000
Supply Fund	957	1,115	1,135
Franchise Fund	1,383	1,928	2,140
Other Functions of the Department	3,085	3,541	3,395
Total Veterans Affairs	**363,362**	**379,998**	**393,803**

Source: DVA 2020 Budget Proposal

Disability Income and health care benefits comprise the largest portion of the VA budget which for 2020 will be about $216.2 billion. Projected spending for medical care in 2020 will be $80.93 billion. Another $95 billion is for Disability Compensation benefits including DIC. Another $5.4 billion is for Pension including Survivors (Death) Pension. These 3 specific expenditures represent a total of about $181.33 billion and encompass about 84% of the entire VA budget.

Department Of Veterans Affairs Yearly Budget

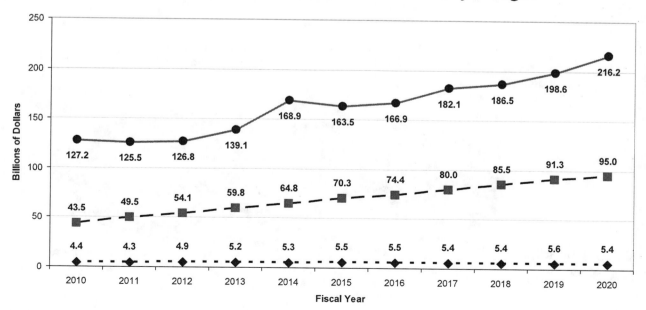

VA 2019 Estimated Budget in Billions of Dollars – $197.51 Billion Total

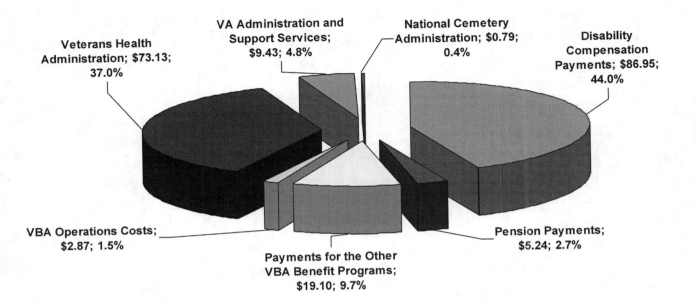

Veterans Health Administration; $73.13; 37.0%

VA Administration and Support Services; $9.43; 4.8%

National Cemetery Administration; $0.79; 0.4%

Disability Compensation Payments; $86.95; 44.0%

VBA Operations Costs; $2.87; 1.5%

Payments for the Other VBA Benefit Programs; $19.10; 9.7%

Pension Payments; $5.24; 2.7%

VA 2020 Proposed Budget in Billions of Dollars – $216.19 Billion Total

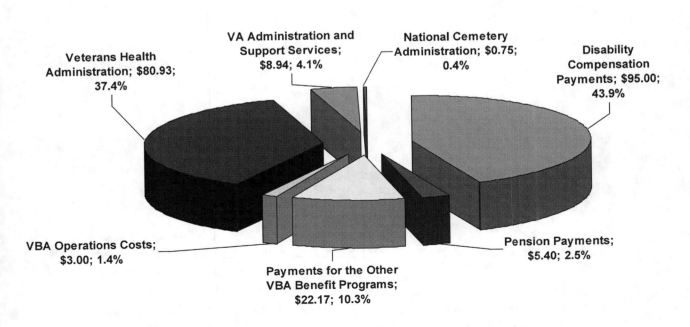

Veterans Health Administration; $80.93; 37.4%

VA Administration and Support Services; $8.94; 4.1%

National Cemetery Administration; $0.75; 0.4%

Disability Compensation Payments; $95.00; 43.9%

VBA Operations Costs; $3.00; 1.4%

Payments for the Other VBA Benefit Programs; $22.17; 10.3%

Pension Payments; $5.40; 2.5%

SUMMARIES OF BENEFITS COVERED IN THIS BOOK

Number of Beneficiaries – 2018	Younger than 65	Age 65 and Older	Total all Ages	Percent of All Claims
Disability Compensation	3,150,664	1,592,444	4,743,108	84.7%
DIC for Surviving Spouse	149,915	255,632	405,547	7.2%
Veterans Pension	65,124	194,965	260,089	4.6%
Survivors Pension for Spouse	24,580	168,243	192,823	3.4%
Fiduciary Beneficiaries (Compensation, Pension and DIC)			190,540	3.4%
100% Disabled			684,851	12.2%
Individual Unemployability (Paid at 100% Disabled Rate)			356,668	6.4%
Special Monthly Compensation (SMC)			691,708	12.3%
Tinnitus and Hearing Loss – Most Prevalent Disabilities			3,363,237	60.0%
Total Beneficiaries – Compensation, DIC and Pension			5,601,567	
Healthcare System Enrolled			9 million +	

Source: VA Annual Benefits Report 2018, DVA 2020 Budget Proposal

Disability Compensation

Disability Compensation is a tax-free benefit paid to a veteran for a service-connected disability that happened as a result of injury, aggravation or disease during active duty, active duty for training, inactive duty for training or injury from VA healthcare or vocational rehab. Cash income payments for Compensation range from a low of $142.29 a month to a high of about $3,600 a month in 2020. Special benefits, like grants for new automobiles or modifying existing automobiles, grants for constructing or modifying homes, clothing allowances and so on are payable for certain severe service-connected disabilities. A veteran cannot receive Pension and Compensation at the same time and a surviving spouse cannot receive Death Pension and DIC at the same time. A choice must be made which benefit the beneficiary wants to receive.

An aid and attendance or housebound benefit in the form of Special Monthly Compensation (SMC) is available to the veteran who is 100% disabled. Without SMC, a single veteran rated for 100% disability will receive a check for $3,106.04 a month in 2020 and if the veteran has a spouse the amount is $3,279.22 a month. A 100% disabled veteran meeting the SMC Schedule (L) for aid and attendance can receive $3,864.90 a month in 2020 and if that veteran has a spouse, the amount can be $4,038.08 a month. Higher amounts are possible if the aid and attendance involves certain severe disabilities. An SMC benefit is also available to a veteran who is housebound.

This aid and attendance allowance with SMC is not an automatic benefit and most veterans don't even know about this special assistance and never apply for it. If the veteran receiving Compensation is not 100% disabled, it may be possible to increase the rating up to 100% or be paid at 100% due to unemployability. Even retired veterans can be considered unemployable.

Most veterans receiving Compensation don't have a clue as to their eligibility for aid and attendance or housebound benefits that are not related to the Pension benefit.

Also, an aid and attendance allowance is available due to the need for these services for a disabled spouse of a veteran where the veteran is 30% or more disabled. The amount goes up as the disability rating goes up. For example, for 2020, a 30% disabled veteran can generate an aid and attendance allowance of $48.00 a month benefit as a result of his or her disabled spouse needing aid and attendance. A 100% disabled veteran can generate an aid and attendance allowance of $158.82 a month for his or her spouse. Again, it is not common knowledge these additional aid and attendance allowances are available and VA does not normally notify people of their existence.

Of particular note for Disability Compensation are Agent Orange claims for each and every veteran who was stationed in Vietnam – or other locations this herbicide was stored or used – and who has developed presumptive health conditions such as certain forms of cancer, type II diabetes, ischemic heart disease (lack of proper blood flow to the heart), B cell leukemia and Parkinson's disease. There are 12 presumptive health conditions for Agent Orange exposure.

Veterans with service-connected hearing loss can also make claims and receive free hearing aids and a lifetime supply of free batteries. This hearing disability rating will also get them into the health care system. Many veterans don't know of the existence of Agent Orange claims or the fact that they might be eligible for service-connected disability for hearing loss.

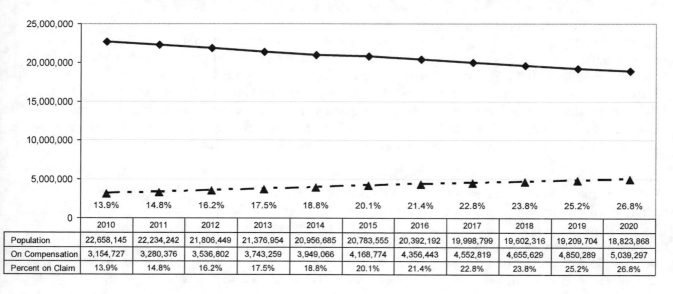

Population of Living Veterans vs Veterans Receiving Compensation – 2010 to 2020

	2010	2011	2012	2013	2014	2015	2016	2017	2018	2019	2020
Population	22,658,145	22,234,242	21,806,449	21,376,954	20,956,685	20,783,555	20,392,192	19,998,799	19,602,316	19,209,704	18,823,868
On Compensation	3,154,727	3,280,376	3,536,802	3,743,259	3,949,066	4,168,774	4,356,443	4,552,819	4,655,629	4,850,289	5,039,297
Percent on Claim	13.9%	14.8%	16.2%	17.5%	18.8%	20.1%	21.4%	22.8%	23.8%	25.2%	26.8%

The biggest challenge with disability benefits for the Department of Veterans Affairs is the ever increasing number of claims for Compensation. The volume for Pension and DIC claims has remained about the same over the years with Pension projected to decline as there are fewer and fewer living veterans of war. On the other hand Compensation applications have skyrocketed.

The population of living veterans from 2010 to 2020 is projected to go from about 22.7 million to 18.8 million – a decline of about 4 million veterans. On the other hand, the number of submissions for compensation will double over this period of time. This means that fewer veterans are filing more claims for benefits. You can also see from the graph that the percentage of veterans receiving compensation from 2010 through 2020 will almost double from 13.9% to 26.8%. Well over a quarter of all veterans will be receiving benefits.

The complexity of claims is also changing. A growing percentage of current returning war veterans are applying for 12 are more different disabilities. It is unlikely anyone has that many service-connected disabilities at one time but it appears the veterans are trying to get as much as they can by throwing everything against the wall to see what will stick. This may be a simple task for the veterans but VA has to expend more effort for all of these claimed disabilities whether they are valid or not. Applications for secondary disability and requests for increases in rating are also going up. In 2020 VA expects 76% of claims to be from veterans already on benefit and the other 24% to be original claims. Many of the applications for veterans already on claim are for secondary disability or for increase in rating. In 2000 the average number of disabilities per veteran receiving compensation was 3.2 and by 2017 was almost double to 5.11 disabilities per veteran.

As a final note VA's budget for paying compensation claims from 2010 to 2020 will go from $38 billion to $95 billion even though the number of living veterans will have gone down by 4 million.

Veterans on Claim for Compensation

	Total Number of Veterans on Claim	Average Yearly Amount of Benefit	Total Amount Paid out in Billions of Dollars
2010	3,154,727	$12,075	$38.09
2011	3,280,376	$13,355	$43.87
2012	3,536,802	$12,542	$44.36
2013	3,743,259	$13,131	$49.15
2014	3,949,066	$13,732	$54.23
2015	4,168,774	$14,444	$60.21
2016	4,356,443	$14,855	$64.71
2017	4,552,819	$15,373	$69.99
2018	4,655,629	$16,808	$78.25
2019	4,850,289	$17,553	$85.14
2020	5,039,297	$18,320	$95.00

Veterans Pension and Survivors Pension with Aid and Attendance

Commonly called "aid and attendance," these twin benefits provide monthly tax-free payments to veterans who served during a period of war or to their single surviving spouses. Pension can help cover the cost of home care, assisted living and nursing home services. Pension is also available to veterans or surviving spouses with very low income and who do not have long-term care costs. Cash income payments from Pension in 2020 range from $768 a month to $2,266 a month depending on the type of claim and the medical rating involved. Many people don't even know of the existence of this benefit. VA does not advertise any of its benefits very well and as such many eligible people never apply.

It is unfortunate Pension has been misnamed "aid and attendance." "Aid and attendance" and "housebound" are medical ratings and allow for additional monetary allowances provided with Pension if the recipient of Pension needs the regular aid and attendance of another person or is considered housebound. The misnomer creates confusion because aid and attendance assistance allowances are also available for service-connected disabilities (Disability Compensation) and to a spouse of a service connected disabled veteran and also an aid and attendance allowance is available to a surviving spouse of a veteran if the surviving spouse is receiving DIC (Dependency and Indemnity Compensation). There are 18 different monetary levels of aid and attendance or housebound allowances available with non-service-connected and service-connected disability programs for veterans or their surviving spouses.

Number of Beneficiaries – 2018	Younger than 65	Age 65 and Older	Total all Ages	Percent of All Claims
Disability Compensation	3,150,664	1,592,444	4,743,108	84.7%
DIC for Surviving Spouse	149,915	255,632	405,547	7.2%
Veterans Pension	65,124	194,965	260,089	4.6%
Survivors Pension for Spouse	24,580	168,243	192,823	3.4%
Fiduciary Beneficiaries (Compensation, Pension and DIC)			190,540	3.4%
100% Disabled			684,851	12.2%
Individual Unemployability (Paid at 100% Disabled Rate)			356,668	6.4%
Special Monthly Compensation (SMC)			691,708	12.3%
Tinnitus and Hearing Loss – Most Prevalent Disabilities			3,363,237	60.0%
Total Beneficiaries – Compensation, DIC and Pension			5,601,567	
Healthcare System Enrolled			9 million +	

Source: VA Annual Benefits Report 2018, DVA 2020 Budget Proposal

DIC (Dependency and Indemnity Compensation)

Dependency and Indemnity Compensation (DIC) is payable to eligible survivors of a military service member who died on active duty or whose death after service resulted from a service-connected injury or disease. It is also available due to improper treatment of the deceased veteran from VA healthcare or rehabilitation services. DIC is automatically granted to a surviving spouse for a veteran who was permanently and totally disabled for 10 years or more. DIC pays $1,340.14 a month in 2020 to a surviving spouse. Additional amounts are available if there are dependent children. A dependent child is one who is 18 years old or younger or 23 years old or younger and enrolled full-time in school or is an adult who became totally dependent prior to the age of 18. If the veteran was 100% continuously disabled at least 8 years immediately preceding death, the amount is $1,624.71.

If the surviving spouse needs the aid and attendance of another person such as home care, assisted living or nursing home care, an additional $332.00 a month assistance benefit will be paid. This DIC with aid and attendance benefit is about $400 more a month than a surviving spouse can receive from Survivors Pension. This additional benefit is not automatic and most individuals receiving DIC do not even know it is available. An additional monthly benefit for being housebound is also available.

Health Care Benefits

The VA health care system is the largest single provider of health care in the United States. It has also been recognized by numerous surveys as being one of the best providers of health care as well. Not all veterans can receive care in the system. Eligibility requires either service-connected disability, receipt of Pension, special service recognition such as prisoner of war or Purple Heart or low income and less than $80,000 in assets. Iraq and Afghanistan veterans are also covered for 5 years after discharge. And, in-country Vietnam veterans are also covered.

For all beneficiaries – not to include those who are means tested –services are free and medications for most veterans are $5.00 per 30 day supply for generic drugs, $8.00 per 30 days for non-preferred generic and over-the-counter and $11.00 per 30 days for brand-name. For veterans rated 50% or more for Compensation, medications are free. Means tested veterans provide a copay for services. There are no other out-of-pocket costs such as health care premiums. Assistance can also be provided with disability-required home renovation grants of $2,000 or $6,800. Orthotics, prosthetics and in certain cases hearing aids and glasses are also available to many in the system. Specialized benefits such as dental care for certain veterans and geriatric care services are also available. VA outpatient clinics are also available.

Burial Benefits

Money is available for burial costs for veterans who were service disabled, receiving Pension or died under VA care. If the death was a result of service-connected disability, $2,000 is available. If the death was non-service related, and the veteran was receiving Pension or Compensation or was entitled to either of these, up to $796 is available for plot allowance and burial and $300 in funeral expense allowances in 2020. All veterans also receive free burial in State and Federal VA cemeteries. Under certain conditions, spouses and other family members can receive free burial in State and Federal VA cemeteries. All veterans – service or non-service connected included – are eligible for a grave marker (or equivalent monetary allowance of $195), a flag for the coffin, a graveside honor guard and a letter from the President of the United States.

Burial and Plot Rate Table 2020 – Effective October 1, 2019

SERVICE CONNECTED DEATH	$2,000
NON-SERVICE CONNECTED DEATH (Reimbursement; veteran dies while hospitalized by VA)	$796
NON-SERVICE CONNECTED DEATH (Reimbursement for Veterans not hospitalized by VA)	$300
NSC DEATH STATE CEMETERY (Paid to a state veterans cemetery for the plot/burial)	$796
NSC DEATH PLOT ALLOWANCE (This amount will be paid to reimburse for a private-paid plot)	$796
NSC HEADSTONE OR MARKER ALLOWANCE (If not provided by the Department)	$195

A service-connected death is one where the veteran was receiving monthly payments for Disability Compensation and the death was due to the disability or condition for which the veteran was receiving pay. It is also possible to receive a service-connected death if the disability or condition was not the direct cause but the disability or condition contributed substantially to the death.

A non-service-connected death is one where the veteran was receiving monthly payments for Disability Compensation or Veterans Pension but the death was due to some other cause not related to the disabilities or conditions for which the veteran was receiving pay.

It should be noted that generally a non-service-connected death can produce $1,096 a month if the survivors have to pay for a funeral plot. Note that if the veteran died while hospitalized by VA and the survivor has to pay for a funeral plot the total amount available is $1,876.

Special Benefits

SAH Grant, Eligibility for up to $90,364 for 2020
VA may approve a grant of not more than 50 percent of the cost of building, buying, or adapting existing homes or paying to reduce indebtedness on a currently owned home that is being adapted, up to a maximum of $90,364. In certain instances, the full grant amount may be applied toward remodeling costs. Veterans and service members must be determined eligible to receive Compensation for permanent and total service-connected disability due to one of the following:

- Loss or loss of use of both lower extremities, such as to preclude locomotion without the aid of braces, crutches, canes or a wheelchair.
- Loss or loss of use of both upper extremities at or above the elbow.
- Blindness in both eyes, having only light perception, plus loss or loss of use of one lower extremity
- Loss or loss of use of one lower extremity together with (a) residuals of organic disease or injury, or (b) the loss or loss of use of one upper extremity which so affects the functions of balance or propulsion as to preclude locomotion without the use of braces, canes, crutches or a wheelchair.
- Severe burn injuries

SHA Grant, Eligibility for up to $18,074 for 2020
VA may approve a grant for the cost, up to a maximum of $18,074, for necessary adaptations to a veteran's or service member's residence or to help them acquire a residence already adapted with special features for their disability, to purchase and adapt a home, or for adaptations to a family member's home in which they will reside.

To be eligible for this grant, veterans and servicemembers must be entitled to Compensation for permanent and total service-connected disability due to one of the following:

- Blindness in both eyes with 5/200 visual acuity or less.
- Anatomical loss or loss of use of both hands.
- Severe burn injuries.

Temporary Residence Adaptation (TRA)

A temporary grant may be available to SAH/SHA eligible Veterans and Servicemembers who are or will be temporarily residing in a home owned by a family member. **The maximum amount available to adapt a family member's home for the SAH grant is $39,669 and for the SHA grant is $7,083 for 2020.**

The first adjustment occurred on Oct. 1, 2009, with future adjustments each Oct. 1 thereafter. These adjustments will increase the grant amounts or leave them unchanged; they will not decrease the grant amounts. The maximum amount for a TRA grant is not indexed and remains unchanged.

The property may be located outside the United States, in a country or political subdivision which allows individuals to have or acquire a beneficial property interest, and in which the Secretary of Veterans Affairs, in his or her discretion, has determined that it is reasonably practicable for the Secretary to provide assistance in acquiring specially adapted housing.

Vocational Rehabilitation and Employment (VR&E) – Housing Adaptation Assistance

VR&E may provide home adaptations to individuals who are not currently able to work because of the effects of their service-connected disabilities, or who require adaptations to achieve a vocational goal. The benefits are limited to those required to improve independence at home and/or in the community. Home adaptations up to $90,364 may be provided as part of an approved rehabilitation plan.

Supplemental Financing

Veterans and service members with available loan guaranty entitlement may also obtain a guaranteed loan or a direct loan from VA to supplement the grant to acquire a specially adapted home.

Hisa Grants

A Home Improvements and Structural Alterations (HISA) grant provides assistance for any home improvement necessary for treatment or disability access. Eligible Veterans and Service members can receive a HISA grant, as well as either a SAH or SHA grant. This program is available for both Veterans with service-connected disabilities and non-service-connected disabilities:

- Service-connected disabilities: home improvement benefits up to $6,800
- Non-service-connected disabilities: home improvement benefits up to $2,000

Special Benefit Allowances

Other benefits may be available after an award for Compensation has been received. Here is a list of these special benefits.

Benefit	Rate	Date Rate Changed
Automobile Allowance	$21,488.29 once	10-01-19
Clothing Allowance	$830.56	12-01-19
Medal of Honor Pension	$1,388.68	12-01-19

State Veterans Benefits

Various states offer specific state veterans benefits that are not part of the Federal VA benefits program. Perhaps the most important are state veterans homes which are funded jointly by states and VA. There are approximately 161 homes in every state offering over 32,000 beds. Some states have as many as 8 veterans homes scattered geographically across the state. All states also offer various additional benefits to veterans to include state veterans cemeteries, special recognition license plates, property tax reduction, free hunting and fishing, state school tuition subsidies, state government hiring preferences and state parks admission as well as a whole host of other benefits. Some states are more generous than others and in some states veterans can receive a one-time cash stipend.

Loan Guaranty Program

Veterans, and eligible surviving spouses can become homeowners under the loan guaranty program. VA offers a home loan guaranty benefit and other housing-related programs to help buy, build, repair, retain, or adapt a home for personal occupancy. VA Home Loans are provided by private lenders, such as banks and mortgage companies. VA guarantees a portion of the loan, enabling the lender to provide the applicant with more favorable terms.

Education Benefits

Many benefits are available to advance the education and skills of veterans and service members. Spouses and family members may also be eligible for education and training assistance. In fact, 25 percent of those benefitting from VAs education programs are non-Veterans. Some might find they're eligible for more than one benefit or that one program is more suited to certain education and training goals than another. Here are the current education programs:

- The Post-9/11 GI Bill offers higher education and training benefits to Veterans, Servicemembers, and their families who served after Sept. 10, 2001.
- The Montgomery GI Bill assists active duty and Reservists with the pursuit of higher education degrees, certificates, and other education and training.
- Reserve Educational Assistance Program
- Veterans Educational Assistance Program
- Survivors and Dependents Educational Assistance Program
- National Testing Program
- National Call to Service Program

Vocational Rehabilitation

A veteran may receive Vocational Rehabilitation and Employment (VR&E) services to help with job training, employment accommodations, resume development, and job seeking skills. Other services may be provided to assist Veterans in starting their own businesses. Independent living services are for those who are severely disabled and unable to work in traditional employment. VA's Education and Career Counseling program is a great opportunity for veterans and service members as well as eligible family members to get personalized counseling and support to guide their career paths, ensure effective use of their VA benefits, and achieve their goals.

Homeless Veterans Program

No veteran should be without a place to call home. VA is committed to ending homelessness among veterans. The focus is threefold:

- Conducting coordinated outreach to proactively seek out veterans in need of assistance.
- Connecting homeless and at-risk veterans with housing solutions, health care, community employment services and other required supports.
- Collaborating with federal, state and local agencies; employers; housing providers, faith-based and community nonprofits; and others to expand employment and affordable housing options for veterans exiting homelessness.

The Right to an Appeal

Appealing a Veterans Benefits Administration Decision

Title 38 CFR § 3.103 Procedural due process and appellate rights. (a) Statement of policy. Every claimant has the right to written notice of the decision made on his or her claim, the right to a hearing, and the right of representation. Proceedings before VA are ex parte in nature, and it is the obligation of VA to assist a claimant in developing the facts pertinent to the claim and to render a decision which grants every benefit that can be supported in law while protecting the interests of the Government. The provisions of this section apply to all claims for benefits and relief, and decisions thereon, within the purview of this part 3. (Title 38 CFR Part 3)

Appealing a Veterans Health Administration Decision

Patients have the legal right to appeal to the Board of Veterans' Appeals (BVA) for a non-medical decision. The BVA has the power to overturn almost any non-medical decision by a VHA administrator or doctor. However, the appellant must file a Notice of Disagreement with the local VHA facility within one year of the contested decision. If VHA maintains its decision, the appellant will receive a Statement of the Case that will describe the reasons why the decision will be upheld. This then will initiate a formal appeal process with the BVA.

The other way to appeal a non-medical decision is to write a reconsideration request to the director of the local VHA facility within one year of the contested decision. One needs to explain why the decision is incorrect. Any new information that might support the disagreement should be included. If the decision is affirmed, the reconsideration request is considered a notice of disagreement for the BVA appeal process.

For a dispute about a medical decision, a patient has a right to a written notice of the decision and appeal rights. <u>For medical decisions, the BVA doesn't have any legal authority. The VA has created a "clinical appeals" process for contested medical decisions. The outcomes of the clinical appeal process are final. There's no right to judicial review</u>. In addition, there's at least one patient advocate at each VA medical facility. The patient advocate listens to complaints and helps resolve the issue before filing an appeal. However, a patient can directly appeal without using the patient advocate.

DISABILITY BENEFIT RATE CHARTS FOR 2020
EFFECTIVE DECEMBER 1, 2019 THROUGH NOVEMBER 30, 2020

Disability Compensation Rate Table for 2020 (In Dollars)

Disability Percent	10%	20%	30%	40%	50%	60%	70%	80%	90%	100%
Veteran Alone	142.29	281.27	435.69	627.61	893.43	1,131.68	1,426.17	1,657.80	1,862.96	3,106.04
Veteran & Spouse			486.69	696.61	979.43	1,234.68	1,547.17	1,795.80	2,017.96	3,279.22
Vet – Sp – 1 Child			525.69	747.61	1,043.43	1,311.68	1,636.17	1,897.80	2,132.96	3,406.04
Vet – 1 Child			469.69	673.61	950.43	1,200.68	1,507.17	1,749.80	1,966.96	3,221.85
Additional Child			25.00	34.00	43.00	51.00	60.00	68.00	77.00	86.05
Addt. Schoolchild			83.00	111.00	138.00	166.00	194.00	222.00	250.00	277.96
A&A for Spouse			48.00	63.00	80.00	96.00	111.00	127.00	143.00	158.82

If veteran has a spouse who requires A&A, add "A&A for spouse" to the amount of dependency & rate code above.

Special Monthly Compensation (SMC) Rate Table for 2020 (In Dollars)

SMC Schedule	L	L½	M	M½	N	N½	O/P	R.1	R.2/T	S
Veteran Alone	3,864.90	4,064.70	4,265.31	4,558.37	4,852.09	5,137.51	5,423.45	7,749.68	8,889.08	3,476.65
Veteran & Spouse	4,038.08	4,237.88	4,438.49	4,731.55	5,025.27	5,310.69	5,596.63	7,922.86	9,062.26	3,649.83
Vet – Sps – 1 Child	4164.90	4364.70	4565.31	4858.37	5152.09	5437.51	5723.45	8049.68	9189.08	3776.65
Vet – 1 Child	3980.71	4180.51	4381.12	4674.18	4967.90	5253.32	5539.26	7865.49	9004.89	3592.46
Additional Child	86.05	86.05	86.05	86.05	86.05	86.05	86.05	86.05	86.05	86.05
Addt. Schoolchild	277.96	277.96	277.96	277.96	277.96	277.96	277.96	277.96	277.96	277.96
A&A for Spouse	158.82	158.82	158.82	158.82	158.82	158.82	158.82	158.82	158.82	158.82
K	110.31	Usually added to other rate or paid as the rate when percentage is zero.								
Q	67.00	Paid in place of a rate.								

If veteran has a spouse who requires A&A, add "A&A for spouse" to the amount of dependency & rate code above

Dependency and Indemnity Compensation (DIC) for 2020

Basic Monthly Rate = $1,340.14, with 1 Child $1,672.14, with 2 Children $2,004.14, etc.

Allowances: with A&A $1,672.14, with Housebound $1,495.67, with 8 Yrs Continuous Disabled $1,624.71

1. Add **$284.57** for veteran's death, if veteran was in receipt of or entitled to receive compensation for a service-connected disability rated totally disabling (including a rating based on individual unemployability) for a continuous period of at least 8 years immediately preceding death AND the surviving spouse was married to the veteran for those same 8 years. (38 U.S.C. 1311(a)(2))
2. Add the following allowance for each dependent child under age 18: Effective 12/1/14 **$332.00** per child (38 U.S.C. 1311(b))
3. If the surviving spouse is entitled to Aid and Attendance, add **$332.00**. (38 U.S.C. 1311(c))
4. If the surviving spouse is entitled to Housebound, add **$155.53** (38 U.S.C. 1311(d))
5. If the surviving spouse has one or more children under the age 18 on the award, add the 2-year transitional benefit of **$286.00** effective, December 1, 2014 (38 U.S.C. 1311(f))

2020 Maximum Annual Veterans Pension Rates (MAPR)
Effective December 1, 2019 – 1.6% COLA Increase

If you are a veteran...	Annual	Monthly
Without Spouse or Child	$13,752	$1,146
No dependents, medical expenses must exceed 5% of MAPR	$687	$57
With One Dependent	$18,008	$1,500
With dependents, medical expenses must exceed 5% of MAPR	$900	$75
Housebound Without Dependents	$16,805	$1,400
Housebound With One Dependent	$21,063	$1,755
A&A Without Dependents	$22,939	$1,911
A&A With One Dependent	$27,195	$2,266
Two Vets Married to Each Other	$18,008	$1,500
Two Vets Married to Each Other One H/B	$21,063	$1,755
Two Vets Married to Each Other Both H/B	$24,114	$2,009
Two Vets Married to Each Other One A/A	$27,195	$2,266
Two Vets Married to Each Other One A/A One H/B	$30,241	$2,520
Two Vets Married to Each Other Both A/A	$36,387	$3,032
Add for Each Additional Child to any category above	$2,351	$195

2020 Maximum Annual Survivors Pension Rates (MAPR)
Effective December 1, 2019 – 1.6% COLA Increase

If you are a surviving spouse...	Annual	Monthly
MAPR Without Dependent Child	$9,224	$768
No dependents, medical expenses must exceed 5% of MAPR	$461	$38
MAPR With One Dependent Child	$12,072	$1,006
With dependents, medical expenses must exceed 5% of MAPR	$603	$50
Housebound Without Dependents	$11,273	$939
Housebound With One Dependent	$14,116	$1,176
A&A Without Dependents	$14,742	$1,228
A&A Without Dependents (SAW Veteran's Surviving Spouse)	$15,339	$1,278
A&A With One Dependent	$17,586	$1,465
A&A With One Dependent (SAW Veteran's Surviving Spouse)	$18,119	$1,509
SBP/MIW Annuity Limitation	$9,224	$768
Add for Each Additional Child	$2,351	$195
MAPR FOR CHILD ALONE	$2,351	$195
Child Earned Income Exclusion effective 1/1/2000	$7,200	$600

Chapter 2
Determining Eligibility and Entitlement

IN THIS CHAPTER:

ELIGIBILITY ISSUES

ENTITLEMENT ISSUES

ELIGIBILITY ISSUES

To be eligible for veterans benefits the applicant must meet the definition of a veteran, meet specified requirements for active duty and must have a discharge other than dishonorable. Reserve and Guard members are generally not eligible for benefits except under certain circumstances.

Definition of a Veteran

One must be a veteran in order to receive veterans benefits. Likewise, the benefit for a survivor must be linked to someone who was a veteran.

- "The term "veteran" means *a person who served in the active military, naval, or air service, and who was discharged or released therefrom under conditions other than dishonorable.*" 38 U.S.C. §101(2); Active military includes the Army, the Navy, the Marines, the Air Force and the Coast Guard
- National Guard and Reserve members are not considered veterans unless they were called up to active duty by the President of the United States and served the appropriate length of time to receive an award for a benefit or they honorably completed the length of obligation for which they were called.
- Disability Compensation and DIC are available to Reserve and Guard members who were not on active duty but sustained injury and certain medical conditions from active duty for training and injury from inactive duty for training

We often receive inquiries from would be veterans or family members of these people who want to know if they qualify for VA benefits. The first thing we have to determine with these inquiries is if the person for whom direct benefits or survivors benefits are available is actually a veteran. Of particular interest, we receive phone calls from former Reserve or Guard members who are senior citizens and who believe that they are veterans due to their active duty training to get into the Reserve or Guard. Not so. Others who spent 20 or more years and retired from the Reserve or Guard and have commissary privileges at a local military installation as well as receiving a military retirement income from their service often assume that they are eligible for VA benefits. It's just not so.

Title 38 USC Chapter 101 defines what a veteran is. As we will learn further on this is a rather narrow definition and there are numerous groups of people who have offered service to the country who are considered veterans for benefit purposes. Unfortunately, National Guard and Reserve members only qualify as veterans if they were called up under Title 10 of the US code by the president of the United States for active duty service. Since the Gulf War in 1990, 64% of all 1.2 million National Guard and reserve troops have been called up – some more than once. Between 2001 and 2003 alone, President Bush called up more than 300,000 Guard and Reserve members.

To be eligible for veterans benefits, members of the Guard or Reserves have to have completed their duty obligation or have completed at least 24 months on active duty – whichever is less. There is one exception to veterans benefits that are available to Reserve and Guard members regardless of whether they served before the Gulf War or since. If these people were injured or contracted certain diseases while engaged in training for inclusion in the Guard or Reserve, they are may be eligible for Disability Compensation or Dependency and Indemnity Compensation – DIC – caused by the illnesses or injuries. This is one exception where they don't have to be classified as veterans in order to get benefits.

In June 2015, Congress authorized that approximately 2,000 National Guard flight crews assigned to C123 aircraft that were used to disperse Agent Orange in Vietnam are also eligible for Disability Compensation benefits. Even though these pilots were not on active duty, the planes they flew were considered to be contaminated by agent orange and as such the pilots and crew would be eligible for any agent orange Disability Compensation benefits.

Other Groups Eligible for Veterans Benefits

There are others who are also considered veterans who have served in uniformed capacity.

- Aliens (non-US citizens) who did not request discharge during a period of hostilities
- full-time duty as a commissioned officer of the Public Health Service
- full-time duty as a commissioned officer of Coast and Geodetic, Environmental Science Services Administration and the National Oceanic and Atmospheric Administration (previous two organizations are now part of NOAA)
- full-time Reserve duty
- Merchant Marines who served during World War 2 and burial benefits and Pension for other Merchant Marines who served from August 15, 1945 through December 31, 1946
- service as a cadet in any of the 3 military academies
- other specialized active military service as specified in regulations or by the Secretary
- a very long list of Active military service participants (not active duty) in World War 2 (see Title 38 CFR Part 3)

It is surprising to many people that large numbers of aliens or non-US citizens have served honorably in the active military. As long as these service members did not request discharge during a period of war and received a discharge other than dishonorable, they are typically eligible for veterans benefits. But they must also meet the service periods for most benefits that are discussed further on.

Time spent in preparatory schools such as those for the Air Force, the Military Academy Preparatory School, the Naval Academy Preparatory School, the preparatory school for the Coast Guard and others are not considered veterans unless they continue on to active duty after the schooling. If so, then their time spent in the schooling is considered active duty. Otherwise the preparatory school can be considered active duty for training.

Historically immigrants who were not yet citizens of the United States represented 18% of the Union army in the Civil War. During World War I, 192,000 alien service members received citizenship during their service. Since World War 2 and up until the advent of the all-volunteer service in July 1973, not that many aliens served. Since the all-volunteer service was started and conscription known as the draft was dropped in 1973, aliens have been sought out to fill gaps in recruiting quotas. Mostly these are people who carry green cards from the Philippines or Mexico. By joining the service, they are given the opportunity to become naturalized citizens.

Recently, undocumented aliens with special skills have been recruited into the service. Since 2014, those who have completed basic training are given the opportunity to become naturalized citizens. From 1907 to 2010 more than 710,000 individuals were naturalized through military service. However, it should be remembered that there are a great number of individuals who served in the military who may not be citizens.

Besides members of the active military which includes the Army, the Navy, the Marines, the Air Force and the Coast Guard, there are 2 other uniformed services in the United States. Seven uniformed services in all. These other 2 are the commissioned officer corps of the Public Health

Service and the commissioned officer corps of the National Oceanic and Atmospheric Administration (NOAA). The Public Health Service is part of the Department of Health and Human Services. There are about 6,500 active commissioned officers in the Public Health Service and about 320 active commissioned officers in NOAA. They use naval uniforms and employ naval rank.

NOAA commissioned officers are pilots and naval officers who command NOAA aircraft and vessels. The Public Health Service is comprised of doctors and nurses and other health specialists who provide special services to public health and are be ready to respond to crises of public help all over the world. For example, officers of the Public Health Service were called into action to help combat the Ebola virus in Africa. The head of the Public Health Service is the Surgeon General of the United States who is a Rear Admiral.

There are likely scores of thousands of retired Public Health Service officers and perhaps thousands of NOAA retired officers. These commissioned officers have special assignments to be called up under military orders to serve all over the United States and when needed all over the world. They are considered veterans for VA benefits

We don't often think of Merchant Marines as being eligible for veterans benefits. Currently, only those who served on sea duty during World War 2 are eligible. It is interesting that World War 2 Merchant Mariners had a higher per capita casualty rate than the uniformed armed services. The Merchant Marine represents merchant ships flying the flag of America. Currently, out of about 1,300 bluewater merchant vessels owned by Americans only about a third fly the flag of the United States. The others are registered in foreign countries. During time of war, the Navy can press into service the Merchant Marine. This has happened during World War 2, Vietnam and Korea and to some extent the current Middle East conflicts. Members of the Merchant Marine who were pressed into service in combat zones since World War 2 have been trying to gain recognition as veterans for 50 years but have had no success.

Certain members of the Reserve compliments are employed full-time by their units to serve the readiness needs of the unit. They wear military uniforms and operate under a military hierarchy and put in a full work load for the unit every day. They are considered active duty and are eligible for veterans benefits. The National Guard also has such a program but they are not considered active duty or eligible for veterans benefits.

Additional Requirements for Receiving VA Benefits

Here are the basic requirements for receiving VA benefits which we will discuss in more detail in the rest of this chapter.

- Must meet definition of a veteran or considered as a veteran
- Must meet active duty requirements
- Must meet the period of active duty service requirements
- Service-connected disabilities cannot be a result of willful misconduct
- Pension is not available if discharge was due to willful misconduct
- Must have received an other than dishonorable discharge

We have already discussed the definition of a veteran and other individuals who are considered veterans. We will discuss further on more about the character of a discharge. Active duty and active duty for training and inactive duty for training will be addressed and what benefits are available. Also, since 1980, in order to receive most veterans benefits such as the education benefits, the loan guarantee, Pension, DIC, healthcare and other categories of benefits available to veterans, a veteran must serve at least 24 months or have been discharged due to medical conditions or have served the length of service for which the veteran was called up such as Reserve and National Guard members called to active duty. Life insurance benefits are the exception as they are always available regardless of character of discharge or period of service.

We will also discuss the special exception that applies to Disability Compensation eligibility. Finally, we will address the special case of willful misconduct. Occasionally, a discharge document will identify willful misconduct as a reason for discharge which may or may not be a discharge other than dishonorable. There are special rules pertaining to what is and is not willful misconduct and VA reserves the right to make the ultimate decision on qualification for certain benefits. As a general rule, willful misconduct is a bar to any veterans disability benefits but it may not be a bar to health care benefits.

Active Duty, Active Duty for Training and Inactive Duty for Training

Active duty is any active military naval and air service and includes a certain number of days of travel time after discharge. For purposes of qualifying for Disability Compensation or DIC, active duty can also include a special duty service called active duty for training, ACDUTRA, and inactive duty for training, IADT. ACDUTRA and IADT generally apply to Reserve and Guard components as well as ROTC participants and cadets of preparatory academies such as the Merchant Marine Academy. Please note that Cadets of the 3 military academies at West Point, Annapolis and Colorado Springs are considered active duty.

Disability Compensation and DIC are available to non-active duty participants under the following conditions.

- any period of Active Duty for Training during which a person in the line of duty is disabled or dies from a disease or injury incurred or aggravated in the line of duty, or
- any period of Inactive Duty Training during which a person in the line of duty is disabled or dies from an
  - injury incurred or aggravated in the line of duty, or from
  - an acute myocardial infarction, a cardiac arrest, or a cerebrovascular accident that occurred during such training .
  -

As we already know, Reserve and Guard members are not considered veterans for VA benefits unless they are actually called up to active service by the president. On the other hand, the basic training that all Reserve and Guard units go through when they first join can be considered active duty for purposes of veterans Disability Compensation benefits or DIC if the trainee is disabled or dies from a disease or injury incurred or aggravated in the line of duty while going through this basic training. Active duty for training can also include the extended annual training completed each year – usually in summer – under orders to maintain the units in combat ready status.

Inactive duty for training is generally the type of training from Reserve or Guard members done on weekends or the extended personal training done to learn special skills or to upgrade to another rank.

Please note that Inactive Duty for Training only allows for <u>disability or death as a result of injury while disability or death as a result of disease is limited to only 3 conditions – an acute myocardial infarction, a cardiac arrest or a cerebrovascular accident.</u>

Period of Active Duty Service

There is some confusion as to how much time a veteran had to have spent in active duty service in order to be eligible for any benefits. The rules below pertain primarily to Pension, education benefits and loan guarantees but as a general rule are applied to all benefits. But there are exceptions such as eligibility for Disability Compensation, life insurance and VA healthcare as well as full benefits for survivors of individuals who died on active duty regardless of how long they were in the service.

- Prior to (1981) generally each benefit defined its own length of duty service
- After 1981 – 24 months or more of active duty service or successful completion of the term of commitment for service
- Disability Compensation and DIC are some of a few exceptions from the 24 month rule

To be eligible for most veterans benefits, a minimum period of active duty of 24 continuous months or the full period for which a person is called or ordered to active duty must be completed. This rule has been in effect since October 16, 1981 for new enlistees. Prior to this date, there is no regular rule of length of service duty that applies for benefits and each benefit generally had its own rules.

Here are a few of the exceptions to this minimum period of active duty for benefits. However, there are more rules than just these.

- Benefits in connection with a service-connected disability or death do not have any prescribed length of service. If injury or illness occurs any time on active duty and results in a disability after discharge, the veteran or surviving spouse is eligible for Disability Compensation or DIC.
- If death occurs while on active duty, life insurance benefits are provided to named beneficiaries. Survivors may also be eligible for DIC from death in service.
- Any monies that have been contributed for educational benefits programs prior to discharge from service or death during service will be refunded to the participant or to the survivors.

In the Line of Duty and Willful Misconduct

In order to be eligible for a claim related to disability or death, the claimant had to have been in the line of duty when that injury or illness or death or occurred. It is important to note that a claimant may make a valid claim when he or she was in the line of duty even though a different injury or illness may have occurred when the veteran was not in the line of duty. Only a claim related to failure to be in the line of duty comes under scrutiny for being valid or not.

VA uses a circular definition to define in line of duty and it is best understood what line of duty is not. Not being in the line of duty includes actions such as willful misconduct, desertion, absent without leave, illness or injury in service caused by drug or alcohol or tobacco use after 1990 as well as injury or illness incurred while confined under a sentence of court-martial or being confined in a civilian jail for a committed felony while in the service. Absent without leave also requires careful scrutiny under a claim as the motives relating to AWOL must be examined and determination could be made that being absent without leave would still result in a valid claim. Exceptions usually apply only to absent without leave of less than 180 days. Specific rules in 38 CFR 3.301 cover the various contingencies associated with in line of duty.

For any claim related to a service-connected disability or death which would include Disability Compensation and DIC, the veteran service representative in the Regional Office for that claim must determine whether the disability or death was incurred in the line of duty. If the service records do not reflect willful misconduct or any other violation of the line of duty requirements but the nature of the claim raises suspicion that line of duty was avoided either through willful misconduct or other actions, the adjudicator has a responsibility to investigate.

On the other hand if the service records indicate that the disability or death was incurred in the line of duty, or flying in a military aircraft while on duty or was accidental such as vehicular accidents and no willful misconduct from police reports or medical records is indicated, VA must accept these findings and determine that the disabling condition or death was in the line of duty. Willful misconduct is covered in great detail in 38 CFR 3.301. It should also be noted that any service member on leave is considered on active duty and anything that happens during that period would be in the line of duty unless a line of duty determination soon after the incident determines otherwise.

> 38 CFR 3.301 (n) Willful misconduct means an act involving conscious wrongdoing or known prohibited action. A service department finding that injury, disease or death was not due to misconduct will be binding on the Department of Veterans Affairs unless it is patently inconsistent with the facts and the requirements of laws administered by the Department of Veterans Affairs.
>
> > (1) It involves deliberate or intentional wrongdoing with knowledge of or wanton and reckless disregard of its probable consequences.
> > (2) Mere technical violation of police regulations or ordinances will not per se constitute willful misconduct.
> > (3) Willful misconduct will not be determinative unless it is the proximate cause of injury, disease or death.

Perhaps one of the most common challenges for VA service representatives are injuries or death incurred while under the influence of alcohol or drugs. Under certain conditions, injuries from the use of alcohol or drugs constitute willful misconduct but only to the extent that judgment and abilities were impaired. For alcohol use, VA will determine a blood alcohol level of .08 or greater to constitute willful misconduct.

Vehicular accidents either caused by reckless behavior or violating rules or laws or being under the influence are a common in line of duty determination challenge for VA adjudicators. Police reports and medical records must be examined to determine if blood alcohol levels contributed to the accident. For example an enlisted man consumes several beers at the NCO club and subsequently is driving off-base and is involved in an automobile accident . The service member is injured resulting in a disability claim after that person was discharged from service. The accident report alcohol level was not above VA's established limit for willful misconduct. However the service member was determined by the police report to be at fault by driving recklessly. This claim would probably be classified as willful misconduct and be denied.

Prior to October 31, 1990 diseases directly caused by abuse of alcohol, drug abuse or tobacco use while in the service could be covered as service-connected. After this date, conditions caused or aggravated by these usages while in service are considered willful misconduct and are not covered. This also applies to any death caused by addiction to these substances for purposes of paying DIC – even if the death was in service. It should be noted however that if a different service connection condition after service resulted in drug or alcohol abuse, a newly arising disability due to secondary conditions causing drug or alcohol abuse would be considered service-connected – but only if that underlying service-connected disability caused the abuse.

Contracting a sexually transmitted disease such as venereal disease is not considered willful misconduct by VA. Suicide for willful misconduct is covered in 38 CFR 3.302.

Recreational use of alcohol or drugs in the service is not considered willful misconduct. However, alcohol abuse or drug abuse – not recreational use – as defined by VA in 38 CFR 3.301 is willful misconduct and could result in a discharge from service due to willful and persistent misconduct. Such a discharge will often be justified by mentioning willful and persistent misconduct on the discharge form. Here is a summary from the regulation pertaining to abuse. *"Drug abuse is the use of illegal drugs including prescription drugs illegally obtained for a purpose other than medically intended use or for intoxicating purposes."* Isolated use of drugs is not willful misconduct unless it results in a disabling condition or unless it can be shown is due to addiction. Contracting a venereal disease is not evidence of willful misconduct.

<u>A discharge that includes willful misconduct will bar a veteran from receiving Pension benefits and vocational rehabilitation benefits.</u>

Character of the Discharge

The requirement that a valid discharge from service must be other than dishonorable in order to qualify for VA benefits seems rather simple on the surface. In reality, there are a variety of different discharges that are characterized between an honorable discharge and a discharge that uses the word dishonorable. In some cases, VA will consider these other than honorable discharges as dishonorable even though the word dishonorable is not used. In other cases these discharges are considered as other than dishonorable.

As a general rule, discharges that are classified as general discharges are considered as other than dishonorable. But a general discharge is still a blight on a serviceman's application for civilian work. General discharges that reflect negative aspects of military conduct will jeopardize a veteran's ability to use education benefits or to be able to reenlist after discharge. Education benefits specifically require an honorable discharge and any other discharge will disqualify for those benefits.

A discharge carrying the words "dishonorable" is very rare as such a discharge can only be handed down to an enlisted member by a general court-martial.

Some discharges are characterized as other than honorable with the reason for separation based on a pattern of behavior that constitutes a significant departure from conduct expected of members of military services. Such discharges may be based on absent without leave, drug use the use of force or violence to produce serious bodily injury or death, abuse of a special position of trust, disregard by a superior of customary superior subordinate relationships, acts or omissions that endanger the security of the United States or the health and welfare of other members of the military services and deliberate acts or omissions that seriously endanger the health and safety of other persons. Depending on the specific facts of the history of such behavior, VA can choose whether to classify such a discharge as other than dishonorable or dishonorable.

The following discharges are specifically mentioned in the regulations as barring the payment of benefits and would thus be classified as dishonorable.

1. As a conscientious objector who refused to perform military duty, wear the uniform, or comply with lawful order of competent military authorities.
2. By reason of the sentence of a general court-martial.
3. Resignation by an officer for the good of the service.
4. As a deserter.
5. As an alien during a period of hostilities, where it is affirmatively shown that the former service member requested his or her release.
6. Acceptance of an undesirable discharge to escape trial by general court-martial.
7. Mutiny or spying.
8. An offense involving moral turpitude. This includes, generally, conviction of a felony.
9. Willful and persistent misconduct
10. Homosexual acts involving aggravating circumstances or other factors affecting the performance of duty.

Examples of homosexual acts involving aggravating circumstances or other factors affecting the performance of duty include child molestation, homosexual prostitution, homosexual acts or conduct accompanied by assault or coercion, and homosexual acts or conduct taking place between service members of disparate rank, grade, or status when a service member has taken advantage of his or her superior rank, grade, or status.

It should be noted that officers are generally not discharged from service by a court-martial. Officers who are convicted of a court-martial with a recommendation for dismissal are forced to resign for the good of the service. Such a discharge for officers is considered dishonorable. There may be other reasons why officers are forced to resign for the good of the service as well.

Certain discharges are administrative discharges and are not characterized by any wrong behavior. VA will examine each type of discharge and determine whether that discharge constitutes other than dishonorable or dishonorable. These include the following type of separations.

1. Entry level separation. Uncharacterized administrative separations of this type shall be considered under conditions other than dishonorable.
2. Void enlistment or induction. Uncharacterized administrative separations of this type shall be reviewed based on facts and circumstances surrounding separation, with reference to the provisions of §3.14 of this part, to determine whether separation was under conditions other than dishonorable.
3. Dropped from the rolls. Uncharacterized administrative separations of this type shall be reviewed based on facts and circumstances surrounding separation to determine whether separation was under conditions other than dishonorable.

For education benefits the discharge must be honorable. There is no other option to get education benefits under the G.I. Bill.

Appealing the Character of the Discharge

One opportunity for any attorney is to represent a veteran client with a military review board. All discharges that have an undesirable characterization can be challenged with the intent of changing the characterization of that discharge. An attorney can charge a fee for representing veteran clients for the purpose of changing a discharge as this is not part of the prohibition on charging a fee for assisting with an initial claim. Or if you are an attorney and this type of representation is outside of your specialty, there are many law firms that specialize in this area that you can contact on behalf of your client and who will help with a correction of a discharge or a discharge upgrade.

Each of the military services maintains a discharge review board with authority to change, correct or modify discharges or dismissals not issued by a sentence of a general court-martial. The board has no authority to address medical discharges.

Veterans with disabilities incurred or aggravated during active duty may qualify for medical or related benefits regardless of separation and characterization of service. Veterans separated administratively under other than honorable conditions may request that their discharge be reviewed for possible re-characterization, provided they file their appeal within 15 years of the date of separation. Questions regarding the review of a discharge should be addressed to the appropriate discharge review board at the address listed on DD Form 293.

The veteran or, if the veteran is deceased or incompetent, the surviving spouse, next of kin or legal representative, may apply for a review of discharge by writing to the military department concerned, using DD Form 293, "Application for the Review of Discharge from the Armed Forces of the United States."

If more than 15 years have passed since discharge, appeals must be directed to the Board for Correction of Military/Naval Records of the respective service. The BCM/NR hears a wide array of appeals and correction requests, and can be utilized by Active Duty, Reserve, National Guard, retired and discharged veterans alike. Normally, an appeal must be filed within 3 years of the occurrence of an error or injustice; however, exceptions are often made.

Any veterans can request that VA itself conduct a discharge review when making application for benefits. Based on feedback from attorneys who help veterans with reclassification of discharge, VA is usually not as accommodating in reviewing and allowing a different interpretation of the character of an undesirable discharge for benefit purposes. VA cannot actually change the character of the discharge, only interpret whether benefits can be permitted under that discharge.

Providing Proof of Service

38 CFR § 3.203 requires that a claimant for benefits submit evidence of service before entitlement to benefits can be established . This evidence must also be submitted before VA will institute its "duty to assist" which is discussed in a subsequent chapter. The evidence must include the length, time and character of service. In all cases, this is the DD 214 issued since 1950 and other various service discharge documents issued prior to that date. The regulation requires that the document has to be an original or a certified copy of an original.

Technically, if any document is submitted that indicates the claimant could be eligible for veterans benefits, VA should follow through and find the eligibility documents on its own. This never happens and the Regional Office will generally delay the application unless an original or certified copy of the discharge is sent in with the claim. We have found over the years that the Regional Office may be lax on this rule and an uncertified copy can be submitted. However, you should not take a chance that the service representative on the other end will demand a certified copy which will significantly delay the claim process.

For any discharges after October 1, 1979, the DD 214 consisted of multiple pages. Submitting an uncertified copy of page 4 of the DD 214 after 1979 is sufficient for evidence and the original document or a certified copy is not required. Submission of claims through the online eBenefit process also does not require submission of the discharge because VA will search its database for the appropriate discharge document and even produce an online certificate that substitutes for the discharge.

Documents pertaining to veterans benefits are kept at The National Personnel Records Center which is part of the National Archives of the United States. It is located in St. Louis Missouri and contains the records for over 60 million former service members. These records include Copies of all DD 214 discharge records after 1950 and applicable discharge documents prior to 1950. Since 1995, all discharges have been stored electronically under the joint DoD and VA DEERS system. They are now available through eBenefits online – the online veterans application and records management system for individual veterans. VA has also gone back to Vietnam veterans and earlier and stored discharges in this system as well. Most of these records can now be obtained online.

Official military personnel files of veterans and inpatient hospital records of former active-duty service members, as well as outpatient and other health treatment records of veterans and dependents and retirees at military healthcare facilities are also archived. These latter outpatient treatment records are called by VA "service treatment records." From the 1990s through 2012, medical records and personnel records had been turned over to the Department of Veterans Affairs Records Management Center in St. Louis which shares its documents with the Personnel Records Center upon request when an SF 180 form is submitted. The RMC still maintains these previous records, but has found a new task by providing FOIA (Freedom of Information Act) requests for records in the VBMS database.

Obtaining personnel and service treatment records from the National Records Center is often a vital part of any claim for service-connected disability or for the discharge document which has been lost or for discharges that are not on the Department of Defense database. This is done through Form SF 180. Records in VBMS cannot be retrieved through the SF 180. They must be requested through a FOIA letter or through a local Regional Office FOIA representative.

Federal law requires that requests through SF 180 must be signed as hard copy and dated by the veteran or next of kin. Even though you can request the records online, it does you little good because the records center will still require a printed copy for you to sign. If you do it online, you can print out the signature page and either fax or mail it to the address on the form. If it is a next of kin of a deceased veteran submitting an SF 180, that person must provide proof of death such as a copy of a death certificate, a letter from a funeral home or a published obituary. It may take a number of weeks to get copies of the records requested.

If records are required more quickly, you can use the Aardvark Research Group. This private company is located near the National Personnel Records Center and will provide certified copies of original DD 214's, usually within a week for $89. Records can be ordered online through the company's website at www.aardvarkresearchgroup.com. We also provide a large list of other records researchers who are authorized through the records center on our Claim Support Disc.

If you have submitted Form SF 180 and it has been months and you have received nothing back, unfortunately you are stuck. You cannot then go to an expediter like Aardvark Research Group to go around the system. The records center will only recognize one request at a time. If you need the DD 214 in a hurry you must use the expediter before you submit the SF 180.

The records center experienced a difficult-to-extinguish fire in 1973 which damaged or destroyed service records for 16 to 18 million Army and Air Force veterans who were discharged between 1912 through 1964. The damage was not due to fire but due to water damage from massive amounts of water needed to contain the fire which occurred on a floor above the floor where these records were kept. Because so many records were involved, they could not be dried out soon enough and mold took over and destroyed them. In some cases the service records can be reconstructed from alternate sources such as base or unit level records, though in some cases, some records are completely irretrievable. You can also contact the researchers on our list on the Claim Support Disc as many of them specialize in uncovering archive records that can substantiate service when discharges are not available.

Records which were damaged or lost due to the fire can take several months or longer to research and complete. From our experience the time is more likely several months. Generally records can be reconstructed if the veteran or the family can provide information regarding the place of discharge, the last unit of assignment and the place of entry into the service.

Some states maintain archives of discharge documents that were recorded with the county recorder when the veteran was discharged from service. Usually the state Department of Veterans Affairs will know where these records are kept or will maintain the records themselves. Always try and find the records this way if the records center in St. Louis indicates that it cannot find a discharge or other service records.

If the Regional Office is also aware that records were destroyed in the fire it can become involved in the search through its systems. In order to facilitate searches of auxiliary records, the veteran or claimant normally will need to complete *NA Form 13055*, so the Regional Office has sufficient information to submit a request through its sources.

ENTITLEMENT ISSUES

There are specific entitlement requirements inherent to each of the following benefits: Compensation, SMC, Pension, DIC, Aid and Attendance and Housebound Allowances, VA Healthcare and Burial Benefits.

Besides the benefits above, there are other benefits available to veterans or their survivors such as parents DIC, education assistance, loan guaranty, vocational rehabilitation, life and disability insurance and a number of other support programs. We do not address entitlement these other benefits in this chapter, however we cover them as separate issues in subsequent chapters.

Submitting an Intent to File – VA Form 21-0966

The Intent to File Has a Number of Advantages
Submitting an "Intent to File" is an important focus of this book because the Intent to File goes hand-in-hand with the key feature of this publication which is a reliance on filing "Fully Developed Claims." We will go into a more detail on the Fully Developed Claim (FDC) further on. The big difference between an FDC and a standard claim is it takes much more effort and time to collect the evidence for an FDC. On the other hand, the Fully Developed Claim Program produces a much faster decision that is more likely to result in an award.

Submitting an Intent to File allows you to lock in an effective date for payment while you are working on the details of the claim. In fact, you have a whole year from submitting the intent to submit your evidence. We hope that information in this book will help you avoid taking up to one year to submit evidence and we will help you understand how to collect information more expeditiously so that you can get the complete claim filed as soon as possible.

There is one major disadvantage, however, to submitting an Intent to File with a Pension claim. If you are relying on medical deduction costs to entitle you to Pension benefits, where you would otherwise not be entitled, you need to demonstrate to VA that you have actually experienced those costs prior to application. By submitting the application early without evidence, VA will come back and either deny the claim or ask for the evidence that you did not submit. Best not to submit an Intent to File until you're actually entitled to benefits.

Three Ways to File
An "Intent to File" can be submitted in one of the following three ways (38 CFR 3.155):

(i) Saved electronic application. When an application otherwise meeting the requirements of this paragraph (b) is electronically initiated and saved in a claims-submission tool within a VA web-based electronic claims application system prior to filing of a complete claim, VA will consider that application to be an Intent to File a claim. (Currently the system used by VA for initiating an Intent to File electronically is the eBenefits program which we discuss below.)

(ii)   Written intent on prescribed Intent to File a claim form. The submission to an agency of original jurisdiction of a signed and dated Intent to File a claim, on the form prescribed by the Secretary for that purpose, will be accepted as an Intent to File a claim. VA Form 21-0966

(iii)   Oral intent communicated to designated VA personnel and recorded in writing. An oral statement of Intent to File a claim will be accepted if it is directed to a VA employee designated to receive such a communication, the VA employee receiving this information follows the provisions set forth in § 3.217(b), and the VA employee documents the date VA received the claimant's Intent to File a claim in the claimant's records.

Forms to Use for a Paper Filing

Once you feel that you can justify a claim for benefits and not waste your time or VA's time, you should proceed to submit an "Intent to File." An "Intent to File," before March of 2015, was known as an "informal claim" for benefits. An informal claim could be submitted just that way – informally. This means that any notification that was sent to VA with an intention to file a claim and with enough information on the veteran and with a description of the benefit sought, would create an effective date. That is no longer the case and the prescribed system outlined above must now be used or you do not get an effective date.

An "Intent to File" is typically used for application for new benefits. If you are applying for a revaluation of existing benefits or a change in existing benefits, you should use a formal request on the appropriate VA form to establish an effective date. Here is the information that you should send to establish an effective date for an original claim.

- VBA Form 21-0966 INTENT TO FILE
- A copy Veteran's Discharge (DD 214 or equivalent; although this is not required it is helpful

We have provided the VBA 21-0966 INTENT TO FILE for you on the "Claim Support Disc" under the folder name "2 Application for Compensation and DIC." On the 0966, ignore #15 entirely. It is a huge hassle to have the claimant's Representative sign. The claimant should be the only one signing. Also, do not use the electronic signature under #14a.

<u>Try to include a copy of the veteran's honorable discharge (DD 214 or equivalent) when you fax or deliver the "Intent to File" to a Regional Office. Sometimes, with only a 0966 in hand, the Regional Office struggles to locate the veteran's records and establish his or her identity and service. Including the discharge will help VA immensely.</u>

It is extremely important that you check one of the boxes on item #13 on the Intent to File form. You have three choices: COMPENSATION, PENSION and SURVIVORS PENSION AND OR DEPENDENCY AND INDEMNITY COMPENSATION (DIC). If you do not check one of these boxes, the form is considered incomplete and you will not receive your effective date. Sometimes, you don't receive notice of this until several weeks later and you have perhaps lost a month on your effective date.

Importance of Filing to Get an Effective Date

Again, the primary purpose of an Intent to File is to establish an effective date. When the Intent to File is received, it will be date stamped and that date will become your Date of Claim. The effective date could be the Date of Claim but not always. We discuss effective dates in a section below. Remember, do not submit an Intent to File unless you are sure that you do have a valid claim for benefits.

You will fax or mail the form to VA's Evidence Intake Center in Jainesville, Wisconsin. If it is close to the end of the month you may have to hand carry your Intent to File into your Regional Office to get a date stamp. VA will not use a postal date or a delivery receipt or a mailroom diary for an effective date. The Intent to File must officially be handled by an authorized representative of the VA and stamped by hand with the date stamp machine.

You can also use eBenefits to submit the Intent to File online. As soon as you complete and save your personal information online with eBenefits , VA will recognize the date and time you submitted the information as an Intent to File. If you use eBenefits for an Intent to File, don't complete the application and submit it online. That could end up being a disaster. Just leave the incomplete application and if you decide to use eBenefits after you have developed your claim, you can go back and do so and submit all of the evidence as well. You cannot use eBenefits to file a Pension claim, but you can use it in the manner in which we described above, as VA will not know what you are filing for if you fill out an incomplete claim. As with any other form of Intent to File, you now have 1 year to complete your claim. We discuss the pros and cons of eBenefits further on.

We highly recommend faxing a few working days before the month's end. Save the original or certified copy of the discharge as well as the original 0966 and fax report to include in the fully developed claim you will submit later on. The fax report will act as your evidence in case the department loses it. See the Claim Support Disc for fax information.

Verification of Active Duty Service and Character of the Discharge

In order to receive benefits, the Regional Office must verify that the person making application is a veteran and completed required active duty service with a discharge other than dishonorable. We discussed what it means to be a veteran in a section above and went into detail on active duty, active duty for training, inactive duty for training, willful misconduct and characterization of discharges. Please review if you have any questions on all of this. In this section we will discuss how VA verifies what was discussed above.

Active service includes the following:

- active duty
- any period of active duty for training (ADT) during which a person is disabled or dies from a disease or injury incurred or aggravated in the line of duty, or
- any period of inactive duty for training (IADT) during which a person is disabled or dies from an injury incurred or aggravated in the line of duty or from any of the following conditions that occurred during training:
  - acute myocardial infarction
  - cardiac arrest, or
  - a cerebrovascular accident and
  - sexual assault constitutes an injury for the purposes of this block.

Time spent proceeding directly to and from active duty for training is also considered as part of the active or inactive duty for training as specified in 38 CFR 3.6(e).

We addressed the need for VA to verify veteran status for active duty and discharge characterization before the Regional Office will proceed with a claim. For the Army, Navy, Coast Guard, Marines and Air Force since 1950, this is done through examining the discharge document DD 214. For these military services prior to 1950 there were a variety of different documents used that verified service. Other uniformed services provide various documents to verify discharge from active duty. Here are examples of acceptable documentary evidence of service for eligibility determinations.

- DD 214 printed prior to July 1, 1979 for Army, Navy, Coast Guard, Marines and Air Force – either the original or a certified copy
- A certified abstract or copy of the discharge from the National Records Center in St. Louis
- PHS 1867 for service by commissioned officers of the US Public Health Service – original or certified copy
- NOAA 56-16 report of transfer or discharge for uniformed members of the NOAA – original or certified copy
- NGB for separation and service from the National Guard – original or certified copy
- DD 214 or DD 215 as a digitally signed online form issued since August 1, 2008
- DD 214 certified copy from a state archive that recorded the document for the discharged veteran as a service provided by some states
- DD 214 issued after July 1, 1979 – any carbon copy from the document

- DD 214 for active duty by reservists or guard – original or certified copy

It should be noted that you should never submit an original copy of your discharge. Years ago, VA was required to return your original copy. With the new scanning process for all documents at the Janesville, Wisconsin scanning center there is no procedure in place for sending back scanned documents and they are instead transferred to a storage facility after scanning. However, once scanned into VBMS, you should technically never have to submit a discharge ever again. But don't leave that to chance.

You will not receive back your original copy of your discharge under the new procedures. You should also never submit original copies of court records and papers, and marriage, birth, and death certificates. For the same reason, the scanning center will not return them to you and they will be transferred to some obscure storage facility as in Raiders of the Lost Ark, never to be seen again. VA will accept uncertified copies of all of official documents and may accept uncertified copies of discharges.

We have found that uncertified copies of discharge documents can be accepted. This does not seem to be a consistent behavior from the Regional Offices, but we suspect now that the Regional Offices have access to all discharge information in the common database from DoD/VA, the Veterans Service Representative can easily compare discharge information on the computer with the uncertified copy.

If the discharge was destroyed in the fire at the Records Center, many veterans have other evidence of service such as discharge certificates from their service. If these certificates contain enough information to verify the name of the veteran or the name under which the veteran served, the date of birth, the Social Security number and the dates of service, these certificates can be submitted as alternative evidence to the Regional Office. The Veteran Service Representative would then verify service by reconstructing the discharge. If this alternative evidence is not adequate, the benefit applied for will be denied until proper evidence has been produced.

Priority Claims

The Department of Veterans Affairs recognizes that certain claims for disability need to be processed more quickly than other claims. The reasons for this are based on hardship or status or impending death or severe illness or injury. Fully Developed Claims and claims for POWs and Medal of Honor recipients are also recognized as priority claims and receive priority treatment as well. Here are the rules from the 2018 adjudication manual M21-1 pertaining to priority claims.

General Information about Claims That Require Priority Processing
Listed below are the types of claims that require priority processing:

Claims from any claimant who is

- a participant in the Fully Developed Claim (FDC) Program
- homeless or experiencing extreme financial hardship
- terminally ill
- more than 85 years old, or
- a survivor of a former Prisoner of War (FPOW).

Claims from any current or former member of the Armed Forces who

- became very seriously ill or injured/seriously ill or injured (VSI/SI) during service and is not already receiving Department of Veterans Affairs (VA) disability benefits
- is diagnosed with Amyotrophic Lateral Sclerosis (ALS) or Lou Gehrig's Disease
- is an Former Prisoner of War (FPOW), or
- received the Medal of Honor.

Priority treatment from the BVA. The Board of Veterans' Appeals (BVA) allows a case to advance on the docket of appeals if there is good cause. BVA determines whether good cause exists to warrant advancing a case on the docket. This good cause would likely include any of the priority handling issues above except for fully developed claims which would not be included.

Upon receipt of one of the types of claims identified above, Regional Offices (ROs) must take any action on the claim that is necessary to move it to the next stage in the claims process before taking action on any other non-priority claim. To ensure a claim requiring priority processing is expedited at all stages of the claims process, ROs must also case-manage such claims by

- frequently following up on pending actions
- utilizing issue-specific coordinators, such as Military Records Specialists, when applicable
- using the telephone to contact homeless Veterans and to conduct development activities with other types of claimants, whenever possible, and
- collaborating with the Veterans Health Administration (VHA) and other involved counterparts.

Priority Processing of Claims from Homeless Veterans

Upon receipt of an application for benefits that contains a telephone number but no mailing address; attempt to contact the claimant by telephone to obtain a current mailing address. All ROs are required to have either a Homeless Veterans Claims Coordinator (HVCC) or a Homeless Veterans Outreach Coordinator (HVOC).

Claims from homeless Veterans and from Veterans who are at immediate risk of homelessness are monitored and tracked by the local HVCC or designee.

Claims Requiring Priority Processing Because of Extreme Financial Hardship

If a claimant states that he/she is experiencing extreme financial hardship and submits documentation to support the assertion, accept the claimant's statement as factual.

Documentation to support the assertion of extreme financial hardship includes, but is not limited to,

- an eviction notice or statement of foreclosure
- notices of past-due utility bills, and/or
- collection notices from creditors.

A Veterans Service Center Manager (VSCM) or Pension Management Center Manager (PMCM) may designate that a claim requires priority processing because of extreme financial hardship even though the documentation described in this block does not exist.

Priority Processing of Claims From VSI/SI Claimants

For the purposes of this topic, a serious illness or injury is defined as a disability that

- occurred as a result of participation in a military operation, and
- will likely result in discharge from military service.

The Department of Defense (DoD) determines whether a service member is:

- VSI
- SI, or
- not seriously ill or injured (NSI).

> All service members categorized by DoD as VSI or SI are considered seriously disabled for VA purposes.
> In the absence of an indicator from DoD that a claimant is VSI/SI, a VSI/SI Coordinator may decide whether a claimant has a serious illness or injury.
> Although VSI/SI Coordinators should contact and assist individuals that DoD has categorized as NSI, their claims do not require case management and priority processing unless they are one of the other types of claims identified in M21-1, Part III, Subpart ii, 1.D.1.a.

All ROs must designate a VSI/SI Coordinator, and VSCMs/PMCMs are responsible for ensuring claims from VSI/SI claimants are case-managed by the Special Operations Team. Duties of the VSI/SI Coordinator include, but are not limited to,

- ensuring the Very Seriously Injured/Seriously Injured claim flash is appended to the claimant's record
- acting as a liaison with VA medical facilities, military facilities, and RO divisions, and
- acting as a direct point of contact for VSI/SI claimants and their dependents.

Prior to awarding benefits to a claimant, ensure he/she is discharged from service.

- A service member may receive treatment at a VA or DoD medical facility for several months before actual separation from service.
- Pre-discharge sites do not process claims requiring case management, including claims from VSI/SI claimants. Per M21-1, Part III, Subpart iii, 2.A.1.e, the station of origination (SOO) is responsible for processing these types of claims.

Claims Requiring Priority Processing Because of Terminal Illness
Upon receipt of medical evidence showing a claimant has an illness that is likely terminal in nature, present the evidence to a Coach or Assistant Coach for a determination as to whether or not priority processing of the associated claim is warranted. When determining whether priority processing is warranted, consider

- the likelihood the claimant will pass away before completion of the claims process, and
- the probable need for additional benefits, such as the benefits payable based on a claimant's need for aid and attendance.

Alerting the Regional Office to a Priority Claim
There is no specific form for alerting your Regional Office that your claim should receive priority status. Some of the older claims forms provided for a comments section where someone could put in that information, but the newer forms do not have that. We recommend you provide A VA Form 21-4138 with the title "I AM REQUESTING PRIORITY HANDLING OF MY CLAIM." Then you could indicate on the form that evidence has been submitted in those cases where evidence needs to be submitted. In those cases where you simply need to point out to VA that the claimant fits the category, then include that instead of identifying evidence.

Under the new paperless system, priority requests often get lost or ignored. We have found that after the claim has been filed, we must go back and verify with VA – typically with a phone call – to reaffirm priority handling or it just doesn't happen.

Understanding Effective Dates

IN THIS SECTION:

- Date of Payment
- General Effective Date Rules
- Effective Date of Claim Made within 1 Year of Discharge
- Effective Date with Correction of Military Records
- Effective Date under Liberalizing Laws or Issues Approved by the Secretary
- Effective Date for Reopened Claims
- Effective Date for Reevaluation for Increased Rating Claims
- Effective Date for Pending Claims with No Adjudication
- Effective Date for Claims Involving Clear and Unmistakable Error (CUE)
- Effective Date for Newly Obtained Service Records
- Nehmer Effective Date Rules
- Effective Dates for Death Benefits
- Effective Dates and Benefit Payments Unique to Pension Claims

Establishing an effective date for your claim is an extremely important part of the claim. The effective date determines when VA will start paying you when a claim is approved. For any formal application for benefits, the date that service representatives receive the application or Intent to File, either at the scanning center or in the Regional Office, becomes the "Date of Claim." Usually, the Date of Claim is also the effective date but not always. We will discuss other effective date options further on in this section.

As a general rule, benefits are paid from the first day of the month following the month of the effective date. (See the regulation below)

If the applicant did not meet the entitlement criteria for the benefit at the effective date but met those criteria at a later date, the later date becomes the effective date and benefits will be paid from the first day of the month following that later date.

For veterans who died and for their survivors' benefits, the benefit will start the first day of the month following the month of death as long as a claim is submitted within one year of the death.

Consider this example. An application for Compensation is made based on a condition that resulted from an injury in service, but the veteran is not currently experiencing any chronic disabling symptoms. In other words, the Regional Office determines that the condition for establishing service connection does exist but does not meet chronicity rules for establishing service connection. This will generally result in a denial of benefits. Evidence must be submitted within a year of the denial that the chronicity test has been met. Medical evidence indicating the date when the condition became chronic is the point at which entitlement for granting a benefit would occur and this would be the defining date for payment of benefits. Failure to submit evidence within one year of the denial will require reapplying for the benefit.

Another example might be an application for Pension where the war veteran was 64 ½ years old and could not provide evidence of being totally disabled. This will generally result in a denial. Evidence must be submitted within one year of the denial to substantiate entitlement. In this case, when the veteran turns 65, entitlement is met and that becomes the effective date.

For any application where qualification for benefit is otherwise assumed – unlike the examples above – you should always establish an effective date at the earliest possible date. This can be done through a an "Intent to File," Submitting an "Intent to File" – generally via VA Form 21-0966 – allows the applicant to notify VA that the applicant or claimant will be turning in a formal claim for a benefit at a future date. VA recognizes an "Intent to File" for establishing an effective date for back-pay purposes.

For example, the veteran is assembling a rather complicated application for Compensation that may take three or four months to get all of the medical information as well as lay testimonies. The veteran should, at the earliest possible point in the current month, submit an Intent to File to establish an effective date. When the benefit is approved, payment will start from the first day of the month following the month of the effective date. Failure to do this could result in the loss of benefit payments. We discussed Intent to File in detail in a previous section of this chapter.

There is another decided advantage to submitting an Intent to File. You have an entire year after the effective date of the of the filing to provide all of the information to the Regional Office in the form of a fully developed claim but still keep the benefit payment stream as if you had filed a formal claim at the time you submitted the Intent to File. In other words, when the benefit is approved, you will receive a sizable retroactive benefit to the first day of the month following the month in which you filed filed for and received the Date of Claim stamp.

Date of Payment

> 38 CFR §3.31 Commencement of the period of payment.
> Regardless of VA regulations concerning effective dates of awards, and except as provided in paragraph (c) of this section, payment of monetary benefits based on original, reopened, or increased awards of Compensation, Pension, dependency and indemnity Compensation, or a monetary allowance under 38 U.S.C. chapter 18 for an individual who is a child of a Vietnam veteran or a child of a veteran with covered service in Korea may not be made for any period prior to the first day of the calendar month following the month in which the award became effective. However, beneficiaries will be deemed to be in receipt of monetary benefits during the period between the effective date of the award and the date payment commences for the purpose of all laws administered by the Department of Veterans Affairs except that nothing in this section will be construed as preventing the receipt of retired or retirement pay prior to the effective date of waiver of such pay in accordance with 38 U.S.C. 5305.

Almost always, according to the rule above, payment starts on the first day of the month following the month of the effective date. As outlined above, there are some exceptions to this rule. For example there is a liberalizing Law under Pension that allows for payment of benefits for up to 1 year prior to the Date of Claim. Also rules allow for payments for certain survivor benefits for a one-time outlay for the month of death of the veteran. We will discuss these exceptions in further detail below

For the rest of this section we will address specific rules pertaining to different types of effective dates that are recognized in the regulations.

General Effective Date Rules

The Department of Veterans Affairs does not want to create a situation where benefits for claims can be paid retroactively for a large number of years prior to the actual application for a benefit. It is irrelevant whether the claimant actually was entitled years prior to making the claim, the intent is to avoid retroactive payments. It is understandable that creating a precedent for back payments could bankrupt not only VA but also create a huge entitlement obligation for the US government. Therefore, the rules pertaining to effective dates and payment dates generally try to restrict any retroactive payments to no more than a year before application. In most cases, payment dates are the first day of the month following the Date of Claim or the first day of the month after the date of application in which entitlement actually arises.

On the other hand, it could take a great deal of time before a final decision on a benefit claim, including an appeal process, is made and that would create several years of back payments. The Regional Office will try everything it can to avoid a lengthy decision on a claim. Decisions on appeals are a different matter. A Board of Veterans Appeals decision could take 5 years or longer and if the claim then goes to the Court Of Appeals for Veterans Claims or on to the US District Court for Appeals it could be many many years before a final decision is made.

The general rule for an effective date is it cannot be a date earlier than the receipt of an application for benefits. (38 USC Section 5110). If the claimant was not entitled to benefits at the Date of Claim then the effective date is the date after the Date of Claim when the applicant is actually entitled. We discussed this rule somewhat in previous paragraphs of this section with some examples. For Disability Compensation claims a delayed date typically means that the service connection did not exist at the time of claim but manifested later or a change in the law authorized benefits at a date later than the initial claim. An example of this could be an Agent Orange claim where a veteran made claim for type II diabetes in 2008 but diabetes was not recognized as a presumptive condition for Agent Orange until 2010.

For Veterans Pension claims, there are really only two entitlement requirements – assuming the veteran meets the required veteran status. The veteran had to be a war veteran meeting that definition and be totally disabled prior to age 65 or age 65 and older. The requirement for Survivors Pension does not even require the disability or age test for the deceased veteran but there is a marriage test for the surviving spouse. Most effective dates for Pension claims are black and white. The claimant meets the requirement for effective date or there's no claim.

Effective Date of Claim Made within 1 Year of Discharge

For Disability Compensation requiring service connection, the effective date is the day following separation from active service or date entitlement arose if the claim is received within 1 year after separation from service. If the claim is filed after the one year deadline the effective date is the Date of Claim, or date entitlement arose, whichever is later. Separation from service means separation under conditions other than dishonorable from continuous active service which extended from the date the disability was incurred or aggravated.

For a presumptive service connection the effective date is is the date the entitlement arose, if the claim is received within 1 year after separation from active duty; otherwise it is the Date of Claim, or date entitlement arose, whichever is later. Where the requirements for service connection (presumptive service connection) are met during service, the effective date will be the day following separation from service if there was continuous active service following the period of service on which the presumption is based and a claim is received within 1 year after separation from active duty.

Effective Date with Correction of Military Records
Where entitlement is established because of the correction, change or modification of a military record, or of a discharge or dismissal, by a Board established under 10 U.S.C. 1552 or 1553, or because of other corrective action by competent military naval, or air authority, the award will be effective from the latest of these dates:

> (1) Date application for change, correction, or modification was filed with the service department, in either an original or a disallowed claim;

> (2) Date of receipt of claim if claim was disallowed; or

> (3) One year prior to date of reopening of disallowed claim.

Effective Date under Liberalizing Laws or Issues Approved by the Secretary

> 38 CFR §3.114 Change of law or Department of Veterans Affairs issue.

> (a) Effective date of award. Where Pension, Compensation, dependency and indemnity Compensation, or a monetary allowance under 38 U.S.C. chapter 18 for an individual who is a child of a Vietnam veteran or child of a veteran with covered service in Korea is awarded or increased pursuant to a liberalizing law, or a liberalizing VA issue approved by the Secretary or by the Secretary's direction, the effective date of such award or increase shall be fixed in accordance with the facts found, but shall not be earlier than the effective date of the act or administrative issue. Where Pension, Compensation, dependency and indemnity Compensation, or a monetary allowance under 38 U.S.C. chapter 18 for an individual who is a child of a Vietnam veteran or child of a veteran with covered service in Korea is awarded or increased pursuant to a liberalizing law or VA issue which became effective on or after the date of its enactment or issuance, in order for a claimant to be eligible for a retroactive payment under the provisions of this paragraph the evidence must show that the claimant met all eligibility criteria for the liberalized benefit on the effective date of the liberalizing law or VA issue and that such eligibility existed continuously from that date to the Date of Claim or administrative determination of entitlement.

The provisions of this paragraph are applicable to original and reopened claims as well as claims for increase.

(1) If a claim is reviewed on the initiative of VA within 1 year from the effective date of the law or VA issue, or at the request of a claimant received within 1 year from that date, benefits may be authorized from the effective date of the law or VA issue.

(2) If a claim is reviewed on the initiative of VA more than 1 year after the effective date of the law or VA issue, benefits may be authorized for a period of 1 year prior to the date of administrative determination of entitlement.

(3) If a claim is reviewed at the request of the claimant more than 1 year after the effective date of the law or VA issue, benefits may be authorized for a period of 1 year prior to the date of receipt of such request. (Authority: 38 U.S.C. 1805, 1815, 1821, 1832, 5110(g))

(b) Discontinuance of benefits. Where the reduction or discontinuance of an award is in order because of a change in law or a Department of Veterans Affairs issue, or because of a change in interpretation of a law or Department of Veterans Affairs issue, the payee will be notified at his or her latest address of record of the contemplated action and furnished detailed reasons therefor, and will be given 60 days for the presentation of additional evidence. If additional evidence is not received within that period, the award will be reduced or discontinued effective the last day of the month in which the 60-day period expired. (Authority: 38 U.S.C. 5112(b)(6))

Effective Date for Challenges within One Year of a Previous Final Decision
It is fairly common for VA to issue a final decision on a claim resulting in denial due to evidence that was not persuasive enough to make a favorable decision. This often happens as a result of a claimant not really understanding the type of evidence necessary for a favorable decision. The claim becomes a "dead" claim from one year after the final decision which is the allotted period of time for challenging that decision under the "New Review Process." After that, no benefit is possible unless a new claim is filed. There are two notable exceptions if more than one year has passed. 1) If service department records were available to the Regional Office and were not used when the claim was denied or 2) there is clear and unmistakable evidence that the denial was due to malpractice of the adjudicating authority. We will discuss both of these exceptions further on.

If the claimant or the person assisting the claimant can find somebody knowledgeable enough to to recognize that there was enough evidence to substantiate a favorable decision, this new evidence can be submitted and the claim will be reopened. The evidence has to meet the standard of "new and relevant evidence" which we will discuss in more detail in further on in this book. If the new evidence results in a favorable decision, the effective date will be the the date of the original claim as long as the evidence was submitted prior to the end of the 1 year period of appeal. If the evidence is submitted after 1 year, the effective date is the date of the new evidence submitted as it is considered a new claim.

Effective Date for Reevaluation for Increased Rating Claims

Many veterans receiving Compensation experience a worsening of the disabling conditions as they age. If the worsening condition creates a trigger for a higher disability rating, the veteran can make application for reevaluation of the condition for the purpose of a higher rating. In general, the effective date for an increased rating will be either the date of the claim or the date entitlement to the higher rating arose. Unlike the effective date for an original claim where the entitlement arising has to be a later date. The entitlement – and thus the effective date – for a higher rating can be awarded up to 1 year previous to submission of the claim.

It should also be noted that if an increase for rating is submitted and there is no medical evidence submitted to substantiate the claim, the effective date will likely be the date where a VA medical examination determined there was an increase in disability. This could be many months after the claim is submitted. If there is any medical evidence indicating an increase in the disability prior to the Date of Claim, this evidence can be used to refute the VA medical examination along with lay evidence. It would typically require filing a Notice of Disagreement and starting an appeal based on the effective date as the area of disagreement. This also brings up an important issue for filing effective claims.

The veteran should not submit an increase for rating claim unless evidence is submitted along with that claim. Relying on VA to substantiate the increase in rating can result in a later effective date from the Date of Claim. Not only should medical evidence be submitted, but detailed lay testimony from the claimant as well as lay testimony from others should also be submitted to substantiate the application.

Medical evidence for the increase in rating can consist of hospital admission records or medical records in the possession of VA or private doctors. If hospital admission records alone are used, only those from a VA hospital will qualify for the earlier effective date. Hospital records from a non-VA hospital will not qualify for the earlier effective date. Private doctors records should not be subject to the date rule mentioned here.

There is also one other trap involved in a filing for increased rating. If the medical evidence for the increase is beyond 1 year prior to to the claim and that evidence is used to substantiate the claim, this violates the rule that the increase had to have occurred no more than 1 year prior to the claim. In this case, the effective date will now be the Date of Claim. Medical records beyond 1 year prior to claim should not be submitted. If there are any medical records substantiating the rating increase that are within the 1 year previous period, these are the records that should be submitted.

Effective Date for Pending Claims with No Adjudication

A pending claim is one for which no final decision has been issued. The Regional Office has no requirement to issue a decision on a pending claim within a year of the effective date. Sometimes because of need for further development, ordering VA medical examinations and submission of new and material evidence by the claimant, a decision could take years. In this section, we are not talking about this kind of claim. Here we are addressing a pending claim that appears to have been lost in the system for many years with no development at all.

Losing track of the claim could happen in several ways. One way might simply be a clerical error in the Regional Office where the claim disappears. This is highly unlikely as claim files are tracked on the computer system in the Regional Office. It would require either a malicious act of computer sabotage or a failure of the computer storage system with no backup. The usual way that a claim appears to be lost in the system is when a claimant methodically files the same claim for the same condition over a number of years. VA is required to address all such claims in development letters to the claimant and to resolve those claims so that older claims for the same condition are not left pending without a decision. Apparently, it seems that confusion over which claim is which can lead to a previous pending claim with no decision.

If one of the more recent effective date claims for the same condition is awarded, then VA should move the effective date to the original claim for the same condition that was not considered. However, numerous court cases have resulted in the so-called "implicit denial rule." This rule allows that any unadjudicated claim remains pending unless that claim was discussed in a development letter where the pending claim was being considered and likely would be rejected. In other words, the Regional Office does not have to explicitly issue a denial letter for a pending claim as long as that claim is discussed in development letters and it is implicit that there is insufficient evidence for an award.

Another argument for a different pending claim effective date is that a rating service officer must infer entitlement to a benefit allowed under the law if evidence indicates that the claimant could be entitled to that benefit even though no claim was made. For example, a veteran who was stationed in Southeast Asia, is making claim for a musculoskeletal condition and the medical records also indicate the claimant has type II diabetes. Since type II diabetes is a presumed condition for service in Vietnam, the adjudicator must raise this issue and notify the claimant there is a potential claim for this new condition as well.

If this procedure is not followed and the claimant subsequently makes application for type II diabetes, presumably VA must accept the effective date of the original claim that was not for type II diabetes. The burden of proof, however lies with the claimant to show that VA did not have a record of why the additional claim was not considered. In other words, the record may show why the the additional claim was deliberately not considered even though the veteran was never notified.

Effective Date for Claims Involving Clear and Unmistakable Error (CUE)
Allowing for an earlier effective date due to clear and unmistakable error is the Holy Grail of many attorneys who represent veterans with claims appeals. Denials for previous applications can go back years and years – sometimes 10 or 20 or 30 years. Proving CUE to get a previous decision reversed could result in hundreds of thousands of dollars of back payments for an award with the original effective date of the original claim. On the next page is the definition of clear and unmistakable error.

38 CFR § 20.1403 Rule 1403. What constitutes clear and unmistakable error; what does not.

(a) General. Clear and unmistakable error is a very specific and rare kind of error. It is the kind of error, of fact or of law, that when called to the attention of later reviewers compels the conclusion, to which reasonable minds could not differ, that the result would have been manifestly different but for the error. Generally, either the correct facts, as they were known at the time, were not before the Board, or the statutory and regulatory provisions extant at the time were incorrectly applied.

(b) Record to be reviewed -

(1) General. Review for clear and unmistakable error in a prior Board decision must be based on the record and the law that existed when that decision was made.

(2) Special rule for Board decisions issued on or after July 21, 1992. For a Board decision issued on or after July 21, 1992, the record that existed when that decision was made includes relevant documents possessed by the Department of Veterans Affairs not later than 90 days before such record was transferred to the Board for review in reaching that decision, provided that the documents could reasonably be expected to be part of the record.

(c) Errors that constitute clear and unmistakable error. To warrant revision of a Board decision on the grounds of clear and unmistakable error, there must have been an error in the Board's adjudication of the appeal which, had it not been made, would have manifestly changed the outcome when it was made. If it is not absolutely clear that a different result would have ensued, the error complained of cannot be clear and unmistakable.

(d) Examples of situations that are not clear and unmistakable error -

(1) Changed diagnosis. A new medical diagnosis that "corrects" an earlier diagnosis considered in a Board decision.

(2) Duty to assist. The Secretary's failure to fulfill the duty to assist.

(3) Evaluation of evidence. A disagreement as to how the facts were weighed or evaluated.

(e) Change in interpretation. Clear and unmistakable error does not include the otherwise correct application of a statute or regulation where, subsequent to the Board decision challenged, there has been a change in the interpretation of the statute or regulation.
(Authority: 38 U.S.C. 501(a), 7111)

Meeting the threshold for CUE is difficult and should only be attempted by an attorney who has the knowledge and expertise to pursue these types of court challenges. This would not be something that should be attempted by just any accredited agent or accredited attorney.

Effective Date for Newly Obtained Service Records

This issue is one of a few exceptions to going back to an effective date beyond a year prior to a Date of Claim. Here is the regulation governing this exception. The information pertaining to newly obtained service records starts with paragraph (c). The procedures in the regulation are self-explanatory.

38 CFR § 3.156 New and material evidence.

(a) General. A claimant may reopen a finally adjudicated claim by submitting new and material evidence. New evidence means existing evidence not previously submitted to agency decisionmakers. Material evidence means existing evidence that, by itself or when considered with previous evidence of record, relates to an unestablished fact necessary to substantiate the claim. New and material evidence can be neither cumulative nor redundant of the evidence of record at the time of the last prior final denial of the claim sought to be reopened, and must raise a reasonable possibility of substantiating the claim.
(Authority: 38 U.S.C. 501, 5103A(f), 5108)

(b) Pending claim. New and material evidence received prior to the expiration of the appeal period, or prior to the appellate decision if a timely appeal has been filed (including evidence received prior to an appellate decision and referred to the agency of original jurisdiction by the Board of Veterans Appeals without consideration in that decision in accordance with the provisions of § 20.1304(b)(1) of this chapter), will be considered as having been filed in connection with the claim which was pending at the beginning of the appeal period.
(Authority: 38 U.S.C. 501)

(c) Service department records.

(1) Notwithstanding any other section in this part, at any time after VA issues a decision on a claim, if VA receives or associates with the claims file relevant official service department records that existed and had not been associated with the claims file when VA first decided the claim, VA will reconsider the claim, notwithstanding paragraph (a) of this section. Such records include, but are not limited to:

(i) Service records that are related to a claimed in-service event, injury, or disease, regardless of whether such records mention the veteran by name, as long as the other requirements of paragraph (c) of this section are met;

(ii) Additional service records forwarded by the Department of Defense or the service department to VA any time after VA's original request for service records; and

(iii) Declassified records that could not have been obtained because the records were classified when VA decided the claim.

(2) Paragraph (c)(1) of this section does not apply to records that VA could not have obtained when it decided the claim because the records did not exist when VA decided the claim, or because the claimant failed to provide sufficient information for VA to identify and obtain the records from the respective service department, the Joint Services Records Research Center, or from any other official source.

(3) An award made based all or in part on the records identified by paragraph (c)(1) of this section is effective on the date entitlement arose or the date VA received the previously decided claim, whichever is later, or such other date as may be authorized by the provisions of this part applicable to the previously decided claim.

(4) A retroactive evaluation of disability resulting from disease or injury subsequently service connected on the basis of the new evidence from the service department must be supported adequately by medical evidence. Where such records clearly support the assignment of a specific rating over a part or the entire period of time involved, a retroactive evaluation will be assigned accordingly, except as it may be affected by the filing date of the original claim.
(Authority: 38 U.S.C. 501(a))

Although § 3.156(c)(1) states that a service department record only counts if it existed when VA first decided the claim, this should not be taken literally.

- A newly created service department record is considered to have existed when VA first decided the claim if the new writing is based on analysis of service department records that existed when VA first decided the claim.

- If VA did not ask for, or give the claimant notice that it needed, additional information from the claimant for the service department record to be located, the claimant should argue that § 3.156(c) still applies because the reason the claimant failed to provide sufficient information was that VA failed to comply with its duty to assist because it failed to ask for sufficient identifying information.

Effective Dates and Benefit Payments Unique to Pension Claims
The effective date for a living veteran filing a Pension claim is generally the Date of Claim or the date of entitlement whichever is later. There are however some exceptions that will be discussed below. The effective date for a survivor filing for Survivors Pension is the first day of the month of the veteran's death as long as the claim is filed within one year of the death. Otherwise if one year has elapsed, the effective date is the Date of Claim.

Earlier Effective Date Option #1
Under 38 CFR 3.400(b)(1), if all of the conditions listed below are met, a Pension award may be retroactive for up to one year prior to the date of receipt of the claim, but not earlier than the date of permanent and total disability.

- The Veteran files a claim for a retroactive award within one year from the date of permanent and total disability.
- The Veteran was prevented from applying for Pension by a disability. The preventing disability
  - must not be of misconduct in origin, and
  - need not be the the permanent and total disability required for Pension.
- The disability prevented the Veteran from filing the Pension claim for at least the first 30 days immediately following the date on which he/she acquired permanent and total disability.

Earlier Effective Date Option #2

Under Public Law 107-103 subject to 38 CFR 3.114, Pension may be awarded to a Veteran retroactive for up to one year prior to the date of receipt of the claim if any of the following criteria are continuously met from September 17, 2001 until the Date of Claim:

- Age 65; or
- Found disabled by Social Security Administration (SSA) for the purpose of Social Security disability benefits; or
- a patient in a nursing home for long-term care because of disability

"M21-1 After entitlement to Pension has been granted a VSR should send a development letter to request income and expense information to determine entitlement from one year prior to the date of receipt. Do not establish an end product for control. Inform the Veteran that he/she has one year to establish entitlement to the earlier date. "

What this means is, the Pension benefit must be awarded before VA considers applying the retroactive date.

Signatures and VA Power Of Attorney

Signatures

Deciding who is to sign an application and/or other documents associated with an application is one of the most confusing parts of filing a claim. No one can sign an application for benefits other than the claimant or a legally recognized attorney-in-fact for the claimant.

There is no mental competency test for the claimant for signing the original application. If the person can move his or her hand, that is all that is necessary. Obviously if the person is not conscious or not capable of making a mark, then the only other person who can sign is an attorney-in-fact identified further on. Most families figure out how to get the claimant to sign the application. Any other documents pertaining to a claim where the VA form indicates the signature of the veteran or the claimant is required, must be signed by the claimant.

VA Power Of Attorney
VA will also recognize another individual representing the interest of the claimant with an application before the agency for benefits. The department calls this individual a "VA power of attorney." (POA) This can be any individual on a once-in-a-lifetime claim, or it can be any accredited claims agent, or accredited attorney or accredited service officer for an unlimited number of claims. VA will not recognize a state law power of attorney for this purpose. Under Public Law (PL) 112-154 a VA Power Of Attorney (POA) can now sign any documents for the claimant that require a claimant's signature.

VA will only recognize a VA Power Of Attorney for approval by submitting the appropriate signed document (VBA Form 21-22a) furnished by the Department. The claimant must sign the VA power of attorney. The person acting as power of attorney can be any individual such as a family member, friend or an accredited agent or an accredited attorney. The VA Power Of Attorney can act on behalf of the veteran in responding to inquiries from the Regional Office.

The POA does not have authority to answer questions on the application pertaining to facts known by the claimant. The claimant must answer these missing facts and sign the correspondence or be represented by a caregiver, care facility or court appointed guardian.

It is our understanding that a VA power of attorney can sign any document on behalf of the claimant, including original applications for Disability Compensation. We do not at this time believe that representatives can sign an original application for DIC or survivors pension.

How the Rating Activity in the Regional Office Makes a Decision

The Job of the Rating Activity
When performing a rating evaluation, Rating Veterans Service Representatives (RVSRs) consider all evidence associated with the claim. This includes service medical records, VA medical examination records, clinical summaries from VA medical centers where treatment has been provided to the veteran, and evidence provided from private sources, such as the veteran's treating physician.

The job of the rating service representative consists primarily of interpreting medical records in deciding if the medical evidence is sufficient enough to result in a favorable or unfavorable decision. First of all, medical evidence must show a disabling condition that is ratable and that is ongoing and not acute. Second, medical evidence from service records or evidence of duty assignment or statements from others or corroborative history must show that an illness or injury that could have resulted in the current condition was incurred in service. Finally, the medical evidence must tie together such that there is a link established between the current chronic disability of the claimant and the illness or injury or exposure that occurred in the service.

Rating Decisions Are Not Made by Individuals with a Medical Background
It is interesting to note that RVSR's are not required to have a medical background, although some of them might be nurses or have served as medics in the service. The raters pay scale is from GS 11 through GS 12. Most doctors would not work for this pay scale and so that is likely

why very few doctors work in the rating activity. Not using doctors seems counterintuitive as rating decisions are primarily based on an understanding of medical terminology and a thorough reading of medical records as well as some understanding of the nature of medical conditions and factors associated with disability. At one time, rating decisions were made by a so-called "rating board" that consisted of two non-medical rating experts along with a physician. In fact, an analog to veterans disability is Social Security disability where decisions regarding disability are made involving a doctor.

Rating boards were replaced in the early 1990s by several non-medical individuals making the decision and more recently by a single non-medical rater making a decision. This removal of medical personnel is due to a ruling by the Court of Appeals for Veterans Claims which has become famous, not only for its impact on not using in-house medical personnel, but also for its impact on the concept of new and material evidence in rating and appeal decisions.

Colvin v. Derwinski, 1 Vet. App. 171 (1991) CAVC
Taken from The Veterans Advocate, January-June 2008

Colvin stands for a now deeply embedded and fundamental principle of veterans law — that VA may use only independent medical evidence to support its benefits decisions. The VA may not use the medical opinion or judgment of the VA rater or BVA Veterans Law Judge to support a decision.

For many years prior to Colvin, VA decisions were based on the findings of VA physicians who were part of the decision-making process. A doctor employed by VA would not only provide the medical opinion that would be used to decide the claim, he or she would participate in deciding whether to grant or deny benefits.

This practice of having VA doctors play a decision making role was ended by Colvin. The Court held that:

"If the medical evidence of record is insufficient, or, in the opinion of the BVA, of doubtful weight or credibility, the BVA is always free to supplement the record by seeking an advisory opinion, ordering a medical examination or citing recognized medical treatises in its decisions that clearly support its ultimate conclusions . . . . This procedure ensures that all medical evidence contrary to the veteran's claim will be made known to him and be part of the record before this Court. Colvin, 1 Vet.App. at 175."

Potential Conflicts with the Rating Activity

Even though the formal procedure of having a VA doctor play a decision making role stopped after Colvin, VA raters and BVA Veterans Law Judges persist in relying on their own medical judgments to decide claims. For example, the VA and BVA may often make a determination that an in-service injury was "acute, without chronic residual disability." However, the degree of injury and whether any disabilities resulted from the injury are medical assessments that the VA and the Board are not competent to make unless there is independent medical evidence to support that conclusion. This means that in many cases the VA's determination that an in-service injury was acute and did not result in chronic disability may violate Colvin.

Another common problem is that VA may dismiss favorable medical evidence of record without citing to medical evidence in the record or medical literature to support its rejection.

A good rule of thumb based on Colvin is that if there is a VA-made medical conclusion – not directly based on a medical examination report, advisory opinion, or medical literature – the conclusion may be erroneous because VA has no independent medical support for its findings. Decisions containing unsupported medical conclusions should be appealed.

The Principle of Preponderance of Evidence

The rating representative uses the principle of preponderance of evidence which is defined as the following: *"The greater weight of the evidence required in a civil (non-criminal) lawsuit (in this case a claim for benefits) for the trier of fact (jury or judge without a jury) to decide in favor of one side or the other. This preponderance is based on the more convincing evidence and its probable truth or accuracy, and not on the amount of evidence."*

What this means is the more probative and credible the evidence that you submit on behalf of your claim, the more likely you will receive a favorable decision. It's not the amount of evidence that you submit but the credibility, probative value and competence of the evidence.

Generally, VA does little research or development of evidence beyond that required by law to substantiate reasons for not approving a claim. In fact, development teams are not allowed to seek out negative evidence if they have personal opinions about a claim. Any negative evidence that VA would generate – resulting in a denial of a claim – would come from discrepancies and inconsistencies in statements from claimants as well as discrepancies in the record itself. Negative evidence could also include a lack of evidence to substantiate entitlement. You have the advantage. Meet this standard and you will likely win.

VA's Principle or Rule of Reasonable Doubt

This principle is an important issue when a decision is made concerning an approval or a denial of a claim. With many Compensation claims for older veterans, and DIC claims, there is often very little evidence substantiating the link between service and the actual disability. In many cases, the rating service officer must make a decision based on weighing inconclusive evidence and then deciding which way to go – either denial or award. A number of claims for older veterans are often made using this principle. Here is the regulation that governs it.

> 38 CFR § 3.102   Reasonable doubt.
> It is the defined and consistently applied policy of the Department of Veterans Affairs to administer the law under a broad interpretation, consistent, however, with the facts shown in every case. <u>When, after careful consideration of all procurable and assembled data, a reasonable doubt arises regarding service origin, the degree of disability, or any other point, such doubt will be resolved in favor of the claimant</u>. By reasonable doubt is meant one which exists because of an approximate balance of positive and negative evidence which does not satisfactorily

prove or disprove the claim. It is a substantial doubt and one within the range of probability as distinguished from pure speculation or remote possibility. It is not a means of reconciling actual conflict or a contradiction in the evidence. Mere suspicion or doubt as to the truth of any statements submitted, as distinguished from impeachment or contradiction by evidence or known facts, is not justifiable basis for denying the application of the reasonable doubt doctrine if the entire, complete record otherwise warrants invoking this doctrine. The reasonable doubt doctrine is also applicable even in the absence of official records, particularly if the basic incident allegedly arose under combat, or similarly strenuous conditions, and is consistent with the probable results of such known hardships.
(Authority: 38 U.S.C. 501)

This rule is extremely important when you are preparing your claim. You must provide enough positive evidence for your claim in order to offset any contrary assertions from the rating service representative that you do not deserve the claim. Generally, the rating authority will not base a decision on whether it has a medical reason to back up that decision. The decision will usually be based on a lack of evidence on your part that the condition meets the requirement for being service-connected. That's where this principle comes in. If VA has no credible evidence on its part denying the benefit and you have enough evidence that would raise the probability that you could be eligible, VA must rule in your favor.

Marriage Issues, Evidence of Marriage and Evidence of Death

We have included all of this information in the Appendix that comes with the Claim Support Disc or is available online at www.supportdisc.com. This information will have the same title as above in the Appendix.

Resources That Are Useful in Understanding and Preparing Successful Claims

CONTACTS

- ➤ National Personnel Records Center (1-866-272-6272)
- ➤ Janesville Scanning Center Disability Compensation Claims
  Department Of Veterans Affairs Claims Intake Center
  PO Box 5235 Janesville, WI 53547-5235
  Toll Free Fax: 844-822-5246
- ➤ If you received a letter from VA requesting additional evidence for your claim or appeal, you can mail/fax to the following address or fax number (also address for FOIA requests):
  Department Of Veterans Affairs Evidence Intake Center
  PO Box 4444 Janesville, WI 53547-4444
  Toll Free Fax: 844-822-5246
- ➤ National Hotline 855-225-0709 must be accredited and have power of attorney to use it

- ➤ Contact Person for Setting up VBMS
  - Jackie Imboden
  - VA Central Office, Compensation Service
  - Lead Consultant, Policy Staff
  - Nashville, TN
  - Jacqueline.imboden@va.gov
  - (615) 279-2913

ONLINE RESOURCES

National Personnel Records Center
https://www.archives.gov/veterans

Board of Appeals Database
https://www.index.va.gov/search/va/bva.jsp

Evidence Requirements for Compensation Claims
https://www.benefits.va.gov/Compensation/evidence.asp

VA Employees Union
http://afgenvac.org/?page_id=763 employees Union

VA Administration Reports
https://www.benefits.va.gov/reports/

Data on Claims Processing – Monday Morning Workload Reports
https://www.benefits.va.gov/reports/detailed_claims_data.asp

VA Office of Budget and Budget Requests
https://www.va.gov/budget/products.asp

Board of Veterans Appeals Rulings
http://www.index.VA.gov/search/VA/BVA.jsp

Court Of Appeals for Veterans Claims
http://search.UScourts.CAVC.gov

Board of Veterans Appeals Rulings
http://www.index.VA.gov/search/VA/BVA.jsp

VA Office of General Counsel Precedent Opinions
http://www.VA.gov/ogc/PrecedentOpinions.asp

Accreditation List
www.acreditlist.com

M21-1 Adjudication Manual Online
https://www.knowva.ebenefits.va.gov/

Board of Veterans Appeals Homepage
https://www.bva.va.gov/index.asp

CLAIM SUPPORT DISC THAT COMES WITH THE BOOK

- All Forms Necessary for a Claim
- Checklist – "Elements of the Fully Developed Claim Process for Disability Compensation"
- M21-1 as of 2018
- VASRD (38 CFR part 4)
- VBMS Annual Report
- List of Nexus Opinion Providers
- BVA Annual Report
- Regional Office Contacts for Setting up VBMS for Accredited Representatives
- Two case studies that apply the principles of this chapter

Chapter 3
Aid and Attendance and Housebound Allowances

IN THIS CHAPTER:

Understanding Aid and Attendance or Housebound Allowances

If a claimant is receiving the aid and attendance of another person because the claimant is so helpless as to be unable to perform certain activities of daily living independently, or the claimant is considered housebound, meaning he or she is basically confined to living quarters for life, there are additional payments available as monetary allowances.

Please do not confuse the meaning of "aid and attendance" or "housebound." These phrases pertain to medical ratings and 18 different monetary allowances available with Veterans Pension, Survivor's Pension, Disability Compensation, Dependency and Indemnity Compensation (DIC) and certain forms of Special Monthly Compensation (SMC). The phrase "aid and attendance" is especially confusing because most individuals have been led to believe this is the name for Veterans Pension or Survivor's (Death) Pension. Unfortunately, the media has chosen to call both forms of Pension "Aid and Attendance."

There is no such VA disability benefit as an "Aid and Attendance Benefit."

When we talk about aid and attendance or housebound benefits with Compensation or DIC or SMC, most people think we are talking about Pension. This is not the case.

Aid and attendance and housebound allowances are medical ratings and additional amounts of money available with all VA disability income benefits to help individuals receiving these benefits cope with the added burden of helplessness or being housebound.

Aid and attendance and housebound allowances require a Rating Veterans Service Officer in the Regional Office to determine the need and issue a rating for either category.

Criteria for the Need for Aid and Attendance

The criteria for a need for aid and attendance is found in the following:

38 CFR § 3.352   Criteria for determining need for aid and attendance and "permanently bedridden."

(a) Basic criteria for regular aid and attendance and permanently bedridden. The following will be accorded consideration in determining the need for regular aid and attendance (§3.351(c)(3):

- inability of claimant to dress or undress himself (herself), or to keep himself (herself) ordinarily clean and presentable;
- frequent need of adjustment of any special prosthetic or orthopedic appliances which by reason of the particular disability cannot be done without aid (this will not include the adjustment of appliances which normal persons would be unable to adjust without aid, such as supports, belts, lacing at the back, etc.);
- inability of claimant to feed himself (herself) through loss of coordination of upper extremities or through extreme weakness;
- inability to attend to the wants of nature;
- or incapacity, physical or mental, which requires care or assistance on a regular basis to protect the claimant from hazards or dangers incident to his or her daily environment.
- "Bedridden" will be a proper basis for the determination (need for aid and attendance). For the purpose of this paragraph "bedridden" will be that condition which, through its essential character, actually requires that the claimant remain in bed. The fact that claimant has voluntarily taken to bed or that a physician has prescribed rest in bed for the greater or lesser part of the day to promote convalescence or cure will not suffice.

It is not required that all of the disabling conditions enumerated in this previous paragraph be found to exist before a favorable rating may be made. The particular personal functions which the veteran is unable to perform should be considered in connection with his or her condition as a whole. It is only necessary that the evidence establish that the veteran is so helpless as to need regular aid and attendance, not that there be a constant need.

Determinations that the veteran is so helpless, as to be in need of regular aid and attendance will not be based solely upon an opinion that the claimant's condition is such as would require him or her to be in bed. They must be based on the actual requirement of personal assistance.

(Regular Aid and Attendance Provided by Relative (not the higher level))
(c) Attendance by relative. The performance of the necessary aid and attendance service by a relative of the beneficiary or other member of his or her household will not prevent the granting of the additional allowance."

Almost without exception, ratings received in conjunction with long term care services in the home or in a care facility are ratings for aid and attendance. This must be obvious because these are the type of services that these care providers offer. They provide professional help with activities of daily living. Or they provide supervision for individuals who are cognitively impaired or have severe physical disabilities and could injure themselves without supervision.

Assistance with Activities of Daily Living (ADLs) and potential Instrumental Activities of Daily Living (IADLs) involve the services of a person to provide the regular aid and attendance to a resident or a client receiving this care. It may be possible that a claimant residing in one of these care settings is housebound and does not need any assistance. This would then generate a rating for housebound which is always a lesser amount of allowance. It is more likely that a rating for housebound would be considered for someone who is living in his or her own home. The need for IADLs by themselves is not sufficient enough to trigger a rating for aid and attendance.

Definition of Housebound

The definition of housebound from 38 CFR § 3.350(i) (1)(2) is the following:

(1) Has additional service-connected disability or disabilities independently ratable at 60 percent, separate and distinct from the 100 percent service-connected disability and involving different anatomical segments or bodily systems,

OR

(2) Is permanently housebound by reason of service-connected disability or disabilities. This requirement is met when the veteran is substantially confined as a direct result of service-connected disabilities to his or her dwelling and the immediate premises or, if institutionalized, to the ward or clinical areas, and it is reasonably certain that the disability or disabilities and resultant confinement will continue throughout his or her lifetime.

Most veterans are going to qualify for being "housebound" under the second option above. Not very many veterans are going to qualify by being 100% rated disabled for Compensation and then having VA say that they have an equivalent combined rating of 60% from other disabilities. Please note that any veteran in this situation would not have a final rating of 160%. The most available is 100%. What this is saying is that VA has determined there are additional disabilities that could be rated at 60% independently without actually paying the veteran for those disabilities since the veteran is already being paid at 100%.

A number of appeals in the past have addressed what "substantially confined" means. Previous board decisions had determined that substantially confines means that the claimant is restricted to his or her house and even restricted to leaving for medical treatment purposes. The Court of Appeals for Veterans Claims overturned those previous BVA decisions.

> *Howell versus Nicholson, March 23, 2006 number 04-0624 CAVC*
> *"The term "substantially confined" is not defined by statute or regulation. See id. Because the meaning of the term "substantially confined" is ambiguous and there is no regulatory interpretation, "the Court must determine the meaning" of the term "and the Board's obligation" thereunder. Thompson v. Brown, 8 Vet. App. 169, 175 (1995); see also Jackson and Cropper, both supra. The Secretary submits that the clear implication of this term is that the requirement that one be "substantially confined" is met when the claimant is restricted to his house except for medical treatment purposes. The Secretary, citing to Senate Report No. 1745 (June 27, 1960), notes that in passing section 1114(s) Congress intended to provide additional Compensation for veterans who were unable to overcome their particular disabilities and leave the house in order to earn an income as opposed to an inability to leave the house at all. Mr. Howell does not contest this interpretation.*
>
> *To the extent substantial confinement does not include departures for medical purposes, we agree that the interpretation that the Secretary presents in his supplemental briefing is reasonable and consistent with statute and regulations. See Jackson, Thompson, and Cropper, all supra.*
>
> *Accordingly, we hold that leaving one's house for medical purposes cannot, by itself, serve as the basis for finding that one is not substantially confined for purposes of SMC-HB benefits, and the Board's interpretation of section 1114(s) to preclude the grant of SMC benefits on the basis of Mr. Howell's leaving his house in order to attend VA medical appointments was erroneous as a matter of law.*

There are no housebound allowances for regular Disability Compensation. The only allowances are for aid and attendance. There are 4 housebound possibilities concerning Veterans Pension, Survivor's Pension, Disability Compensation or DIC for housebound allowances.

1. The first of these are housebound allowances for a veteran receiving Veterans Pension.

2. The second are housebound allowances for a surviving spouse receiving Survivor's Pension.

3. The third is an alternative higher level of payment under SMC Schedule S where a veteran who is totally disabled can get an additional monthly income if that veteran is considered housebound but is not in need of aid and attendance.

4. The fourth is an allowance for a surviving spouse receiving Dependency and Indemnity Compensation (DIC) who is rated housebound.

Interpreting the Regulation for the Requirement for Aid and Attendance

We have taken the rules from 38 CFR §3.352 and applied them to more modern terminology of providing assistance. Here is our list based on the regulation.

1. Assistance with bathing or showering
2. Assistance with toileting
3. Assistance with feeding (having a need to be fed by someone else)
4. Assistance with dressing or undressing
5. Assistance with transferring in or out of a bed or chair
6. Assistance with incontinence
7. Assistance with ambulating (walking)
8. Assistance with keeping oneself ordinarily clean and presentable, including hygiene
9. Assistance with frequent need of adjustment of special prosthetic or orthopedic devices which cannot be done without the aid of another person
10. Having an incapacity (physical or mental) requiring care or assistance on a regular basis to protect the patient from hazards or dangers incident to his or her daily environment
11. Is blind or so nearly blind as to have corrected visual acuity of 5/200 or less, in both eyes, or concentric contraction of the visual field to 5 degrees or less in both eyes
12. Is a patient in a nursing home because of mental or physical incapacity
13. Meets the criteria of being totally bedridden as defined in the regulation

As is mentioned in the regulation, there does not need to be a certain number of these incapacities in order to determine a rating for aid and attendance. The rating service representative simply must determine from the evidence whether the claimant is so helpless as to require the regular aid and attendance of another person based these conditions.

From our experience with the rating authority, the veteran who is applying or the spouse of the veteran who is applying should exhibit the need for and be receiving at least two or more of the services from #1 through #8 above and from #9 through #13, only one of these need apply.

It is also important to note that a relative or a member of the household providing aid and attendance services is acceptable to VA for granting the additional r`egular – not the higher amount – allowance for aid and attendance. (The so-called higher amount is only available with SMC Schedule R.2.)

Since Compensation, DIC and SMC are not means tested programs – unlike Veterans Pension or Survivor's (Death) Pension – VA does not require a caregiver or relative or member of the household to be paid for services. For non-Pension benefits, VA would probably grant the allowance without evidence that anyone is providing services. The Regional Office would rely primarily on *VA Form 21-2680* for granting the additional allowance.

We have found it useful to provide the Regional Office with evidence that care for aid and attendance is also being provided. This helps if there is a question on the 2680 whether or not the beneficiary actually meets the medical criteria to grant the rating. If a question is raised about the suitability for a rating, then submitting evidence of care being provided will help VSRs make the decision. Service Representatives will likely note the discrepancy between an inadequate 2680 and evidence of care and ask for more information, or for a 2680 that provides more detailed information for a rating decision.

Allowances Available for Disability Compensation, DIC, SMC and Pension

Here is the authorization for the allowances for Disability Compensation, DIC and Pension.

> **38 CFR §3.351 Special monthly dependency and indemnity Compensation, death Compensation, Pension and spouse's Compensation ratings.**
>
> (a) *General.* This section sets forth criteria for determining whether:
> (1) Increased Pension is payable to a veteran by reason of need for aid and attendance or by reason of being housebound.
> (Authority: 38 U.S.C. 1521(d), (e))
> (2) Increased Compensation is payable to a veteran by reason of the veteran's spouse being in need of aid and attendance.
> (Authority: 38 U.S.C. 1115(1)(E))
> (3) Increased dependency and indemnity Compensation is payable to a surviving spouse or parent by reason of being in need of aid and attendance.
> (Authority: 38 U.S.C. 1311(c), 1315(h))
> (4) Increased dependency and indemnity Compensation is payable to a surviving spouse who is not in need of aid and attendance but is housebound.
> (Authority: 38 U.S.C. 1311(d))
> (5) Increased Pension is payable to a surviving spouse by reason of need for aid and attendance, or if not in need of aid and attendance, by reason of being housebound.
> (Authority: 38 U.S.C. 1541(d), (e))

(6) Increased death Compensation is payable to a surviving spouse by reason of being in need of aid and attendance.
(Authority: 38 U.S.C. 1122)

(b) *Aid and attendance; need.* Need for aid and attendance means helplessness or being so nearly helpless as to require the regular aid and attendance of another person. The criteria set forth in paragraph (c) of this section will be applied in determining whether such need exists.

(c) *Aid and attendance; criteria.* The veteran, spouse, surviving spouse or parent will be considered in need of regular aid and attendance if he or she:
> (1) Is blind or so nearly blind as to have corrected visual acuity of 5/200 or less, in both eyes, or concentric contraction of the visual field to 5 degrees or less; or
> (2) Is a patient in a nursing home because of mental or physical incapacity; or
> (3) Establishes a factual need for aid and attendance under the criteria set forth in §3.352(a).
> (Authority: 38 U.S.C. 1502(b))

(d) *Housebound, or permanent and total plus 60 percent; disability Pension.* The rate of Pension payable to a veteran who is entitled to Pension under 38 U.S.C. 1521 and who is not in need of regular aid and attendance shall be as prescribed in 38 U.S.C. 1521(e) if, in addition to having a single permanent disability rated 100 percent disabling under the Schedule for Rating Disabilities (not including ratings based upon unemployability under §4.17 of this chapter) the veteran:
> (1) Has additional disability or disabilities independently ratable at 60 percent or more, separate and distinct from the permanent disability rated as 100 percent disabling and involving different anatomical segments or bodily systems, or
> (2) Is "permanently housebound" by reason of disability or disabilities. This requirement is met when the veteran is substantially confined to his or her dwelling and the immediate premises or, if institutionalized, to the ward or clinical area, and it is reasonably certain that the disability or disabilities and resultant confinement will continue throughout his or her lifetime.
> (Authority: 38 U.S.C. 1502(c), 1521(e))

(e) *Housebound; dependency and indemnity Compensation.* The monthly rate of dependency and indemnity Compensation payable to a surviving spouse who does not qualify for increased dependency and indemnity Compensation under 38 U.S.C. 1311(c) based on need for regular aid and attendance shall be increased by the amount specified in 38 U.S.C. 1311(d) if the surviving spouse is permanently housebound by reason of disability. The "permanently housebound" requirement is met when the surviving spouse is substantially confined to his or her home (ward or clinical areas, if institutionalized) or immediate premises by reason of disability or disabilities which it is reasonably certain will remain throughout the surviving spouse's lifetime.
(Authority: 38 U.S.C. 1311(d))

(f) *Housebound; improved Pension; death.* The annual rate of death Pension payable to a surviving spouse who does not qualify for an annual rate of death Pension payable under §3.23(a)(6) based on need for aid and attendance shall be as set forth in §3.23(a)(7) if the surviving spouse is permanently housebound by reason of disability. The "permanently housebound" requirement is met when the surviving spouse is substantially confined to his or her home (ward or clinical areas, if institutionalized) or immediate premises by reason of disability or disabilities which it is reasonably certain will remain throughout the surviving spouse's lifetime.
(Authority: 38 U.S.C. 1541(e))
[44 FR 45939, Aug. 6, 1979]

Here is the authorization for the aid and attendance or housebound allowances under Special Monthly Compensation (SMC).

38 CFR §3.350 Special monthly Compensation ratings.

(b) *Ratings under 38 U.S.C. 1114(l).* The special monthly Compensation provided by 38 U.S.C. 1114(l) is payable for anatomical loss or loss of use of both feet, one hand and one foot, <u>blindness in both eyes with visual acuity of 5/200 or less or</u> <u>being permanently bedridden or so helpless as to be in need of regular aid and attendance.</u>

(l) *Special aid and attendance benefit; 38 U.S.C. 1114(r)*—(1) Maximum Compensation cases. A veteran receiving the maximum rate under 38 U.S.C. 1114 (o) or (p) who is in need of regular aid and attendance or a higher level of care is entitled to an additional allowance during periods he or she is not hospitalized at United States Government expense. (See §3.552(b)(2) as to continuance following admission for hospitalization.) Determination of this need is subject to the criteria of §3.352. The regular or higher level aid and attendance allowance is payable whether or not the need for regular aid and attendance or a higher level of care was a partial basis for entitlement to the maximum rate under 38 U.S.C. 1114 (o) or (p), or was based on an independent factual determination.

(s) *Total plus 60 percent, or housebound; 38 U.S.C. 1114(s).* The special monthly Compensation provided by 38 U.S.C. 1114(s) is payable where the veteran has a single service-connected disability rated as 100 percent and,
> (1) Has additional service-connected disability or disabilities independently ratable at 60 percent, separate and distinct from the 100 percent service-connected disability and involving different anatomical segments or bodily systems, or
> (2) Is permanently housebound by reason of service-connected disability or disabilities. This requirement is met when the veteran is substantially confined as a direct result of service-connected disabilities to his or her dwelling and the immediate premises or, if institutionalized, to the ward or clinical areas, and it is reasonably certain that the disability or disabilities and resultant confinement will continue throughout his or her lifetime.

HOW VA APPLIES THE ALLOWANCES IN PRACTICE

Aid & Attendance / Housebound Allowances for Spouses or Surviving Spouses

1. Incrementally larger allowances for the spouse of a veteran where the spouse needs aid and attendance and the veteran is at least 30% disabled. A different benefit corresponds to each 10% rating increase from 30% up to 100%. See applicable rate table below.
2. An aid and attendance or housebound allowance for a surviving spouse receiving Dependency and Indemnity Compensation (DIC). See applicable rate table below.
3. An allowance for the spouse of a veteran where the spouse needs aid and attendance and the veteran is receiving Special Monthly Compensation (SMC).

See applicable rate table below.

Disability Compensation Rate Table for 2020

Disability Percent	30%	40%	50%	60%	70%	80%	90%	100%
Spouse Aid and Attendance Allowance	$48.00	$63.00	$80.00	$96.00	$111.00	$127.00	$143.00	$158.82

Dependency and Indemnity Compensation (DIC) for 2020

Basic Monthly Rate = $1,340.14, with 1 Child $1,672.14, with 2 Children $2,004.14, etc.

Allowances: with A&A $1,672.14, with Housebound $1,495.67, with 8 Yrs Continuous Disabled $1,624.71

1. Add **$284.57** for veteran's death, if veteran was in receipt of or entitled to receive compensation for a service-connected disability rated totally disabling (including a rating based on individual unemployability) for a continuous period of at least 8 years immediately preceding death AND the surviving spouse was married to the veteran for those same 8 years. (38 U.S.C. 1311(a)(2))
2. Add the following allowance for each dependent child under age 18: Effective 12/1/14 **$332.00** per child (38 U.S.C. 1311(b))
3. If the surviving spouse is entitled to Aid and Attendance, add **$332.00.** (38 U.S.C. 1311(c))
4. If the surviving spouse is entitled to Housebound, add **$155.53** (38 U.S.C. 1311(d))
5. If the surviving spouse has one or more children under the age 18 on the award, add the 2-year transitional benefit of **$286.00** effective, December 1, 2014 (38 U.S.C. 1311(f))

Special Monthly Compensation (SMC) Rate Table for 2020

SMC Schedule	L	R.1	R.2 or T	S
Aid and Attendance Allowance for Spouse	$158.82	$158.82	$158.82	$158.82

Aid and Attendance or Housebound SMC for Veterans who are Totally Disabled

1. An income under SMC Schedule L is available for a veteran who needs aid and attendance and is receiving Disability Compensation at 100% disability under a single disability rating. Generally this cannot be a combined 100% rating, but under certain circumstances it can be if the same underlying condition contributes to the various disabilities in the combined rating. The condition rated 100% or the combined 100% due to contributing impairments from the same condition must be all or partly responsible for the need for aid and attendance. If this is not the case, SMC under Schedule L is not allowed. We will discuss in more detail further on how VA evaluates the need for aid and attendance under Schedule L and how to apply for the additional income. Also look at the applicable rate table below.

2. An income under SMC Schedule S is available for veterans 100% disabled with an additional single rating of 60% or more, or who are permanently confined to their residence and are considered housebound. This is an alternative benefit for veterans who do not meet criteria for aid and attendance but do meet criteria for being housebound. Generally this requires a 100% disability under a single disability rating. However, court rulings have allowed the 100% rating under Individual Unemployability (IU) which requires a single rating of 60% or more to be paid at the 100% IU rate. ***The combined rating option of 70% for qualifying for IU is not applicable for qualifying for SMC Schedule S – only the 60% single disability option***. The condition or conditions rated 100% or 100% IU must be all or partly responsible for the need for being housebound. If this is not the case, SMC under Schedule S is not allowed. We will discuss in more detail further on how VA evaluates the need for housebound under Schedule S and how to apply. See the applicable rate table below.

3. Two special increased aid and attendance allowances are available for severely disabled veterans receiving SMC under Schedule (R.1) and Schedule (R.2) under very specific conditions. These special ratings require daily intensive home care under certain conditions and there are only a few score thousand veterans who are receiving this special benefit which could be as much as $8919.54 a month for a veteran with dependents. See table below.

4. An income under SMC Schedule T due to residuals from traumatic brain injury (TBI) is available. The benefit is available for TBI injury that requires aid and attendance. We will discuss this option below. This benefit is paid at the applicable rate of SMC Schedule R.2

You may be interested to know how many veterans on claim for Disability Compensation would meet the criteria above. On the next page we provide a table of the most current statistics for veterans in this category as of 2018.

According to the table, 1,041,519 claimants were 100% disabled or being paid at 100% due to individual unemployability. Some of these may not know that they are entitled to an additional allowance for aid and attendance or housebound. Also from the same table you will see that 691,708 claimants are receiving SMC. But, there are various categories of SMC and not all of these beneficiaries are receiving it because of the need for aid and attendance or housebound. There may be an opportunity here to apply for increased benefits.

Number of Beneficiaries – 2018	Younger than 65	Age 65 and Older	Total all Ages	Percent of All Claims
Disability Compensation	3,150,664	1,592,444	4,743,108	84.7%
DIC for Surviving Spouse	149,915	255,632	405,547	7.2%
Veterans Pension	65,124	194,965	260,089	4.6%
Survivors Pension for Spouse	24,580	168,243	192,823	3.4%
Fiduciary Beneficiaries (Compensation, Pension and DIC)			190,540	3.4%
100% Disabled			684,851	12.2%
Individual Unemployability (Paid at 100% Disabled Rate)			356,668	6.4%
Special Monthly Compensation (SMC)			691,708	12.3%
Tinnitus and Hearing Loss – Most Prevalent Disabilities			3,363,237	60.0%
Total Beneficiaries – Compensation, DIC and Pension			5,601,567	
Healthcare System Enrolled			9 million +	

Source: VA Annual Benefits Report 2018, DVA 2020 Budget Proposal

Special Monthly Compensation (SMC) Rate Table for 2020 showing the extra allowances for A & A and housebound

SMC Schedule	L	R.1	R.2 or T	S
Veteran SMC Alone	$3,864.90	$7,749.68	$8,889.08	$3,476.65
Veteran Alone Rated 100%	$3,106.04	$3,106.04	$3,106.04	$3,106.04
Difference between SMC and Rated 100%	**$758.86**	**$4,643.64**	**$5,783.04**	**$370.61**
Veteran & Spouse SMC	$4,038.08	$7,922.86	$9,062.26	$3,649.83
Veteran & Spouse Veteran Rated 100%	$3,279.22	$3,279.22	$3,279.22	$3,279.22
Difference between V&S SMC and 100%	**$758.86**	**$4,643.64**	**$5,783.04**	**$370.61**
Aid and Attendance Allowance for Spouse	$158.82	$158.82	$158.82	$158.82

Pension with Aid and Attendance or Housebound Allowances

We discuss these allowances along with the very complicated applications associated with the allowances for Veterans Pension and Survivors Pension in Chapter 6.

2020 Maximum Annual Pension Rates (MAPR)
Showing Aid and Attendance and Housebound Allowances

FOR A VETERAN	Annual	Monthly
Basic MAPR without Spouse or Child	$13,752	$1,146
Basic MAPR with One Dependent	$18,008	$1,500
Basic MAPR Plus Housebound Allowance without Spouse or Child	$16,805	$1,400
Amount of Housebound Allowance without Spouse or Child	**$3,053**	**$254**
Basic MAPR Plus Aid and Attendance Allowance without Spouse or Child	$22,939	$1,911
Amount of Aid and Attendance Allowance without Spouse or Child	**$9,187**	**$765**
Basic MAPR Plus Housebound Allowance with One Dependent	$21,063	$1,755
Amount of Housebound Allowance with One Dependent	**$3,053**	**$254**
Basic MAPR Plus Aid and Attendance Allowance with One Dependent	$27,195	$2,266
Amount of Aid and Attendance Allowance with One Dependent	**$9,187**	**$766**
FOR A SURVIVING SPOUSE	Annual	Monthly
Basic MAPR Without Child	$9,224	$768
Basic MAPR With One Dependent Child	$12,072	$1,006
Basic MAPR Plus Housebound Allowance without Child	$11,273	$939
Amount of Housebound Allowance without Child	**$2,049**	**$171**
Basic MAPR Plus Aid and Attendance Allowance without Dependent Child	$14,742	$1,228
Amount of Aid and Attendance Allowance without Child	**$5,518**	**$460**
Basic MAPR Plus Housebound Allowance with One Dependent Child	$14,116	$1,176
Amount of Housebound Allowance with One Dependent Child	**$2,049**	**$171**
Basic MAPR Plus Aid and Attendance Allowance with One Dependent Child	$17,586	$1,465
Amount of Aid and Attendance Allowance with 1 Dependent Child	**$5,518**	**$460**

The Application Process for Aid and Attendance or Housebound Allowances

Under the new rules effective February 19, 2019, any applications for benefits, whether they be applications for initial claims or applications for individuals already on claim, must use the appropriate forms for those applications. In the past, any request for the allowances discussed in this chapter could generally be submitted using VA Form 21-4138 and that would initiate duty to assist from the Regional Office. Informally, this may still be true, but we recommend following the new requirements by submitting on the proper application form. We generally get better results by following the new rules.

If the benefit for Pension, Compensation or DIC has been awarded within one year of applying for one of these allowances, the requirement is to use VA Form 20-0995 which is known as a "Supplemental Claim." Any request after one year of receiving an award should be filed on the appropriate form for that particular benefit such as VA Form 21-526 EZ for Special Monthly Compensation or VA Form 21-534 EZ for DIC. Applications for allowances with Pension are discussed in Chapter 6 and procedures for requesting increases for those allowances are covered in that chapter.

We have found, that the Supplemental Claim Form is much simpler to use whether an award has been made within the last year or it has been longer than one year after receiving a favorable decision. And, VA does not seem to mind if we use this form instead of using the other forms listed in the paragraph above. Here are the criteria to use this form as found on the form itself.

> *"In choosing this option, you're adding new evidence that supports your case or identifying new evidence for review. A reviewer will look at all the evidence and determine whether it evidence changes the decision. Use this form to request a SUPPLEMENTAL CLAIM of the decision you received that you disagree with. A SUPPLEMENTAL CLAIM is a new review of an issue(s) previously decided by the Department of Veterans Affairs (VA) based on submission of new and relevant evidence."*

However, be careful in using a supplemental claim form for an increase in the benefit where the final decision has been longer than one year. You cannot submit an "intent to file" with a supplemental claim and thus you cannot capture an effective date if you use this method.

If you need some time to gather the VA Form 21-2680 or the Form FV13, and it has been one year since the most recent final decision, then use an original claim form that pertains to the particular benefit for which you are filing an increase. For Compensation with SMC or spousal aid and attendance allowance with compensation it is VA form 21-526 EZ. For DIC it is VA Form 21-534 EZ.

Following is how we use this supplemental claim form or if necessary the more complete initial application form. Below you will see a partial screenshot of the first page of form itself. We use it because it is very simple and because the Regional Office already has all of the information necessary in the eFolder to process a new request. Using one of the initial application forms is just a redundant process. You must put the VA case number on this form that pertains to the benefit that is already being received.

Unlike the forms for initial application, this one has only 2 pages and is pretty straightforward. We also believe that it will receive a quicker response on a decision from the Regional Office.

Expiration Date: 2/28/2022

Department of Veterans Affairs

DECISION REVIEW REQUEST: SUPPLEMENTAL CLAIM

VA DATE STAMP
DO NOT WRITE IN THIS SPACE

INSTRUCTIONS: PLEASE READ THE PRIVACY ACT NOTICE AND RESPONDENT BURDEN INFORMATION ON PAGE 2 BEFORE COMPLETING THIS FORM.

PART I - CLAIMANT'S IDENTIFYING INFORMATION

NOTE: You can either complete the form online or by hand. If completed by hand, print the information requested in ink, neatly, and legibly to expedite processing the form.

1. VETERAN'S NAME (First, Middle Initial, Last)

2. VETERAN'S SOCIAL SECURITY NUMBER

3. VA FILE NUMBER (If applicable)

4. VETERAN'S DATE OF BIRTH (MM/DD/YYYY)
Month   Day   Year

5. VETERAN'S SERVICE NUMBER (If applicable)

6. INSURANCE POLICY NUMBER (If applicable)

7. CLAIMANT'S NAME (First, Middle Initial, Last) (If other than veteran)

8. CLAIMANT TYPE:
☐ VETERAN   ☐ VETERAN'S SPOUSE   ☐ VETERAN'S CHILD   ☐ VETERAN'S PARENT   ☐ OTHER (Specify)

9. CURRENT MAILING ADDRESS (Number, street or rural route, City or P.O. Box, State and ZIP Code and Country)

No. & Street

Apt./Unit Number   City

State/Province   Country   ZIP Code/Postal Code

10. TELEPHONE NUMBER (Include Area Code)

11. E-MAIL ADDRESS (Optional)

12. BENEFIT TYPE: PLEASE CHECK ONLY ONE (If you would like to file for multiple benefit types, you must complete a separate request form for each benefit type.)
☐ COMPENSATION   ☐ PENSION/SURVIVORS BENEFITS   ☐ FIDUCIARY   ☐ INSURANCE   ☐ VETERANS HEALTH ADMINISTRATION
☐ VOCATIONAL REHABILITATION AND EMPLOYMENT   ☐ LOAN GUARANTY   ☐ EDUCATION   ☐ NATIONAL CEMETERY ADMINISTRATION

PART II - ISSUE(S) FOR SUPPLEMENTAL CLAIM

Here is the rest of the front page from the Supplemental Claim Form. This is called Part II and you will fill out what you are requesting in this section. Please note that you must check the appropriate box such as Compensation or Pension/Survivor's Benefits (DIC). Next, type into this form the statement that we show in the screenshot below – "Please read attached VA Form 21-4138 that explains this claim." For the date, use the date of the original award or guess at that date if you can't remember. You would enter similar information on an initial application form.

---

12. BENEFIT TYPE: PLEASE CHECK ONLY ONE *(If you would like to file for multiple benefit types, you must complete a separate request form for each benefit type.)*

- ☐ COMPENSATION
- ☐ PENSION/SURVIVORS BENEFITS
- ☐ FIDUCIARY
- ☐ INSURANCE
- ☐ VETERANS HEALTH ADMINISTRATION
- ☐ VOCATIONAL REHABILITATION AND EMPLOYMENT
- ☐ LOAN GUARANTY
- ☐ EDUCATION
- ☐ NATIONAL CEMETERY ADMINISTRATION

PART II - ISSUE(S) FOR SUPPLEMENTAL CLAIM

13. YOU MUST LIST EACH ISSUE DECIDED BY VA THAT YOU WOULD LIKE VA TO REVIEW AS PART OF YOUR SUPPLEMENTAL CLAIM. *Please refer to your decision notice(s) for a list of adjudicated issues. For each issue, please identify the date of VA's decision. (You may attach additional sheets of paper, if necessary. Include your name and file number on each additional sheet.*

Check this box if any issue listed below is being withdrawn from the legacy appeals process. ☐ OPT-IN from SOC/SSOC

13A. SPECIFIC ISSUE(S)	13B. DATE OF VA DECISION NOTICE
Please read attached VA Form 21-4138 that explains this claim	09/25/2019

VA FORM FEB 2019 **20-0995**

In subsequent sections of this chapter, we furnish the appropriate language to include on the VA Form 21-4138 that you will submit with the 20-0995 or with one of the initial application forms.

How to Apply for Spouse Aid and Attendance with Compensation or SMC

As mentioned above, for a veteran who is receiving Disability Compensation of at least 30% or higher or is on Special Monthly Compensation, and who has a spouse who needs aid and attendance, the veteran claimant can get an additional monthly allowance to help offset the cost of aid and attendance for his or her spouse. Following are the directions for this type of claim. All of the forms that you need are found on the "Claim Support Disc" that comes with this book.

1. If it is going to take you awhile to assemble the evidence for the need for aid and attendance, do an "Intent to File" using the following form (you can only use this with an initial application form):

> VA Form 21-0966 INTENT TO FILE (found on the Claim Support Disc)

2. You must provide medical evidence that the spouse of the veteran is in need of the aid and attendance of another person. Use VA Form 21-2680 for this and have the physician treating the spouse who needs aid and attendance, fill out the form. <u>VA Form 21-2680 must be signed by a M.D. Nurse Practitioner or D.O. and not by a nurse or physician's assistant.</u>

> VBA-21-2680-ARE – Exam for Housebound Status or Permanent Need for Regular A&A

3. Although it is not necessary to show that someone is providing A&A services we recommend providing evidence for those services. The reason for this is if the 2680 form makes a weak case for the need for aid and attendance, the fact that somebody is providing aid and attendance will clue in the Regional Office that perhaps more information is needed from the doctor. This might then facilitate redoing the form or getting a supplementary statement from the doctor in addition to the 2680 as to why the spouse needs aid and attendance. Here is the form for this purpose.

> FV13 – Care Provider Certification of Services (found on the Claim Support Disc)

If the spouse is confined to a nursing home use this form instead of the FV13.

> VBA-21-0779-ARE – Request for Nursing Home Info in Connection with Claim for Aid and Attendance (found on the Claim Support Disc)

4. Complete VA Form 20-0995 – Supplemental Claim, based on the instructions provided in a previous section. Or use VA Form 21-526 EZ.

Use VA Form 21-4138 to Provide Further Detail with the Supplemental or Initial Claim

> VBA-21-4138-ARE – Statement in Support of Claim (found on the Claim Support Disc)

On the VA Form 21-4138, enter the name of the veteran who is on claim and enter the VA case number for the Disability Compensation or SMC claim. If you can't find the case number, you can enter the Social Security number. Enter the following text in the form area for text. The title of this text area is is: *"The following statement is made in connection with a claim for benefits in the case of the above-named veteran:"*

> I am the above name veteran, I am currently receiving *(use either "Disability Compensation" or "SMC" here whichever applies)* benefits from the Department of Veterans Affairs. I am requesting the spouse aid and attendance allowance available to me under my current award. My current living spouse, *(insert the full name of the spouse)*, is in need of the aid and attendance of another person. She is my legal spouse and we have been living together continuously up to this current date. I now

qualify for the aid and attendance allowance under *(use"Disability Compensation" or "SMC" whichever applies here).* I am enclosing VA Form 21-2680 as medical evidence of the need for the aid and attendance of another person for my spouse as well as a certification of service by the caregiver who is providing aid and attendance for my spouse.

5. Include the following form with a request for aid and attendance if the veteran was single or married to a different spouse and not married to the current spouse at the time of the award for Disability Compensation or SMC. Otherwise do not include this form.

VBA-21-686c-ARE – Declaration of Status of Dependents (Claim Support Disc)

6. The veteran on claim for Disability Compensation or SMC has to sign the VA Form 21-4138.

Submit all of the forms to the claims center in Janesville Wisconsin. See the Claim Support Disc that comes with this book for the forms listed above as well as instructions for submitting to the VA's Claims Intake Center at Janesville Wisconsin

How to Apply for Aid and Attendance or Housebound with DIC

A Sad Commentary on DIC Recipients Who Should Be Receiving Allowances but Aren't
As discussed previously, a surviving spouse who is currently receiving monthly payments for Dependency and Indemnity Compensation (DIC) is entitled to an additional aid and attendance allowance if that person needs aid and attendance or to an additional housebound allowance if that person is considered housebound. It should be noted from previous material in this book that a large number of surviving spouses are receiving DIC.

In fact, more survivors are receiving DIC than are receiving Survivor's Pension with Aid and Attendance. In 2018, 405,547 individuals were receiving DIC and **less than half of that amount – 192,823** individuals were receiving Survivor's Pension with Aid and Attendance. It is a sad commentary that so much attention in the community is placed on getting Survivor's Pension with Aid and Attendance for older individuals and no attention is given at all to increasing monthly DIC payments for the same reason. DIC with aid and attendance is **$1,672.14** a month and is not subject to any means testing. Survivor's Pension with Aid and Attendance is **$1,228** a month and is subject to constant scrutiny from VA to make sure that the means testing is being met. DIC with housebound is **$1,495.67** a month.

Number of Beneficiaries – 2018	Younger than 65	Age 65 and Older	Total all Ages	Percent of All Claims
Disability Compensation	3,150,664	1,592,444	4,743,108	84.7%
DIC for Surviving Spouse	149,915	255,632	405,547	7.2%
Veterans Pension	65,124	194,965	260,089	4.6%
Survivors Pension for Spouse	24,580	168,243	192,823	3.4%
Fiduciary Beneficiaries (Compensation, Pension and DIC)			190,540	3.4%
100% Disabled			684,851	12.2%
Individual Unemployability (Paid at 100% Disabled Rate)			356,668	6.4%
Special Monthly Compensation (SMC)			691,708	12.3%
Tinnitus and Hearing Loss – Most Prevalent Disabilities			3,363,237	60.0%
Total Beneficiaries – Compensation, DIC and Pension			5,601,567	
Healthcare System Enrolled			9 million +	

Source: VA Annual Benefits Report 2018, DVA 2020 Budget Proposal

It is most likely that perhaps 15% to 20% or more of the number of those on DIC might be eligible for the aid and attendance or housebound allowances but are not receiving this extra income simply because the beneficiaries don't know the allowances exist. Probably only a paltry percentage of these beneficiaries are actually receiving allowances currently. The reason we estimate so many could be eligible is because more than 60% of all of those on DIC are age 65 and older and many of them are probably in their 70s, 80s or even 90s because they are survivors of World War 2, Korea and Vietnam veterans – the largest cohort of any veterans in recent history. Statistically, people that old are often housebound or in need of aid and attendance.

Aid and attendance or housebound allowances with DIC are not advertised anywhere. VA does not send out notices to beneficiaries of DIC that they might be eligible simply because it would be a huge commitment of resources and besides VA would have no way of knowing if any of these beneficiaries would qualify or not. There is no requirement for someone on DIC to report back to VA on a regular basis to notify of the need for aid and attendance or housebound. We believe – and it is a sad commentary – that those who would be eligible have no clue that they can get this extra money to help them in with their needs.

Filling out the Application

Below are the directions for this type of claim. All of the forms that you need are found on the "Claim Support Disc" that comes with this book.

1. If it is going to take you awhile to assemble the evidence for the need for aid and attendance or housebound, submit an "Intent to File" using the following form (you can only use this with an initial application form)::

  VA Form 21-0966 INTENT TO FILE (on Claim Support Disc)

2. You must provide medical evidence that the DIC beneficiary is in need of the aid and attendance of another person or is housebound. Please read the section in this chapter on what constitutes housebound and aid and attendance if you are not sure. Use VA Form 21-2680 for the medical evidence and have the physician treating the DIC beneficiary who needs aid and attendance or is housebound, fill out the form. VA Form 21-2680 must be signed by a doctor or nurse practitioner and not by a nurse or physician's assistant.

It is important to note that the DIC claim will be under the veterans claim file. Make sure that the veteran information is provided on the 21-2680 and that the spouse of the veteran receiving DIC is indicated as the claimant on this form. The relationship to the veteran on the form is "surviving spouse."

  VBA-21-2680-ARE – Exam for Housebound Status or Permanent Need for Regular A&A (on Claim Support Disc)

3. Although it is not necessary to show that someone is providing services for aid and attendance, we recommend providing evidence for those services. The reason for this is if the Form 21-2680 makes a weak case for the need for aid and attendance, the fact that somebody is providing aid and attendance will clue in the Regional Office that perhaps more information is needed from the doctor. This might then facilitate redoing the form or getting a supplementary statement from the doctor in addition to the 2680 as to why the spouse needs aid and attendance. If the 2680 is not strong enough to substantiate aid and attendance or housebound, you can always go back to the doctor and explain what the form is for and that the doctor needs to be more specific about whether his or her patient on DIC is really in need of aid and attendance or housebound based on the definition in this chapter which is "substantially confined to his or her

residence for life." The housebound residence can include a personal residence or a care community or a nursing home. Here is the form for providing evidence of aid and attendance.

FV13 – Care Provider Certification of Services (on Claim Support Disc)

If the DIC beneficiary is confined to a nursing home use this form instead of the FV13.

VBA-21-0779-ARE – Request for Nursing Home Info in Connection with Claim for Aid and Attendance (on Claim Support Disc)

4. Complete VA Form 20-0995 – Supplemental Claim, based on the instructions provided in a previous section or use an initial application form VA Form 21-534 EZ if you are going to capture an effective date.

Use VA Form 21-4138 to Provide Further Detail with the Supplemental Claim

VBA-21-4138-ARE – Statement in Support of Claim (found on the Claim Support Disc)

On the 21-4138 form enter the name of the deceased veteran. The DIC claim will be under the name of the veteran and not the surviving spouse. Enter the veterans claim file number or Social Security number of the veteran. Enter the following text in the form area for text. The title of this text area is: *"The following statement is made in connection with a claim for benefits in the case of the above-named veteran:"*

The above named veteran is deceased. I am the legal surviving spouse of this veteran and I have been receiving DIC based on the veteran's death. My name and SSN are (*put in the name and Social Security number of the DIC beneficiary*) and I now qualify for the (*use here either the words "aid and attendance allowance" or "housebound allowance"*) available to me under DIC. I am enclosing VA Form 21-2680 as medical evidence of the need for this additional allowance.

5. The beneficiary receiving DIC should sign the VA Form 21-4138.

6. Submit all of the forms to the claims center in Janesville Wisconsin. See the Claim Support Disc that comes with this book for the forms listed above as well as instructions for submitting to the VA's Claims Intake Center at Janesville Wisconsin.

How to Apply for the SMC Schedule S Housebound Benefit

An income under SMC Schedule S is available for veterans who are

- 100% disabled with an additional single rating of 60% or more, **OR**
- 100% and permanently confined to their residence and are considered housebound.

Special Monthly Compensation (SMC) Rate Table for 2020 (In Dollars)

SMC Schedule	L	L½	M	M½	N	N½	O/P	R.1	R.2	S
Veteran Alone	3,864.90	4,064.70	4,265.31	4,558.37	4,852.09	5,137.51	5,423.45	7,749.68	8,889.08	3,476.65
Veteran & Spouse	4,038.08	4,237.88	4,438.49	4,731.55	5,025.27	5,310.69	5,596.63	7,922.86	9,062.26	3,649.83

This is an alternative benefit for veterans who do not meet criteria for aid and attendance under SMC Schedule L but do meet criteria for being housebound under Schedule S. Generally this requires a 100% disability under a single disability rating. However, court rulings have allowed

1. a 100% equivalent rating under Individual Unemployability (IU) WHICH IN TURN
2. requires a single rating of 60% or more to be paid at the 100% IU rate AND
3. the optional combined rating option of 70% for qualifying for IU is disregarded for qualifying for SMC Schedule S – only the 60% single disability option is considered.

The condition or conditions rated 100% or 100% IU must be all or partly responsible for the need for being housebound. If this is not the case, SMC under Schedule S is not allowed. We will discuss in more detail below how VA evaluates the need for housebound under Schedule S. Note the large number of individuals in 2015 who are receiving Special Monthly Compensation.

Number of Beneficiaries – 2018	Younger than 65	Age 65 and Older	Total all Ages	Percent of All Claims
Disability Compensation	3,150,664	1,592,444	4,743,108	84.7%
DIC for Surviving Spouse	149,915	255,632	405,547	7.2%
Veterans Pension	65,124	194,965	260,089	4.6%
Survivors Pension for Spouse	24,580	168,243	192,823	3.4%
Fiduciary Beneficiaries (Compensation, Pension and DIC)			190,540	3.4%
100% Disabled			684,851	12.2%
Individual Unemployability (Paid at 100% Disabled Rate)			356,668	6.4%
Special Monthly Compensation (SMC)			691,708	12.3%
Tinnitus and Hearing Loss – Most Prevalent Disabilities			3,363,237	60.0%
Total Beneficiaries – Compensation, DIC and Pension			5,601,567	
Healthcare System Enrolled			9 million +	

Source: VA Annual Benefits Report 2018, DVA 2020 Budget Proposal

Also, note from the previous chart how many veterans are 100% disabled added to how many surviving spouses are receiving DIC. The total is more than twice the number of total beneficiaries for Veterans Pension and Survivor's Pension combined.

We think SMC Schedule S and DIC eligible beneficiaries are an overlooked area in which to assist veterans and their survivors. Many accredited agents and accredited attorneys seem to be concentrating on getting Pension benefits for veterans and their survivors but likely have as much potential or more in helping surviving spouses with DIC and 100% disabled veterans receive aid and attendance or housebound benefits under SMC as well. We doubt that very few accredited attorneys ever bother to ask their clients if those clients are on DIC or 100% disabled or have a worsening disability that might increase their rating to 100%.

<u>We believe a large number of spouses receiving DIC and veterans rated 100% are completely unaware of the housebound and aid and attendance incomes that they could be receiving.</u>

There is also a possible additional option for veterans on Disability Compensation and not rated 100%. It may be quite possible for an older claimant to request an increase in rating and possibly get 100% or get 60% and then further apply for Individual Unemployability. Remember, the second option for receiving IU where the veteran is at least 70% combined rating does not apply here. Courts in the past have ruled that the code only applies to a veteran who is 60% or more disabled and then applies for IU at 100%. For more information on how to apply for IU see Chapter 5.

Follow the instructions below for a veteran who is being paid at 100% rated and who wishes to apply for SMC Schedule S.

1. If it is going to take you awhile to assemble the evidence for housebound, submit an "Intent to File" using the following form (you can only use this with an initial application form):

    VA Form 21-0966 INTENT TO FILE (found on the Claim Support Disc set)

2. You must provide medical evidence that the applicant is housebound. We cover this in a previous section in this chapter but here's the definition according to regulation and court rulings.

The definition of housebound from 38 CFR § 3.350(i) (1)(2) is the following:

(1) Has additional service-connected disability or disabilities independently ratable at 60 percent, separate and distinct from the 100 percent service-connected disability and involving different anatomical segments or bodily systems,

OR

(2) <u>Is permanently housebound by reason of service-connected disability or disabilities. This requirement is met when the veteran is substantially confined as a direct result of service-connected disabilities to his or her dwelling and the immediate premises or, if</u>

<u>institutionalized, to the ward or clinical areas, and it is reasonably certain that the
disability or disabilities and resultant confinement will continue throughout his or her
lifetime.</u>

Most veterans are going to qualify for being "housebound" under the second option above. Not very many veterans are going to qualify by being 100% rated disabled and then having VA say that they have an equivalent combined rating of 60% from other disabilities. Please note that any veteran in this situation would not have a final rating of 160%. The most available is 100%. What this is saying is that VA has determined there are additional disabilities that could be rated at 60% independently without actually paying the veteran for those disabilities since the veteran is already being paid at 100%.

A number of appeals in the past have addressed what "substantially confined" means. Previous board decisions had determined that substantially confines means that the claimant is restricted to his house and could not leave even for medical treatment purposes. The Court of Appeals for Veterans Claims overturned those previous BVA decisions.

> *Howell versus Nicholson, March 23, 2006 number 04-0624 CAVC*
> *"The term "substantially confined" is not defined by statute or regulation. See id. Because the meaning of the term "substantially confined" is ambiguous and there is no regulatory interpretation, "the Court must determine the meaning" of the term "and the Board's obligation" thereunder. Thompson v. Brown, 8 Vet. App. 169, 175 (1995); see also Jackson and Cropper, both supra. The Secretary submits that the clear implication of this term is that the requirement that one be "substantially confined" is met when the claimant is restricted to his house except for medical treatment purposes. The Secretary, citing to Senate Report No. 1745 (June 27, 1960), notes that in passing section 1114(s) Congress intended to provide additional Compensation for veterans who were unable to overcome their particular disabilities and leave the house in order to earn an income as opposed to an inability to leave the house at all. Mr. Howell does not contest this interpretation.*
>
> *To the extent substantial confinement does not include departures for medical purposes, we agree that the interpretation that the Secretary presents in his supplemental briefing is reasonable and consistent with statute and regulations. See Jackson, Thompson, and Cropper, all supra.*
>
> *Accordingly, we hold that leaving one's house for medical purposes cannot, by itself, serve as the basis for finding that one is not substantially confined for purposes of SMC-HB benefits, and the Board's interpretation of section 1114(s) to preclude the grant of SMC benefits on the basis of Mr. Howell's leaving his house in order to attend VA medical appointments was erroneous as a matter of law.*

3. Use VA Form 21-2680 for medical evidence of being housebound. Make sure that the physician signing this form understands that the form is being used for a disability benefit. Medical evidence must reflect that the person is substantially confined to his or her residence permanently and for life. You should encourage the doctor to make a statement to this effect on

the form. <u>VA Form 21-2680 must be signed by a doctor or nurse practitioner and not by a nurse or physician's assistant.</u>

VBA-21-2680-ARE – Exam for Housebound Status or Permanent Need for Regular A&A (found on the Claims Support Data Disk)

PLEASE NOTE THAT THE DISABILITY COMPENSATION CONDITION THAT ALLOWS THE APPLICANT TO BE 100% RATED MUST BE PARTLY RESPONSIBLE FOR OR BE A DIRECT REASON FOR WHICH THE VETERAN IS HOUSEBOUND. In the case where the veteran is receiving 100% because of IU, Individual Unemployability would not be the reason. It would be the underlying single condition that was rated 60% or more. Make absolutely sure that the medical report the doctor provides indicates the need for being housebound is a result of the service-connected condition for which the veteran is receiving Compensation. Without this important information, the claim will be denied.

4. Complete VA Form 20-0995 – Supplemental Claim, based on the instructions provided in a previous section or use VA Form 21-526 EZ if you submit an intent to file.

Use VA Form 21-4138 to Provide Further Detail with the Supplemental Claim

VBA-21-4138-ARE – Statement in Support of Claim (found on the Claim Support Disc)

Fill in all the appropriate boxes that pertain to the veteran who is making application. In the text section on the 4138 with the following information

"I am applying for Special Monthly Compensation Schedule S due to being housebound. I have provided you a completed VA Form 21-2680 signed by a licensed health-care professional that substantiates my being housebound. I also provide another form – FV 13 – that substantiates care support that I am receiving as a result of being housebound. My being housebound is a direct result of the condition(s) for which I am currently rated"

5. <u>You may wish to include the following form with a request for aid and attendance if the veteran was single or married to a different spouse and not married to the current spouse at the time of the original award for Disability Compensation. Otherwise do not include this form.</u>

VBA-21-686c-ARE – Declaration of Status of Dependents

6. Remember to complete the signature blocks on the 21-526 EZ. Submit all of the forms to the claims center in Janesville Wisconsin. See the Claim Support Disc that comes with this book for the forms listed above as well as instructions for submitting to the VA's Claims Intake Center at Janesville Wisconsin.

How to Apply for the SMC Schedule L Aid and Attendance Benefit

An income under SMC Schedule L is available for a veteran who needs aid and attendance and is receiving Disability Compensation and is

- at 100% disability under a single disability rating OR
- has a combined 100% disability rating where the individual ratings causing impairment are due to the same underlying condition

Special Monthly Compensation (SMC) Rate Table for 2020 (In Dollars)

SMC Schedule	L	L½	M	M½	N	N½	O/P	R.1	R.2	S
Veteran Alone	3,864.90	4,064.70	4,265.31	4,558.37	4,852.09	5,137.51	5,423.45	7,749.68	8,889.08	3,476.65
Veteran & Spouse	4,038.08	4,237.88	4,438.49	4,731.55	5,025.27	5,310.69	5,596.63	7,922.86	9,062.26	3,649.83

The condition or conditions rated 100% must be all or partly responsible for the need for being housebound. If this is not the case, SMC under Schedule L is not allowed. Note from the chart the large number of individuals in 2018 who were receiving Special Monthly Compensation.

Number of Beneficiaries – 2018	Younger than 65	Age 65 and Older	Total all Ages	Percent of All Claims
Disability Compensation	3,150,664	1,592,444	4,743,108	84.7%
DIC for Surviving Spouse	149,915	255,632	405,547	7.2%
Veterans Pension	65,124	194,965	260,089	4.6%
Survivors Pension for Spouse	24,580	168,243	192,823	3.4%
Fiduciary Beneficiaries (Compensation, Pension and DIC)			190,540	3.4%
100% Disabled			684,851	12.2%
Individual Unemployability (Paid at 100% Disabled Rate)			356,668	6.4%
Special Monthly Compensation (SMC)			691,708	12.3%
Tinnitus and Hearing Loss – Most Prevalent Disabilities			3,363,237	60.0%
Total Beneficiaries – Compensation, DIC and Pension			5,601,567	
Healthcare System Enrolled			9 million +	

Source: VA Annual Benefits Report 2018, DVA 2020 Budget Proposal

Also, note from the chart above how many veterans are 100% disabled and add this to how many surviving spouses are receiving DIC. The total is more than twice the number of total beneficiaries for Veterans Pension and Survivor's Pension. We think this is an overlooked area to assist veterans and their survivors. Many accredited agents and accredited attorneys seem to be concentrating on getting Pension benefits for veterans and their survivors but likely have as much potential or more in helping surviving spouses with DIC and 100% disabled veterans receive aid and attendance or housebound benefits as well. We doubt that very few accredited attorneys ever bother to ask their clients if those clients are on DIC or 100% disabled or have a worsening disability that might increase their rating to 100%.

We believe a large number of spouses receiving DIC and veterans rated 100% are completely unaware of the housebound and aid and attendance allowances that they could be receiving.

Follow the instructions below for a veteran who is 100% rated and who wishes to apply for SMC Schedule L

1. If it is going to take you awhile to assemble the evidence for aid and attendance, do an "Intent to File" using the following form (you cannot submit an intent to file with a supplemental claim):

VA Form 21-0966 INTENT TO FILE (found on the Claim Support Disc)

2. You must provide medical evidence that the applicant needs aid and attendance. We cover criteria for aid and attendance in a previous section in this chapter. Use VA Form 21-2680 for medical evidence of needing aid and attendance. Make sure that the physician signing this form understands the form is being used for a disability benefit. Medical evidence must reflect that the applicant meets the criteria discussed earlier in this chapter for needing aid and attendance. You should encourage the doctor to even specifically state that the applicant is in need of aid and attendance on the form. VA Form 21-2680 must be signed by a doctor or nurse practitioner and not by a nurse or physician's assistant.

VBA-21-2680-ARE – Exam for Housebound Status or Permanent Need for Regular A&A (found on the Claim Support Disc)

PLEASE NOTE THAT THE DISABILITY COMPENSATION CONDITION OR THE RELATED SYMPTOMS DUE TO ONE CONDITION UNDER A COMBINED RATING THAT ALLOW THE APPLICANT TO BE RATED 100% MUST BE PARTLY RESPONSIBLE FOR OR BE A DIRECT REASON FOR WHICH THE VETERAN NEEDS AID AND ATTENDANCE. Make absolutely sure that the medical report the doctor provides indicates that the need for aid and attendance is a result of one or more of the related service-connected impairments for which the veteran is receiving Compensation. Without this important information, the claim will be denied.

4. Complete VA Form 20-0995 – Supplemental Claim, based on the instructions provided in a previous section. Or use VA Form 21-526 EZ if you submit an intent to file.

Use VA Form 21-4138 to Provide Further Detail with the Supplemental Claim

VBA-21-4138-ARE – Statement in Support of Claim (found on the Claim Support Disc)

Fill in all the appropriate boxes that pertain to the veteran who is making application. In the text section on the 4138 enter the following information

"I am applying for Special Monthly Compensation Schedule L due to needing the aid and attendance of another person. I have provided you a completed VA Form 21-2680 signed by a licensed health-care professional that substantiates my being housebound. I also provide another form – FV 13 – that substantiates care support that I am receiving as a result of my needing aid and attendance. This need for aid and attendance is a direct result of the condition(s) for which I am currently rated"

5. <u>You may wish to include the following form with a request for aid and attendance if the veteran was single or married to a different spouse and not married to the current spouse at the time of the original award for Disability Compensation. Otherwise do not include this form.</u>

VBA-21-686c-ARE – Declaration of Status of Dependents

6. Remember to complete the signature blocks on the 21-526 EZ. Submit all of the forms to the claims center in Janesville Wisconsin. See the Claim Support Disc that comes with this book for the forms listed above as well as instructions for submitting to the VA's Claims Intake Center at Janesville Wisconsin.

Comments on SMC Schedule R.1, R.2 and Schedule T

The Basic Concept of SMC

We have not gone into any detail in this chapter on exactly what SMC is and the scope of disabilities it covers. The definition of Special Monthly Compensation is found in Title 38 USC 1114. In essence, VA can pay additional Compensation to a Veteran who, as a result of military service, incurred the loss or loss of use of specific organs or extremities. This is called Special Monthly Compensation.

Loss, or loss of use, is described as either an amputation or, having no effective remaining function of an extremity or organ. The disabilities VA can consider for SMC include:

- loss, or loss of use, of a hand or foot
- immobility of a joint or paralysis
- loss of sight of an eye (having only light perception)
- loss, or loss of use, of a reproductive organ
- complete loss, or loss of use, of both buttocks
- deafness of both ears (having absence of air and bone conduction)
- inability to communicate by speech (complete organic aphonia)
- loss of a percentage of tissue from a single breast, or both breasts, from mastectomy or radiation treatment

Higher Level of SMC for Combined Disabilities

VA will pay higher rates for combinations of these disabilities such as loss or loss of use of the feet, legs, hands, and arms, in specific monetary increments, based on the particular combination of the disabilities. There are also higher payments for various combinations of severe deafness with bilateral blindness.

Additional SMC is available if a Veteran is service-connected for paraplegia, with complete loss of bowel and bladder control. In addition, other service-connected disabilities that, in combination with the above special monthly Compensation, meet certain criteria, result in a higher amount of SMC.

SMC Schedule R.1, Schedule R.2 and Schedule T are the higher levels of SMC for combined disabilities as they also include the need for aid and attendance in the form of daily home care.

It would not be possible for us to go into how to submit applications for these particular benefits in the sentence above that incorporate aid and attendance, because the application would also have to be for the other underlying disabilities.

Claims for these particular aid and attendance related SMC Schedules would be incorporated into an original claim that would result in an award of any of these particular types of SMC. We simply can't go in and ask for an allowance with these benefits for someone who is already rated 100%. They are all tied together with specific requirements for certain disabilities and services.

Also SMC under Schedule R.2 has become a target for budget reduction by Congress. Currently, even though a veteran may qualify for this particular benefit, the total amount of money at the Scheduled rate is not being applied and paid to the veteran.

In 2017 VA was seeking a technical amendment to 38 U.S.C. § 1114(r) in order to restore eligibility for the additional aid and attendance allowance for Veterans receiving the high level of Special Monthly Compensation (SMC) Schedule R.2. Veterans at these specific levels of SMC were initially entitled to consideration for the maximum level of SMC when it was created by Congress, but due to legislative increases in Compensation rates over a period of time, they are no longer eligible for entitlement to this maximum level of SMC. This amendment would not automatically result in an increase in payment rates for these levels of SMC but would allow a Veteran at these levels to be considered for the maximum level of SMC

SMC Schedule T

In 2008, VA did an overhaul of the rating system for TBI, and added a new section to 38 CFR § 3.310. Under the new rating Schedule, veterans can be compensated for TBI in the following rating categories under 38 CFR Part 4:

- Emotional/Behavioral residuals
- Physical (neurological) dysfunction
- Subjective symptoms
- Cognitive impairment residuals

In assigning ratings for TBI, VA also recognized there are caregiving costs associated with TBI-related care. This resulted in a Special Monthly Compensation benefit specifically for TBI cases – SMC Schedule T – under 38 USC 1114 (t). Schedule T pays at the highest possible level of Special Monthly Compensation – SMC R.2, but without the stringent requirements of the SMC R.2 benefit. In order to be eligible for this special monthly Compensation, the veteran must be able to prove that, due to TBI residuals:

- The veteran is in need of in-home aid and attendance OR
- The veteran would require hospitalization, nursing home care, or other residential institutional care in the absence of regular in-home aid and attendance. AND
- The veteran does not otherwise qualify for a higher level of Aid & Attendance under 38 U.S.C.S. § 1114 (R-2).

In order to be considered in need of Aid & Attendance, the veteran must demonstrate:

- Inability to dress/undress without assistance
- Inability to keep clean and presentable without assistance
- Inability to feed oneself without assistance
- Inability to attend to the wants of nature
- Exposure to hazards/dangers incident to daily environment

We also need to point out with Schedule T that it would not be possible to make application for a veteran rated 100% and needing aid and attendance or being housebound as is the case with Schedules L and S. Getting this benefit would require a complete original application.

Chapter 4
Understanding How Claims Are Processed

IN THIS CHAPTER:

- The Regional Office Claims Processing Model; pg. 101
- Deficiencies with the Claims Processing Model; pg. 122
- Understanding Undeveloped and Fully Developed Claims; pg. 131
- The Elements of a Fully Developed Claim for Compensation; pg. 133
- The Elements of a Fully Developed Claim for Pension; pg. 137
- Assistance with Submitting an Application for Benefits; pg. 141
- Services of the Senior Veterans Service Alliance; pg. 143

The Regional Office Claims Processing Model

Definition of Original, Initial and Supplemental Claims

Under the "Veterans Appeals Improvement and Modernization Act" of 2017 Congress redefined definitions of the claims process. For a long time, prior to the new law, the Department had been using the terms "original" and "supplemental" to differentiate between the types of applications that are submitted for disability benefits. Previously, "original claims" meant those submitted by Veterans of all eras who are claiming Disability Compensation or Pension from VBA for the first time. "Supplemental claims" were those submitted by Veterans of all eras who had previously filed for Disability Compensation or Pension with VBA. These definitions have changed.

VA has changed 38 CFR § 3.1 to define the terms "initial claim" and "supplemental claim." Essentially an "initial claim" is a claim for a benefit other than a supplemental claim, including the first filing by a claimant – "an original claim." An initial claim is also a subsequent claim filed by a claimant for an increase in a disability evaluation, a new benefit, or a new disability. These last three categories were previously defined as supplemental claims by VA. Under the new rules, a "supplemental claim" is any claim for benefits under laws administered by the Secretary filed by a claimant who had previously filed a claim for the same or similar benefits on the same or similar basis. Basically, a supplemental claim pertains to an initial claim that needs to be looked at again.

The inclusion of this requirement for a supplemental claim is consistent with the language of revised 38 U.S.C. 5108 under the new law, which requires the Secretary to "readjudicate" a claim where "new and relevant evidence is presented or secured with respect to a supplemental claim." This language presupposes that VA has already adjudicated the claim and issued a notice of decision before a supplemental claim is filed.

VA has amended § 3.103 to require that the evidentiary record for a claim before the agency of original jurisdiction closes when VA issues a decision notice on said claim. The new law allows a claimant to reopen the evidentiary record by submitting a supplemental claim or claim for an increase on the prescribed application form. Submission of a substantially complete initial or supplemental claim also triggers VA's duty to assist in the gathering of evidence under § 3.159. The evidentiary record also reopens when a claim must be readjudicated due to identification of a duty to assist error on higher-level review or by the Board. Whenever the record reopens, evidence submitted to the agency of original jurisdiction while the record was closed will become part of the record to be considered for a subsequent adjudication but nothing will happen with this evidence until a claim is submitted. Unlike previous rules where a claim could be reopened at any time along the process, the new rules only allow reconsideration of a claim when a supplemental claim on VA Form 20-0995 with new and relevant evidence has been submitted.

These new rules are important, because when a "decision notice" is issued the claimant can keep his or her application alive by submitting new evidence and triggering a reconsideration of the decision. Likewise, an initial ruling from the Board of Veterans Appeals also allows the claimant to go back to the Regional Office, submit a supplemental claim with new and relevant evidence and receive a new adjudication decision. Board rulings are now no longer final as long as there is new and relevant evidence. As long as the claimant can uncover new and relevant evidence that is proven to be "new and relevant," the claimant could keep his or her application alive forever in the Regional Office and never have to go to an appeal. Or even go to an appeal, receive a ruling and then find new and relevant evidence and come back and receive reconsideration of the claim from the Regional Office.

The "Intent to File" provisions do not apply to supplemental claims. You cannot submit an Intent to File in anticipation of filing a supplemental claim. This is because the new rules provide that a claimant can maintain the effective date of a potential benefits award by submitting a request for review under any of the three new lanes within one year of the date of the decision denying benefits. Consistent with this requirement, the Intent to File provisions would not apply to supplemental claims as this provision would allow for the submission of a supplemental claim beyond the one-year period provided by statute for protection of effective dates. In other words, if a supplemental claim were submitted after the 1 year protection period from a decision notice, the supplemental claim would be treated as an initial claim and the original effective date would be lost.

Statistics Pertaining to Original and Supplemental Claims

- The number of claims is magnified by growing complexity. There has been a 200 percent increase over the last 10 years in original claims containing eight or more specific medical issues, or contentions.

- The number of individual disabilities claimed has doubled in just the last five years.

- 63% of pending claims are supplemental and 37% are original.

- 81% of Veterans filing supplemental claims are receiving some level of monetary benefit from VBA.

- 10% of Veterans filing supplemental claims already have a 100% disability rating (i.e., they receive $3,000 or more per month) or qualify for Individual Unemployability and are compensated at the 100% disabled rate.

- 48% of Veterans filing supplemental claims are already rated at 50% disability or higher.

- 34% of supplemental claims are from Vietnam-era Veterans and 26% are from Veterans of the Iraq and Afghanistan conflicts.

Forms to Be Used with Each Type of Claim

If you are filing a claim for the first time, you will use VA Form 21-526EZ for Compensation or SMC or VA Form 21-527EZ for Pension or VA Form 21-534EZ for Survivors Pension, accrued benefits or DIC. If you are already receiving a benefit, but you are requesting a reevaluation of the existing rating, an application for secondary service connection based on the existing condition for which you are rated or simply filing for a new benefit, you will use the these same forms for this purpose. The new supplemental application form VA Form 20-0995 is supposed to be used only if you received a decision you did not agree with and you have new evidence to reopen the file for reconsideration and a new decision.

On the other hand we have been using the 20-0995 for requests for reevaluation, secondary disability and increased allowances for Pension, Compensation, DIC and SMC even if we are beyond the 1 year protection period or the claim is in appeal and waiting a decision and we wish to start over. It's a much simpler form than using an original application form. Regional Offices seem to be okay with our using this form for these purposes. However, use this option sparingly. If it will take considerable time to gather the new evidence, you are not allowed to establish an effective date with a supplemental claim by submitting an "intent to file." If you are concerned about establishing an effective date you must use an original application and an "intent to file."

Claims Processing in the Regional Offices

The Veterans Benefits Administration (VBA) is responsible for managing disability claims and payments. VBA operates a national network of 56 Regional Offices in all 50 states. There are also small Regional Offices in San Juan, Puerto Rico and Manila, Philippines. Each state has at least one Regional Office with a few states having more than one. California has 3, Texas 2, Pennsylvania 2 and New York 2. Designated Regional Offices also handle other benefits responsibilities for VBA as listed below.

- 3 Pension Management Centers (PMCs) in St. Paul, Milwaukee and Philadelphia
- 6 Fiduciary Hubs in Salt Lake City, Lincoln, Louisville, Indianapolis, Columbia and Milwaukee
- 3 Education Regional Processing Offices (RPOs) in Muskogee, St. Louis and Buffalo
- 6 Regional Loan Centers (RLCs) in Phoenix, Denver, Houston, Cleveland, Roanoke and St. Petersburg
- The Philadelphia Insurance Center, and
- 8 National Call Centers (NCCs) which are the main contact points for Veterans regarding VBA benefits and services.

Each Regional Office includes a Veterans Service Center (VSC), which is the component that processes Disability Compensation claims. The 3 Pension Management Centers handle Pension claims , DIC and accrued benefit claims.. Regional Offices function under a standardized structure called the claims process improvement (CPI) model, which was first recommended in 2001 by the Claims Processing Task Force appointed by the VA secretary to address the growing backlog of claims. The model was designed to increase efficiency in processing Compensation claims and to reduce the number of errors. The model was substantially changed with the introduction of the paperless claims process and VBMS in 2012 and has seen several revisions.

Failure of the basic claim processing models in the past has resulted in several iterations of models to accommodate mismanagement issues. These failures were largely due to push back from employees and the employees union against poor upper management decisions. Additionally, there have been numerous complaints from veterans and Veterans Service

Organizations about unfavorable decisions, wait times and the failure of VA to implement a well-functioning claims process for Compensation. It is interesting to note that there have been little or no complaints from the claims processing done by the Pension Management Centers.

An Overview of How Claims Are Handled

The claims processing in the Regional Offices is designed around a production line process. Certain teams of employees are assigned to move a claim along that assembly line until it comes out at the end. Perhaps 6 or even 10 people could be involved in processing a single claim.

We provide a schematic of the Compensation model on the next page. The graphic below illustrates the various actions in the production line process once it has been received in the Regional Office. This particular example shows the process under VA's Duty to Assist to develop a Compensation or SMC application for a rating decision. Not all of these steps are necessary as some claims do not require rating decisions or some of these actions below are not needed. A similar process is followed for Pension and DIC claims in the 3 Pension Management Centers, except that the development may not involve as many actions as outlined below.

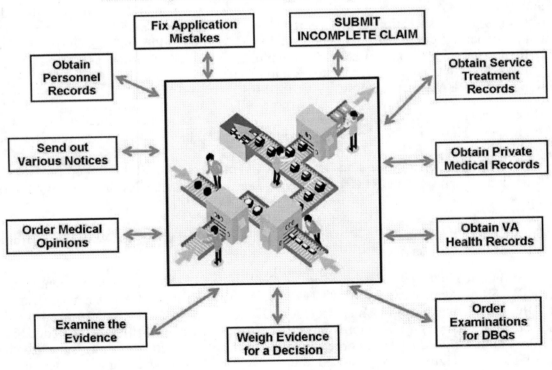

The RO Veterans Service Center Production Line Approach
Development through Duty to Assist

The Most Current Compensation Claims Processing Model in the Regional Offices

On the next page is a schematic of the Compensation processing model. Please refer back to this graphic as subsequent pages will describe the various steps outlined. We will describe the process from initial submission through final decisions and challenges to those decisions.

Regional Office Claims Processing Model as of 2020

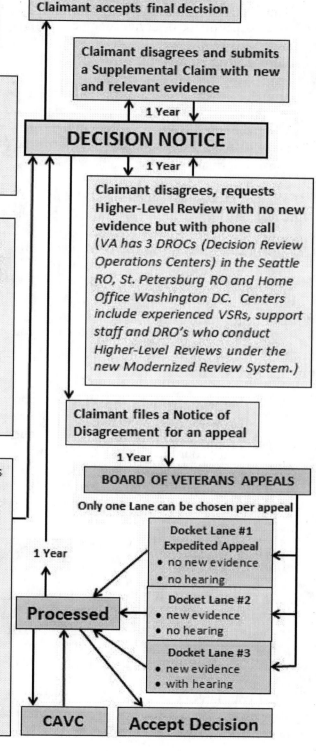

Paper claim sent to Janesville Scanning Center or submitted through eBenefits or vets.gov

Scanned claim uploaded into VBMS through the VA intranet, assigned to a Regional Office through the National Work Queue. (NWQ) eBenefits claim goes directly into the Work Queue. Attempt is made to assign to the Regional Office area where the claimant lives.

Claim is received at the assigned Regional Office (RO) with a VBMS flag and processed by members of the Intake Processing Center (IPC) in the Regional Office Veterans Service Center. The IPC has the following duties.
- Coordinate RO mail room and scanning with the Janesville Scanning Center
- Check claims for accuracy
- Update records for existing claims
- Order Service Treatment Records for new claims
- Workload to Cross Functional Teams

Claim is sent to any of several designated Cross Functional Teams in the VSC.
- Teams are composed of multi-person work queues in the Regional Office
- Work Queue Team is assigned a daily claim workload by Team Coach based on End Product Codes (EP Codes). There are around 30 commonly used codes
- EP Codes determine the amount of time it will take to process each given claim
- Work Queue Teams are flexible – cross functional – and can be organized around certain claim parameters . Generally employees in multiple Regional Offices are working on the same claim

Claimant accepts final decision

Claimant disagrees and submits a Supplemental Claim with new and relevant evidence

1 Year

DECISION NOTICE

1 Year

Claimant disagrees, requests Higher-Level Review with no new evidence but with phone call (*VA has 3 DROCs (Decision Review Operations Centers) in the Seattle RO, St. Petersburg RO and Home Office Washington DC. Centers include experienced VSRs, support staff and DRO's who conduct Higher-Level Reviews under the new Modernized Review System.*)

Claimant files a Notice of Disagreement for an appeal

1 Year

BOARD OF VETERANS APPEALS

Only one Lane can be chosen per appeal

Docket Lane #1
Expedited Appeal
- no new evidence
- no hearing

Docket Lane #2
- new evidence
- no hearing

Docket Lane #3
- new evidence
- with hearing

1 Year

Processed

CAVC

Accept Decision

Filing an Application through eBenefits

eBenefits is a joint VA and Department of Defense web portal that provides resources and self-service capabilities to service members, veterans, and their families. Its purpose is to apply for benefits, do research, and manage VA and military benefits and personal information through a secure Internet connection.

Through eBenefits Veterans can go online to do any of the following: 1) apply for benefits, 2) view their Disability Compensation claim status, 3) access official military personnel documents such as their DD 214, 4) transfer entitlement of Post-9-11 GI Bill to eligible dependents, 5) obtain a VA-guaranteed home loan Certificate of Eligibility, and 6) register for and update direct deposit information for certain benefits. New features are being added regularly.

From our personal experience, an eBenefits account may be more useful to a veteran as a management tool than for an original application for Compensation.

Signing up for the BASIC level with eBenefits is pretty straightforward. To find eBenefits, simply do an online search for "eBenefits." Click on the link that a search brings up and go to the eBenefits homepage then click on the "Register" button on the upper right of any page on the eBenefits website. Click the "Basic Account" link on the left. Follow the online instructions.

The basic account cannot be used for applications and signing up for a PREMIUM account is necessary in order to do a claim or to do about anything else useful with the system. There are several ways to do this.

1. If you are currently on active duty and have a DoD Common Access Card (CAC) or a myPay account you can sign up online with these access options
2. If you are a veteran you can visit your state Regional Office or a TRICARE facility and verify your identity using all of the following
   - A government-issued photo ID such as a driver's license, identification card, or U.S. passport (expired or unexpired)
   - A secondary form of identification such as a birth certificate, social security card, or picture ID
   - An original or certified copy of your DD 214
   - Or if you are already on claim you can go through an at-home verification process

For veterans who were separated after 1995, the eBenefits sign up will automatically lead to a Premium account. You don't have to register for a Basic account first. For these veterans separated from service after 1995, the eBenefits Premium account is valuable for obtaining personnel and health records. For these particular veterans, there is a link on their webpage that connects to NPRIS where all of their records can be obtained electronically.

After you start out with the BASIC account, you will register for the PREMIUM level of access through Norton security access online which requires answering various security questions based on where you live, your credit history and your military history. For older veterans, who are registered in the DEERS database but not already on claim, you will likely have to go to the nearest Regional Office or TRI-CARE office to prove your identity.

To register for the PREMIUM level access online – if you are not automatically registered as PREMIUM because of your more recent veteran status – first go to your BASIC account logon page by using the "login" button at the top of any page on the website. This takes you to the basic login page. On the bottom left you will see a button that says "More DS Logon Options." Click on that button and choose the option "Upgrade My DS Logon." This will then have you logon with your basic logon and then take you to the PREMIUM upgrade procedure.

For older veterans, who are not flagged in the database for initial PREMIUM access, going to the PREMIUM level is not an easy process. If you are only doing it to make application for an FDC Disability Compensation application, it may not be worth it to you. These veterans actually have to make a trip to the Regional Office to prove who they are before they can set up an account.

In some cases, you can certainly use eBenefits to make an original claim for Compensation and in some cases it may be a faster way to do it. In most cases, especially for older veterans, you shouldn't use eBenefits for an application.

An eBenefits application for Compensation is a Fully Developed Claim using VA Form 21-526EZ. In fact, by completing the various online screens to make application and clicking the submit button on the final screen, eBenefits will not only forward the file to a Regional Office for processing, but it will also create a fully completed 526EZ in PDF format for the applicant to print out. eBenefits cannot currently be used for Pension or DIC applications. VA asserts that it is preparing the system to take these claims in the future.

Using eBenefits, you do not have to verify your veteran status or your eligibility for VA benefits if you are in the DEERS system. Most veterans – going back to the Korean War – have been put into that system. The system will automatically recognize you and let you know whether you are eligible or not. You can even print out a one page certification of your veteran status or your discharge once you complete the application process.

A decided advantage in using eBenefits is that when you complete the screen that includes all of your personal and contact information – which may already have been downloaded to your account from DEERS – and click the "save and continue" button, you will have automatically initiated an Intent to File based on the time and date that you clicked the button (Eastern time). This is a legitimate "Intent to File" and regardless of whether you discontinue the application at that point or fail to ever submit the final application, you have 1 year from the date you completed the entry screens but did not click the final submit button.

The biggest disadvantage that we see from using eBenefits for claims is it is not well designed for Fully Developed Claim applications that require significant evidence from private medical records, private opinions and lay statements. Once you complete the application screens online and choose the final submission button, you must decide whether the claim is truly an FDC application or not. Obviously you do not want to reject the FDC option as this will put your claim on the standard claims track. The whole purpose of this course is to help you submit FDC applications, not applications that could take forever and run the risk of denials.

But, choosing the FDC option is not a suitable approach either. If you choose the FDC application option, you have now started the process in the Regional Office for a timely decision. Veterans Service Representatives will do their best to order pertinent federal records and schedule an exam, if necessary, to provide the evidence for a claim that you have told VA must be prioritized.

Here is the problem. If you have to provide additional private record evidence in order to ensure a favorable decision for a claim, you must upload that to your eBenefits account as soon as possible. Otherwise, the Regional Office will not ask you for additional information unless there are some outstanding issues on your application. If you take too long to submit the additional evidence, your application may already be on the desk of a Rating Veterans Service Representative for a decision and you are likely looking at a denial.

Another huge problem for using eBenefits is that it is not useful for individuals who do not have computers at home or are challenged by using computers. Uploaded documents should be in PDF format. Scanning and converting paper documents into PDF requires equipment, expertise or assistance from someone who knows how to do it. In addition, scanned paper records should be converted from JPEG to PDF and converted through OCR to make them manageable for editing and organizing. Finally, some existing records will be received in PDF format. They need to be organized and indexed as well. In order to edit and manipulate PDF documents, you need a current copy of Adobe Acrobat or a program similar to that which can delete and add pages, sort and order pages and edit text.

For Compensation claims that require private nexus opinions, private DBQs and private medical records, you should not click the final button to initiate an FDC claim with eBenefits. Instead, when you get to that point just don't do anything more. In order to get to that point, you have already initiated "An Intent to File " and that is probably all you need to use eBenefits for. Complete the application with paper documents including a new paper 526EZ. You have 1 year from the Intent to File to provide your documentation to the scanning center in paper form.

Currently eBenefits cannot be used to file applications for Pension, Survivors Pension, DIC or accrued benefits. VA wants to use it for this purpose but the option is not yet available.

Filing an Application as a Paper Claim
In order to facilitate the new paperless records system, the Department scans almost every single disability claims document that is sent in paper form into digital PDF format. This also includes documents pertaining to correspondence, evidence and also documents pertaining to appeals. The scanning is done by a private vendor – Data Dimensions – located in Janesville, Wisconsin. On the next page is a picture of the scanning center. Various paper documents pertaining to various types of claims or appeals are sent to various post office boxes at the Janesville scanning center before the Regional Offices can process them. VA would like to avoid paper claims altogether and is actively pushing the eBenefits process for claims.

From Janesville, scanned records are sent electronically to any one of the 56 Regional Offices in the United States where the National Work Queue assigns that claim. Preference is given to the claimant's Regional Office of Jurisdiction that serves the geographic area where the claimant lives. If the claimant's local Regional Office does not have the capacity to process the claim at that time, then the claim is sent to an office that does have the resources to process it.

Data dimensions originally contracted with the Department Of Veterans Affairs in 2012 when the initiative to convert everything to digital format was undertaken. In 2015, VA extended a new five-year contract to Data Dimensions to continue the scanning project. In 2016 Data Dimensions completed construction of the new 23,000 square square foot building you see below in Janesville, Wisconsin and has hired additional new employees. Original paper records will also be stored in this building. The company has over 100 employees in Janesville.

In addition, when a Regional Office orders Service Treatment Records and personnel records from the National Personnel Records Center or the Records Management Center both in St. Louis, those files are sent to Janesville to be scanned. The files are not returned to St. Louis and future attempts to obtain these paper files will result in a letter from the records center indicating they are not available. We discuss in Chapter 5 obtaining records for Compensation claims.

We have provided on the "Claim Support Disc" the addresses and or fax numbers for Compensation, Pension and DIC claims and for correspondence sent to the intake center. If you can, you should always fax the documents as you will have the fax scanning record as proof that they were sent. Documents do get lost.

The Document Intake Scanning Center in Janesville Wisconsin

VA has redesigned all of its forms so that vital information on the form such as names, addresses, Social Security numbers and so forth are scanned directly into the database through optical character recognition (OCR). On the next page is a screenshot of the OCR portion of a typical VA form that requires putting a letter or number in an individual box. The purpose is to bypass human intervention and allow the scanning function to feed the vital information directly into the computer system for distribution through the National Work Queue (NWQ).

Department of Veterans Affairs

VA DATE STAMP
(DO NOT WRITE IN THIS SPACE)

INTENT TO FILE A CLAIM FOR COMPENSATION AND/OR PENSION, OR SURVIVORS PENSION AND/OR DIC
(This Form Is Used to Notify VA of Your Intent to File for the General Benefit(s) Checked Below)

NOTE: Please read the Privacy Act and Respondent Burden below before completing the form.

SECTION I: CLAIMANT/VETERAN IDENTIFICATION

NOTE: You can either complete the form online or by hand. If completed by hand, print the information requested in ink, neatly and legibly to expedite processing of the form.

1. CLAIMANT'S NAME (First, Middle Initial, Last)

2. CLAIMANT'S SOCIAL SECURITY NUMBER

3. VA FILE NUMBER (If applicable)

4. VETERAN'S DATE OF BIRTH (MM,DD,YYYY)
Month   Day   Year

5. VETERAN'S NAME (First, Middle Initial, Last) (If different from claimant)

6. VETERAN'S SOCIAL SECURITY NUMBER

7. VETERAN'S SEX
☐ MALE   ☐ FEMALE

8. VETERAN'S SERVICE NUMBER (If applicable)

9. CURRENT MAILING ADDRESS (Number and Street or rural route, P.O. Box, City, State, ZIP Code and Country)

No. & Street

Apt./Unit Number   City

State/Province   Country   ZIP Code/Postal Code

10. HAS THE VETERAN EVER FILED A CLAIM WITH VA?
☐ YES   ☐ NO

11. TELEPHONE NUMBER (Include Area Code)

12. EMAIL ADDRESS (If applicable)

SECTION II: GENERAL BENEFIT ELECTION

IMPORTANT: You may not be able to use this form to establish an effective date for benefits if you do not select one or more of the general benefits listed below.

13. I intend to file for the general benefit(s) checked below. (Choose all that apply)

☐ COMPENSATION   ☐ PENSION

NOTE: Only check the box below if you are a surviving dependent of the veteran.

☐ SURVIVORS PENSION AND/OR DEPENDENCY AND INDEMNITY COMPENSATION (DIC)

IMPORTANT: After receiving this form, VA will give you the appropriate application to file for the general benefit you select above. You can also apply for VA disability compensation online through eBenefits at www.ebenefits.va.gov. If you give VA a completed application for the selected general benefit within **one** year of filing this form, your completed application will be considered filed as of the date of receipt of this form. Only the **first** completed application for each selected general benefit that is received after you file this form will be considered filed as of the date of receipt of this form. You may indicate your intent to file for more than one general benefit on this form or you may submit a separate intent to file for each general benefit. Please complete as many fields in Section II as possible. VA cannot process this form if we cannot identify the claimant and veteran.

SECTION III: DECLARATION OF INTENT

By filing this form, I hereby indicate my intent to apply for one or more general benefits under the laws administered by VA. I acknowledge that: (1) this is **not a claim for benefits**; (2) I must file a complete application for each general benefit with VA before VA will process my claim; and (2) a complete application for the same general benefit(s) as indicated on this form must be received within one year of the date VA receives this form for my application to be considered filed as of the date of this form.

14A. SIGNATURE OF CLAIMANT/AUTHORIZED REPRESENTATIVE

14B. DATE SIGNED (MM,DD,YYYY)

15. NAME OF ATTORNEY, AGENT, OR VETERANS SERVICE ORGANIZATION (Please Print)
(NOTE: This form may only be completed by a Veterans Service Organization, attorney, or agent if a valid power of attorney has been completed.)

VA FORM
MAR 2017   **21-0966**

EXISTING STOCK OF VA FORM 21-0966, JUL 2015, WILL BE USED.

110

The National Work Queue

In May 2016, VBA completed implementation of the National Work Queue—an electronic workload management initiative that prioritizes and distributes claims across Regional Offices. Previously, a veteran's claim was processed from start to finish by the veteran's local Regional Office of Jurisdiction, and the Regional Office's workload generally depended on how many claims were filed by veterans within its area of jurisdiction. Now, a claim can be processed by multiple Regional Offices, and claims are distributed based on Regional Office Capacity (see figure below).

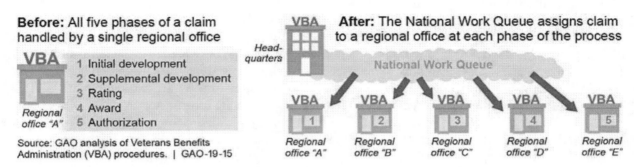

Before: All five phases of a claim handled by a single regional office

VBA

1 Initial development
2 Supplemental development
3 Rating
4 Award
5 Authorization

Regional office "A"

Source: GAO analysis of Veterans Benefits Administration (VBA) procedures. | GAO-19-15

After: The National Work Queue assigns claim to a regional office at each phase of the process

Headquarters

National Work Queue

VBA 1 — *Regional office "A"*
VBA 2 — *Regional office "B"*
VBA 3 — *Regional office "C"*
VBA 4 — *Regional office "D"*
VBA 5 — *Regional office "E"*

The National Work Queue (NWQ) was designed to even out the differences in claims workload across Regional Offices by having multiple offices complete parts of a claim and allocating claims based on each office's capacity. For example, as shown in the figure below, in fiscal year 2017, about 88 percent of all disability Compensation claims were processed by more than one office, and over 75 percent were processed by three or more offices. This distribution method is intended to keep all offices working at their capacity, regardless of the volume of claims filed by veterans in each region. Originally VA intended the NWQ to assign a majority of claims to the veterans' local Regional Offices, but VA determined the system operates more effectively if a veteran's location is a lower priority factor for claims distribution. Thus, few claims are processed entirely at a veteran's local Regional Office.

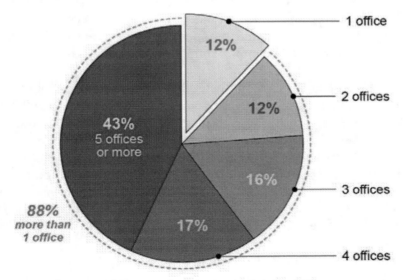

- 1 office: 12%
- 2 offices: 12%
- 3 offices: 16%
- 4 offices: 17%
- 5 offices or more: 43%
- 88% more than 1 office

Source: GAO analysis of Veterans Benefits Administration data. | GAO-19-15

Once the National Work Queue allocates claims to a Regional Office, the office has some discretion in managing the distribution of claims to its staff and managing the claims review process. For example, while VBA determines how the claims workload is allocated across offices, Regional Office Managers decide which claims within the office's queue to work first, how to program the office's queue for distributing claims to individual claims processors' electronic work queues, and whether any changes to distribution are needed throughout the day.

While having discretion in workload management can be beneficial, such discretion can also lead to inconsistent handling of the claims workload. In particular there appears to be no guidance for managing deferrals—actions taken by claims processors in VBA's electronic claims management system (VBMS) – when they identify claims errors that occurred earlier in the claims process. The deferral process begins with the National Work Queue since claims are currently, for the first time, routinely being processed by multiple Regional Offices. Through deferrals, when claims processors identify errors in a claim, they can use the National Work Queue to return the claim for correction to the office that made the error. According to VBA, in fiscal year 2017, VBA claims processors deferred claims in 450,305 instances. The deferral process represents a squandering of employee resources and results in handling of the same action over and over again by different employees. Instead of creating more efficiency, deferral claims handling under the NWQ results in more time spent per claim and less efficiency.

The Intake Processing Center and Assignment of End Product (EP) Codes
Although paper claims should go directly to the scanning center in Jainesville, Regional Office mailrooms still occasionally receive copies of paper claims or other evidence relating to paper claims. These are sent on to the scanning center to be entered into VBMS along with all other claims that are aggregated through the scanning center either through online submission or through paper submission.

Once a substantially complete claim is in the VBMS database, action is taken within an hour or so to assign the claim to a Regional Office through the National Work Queue software program. We have not been able to find out exactly how this works and maybe it isn't that important. Perhaps the system automatically assigns the workload based on the processing capabilities of the 56 Regional Offices at the time of assignment, or perhaps a software switch is initiated once the claim is in VBMS and is substantially complete and the assignment is then made.

All Regional Offices have an Intake Processing Center that accommodates incoming workload assignments. For Compensation claims, all 56 Regional Offices have an organizational structure called the Veterans Service Center which is organized around the assembly line process for Compensation claims. For Pension, DIC and accrued benefit claims, there are 3 designated Regional Offices in St. Paul, Minnesota, Milwaukee, Wisconsin and Philadelphia, Pennsylvania that have dedicated staff that have been trained to handle only these types of claims.

Even though Veterans Service Centers have a great deal of latitude over their claims processing procedures, the general duties of the Intake Processing Center usually include the following

- ensuring the claim or legacy appeal is substantially complete
- verifying that basic eligibility exists

- processing all submitted documents properly, and
- updating the records in the computer system

Specifically the Intake Processing Center looks for the following

- checking for blank spaces or insufficient information on the application and taking appropriate action
- determining the type of benefit the claimant seeks based on the information, evidence and applications submitted
- consideration of entitlement to other benefits even if the claimant does not request them
- assigning or changing End Product Codes (EP) related to the claimed benefit or benefits
- checking for proper signature on paper documents which includes VA recognized signatories; however, signatures are not required on electronically submitted claims
- checking for basic eligibility for the benefit sought such as minimum service duty, in the line of duty or war time service duty or means testing for Pension claims
- checking the character of the discharge and handling discharges that are other than honorable
- determining dependency status such as marriages, dependent children and so forth
- checking for duplicate claims for the same benefit already in the system or in appeal and taking the appropriate action

Once the End Product Code or EP has been assigned along with all of the actions above having been reviewed and the claim is considered substantially complete based on the actions above, the claim is handed off to the adjudication team in the assigned Regional Office. Apparently at some point, which is not clear to us from reading M21 instructions, additional Regional Offices will have become involved in processing certain aspects of the claim. For example the assigned Regional Office may be responsible for the final decision or rating, but teams in other Regional Offices might be assigned developmental responsibilities such as obtaining private medical records, personnel records or service treatment records or ordering contract examinations.

For example with a recent claim that we are processing, the claim itself was assigned to the Salt Lake Regional Office, but the LA Regional Office is responsible for personnel records retrieval and the Milwaukee Regional Office is responsible for other verification issues. As we will point out in a subsequent section, under current practice, there does not seem to be any coordination between these activities in various Regional Offices for the same claim. We believe that this is one of the major flaws of why claims are not being processed properly. Without a responsibility of ownership and oversight for the claim, we have found Intake Processors often misunderstand the nature or theory of some claims and in many cases these people have not even looked at any of the evidence to understand how to properly assign the claim to the adjudication team.

The EP code is an important part of the processing. Basically, certain activities associated with certain claims issues are assigned a time completion task. We include a sample of the many EP codes on the next page. This is just a sample as there are many more EP's that are used. As you can see from the sample, an initial Compensation claim with 8 different disability issues or more is assigned a code of 010 and given 14.87 hours to complete. The most typical Compensation claim is for 7 issues or less and is assigned the most common EP code of 110 and allowed 7.46 hours for completion. In the past, we understand these completion requirements were considered more guideline than actual hard and fast timing rules. In the last few years, VA has been using VBMS to rigidly enforce these timing requirements and as a result, we believe it has affected employee morale as well as the efficiency of getting the claims done properly and contributed to a flawed and unreliable process for Compensation claims.

Sample of Work Rate Standards –End Product Codes – for Adjudication Activities for Compensation and Pension In Fractions of Hours Including Incidental Labor

EP	EP Name	Non-Rating	Rating	Comb.
010	Initial Disability Comp-8 Or More Issues	5.40	9.47	14.87
020	Reopened Compensation	4.14	4.31	8.45
050	Eligibility Verifications	0.49	0.00	0.49
070	Appeal Certifications/SSOCs	1.59	2.6	4.19
095	Ch31 Elig W/Rating	0.83	1.51	2.34
110	Initial Disability Comp-1 To 7 Issues	4.08	3.38	7.46
120	Reopened Pension	2.47	0.74	3.21
130	Disability & Death Dependency	0.90	0.02	0.92
133	REPS Cases (St Louis Only)	2.37	0.00	2.37
135	Hospital Adjustments	1.27	0.05	1.32
140	Initial Death Comp & DIC	3.12	1.27	4.39
150	Income, Estate, Elections	1.13	0.00	1.13
154	Pen & Parent DIC Income Match	2.34	0.00	2.34
155	Entitlement Verifications	0.91	0.00	0.91
160	Burial/Plot/Headstone/Etc	0.97	0.08	1.05
165	Accrued Claims	2.21	1.15	3.36
172	Statements of the Case	3.00	7.09	10.09
180	Initial Disability Pension	2.77	0.76	3.53
190	Initial Death Pension	2.47	0.17	2.64
290	Eligibility Determinations - Other	0.88	0.11	0.99
293	Waiver & Compromise Decisions	1.20	0.00	1.20
295	Chapter 31 Elig W/O Rating	0.08	0.00	0.08
310	Reviews - Future Examinations	1.29	2.13	3.42
314	SC Unemployability Wage Match	3.48	2.16	5.64
320	Reviews - Due Hosp/Outpatient	1.00	1.73	2.73
400/1520	Correspondence - Non-Controlled	0.63	0.00	0.63
500/1500	Correspondence - Controlled	3.02	0.00	3.02
510/1510	Correspondence - PA/FOIA	0.84	0.00	0.84
600	Predetermination Notice Cases	1.37	0.09	1.46

Applications for Pension, DIC and Accrued Benefits

The National Work Queue is used, as well, to distribute claims to the 3 Pension Management Offices which are housed in 3 Regional Offices – Milwaukee, St. Paul and Philadelphia. However, the process by which these particular applications are handled is somewhat different from the way Compensation claims are handled.

Pension and DIC claims are based primarily on submitted evidence. There is generally no requirement for further development such as obtaining personnel records, obtaining service treatment records, obtaining private medical records, ordering DBQs or medical opinions and so forth. It is a much more straightforward process than application for Compensation. As such, the complicated process that we introduced in a graphic near the beginning of this chapter is not needed for Pension claims.

The National Work Queue assigns Pension claims to the applicable Pension Management Center that is responsible for claims from the geographic area where the claimant resides. We understand that recently there has been an attempt to equalize workloads by violating this principle and moving the claim to whichever PMC can handle it. We also understand that some Pension claims are even being assigned to Regional Offices that do not have a PMC.

The Intake Processing Center (IPC) at the PMC is primarily responsible for putting claims under EP (End Product) control. As a local option, the IPC may include claims processors who may handle cases that do not generally require a claims folder review. Work that is not retained by the IPC for processing is handled by claims processors on general processing teams.

General processing team responsibilities in the PMC include, but are not limited to

- initiating development, if needed, to resolve the issue
- making claims ready for the rating activity, and
- taking any necessary award action.

As of June 10, 2019, all rating decisions for PMC inventory are completed by only the St. Paul and Milwaukee PMCs. The Philadelphia PMC will no longer make rating decisions.

Challenges to a PMC decision such as a supplemental claim are handled by the same PMC of original jurisdiction. Because PMCs are specialized processing sites, Higher-Level Reviews (HLR) can be assigned to any PMC, regardless of which office issued the prior decision that is now under review. However, claimants can request an HLR be conducted by the PMC that issued the decision in question. That request must be honored, unless there is good cause to deny – for example the office rendering the prior decision does not have higher-level review capacity to conduct the review

Applications for Compensation

Each Veterans Service Center (VSC) is individually structured to process claims for Compensation benefits in support of the overall mission of the Veterans Benefits Administration. A VSC may support one or more special missions in addition to a traditional VSC workload. The basic components of the VSC include

- an intake processing center (IPC)
- adjudication teams (performing the actions of the development, rating, and authorization activities), and
- a Public Contact Team (PCT).

The primary functions of the IPC include, but are not limited to,

- processing and controlling mail received by the Regional Office (RO)
- managing outgoing paper mail
- establishing new records and claims folders when warranted, and
- performing record maintenance actions, as directed within the M21-1 or by the Office of Field Operations.

Each IPC is composed of a Coach (supervisor) and Claims Assistants (CAs). If deemed necessary by the VSC, the IPC may also include

- an Assistant Coach
- Veterans Service Representatives (VSRs)
- File Clerks or Program Support Clerks, and
- Mail Clerks (if the VSC is responsible for mailroom operations).

An adjudication team is responsible for the development, rating, and authorization activities necessary to process a claim. The primary functions of the adjudication team include, but are not limited to,

- initial and supplemental claim development
- preparation of a rating decision, if necessary
- decision notice
- award promulgation, and
- award authorization.

The composition of an adjudication team is structured and staffed to process claims for benefits in support of the overall mission of VBA. The team is composed of, but not restricted to,

- a Coach (supervisor)
- an Assistant Coach (if deemed necessary by the VSC)
- a Claims Assistant – CA (if deemed necessary by the VSC)
- Veteran Service Representatives (VSRs) and Rating Veterans Service Representatives (RVSRs).

We will not discuss here the function of the Public Contact Team. With the advent of online communication, accredited representative access to VBMS and the availability of the National Call Center, Public Contact Teams don't seem to be very relevant anymore. The primary function appears now just to help anyone actually going to a Regional Office with a claim. On the other hand, most Regional Offices now house Veteran Service Officers from Veterans Service Organizations and they handle claims submissions instead.

In past years the claims handling structure of the Veterans Service Center was more rigidly defined in the M21-1. We believe many Regional Offices are still organized around that more defined structure. This is because it was the just in the summer of 2019 that the very detailed organization of the VSC was officially relaxed for the less defined description we offer above.

Under the previous system, claims are organized under processing lanes depending on the type of claim. Examples of these would be an initial claim for Compensation or a request for adding dependents or declaring the death of a claimant, or reevaluation issues or claims for special benefits or claims that are restricted or a bunch of different non-rating issues related to existing claims. Veteran Service Representatives and Claims Assistants could be assigned temporarily to any of these processing lanes depending on the workload. The idea is to be flexible and to always have employees engaged in a particular assigned task.

In addition, certain teams consisting of one or more Coaches (supervisors) Claims Assistants, VSRs and RVSRs are assigned to the particular function of developing and completing applications for Compensation. The teams are organized around particular types of applications and the team member expertise required. These are called cross functional teams and are responsible for

- assigning incoming claims to certain experienced individuals
- initial and supplemental claim development
- preparation of a rating decision, if necessary
- award promulgation, and
- award authorization.

The Coach or Assistant Coach assigns claims to individuals by

- assigning terminal digit responsibilities
- auto assigning claims to work queues in the Veterans Benefits Management System (VBMS), and/or
- manually assigning claims to work queues.

The duties of a Veteran Service Representative (VSR) include

- determining what evidence is necessary to decide a claim
- undertaking development action to obtaining necessary evidence
- ensuring VBA electronic systems accurately reflect
- suspense dates and reasons

- contentions associated with a claim
- development undertaken in connection with a claim
- evidence received in connection with a claim, and
- claim status
- determining when a claim is ready for a decision
- notifying beneficiaries of proposed adverse actions
- deciding claims/issues that do *not* require a rating decision
- entering award data into VBA electronic systems, and
- notifying claimants of decisions on their claims.

The duties of a Rating Veterans Service Representative (RVSR) include

- preparing complex medical opinion requests
- determining whether medical evidence received in connection with a claim justifies the granting of entitlement to VA benefits
- ensuring all recent and relevant treatment records found in the Compensation and Pension Records Interchange (CAPRI) and the Joint Legacy Viewer (JLV) have been associated with the claims folder and if necessary, associating the records, and
- preparing rating decisions that discuss the evidence reviewed and the decision narrative behind a decision to grant or deny entitlement.

When an RVSR determines additional development is required in order to decide a claim, he/she should collaborate with a VSR on his/her team to determine how long it will take to complete the development. If the VSR *cannot* complete the development action quickly, the RVSR must prepare a deferred rating decision, and return the claim to the VSR. If the VSR *can* complete the development action quickly, the VSR must take the action as soon as possible and notify the RVSR when it is complete.

Section 5103 Notices and Decision Notices
VA is required by law to respond to certain issues concerning a pending claim. These notices have traditionally been called development letters and we will continue to use that term interchangeably in this section. It is a logical reference as perhaps the most frequent words used in the adjudication manual are "development" or "develop" which refer to the evidence gathering process required to make a decision. Officially, notices about a pending claim are called "Section 5103 Notices." You may see reference to this official name in the notices you receive. Below is a description of these required 5103 notices and how the requirements have undergone significant changes in recent years.

Background on the Requirements for Notification
On November 9, 2000, Congress enacted the Veterans Claims Assistance Act (VCAA), which provided that VA has a duty to assist a claimant who files a substantially complete application in obtaining evidence to substantiate his or her claim before making a decision on the claim. The law eliminated the concept of a well-grounded claim, redefined VA's duty to assist, and mandated specific notification requirements.

The well-intentioned requirements of the VCAA have presented VA with significant challenges. In the past many claimants received multiple notices addressing the same condition, or addressing different conditions or claims at various stages of development. Although sent in an effort to help the claimant, the practice of issuing multiple notices did not necessarily enhance the claimant's understanding of the claims process. In 2013, Congress enacted PL 112-154 which represents a valuable step to streamline VA's duty-to-notify or assist responsibilities. The new procedures address claims processing delays that occur due to the VCAA.

Previous notifications sent out under the VCAA were appropriately called VCAA notices. Internally in the Regional Offices they were often referred to as development letters. New nomenclature in the adjudication manual now refers to these notifications as "section 5103 notices." This new name refers to the codification of the 2013 law in Title 38 USC § 5103. It is important to note that PL 112-154 does not change the content of VA's previous VCAA notices, but instead affords VA flexibility under the law to deliver § 5103 notices in a more efficient manner and to include the transmission of the notice through electronic communication. It also provides VA the authority to engage claimants in taking a more active role in claims development.

Flexibility in How and When VA Delivers the §5103 Notice

The amended 38 U.S.C. § 5103 no longer requires § 5103 notices to be sent after receipt of a claim. Instead, VA is authorized to place such notices on claims application forms, thereby making the § 5103 notice information available to the claimant prior to claim submission. This is currently accomplished through the use of VA Forms 21-526EZ, 21-527EZ, and 21-534EZ. Although these forms are currently designated for the Fully Developed Claim (FDC) program, it is important to remember that the § 5103 notice requirements are satisfied for a claim filed on the appropriate claimant-signed EZ form, regardless of whether or not the claim is ultimately found to meet FDC criteria.

This change in notice procedures is a significant improvement. Previously, claimants would receive an acknowledgment letter that detailed what the claimant had provided as far as evidence and forms and then detail what was required as far as evidence and forms. This was totally confusing as the applicant never knew whether the Regional Office was again requesting all of the documentation that had been already submitted. On the other hand, since no notification is now required, anyone applying for benefits might not know if a paper application had actually been received. For various reasons, VA has opted not to use email for verifications.

Providing §5103 Notices Electronically through eBenefits

PL 112-154 amends 38 U.S.C. § 5103 to allow VA to deliver the § 5103 notice by the most effective means available, to include electronic communication. By providing the § 5103 notices electronically, rather than exclusively through paper-based correspondence, VA will continue to improve performance and customer service to our claimants. The electronic notification is currently accomplished through the VONAPP Direct Connect (VDC) portal in eBenefits. The VDC portal allows claimants to file claims in a paperless environment using the VA Form 21-526EZ and receive the legally required § 5103 notice electronically. Although VDC utilizes the 526EZ, not all claims submitted through VDC are FDCs. The electronic notification provided to claimants through VDC is sufficient, regardless of whether or not the claim is ultimately found to meet FDC criteria.

Although the new law authorizes VA to utilize email as a way to transmit the § 5103 notice, this is currently not considered a viable option due to privacy and security concerns.

There are unique § 5103 requirements for claims that were previously denied service connection and for which the appeal period has expired. Therefore, regardless of whether the claim is received on an EZ form or through VDC, Regional Offices and Pension Management Centers must send the claimant a subsequent notice containing, "What the evidence must show specific to new and material evidence, including the date of and reasons for a prior denial." See Kent v. Nicholson, 20 Vet.App.1, 10 (2006).

VA has also adopted special development features to keep eBenefits claimants informed as to the progress of the claim. These are referred to as the 3 phases of the claims status in eBenefits. Here are the phases

Phase	Definition
Development	This is the initial part of the claims process. The claimant is provided information as to what information is needed for the claim and an opportunity to provide or identify any additional evidence to support the claim. All appropriate evidence is gathered and reviewed.
Decision	All information and evidence are carefully reviewed to ensure we have everything we need to make an informed decision on the claim. If something is missing, the claim returns to the development phase to obtain that missing information. If all the needed evidence is received, a proposed decision will be made.
Notification	Once the decision is reviewed carefully and approved, a notification letter is sent to the claimant.

Section 5103 Notices Are Not Required in Certain Instances
In accordance with amended 38 U.S.C. § 5103(b)(4), Regional Offices are no longer required to send a § 5103 notice for subsequent claims that are filed while previous claims are pending, if the previous notice provided sufficient notice of the information and evidence necessary to substantiate such subsequent claims. However, ROs must still send a § 5103 notice if over one year has passed since any notice was sent and a subsequent claims is received. Issuing § 5103 notices unnecessarily diverts valuable resources from more productive efforts within Veterans Service Centers.

The following examples are provided to highlight changes described above:

Example 1: Veteran submits a claim for increased evaluation for left knee condition on a VA Form 21-4138. VA sends initial § 5103 notice to claimant. After three months and while the claim for left knee is pending, the claimant sends in a claim for increase for right hip. A second § 5103 notice for the right hip claim is not required.

Example 2: Veteran submits a claim for increased evaluation for low back condition on a VA Form 21-526EZ. Nine months later, while the previous claim is still pending, the Veteran submits a new claim for service connection for migraine headaches on a VA Form 21-526 EZ. In this case, no § 5103 notice is required for the claim for migraine headaches because the previous notice (i.e., attachment on the VA Form 21-526EZ) contains sufficient notice of the information necessary to substantiate a claim for service connection.

The amended law indicates that VA's duty-to-notify and duty-to-assist responsibilities no longer apply when VA can award the "maximum benefit" based on the evidence of record.

Responding to Development Letters for Veterans Pension and Survivor Benefits
VA will send a claimant a development letter for Pension when it needs more information to help decide a claim. Development letters may be sent for a number of reasons, including:

- insufficient marital history for all marriages
- insufficient income information including interest and dividends from all sources
- lacking evidence of a property's market value
- lacking care service information
- possible unreported assets or income
- insufficient proof of payment for a certain medical expense
- possible re-imbursements for care or funeral expenses
- clarification of tax events from past years' statements
- insufficient medical evidence to determine a rating
- incomplete forms
- poor quality or photo-copied discharge records

If a development letter is sent to you or a claimant you are assisting, do not initiate an action under the new review system. We warn you to use options like "appeal" and "disagree" cautiously and only as a last resort. Generally, a response with the proper additional evidence will satisfy an inquiry and give Pension management enough reason to continue processing a claim. Read the development letter thoroughly and pay attention to any response requirements.

To respond to a development letter, use *Form 21-4138* as a cover letter. Complete any other form the letter asks for. Also consider including outside evidence to support any new information you need to give VA. Remember, the more detailed your response, the more likely VA can continue processing the claim. Ask yourself, "did I cover the who, what, when, where and why of the items in questions?"

Changes from the Veterans Appeals Improvement and Modernization Act of 2017
On February 19, 2019, changes went into effect based on PL 115-55, "Veterans Appeals Improvement and Modernization Act of 2017." The public law and associated regulatory changes impacted both VA's duty to assist and duty to notify requirements. PL 115-55 revised Section 5103 to state that the notice requirement for a substantially complete claim applies to

initial and supplemental claims; however, <u>VA is not required to provide that notice with respect to a supplemental claim filed within one year of an agency of original jurisdiction or Board decision on an issue.</u> VA's duty to assist is reinstated when a substantially complete initial claim or supplemental claim is filed or when a claim is returned to correct a "duty to assist" error in a prior decision.

VA's duty to assist in the gathering of evidence begins upon receipt of a substantially complete application for an initial or supplemental claim and ends once VA issues a decision on the claim. The definition of a substantially complete application in 38 CFR 3.159 has been amended to add the requirement that a supplemental claim application include or identify potentially new evidence. However, the duty to assist does not apply to higher-level reviews (HLRs).

Decision Notices
PL 115-55 required a change to 38 CFR 3.103(f). Effective February 19, 2019, 38 CFR 3.103(f) requires VA's written decision notices to include all of the following elements:

- identification of the issues adjudicated
- a summary of the evidence considered
- a summary of the applicable laws and regulations
- identification of findings favorable to the claimant
- in the case of a denial, identification of elements not satisfied leading to the denial
- an explanation of how to obtain or access evidence used in making the decision
- if applicable, identification of the criteria that must be satisfied to grant service connection or the next higher level of Compensation, and
- a summary of the applicable review options under 38 CFR 3.2500 available for the claimant to seek further review of the decision.
- these elements can be satisfied through a combination of the decision notice and its enclosures.

Deficiencies with the Claims Processing Model

Deficiencies with the Physical Structure of Claims Processing
Not all Regional Offices are the same size, employee-wise. If one were to look at the photos of offices in North Dakota or South Dakota or Montana or Wyoming none of these offices could house more than 100 people at most. On the other hand, the photograph of the Philadelphia Office shows a very large building that probably houses up to 2,000 employees or more.

It might have made sense 50 or 60 years ago for Regional Offices to be in every state and be accessible by veterans who might want to go into that Regional Office for various reasons. Nowadays, accessibility can be attained through email or through the new Veterans Call Center at 800-827-1000, which usually responds to a phone call within a reasonable amount of time. We can affirm that after many years of poor service, the call center now offers excellent support. In fact, Regional Offices have cut back on accessibility and there are very few employees who interact directly with the public. <u>No longer can anyone just go into the office to review records. Staff is not available and this records review policy is no longer supported.</u> There might be only a handful of people in the Regional Office to serve the public, primarily by accepting documents or helping get started with an application.

Fragmenting itself into 56 different offices is a highly inefficient way for VBA to operate. Each office requires a management staff, training staff, IT people, security and maintenance staff and a whole host of other people who are not critical to the processing of claims. Providing this type of support for a small office of 100 people or less is highly inefficient. By the way, there are 2 additional Regional Offices in Manila, Philippines and San Juan, Puerto Rico, but they do not participate in the claims processing model that we describe in this chapter.

Communication with headquarters and other Regional Offices is made more difficult by keeping 56 different Regional Office Directors with equal authority in the loop and due to different management styles, every office is going to have a different culture. And then of course there's the additional cost of physically remodeling and physically maintaining 56 different work center buildings scattered all over the United States. It would make much more sense to consolidate all of the claims processing into perhaps 3 regional centers where training, oversight, maintenance of the buildings and so forth would be centralized. Likewise, having the resource of a large group of employees at one location allows for greater efficiency in assignments and workloads.

Admittedly, the National Work Queue has made a decided difference in making sure that workloads between the various offices have been distributed so as to make maximum use of all of the employees. This is done electronically by assigning claims cases to the various Regional Offices who have the capacity, at any given moment, to handle those claims. In addition, claims are often broken up and various aspects of the handling process for the same claim are typically done in different Regional Offices with the results being kept track of in VBMS. Despite this attempt to overcome an already deficient processing structure, allocation of workloads through the NWQ does not represent an effective strategy for handling claims but instead only reflects an attempt to correct an already inefficient operating deficiency. In fact, this allocation strategy of making sure everyone is operating at full capacity, is not working and in our opinion results in just the opposite. We believe that a claim that could take 10 hours to develop and adjudicate under the old system is probably taking 20 or 30 hours due to the deficiencies in the new system.

One can certainly argue that it is not necessary in our age of Internet communication for employees to gather together physically in one building. This is evident in the fact that many large companies such as IBM maintain office buildings that are almost empty of employees because everyone is working at home. And yes, VA allows employees to work at home. This still does not substitute for consolidating management, training, oversight, evaluations and so forth into one large regional processing center instead of fragmenting it all across the country.

Numerous complaints from Veterans Service Organizations have identified that fragmenting claims through 56 different Regional Offices results in confusion, lost claims in the system, poor oversight and lack of accountability. Imagine if a private company with about 20,000 employees split itself into 56 different independent entities each with a director over that entity and with each director having equal authority with the other 55 directors, but yet each of these offices was producing the same product. The communications problems, the different management styles, the potential friction between directors, the maintenance costs of 56 different structures to house employees are all additional challenges that don't need to exist. It is our opinion that the Regional Office structural approach to handling claims is an inefficient model and a more efficient approach would be to consolidate operations. This would lead to more efficient production output and control.

A Frustrating Experience for Anyone Submitting a Claim

VA is obsessed with completing applications in 125 days or less. In 2019, the Department will complete a projected 1.3 million disability Compensation rating claims, with an average of 107 days for completion, well under the 125 day limit. They anticipate an inventory of claims pending more than 125 days at 59,000. Claims completed in less than 125 days represents about 95.5% of submissions in 2019. That's pretty good success – at least on paper. VA asserts there are numerous issues associated with that 4.5% claims going over 125 days that the Regional Offices can't control. <u>We don't experience this 107 day timeliness with any of our claims.</u>

<u>Our experience with submitting hundreds of applications a year and in talking with others who file applications is the 125 day limit doesn't seem to apply to any of our claims or to the claims from other representatives we work with. We seldom have a Compensation claim with a decision notice less than 4 months. Fully Developed Pension claims where no additional evidence is required are now taking 5 to 7 months or longer.</u> We used to get them approved more quickly and sometimes within a matter of weeks, but that no longer happens. Fully Developed Claims currently don't receive any faster priority consideration than any other claims. Other priority claims based on age, illness or lack of income only get priority handling if we notify the Regional Office after submission with a heads up that it is a priority claim. <u>What is supposed to be happening in theory and with assertions from VA to Congress that the 125 day deadline is being met doesn't connect with the reality of what we experience.</u>

Perhaps our experience is based on the types of claims that we submit. We mostly deal with older veterans and these claims require significantly more evidence such as private medical opinions and personal medical records as well as detailed descriptions of the theory of the claim and personal lay statements. We just don't know. Other delay issues might include the fact that we definitely know there is a backlog with the scanning center for paper applications which we use. Currently, we believe it is about a 6 week delay in getting those claims into VBMS.

But that does not explain the delay in processing Pension applications. The types and ages of people we represent with Pension applications have not changed over the years. In past years the average approval time was about 3 or 4 months and sometimes we could get priority claims within a matter of weeks. That no longer happens. VA seems to ignore Pension priority claims altogether and the average approval time is anywhere from 5 to 7 months.

<u>Our conclusion is that the assertion by VA that 95.5% of all claims are processed in less than 4 months is a fairytale based on our own experience.</u>

Other Identifiable Problems with Compensation Claims

The National Work Queue and Lack of Oversight

The deficiencies with the National Work Queue that we have pointed out earlier do not seem to affect simple applications for Compensation. These would be applications for 1) one or two disability issues or for 2) presumptive service connection or for 3) simple direct service connection representing applications such as hearing loss or musculoskeletal disabilities that are easy to define and to connect to service or for 4) requests for increase or requests for secondary disability. We don't typically have any major challenges with the processing of these types of applications other than dealing with an inefficient and frustrating system that takes much longer than it should and demonstrates deficiencies all along the way.

The problem seems to be with complex claims that appear to challenge the competence and training level of the Input Processing Center employees. We believe that many of these employees don't understand the intricacies of complex claims or claims with many apparently disparate disability issues and therefore they simply screw up these kinds of claims.

Here is an example from one of our more recent claims. We submitted this application in April 2019 and 9 months later VA is still developing for evidence even though we furnished all the evidence necessary to make a decision. The veteran was stationed in Vietnam and developed prostate cancer 7 years ago for which he had a radical prostatectomy to remove the prostate. After follow-up treatment with radiation, he has been in remission with the cancer. On the other hand, he has at least 4 residual medical issues as a result of that surgery that are debilitating and in some cases disabling and warrant ratings. He also developed type II diabetes a number of years ago and it is currently being controlled with medication and diet. However, he also has at least 5 residual medical problems due to the diabetes such as high blood pressure, erectile dysfunction, severe diabetic neuropathy and so on. Most of these are ratable issues

We submitted the claim using our own method as is outlined in Chapter 5 of this book by detailing on a separate Form 21-4138 that we were claiming presumptive service connection for the prostate cancer and the diabetes and we listed 9 secondary disability issues which we stated were directly caused by either the diabetes or the prostate cancer. As a harbinger of what was to come we could not find the claim in VBMS after 3 months. The scanning center lost the claim and we had to resubmit it. Next, we found it was assigned to 3 different Regional Offices for development. We had already furnished the necessary DBQs and other medical evidence and there was no need for any development. Next we found that the Regional Office ordered 9 different medical opinions from an examiner to opine whether the 9 secondary disability issues were direct service-connected. Either the person ordering the examinations was totally incompetent in understanding the difference between presumptive service connection, direct service connection and secondary service connection or he or she just didn't care.

Obviously, the veterans secondary service connection disabilities are not direct service-connected. This the opinions confirmed. We also submitted enough evidence including his DD214 and other material in his possession that proved he was in Vietnam. That was also ignored. It has been over 4 months with an open request for his personnel records from the NPRC. The last look into VBMS shows the open request, yet the personnel records are there. This claim is a total mess, not due to our fault, but because of total incompetency, most likely from lack of coordination and oversight from the National Work Queue.

Other Issues – Employee Workload Deadlines
There is tremendous pressure on employees to meet the 125 day workload goal. VSRs and RVSRs have a point system for their performance evaluations. If they fail to meet the processing

workload goals they lose points and this affects their bonuses, wage increases and promotions and can also result in reprimands.

Employees are rigidly timed by VBMS on various actions taken on a given claim. For example, the most common Compensation application with less than 7 issues is assigned an EP code of 110. The EP chart sample in a previous section allows 7.6 hours for completion of EP code 110. If the adjudication team exceeds this limit and they can't make up this overage with other claims that go shorter than 7.6 hours they are docked performance points. Complex claims with a lot of evidence could easily disrupt the average processing allocation limits.

What we are finding is the adjudication team figures out a way to process these complex applications without reading all of the evidence. This is not allowed under regulations, but it appears to be happening. Failure to read all of the evidence can often lead to the wrong decision or a denial.

Finally, employees are not valued for their efforts. For example, in one Regional Office, a VSR is given 37 minutes to complete an order for a C&P exam. If it takes longer, the VSR must abandon the task or risk losing performance points. VA refers to this process as "deferral. " Someone else has to take up the action later on which not only exceeds workload limits but also does not give credit to the original VSR. This multiple handling of the same action happens more frequently than not and in addition the important incentive of giving the team ownership of the claim is lost. This ownership incentive in the past has been important to employee morale.

All of this adds up to a muddled system with multiple handling of the same claims issues by different employees and lack of accountability due to fragmenting the claim process. <u>Regardless of what VA asserts is an efficient handling in 107 days or less, claims are taking in reality much longer to decide.</u>

Additional Compensation Claims Processing Deficiencies
It would take many more pages to home in more accurately on deficiencies with Compensation claims processing in the Regional Offices. Below are some bullet points that are generated from hours and hours of research on trying to understand the challenges faced by VA employees.

1. It appears that the processing model was devised by upper management alone without input from the employees themselves. There are employee complaints that many of these upper management people have not come up through the ranks and have no understanding of how things actually function in the Regional Office. Reliance has been entirely on contract consultants, hired by VA, who come in and do studies and make recommendations and these organizations as well do not work with the lower ranks.

2. It appears that management is relying too much on technology to solve the challenges from a year-to-year increase in application submissions from veterans and dependents – not just for original claims but for all kinds of issues. This continually-increasing volume of submissions created a huge backlog of unprocessed actions approaching at least 1 million. By 2012 many of these actions were going well beyond a year from original submission. Also original claims themselves have become each year much more complex involving multiple disability issues. The technology solution was to go to a

126

paperless system and rely on an all-encompassing database that theoretically could take over most of the human functions under the old paper-based system. Incorporating this complex new system took 5 years and was naturally a challenge, resulting in many disrupting processing issues. Now, the system is considered mostly complete, but the processing issues persist. Apparently a one-size-fits-all technology approach does not work for the extremely complicated Compensation adjudication process. Human input is important. It appears upper management is treating the human components of the system as machine cogs of an assembly line conveyor belt and as such, management doesn't recognize employee input or their ability to adapt to make the system work better.

3. In 2010, the Secretary of the Department of Veterans Affairs came up with an inviolate goal of not allowing claims to go beyond 125 days in the system unless there were extenuating circumstances. This 125 day goal line has become such an obsessive focus of the Department that violation of this bright line barrier is to be avoided at all costs. This obsession may be due to political pressure from Congress, but the overall result has been an unnecessary focus on moving claims through the system quickly regardless of whether those claims are given a fair evaluation or not. It is not surprising that this organizational objective has resulted in many unfair or unfavorable decisions or denials.

4. Sometime around 2012 VBA came up with an excellent idea called the "Fully Developed Claim." Prior to this, VA's duty to assist was absolute, based on legislation passed in the early 1990s. Duty to assist could not be avoided. The Fully Developed Claim allows an applicant to disavow his or her right to duty to assist and to pass the claim with all of the attending evidence directly to the decision-maker. This avoids months of records requests, unnecessary notices and other activities that are not needed for a claim that is complete and ready for a decision. Fully Developed Claims allow processing teams in the Regional Office to meet their time constraints under the processing model. It is a win-win for the employee and for the applicant. New EZ forms were developed for this purpose and currently these are the preferred forms that should be used for any application. Unfortunately, our experience is that VA has lost sight of the Fully Developed Claim process and is ignoring evidence submitted under this process and continuing to develop claims as not Fully Developed Claims. It is demoralizing to many of us to take the time to develop a claim to the point where it is credible and likely will result in a favorable decision, only to have VA mess it all up with their own development, their own shoddy medical opinions and their refusal to read important evidence supporting the claim. As a result, many of the claims that we do require challenges to final decisions to fix the unfair treatment.

5. **We don't have any specific statistics, but based on empirical evidence, hardly any applicants are submitting Compensation claims that are Fully Developed. There are probably 2 reasons for this. First, a claimant who is submitting an application for the first time – without any assistance from someone who is experienced, will likely not understand how to do a Fully Developed Claim. Even though instructions are on the form – and they are very good instructions – the process is complicated and intimidating. Second, if a claimant is using the assistance of an accredited representative of a veterans service organization, that representative may very well**

know how to do a Fully Developed Claim but will not take the time to do it. Service officers of VSOs are paid by how much paperwork they can generate in a given month or year. If they don't produce, they don't have a job. Putting together a Fully Developed Claim takes a great deal of time, but doesn't result in any more paperwork than submitting a form that is not Fully Developed and takes only a few minutes. Veteran Service Officers often have people waiting for their assistance and they don't have time for anything else other than filling out forms. Also based on our observations, claims processors do not respect Fully Developed Claims and routinely ignore the evidence that substantiates a Fully Developed Claim. Unfortunately, as a result, we often have to challenge decision notices to get the results we are seeking.

6. VBA's attitude towards employees being only automatons has affected employee morale. Under the prior system, the development and rating team would work together and stick with a particular claim by developing it and getting it ready for a final decision. Each member of the team would receive satisfaction by knowing that they had helped another claimant possibly get some benefits he or she deserved. Under the new system, credit for a particular claim is rarely earned. Because of time constraints, each employee can only handle a certain claim for a certain period of time and if that time is exceeded, the claim gets put on hold until another employee can pick it up. Fragmenting the claim among various Regional Offices also creates a lack of ownership and the responsibility for that claim. A system that was designed for 3 or 4 people on the team to develop for the decision often results in the equivalent handling of 10 or more people involved even if it is the same person doing it over and over again. Redundant handling of the same actions over and over is a major problem with the new system. Under the new system, no particular person gains any satisfaction by seeing a claim through the entire process. The original principle of ownership of the claim under the old system has been lost and employees don't get the feeling of accomplishment that they used to get. In fact, it is just the opposite. Failure to meet the time constraints can result in the loss of performance points for employee evaluations. Failure to meet the required performance points in a given period of time can result in reprimands, loss of promotion, loss of bonuses and even perhaps employment discharge.

7. Assignment of a particular claim to an adjudication team is not an exact science. The team Coach must be able to determine how long a particular claim will take as there are daily work load assignments. For example one Regional Office may require a team handling Compensation claims with 7 or less disability issues to deliver 3 rating decisions a day. Some claims of this type may only require a total of 4 or 5 hours of development and others may require 10 or 12 hours of development. Sometimes it is hard to determine upfront how long it will take. This uncertainty in the model also creates a great deal of stress and conflict on the adjudication teams. This uncertainty also leads to an important strategy for submitting successful Compensation claims. Knowing about this issue, allows you to notify the Intake Processing Center and the team Coach in clear and unmistakable language exactly what your claim entails, the fact that it is Fully Developed for a decision, what evidence there is and how well you have organized it for a decision. You can give the team a better idea of how long it would take to get through it.

What We Learn from the Deficiencies with Compensation Claims Processing

Hours and hours of research trying to understand the problems plaguing the Compensation claims processing system have led us to some conclusions. However, we are still not certain that we understand all of the dysfunction as trying to uncover what is going on is like trying to gain access to a locked building by peering through tiny windows to try to see what is going on inside. As a result, the list below is our best attempt to help you get around the faulty Compensation claims process and have greater success with your application.

- If the initial application is for a number of disparate disability issues that are not direct service-connected but are secondary service-connected, don't expect the intake processing employees to understand the difference between direct service connection and secondary service connection (even though they should); establish the direct service connection issues or presumptive service connection issues first and then refile for an increase in rating. (See Chapter 5 to understand this)
- Don't allow the Intake processors to identify the theory of the claim from the application form itself, but force them from the application to read a more thorough (but brief) explanation of the claim on a VA Form 21-4138 but be aware they may not understand complex theories anyway due to a general lack of knowledge of medical issues
- Make sure that the adjudication team knows the claim is Fully Developed and does not need any development from them as this will save a great deal of time by avoiding duty to assist and in turn not cause the claim to come up against the 125 day bright line barrier (be aware however that they often ignore your evidence and develop for the same evidence anyway)
- Summarize exactly what the claim is about and what the service connection is so that they know exactly what evidence they are supposed to look at and save some time
- Organize and index the medical records with a table of contents and brief description of each issue to make it easy for the rating team to review this evidence and understand the important medical issues relating to the claim so that they don't have to waste time ferreting out those issues from the record and also circle with a black felt pen those particular medical issues you want them to read. (Accept the fact that they will not take the time to actually read all of the medical evidence as regulations require so you must hold their hands and put the medical evidence you want them to read directly in their faces)
- Organize, index and correlate all other evidence with tables of contents and brief descriptions to make it easy for the rating team to understand the purpose of that evidence and circle with a black felt pen any particular points of evidence that prove the claim
- Write a well-organized and thorough lay statement that includes a detailed explanation of the theory of the claim, a well-defined list of evidence, a detailed description of the current disabilities, an explanation of why the evidence leads to service connection and finally a thorough history of the incident in service and how it ties to the current disabilities
- Be detailed but keep it simple as too much paperwork will be stored in VBMS, but no one will ever look at it even though it is important evidence and even though regulations require Rating VSRs to read all the evidence; assume they won't do that even though they state on the decision notice that they have read all the evidence

Maintain Personal Control over the Claim Process

We have already discussed the most important principle strategy for overcoming the current flawed system – <u>Do not give up your personal control to VA's duty to assist.</u> <u>This means that your claim has to be Fully Developed, well documented, well organized and ready for a decision.</u>

VA apologists would argue that the purpose of the Department's paternalistic assistance with duty to assist is to not put a burden on the claimant, especially for incurring out-of-pocket costs. The issue is the veteran or survivor simply can't afford to pay for preparation of an application. Unfortunately, as we have pointed out, the claim system is flawed. Not only that, we believe employees in the veterans service center are somewhat jaded. They see the same questionable claims with little evidence, coming through every day and it probably causes employees to feel some reluctance for development knowing many of these claims are meritless.

As a result, the veteran or survivor must defend himself or herself against adverse actions that the adjudication team in the Regional Office will take; possibly because of this attitude. If you really want to get a favorable decision with the best possible disability rating, you have to put some time and money into it. In reality, that's the way it works.

It's not that the people in the Regional Office are deliberately trying to take your benefits away. On the contrary, they rightly believe they are doing their job by questioning evidence that appears to be suspicious or lacking. Even though they are paid to be advocates for the veteran, it often appears to these people who work for VA – from many years of experience –that many veterans are trying to get something for nothing. And in many cases this is probably true. VA employees probably act adversely because of their experience in trying to prevent someone from getting a benefit to which that person is not entitled.

The suspicion from the Regional Office is not due to policy. Regulations prohibit adjudicators from exhibiting bias. It is due to questionable evidence from many years of experience dealing with this issue. One important strategy to win the confidence of the development and rating team is to submit a claim that commands their respect. You do this through

1. detailed and well-argued lay statements,
2. credible and probative medical evidence
3. well-reasoned and well-documented medical opinions and
4. support from credible medical literature where necessary

We will discuss in more detail further on in this chapter and in Chapter 5 on Compensation and Chapter 6 on Pension how to go about gathering and creating the material for a persuasive, well-developed claim.

<u>We provide several case studies for you that are found on the Claim Support Disc.</u> <u>These studies represent the principles that are covered in this book.</u> <u>The cases include detailed lay statements, convincing medical evidence, strongly worded nexus opinions and support from medical literature.</u> <u>If you study these cases you will understand the issues we are stressing in this chapter.</u>

Understanding Undeveloped and Fully Developed Claims

What Developing a Claim Means

"Developing a claim" is VA-speak for the time and effort that employees in the Regional Office take to gather evidence and obtain medical evaluations on behalf of individuals who have made application for Compensation or Pension. Whenever an application is made, these employees are required under law to pursue this development process. VA must make an effort to obtain a variety of certain forms and evidence with Pension claims. With Compensation claims an effort must be made to obtain service treatment records and service clinical records where needed, personnel records from the service when needed, government health facility medical records, DBQ evaluations, medical opinions when necessary and at least 2 attempts to obtain private sector medical records. This process can take months and uses up a great deal of the time that is allotted to the adjudication team for processing claims.

When we discuss further on what we call "undeveloped claims" we are describing the process discussed above. In particular, most applications fail to provide all of the evidence that is necessary to make a decision and instead place the burden on the Regional Office to find this evidence or in other words to "develop the claim." An undeveloped claim can be submitted in a matter of minutes by simply filling the 21-526 EZ form for Compensation or either of the 2 forms for Pension – 21-527 EZ or 21-534 EZ. Unfortunately, just filing the forms is not enough to generate a decision. With Compensation or Pension there is a lot more evidence and supporting documentation that is required. The burden now falls on the Regional Office to request this additional information from the applicant or to generate it on behalf of the applicant.

Understanding VA's Duty to Assist

In 2000 the Veterans Claims Assistance Act (VCAA) created a change in the Department of Veterans Affairs' duties to notify and assist claimants for VA benefits. The law is codified into the regulations in Title 38 CFR 3.159.

Prior to the passage of the VCAA, the process of applying for Disability Compensation benefits and Pension benefits was adversarial. In other words, the claimant had to provide enough evidence to convince VA that the claim was "well grounded" so that VA would assist in developing for further evidence by ordering records and arranging for medical examinations. With the VCAA Congress recognized this adversarial process and did away with "well grounded" claims. Under the new rules, a veteran need only to submit enough information to trigger the "duty to assist" found in the new law by submitting a simple application called a "substantially complete claim."

Duty to assist may actually be a detriment for veterans submitting applications. What we mean by this is the typical veteran claimant or the survivor claimant puts his or her full trust in the capabilities of the Department to adequately develop the claim for a decision by gathering all of the evidence on behalf of the claimant. The assumption is the adjudication team in the Regional Office will do the best job possible for developing evidence and provide the best decision under these circumstances. As many applicants have found out over the years, putting their full trust in VA can result in undesirable decisions or denials.

The process of "duty to assist" is well-meaning. Congress did not want to put an additional burden on those applying for benefits by forcing them to take the time and spend money to gather the evidence for their applications. Unfortunately, duty to assist has often resulted in just the opposite effect. Applicants have found it so easy to take a few minutes and submit an application without any additional effort to support their applications, that the Department has been burdened with hundreds of thousands of superfluous claims over the years. Many applicants simply turn in an application to see what will happen. Like playing the lottery, many applicants hope they might just get an award if they try. In other words they are throwing whatever they can against the wall and hoping something will stick. This attitude from claimants has gummed up the system with hundreds of thousands of claims and made it more difficult for legitimate claims to get through.

The Fully Developed Claim
In 2012 VA came up with an excellent idea called the "Fully Developed Claim." Prior to this, VA's duty to assist was absolute – based on the Veterans Claims and Assistance Act of 2000. Duty to assist could not be avoided. Fully Developed Claims work equally well for Pension applications and for Compensation applications. Fully Developed Claims (FDC) for Compensation and Pension have the same goal of a timely decision but the underlying approach between the two is different due to the type of evidence and documentation that is required for each type of benefit.

The Fully Developed Claim process allows an applicant to develop his or her claim with little assistance from the Regional Office. This avoids months of records requests, unnecessary notices and other activities by the Regional Office that are not needed as the FDC claim is complete and ready for a decision. Fully Developed Claims allow processing teams in the Regional Office to meet their time constraints under the claims processing model. It is a win-win for the employee and for the applicant. New EZ forms were developed for this purpose and currently these are the forms to use for all applications whether Fully Developed are not.

Notwithstanding that the EZ form tells VA the claim is Fully Developed this does not necessarily mean that application will get priority handling. The information provided with the application must be sufficient to meet the definition of a Fully Developed Claim. A legitimate Fully Developed Claim is put on a fast-track for a decision. It is treated as a priority claim. That is the primary purpose as it saves a great deal of time in developing evidence in the Regional Office. On the other hand the EZ forms are now the only way to make application for Compensation, Pension or DIC. If the form is submitted without all of the supporting documentation that is required for a Fully Developed Claim, VA will designate that claim as incomplete and will take it off of the priority track and put it on what they call the standard track for further development. This not only slows down the decision process, but more importantly it could cause the claim to push up against the 125 day deadline for decisions and more likely result in a denial or an award for less than was expected.

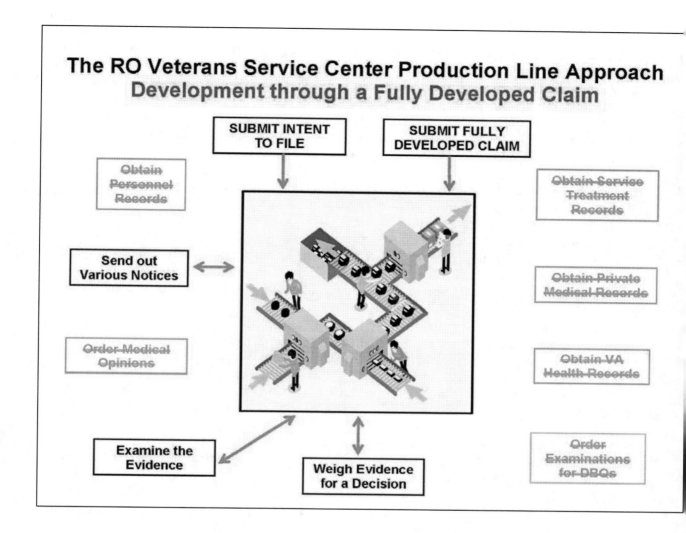

The RO Veterans Service Center Production Line Approach
Development through a Fully Developed Claim

The Elements of a Fully Developed Claim for Compensation

Help Veterans Service Representatives Understand the Theory of the Claim
Oftentimes, for a complex claim with a number of disability issues, there is an underlying theory of the claim that produces those disabilities. For example, a back injury in service can lead to all kinds of secondary disabilities such as stenosis, sciatica, neuropathy pain, weakness and static pain. The application for Disability Compensation, VA Form 21-526 EZ, does not provide enough space on the form to develop a theory or multiple theories of the claim. On the contrary, the application focuses entirely on the disability issues and treats them as separate issues instead of relating to a single event or multiple events that caused them.

Under duty to assist, the adjudicator is supposed to infer a theory of the claim from the evidence. The problem here is that for complex claims the theory is not always evident and the other problem is that due to time constraints, adjudicators rarely review all of the medical evidence and so they have no opportunity to see the "big picture."

133

It is essential that you identify the theory of the claim right up front and put it in the adjudicator's face. If you allow the adjudicator to determine his or her own theory of the claim you have just gone down a path from which you cannot return. In other words, once the adjudication team in the Regional Office have determined what they think the theory of the claim is, they will not deviate from that course no matter how much new evidence you give them to show that they are on the wrong path. As a result, a denial of your claim is often inevitable no matter what you try to do to forestall it.

Use VA Form 21-4138 to Summarize a Claim for Compensation

Summarizing the entire claim on a separate VA Form 21-4138 allows you to bypass the restrictive entry options on the application form itself – VA Form 21-526 EZ. You will have ample space to discuss and identify all of the issues pertaining to your claim by tying together all of the evidence and identifying the theory of the claim. Using this approach, you can provide sufficient detail with several paragraphs of information. The form itself only gives you a space of 76 individual characters to type all of the information pertaining to the issue you are claiming.

The key to any summary is not to overdo it. Providing too much information is just as bad as not providing enough. If you overload the adjudication team with pages and pages of summary, they will likely not read it as they are under time constraint. On the other hand, if you are too sketchy, they will not understand what you are claiming. We recommend no more than two or three paragraphs. You must work hard to communicate your claim in as few words as possible. Writing a summary can often be one of the more challenging aspects of filing an application.

Obtain and Organize Your Medical Records

It is essential that you obtain your own medical records. If your medical records from the service and your current medical records are extensive, there is no way the team in the Regional Office will read all of that information. You must obtain your own records and organize them for the adjudication process. You will point out or extract the pertinent information in your records that will lead to the proper decision. Theoretically, Veteran Service Representatives must review all of the pertinent evidence that relates to that claim. In reality, this just doesn't happen. For those claims where there is a great deal of medical evidence to pour through, that evidence is never thoroughly reviewed. We have seen cases where medical records constitute anywhere from 800 pages to 3,000 pages or more. With this sort of challenge the service representative will abstain from pouring through the records and instead take a shortcut by ordering a medical exam and an opinion. The medical examiners hired by VA for opinions are only given about a half hour to carry out their assigned task. As far as we can tell, they never review the medical records.

Currently, all medical examinations and opinions ordered by VA are through 5 large national contractors who in turn contract with local physicians assistants and nurse practitioners and sometimes medical doctors to do these examinations. This system is flawed. Examiners are only given a certain amount of time to do the examination and in most cases, they are not even required to write adequate opinions but simply to check off a number of boxes. This system is likely in violation of the intent of the regulations and someday may be challenged in court, but in the meantime we have to put up with it.

As an example, a claims file that may have 1,000 pages or more of medical records, can be organized and indexed properly so that only about 10 or 20 of those pages that are necessary for a decision are presented to the adjudicator. If the medical evidence is extensive enough, you should organize a table of contents and provide an explanation for each item under that table of contents. By going through this process, it is more likely the VSRs in the Regional Office will take the time to read that evidence. It is best to summarize the medical information for them in a few paragraphs and then reference the page numbers of the actual medical record file itself.

Organize All Other Evidence

The same method that we described in the section above is used for all other evidence. This includes personnel records, pertinent medical literature, personally procured DBQs and personally procured medical opinions or other evidence necessary for a Fully Developed Claim.

Just as with medical records, this material must be organized with tables of content and cover pages identifying what it is and a short description on the cover page pertaining to the nature of the evidence.

Write a Concise Lay Statement When Needed

A well-written and detailed personal lay statement is often essential to winning an award. A lay statement is a narrative of your claim which describes in detail the incident or incidents that were incurred in service, the history since discharge pertaining to the medical repercussions from the experience in service and a description of the current disability or disabilities. Lay statements can come from the claimant or from fellow service members who were present and observed the particular incident or from a spouse or family member who has observed symptoms over the years and verifies continuity of those symptoms.

It's important to know that a lay statement cannot contain a medical nexus opinion unless the person writing the statement is a licensed medical provider and is competent to provide that opinion. However, this does not preclude the person who is writing this statement from testifying of known facts from a source that is qualified to support a nexus opinion. For example the claimant can testify of diagnoses or other conditions that were given to the claimant either orally by treating physicians or through medical records that no longer exist.

The claimant can also testify to contemporaneous opinions that were offered by treating medical providers. In addition, the claimant can provide substantial evidence from competent medical literature that supports his or her assertions for service connection or a disability rating decision. When using medical literature evidence, the lay statement should point out why that literature supports the service connection rating or disability rating.

Lay evidence in a VA Compensation Claim has zero evidentiary value if the adjudicator in the Regional Office or the BVA Judge does not think it is credible and competent. When considering lay evidence, the Board or adjudicator should determine whether the veteran's disability is the type of disability for which lay evidence is competent. See Jandreau, 492 F.3d at 1377. If the disability is of the type for which lay evidence is competent, the adjudicators must weigh that evidence against the other evidence of record in making a determination regarding the existence of a service connection. Buchanan, 451 F.3d at 1334-37. Here are the criteria for determining that.

- It must determine if the lay evidence is competent and provides an adequate explanation of determination (Jandreau v. Nicholson, 492 F.3d 1372 Fed. Cir. 2007)
- It must weigh the lay evidence against other evidence to make a determination of its value on the claim (Buchanan v. Nicholson, 451 F.3d 1331, 1334-1337 Fed. Cir. 2006)
- It must make a credibility determination as to whether the evidence supports a finding of service connection and a continuity of symptomology (Barr v. Nicholson, 21. Vet App. 303 2007)

Submit Your Own Medical Opinion from a Competent Licensed Health Provider
If a medical opinion is needed to support the claim, you can go about obtaining your own medical opinion from a competent licensed health provider in two ways. The first is to submit it with the initial claim. Theoretically, if it is an adequate opinion, VA should accept it at face value and make a decision based on that opinion.

Unfortunately adjudicators have developed an adversarial approach to privately produced medical opinions. If a DBQ (Disability Benefits Questionnaire) is needed, which with most Compensation claims it is, then as part of that DBQ examination VA will usually order an opinion and disregard your opinion that has been submitted with the claim. Please note that they also routinely ignore privately produced DBQ's. The process of the Regional Office ordering its own medical opinion also occurs as we've pointed out when the medical record evidence is too extensive. Adjudicators will find an excuse to order an opinion based on that record from a contract examiner to avoid examining the record themselves. Unfortunately, the examiners do not look at the record either. They don't have enough time. Opinions from contract examiners routinely lack detailed reasoning for the conclusion or fail to provide supporting citations from medical literature. As such they typically have no probative value for a fair decision.

Nevertheless, adjudicators will accept an incompetent opinion from a paid examiner hired for this purpose regardless of its value. Even though a more adequate opinion may have been furnished by you, adjudicators usually ignore it and will never read it. Of course, in the decision letter that you receive based on the examination of the evidence, the adjudicator will always state that he or she has read all of your evidence which would include your own private medical opinion. If this were really true, then many of the claims that we have submitted should have been decided based on the more probative opinion. This typically has not been the case and so it is obvious that the VSR has ignored the more competent conclusion.

The second way for you to submit your own privately produced opinion is to allow the Regional Office to follow the procedure outlined above and allow the VSRs from VA to follow their predetermined course of ordering their own medical opinions. Examiners hired by VA to do DBQs and to offer medical opinions are only given a certain amount of time for the examination. In many cases this might only be 30 minutes and most of that time would be consumed filling out the DBQ or DBQ's. The examiner has little time for anything else.

When writing an opinion, the examiner is supposed to review the claimant's record in his or her eFolder. In fact, the contract examiner is required to state on the form furnished from VA whether he or she has reviewed the record. A review is not mandatory. On the other hand, how can the examiner come to a competent conclusion without understanding the history of the claim? Examiners almost always check the box that they have reviewed the medical record, but in most cases, due to time constraints or more typically due to inability to access those records from their personal office computers, they have not. Without any knowledge of the underlying medical issues, an examiner will often issue an opinion for service connection based primarily on his or her gut feelings or how he or she relates to the claimant.

The majority of these examiners are physicians assistants or nurse practitioners who generally have no specialized training for the particular medical condition for which they are offering an opinion. To date, we have not seen any opinion from a VA contract examiner where the conclusion was based on a well reasoned discussion of the issues due to the examiner's own experience or on citations from medical literature to back up that reasoning. Generally, these conclusions reflect a lack of professionalism. In most cases, the conclusion is a simple statement of whether there is service connection or not without a detailed explanation for that conclusion.

The Challenge with a "Development to Deny"
Don't be surprised by the conflict of interest we have discussed above. This process of fighting VA with medical opinions is totally adversarial and sometimes there is really little difference between what you are accomplishing with the adjudicator in the Regional Office and what you have to do to make your case in the traditional court system. The VA adjudication system is not supposed to work that way. According to the regulations the adjudication process is deliberately non-adversarial. Sometimes Veteran Service Representatives get carried away and think that they are acting as judges, which they are not. Their only requirement is to balance evidence on a scale and determine by the Preponderance Rule which way the evidence points. VA wants you believe the rating team is your advocate, but when it comes to medical opinions that's not true.

We have discussed above the possibility of a conflict when you are the first to provide the medical or nexus opinion. Even though he or she may have an adequate opinion in the file, the VSR in the Regional Office will order his or her own opinion. Regulations don't specifically prohibit the practice, but it is inconsistent with VA's duty to assist as an advocate to the veteran. Unfortunately, it happens a lot. In fact, it happens so frequently that accredited attorneys and accredited claims agents have a name for it. They call it "Development to Deny."

The Elements of a Fully Developed Claim for Pension

Application for Pension
VBA-21P-527EZ – This is the application a married or single veteran will use to apply for Veterans Pension – with or without the aid and attendance or housebound allowance. The veteran is always the claimant if he or she is alive even if the veteran is claiming expenses from the spouse's care.

It is especially important to remember the marriage and income sections must be filled out completely. Complete marriage information includes month and year dates, city state and county locations , full names, and the type of marriage. Basically, no information can be missing and partial answers are not tolerated. If you are not absolutely thorough with this form, Pension

Management will return it to you to be completed accurately and you will have lost 30 - 60 days. In processing time.

Application for DIC, Survivors Pension, and/or Accrued Benefits
VBA-21-534EZ is the application a surviving spouse will use to apply for Survivor's (Death) Pension, DIC or accrued benefits. You must fill out every applicable section of the 534EZ. Sections that don't apply do not have to be completed.

If you leave questions unanswered, VA will send a development letter asking for explanations. It is especially important to remember the marriage and income sections must be filled out completely.

Appointment of Individual as Claimant's Representative
VBA-21-22a allows an individual to act as a claimant's representative. As we discuss at the end of this chapter, the staff at the Senior Veterans Service Alliance could be your most effective advocate for a Pension application due to vest experience with these claims.

Exam for Housebound Status or Permanent Need for Regular Aid and Attendance
VBA-21- 2680 is essential for earning a rating for aid and attendance or housebound. With a rating, a claimant can qualify for improved Pension rather than just basic Pension. For example, basic Pension will pay up to only $1,146 per month for a single veteran. If that same veteran can earn a rating for aid and attendance, the veteran is eligible for up to $1,991 a month from improved Pension.

The signing physician must understand the form is for a disability rating particularly directed towards activities of daily living. In short, VA is looking for language that justifies custodial care needs and highlights specific activities of daily living (ADLs) like bathing, walking, dressing, toileting, hygiene, feeding, protected environment, etc… Statements like "patient requires assistance with bathing and dressing" are far more convincing then vague statements like "poor motor skills and general weakness due to age."

The basic criteria VA follows to determine if a claimant requires the regular aid and attendance of another person or is permanently bedridden can be found in 38 CFR § 3.352.

Request for Nursing Home Information in Connection with Claim for Aid and Attendance
If the veteran is a patient in a skilled nursing home, a rating for aid and attendance is automatic. VBA-21-0779 is a form the nursing home fills out to verify the applicant is a patient. As long as #13 is marked "Skilled Nursing Care" there is no need for the doctor's exam, made on *Form 21-2680*, nor for any caregiver to certify that the caregiver is providing custodial care. This form takes the place of that evidence. VA may ask for additional evidence if #13 is marked "Intermediate Nursing Care." This form is not applicable where the spouse of a living veteran is the one who is receiving care.

Income and Asset Statement
The new application for Veterans Pension on VA Form 21-527EZ includes the new questions concerning assets. The new application for Survivors Pension on VA Form 21-534EZ also

contains the same questions although they are numbered differently. Any questions that are answered "yes" on this portion of the 527EZ from question 29A through question 29E requires filling out the new VA Form 21-0969. Likewise any questions that are answered "yes" on this portion of the 534EZ from question 43A through question 43D also requires a 21-0969.

Doctor Report Addendum

Form FV 12 is used for the veteran or spouse and acts as a wonderful supplement to *VA Form 21-2680*. It is especially useful to help certify a "protected environment" need because of a cognitive condition.

Care Provider Certification of Services

Form FV13 is very important. Even though the doctor is required to produce medical evidence for the claimant to meet the criteria for aid and attendance or housebound outlined above, <u>without evidence the claimant is receiving and paying for these services there is likely no benefit</u>. This general-purpose form covers all types of care services from facilities to family members providing care. The form must be completed accurately, backspace and the proper sections are filled out and the need for two or more activities of daily living must be checked off. It must be signed by the provider. VA may reach out to the care provider to verify what is reported here.

You may be seeking to deduct unreimbursed medical expenses (UMEs) from the claimant's household income. This form will provide further evidence of these expenses, which are likely the claimant's biggest expense. After you submit the application, if the costs you report on this form change or if the claimant moves, notify VA immediately.

Independent Living Community Certification of Services

Form FV13 must be completed by an administrator of the community if the veteran or surviving spouse resides in Independent Living. Remember, Independent Living room and board costs alone are not considered to be unreimbursed medical expenses (UMEs). Housing, meals, room maintenance, emergency pull cords, 24-hour staffing, and locked exterior doors are not medical or nursing services (custodial care) by themselves.

VA will deduct Independent Living room and board when, due to poor health, the veteran or unhealthy spouse hires additional 3rd party care to meet their care needs AND the doctor certifies this arrangement.

For all claims involving Independent Living, include an *FV13* Form completed by the contracted 3rd party care and a letter from the doctor, signed, with this specific language:

> "I, the signing medical practitioner, certify that _____ (claimant) must reside in _____ (the Independent Living Community) to receive _____'s (the Contracted 3rd Party Care Provider) assistance with their Activities of Daily Living (ADLs) and custodial care needs. I prescribe the care outlined in the application that the 3rd Party Care Provider will offer the claimant in that facility."

If ALL of the above criteria are met, VA will deduct the room and meal costs and the 3rd party care costs. If not, VA will only deduct the 3rd party care costs. If there is no apparent need for third party care, do not bother making application for Pension if residing in independent living.

Cover Letter for Submission
It is a good idea to create a cover letter to organize all of the claim's forms and supporting evidence and to identify the claim as Fully Developed for the veteran service representatives who will adjudicate the claim.

Other Necessary Forms
Other possible necessary documentation might include supporting documents like:

- a marriage certificate,
- a death certificate <u>with a cause of death shown</u> (VA must be able to clearly read the cause of death. Adjudicators are required to look for instances of suspicious death, homicide, and whether or not the death was service connected). Adjudicators will also check to see if the veteran was married at the time of death.
- name change records,
- recently paid receipts/invoices from care providers
- a current bank statement, social security statement, insurance statement, asset statement(s), or supplemental insurance statement.

Submitting an "Intent to File"
Before applying for benefits, a veteran claimant or a surviving spouse claimant may wish to establish an Effective Date by submitting an "Intent to File" on VBA Form 21-0966. Formerly known as an "Informal Claim" An "Intent to File" can be submitted in three different ways (see 38 CFR 3.155).

Using an "Intent to File" to establish an effective date before the claimant has sufficiently prepared his or her application will allow the claimant to receive a larger lump sum retroactive payment than he or she otherwise would have.

For Pension and Survivor Pension claims with the aid and attendance allowance, if the applicant meets all of the following

- meets the medical requirement for a rating,
- is receiving aid and attendance services,
- can demonstrate having paid at least one month's worth of unfavorable services,
- in addition meets the war service test,
- meets the Net Worth limit (asset test) and
- meets the income test,

you should submit an "Intent to File" as soon as possible. This will establish an effective date. Don't submit an intent to file if you don't meet the criteria above. It messes things up.

Assistance with Submitting an Application for Benefits

Claimant Makes Application without Any Assistance
As mentioned above, some veteran claimants will fill out one of the EZ forms and send it in hoping to get some sort of benefit. These applications are almost without exception undeveloped claims. Unless an individual applicant is an expert on how to file for veterans benefits or that person has received detailed instructions from a competent source such as this book, the process for a Fully Developed Claim is just simply too complicated for the average layperson.

Without understanding the process that an undeveloped claim will go through, the hopeful applicant sits back and waits for the money to come in. VA has imposed upon itself a deadline of 125 days to process claims. According to VA, more than 90% of claims do receive a decision within 125 days or less of submission. Unfortunately, claims that are not Fully Developed often receive a denial or an award of benefits that is far less than the applicant was expecting because the deadline interferes with adequate development and a subsequent fair decision. The Regional Office simply runs out of time to develop all of the evidence and has to make a decision. Or in some cases as with Pension, the award may not be the maximum benefit allowed, but the claimant really doesn't know that and accepts a far lesser amount.

Claimant Makes Application Based on Instructions in This Book
If you understand all of the material in this book pertaining to the type of application you want to file, you should be more successful than doing it any other way. We have given you numerous tips and other strategies to help you get a successful decision notice.

Claimant Makes Application with the Help of a Service Organization
It has been the intent of Congress for the past century to make it easy for veterans or survivors to submit claims for benefits. In order to facilitate this process, Congress created a designation called called "accredited claim representative." Accredited representatives are the only individuals who have authority under the law to assist potential applicants with their claims. This does not mean that an individual has to use an accredited claim representative or that individual can enlist the assistance of someone who is not accredited. However, under the law, that person who is assisting and who is not accredited can only provide that assistance one time in that person's lifetime.

There are three types of accredited representatives – accredited representatives of Veterans Service Organizations, accredited attorneys and accredited agents. In order to represent the interests of veterans, Congress allowed, beginning in the early 1900s, for establishment of Veterans Service Organizations such as State Veterans Departments from all 50 states, the American Legion, the DAV, the Veterans of Foreign Wars, Vietnam Veterans of America, AMVETS and many more smaller organizations. There are roughly 30 of these service organizations allowed to process claims and they are typically called VSOs. These VSOs are allowed to provide training to accredit individuals in their organizations to assist with claims. There are about 10,000 accredited representatives of VSOs across the country. They are typically called "Veteran Service Officers." The majority of them are employed as state and county Veteran Service Officers. And the majority of all claims are processed by these state and county accredited employees.

Claim representatives of VSOs are paid a salary directly or indirectly by the service organization to assist with applications for benefits. Their services are absolutely free to potential claimants. It is the intent of Congress that no one should have to pay for assistance with submitting a claim. In fact, the law specifically prohibits service officers from receiving any kind of renumeration – other than their salary – such as a fee, or a gift or even an exchange of goods with a claimant.

If a claimant is using the assistance of an accredited representative of a veterans service organization, that representative may very well know how to do a Fully Developed Claim but will usually not take the time to do it. Service officers of VSOs are typically paid by how many claims they can generate in a given month or year. As a general rule, if they don't produce, they don't have a job. Putting together a Fully Developed Claim takes a great deal of time, but doesn't result in any more claims forms, for which employment credit is judged, than submitting an application that is not Fully Developed and takes only a few minutes to fill out. There is no incentive to submit a Fully Developed Claim and in fact for a service officer to do so on a regular basis could result in that service officer losing his or her job. As an added disincentive for submitting Fully Developed applications, service officers often have people waiting for their assistance and they don't have time for anything else other than filling out application forms.

Claimant Makes Application with the Help of an Accredited Attorney or Agent

The other two types of accredited representatives authorized by Congress are accredited attorneys and accredited agents. There are approximately 17,000 accredited attorneys and about 500 accredited agents. These individuals are also prohibited by law from charging fees for assistance with initial claims for benefits. On the other hand, the law is more liberal with these individuals concerning charging fees when it is not an initial claim. For example, VA policy allows for charging a fee for what is called a "prefiling consultation." A fee can also be charged by attorneys or agents after a claimant receives an unfavorable decision.

Because attorneys and agents are not paid any salaries for assisting with initial claims, and because they must assist with these claims for free, there is little incentive for these accredited representatives to do this. If they assist with a filing, they must find some other way to make money as it is difficult for any individual to abstain from any renumeration on a regular basis unless that person has some other source of income.

Thus, the primary motivation for accredited attorneys and accredited agents is to generate some source of income in conjunction with providing assistance with claims. Sometimes this is done through prefiling consultations, sometimes money is made by providing other services to the claimant that are not tied to the application itself, and in some cases, income is made by legitimately receiving a fee from the claimant through representing that claimant with an unfavorable decision.

As a general rule, not many initial claims – that are entirely cost free or not tied to any other services – are processed by accredited attorneys or accredited agents. But there are exceptions. Some accredited attorneys and a number of accredited agents offer their services without expecting any renumeration for initial applications. They provide their services free of any renumeration out of a genuine desire to help veterans receive benefits.

Claimant Makes Application with the Help of the Senior Veterans Service Alliance
Claim representatives from the Senior Veterans Service Alliance (SVSA) are accredited through the Department of Veterans Affairs. These claim representatives do not charge any fees for assistance with initial applications, nor do they have any hidden agendas for making income from claimants with an initial application. The SVSA is a nonprofit organization that derives its operating revenues from other sources. The staff provide their services without being paid by the SVSA. Claimants may have to submit their evidence to another organization for a prefiling consultation determination of eligibility, but that is a separate service from what the SVSA provides free for Fully Developed initial claims.

The SVSA has been very successful with its cost free Fully Developed Claims program for initial claims and if a determination has been made that a potential application has merit and has a chance of being approved, the success rate is very high.

For any claimants who come to the SVSA with previous unfavorable decisions which were a result of filing an application themselves or were a result of the services of some other accredited representatives, these unfavorable decisions will be accommodated by the SVSA for corrective action if the claim has any merit. At the Senior Veterans Service Alliance, we have handled numerous cases of incomplete and undeveloped claims and we have rescued many of these claims. With many of these cases, we have been able to produce favorable decisions where otherwise these claims would have met a dead-end.

Services of the Senior Veterans Service Alliance
The Senior Veterans Service Alliance was organized in 2011 to educate veterans and their survivors on all benefits that are available to them. Our website contains a vast amount of information about these benefits. The website is a popular destination for individuals across the country who are searching for information and assistance with veterans benefits.

Accredited representatives who provide their services to our nonprofit organization, have years of experience with submitting successful Fully Developed Claims for Compensation, Pension and DIC. Our representatives also stand ready to help any applicants who have received denials or have received decisions less favorable than they anticipated to represent those claimants against VA and hopefully turn around those unwanted decisions. If it is a valid claim, we have been successful in most cases in winning challenges and getting the benefits that were desired.

If you are a veteran, a family member of a veteran or an accredited claims representative, you become a member of the Senior Veterans Service Alliance at no cost. As a member you will receive a biweekly newsletter and you can call any time with a claim question.

Chapter 5
Applying for Disability Compensation

IN THIS CHAPTER:

This chapter serves 3 types of users. The first user is any individual who wants to win a successful claim for Compensation benefits. The next user is an accredited representative who wants to win benefits on behalf of a claimant. The third user is any individual or an accredited representative challenging VA with an unfavorable decision by using the new VA review process for unfavorable decisions. Even though we don't discuss the review and appeals process in this chapter and instead discuss it in Chapter 8, winning on review or appeal is no different than winning a well-developed initial claim. It is the same process.

If you understand the issues covered in this chapter, you will understand how to win a successful challenge to an unfavorable decision. The strategies discussed in this chapter will result in favorable decisions for either initial claims, supplemental claims, request for higher-level review or appeals – the process is the same for all.

We would like to point out that the application process we give you in this chapter is primarily designed for the following types of claims.

1. Initial claims for direct service connection or presumptive service connection
2. Requests for increase
3. Secondary service connection claims

We discuss challenges to unfavorable decisions as well as appeals to the Board of Veterans Appeals in Chapter 8 of this book.

PART 1 – UNDERSTANDING DISABILITY COMPENSATION

Entitlement Requirements

There are four requirements that are necessary for an application for Disability Compensation. With the exception of presumptive service connection, all four must apply or there is no benefit.

1. The veteran, alive or deceased, must meet service requirements for the requested benefit

2. With the exception of presumed service-connected conditions or diseases, evidence must establish an illness, injury, exposure or aggravation that happened while in service.

3. Evidence must establish that the veteran is currently suffering from a disabling condition or disease that could be a result of the illness, injury, exposure or aggravation that occurred in service and generally this condition or disease must be chronic.

4. With the exception of presumed service-connected conditions or diseases, there must be convincing evidence of a causative link or nexus between the current disabling condition or disease and the illness, injury, exposure or aggravation that happened in service.

WE DISCUSS EACH OF THESE FOUR REQUIREMENTS BELOW

1. Meeting Service Requirements for Veterans Benefits

Establishing service requirements is covered in "Chapter 2 Determining Eligibility and Entitlement." Please go back and reread that information if you have any questions concerning what it means to be a veteran and meeting duty requirements for benefits.

2. Establishing Evidence of Illness, Injury, Exposure or Aggravation Incurred in Service

In this chapter, we cover 17 various of Disability Compensation or Compensation related claims. Using these 17 types is a classification system we came up with. Other handbooks may come up with their own dichotomies as to how to approach various categories of claims. Our approach is simply a way to try and make it all a little more understandable from our point of view. It is important to remember that every claim is unique. There are thousands of different combinations of disabilities and underlying reasons for those disabilities that result in the benefits packages for roughly 4.6 million claimants receiving Disability Compensation.

There are 3 major issues for service connected disabilities that could result in a claim for disability benefits after service. The current disability after service could be due to any or all of the following three: 1) in-service injury, 2) in-service illness or 3) aggravation of an existing condition that was noted in the induction physical. A claimant must provide evidence of these incurrences in service either through medical records, personnel records, buddy statements or other credible evidence. There are however exceptions. The first of these exceptions are what are called presumed service-connected conditions where evidence only of a certain duty assignment is necessary in order to establish service connection. In addition, injuries or illnesses incurred in combat generally don't require evidence if the injury or illness was consistent with combat duty and the circumstances of combat that resulted in injury or illness.

3. Establishing Evidence for a Current Disabling Illness or Condition

Medical evidence is required for proving existence of a current disabling illness or condition. The Regional Office may want to see the VA healthcare medical file or the current private medical file of the claimant pertaining to the disabling illness or condition that is being claimed. You should be aware that the Regional Office does not want to see medical records that are not pertinent. They are useless and end up bogging down the decision process. It is important the condition be persistent or long-lasting and not temporary in nature. VA wants to see evidence of the continuity of the disability or condition from discharge or reasons why that is not the case.

Your current medical records pertaining to the disability may not actually identify disability associated with your current illness or other condition. In other words, your doctors may devote a great deal of information pertaining to diagnosis, treatment and prognosis but not even mention disability. This is also not always useful information as it requires VA to infer from the records that there may be a disability or there may not be. On the other hand, such conditions as stage IV cancer or congestive heart failure or other debilitating conditions, carry with them an inferred disability and it is not necessary to know the symptoms resulting from these conditions as long as the specific treatment is listed which will be used for assigning a disability rating. For most rating decisions, the rater has to determine a level of disability in percentage amounts. Many of the disability rating tables identify certain symptoms that relate to a level of disability such as 40%, 60% or 100%. In order to do the rating for certain conditions, the rating authority needs a listing of disability symptoms or what VA calls symptomology.

As a general rule, if medical records cannot establish the continuity and the nature of and chronicity of symptoms, the Regional Office will order a medical examination to produce an assessment of the condition or illness. The examiners are required to use forms for these assessments called Disability Benefit Questionnaire (DBQ's). There are 69 of these forms, each corresponding to different types of diseases, illnesses or disabilities. We will discuss the use of DBQ's further on in this chapter. The claimant also can submit his or her own DBQ's from treating doctors avoiding the need for VA to order an exam for this purpose.

You are not eligible for benefits if you are not currently suffering from disability or a condition that is inferred to produce disability. All Disability Compensation claims require a rating, but without disabling symptoms or treatments that infer disability the rating will be 0%. As an example, most hearing loss awards without profound hearing loss and without tinnitus are rated at 0%. Or as an example a presumptive condition for Agent Orange exposure, type II diabetes, will receive a 0% rating if the diabetes is under control through exercise and proper diet. Don't make application if your condition is acute (temporary) or is not principally chronic – meaning that it persists over a long period of time. Your medical records or the medical assessment must reflect the continuity of your condition.

It is important to note that if you have a disabling condition that can be rated at 0%, you should definitely make application, as you have established service connection even though you will receive no money. This service connection could be very valuable later if your condition gets worse or causes a secondary disability that could be ratable and result in an award. It saves your going back and establishing service connection.

4. Establishing a Link or Nexus between the Current Disability or Disease and the Illness, Injury or Aggravation That Occurred in Service.

It should be noted that for presumptive service-connected disability, this fourth step is not necessary. Notwithstanding, in order to establish presumptive service connection, the claimant must have been in the right place at the right time. Evidence of this assignment is required.

For all other service-connected disability claims, a connective causative link or Nexus between the incurrence in service and the current condition or conditions must be proven through medical records or personnel records or service treatment records or inference that the particular assignment or incident in service could have resulted in the current condition or conditions. In some cases where a continuation of symptoms from discharge cannot be shown with medical evidence or other credible evidence, VA will require a medical opinion called a Nexus opinion from a licensed health care provider. The purpose of this opinion is for the medical professional to explain when, how and why the current condition or conditions are connected to what occurred in service.

3 types of service connection

Direct Service Connection
Direct service-connected claims require that the veteran or the survivor on behalf of the veteran must provide some sort of evidence that a particular injury, exposure or disease resulting in disability was incurred while serving in the Armed Forces OR if that condition was pre-existing to entry in the service, it was aggravated through service. These claims do not require any specific amount of duty time as do the presumptive service connected claims.

Service Induction Examination – Presumption of Soundness
The veteran is presumed to be in sound condition after the induction examination except when defects, infirmities or disorders were noted in the records at entrance into service. Nevertheless, even though pre-existing conditions are not noted at entrance, VA still must provide clear and unmistakable evidence that the disease or injury did not exist prior to service and was not aggravated by service.

For those conditions that were known at entry, the Regional Office will establish a baseline for determining whether the pre-existing condition was aggravated by service based on the veteran's entwere history of service medical records for that condition.

Accident, Injury or Illness as a Matter of Record – Personnel/Service Treatment Records STR

The Regional Office must review the evidence of record to include personnel and medical records, or as they are called "Service Treatment Records" (STR's), to ensure the injury or illness occurred during service and in the line of duty. If the record does not exist, corroborative evidence can be used if it is consistent with the conditions that would have caused the accident injury or illness. Perhaps the veteran was treated for the injury or illness at a civilian location. If records can be found, this can provide the proper evidence. A sworn statement by the veteran is usually not acceptable unless other written evidence can corroborate the sworn statement.

Unreported Accident, Injury or Illness

A discharge medical evaluation may uncover unreported accidents injuries or illnesses. It is not unreasonable to assume that the rigors of military service for certain assignments would result in back injuries, muscle injuries or other joint injuries. For various reasons, these injuries might go unreported. Perhaps illnesses are also unreported that could have a chronic effect many years after discharge. Where any evidence from service records is lacking, it is up to the claimant to try and come up with enough evidence to provide a reasonable assumption that the existing disability was due to an unreported accident, injury or illness. This is a large burden of proof and it may not always be possible to win these kinds of claims. A sworn statement by the veteran alone without other evidence, is typically not acceptable unless accompanied by documents such as personnel records, squadron or battalion duty records showing temporary duty due to injury or illness or other medical records that might point to complications caused by the unreported accident, injury or illness even though medical records for the primary injury do not exist.

Exposure to Hazards or Stressors Resulting in Post Service Disability

Some exposures are already covered under presumptive service connection. These would include ionizing radiation, tropical diseases, prisoner of war, Agent Orange and other herbicide exposures, and to some degree posttraumatic stress syndrome which is not presumptive but in some respects is often acknowledged as occurring in service because of combat stress or the fear of imminent danger. Other exposures such as asbestos, loud noises, fumes, fuels and solvents, vibration, extreme heat, extreme cold and so forth are not considered presumptive.

On the other hand, when it can be shown that a current disabling condition is at least as likely as not the result of one of these kinds of exposures and that the claimant was indeed exposed because of duty assignment, these kinds of disability conditions can often result in an award. A sworn statement by the veteran is usually not acceptable by itself unless accompanied by other evidence. One example of this type of claim is a veteran who develops bladder cancer due to exposure to carbon tetrachloride. Bladder cancer is a known type caused by this carcinogen. If the veteran can provide lay statements as to working with the carbon tetrachloride – for example cleaning engine parts as the duty assignment of a diesel mechanic – and personnel records can back up this claim, that is likely enough evidence, along with a doctor's opinion for service connection, to result in a claim. Another example of exposure to hazards is a hearing loss claim. In Part 4 of this chapter, we provide a table of assignments where hearing loss could be expected because of the duty required. Matching the duty assignment to the probability of hearing loss is a huge step in getting a hearing loss claim even if service treatment records for hearing loss don't exist because the hearing loss was not manifest at the time.

Combat

Illnesses, conditions or injuries that are incurred in combat are generally treated in a more liberal manner as far as evidence of incurrence in service. Scars may be used as evidence of wounds, but they may not always be due to combat and thus corroborating evidence is necessary. If the veteran participates in the Separation History and Physical Examination Program (SHPE). Or through the Department of Defense Separation Retirement, combat injuries or illnesses may show up in this evaluation. In the absence of any Service Treatment Records or discharge evaluations, lay statements from the veteran or other individuals corroborating the statements will be accepted that an injury or disease was incurred. Lay statements also apply to conditions aggravated in combat, if the evidence is consistent with circumstances, conditions, or hardships of such service even though there is no official record of such incurrence or aggravation. For conditions incurred in combat, lay evidence should be sufficient by itself if it is consistent and plausible and not refuted by clear and convincing evidence to the contrary.

Aggravation of an Existing Condition during Service

Aggravation is covered under 38 CFR 3.306 and 38 CFR 3.307. Service Treatment Records must indicate an aggravation during the period of service. Temporary or intermittent flare ups of pre-existing injury or disease are not sufficient to be considered aggravation in service unless the underlying condition has worsened. Rehabilitation from surgery shall not be considered as an aggravation. For a veteran entering the service with a hereditary disease, aggravation and thus service connection can be established if the disease manifests itself after entry on duty. A genetic disease such as Huntington's Disease that is predisposed for development is not service-connected under the aggravation rules.

Establishing Direct Service Connection

<u>Because direct service connection is not presumptive, a direct nexus or link between the current disability and any injury or illness or exposure in service that is claimed as the cause of the current disability must be established.</u> There is no required time in service for receiving an award through direct service connection.

The disabling condition that the veteran is currently experiencing could have been caused by an illness, injury, or aggravation in the service. It could also have been caused caused by exposure to hazardous material or hazardous environment. A veteran seeking service connection for an existing condition, has several ways to prove the connection based on the place, the timing, or the circumstances of his service. The evidence required can include lay statements, Service Treatment Records, private medical records, personnel records, naval group, squadron or battalion records, Disability Benefits Questionnaire and medical nexus opinion letters. Service medical treatment records (STRS) and personnel records are available from the National Records Center in St. Louis for providing this evidence.

As with presumptive service-connected conditions or diseases, you may also be required to show evidence of a continuity of symptoms if there is no record of those symptoms from previous years and the symptoms manifest many years after discharge – perhaps 30 or 40 years later. If there is no corroborating evidence from VA healthcare records or from private physician records, lay testimony can be very helpful here.

With some claims, a principal used by the rating activity in the Regional Office could come to your aid. It is called "reasonable doubt" and is found in 38 CFR 3.102.

"It is the defined and consistently applied policy of the Department Of Veterans Affairs to administer the law under a broad interpretation, consistent, however, with the facts shown in every case. When, after careful consideration of all procurable and assembled data, a reasonable doubt arises regarding service origin, the degree of disability, or any other point, such doubt will be resolved in favor of the claimant. By reasonable doubt is meant one which exists because of an approximate balance of positive and negative evidence which does not satisfactorily prove or disprove the claim. It is a substantial doubt and one within the range of probability as distinguished from pure speculation or remote possibility. It is not a means of reconciling actual conflict or a contradiction in the evidence. <u>Mere suspicion or doubt as to the truth of any statements submitted, as distinguished from impeachment or contradiction by evidence or known facts, is not justifiable basis for denying the application of the reasonable doubt doctrine if the entwere, complete record otherwise warrants invoking this doctrine. The reasonable doubt doctrine is also applicable even in the absence of official records, particularly if the basic incident allegedly arose under combat, or similarly strenuous conditions, and is consistent with the probable results of such known hardships.</u>"

Presumptive Service Connection

Over the years, Congress has felt that certain disabling conditions – presumably developed as a result of service – are automatically considered to be a result of service. These are called presumptive service-connected conditions, diseases or disabilities. The list of these conditions, illnesses or diseases amounts to more than 120 different presumptive disease categories. With these particular types of claims, the veteran does not have to prove that an illness or injury or aggravation of an existing disability was incurred in the service. It is presumed to have been incurred. Evidence need only be provided to show that the claimant currently has one of these presumptive conditions and meets the service conditions for presumption. A benefit is usually awarded. With presumptive service connection, the burden for the claimant to prove service connection has been eliminated, and makes it much easier for these claims to be approved.

Ninety days of service is required for certain defined presumptive conditions manifesting within one year after service and for tropical diseases. If a current disease or condition is considered presumptive service-connected, there is no need to establish a nexus or link between that disease or condition and active duty service. It is automatically considered to be caused by service.

It is important to note that some VA-listed presumptive conditions may not actually be the result of service, but many years after discharge may be the result of other non-service health developments. In order to be service-connected, many of the presumptive conditions must have manifest within a certain period of time after leaving the service – usually to a degree of 10% disability within the first year. For other presumptive conditions where there is no time limit, and the condition has been recently diagnosed and the time between discharge and the claim is significant, the Regional Office will be forced to acknowledge that the condition or conditions are service-connected regardless of when they manifested. The only requirement is that the current disabilities or diseases are chronic – meaning that the symptomology from injury or disease is experienced on a regular basis. In addition, any conditions that are currently under treatment, such as cancer, that is considered presumptive for service, will warrant a rating for at least a year or longer while the treatment is being administered. The rating may be reduced to 0% when the treatment is stopped and the disease or illness has gone into remission or the injury no longer exhibits symptoms.

Secondary Service Connection
Often a service-connected condition will result in a disability or disease that was not incurred in service but because the service connected condition caused it, VA will also pay a benefit. This is called secondary service connection. We cover applications for secondary disability in Part 4 of this chapter.

Secondary service-connected claims and requests for increase in rating are the most prevalent types of claims VA receives for compensation. In 2019 the department anticipates that 74% of all applications will come from veterans who are already receiving benefits. The other 26% of applications are original claims or other issues that need to get solved. Many of those 74% of applications from veterans who are already on claim will be for secondary disability.

Summary of the Rules Pertaining to Secondary Disability
Currently there are two categories of claims that can be granted secondary service connection under Title 38 CFR 3.310 (a) and (b). The first category includes claims for which there is an existing service connected disability and a subsequent disability or disabilities is found to be proximately due (caused by) the service-connected disability. One example of this type of claim could be loss of a limb due to amputation occurring subsequent to presumptive service-connected diabetes. Disability due to the loss of a limb should be service-connected in addition to the diabetes, because the amputation may not have been needed had the veteran not developed diabetes which was service-connected.

The second category of secondary disability is granted in accordance with a 1995 court decision (Alan v Brown 7vet. app. 439). This ruling forces VA to grant service connection under 38 CFR 3.310 (b) in claims where there is an increase in the severity of a non-service-connected disability that is found to be due to aggravation by a service-connected disability. The non-service connected disability can exist prior to establishing service connection for the disability that aggravates it. This second category is called secondary service connection by aggravation.

The baseline of the non-service connected disability which was aggravated by a service-connected disability must be established by medical evidence created before the onset of aggravation. Or if this is not possible, the earliest medical evidence that can be created between the onset of aggravation and receipt of medical evidence establishing the current level of severity of the non-service connected disability.

If it is impossible to establish a baseline to determine the severity of aggravation, it is unlikely that there will be an award. Medical records are critical to this type of claim. The veteran must furnish medical evidence of the current level of severity of the non-service connected disability and medical evidence of its level of severity prior to the point at which it was being aggravated by the service-connected disability.

Once the rating authority has this information, a medical examination will be requested directing an opinion by the examiner to establish whether the examiner feels that the severity of the non-service connected disability is proximately due to the service-connected disability. The examiner must have all of the private records of the veteran establishing the baseline for review when providing an opinion on the issue of aggravation. The examiner's report must separately address all of the following medical issues in order to be considered adequate for rating a claim for secondary service connection based on aggravation:

- the current level of severity of the non-service connected disease or injury
- an opinion as to whether a service-connected disability proximately caused the non-service connected disability to increase in severity, and
- the medical considerations supporting this opinion.

The rating activity will use this information as the primary source of evidence for making a decision whether there was aggravation or not and whether it is ratable or not.

If enough evidence is produced to show that there is a reasonable assumption or inference that the non-service connected secondary disability is due to the service-connected disability, then a strong opinion letter from a licensed medical provider might sway VA to make a favorable decision. With these particular kinds of claims you may also want to provide your own private doctor's opinion and not rely on an opinion ordered by VA.

Establishing Secondary Disability with an Initial Claim
Secondary disability can be awarded for a claimant who has never made application and thus never received an award for direct service connection. The service-connected disability that has led to that non-service-connected secondary disability or that has aggravated an existing non-service-connected disability does not have to be awarded first, followed by a second application for secondary service submitted at a later date. They generally can be awarded together. Both the underlying condition for service connection and the secondary disability can be applied for at the same time. Even if the underlying condition is rated at 0%, the secondary disability can be rated and produce a monthly benefit.

For example suppose a veteran develops diabetes from exposure to herbicide while serving in the Republic of Vietnam. He has never made a claim for disability compensation. However, his diabetes is severe enough to have caused development of diabetic neuropathy. He makes an initial application based on his neuropathy and the presumption of diabetes due to herbicide exposure. He will receive an award based on the neuropathy. VA will also grant service connection for his diabetes even though he never initiated a claim for diabetes

Another way secondary service connection can be established, where the veteran is not receiving a monetary benefit is, when a rating for service connection has already been issued at 0%, and the service-connected condition has subsequently resulted in a secondary disability that can be rated. A rating for service connection can be based on secondary disability as long as it is caused by a service-connected disability.

Most Common Claims for Secondary Disability
Here are the 10 most common types of claims for secondary disability in order of importance.

1. sciatic nerve damage
2. erectile dysfunction
3. median nerve damage (paralysis)
4. external popliteal nerve damage
5. arteriosclerotic heart disease
6. arterial sclerosis obliterans
7. hypertensive vascular disease
8. renal involvement in systemic diseases
9. sciatic nerve (neuritis)
10. degenerative arthritis of the spine

Benefit Payment Issues

Disability Compensation is a tax free monetary benefit paid to veterans with disabilities that are the result of a disease or injury incurred or aggravated during active military service. Compensation may also be paid for post-service disabilities that are considered related or secondary to disabilities occurring in service and for disabilities presumed to be related to circumstances of military service, even though they may arise after service. Increasing designated payments for degrees of disability in 10% increments from 0% to 100% are designed to compensate for considerable loss of working time from exacerbations or illnesses. A rating for 0% is also available but results in no payments.

We have provided some pertinent charts and graphs for you in Chapter 1 of this book to help you understand how veterans' disability benefits fit in with the population and the cost of these benefits. If you are an accredited agent or an accredited attorney and you are assisting veterans or their survivors with benefits, these charts might be useful to help you understand the people you are serving. In addition, we provide on the DVD Claim Support Disc a number of charts and graphs from all of the programs that we discuss in this book. For those of you who like this kind of information to gain a perspective on things, we hope this will satisfy that need.

Most veterans receive their disability benefit payments by direct deposit to a bank, savings and loan or credit union account. Other veterans may still be receiving benefits by paper check. Compensation and Pension beneficiaries can establish direct deposit through the Treasury's Go Direct helpline or through eBenefits. Veterans also have the option of receiving their benefits via a prepaid debit card, even if they do not have a bank account. There is no credit check, no minimum balance required, and basic services are free.

Veterans with disability ratings of at least 30 percent are eligible for additional allowances for dependents, including spouses, minor children, children between the ages of 18 and 23 who are attending school, children who are permanently incapable of self-support because of a disability arising before age 18, and dependent parents. The additional amount depends on the disability rating and the number of dependents

All veterans who develop Amyotrophic Lateral Sclerosis (ALS), also known as Lou Gehrig's Disease, at any time after separation from service, are eligible for Compensation for that disease by only providing proof of the disorder. No other evidence is required. The disability rating is 100%.

Disability Compensation Payments and Military Severance or Disability Pay
The payment of military retirement pay, disability severance pay and separation incentive payments, known as SSB (Special Separation Benefits) and VSI (Voluntary Separation Incentives) typically affect the amount of VA Compensation paid to disabled veterans. Reductions or possible elimination of Compensation Payments will be made if other benefits related to military disability from active duty are being received.

Concurrent Retirement and Disability Payments (CRDP)
Veterans receiving military retirement income cannot receive Disability Compensation at the same time except under certain conditions. This rule does not apply to veterans receiving military retirement and who are also receiving Pension. There is no such prohibition. Typically, the veteran receiving Disability Compensation will choose not to receive the equivalent amount from his or her military retirement. This is called an offset election. The reason for preferring Disability Compensation to retirement is that Compensation is nontaxable and retirement is.

CRDP does not restrict payment of military retirement for retwerees with ratings from 50% to 100% . In other words, veterans rated 50% or higher have no offsetting income from their retirement pay.

To qualify for no reduction, under CRDP you must also meet the following criteria:

- You are a regular retiree with a VA disability rating of 50 percent or greater.

- You are a reserve retiree with 20 qualifying years of service, who has a VA disability rating of 50 percent or greater and who has reached retirement age. (In most cases the retirement age for reservists is 60, but certain reserve retirees may be eligible before they turn 60. If you are a member of the Ready Reserve, your retirement age can be reduced below age 60 by three months for each 90 days of active service you have performed during a fiscal year.)

- You are retired under the Temporary Early Retirement Act (TERA) and have a VA disability rating of 50 percent or greater.

- You are a disability retiree who earned entitlement to retired pay under any provision of law other than solely by disability, and you have a VA disability rating of 50 percent or greater. You might become eligible for CRDP at the time you would have become eligible for retired pay.

Retirees do not need to apply for CRDP. Payment is coordinated between VA and the Department of Defense (DoD).

Combat-Related Special Compensation (CRSC)

CRSC provides tax-free monthly payments to eligible returned veterans with combat-related injuries. With CRSC, veterans can receive both their full military retirement pay and their VA Disability Compensation if the injury is combat-related. Of course, it should be noted that if the veteran is 50% or higher rated he or she is automatically entitled to full retirement pay under the concurrent rule above.

Returned veterans with combat-related injuries must meet all of the following criteria to apply for CRSC:

1. Active or Reserve component with 20 years of creditable service or medically returned.
2. Receiving military returned pay.
3. Have a 10 percent or greater VA-rated injury.
4. Military returned pay is being reduced by VA disability payments (VA Waiver).

In addition, veterans must be able to provide documentary evidence that their injuries were a result of one of the following:

- Training that simulates war (e.g., exercises, field training)
- Hazardous duty (e.g., flight, diving, parachute duty)
- An instrumentality of war (e.g. combat vehicles, iapons, Agent Orange)
- Armed conflict (e.g. gunshot wounds, Purple Heart)

The Rating Activity in the Regional Office

The Job of the Rating Activity

After all development actions for a claim are complete, the adjudication team VSRs (Veteran Service Representatives) refer the claim to the team RSVR (Rating Veterans Service Representative) for a rating. The RSVR reviews all the evidence associated with the claim, makes decisions on issues raised by the claimant, and identifies any inferred issues that should be addressed. The rater documents the rating decision in a standard format, using an automated rating preparation system called Rating Board Automation (RBA) 2000. The system automatically calculates the disability rating. After completing the rating decision, the other members of the adjudication team complete the claim for follow-up and issue. This process implements the rating decision by preparing either a monetary award or a denial. It also prepares notification letters for the claimant and representative.

When performing a rating evaluation, RVSRs consider all evidence associated with the claim. This includes service medical records, VA medical examination records, clinical summaries from VA medical centers where treatment has been provided to the veteran, and evidence provided from private sources, such as the veteran's treating physician.

The job of the Rating Veterans Service Representative consists primarily of interpreting medical records in deciding if the medical evidence is sufficient enough to result in a favorable or unfavorable decision. First of all, medical evidence must show a disabling condition that is ratable and that is ongoing and not acute. Second, medical evidence from service records or evidence of duty assignment or statements from others or corroborative history must show that an illness, aggravation or injury that could have resulted in the current condition, was incurred in service whether this is for presumptive or direct service connection. Finally, the medical evidence must tie everything together such that there is a link established between the current condition of the claimant and the illness or injury or aggravation incurred in service.

Rating Decisions Are Not Made by Individuals with a Medical Background
It is interesting to note that RVSR's are not required to have a medical background, although some of them might be nurses or have served as medics in the service. Medical doctors are not prohibited from being raters, but the pay scale of GS 12 would likely not attract very many medical doctors. Unfortunately, many adjudicators often don't understand medical terminology or complex medical conditions.

At one time, rating decisions were made by a so-called "rating board" that consisted of two non-medical rating experts along with a physician. In fact, an analog to veterans disability is Social Security disability where decisions regarding disability are made involving a doctor. Rating boards were replaced in the early 1990s by several non-medical individuals making the decision or in recent years by a single non-medical rater making a decision. This removal of medical personnel is due to a ruling by the Court of Appeals for Veterans Claims which is often cited, not only for its impact on not using in-house medical personnel, but also for its impact on the concept of new and material evidence in rating and appeal decisions.

Colvin v. Derwinski, 1 Vet. App. 171 (1991) CAVC
Taken from The Veterans Advocate, January-June 2008

Colvin stands for a now deeply embedded and fundamental principle of veterans law – that VA may use only independent medical evidence to support its benefits decisions. The VA may not use the medical opinion or judgment of the VA rater or BVA Veterans Law Judge to support a decision.

For many years prior to Colvin, VA decisions were based on the findings of VA physicians who were part of the decision-making process. A doctor employed by VA would not only provide the medical opinion that would be used to decide the claim, he or she would participate in deciding whether to grant or deny benefits.

This practice of having VA doctors play a decision making role was ended by Colvin. The Court held that:

"If the medical evidence of record is insufficient, or, in the opinion of the BVA, of doubtful weight or credibility, the BVA is always free to supplement the record by seeking an advisory opinion, ordering a medical examination or citing recognized medical treatises in its decisions that clearly support its ultimate conclusions . . . . This procedure ensures that all medical evidence contrary to the veteran's claim will be made known to him and be part of the record before this Court. Colvin, 1 Vet.App. at 175."

158

But advocates must watch out . . . even though the formal procedure of having a VA doctor play a decision-making role stopped after Colvin, VA raters and BVA Veterans Law Judges persist in relying on their own medical judgments to decide claims. For example, the VA and BVA may often make a determination that an in-service injury was "acute, without chronic residual disability." However, the degree of injury and whether any disabilities resulted from the injury are medical assessments that the VA and the Board are not competent to make unless there is independent medical evidence to support that conclusion. This means that in many cases VA's determination that an in-service injury was acute and did not result in chronic disability may violate Colvin.

Another common problem is that VA may dismiss favorable medical evidence of record without citing to medical evidence in the record or medical literature to support its rejection. This often reflects the lack of medical knowledge by the rating authority.

A good rule of thumb based on Colvin is that if there is a VA-made medical conclusion – not directly based on a medical examination report, advisory opinion, or medical literature – the conclusion may be erroneous because the VA has no independent medical support for its findings. Decisions containing unsupported medical conclusions should be challenged.

The Rating Decision May Lead to Granting a Benefit Which Was Not Applied for
When submitting a claim for disability benefits, the Regional Office does not require the claimant to articulate every benefit that he or she is seeking. The claimant probably has no idea of what is available based on his or her evidence. The Regional Office is required to examine every claim including all of the evidence and testimony and determine if other benefits are applicable. For example a claim for Disability Compensation might end up being awarded for SMC or 100% for unemployability or providing aid and attendance or housebound allowances or providing retroactive benefits or housing allowances or clothing allowances or automobile adaptations and the list goes on and on.

The Disability Rating System

Disability Ratings

If a claim is approved, VA will assign a disability rating from 0% to 100%. A 0% disability rating does not pay any benefit. Why then would one want such a rating? The answer is that by receiving a 0% rating, your Regional Office Veterans Service Center has recognized that the disability is service-connected. You have already overcome a large hurdle towards getting a benefit. If, in the future, the disability worsens or causes a secondary disability, then service connection is already established and you now only have to provide evidence that the condition has worsened or that it has caused a secondary condition. We post the rates for 2020 below. You will notice that the difference between 90% and 100% is significant. This represents the loss of earnings capacity between someone who might possibly still be employed and someone who at 100% is considered unemployable.

Disability Compensation Rate Table for 2020 (In Dollars)

Disability Percent	10%	20%	30%	40%	50%	60%	70%	80%	90%	100%
Veteran Alone	142.29	281.27	435.69	627.61	893.43	1,131.68	1,426.17	1,657.80	1,862.96	3,106.04
Veteran & Spouse			486.69	696.61	979.43	1,234.68	1,547.17	1,795.80	2,017.96	3,279.22
Vet – Sp – 1 Child			525.69	747.61	1,043.43	1,311.68	1,636.17	1,897.80	2,132.96	3,406.04
Vet – 1 Child			469.69	673.61	950.43	1,200.68	1,507.17	1,749.80	1,966.96	3,221.85
Additional Child			25.00	34.00	43.00	51.00	60.00	68.00	77.00	86.05
Addt. Schoolchild			83.00	111.00	138.00	166.00	194.00	222.00	250.00	277.96
A&A for Spouse			48.00	63.00	80.00	96.00	111.00	127.00	143.00	158.82

If veteran has a spouse who requires A&A, add "A&A for spouse" to the amount of dependency & rate code above.

Combined Ratings

A single rating percentage can also be a combination of a number of disabilities rated at different percentages. For example, suppose a veteran has a rating of 40% for PTSD, a rating of 10% for hearing loss and a rating of 20% for back injury. These are all plausible ratings for a veteran exposed to the rigors of combat. The combined rating is not the sum of the individual ratings resulting in a total rating of 70%. It is a little more complicated.

Here's how it works. To calculate the combined rating, you sort the percentages descending from the largest to the smallest. In this case the order is 40%, 20%, 10%. Next subtract the largest (40%) from 100% which yields 60%. This is the first calculation that is used to determine the combined rating. VA assumes that if the veteran is 40% disabled he or she only has the remaining efficiency to perform work at a 60% level (100% - 40%.) Therefore if a veteran is 20% disabled from back injury on top of being 40% for PTSD then the veteran can only perform 20% times the 60% of the remaining efficiency. Multiplying 20% by 60% yields 12%. The next step is to add this remaining efficiency rating of % on to the very first rating of 40% yielding a first stage combined rating of 52%.

The next step is to account for the 10% rating for hearing loss. To do this we subtract the new first step combined rating of 52% from 100% which gives us a remaining efficiency to perform work of 48%. Multiply this remaining efficiency of 48% times 10% for hearing loss and you get 4.8% which represents the remaining efficiency times the disability for hearing loss. Now we add the first stage combined rating of 52% to the second stage calculated remaining efficiency rate of 4.8% to obtain the second stage combined rating. The total is 56.8%.

The final stage combined rating is rounded up or rounded down to the nearest 10% multiple. If the total combined rating calculation results in a number with 5% in it, you always round up to the next 10% value. Because our calculated rating of 56.8%, we will round up and the combined disability is 60% for our example. It is not the 70% that you would expect by simply adding all three ratings together. Cumulative ratings can never exceed a combined rating of 100%.

If there are 4 individual ratings or 5 individual ratings or more, we just keep completing the steps and going to the next stage of combined rating. For 4 individual disability ratings there would be 3 stages of combined rating calculations. For 5 individual disability ratings there would be 4 stages of combined rating calculations. Based on how combined ratings are calculated, a combined rating will never exceed 100%.

If this is all confusing, we have included on the Claim Support Disc, "38 CFR Part 4 – Schedule for Rating Disabilities." This portion of 38 CFR is often referred to as the VASRD – standing for VA Schedule for Rating Disabilities. This 243 pages of material covers over 700 different conditions and how they are assigned various disability ratings. Each of these 700 or so different conditions is assigned a four digit code which VA calls a "Disability Code" (DC). For instance tremor has one of either of these codes: Tremor 8105 or 8103

VASRD also contains information how to use the rating schedule and how to calculate a combined rating. For those who don't want to calculate a combined rating as described above, the rating schedule includes rating tables for you that remove a few steps from the hand calculation and help you determine what the final combined rating is from a combination of different ratings. Rating service officers in the Regional Office, in the past, had to manually determine what the rating was for each condition and then derive them from the table if they were combined ratings. Now they have a computer program that does it for them.

We believe that the schedule for rating disabilities can be useful to you if you want to see what sort of rating you will get for any given condition and how much you expect to be paid and that is why we have included it for you on the Claim Support Disc.

If you wish to use it, you need to understand that this system was created in 1946 and has only been partially revised since then. Many of the medical conditions referred to in the rating schedule have different names now and some of them did not even exist as far as being recognized in 1946. We have provided 2 indexes for you to help you use the rating schedule. The first of these is entitled the "c-index" which is used to find actual titles of all of the conditions in the rating schedule and the codes that pertain to them. The second index is called "Analogous and Equivalent Codes." The rating schedule has some inherent faults because it is so old. First of all how do you rate a condition that now has a name that doesn't appear in the rating schedule? Second how do you find something with a modern name that has an antiquated name? This analogous index helps you. If the condition can't be found, VA uses what they call an analogous rating which uses one of the antiquated names in the rating schedule as an equivalent for the more modern condition. The index identifies these equivalents. VA is currently working on updating the VASRD to reflect more modern medical issues.

Protected Ratings

Protection of a Scheduled Disability Rating
Preservation of disability evaluations – the protection of certain long-standing evaluations from reduction – derives from 38 U.S.C. 110 and is implemented in 38 CFR 3.951(b). The regulation provides that a Disability Compensation evaluation of any level that has been continuously in effect for 20 years or more will not be reduced to a lower evaluation except upon a showing that the higher evaluation was based upon fraud.

Example:
A Veteran files a claim for increase in his service-connected (SC) sinusitis, evaluated at 30 percent for over 20 years. The Department Of Veterans Affairs (VA) exam on which the 30% evaluation was based showed that the Veteran did not have incapacitating episodes, but did suffer three non-incapacitating episodes per year. This warranted only a 10% evaluation but the VA exam was misread by the Rating Veterans Service Representative (RVSR) as involving three incapacitating episodes. The current VA exam still shows symptomatology warranting a 30% evaluation. However, the 30% cannot be reduced because it is protected.

PL 102-86 states that a rating evaluation cannot be reduced solely because of a change to the rating schedule subsequent to August 13, 1991. 38 CFR 3.951(a) provides that a readjustment to the Schedule for Rating Disabilities shall not be grounds for reduction of a disability rating in effect on the date of the readjustment unless medical evidence establishes that the disability to be evaluated has actually improved. If the disability rating system changes the percentage of current single or combined rating of the veteran to a lower rating because of a change in the law, and the 20 years has not been achieved, the lower rating will apply.

The rating protection for a disability rating applies even if the veteran has elected not to receive a monetary award, due to offsetting from military retirement. This rating protection also applies to combined ratings and the individual ratings that make up that combined rating.

A protected disability rating is important, because for some awards, the computer system has been flagged to order examinations in the future to reevaluate that particular disability. VA has the right at any time before the 20 year guarantee kicks in, to reduce a disability rating based on a reevaluation. Sometimes a reevaluation comes into play when a veteran on claim makes a request for an increase in rating. There is a distinct possibility a medical examination from that request could actually result in a reduction of the rating and not an increase. Veterans on claim should be very careful about requesting changes to ratings unless they are sure that their condition has gotten worse instead of better. This would also apply to applications for secondary disability, where the primary service-connected disability will also be reevaluated medically.

Protection of a Rating for Service Connection
If service connection for disability or cause of death has been in effect 10 or more years, the rating for service connection is guaranteed except for the following: *Service connection can be removed if the original grant was based on fraud, or it is clearly shown that the person concerned did not have the requisite service or character of discharge.* Protection against removing service connection does not only require continuation of service-connected status after

10 years. VA must also continue to pay Compensation at the appropriate evaluation for the protected condition as if service connection was not erroneous. However, the disability benefit amount will not be paid due to willful misconduct or alcohol or drug abuse.

Service connection for a disability is not severed simply because the bodily siting of a disability, or disability code associated with it, is corrected to more accurately describe the correct disability. For example disability evaluation for degenerative arthritis under 38 CFR 4.71a, Disability Code 5003 that has been in place for over 10 years can be recharacterized as traumatic arthritis under 38 CFR 4.71a, Disability Code 5010, but the service connection for the original disability is maintained.

So exactly what does this mean? If for some reason VA decides to reevaluate a claim and finds out that due to not meeting the level of entitlement for service connection for some reason due to misinterpretation of the evidence or lack of corroborating evidence, if this new development occurs before the end of 10 years from the effective date of the claim, the veteran will lose all benefits due under a service connection rating. In essence, this is sort of a statute of limitations that protects the veteran from losing everything if VA does not challenge the award of service connection prior to 10 years.

Special Monthly Compensation (SMC)

VA can pay additional Compensation under Special Monthly Compensation (SMC) to a veteran who, as a result of military service, incurred the loss of or loss of use of specific organs or extremities. The governing code for SMC is Title 38 USC 1114. We include a summary of this code below below. To understand all of the various combinations look up Title 38 USC 1114.

Loss, or loss of use, is described as either an amputation or, having no effective remaining function of an extremity or organ. The disabilities VA can consider for SMC include:

- loss, or loss of use, of a hand or foot
- immobility of a joint or paralysis
- loss of sight of an eye (having only light perception)
- loss, or loss of use, of a reproductive organ
- complete loss, or loss of use, of both buttocks
- deafness of both ears (having absence of air and bone conduction)
- inability to communicate by speech (complete organic aphonia)
- loss of a percentage of tissue from a single breast, or both breasts, from mastectomy or radiation treatment

The Department will pay higher rates for combinations of these disabilities such as missing or loss of use of the feet, legs, hands, and arms, in specific monetary increments, based on the particular combination of the disabilities. There are also higher payments for various combinations of severe deafness with bilateral blindness. Additional SMC is available if a veteran is service connected for paraplegia, with complete loss of boil and bladder control. If the veteran has other service-connected disabilities that, in combination with the above special monthly Compensation, meet certain criteria, a higher amount of SMC can also be considered.

If a veteran is receiving Disability Compensation and is service connected at the 100% rate or is Individually Unemployable and is housebound, bedridden, or is so helpless as to need the aid and attendance of another person, then an additional SMC rate is also available. An aid and attendance allowance is also available to a veteran receiving SMC for whom a spouse needs aid and attendance or is housebound.

Number of Beneficiaries – 2018	Younger than 65	Age 65 and Older	Total all Ages	Percent of All Claims
Disability Compensation	3,150,664	1,592,444	4,743,108	84.7%
DIC for Surviving Spouse	149,915	255,632	405,547	7.2%
Veterans Pension	65,124	194,965	260,089	4.6%
Survivors Pension for Spouse	24,580	168,243	192,823	3.4%
Fiduciary Beneficiaries (Compensation, Pension and DIC)			190,540	3.4%
100% Disabled			684,851	12.2%
Individual Unemployability (Paid at 100% Disabled Rate)			356,668	6.4%
Special Monthly Compensation (SMC)			691,708	12.3%
Tinnitus and Hearing Loss – Most Prevalent Disabilities			3,363,237	60.0%
Total Beneficiaries – Compensation, DIC and Pension			5,601,567	
Healthcare System Enrolled			9 million +	

Source: VA Annual Benefits Report 2018, DVA 2020 Budget Proposal

Special Monthly Compensation (SMC) Rate Table for 2020 (In Dollars)

SMC Schedule	L	L½	M	M½	N	N½	O/P	R.1	R.2/T	S
Veteran Alone	3,864.90	4,064.70	4,265.31	4,558.37	4,852.09	5,137.51	5,423.45	7,749.68	8,889.08	3,476.65
Veteran & Spouse	4,038.08	4,237.88	4,438.49	4,731.55	5,025.27	5,310.69	5,596.63	7,922.86	9,062.26	3,649.83
Vet – Sps – 1 Child	4164.90	4364.70	4565.31	4858.37	5152.09	5437.51	5723.45	8049.68	9189.08	3776.65
Vet – 1 Child	3980.71	4180.51	4381.12	4674.18	4967.90	5253.32	5539.26	7865.49	9004.89	3592.46
Additional Child	86.05	86.05	86.05	86.05	86.05	86.05	86.05	86.05	86.05	86.05
Addt. Schoolchild	277.96	277.96	277.96	277.96	277.96	277.96	277.96	277.96	277.96	277.96
A&A for Spouse	158.82	158.82	158.82	158.82	158.82	158.82	158.82	158.82	158.82	158.82
K	110.31	Usually added to other rate or paid as the rate when percentage is zero.								
Q	67.00	Paid in place of a rate.								

If veteran has a spouse who requires A&A, add "A&A for spouse" to the amount of dependency & rate code above

The various rates of payment in the table above correspond to the paragraph letter identifications found in Title 38 USC 1114.

PART 2 – PREPARING FOR THE CLAIM

- Obtaining Service Treatment and Personnel Records; pg. 165
- Obtaining Post-Service Medical Records; pg. 169
- Obtaining Medical Opinions; pg. 171
- Obtaining Disability Benefits Questionnaires; pg. 182
- Writing a Personal Lay Statement; pg. 184

Obtaining Service Treatment Records and Personnel Records

In order to take charge of your own application, it is essential to obtain your own military records instead of allowing VA to obtain those records for you. Incidentally, VA may obtain the records anyway, <u>but your having your own copies allows you to analyze the contents, organize them and prepare them in a manner that will present your case through logical and persuasive arguments.</u>

You should order your records as the very first thing you do – before you even file a claim and before you submit an Intent to File. If your records are still paper-based and are available through the National Personnel Records Center (NPRC) in St. Louis, it's a matter of first come first serve. With the new paperless claims process, if VA orders any NPRC paper records before you do, the Records Center will remove those particular documents from your folder and send them to the Jainesvwelle Document Intake Scanning Center to be scanned into VBMS. The paper documents will not be returned to the NPRC. If you subsequently apply for those records, using an SF 180 – after the lengthy period of time it takes for the Center to respond – you will be told that your records do not exist. Of course they do, but they no longer exist as paper but are in VBMS. The dilemma you now have is trying to get those files from the VBMS system. We will discuss this a little further on.

The military records that you want to obtain are almost always Service Treatment Records (service medical records) and possibly clinical records from military hospital stays. In some cases, you may also want to retrieve personnel records. Personnel records are needed for those claims where you have to prove that you had a certain duty assignment or you were stationed at a certain location at a certain time. For example a claim for exposure to hazards or trauma resulting in Gulf War syndrome, PTSD, cancer or Agent Orange presumptive conditions often requires evidence from personnel records. On the other hand, you may have these records in your possession that substantiate this and you won't need personnel files.

The important consideration for where your records are is the date of your discharge. As a general rule, if you were discharged between 1994 and 2004, your records could either be available through the NPRC or through the Defense Personnel Records Information Retrieval System (DPRIS), depending on which military service you were in. Except for the Coast Guard, discharge after 2004 means your records are with DPRIS. If your files are in DPRIS, you can obtain them through eBenefits for which you need a Premium account. For most older veterans, an eBenefits Premium is hard to set up. For those of you who have discharges from 1995 on, you are automatically entitled to a Premium account. Here are the discharge start dates for DPRIS records.

Going forward – OMPF Records Availability Start Dates for DPRIS	
Service Branch	**Discharge or Retirement Cutoff Date**
Air Force	1 October 2004
Marine Corps	1 January 1999
Navy	1 January 1995
Army	1 October 1994
Coast Guard	Not available via DPRIS at this time

Records Which Can Be Obtained through Standard Form 180
The Standard Form 180, "Request Pertaining to Military Records" (SF180) is used to request information from military records. The last page of this form will give you the address where you should mail the request. The mailing addresses are based on the discharge dates from each branch of military service which determine where the records are being kept. It is important to remember that beginning in the 1990s, personnel records were returned to the NPRC but health records were sent over to the VA Records Management Center, 6 miles down the road. This process continued until 2014, when this function of the Records Management Center became obsolete and the military service branches stored their own records.

As a general rule, any records pertaining to discharges before the dates in the table above, are generally available through records requests with the National Personnel Records Center or the VA Records Management Center for health records for discharges since the 1990s.
It is important to remember that if the documents are supposed to be in the NPRC, but have been requested at any time by VA since 2012, due to a former claim for example, those documents are no longer available through the SF 180. It is also important to know that any records that were not requested by VA in paper form from the NPRC are still available from the Center. Additionally if only medical files were requested, the personnel files should still be there.

The Form SF 180 is designed to retrieve your records regardless of whether they are in the National Personnel Records Center, the VA Records Management Center or they are being stored electronically through departmental records maintained by each branch of service.

Records Which Are in the Possession of Veterans Benefits Administration on VBMS
we have already discussed your not allowing, if possible, VA to beat you to your paper records in the St. Louis Records Center. To avoid a lot of headache and wasted time, go for those files first, before you file the claim. If for some reason, those files had been already requested since 2012, you now have to obtain them through a request to the VA Records Management Center which is also located in St. Louis about 6 miles down the road from the NPRC. This is done through a Freedom of Information Act Request/Privacy Act Request submitted to the Janesville scanning center or you can mail your request to the Records Management Center directly. This is now the standard procedure for requesting records in the possession of the VBA. The Records Management Center claims that it fulfills 125,000 to 150,000 of these requests a year.

If you had an inactive claim in paper form in the VA system which was submitted before scanning began in 2012, this paper folder or C File should have been sent either to Janesville or to the RMC in St. Louis for scanning into VBMS. <u>With the exception of certain files that are so sensitive that they must be maintained and locked in cabinets as paper files, all inactive paper files that were kept in the Regional Offices have been shipped out and all inactive claims should now be available on VBMS.</u> This is actually very helpful if you are filing an appeal or if you are an accredited representative helping a veteran with an appeal. All of those existing records that you would have requested years ago in paper form or in copy machine form, are now available on a disc sent to you in PDF format through a FOIA request.

If you seek Compensation benefits records contained within a VA claims folder, or military service medical records in VA's possession, your request will be fulfilled by the VA Records Management Center as part of its new Centralized FOIA/PA Initiative.

Mail or fax Privacy Act or FOIA requests to the Intake Center in Janesville, Wisconsin:

Department of Veterans Affairs
Claims Intake Center
P.O. Box 4444
Janesville, WI 53547-4444
Fax: 844-531-7818

You can also mail the request directly to the Records Management Center and avoid the scanning center as we have had experience with employees in Janesville who don't seem to understand the purpose of various forms.

Here is an example of a cover letter that was the result of a recent FOIA request for records. The cover letter and the documents were received on a disc in PDF format about 6 months after the request was submitted. Unfortunately, it is taking that long.

The letterhead is from the VA Records Management Center at 4300 Goodfellow Blvd., Building 104 in St. Louis Missouri. On the page following is a copy of what was contained in the letter.

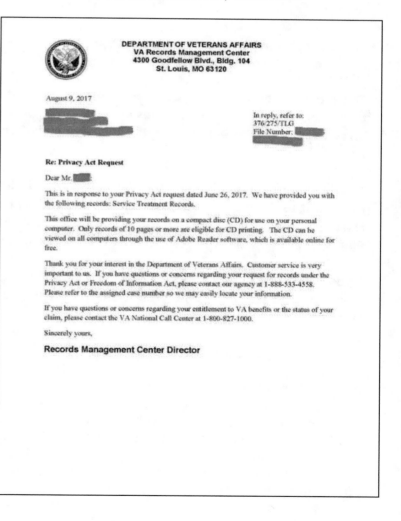

August 9, 2019

DEPARTMENT OF VETERANS AFFAIRS
VA Records Management Center
4300 Goodfellow Blvd., Bldg. 104
St. Louis, MO 63120

In reply, refer to:
File Number:

Re: Privacy Act Request

Dear Mr. ▉ :

This is in response to your Privacy Act request dated June 26, 2017. I have provided you with the following records: Service Treatment Records.

This office will be providing your records on a compact disc (CD) for use on your personal computer. Only records of 10 pages or more are eligible for CD printing.   The CD can be vieid on all computers through the use of Adobe Reader software, which is available online for free.

Thank you for your interest in the Department of Veterans Affairs. Customer service is very important to us. If you have questions or concerns regarding your request for records under the Privacy Act or Freedom of Information Act, please contact our agency at 1-888-533-4558. Please refer to the assigned case number so i may easily locate your information.

If you have questions or concerns regarding your entitlement to VA benefits or the status of your claim, please contact the VA National Call Center at 1-800-827-1000.
Sincerely yours,

Records Management Center Director

Please note that the agency has provided a phone number. As far as we know, this number is not generally available to the public. It could be very useful to you if you have some difficulty recovering information that you feel is necessary to a claim or an appeal, and you have someone to talk to. We have used this contact number on several occasions. The staff was quick to answer the phone and they attempted to get us to the right person to solve our problems. One such request was for expediting release of the records due to a pending hearing. They did comply and the records were sent. Currently, requests are taking about six months to fulfill.

It should be noted that VA insists on tying FOIA requests to privacy requests. This is a deliberate attempt to avoid the 20 day deadline for any FOIA request as privacy requests have no deadline. Doing so, gives VA more time to respond to these requests as it is unlikely the Department has the resources to respond to records requests in 20 days or less. There is no prescribed form for a request. We offer a format that provides enough information to process the request. We have provided that sample Privacy Act/FOIA request below. This document is also found on the Claim Support Disc under the title "Sample FOIA Request."

SUBJECT: Privacy Act/FOIA request for VBA records at the Records Management Center
<<Your Street Address>>
<<Your City, State, Zip>>
<<Date of request>>

DEPARTMENT OF VETERANS AFFAIRS
VA Records Management Center
4300 Goodfellow Blvd., Bldg. 104
St. Louis, MO 63120

Dear FOIA Officer:

This is a request under the Freedom of Information Act and pursuant to the Privacy Act.

I request that you submit a copy of <<the document you seek>>, or documents containing << the information you seek>>. <<Be very specific about dates and types of documents.>>

The records I am requesting are archived with the following identification:

<<your full name or the full name of the veteran if you are a claimant under the veteran>>
<<your date of birth or date of birth of the veteran>>
<<Social Security number or Social Security number of the veteran>>
<<VA file number – if available>>
<<your relationship to the veteran if you are not the veteran and the reason you are requesting the records if you are not the veteran>>

If you have any questions, I may be reached at <<your phone number>> or by email at <<your email address>>.

Sincerely,

<<Sign your request>>

Obtaining Post-Service Medical Records

Obtaining Medical Records from VA Medical Facilities

The Department of Veterans Affairs, Veterans Health Administration was an early innovator of electronic medical records systems. As early as 1977, the Department had operating software in many locations. Over the years the record system has evolved into a program called VistA. The VistA system is highly rated by physicians, receiving the highest overall score in Medscape surveys of over 15,000 physicians in 2014 and again in 2016, and receiving particularly high marks for connectivity and utility as a clinical tool.

Because the system has been around a long time and is highly functional, it is relatively easy to get copies of your VA healthcare records from your local medical center. Most centers respond to requests within 20 days and you should have a copy of your records within 30 days. The records arrive in the form of a disc which contains your healthcare documents you requested in PDF format. Unfortunately, the records are not very well organized when you receive them.

There are 2 forms that are used for obtaining VA medical records. The first of these forms is for you personally as the veteran to request your own records. This form is VA Form 10-5345a. Be very specific when you fill out this form and we would suggest that you check all of the boxes pertaining to your medical records. Provide the dates and the names of the clinics or the medical centers where you were treated. We include this form on the Claim Support Disc.

The second form, VA Form 10-5345, is for an individual representing the veteran's interests to obtain the veteran's medical records. If you are representing a veteran for a claim, this form allows the veteran to give you permission to obtain his or her records. We also include this form on the Claim Support Disc.

Obtaining Private Medical Records

If you are obtaining private medical records and you are not the veteran, you will have to obtain a release form from the private medical provider and have the veteran sign it. Almost always you will have to pay copying charges for these records. If you are the veteran, there is also a private provider form associated with the particular provider or providers you have seen. Typically, you will not have to pay anything for obtaining your own records.

Not all private medical providers have adopted electronic records systems. If the records come to you in paper format, you may be able to organize those records sufficiently to make them easy for the RSVR to understand when you submit your claim. If the records are not easily understood, you should arrange to have them scanned to PDF format. Records in PDF format can then be manipulated, cropped, extracted and rearranged in an order that will be more understandable to make your case to the rating team in the Regional Office. If you receive your private records in PDF format – which is more likely – you will also want to organize those records before you submit them. Working with PDF documents requires a version of Adobe Acrobat or a similar program. If you are an accredited representative make sure that you have an appropriate HIPAA release form giving you permission to review a claimant's medical records.

For an example of records that are in PDF format or that have been translated from handwritten records into Microsoft Word and then converted to PDF format, look at examples of these in the two sample cases found on the Claim Support Disc. The sample cases provide you a ialth of insight into how to organize your records in order to make it easier for the RSVR to understand your claim.

Obtaining Medical Opinions

We discuss here the use of opinions for service connection, called nexus opinions or more simply "medical opinions," which use a licensed health care provider to provide an opinion on the connection or link of an existing disability or disease with an injury, illness or other incident that was incurred in service. It is essential for you to understand this information on medical opinions as they are, with some claims, crucial to establishing service connection and obtaining a disability rating. In this section we will address the potential conflict with the Regional Office adjudicator of your claim where you can end up in an adversarial battle . We will also address the difficulty of obtaining your own opinions from private-sector specialists which includes persuading a licensed health care provider to write an opinion for you.

We have found it is best for you to allow the Regional Office to order its own opinion through its network of contract examiners. In many cases, these opinions represent a lack of engagement where the medical practitioner has not taken time to back up his or her assertions and seldom do these examiners provide any probative reasoning for their opinions. A good opinion should also require substantiation from medical literature, review of the medical record and clinical experience which these contract examiners as a general rule will not provide. After receiving a shoddy opinion through a VA examiner, you can now counter with your own adequate well reasoned opinion from a more credible source such as a specialist MD.

Usually VA's opinions are hastily done, are sloppy and are not of sufficient merit. The correct term for an opinion that is not suitable is called an "Inadequate opinion." If this is the case for you, now you have the opportunity of besting the adjudicator by providing a credible and probative opinion of your own. Your own private opinion should be an "adequate opinion." If you use this strategy and produce a significantly more probative opinion on your own, you should win the battle. Letting the Regional Office go first also allows your opinion maker, in his or her response, to discredit the often shoddy opinion provided by the VA examiner.

Adequate Verses Inadequate Medical Opinions

Based on court rulings, an inadequate medical opinion has little or no probative value for making a determination for service connection unless it is the only opinion available. Unfortunately, VA will treat its own opinion as the only one available even if you have provided one with the initial application. In order to counter VA's adversarial approach it is best to let the adjudicator order his or her own medical opinion first and then provide your own private opinion if necessary.

Court rulings have established a standard for determining whether an opinion is adequate or inadequate. Here are the principles. If any of these principles is violated, the opinion can be considered inadequate.

1. Examiners need to consider lay statements describing relevant symptoms
2. Examiners need to provide clear conclusions with supporting data and a reasoned medical explanation concerning the service connection
3. Medical examiners may not decide the veracity of nonmedical facts
4. A medical opinion is inadequate if it is based on inaccurate factual premises
5. A medical opinion is inadequate if the examiner can't reach a conclusion
6. Examiners can't use an evidentiary standard greater than the reasonable doubt principle
7. Examiners need to address all legal theories of entitlement to service connection

It is highly unfortunate that contract examiners who provide medical opinions apparently are not aware of the principles above. We have yet to see an adequate opinion ordered by the Regional Office whether it is favorable to the claimant or not. Any claimant who relies on VA for a medical opinion and does not get a private opinion is at high risk for receiving a denial.

When you do challenge a contract examiner opinion, it is critical that you provide in writing, on a VA Form 21-4138, the reason that opinion is inadequate. Your failure to challenge the opinion based on the elements above, will make it less likely for you to prevail. It is essential that you point out the flaws – if there are any – in the VA opinion. If you cannot do this then you don't have a good case and you might want to give up your claim altogether.

Court Precedent Rulings on Adequate Medical Opinions That Are Binding on VA

When a medical opinion is adequate :

1. Citation #1 *"...where it is based on consideration of the veteran's prior medical history and examinations and also describes the disability, if any, in sufficient detail so that the Board's 'evaluation of the claimed disability will be a fully informed one.'* Stefl v. Nicholson, 21 Vet.App. 120, 123 (2007) (quoting Ardison v. Brown, 6 Vet.App. 405, 407 (1994)). And the opinion *"must support its conclusion with an analysis that the Board can consider and weigh against contrary opinions."* Id. at 124.

2. Citation #2 *"In order to fully inform the Board's decision, an opinion must contain not only clear conclusions with supporting data, but also a reasoned medical explanation connecting the two."* Nieves-Rodriguez v. Peake, 22 Vet.App. 295, 301 (2008).

   "An examination that merely lists facts and conclusions with no reasoned explanation connecting the two therefore lacks probative weight" Id (above)

On the Next Page Is an Example of Challenging an Opinion:
The Regional Office ordered a medical opinion concerning this claim which was signed by a Nurse Practitioner. She was provided a form containing the text on the next page with the checkboxes and preconceived statements as shown in the exactly worded re-creation we provide. It was in electronic format. Although the opinion form may vary depending on which of the 5 examining contract companies that VA employs, the use of of a standardized form as outlined on the next page has become the normal operating procedure when a Regional Office orders its own contract examiner medical opinion.

(Below is an exact wording copy of the report form used by this contract examiner)

Medical Opinion 1 of 5) Are any currently diagnosed condition(s) related to the veteran's claimed right upper extremity peripheral neuropathy with intention tremor, at least as likely as not (50% or greater probability) proximately due to or the result of the veteran's sinusitis?

Medical Opinion 2 of 5) Are any currently diagnosed conditions related to the veteran's claimed left upper extremity peripheral neuropathy with intention tremor, at least as likely as not (50% or greater probability) proximately due to or the result of the veteran's sinusitis?

Medical Opinion 3 of 5) Are any currently diagnosed condition(s) related to the veterans claimed left lower extremity peripheral neuropathy with intention tremor, at least as likely as not (50% or greater probability) proximately due to or the result of the veteran's sinusitis?

Medical Opinion 4 of 5) Are any currently diagnosed condition(s) related to the vetera's claimed right lower extremity peripheral neuropathy with intention tremor, at least as likely as not (50% or greater probability) proximately due to or the result of the veteran's sinusitis?

Medical Opinion 5 of 5) Are any currently diagnosed condition(s) related to the veteran's claimed bilateral knee condition claimed as ligament laxity, at least as likely as not (50% or greater probabiltty) proximately due to or the result of the veteran's lower extremity anti-mag neuropathy?

Was the Veteran's VA claims file revieid?.
[X] Yes []No
If yes, list any records that were revieid but were not included in the Veteran's VA claims file:

If no, check all records revieid:

[] Military service treatment records
[] Military service personnel records
[] Military enlistment examination
[] Military separation examination
[] Military post-deployment questionnawere
[] Department of Defense Form 214 Separation Documents
[] Veterans Health Administration medical records (VA treatment records)
[] Civilian medical records
[] Interviews with collateral witnesses (family and others who have known the veteran before and after military service)
[] No records were revieid

Other:
Complete only the sections below that you are asked to complete in the Medical Opinion DBQ request.

4. Medical opinion for direct service connection
Choose the statement that most closely approximates the etiology of the claimed condition.

a. [] The claimed condition was at least as likely as not (50 percent or greater probability) incurred in or caused by the claimed inservice
injury, event, or illness.
Provide rationale in section c.
b. [] The claimed condition was less likely than not (less than 50 percent probability) incurred in or caused by the claimed in-service
injury, event, or illness.
Provide rationale in section c.
c. Rationale:

5. Medical opinion for secondary service connection

a. [X] *The claimed condition is at least as likely as not (50 percent or greater probability) proximately due to or the result of the Veteran's service connected condition.*
Provide rationale in section c.

b. [X] *The claimed condition is less likely than not (less than 50 percent probability) proximately due to or the result of the Veteran's service connected condition.*
Provide rationale in section c.

c. *Rationale:*

Questions 1-4 of 5: b. The claimed condition, peripheral neuropathy of the upper and lower extremities, is less likely than not (less than 50 percent probability) proximately due to or the result of the Veteran's condition of sinusitis.

Rationale: Sinusitis is a confined condition, within the sinus cavities, that can be acute or chronic. The sinus condition has no ability to affect the peripheral nerves.

Question 5 of 5: a. The claimed condition, knee ligament laxity, is at least as likely as not (50 percent or greater probability) proximately due to or the result of the Veteran's condition of anti-MAG neuropathy.

Rationale: Anti MAG peripheral neuropathy is an auto-immune disease that causes myelin destruction in the distal extremities. Myelin is an important part of the peripheral nervous system. It wraps around the nerve axon much like insulation around an electrical wwere. The nerves extend from the spinal cord to the rest of the body, stimulating muscle contraction and transmitting sensory information back to the nervous system receptors in the skin and joints. This myelin allows electrical impulses to efficiently travel along the nerve axon. When myelin is damaged or removed, these electrical impulses are slowed or lost, and messages transmitted from the brain are disrupted and may never make it to their final destination. As a result, balance disturbance, difficulty walking and sometimes to the person being wheelchair bound are the result of this progressive disease. It is at least as likely as not that the anti-MAG neuropathy could cause looseness and laxity in the knees.

This Opinion Was Inadequate

In a subsequent challenge to the document above, we argued the following:

Based on court rulings, an inadequate medical opinion has no probative value for making a determination for service connection unless it is the only opinion available. In this case, you have in the record, 2 adequate and highly probative medical opinions which were furnished with a supplemental application and which directly contradict the opinion of your contract examiner.

Court rulings have established a standard for determining whether an opinion is adequate or inadequate. Here are the principles. If any of these principles is violated, the opinion can be considered inadequate.

1. *Examiners need to consider lay statements describing relevant symptoms*
2. *Examiners need to provide clear conclusions with supporting data and a reasoned medical explanation concerning the service connection*
3. *Medical examiners may not decide the veracity of nonmedical facts*
4. *A medical opinion is inadequate if it is based on inaccurate factual premises*
5. *A medical opinion is inadequate if the examiner can't reach a conclusion*
6. *Examiners can't use an evidentiary standard greater than the reasonable doubt principle*
7. *Examiners need to address all legal theories of entitlement to service connection*

Your contract examiner violated the following principles: #1, #2 and #7.

#1 – She records that she revieid my claims file but she obviously didn't read my lay statement, because if she had, she would have addressed the actual theory of the claim which is development of an autoimmune disorder in service and not chronic sinusitis directly causing an immune neuropathy after service.

#2 – She failed to provide any supporting data for her opinion and there was no reasoning involved as to why she reached her conclusion.

#7 – She failed to consider whether there might be another theory involved in this claim. In the next section I will argue that had she exercised any amount of intellectual curiosity about this claim, she would have gone to the Internet to see if a chronic sinusitis condition could be related to an autoimmune neuropathy – which in my case it is.

The opinion from (name of nurse practitioner) is not probative for my claim. This is because her opinion is inadequate and the theory of the opinion does not fit the actual claim. We are not claiming that chronic sinusitis leads to development of immune demyelinating neuropathy. The private opinions that we are furnishing with a supplemental claim are probative. They are backed up by both examiners reviewing all of my pertinent records including a lay statement so as to gain an understanding of the claim. The private examiners also provided significant supporting data in the form of medical journal articles and studies. Finally, the examiners provided well-reasoned opinions that were consistent with medical literature the claimant's medical history.

We assert that the opinion from (name of nurse practitioner) be disregarded and provided no evidentiary weight when adjudicating this claim.

IN REFUTING THE INADEQUATE OPINION FROM VA
THE FOLLOWING ADDITIONAL EVIDENCE WAS PROVIDED:

Evidence That the Regional Office Ordered Medical
Opinion Cannot Be Considered As Probative to My Claim

Google search for "chronic sinusitis and autoimmune disorders"

The simple exercise using the search string above with a Google search resulted in countless pages of search title categories that tie together chronic sinusitis and chronic rhinosinusitis with autoimmune disease. There is a ialth of information on the Internet concerning this particular word string search. Other similar word string searches would probably bring up similar search title categories of other articles tying together chronic sinusitis and autoimmunity.

I include only 9 samples from this search (there were many more) to prove that the Regional Office-ordered medical opinion from (name of Examiner), NP, dated 06/19/2018 in which she opined that there is less likely as not a relationship between anti-MAG peripheral neuropathy and chronic sinusitis, is totally inadequate and has no credibility or probative value.

Ms. (name of nurse practitioner) acknowledged in her opinion that anti-MAG neuropathy is an autoimmune disorder. She failed to exercise intellectual curiosity to find out if the two conditions identified in the medical record – the in-service chronic rhinosinusitis and later development of autoimmune anti-MAG neuropathy – could possibly be related through an underlying and common autoimmune disorder which can manifest symptoms of both conditions. Had she conducted some simple online research, she would have discovered that there is a relationship.

Excerpt from an online article article from Mount Sinai Health Network entitled "Sinusitis: Acute and Chronic Sinusitis"

https://www.mountsinai.org/care/ent/services/nasal-sinus-allergy/conditions/sinusitis

Chronic Sinusitis

Chronic sinusitis (CRS) is a condition that has tremendous direct and indirect costs to our healthcare system. Patients experience significant loss in quality of life that is greater than those who suffer from congestive heart failure or coronary artery disease. The negative impact of chronic sinusitis on work productivity is well documented and an underappreciated consequence of this condition.

A critical misunderstanding is that people are under the impression that chronic sinusitis is an infectious process. The reality is that it is an inflammatory disease with occasional exacerbations associated with infection. Patients may have coexisting conditions such as allergies, asthma, or immunodeficiency. In addition severe cases of CRS may be a manifestation of more serious conditions such as autoimmune disease (Sarcoid, Igener's Granulomatosis, Churg-Strauss Syndrome), ciliary dyskinesia or cystic fibrosis.

The diagnosis of CRS requires the presence of symptoms for at least tilve ieks. Patients will experience mucopurulent drainage, nasal congestion, facial pain-pressure-fullness, or a decreased sense of smell. In addition to the subjective symptoms patients must have an endoscopic exam that demonstrates polyps or mucus draining from the sinuses or a CT scan showing inflammation in the sinuses. In patients who have had prior surgery it is critical to perform a complete evaluation of the immune system.

Journal Article from the American Journal of Otolaryngology 2011

Am J Otolaryngol. Author manuscript; available in PMC 2012 Jul 2.
Published in final edited form as:
Am J Otolaryngol. 2011 Sep-Oct; 32(5): 388–391.
Published online 2010 Sep 15. doi: [10.1016/j.amjoto.2010.07.013]
PMCID: PMC3387732
NIHMSID: NIHMS387461
PMID: 20832903

Chronic rhinosinusitis in the setting of other chronic inflammatory diseases[★,★★]

Rakesh K. Chandra, MD,[*] David Lin, MSII, Bruce Tan, MD, Robin Smolak Tudor, PA-C, David B. Conley, MD, Anju T. Peters, MD, Leslie C. Grammer, MD, Robert P. Schleimer, PhD, and Robert C. Kern, MD
Author information Copyright and License information Disclaimer
The publisher's final edited version of this article is available at Am J Otolaryngol
See other articles in PMC that cite the published article.

The objectives of the study were to determine the prevalence of chronic rhinosinusitis (CRS) overall and its 2 phenotypic variants, CRS with and without polyposis (NP), in patients with chronic inflammatory comorbidities including autoimmune disorders, inflammatory boil disease, and atopic dermatitis. These findings were compared with data in patients with asthma. Patients with hypertension were also used as a reference group to estimate the incidence of CRS in a group with regular medical follow-up.

Electronic medical record database prevalence of CRS in patients with hypertension was 4.4%. The prevalence of CRS was 18% in asthma ($P < .0001$), 7% in atopic dermatitis, 3.5% in inflammatory boil disease, and ranged from 1.4% to 5.9% in autoimmune disorders. The frequency of CRS patients exhibiting the NP phenotype was similarly low in patients with autoimmune disease and hypertension, but was significantly greater in patients with asthma ($P < .0001$), inflammatory boil disease ($P = .033$), and atopic dermatitis ($P = .049$),

Conclusions
These findings suggest similar prevalence of overall CRS in patients with autoimmune disease and inflammatory boil disease, and background rates as estimated by observations in hypertension patients. Inflammatory boil disease and atopic dermatitis patients with CRS exhibit some skewing toward the NP phenotype, as do asthmatics, where this association is well known.

Journal article from "Expert Review of Clinical Immunology" 2017

Expert Rev Clin Immunol. Author manuscript; available in PMC 2017 May 12.
Published in final edited form as:
Expert Rev Clin Immunol. 2017 Feb; 13(2): 117–123.
Published online 2016 Aug 18. doi: [10.1080/1744666X.2016.1216790]
PMCID: PMC5429028
NIHMSID: NIHMS857324
PMID: 27500811

Immune deficiency in chronic rhinosinusitis: screening and treatment

Sergio E. Chiarella and Leslie C. Grammer
Author information Copyright and License information Disclaimer

Key issues
Chronic rhinosinusitis (CRS) is a prevalent disease with a high burden in medical costs.
In some patients, immune deficiency contributes to the pathophysiology of CRS.
The most common immune deficiencies associated with CRS are humoral deficiencies such as specific antibody deficiency (SAD) and common variable immune deficiency (CVID).
New immune defects are being identified in patients with CRS such as CD8+ T cell deficiency and multiple defects in the Toll-like receptor (TLR) pathways.
Current treatments for these immune deficiencies include vaccination, antibiotics, immunoglobulin replacement, and surgery.
As i recognize the diversity of immune defects that contribute to the pathophysiology of CRS, new targeted therapies will emerge.

Article from a website called "Self"

Health
|March 6, 2007|
By Indy Shanker
Dealing with autoimmune disease
The enemy within: How do you fight an illness that makes your own body destroy itself? One woman's war with a rare autoimmune disease

I have a severe case of a rare, incurable autoimmune disease called Igener's granulomatosis, which inflames the walls of the blood vessels, depriving the organs of blood and leading to the destruction of tissue and cartilage (in my case, my sinuses, lungs and kidneys). No one knows how you get Igener's, which is in the same family as lupus and multiple sclerosis, or how to cure it. So doctors treat it like cancer, with a combination of steroids and chemotherapy, hoping to force the disease into a long-lasting remission. Of the approximately 23 million Americans who have autoimmune diseases, a disproportionate number are women. Many are in their 20s or 30s, their prime childbearing years. And most of the women I've talked to with mysterious illnesses such as these have had their initial symptoms misdiagnosed or dismissed as hypochondria. The guilt that follows seems so inherently feminine to me. Autoimmune disease: strong enough for a man but made for a woman.

My Igener's debuted in 1998, when I was 27. I had a sinus infection that wouldn't go away. A doctor eventually biopsied a tumor they found in my sinuses, which revealed a mass of inflamed cells identified as Igener's. A rheumatologist started me on a low-dose regimen of the steroid prednisone and a chemo drug called methotrexate, which basically kept symptoms of the disease (sinus problems and joint pain) at bay. I had a few sinus infections and a bit of aching from time to time, but nothing so bad that it stopped me from working at my day job as a TV writer, hitting the gym or living the high life in New York City.

Article from the website sponsored by a Doctor Will Cole

Why You Keep Getting Sinus Infections + Exactly What To Do About It

May 8, 2017 // by Dr. Will Cole
Why You Keep Getting Sinus Infections + Exactly What To Do About It

by Dr. Will Cole

Throbbing pressure in your head, a congested nose, Kleenex for days – nobody thinks sinus infections are a breeze, and yet they affect a whopping 29.4 million of us. But go to a doctor, and what do you get? "Cures" like over-the-counter sinus medications, pharmaceutical antibiotics, and steroids, all with side effects that can be as bad or worse than the infection itself. Sure, sometimes these medications might be necessary, but the truth is that these mainstream options are over-prescribed and often, they don't have any effect on the actual progression and healing of the infection.

So what does a health-conscious sufferer do about the pressure, pain, congestion, fatigue, and all-around discomfort of a sinus infection? Stop them from happening, that's what! The best way to do this is to discover the most common causes of these infections, so you can correct the underlying problem, rather than just masking the uncomfortable symptoms. Here are the causes, and what you can do about them right now:

1. Gut bacteria imbalance.
2. Bad-guy biofilms.
3. Viral infections.
4. Environmental toxins.
5. Immune system dysfunction.
    All of these factors (bacteria, toxic biofilm, viruses, and toxins) can lead your immune system to activate inflammation cascades.

Online article from Standford University Medical School

What causes sinusitis?
Sometimes, a sinus infection happens after an upper respiratory infection (URI) or common cold that 'never seems to go away.'. The URI causes inflammation of the nasal passages that can lead to profound obstruction of the opening of the paranasal sinuses, which can then lead to repeated cycles of infection and inflammation in the sinuses. Allergic disease can also lead to sinusitis because of the swelling of the nasal tissue and increased production of mucus.

There are other possible conditions that can block the normal flow of secretions out of the sinuses and can lead to sinusitis. These may include:

- structural/anatomic abnormalities in the nose and sinuses that physically narrow the sinus passages
- enlarged adenoid tissue in the back of the nose
- diving and swimming
- infections from an upper molar tooth
- trauma to the nose
- foreign objects that are trapped in the nose
- nasal polyps
- obstructing, intranasal scarring after past sinus surgery
- fungal infection of the sinuses
- certain autoimmune diseases
- immunosuppression/compromised immune system
- cystic fibrosis

INTERNATIONAL JOURNAL OF IMMUNOPATHOLOGY AND PHARMACOLOGY Vol. 27, no. 2,155-161 (2014)
EDITORIAL
EVIDENCE AND ROLE OF AUTOANTIBODIES IN CHRONIC RHINOSINUSITIS WITH NASAL POLYPS

G.F. MACRI, A. GRECO, C. MARINELLI, A. GALLO, M. FUSCONI, A. DE VIRGILIO and M. DE VINCENTIIS
Department of Sense Organs, ENT Section, Policlinico "Umberto I",
Sapienza University of Rome, Rome, Italy
Received March 3,2014 -Accepted May 5,2014

In this study, i review our current knowledge of the autoimmune etiopathogenesis of chronic rhinosinusitis with nasal polyps including bacterial infections, viral infections and immunomediated mechanisms and to discuss pathogenesis with relevance for pharmacotherapy. Relevant publications on the etiopathogenesis and treatment of chronic rhinosinusitis with nasal polyps (CRSwNP) from 1977 to 2013 were analyzed. The characteristic signs and symptoms include appearance of relapsing nasal polyps, with typical symptoms such as nasal obstruction, nasal discharge and, usually, loss of the sense of smell. The etiology and pathogenesis remain unknown. Proposed theories of causation include bacterial or viral infections and immunomediated mechanisms. The autoimmune aetiology of of unknown origin or failure to respond to classic pharmacological treatments with nasal and oral steroids is now suspected. At present, the nature of the antigen trigger, the exact role played by BIT cells and anti-dsDNA autoantibodies in the pathogenesis of nasal polyposis remains unclear. Corticosteroids and surgery are the first line of treatment in CRSwNP. In the case of corticosteroid treatment failure, other drugs can be used such as rituximab, belimumab or omalizumab which have demonstrated clinical efficacy in the treatment of nasal polyposis with comorbid asthma. Immunosuppressive drugs such as methotrexate, and cyclophosphamide have also been used with varying degrees of success.

Article from the Washington Post

A Complicated Case

Nancy Kennedy endured years of pain and uncertainty as her symptoms pointed in many directions. (Oin Freeman/For The Washington Post)
By Sandra G. Boodman
April 15, 2013

For someone who had been such a healthy child, Nancy Kennedy couldn't figure out how she had become the kind of sickly adult whose life revolved around visits to a seemingly endless series of doctors.

Beginning in 2005, shortly after a job transfer took her from Northern Virginia to St. Louis, Kennedy, then 47, developed a string of vexing medical problems. Her white blood cell count was inexplicably elevated. Her sinuses were chronically infected, although her respiratory tract seemed unusually dry. She often felt fatigued, and her joints hurt.

During an hour-long appointment, Kennedy described her pain, and she and Johnson revieid her family history of arthritis: An aunt has rheumatoid arthritis (RA), and her father has severe osteoarthritis. Johnson, who had suspected Kennedy might be suffering from an autoimmune disorder, a constellation of diseases in which the body mistakenly attacks its own tissues, ordered another test for RA, although previous screens had been negative. This time, she added tests for an autoimmune disorder that often accompanies RA, Sjogren's syndrome, for which Kennedy had never been checked.

The results of those tests provided the answer that had eluded Johnson and Kennedy. Her joint pain, dryness, chronic sinus infections and fatigue were the result of primary Sjogren's syndrome; tests for RA were negative.

Journal Article

A role for auto-immunity in chronic rhinosinusitis? Lessons learned from sub-epidermal bullous disorders of the skin

- Philippe Lefrançois,
- Hugo Chapdelaine,
- Benoît Côté and
- Martin DesrosiersEmail author

Allergy, Asthma & Clinical Immunology201612:38

https://doi.org/10.1186/s13223-016-0141-1

© The Author(s) 2016

- **Received:** 8 June 2016
- **Accepted:** 13 July 2016
- **Published:** 5 August 2016

Abstract
Chronic rhinosinusitis (CRS) is a frequent chronic condition, which has origins in complex interactions between genetic, immunological and microbial factors. The role of auto-immunity in CRS remains unclear, although recent studies have started to emerge in CRS patient refractory to maximal medical management. I discuss the possible auto-immunity link between CRS and other skin diseases, in particular acquwered bullous dermatoses, and review the current evidence. I raise additional considerations for auto-immunity from both research and clinical standpoints.

VA RESPONDED TO THE PRECEDING CHALLENGE BY ORDERING ANOTHER MEDICAL OPINION:

After a second medical opinion was ordered by VA and the adjudicators continued to ignore the very probative opinions that had been submitted already, we decided to take another approach.

Under its current operating procedures for examinations and medical opinions, VA allows the veteran to personally carry new and relevant evidence into the examination to present to the licensed medical provider. We put together a one page explanation of the theory of the claim for the claimant to present to the examiner as well as having the claimant deliver copies of both highly probative opinions – one from a PhD and MD specialist in the field of neurology and the other from an expert court witness who specializes in medical opinions.

By confronting the examiner with highly probative and well reasoned opinions that also quoted medical literature – if the examiner were truly professional – that person would be required to acknowledge the private opinions and the theory of the claim. This is exactly what happened. The examiner in his report simply averred making an opinion and referred the adjudicators to the previous opinions that were in the file and that he felt adequately expressed his own views. The claim was approved at 100% disability. But this entire process took almost 3 years.

What We Have Learned from Complex Claims with Difficult Theories Requiring Opinions

We believe the incompetent behavior exhibited by adjudicators in the Regional Office pertaining to the claim that we discussed above is a result of the ever changing adjudication procedures over the past years. We discussed the flaws in the system in detail in Chapter 4. Under the new claims model, if an adjudicator does not comprehend the theory of the claim – as was obvious with our previous example –because of time constraints, that person cannot consult with someone who is more experienced and who can explain the medical concepts. This option is simply not built into the system. Remember, almost all adjudicators have no medical background and likely many of them cannot even interpret medical terminology. It was much easier for the adjudicator in our real life example to "pass the buck" by ignoring evidence and by ordering additional medical examinations than trying to comprehend the claim.

You also need to understand that this particular real-life example is an outlier and very few claims have such complex theories of service connection. Nevertheless, you must be wary that there is a significant failure in the current claims processing model to properly and adequately adjudicate any Compensation claims. Any application submission must be done with the expectation that it will likely be mishandled and result in an unfavorable decision. Further on in this chapter, we provide you with a defensive approach to submitting initial applications which is based on treating the adjudicators in the regional office as if they were incompetent and in many cases ignorant of certain medical issues and making sure that every step in the application process has been simplified and deliberately shoved into their faces so that they cannot ignore significant evidence. Even at that, you should probably be prepared for a long battle through challenging the unfavorable decisions that arise from VA's flawed claims processing model.

The Difficulty of Obtaining a Private Medical Opinion

If you are seeking your own private medical opinions, it is often difficult to find a physician, nurse or other medical professional who will provide a strong opinion without being paid for it. Also, the strategy of letting VA go first may take much longer for winning your case and if a VA contract examiner's opinion results in a denial, you will have to submit your own new privately obtained opinion as new evidence and reopen the case for reconsideration. But sometimes coming in after VA with your own Nexus opinion is the only way to win.

It's also difficult to get a probative and well written statement from your private treating physician, PA, nurse or nurse practitioner. They don't know how to write them to be persuasive and if they do, it takes too much time for them to do it without being paid. You may get refusals.

One solution is to research and write the opinion for your professional to review and sign. Sometimes this works and sometimes it doesn't. If you use this approach, you will almost always work with your practitioner's nurse who will review it for the provider, revise as necessary and then recommend that the practitioner sign it. We have also found that it is possible to persuade treating physicians to include opinion statements in routine consultations or examinations as part of the medical record. For example, the following sentence could be included as part of an examination for back pain, "it is my opinion that Mr. Smith's current lumbar radiculopathy is a result of the back injury that he sustained while he was in the Armed Forces on active duty." A copy of the record with the pertinent information circled with a felt tip pen then would be submitted along with an application or a challenge to a decision.

If your private providers cannot produce an opinion or if you cannot on your own write one for your medical practitioner to sign, you will have to pay an expert or medical specialist to provide an opinion for you. If you believe strongly in your claim, you are going to have to fork over a substantial sum of money to make it work. We have provided for you a list of professional nexus opinion professionals. This is found on the Claim Support Disc.

You Might Be Challenged with a Development to Deny

Don't be surprised. This process of fighting VA with medical opinions is totally adversarial and sometimes there is really little difference between what you are attempting to achieve with the adjudicator in the Regional Office and what you have to do to make your case in the traditional court system. The VA adjudication system is not supposed to work that way. According to the regulations the adjudication process is deliberately non-adversarial. Sometimes Veteran Service Representatives get carried away and think that they are acting as judges, which they are not. Their only requirement is to balance evidence on a scale and determine by the Preponderance Rule which way the evidence points. VA wants you believe the rating team is your advocate, but when it comes to medical opinions that's not usually the case.

A conflict usually arises when you are the first to provide the nexus opinion. If for some reason your private opinion is not convincing enough for the RSVR – for whatever reasons – he or she will order his or her own opinion. Regulations don't specifically prohibit the practice, but it is inconsistent with VA's duty to assist as an advocate to the veteran. But it happens a lot. In fact, it happens so frequently that accredited attorneys and accredited claims agents have a name for it. They call it "Development to Deny." Development is VA's terminology for generating evidence for a claim.

Obtaining Disability Benefits Questionnaire

In 2009, based on a contest for improving efficiency in the Regional Offices, an employee in the Pittsburgh Office came up with a suggestion for improving the rating process. The idea was to provide a checklist document for clusters of a variety of medical conditions that would allow the rating authority to directly correlate the information on the form with the disability rating calculator. The suggestion was to be able to input the information on the form directly into the calculator without having to interpret medical information from an examination or from medical records. This process would also allow for a more accurate assignment of disability ratings. Thus the idea of Disability Benefits Questionnaire was born.

The Department now has a series of 69 medical evaluation surveys called Disability Benefits Questionnaire or DBQs for short. Prior to this initiative, if the rating authority needed more input to determine a rating, the rating authority could order an examination in order to provide the information or more likely information from existing medical records would be used. The examiners had a series of evaluation sheets similar to DBQs that they used for the evaluation, but these evaluation sheets were not available to the general public nor were they convenient for the rating authority to assign a disability rating using the computer rating calculator. We provide the 69 DBQs on the Claim Support Disc.

A medical examiner filling out a DBQ does not have to be a licensed physician but can be any licensed healthcare professional who has the training to fill out the form. VA originally intended that most DBQs would be performed by employees of the Veterans Health Administration, but in recent years that is not happening.

Veterans who are in the VA healthcare system can request that their VA primary care physicians fill out these forms; however, Veterans Health Care Administration policy generally dictates not complying with these requests. Most VHA physicians not willing to do this as they are not trained in filling out the forms and they are under a lot of pressure for seeing other patients. It takes 30 minutes to 60 minutes to complete one of these forms as many of the forms require an examination assessing the nature of the condition.

Currently the Department orders these exams through private contractors who have been trained and retained on a contract basis through master agreements with VBA. Due to the inability of the health care side of VA to provide primary care doctors for these examinations, VBA is doing most of the exams through private contractors. However, some exams must be done by VA doctors. These are exams associated with discharge physicals.

In March 2016, VA announced an agreement with 5 private companies to provide contract examinations for VBA. The award was for 12 months with 4 possible contract extensions of another 48 months. The total five-year aggregated cost was $6.8 billion. Most examinations will be done by these companies and not by VA healthcare. Here are the companies.

1. VetFed Resources, Inc., 2034 Eisenhoir Ave., Ste 270, Alexandria, VA
2. Veterans Evaluation Services, Inc., 3000 Richmond Avenue, Ste 540, Houston, TX
3. QTC Medical Services, Inc, 21700 Copley Drive, Ste 200, Diamond Bar, CA
4. Logistics Health, Inc., La Crosse, WI
5. Medical Support Los Angeles, A Medical Corporation, Pasadena, CA

Veterans also have the option of providing their own DBQs from any licensed healthcare provider which might include a nurse, physician's assistant, nurse practitioner, chiropractor, naturopath, physical or occupational therapist or medical doctor. One exception to this is that PhD psychologists or psychiatrists are required for mental disorder evaluations. When DBQs were first introduced, the expectation was that the claimant's private care providers would furnish these documents. In recent years VA has abandoned this approach altogether.

Even though we encourage the applicant to furnish his or her own DBQs, we have found that the current processing model does not recognize DBQs furnished by the claimant. It has been our experience that VA will always order its own DBQs from contract examiners and when necessary, combine that examination with a medical opinion if it is needed. This current procedure violates the time-saving intent of the DBQ, but logical and coherent adjudication responses from the Department do not seem to be the norm under the current system.

Writing a Personal Lay Statement

A personal statement outlining the theory of the claim, the incidents leading up to the injury or illness, the description of current disabilities and continuity of symptoms since discharge and why the claimant believes he or she is entitled to service connection can be an important part of the evidence. This personal statement also called "lay evidence" has zero evidentiary value if the adjudicator in the Regional Office or the BVA Judge does not think it is credible and competent. When considering lay evidence, the Board or adjudicator should determine whether the veteran's disability is the type of disability for which lay evidence is competent. See Jandreau, 492 F.3d at 1377. If the disability is of the type for which lay evidence is competent, the adjudicator must weigh that evidence against the other evidence of record in making its determination regarding the existence of a service connection. Buchanan, 451 F.3d at 1334-37. Here are the criteria

- VA must determine if the lay evidence is competent and provides an adequate explanation of determination (Jandreau v. Nicholson, 492 F.3d 1372 Fed. Cir. 2007)
- VA must weigh the lay evidence against other evidence to make a determination of its value on the claim (Buchanan v. Nicholson, 451 F.3d 1331, 1334-1337 Fed. Cir. 2006)
- VA must make a credibility determination as to whether the evidence supports a finding of service connection and a continuity of symptomology (Barr v. Nicholson, 21. Vet App. 303 2007)

The bottom line – it is better to provide more evidence than less. If you are unsure if the lay evidence is admissible, either confer with your representative or attorney, or submit it and have the RO determine its admissibility based on the above criteria.

A well-written and detailed, yet not overly lengthy, personal lay statement is sometimes essential to winning an award. A lay statement is a narrative of your claim which describes in detail the incident that was incurred in service, the history since discharge pertaining to the medical repercussions from that incident and a description of the current disability. Lay statements can come from the claimant or from fellow soldiers who were present and observed the particular incident or from a spouse or family member who has observed symptoms over the years and verifies continuity of those symptoms.

It's important to know that a lay statement cannot contain a medical nexus opinion unless the person writing the statement is a licensed medical provider and is competent to provide that opinion. However, this does not preclude the person who is writing this statement from testifying of known facts from a source that is qualified to support a nexus opinion. For example the claimant can testify of diagnoses or other conditions that were given to the claimant either orally by treating physicians or through medical records that no longer exist. The claimant can also testify to medical opinions concerning service connection that were offered by treating medical providers. In addition, the claimant can provide substantial evidence from medical literature that supports his or her assertions for service connection or a disability rating decision. When using medical literature evidence, the lay statement should point out why that literature supports the service connection rating or disability rating.

Further on we will provide sample lay statements. In addition, the case studies that are found on the Claim Support Disc contain detailed lay statements. It will help you to go to the case studies and read these statements to see how a persuasive case can be laid out. We should also note that lay statements need not be as detailed as those in the case studies as those statements were perhaps a little bit too detailed. On the other hand, the rater is required to read pertinent evidence and more detail can always help to guide the rater to a better decision.

Citations and Court Precedent Rulings on Lay Statements

The following is taken from the website vetsfirst.org

When adjudicating a claim for veterans benefits, "[t]he Secretary shall consider all information and lay and medical evidence of record." 38 U.S.C. § 5107(b). Lay evidence may be competent to prove the existence of a chronic disease that can be diagnosed or demonstrated without medical expertise in presumptive service-connection claims. See Savage v. Gober, 10 Vet. App. 488, 495 (1997) (for certain chronic diseases, lay evidence may be competent to identify in-service existence of chronic disease and whether current condition is subsequent manifestation of that same chronic disease); 38 C.F.R. §§ 3.303(b), 3.307(a), 3.309(a). The distinction between the use of lay evidence in direct service-connection claims and presumptive service-connection claims for chronic diseases exists because in the latter case the lay evidence is not being used to establish a medical causation or etiology but rather to establish, by evidence of observable symptomatology, that the currently diagnosed chronic disease is the same condition that was present during service or during the presumptive period of § 3.307(a).

In its role as factfinder, the Board must first "determin[e] whether lay evidence is credible in and of itself, i.e., because of possible bias, conflicting statements, etc." Buchanan v. Nicholson, 451 F.3d 1331, 1334-37 (Fed. Cir. 2006); see also Miller v. Derwinski, 3 Vet. App. 201, 204 (1992).

In certain situations, lay evidence may be used to diagnose a veteran's medical condition. See Jandreau v. Nicholson, 492 F.3d 1372, 1377 (2007) (holding that lay evidence may be used to diagnose a condition when

(1) a layperson is competent to identify the medical condition,
(2) the layperson is reporting a contemporaneous medical diagnosis, or
(3) lay testimony describing symptoms at the time supports a later diagnosis by a medical professional");

Barr v. Nicholson, 21 Vet. App. 303, 307 (2007) (stating that "[l]ay testimony is competent ... to establish the presence of observable symptomatology and 'may provide sufficient support for a claim of service connection' " (quoting Layno v. Brown, 6 Vet. App. 465, 469 (1994))); Washington v. Nicholson, 21 Vet. App. 191, 195 (2007) (holding that, "[a]s a layperson, an appellant is competent to provide information regarding visible, or otherwise observable, symptoms of disability").

Further, lay evidence may be competent to show continuity of symptomatology under 38 C.F.R. § 3.303(b). See Davidson v. Shinseki, 581 F.3d 1313, 1315-16 (Fed. Cir. 2009) (rejecting the view that "competent medical evidence is required ... [when] the determinative issue involves either medical etiology or a medical diagnosis." (citing Jandreau, 492 F.3d at 1376-77)); Savage

v. Gober, 10 Vet. App. 488, 497 (1997). When considering lay evidence, the Board should determine whether the veteran's disability is the type of disability for which lay evidence is competent. See Jandreau, 492 F.3d at 1377. If the disability is of the type for which lay evidence is competent, the Board must weigh that evidence against the other evidence of record in making its determination regarding the existence of a service connection. Buchanan, 451 F.3d at 1334-37.

The Board **"cannot determine that lay evidence lacks credibility merely because it is unaccompanied by contemporaneous medical evidence." Buchanan, 451 F.3d at 1337. Section 3.307(b) does not require both medical and competent lay evidence to establish the existence of a chronic disease, and thus, "competent lay evidence can be sufficient in and of itself" to establish entitlement to a benefit**. Buchanan, 451 F.3d at 1335 (citing 38 C.F.R. § 3.307(b) (in claiming chronic disease, "factual basis may be established by medical evidence, competent lay evidence[,] or both.")).

PART 3 – SUBMITTING THE CLAIM

Organizing the Evidence for the Adjudication Team

Organizing the evidence is a very important part of presenting your case in a favorable manner to the Rating Veteran Service Representative in the Service Center where your claim is being processed. Remember, your claim may not be in your own state Regional Office. Workload allocation procedures will try to move your claim to your local office, but if the local office cannot handle it and another office has the resources at that point to handle the claim, it will be sent to that particular office that has the best capacity at the time.

As discussed in Chapter 4 the new paperless system puts a great deal of time constraint on the adjudication team. If you present that team with all kinds of evidence that is not well organized and is not structured to point out the crucial evidence statements that are necessary for a favorable decision, the team may never find that crucial evidence. Once the claim gets through the initial intake process where everything is checked for completeness and then moved on to the adjudication team, a VSR on the team will examine the claim to determine what new evidence needs to be developed. Typically, this involves ordering Service Treatment Records and VA medical records if the application indicates the veteran has such records. If you have submitted your own medical records, the VSR will likely order a DBQ examination. If you provide your own DBQs and you organized the evidence to make it clear that those exams are in the file, the claim should be referred to the Rating VSR of the team for a decision and without ordering any documents. This rarely occurs as VA tends to ignore privately produced DBQ's.

If the claim includes a substantial amount of evidence and a difficult to understand theory along with numerous disability issues related to that theory, the developing VSR on adjudication team may not comprehend what is being claimed. That person may order unnecessary documents or even the wrong DBQs especially if the evidence doesn't specifically identify the nature of the claim. This slows down the process and can even lead to an adverse decision if a wrong DBQ is produced that has nothing to do with the service connection you are requesting a decision on. Unfortunately, we have seen numerous examples of requesting unrelated DBQs and in addition requests for medical opinions that don't even pertain to what is being claimed.

Most of the documents you will be using will be in PDF format from Adobe Acrobat because that is the standard format that VA uses for all of its electronics records system. Any paper documents that you have should be scanned on a scanning printer or a scanner into PDF format and not into JPEG or another image format. All of the documents that you have must be organized in a logical manner that makes it easy for the development VSR on the rating team as well as the Rater to understand the nature of the claim and to be able to review the evidence in an organized and well laid out manner.

In order to organize and work with PDF documents, you need to have a computer such as a laptop or desktop computer with a large enough screen to be able to move documents around. You will also need a software copy of Adobe Acrobat Pro or equivalent newer versions or an equivalent program that can delete pages, insert pages and even edit text. You can rent Adobe Acrobat Pro DC online for a monthly fee and then if you don't need it anymore, cancel your rental contract. You can also find someone to help you who has expertise in this area. <u>If you are a claim representative, you should have Adobe Acrobat. This is a vital tool in organizing claims.</u>

<u>The disability claim case studies on the Claim Support Disc illustrate the issues we are addressing here. You can see how the documents were stitched together using a combination of Acrobat and Microsoft Word files converted to PDF in order to present the evidence in a logical flow and make it easy for the rating team to find the evidence we wanted them to consider.</u>

Preparing the Application for Submission

Here are the conclusions that we reached from Chapter 4 that will allow you to get around the dysfunctional claims processing model in the Veterans Service Center. We are still not certain that we understand all of the dysfunction as trying to uncover what is going on is like trying to gain access to a locked building by peering through tiny windows to try to see what is going on inside. However, the list below is our best attempt to help you get around the faulty process and have greater success with your claim.

1. If the initial application is for a number of disparate disability issues that are not direct service-connected but are secondary service-connected, don't expect the intake processing employees to understand the difference between direct service connection and secondary service connection (even though they should); establish the direct service connection issues or presumptive service connection issues first and then refile for an increase in rating. (See Chapter 5 to understand this)

2. Don't allow the Intake processors to identify the theory of the claim from the application form itself, but force them from the application to read a more thorough (but brief) explanation of the claim on a VA Form 21-4138 but be aware they may not understand complex theories anyway due to a general lack of knowledge of medical issues.

3. Make sure that the adjudication team knows the claim is Fully Developed and does not need any development from them as this will save a great deal of time by avoiding duty to assist and in turn not cause the claim to come up against the 125 day bright line barrier. (be aware however that they often ignore your evidence and develop for the same evidence anyway)

4. Summarize exactly what the claim is about and what the service connection is so that they know exactly what evidence they are supposed to look at and save some time.

5. Organize and index the medical records with a table of contents and brief description of each issue to make it easy for the rating team to review this evidence and understand the important medical issues relating to the claim so that they don't have to waste time.

Ferreting out those issues from the record and also circle with a black felt pen those particular medical issues you want them to read. (Accept the fact that they will not take the time to actually read all of the medical evidence as regulations require so you must hold their hands and put the medical evidence you want them to read directly in their faces)

6. Organize, index and correlate all other evidence with tables of contents and brief descriptions to make it easy for the rating team to understand the purpose of that evidence and circle with a black felt pen any particular points of evidence that prove the claim.

7. Write a well-organized and thorough, but not too lengthy lay statement that includes a detailed explanation of the theory of the claim, a well-defined list of evidence, a detailed description of the current disabilities, an explanation of why the evidence leads to service connection and finally a thorough history of the incident in service and how it ties to the current disabilities.

8. Be detailed but keep your supporting statements simple as volumes of paperwork will be stored in VBMS, but no one will ever look at it even though it is important evidence and even though regulations require Rating VSRs to read all the evidence; assume they won't do that even though they state on the decision notice that they have read all the evidence

We will follow these principles above on subsequent pages and show you how to use them when you submit your application. On the next 10 pages we are going to show you how to apply the principles above with a fictitious sample application for the claimant George A Smith. You will see how we recommend tying it all together.

Organize All of the Evidence with Title Pages, Tables of Contents and Summaries
When the Intake Processing Center in the Veterans Service Center of the Regional Office receives an initial claim, one of the duties of these people is to organize and title all of the documents associated with the claim in VBMS. There are various switches that are used to make sure that the documents show up under proper tabs. Also, there are conventions for titling that are used so that VSRs can recognize what is in the file and whether it is complete or not.

You can title your documents whatever you want, but the titles must reflect accurately the content of those documents. For example, if it is a medical opinion which is critical to your claim, you must identify it as such. Likewise, DBQs are often required so you must identify the particular DBQ that you are submitting. In the next section, we will show you a sample table of all of the documents submitted with our sample claim for Mr. Smith with appropriate titles. On the next page are titles associated with claims forms that should be included in your table of attached documents with the claim.

TITLES OF VBA FORMS TO BE USED IN THE EVIDENCE DOCUMENT TABLE

VA 21-526EZ, Fully Developed Claim (Compensation)
VA 21-686c Declaration of Status of Dependents
VA 21-2680 Examination for Housebound Status or Permanent Need for Regular Aid and Attendance
VA Form 21-0847 – Request for Substitution of Claimant upon Death of Claimant
VA Form 21-4176 – Report of Accidental Injury in Support of Claim for Compensation or Pension
Statement of Witness to Accident
VA Form 21-4192 – Request for Employment information in Connection With Claim for Disability
Benefits
VA Form 21-0781a – Statement in Support of Claim for Service Connection for PTSD Secondary to
Personal Assault
VA Form 21-0781 – Statement in Support of Claim for Service Connection for PTSD
VA Form 21-8940 – Veteran's Application for Increased Compensation Based on Unemployability

All of your evidence documents should have a separate title page with your TITLE OF DOCUMENT heading that will alert the employee in the Veterans Service Center how to identify that particular evidence in VBMS.

For multiple pages of evidence you submit, everything should be organized and you should include a table of contents. You should also provide a brief summary in that table of contents of what is contained in each category. This advice primarily applies to medical records and medical literature evidence more than any of the other evidence that you are providing. Certain statements in the medical record that are critical to proving service connection must be circled with a fine tip black felt tip pen so that they will jump out immediately when the rating service officer is browsing through the records. Remember, if the records are extensive, the rater will not read everything and simply skim to find pertinent information relating to service connection. Other evidence is already going to be organized such as your medical opinions, your lay statement and any other documents. But if not, organize it as well

Organizing your evidence – especially medical records – could end up taking a great deal of time. In the complex claim for neuropathy related to development of autoimmunity in service, which we discussed previously, there were 37 different documents associated with the service treatment records that were pertinent to establishing service connection. These were old records and were all handwritten. When they came in from the National Personnel Records Center, they were all jumbled out of order and had to be organized chronologically. All of the records were scanned in PDF format and were also received in that format, but the organization, translation into text from handwritten and assembling them chronologically took a great deal of time. In fact it took about 12 hours to accomplish this task.

Likewise, the medical records after service were extensive, comprising 840 pages, and had to be organized with a table of contents and a description of each visit and location in the final assemblage of documents. This took another 10 hours to accomplish this task.

Think about this. If these records had been given to the Regional Office in their original disjointed form, the development team and the rater would have been just as challenged trying to decipher everything in the file. It would be a foregone conclusion, that they will have missed something important without those 22 hours of pre-preparation. They probably would have been totally frustrated trying to decipher the handwritten service treatment records as they were written by medical doctors and everyone knows the problem reading the handwriting of doctors. As a final note, the lay statement with this claim also tied everything together for the RO.

CLAIMANT: Frank Katana
SSN: 922-00-1921
DOB: June 31, 1947

TITLE OF THIS DOCUMENT: Outpatient Military Records Pertinent to This Claim

VBMS DOCUMENT CATEGORY: Service Treatment Record

**Disability Compensation Claim Records for
Frank Katana, SSN 922-00-1921, DOB June 31, 1947**

**Service Treatment Records from January 4, 1973 through
August 23, 1973**

**Below is the Text-Translated Content of Attached
Handwritten Service Treatment Records – Sorted Chronologically**

January 4, 1973. Record of Medical Care. Annual physical examination accomplished. Okay. John Bishop Captain – PAGE 27

February 15, 1973. Record of Medical Care. Patient has a cold – typical URI symptoms. Also some fatigue. Patient can perform normal Valsalva. pn looks good. (Unintelligible). Imp: URP. (Unintelligible) 1) Robitussin cough syrup (unintelligible) 2) (unintelligible) 3) (DUTY NOT TO INCLUDE FLYING) (duty not to include flying) 4) more spoke to test negative. Alfred Watson Lieutenant Colonel – PAGE 27

February 15, 1973. Form 1042 removal from flight duty and potential grounding up to last day of May 1973 due to virus infection/unspecified/upper respiratory tract – PAGE 11

February 20, 1973. Record of Medical Care. Follow-up URI. Off meds. No symptoms. VNB. RFD (return to flight duty) – PAGE 28

February 20, 1973. Form 1042 return to flight duty – PAGE 10

March 14, 1973. Record of Medical Care. C/C cold symptoms, congestion runny nose temperature 99°. Ears won't clear. Sore throat. Cough and scant sputum. Nasal congestion. PE: TMs clear. Pharynix slightly red. Chest clear. DX: URI. Plan 1) DNIF (duty not to include flying) no RSU (runway supervisory unit) no link (flight simulator) 2) Actifed TID #15 3) RTC pm 4) Afrin spray. John Bishop Captain – PAGE 28

March 14, 1973. Form 1042 removal from flight duty and potential grounding up to last day of June 1973 due to virus infection, unspecified, upper respiratory tract – PAGE 9

March 20, 1973. Record of Medical Care. Follow-up from F Flight line sick call. Still has nasal congestion and cough with white sputum. Ears stuffy. Has had similar symptoms off and on including sinuses. PE: ears clear. Chart X-ray: WNL. Sinus x-ray: WNL. Chest clear. (The rest of the record is missing on another page) – PAGE 28

March 20, 1973. Record of Medical Care. Plans: continue the same. (Unintelligible something FL sooner.) John Bishop Captain – PAGE 25

Page 1 of 5

Completing the Evidence Document Table

On the following page is a sample table filled out. This table is in a Microsoft Word document entitled **"VA 21-4138 Special Pages 2 through 20."** The 4138 form is found on the claim support disc in a folder called **"Create Your Own Special Compensation VA 21-4138."**

191

List of Documents Submitted with This Claim

TITLE OF DOCUMENT

List of Documents Submitted with This Claim

TITLE OF DOCUMENT
DD-214 for James Smith
VA Form 21-22a
VA Form 21-534EZ
Evidence of Service in Vietnam
Death Certificate for James Smith
Marriage Certificate for James and Eleanor Smith
Medical Opinion for Cause of Death, Roger Moore MD
Medical Records for James Smith

Write a Well Organized Brief Summary of What You Are Claiming

Summary of My Claim for Compensation

I injured my foot severely when I was in the service in 1975 at Fort Benning, Georgia. This required surgery to repair the foot, but it did not heal properly and over the years I have not been able to walk properly because of the foot injury. I am furnishing the service medical records from that incident. The inability to walk properly has put undue pressure on my left hip and my orthopedic doctor tells me that my hip is deteriorating because of this foot injury. He also tells me that this hip deterioration is a direct result of the foot injury that happened while I was in the service. He has provided a letter stating this fact that the foot injury and the hip deterioration are service-connected and detailing my hip condition and the causes of it. I also include my current medical records relating to the foot injury and the hip condition. I also include the pertinent Disability Benefit Questionnawere for hip condition filled out by my orthopedic doctor.

Write a Well Organized and Thorough Lay Statement to Tie Everything Together

My Personal Lay Statement Supporting Service Connection

Under federal law you are required to accept my lay statement as probative evidence if it is competent and credible. In this case, it does meet that test and your requirement to read this evidence is found in federal code – , "[t]he Secretary shall consider all information and lay and medical evidence of record." 38 U.S.C. § 5107(b)

In the summer of 1975, I was stationed at Fort Benning, Georgia undergoing airborne operations training. At one point during a training exercise, a group of us were to egress from a helicopter in a simulated battle situation. I were fully equipped for combat with rifles, ammunition and other gear. There were six of us in the helicopter awaiting the egress point when about 6 feet above the ground, I was pushed out the door by the by someone from behind whom I could not identify, but I suspect it was our trainer. He and I had had some words over the summer and he did not like me. After a formal inquiry, no one admitted to pushing me and the conclusion was that I had lost my balance and fallen out by myself.

I fell about 6 feet and landed in an awkward position with my right leg extended. My right foot twisted at an extreme angle and caused my leg to rotate. I was severely injured and I had heard a cracking sound and suspected that I had broken something. I was taken to the base hospital where I was diagnosed with spiral fractures in the fibula and tibia of the right leg. I was also told that I had detached numerous ligaments in my right foot and it would require surgery to reattach those ligaments. I was told without surgery I would have difficulty walking and would be in pain the rest of my life. I was told that the leg fractures would heal themselves without any lasting repercussions.

After the surgery, I was in the hospital for a number of days and then released with a boot cast on my foot and told that I needed to keep the weight off that foot. I was given a pair of crutches to get around on. Since it would take about 4 to 5 months for the ligament surgery to heal up, I was reassigned to a different duty where I was given a desk job in the procurement section of the base. They wanted me to stay at that location to follow up with my injury.

My foot eventually healed and I had little or no pain in walking on it. However, it did not heal perfectly as my right foot was stiff and I could not rotate it the same way that I could rotate my left foot. I also could not push off my right foot as adequately as I could push off with my left foot when walking. This resulted in a slight limp and caused me to favor my left leg when walking as that was the stronger limb. I could not participate in any running sports, but I was capable of doing most everything else.

I was discharged from the service in 1977 with an Honorable discharge.

Over the years since my discharge, my foot has become more stiff and more unmanageable and my limp has become more pronounced, causing me to rely more on my left leg for walking. I have consulted with numerous orthopedic surgeons who tell me that they can do nothing to correct my condition as they claim that scar tissue and some calcification has occurred and they cannot go in and correct that for this particular injury.

As I have grown older, my favoring of my left leg has caused me to experience pain in my left hip. Most recently, I consulted with an orthopedic doctor who told me that my irregular gait has put undue pressure on that hip and the hip joint has started to deteriorate. He recommended that I elect for a hip replacement surgery, but he says my insurance would not approve it at this point as the hip is still functional and the pain can be controlled with medication.

Most recently I am in constant pain even when I am not putting any pressure on the hip or moving it around. The pain is affecting my ability to function and often times I must resort to crutches to get around especially when I have to walk long distances. At night, I have difficulty sleeping due to the pain and pain pwells work somewhat but do not completely eliminate it.

I was told by a friend that I may qualify for a disability benefit from the Department of Veterans Affairs and so I am submitting an application for this purpose. I am receiving assistance with this application from a trained individual who says he is accredited with the Department of Veterans Affairs.

Prepare a Detailed List of Current Disability Symptoms

This list is important as you want to identify all possible ratable issues. In this case, pain of movement and static pain are two different ratable conditions. The RO may get this from the DBQ as well, but it helps them to see the big picture and possibly improve the rating decision.

Observational Description of My Disabilities

- I am in constant pain whether I put pressure on my hip or not
- The pain becomes more severe when I need to walk and sometimes I use crutches to walk around
- The pain in my left hip lingers even when I am sitting or lying in bed and I would say on a scale of 1 to 10 it is about a 5 without medication.
- I refuse to take opioids and I have found that Celebrex, 100 mg dosage taken twice a day is the most effective as this reduces my pain level to about a 3 when resting and goes up to about 4 or 5 when I walk a lot

Prepare the VA Form 21-526EZ

As part of the effort to avoid the dysfunctional claim system, you do not want to list what you are claiming on VA Form 21-526EZ. If your claim has many moving pieces, they don't give you enough space to describe the claim. As you see on this snippet from the claim form, they only give you a 76 character space to describe your disability. This is highly inadequate for any claim. Providing only a brief description of your service connected condition will probably trigger duty to assist, even though your claim should be fully developed. The development team will go their merry way trying to develop for whatever they think you are claiming and you may end up with a decision notice that has nothing to do with what your claim really is all about.

To avoid this, force them to read a more thorough description of the disabilities that you believe are service-connected. Notice below that you will force them to go to a specially prepared VA 21-4138, where you will provide a detailed description of the service connection theory, a detailed description of your disabilities, a complete list of all of the evidence records submitted and a detailed and thorough lay statement.

SECTION IV: CLAIM INFORMATION

16. LIST THE CURRENT DISABILITY(IES) OR SYMPTOMS THAT YOU CLAIM ARE RELATED TO YOUR MILITARY SERVICE AND/OR SERVICE-CONNECTED DISABILITY
(If applicable, identify whether a disability is due to a service-connected disability; confinement as a prisoner of war; exposure to Agent Orange, asbestos, mustard gas, ionizing radiation, or Gulf War environmental hazards; or a disability for which compensation is payable under 38 U.S.C. 1151)
NOTE: List your claimed conditions below. See the following three examples for guidance on how to complete Section IV.

EXAMPLES OF DISABILITY(IES)	EXAMPLES OF EXPOSURE TYPE	EXAMPLES OF HOW THE DISABILITY(IES) RELATE TO SERVICE	EXAMPLES OF DATES
Example 1. HEARING LOSS	NOISE	HEAVY EQUIPMENT OPERATOR IN SERVICE	JULY 1968
Example 2. DIABETES	AGENT ORANGE	SERVICE IN VIETNAM WAR	DECEMBER 1972
Example 3. LEFT KNEE, SECONDARY TO RIGHT KNEE		INJURED LEFT KNEE WHEN BRACE ON RIGHT KNEE FAILED	6/11/2008
CURRENT DISABILITY(IES)	IF DUE TO EXPOSURE, EVENT, OR INJURY, PLEASE SPECIFY (e.g., Agent Orange, radiation)	EXPLAIN HOW THE DISABILITY(IES) RELATES TO THE IN-SERVICE EVENT/EXPOSURE/INJURY	APPROXIMATE DATE DISABILITY(IES) BEGAN OR WORSENED
1. See attached VA Form 21-4138 entitled "Explanation of My Claim"			
2.			

Preparing a 21-526EZ for Multiple Issue Claims

Over the years the Department has been receiving applications with an ever increasing number of claims issues. In this case claims issues means separate disabling symptoms that each could receive a rating. In many cases, these claims issues are tied to the same event that occurred in service and are not the result of multiple events that occurred in service.

For example, the sample that we have been working on in previous sections and in which you will eventually see the final results in a subsequent section, is a claim for a single event in service – a severe foot injury – that eventually led to at least 4 claims issues that each could warrant a rating. The issues are the foot injury itself which has gotten worse, (issue #1) a secondary disability from the foot injury that has led to hip deterioration which in turn causes limited ability to function (issue #2), static pain that in itself is a disability (issue #3) and pain from motion that results in loss of functionality (issue #4).

The new VA Form 21- 526EZ recognizes that there could be many disability issues and the form provides 15 rows to list at least this number of conditions. But that is really not necessary as most claims issues for a given application usually center around one event or incident that occurred in service. Our approach makes more sense by putting all of these separate disabilities in one place on the 4138 and then tying them altogether with the narrative on that form.

But, not all applications involve just one event, incident or illness that occurred in service. Increasingly, claimants are deciding to apply for as many disabilities as they can think of and hope that some of them will stick. It's kind of like throwing a bowl of spaghetti at the wall and hoping some of it sticks. This is a selfish approach as it takes up a great deal of time for the Regional Office to develop these multiple issue claims and uses up resources for veterans who have valid claims.

On the other hand, we have to recognize that there could have been more than one injury, incidence or illness, that occurred in service and thus there could be multiple disabilities as a result of those. Consider the following example. A combat veteran from the the conflict in Afghanistan is claiming 4 different disability events. The first is a cervical spine injury due to

195

whiplash from a vehicular accident in service, the second is a lumbar spinal injury incurred while moving a wounded comrade out of harms way, the third is PTSD and the fourth is a result of the other 3 – a claim for individual unemployability.

Each of these events has numerous disability issues. The cervical spine injury has resulted in limited motion of the head, static pain, numbness, pain and iakness in the right arm. The lumbar spinal injury has resulted in limited motion from back pain, myofascial pain in the buttocks and down the back of the legs and iakness in the legs. PTSD was a result of a stressor in combat. And finally individual unemployability is a result of not being able to maintain gainful employment because of all of the other issues combined. These combat related disabilities do not require medical evidence from service as long as the lay statement is consistent. This is an exception in the rules for combat veterans only. In this case, we will use 4 different VA 21-4138's for each event.

SECTION IV: CLAIM INFORMATION			
16. LIST THE CURRENT DISABILITY(IES) OR SYMPTOMS THAT YOU CLAIM ARE RELATED TO YOUR MILITARY SERVICE AND/OR SERVICE-CONNECTED DISABILITY *(If applicable, identify whether a disability is due to a service-connected disability; confinement as a prisoner of war; exposure to Agent Orange, asbestos, mustard gas, ionizing radiation, or Gulf War environmental hazards; or a disability for which compensation is payable under 38 U.S.C. 1151)* NOTE: List your claimed conditions below. See the following three examples for guidance on how to complete Section IV.			
EXAMPLES OF DISABILITY(IES)	EXAMPLES OF EXPOSURE TYPE	EXAMPLES OF HOW THE DISABILITY(IES) RELATE TO SERVICE	EXAMPLES OF DATES
Example 1. HEARING LOSS	NOISE	HEAVY EQUIPMENT OPERATOR IN SERVICE	JULY 1968
Example 2. DIABETES	AGENT ORANGE	SERVICE IN VIETNAM WAR	DECEMBER 1972
Example 3. LEFT KNEE, SECONDARY TO RIGHT KNEE		INJURED LEFT KNEE WHEN BRACE ON RIGHT KNEE FAILED	6/11/2008
CURRENT DISABILITY(IES)	IF DUE TO EXPOSURE, EVENT, OR INJURY, PLEASE SPECIFY (e.g., Agent Orange, radiation)	EXPLAIN HOW THE DISABILITY(IES) RELATES TO THE IN-SERVICE EVENT/EXPOSURE/INJURY	APPROXIMATE DATE DISABILITY(IES) BEGAN OR WORSENED
1. See attached VA Form 21-4138 entitled "Explanation of Cervical Spine Injury"			
2. See attached VA Form 21-4138 entitled "Explanation of Lumbar Spine			
3. See attached VA Form 21-4138 entitled "Explanation of PTSD"			
4. See attached VA Form 21-4138 entitled "Explanation of Individual Un			
5.			
6.			

Preparing Single or Multiple VA 21-4138 Forms for Submission

Use these instructions to construct your "Explanation of My Claim" submission that we have discussed in the past several pages. This construction will direct the adjudication team in the Veterans Service Center down an easily recognizable pathway to understanding and adjudicating your application. First of all, you will not allow VA to gain control your application by your submitting any information about what you are claiming on the 21-526EZ itself.

In addition, you will give them the necessary information to put the pieces together with all of the other evidence that you provide by forcing them to read it all in the same document – the 21-4138. On the next page is is the information you will give them in that document.

VA Form 21-4138 – Contents of This Statement (Continued from page 1)

Summary of My Claim for Compensation; see page 2
Observational Description of My Disabilities; see page 3
List of Documents Submitted with This Claim; see page 4
My Personal Lay Statement Supporting Service Connection; see page 5

We have designed a special 4138 Page 1 to help you with this process. The form is a PDF form fill document exactly the same as the existing VA Form 21-4138 except that the **SECTION II: REMARKS** space has been replaced by a message that puts the Regional Office on notice your claim is fully developed and ready for a decision and then leads them to Page 2 of the 4138.

We have also converted Page 2 from the 4138 to a Microsoft Word document, so that you can use MS Word to fill it out and in addition we have added 17 more pages just like it so that you can complete a narrative in the same form style. This allows the development team to recognize that all of the information that you are providing is part of one large 4138.

If you wish to create your own Page 1 of the 4138, we provide you a PDF form fill version of Page 1 of the VA 21-4138 with a blank remarks section. You create the message you want in Word and then insert it into this specially prepared form as a screen capture image. The Word document we furnish is called "Explanation of My Claim Template Blank." You would create your message in Word and then take a screenshot saving it as a JPEG file. You would then insert the JPEG file into the remarks section of the 21-4138 using Acrobat or a similar program.

Here is a list found on the Claim Support Disc of all of the forms to create what we have talked about on previous pages.

- Compensation – Explanation of My Claim Template Blank
- Compensation – VA 21-4138 Page 1 Blank
- Compensation – VA 21-4138 Page 1 Standard
- Compensation – VA 21-4138 Page 1 Waiver of VAMC Records
- Compensation – VA 21-4138 Pages 2 through 20 Blank
- Compensation – VA 21-4138 Pages 2 through 20 Sample
- Compensation – VA 21-4138 Sample Filing

All of these forms are found on the Claim Support Disc in a folder called **"Special 21-4138 Forms for Our Application System."**

OMB Control No. 2900-0075
Respondent Burden: 15 minutes
Expiration Date: 12/31/2020

VA Department of Veterans Affairs

STATEMENT IN SUPPORT OF CLAIM

**VA DATE STAMP
(DO NOT WRITE IN THIS SPACE)**

INSTRUCTIONS: Read the Privacy Act and Respondent Burden on Page 2 before completing the form. Complete as much of Section I as possible. The information requested will help process your claim for benefits. If you need any additional room, use the second page.

SECTION I: VETERAN/BENEFICIARY'S IDENTIFICATION INFORMATION

NOTE: You will *either* complete the form online or by hand. Please print the information request in ink, neatly, and legibly to help process the form.

1. VETERAN/BENEFICIARY'S NAME *(First, Middle Initial, Last)*

George | A Smith

2. VETERAN'S SOCIAL SECURITY NUMBER: 200 – 10 – 1234

3. VA FILE NUMBER *(If applicable)*: none

4. VETERAN'S DATE OF BIRTH *(MM/DD/YYYY)*
Month: 01 – Day: 01 – Year: 1955

5. VETERAN'S SERVICE NUMBER *(If applicable)*: none

6. TELEPHONE NUMBER *(Include Area Code)*: 555-321-1234

7. E-MAIL ADDRESS *(Optional)*: george@email.com

8. MAILING ADDRESS *(Number and street or rural route, P.O. Box, City, State, ZIP Code and Country)*

No. & Street: 524 Deering Street

Apt./Unit Number: 999 | City: Darnville

State/Province: VA | Country: US | ZIP Code/Postal Code: 01020 – 0000

SECTION II: REMARKS
(The following statement is made in connection with a claim for benefits in the case of the above-named veteran/beneficiary.)

Explanation of My Claim

This Is a Fully Developed Claim for Disability Compensation – Ready for a Decision

I HAVE FURNISHED ALL OF THE EVIDENCE YOU NEED FOR A DECISION. You do not need to develop any further as this claim is ready to give to the Rating Veteran Service Representative (RVSR). Any further documentation or evidence which I have not submitted is not required for a rating decision for this particular claim.

A detailed explanation of what I am claiming and a complete list of all of the documents I am submitting is continued on Page 2 of this VA Form 21-4138

SECTION II: REMARKS (Continued)
(The following statement is made in connection with a claim for benefits in the case of the above-named veteran/beneficiary.)

VA Form 21-4138 – Contents of This Statement (Continued from page 1)

Summary of My Claim for Compensation; see page 2
Observational Description of My Disabilities; see page 3
List of Documents Submitted with This Claim; see page 4
My Personal Lay Statement Supporting Service Connection; see page 5

Summary of My Claim for Compensation

I injured my foot severely when I was in the service in 1975 at Fort Benning, Georgia. This required surgery to repair the foot, but it did not heal properly and over the years I have not been able to walk properly because of the foot injury. I am furnishing the service medical records from that incident. The inability to walk properly has put undue pressure on my left hip and my orthopedic doctor tells me that my hip is deteriorating because of this foot injury. He also tells me that this hip deterioration is a direct result of the foot injury that happened while I was in the service. He has provided a letter stating this fact that the foot injury and the hip deterioration are service-connected and detailing my hip condition and the causes of it. I also include my current medical records relating to the foot injury and the hip condition. I also include the pertinent Disability Benefit Questionnaire for hip condition filled out by my orthopedic doctor.

Continued on Page 3

SECTION III: DECLARATION OF INTENT

I CERTIFY THAT the statements on this form are true and correct to the best of my knowledge and belief.

9. SIGNATURE *(Sign in ink)*	10. DATE SIGNED *(MM/DD/YYYY)*

PENALTY: The law provides severe penalties which include fine or imprisonment, or both, for the willful submission of any statement or evidence of a material fact, knowing it to be false.

VA FORM 21-4138, DEC 2017

Page 2

VETERAN'S SOCIAL SECURITY NO. ☐☐☐ – ☐☐ – ☐☐☐☐

Observational Description of My Disabilities

- I am in constant pain whether I put pressure on my hip or not
- The pain becomes more severe when I need to walk and sometimes I use crutches to walk around
- The pain my left hip lingers even when I am sitting or lying in bed and I would say on a scale of 1 to 10 it is about a 5 without medication.
- I refuse to take opioids and I have found that Celebrex, 100 mg dosage taken twice a day is the most effective as this reduces my pain level to about a 3 when resting and goes up to about 4 or 5 when I walk a lot

Continued on Page 4

SECTION III: DECLARATION OF INTENT	
I CERTIFY THAT the statements on this form are true and correct to the best of my knowledge and belief.	
9. SIGNATURE (Sign in ink)	10. DATE SIGNED (MM/DD/YYYY)

PENALTY: The law provides severe penalties which include fine or imprisonment, or both, for the willful submission of any statement or evidence of a material fact, knowing it to be false.

List of Documents Submitted with This Claim

TITLE OF DOCUMENT
DD-214
VA 21-526EZ Fully Developed Claim
VA 21-686c Declaration of Status of Dependents
VA 21-4138 Explanation of My Claim
Military records from Fort Benning, Georgia
Most Recent Personal Medical Records
Opinion for Service Connection, John Crew, M.D.
DBQ 21-0960M-8 Hip and Thigh Conditions
VA Form 21-22 POA Appointment
VA Form 21-0845 Third-Party Information Release
Medical Literature Evidence for My Claim

Continued on Page 5

SECTION III: DECLARATION OF INTENT

I CERTIFY THAT the statements on this form are true and correct to the best of my knowledge and belief.

9. SIGNATURE *(Sign in ink)*	10. DATE SIGNED *(MM/DD/YYYY)*

PENALTY: The law provides severe penalties which include fine or imprisonment, or both, for the willful submission of any statement or evidence of a material fact, knowing it to be false.

SECTION II: REMARKS *(Continued)*
(The following statement is made in connection with a claim for benefits in the case of the above-named veteran/beneficiary.)

My Personal Lay Statement Supporting Service Connection

Under federal law you are required to accept my lay statement as probative evidence if it is competent and credible. In this case, it does meet that test. Your requirement to read this evidence is found in federal code –, "[t]he Secretary shall consider all information and LAY and medical evidence of record." 38 U.S.C. § 5107(b). Court precedents require you to accept and read this evidence.

In the summer of 1975, I was stationed at Fort Benning, Georgia undergoing airborne operations training. At one point during a training exercise, a group of us were to egress from a helicopter in a simulated battle situation. We were fully equipped for combat with rifles, ammunition and other gear. There were six of us in the helicopter awaiting the egress point when about 6 feet above the ground, I was pushed out the door by someone from behind whom I could not identify, but I suspect it was our trainer. He and I had had some words over the summer and he did not like me. After a formal inquiry, no one admitted to pushing me and the conclusion was that I had lost my balance and had fallen out by myself.

I fell about 6 feet and landed in an awkward position with my right leg extended. My right foot twisted at an extreme angle and caused my leg to rotate. I was severely injured and I had heard a cracking sound and suspected that I had broken something. I was taken to the base hospital where I was diagnosed with spiral fractures in the fibula and tibia of the right leg. I was also told that I had detached numerous ligaments in my right foot and it would require surgery to reattach those ligaments. I was told without surgery I would have difficulty walking and would be in pain the rest of my life. I was told that the leg fractures would heal themselves without any lasting repercussions.

After the surgery, I was in the hospital for a number of days and then released with a boot cast on my foot and told that I needed to keep the weight off that foot. I was given a pair of crutches to get around on. Since it would take about 4 to 5 months for the ligament surgery to heal up, I was reassigned to a different duty where I was given a desk job in the procurement section of the base. They wanted me to stay at that location to follow up with my injury.

Continued on Page 6

SECTION III: DECLARATION OF INTENT

I CERTIFY THAT the statements on this form are true and correct to the best of my knowledge and belief.

9. SIGNATURE *(Sign in ink)*	10. DATE SIGNED *(MM/DD/YYYY)*

PENALTY: The law provides severe penalties which include fine or imprisonment, or both, for the willful submission of any statement or evidence of a material fact, knowing it to be false.

PRIVACY ACT INFORMATION: The VA will not disclose information collected on this form to any source other than what has been authorized under the Privacy Act of 1974 or Title 38, Code of Federal Regulations 1.576 for routine uses (i.e., civil or criminal law enforcement, congressional communications, epidemiological or research studies, the collection of money owed to the United States, litigation in which the United States is a party or has an interest, the administration of VA Programs and delivery of VA benefits, verification of identity and status, and personnel administration) as identified in the VA system of records, 58VA21/22/28, Compensation, Pension, Education, and Vocational Rehabilitation and Employment Records - VA, published in the Federal Register. Your obligation to respond is required to obtain or retain benefits. VA uses your SSN to identify your claim file. Providing your SSN will help ensure that your records are properly associated with your claim file. Giving us your SSN account information is voluntary. Refusal to provide your SSN by itself will not result in the denial of benefits. The VA will not deny an individual benefits for refusing to provide his or her SSN unless the disclosure of the SSN is required by Federal Statute of law in effect prior to January 1, 1975, and still in effect. The requested information is considered relevant and necessary to determine maximum benefits under the law. The responses you submit are considered confidential (38 U.S.C. 5701). Information submitted is subject to verification through computer matching programs with other agencies.

RESPONDENT BURDEN: We need this information to obtain evidence in support of your claim for benefits (38 U.S.C. 501(a) and (b)). Title 38, United States Code, allows us to ask for this information. We estimate that you will need an average of 15 minutes to review the instructions, find the information, and complete this form. VA cannot conduct or sponsor a collection of information unless a valid OMB control number is displayed. You are not required to respond to a collection of information if this number is not displayed. Valid OMB control numbers can be located on the OMB Internet Page at www.reginfo.gov/public/do/PRAMain. If desired, you can call 1-800-827-1000 to get information on where to send comments or suggestions about this form.

VA FORM 21-4138, DEC 2017

SECTION II: REMARKS (Continued)
(The following statement is made in connection with a claim for benefits in the case of the above-named veteran/beneficiary.)

Personal Lay Statement Continued from Page 5

My foot eventually healed and I had little or no pain in walking on it. However, it did not heal perfectly as my right foot was stiff and I could not rotate it the same way that I could rotate my left foot. I also could not push off my right foot as adequately as I could push off with my left foot when walking. This resulted in a slight limp and caused me to favor my left leg when walking as that was the stronger limb. I could not participate in any running sports, but I was capable of doing most everything else.

I was discharged from the service in 1977 with an Honorable discharge.

Over the years since my discharge, my foot has become more stiff and more unmanageable and my limp has become more pronounced, causing me to rely more on my left leg for walking. I have consulted with numerous orthopedic surgeons who tell me that they can do nothing to correct my condition as they claim that scar tissue and some calcification has occurred and they cannot go in and correct that for this particular injury.

As I have grown older, my favoring of my left leg has caused me to experience pain in my left hip. Most recently, I consulted with an orthopedic doctor who told me that my irregular gait has put undue pressure on that hip and the hip joint has started to deteriorate. He also told me that my hip condition is directly attributable to the foot injury that I had experienced while I was in the service. He recommended that I elect for a hip replacement surgery, but he says my insurance would not approve it at this point as the hip is still functional and the pain can be controlled with medication.

Most recently I am in constant pain even when I am not putting any pressure on the hip or moving it around. The pain is affecting my ability to function and often times I must resort to crutches to get around especially when I have to walk long distances. At night, I have difficulty sleeping due to the pain and pain pills work somewhat but do not completely eliminate it.

I was told by a friend that I may qualify for a disability benefit from the Department of Veterans Affairs and so I am submitting an application for this purpose. I am receiving assistance with this application from a trained individual who says he is accredited with the Department of Veterans Affairs. (End)

SECTION III: DECLARATION OF INTENT

I CERTIFY THAT the statements on this form are true and correct to the best of my knowledge and belief.

9. SIGNATURE *(Sign in ink)*	10. DATE SIGNED *(MM/DD/YYYY)*

PENALTY: The law provides severe penalties which include fine or imprisonment, or both, for the willful submission of any statement or evidence of a material fact, knowing it to be false.

VA FORM 21-4138, DEC 2017

Submitting the Application

You can submit the application using only eBenefits. This requires you to have the organizational capabilities and the software and the know-how to create PDF documents that can be uploaded into your eBenefits account within a short time of submitting that application. As we have recommended before, you can start an application with eBenefits and get to the final submit button but stop short of submitting. To this point, you have created an application that used DEERS to verify your service without having to submit a DD 214. In addition, you have created an Intent to File as of the date of your application and you now have an effective date going back to when you will be paid. This gives you the option of either submitting the actual claim with a 526EZ as paper to the Janesville scanning center or going back to eBenefits to finish up the claim and upload your documents.

VA will now do nothing towards developing the claim until you actually submit the claim in eBenefits. This gives you a whole year to put together your evidence. This also allows you to get your military records from the NPRC – if that is where they are – without VA beating you to those records – assuming you have not filed another application since 2012. We have already talked about the problem with allowing VA to get your paper records making them no longer available to you except through a FOIA request. Once you have all the documents, you can go back to eBenefits and your original unfinished application will still be there. VA holds onto it for a year. Go in and finish the application by submitting and then upload your documents. Or submit the claim as paper to Janesville. It for you are using paper, you must submit a new 21-526EZ in paper form along with the rest of the paper claim.

If you decide to submit as a paper application only, make sure that you put in an Intent to File before you do anything else. This creates an effective date from which you will be paid. You now have a full year to gather up all of the documents that you need, to do research and to write lay statements. By not submitting the 526EZ you now have access to your paper documents in the NPRC if that is where they are. Likewise, you have access to your STRs with the Records Management Center if that is where they are. If VA beats you to those records, or if you have filed another application since 2012, those paper documents are no longer available to you and you have to file a FOIA request. By not filing the 526EZ until you have all the documents, VA will not develop and not order records.

If you are a claim representative, you should obviously get a VA power of attorney – VA Form 21-22a – from the claimant in order to get feedback on the claim. If you use eBenefits, you will get feedback on actions that require notification when you log into the veteran's account. If you are not a claim representative and want to know all the internal workings of what is going on, you need to have someone such as a claim representative or you yourself have access to VBMS.

Deciding What to Do with an Unfavorable Decision

A well-documented and well-researched application for service connection should not result in a denial. However, Rating Veterans Service Representatives are not infallible and they may have missed some evidence or not understood the evidence. In addition, the faulty claims process currently in existence for compensation claims often results in unfavorable decisions regardless of how well the initial application was put together. If you receive a denial or miss a rating you are expecting, you will be told the basis for that denial. You will also be given information to sign up for the new review system. Don't elect for appeal but come up with new and relevant evidence to refute the decision from the Regional Office. Or if you choose you can ask for a higher-level review. See chapter 8 for more information on the new review system.

A common reason for an unfavorable decision might be that you chose to have VA order its own medical nexus opinion. Often these opinions lead to denials. If you have a strong case, you will have to go after your own opinion to refute the one from VA. You can try and get this opinion from your personal medical providers. Generally, if you are fighting a bad opinion from VA, your own private providers will likely not be any more adept than the VA examiner at writing a credible and probative opinion of their own. That takes an understanding of how to put opinions together as well as a lot of time and even research with citation of medical literature. You may have to write a persuasive opinion yourself and have the provider sign it. If the provider refuses, you may have to pay a professional to provide it. This will likely cost you a lot of money, but if you believe you have a valid claim, this is what you must do and then resubmit to reopen the claim. <u>We provide you a list of medical nexus opinion professionals on the Claim Support Disc.</u>

You may receive an award for service connection but it may not be the disability rating that you anticipated. This might be based on a poorly executed DBQ that was ordered by VA. Again you will likely have to get a better DBQ or multiple DBQs in order to refute those that were created by the contract examiner. These must be new and relevant. This means that they must introduce new information that was not on the original DBQs and this new information must be relevant to awarding a larger disability rating. Otherwise don't bother to try and go for a supplemental claim for reopening as it could be a waste of time.

In Chapter 8 we go into much greater detail on unfavorable decisions and how to deal with them. That chapter also covers the new review and appeals procedures that were affective in February 2019. This new process is a major revision in how unfavorable decisions are now handled. The emphasis is on keeping the claim in the Regional Office and preferably avoiding the BVA by introducing new opportunities for challenging an unfavorable decision. Even if a notice of disagreement is filed and the claim goes to the BVA and the BVA issues an unfavorable decision, the new rules allow going back to the Regional Office with new and relevant evidence for a reopening of that decision. In the past, decisions from the Board of Veterans Appeals were treated as the ultimate authority and these decisions were superior to any decisions made in the Regional Office. The new rules make decisions by either agency coequal in their importance.

PART 4 – EXAMPLES OF VARIOUS COMPENSATION CLAIMS

Using these 17 types of claims is a classification system we came up with. Other handbooks may come up with their own dichotomies on how to approach various categories of claims. Our approach is a way to try and make it all a little more understandable from our point of view. Every claim is unique. There are thousands of different combinations of disabilities and underlying reasons for those disabilities that result in the benefits packages for 4.5 million plus claimants receiving Disability Compensation.

Checklist for Submitting Fully Developed Compensation Claims

We created the checklist on the next page to make sure that you construct a complete and well documented application for your Fully Developed Claim for Disability Compensation. We will apply this checklist to each of the 17 different types of various Compensation applications covered in this chapter. The required steps for a specific type of application will be included for that specific claim. The steps that are not necessary for a specific type of application will also be excluded for that specific claim.

Not all of these steps apply to every type of disability application. In fact, there are not any types of claims that require all 11 steps. We provide a brief description of each step below. But for the purpose of brevity, with each of the 17 different types of applications, we do not include the steps with their descriptions. We just include the steps. If you have any question, simply come back to this page where we have provided the descriptions.

1. **Determine Entitlement Based on Service and the Merit of Your Claim**
   Make sure that you meet the active duty requirements outlined in Chapter 2 as well as character of discharge requirements and any issues with misconduct. Be honest about whether you think your current illness or disability is a result of your service. Don't just submit an application thinking you are entitled to something and hope that perhaps it "sticks." Submitting a claim without merit wastes the resources of the Department of Veterans Affairs and makes it more difficult for those who have legitimate claims.

2. **Submit an Intent to File, VA Form 21-0966, but Don't File a Claim at This Point**
   The Intent to File will establish an effective date for payment and give you a full year to fulfill all of the remaining steps of this checklist. Do not file an application at this point as it will screw up the whole process and destroy any hope of your maintaining control over your claim. If you decide to use eBenefits for your claim, only complete the online application to the point at which you have furnished all of your personal information. **DO NOT CLICK THE SUBMIT BUTTON. Filling out an incomplete application does generate an Intent to File with eBenefits.**

3. **Obtain a Copy of Your Discharge**
   If you do not have a copy of your discharge, follow the instructions in this chapter. If you decide to use eBenefits, a certification of your discharge is available online inside eBenefits and it is not necessary to submit the discharge if you complete the application in eBenefits. Follow the instructions in step #2 and don't submit the application if you use eBenefits. If you decide to do a paper application starting out with eBenefits, you can do that, but you must submit a copy of your discharge with the paper application.

4. **Obtain Copies of Service Treatment Records**
   Service Treatment Records are not required for every one of the 18 different applications i discuss in this chapter. I will let you know which type of application will require these records by including this step in the checklist for that particular application. Follow the instructions in this chapter for obtaining these records.

5. **Obtain Copies of Your Military Personnel File**
   Military personnel records are generally not required for any application for Compensation unless you need to prove a duty assignment or assignment to a particular military facility location. I will let you know for the particular application type whether you should order personnel records or not. Follow instructions in this chapter for obtaining these records.

6. **Obtain of Copies of VA Medical Center Records**
   If you have obtained health care services at a VA Medical Center, the Regional Office will want a copy of these records, whether they apply to your service-connected claim or not. Beat them to these records by following the instructions in this chapter. Every benefit type requires that you do this even if the records are not going to be used by VA. You should follow the instructions in this chapter for organizing those records and provide tables of contents and summaries when you submit your claim.

7. **Obtain Copies of Your Own Private Medical Records**

You are always going to have to provide private or government facility medical records that pertain to your particular disability, illness or disease. If those records are available you must furnish them. Do not allow VA to order the records for you as you want to follow the steps in in this chapter by organizing the documents and making it easy for the rating authority to understand your current condition.

8. **Obtain Your Own DBQs from Private Clinicians**

Not all applications require a DBQ, but for direct service-connected claims you should plan on needing one or more DBQs. We will let you know for the particular application type whether you should obtain your own DBQs. Follow the instructions in in this chapter for obtaining DBQs. Be aware that VA will probably order its own DBQs anyway. However, if the contract examiner DBQ is insufficient, you now have a DBQ that can challenge the one ordered by VA if you end up challenging an unfavorable decision.

9. **Obtain Your Own Private Medical Opinions**

Not all applications require a medical opinion for service connection. We will let you know which application requires this step. Follow the instructions in in this chapter on obtaining private medical opinions.

10. **Write a Detailed and Credible Lay Statement to Describe Your Claim**

Not all applications require a lay statement from you or from buddies or from a member of your family. We will let you know which application requires this step. Follow the instructions in in this chapter on producing lay statements.

11. **Follow Our Instructions in this Chapter for Submitting the Claim**

Parts 2 and 3 in this chapter cover our unique system that we have designed and that we believe will give you better results with your claims applications. Don't attempt an application without reading Part 2 and Part 3, unless you are absolutely certain you know what you are doing without that instruction.

1. Specific Chronic Conditions Presumed Service-Connected with a Time Limit

Details:

The veteran must have 90 continuous days or more of service. Having one or more of these 41 chronic diseases or disorders below is considered to have been caused by service if they manifest themselves to a degree of disability of 10% or more within one year after discharge. Manifesting does not necessarily mean medical diagnosis, only that evidence shows the existence. There are some exceptions to the one year rule which are: Hansen's Disease (leprosy) must have appeared within three years after separation. Tuberculosis must have appeared within three years after separation. Multiple sclerosis must have appeared within seven years after separation.

Amyotrophic Lateral Sclerosis (ALS), also known as Lou Gehrig's Disease can appear any time after separation from service. Because service connection is presumed, it is not required to produce evidence for service connection – only evidence of the manifestation of the disorder or disease. Here's the list.

- Anemia, primary.
- Arteriosclerosis.
- Arthritis.
- Atrophy, Progressive muscular.
- Brain hemorrhage.
- Brain thrombosis.
- Bronchiectasis.
- Calculi of the kidney, bladder, or gallbladder.
- Cardiovascular-renal disease, including hypertension. (This term applies to combination involvement of the type of arteriosclerosis, nephritis, and organic heart disease, and since hypertension is an early symptom long preceding the development of those diseases in their more obvious forms, a disabling hypertension within the 1-year period will be given the same benefit of service connection as any of the chronic diseases listed.)
- Cirrhosis of the liver.
- Coccidioidomycosis.
- Diabetes mellitus.
- Encephalitis lethargica residuals.
- Endocarditis. (This term covers all forms of valvular heart disease.)
- Endocrinopathies.
- Epilepsies.
- Hansen's disease.
- Hodgkin's disease.
- Leukemia.
- Lupus erythematosus, systemic.
- Myasthenia gravis.
- Myelitis.
- Myocarditis.
- Nephritis.
- Other organic diseases of the nervous system.
- Osteitis de Formans (Paget's disease).
- Osteomalacia.
- Palsy, bulbar.
- Paralysis agitans.
- Psychoses.
- Purpura idiopathic, hemorrhagic.
- Raynaud's disease.
- Sarcoidosis.
- Scleroderma.
- Sclerosis, amyotrophic lateral.
- Sclerosis, multiple.
- Syringomyelia.

- Thromboangiitis obliterans (Buerger's disease).
- Tuberculosis, active.
- Tumors, malignant, or of the brain or spinal cord or peripheral nerves.
- Ulcers, peptic (gastric or duodenal) (A proper diagnosis of gastric or duodenal ulcer (peptic ulcer) is to be considered established if it represents a medically sound interpretation of sufficient clinical findings warranting such diagnosis and provides an adequate basis for a differential diagnosis from other conditions with like symptomatology; in short, where the preponderance of evidence indicates gastric or duodenal ulcer (peptic ulcer). Whenever possible, of course, laboratory findings should be used in corroboration of the clinical data.

You do not have to prove service connection with any condition listed above as it is presumed service-connected. Your challenge is, if you have never filed a claim for any of the conditions above, and it has been a number of years since leaving the service, you have to demonstrate some sort of evidence that the conditions manifested themselves within the proper time frame. Otherwise, you can have the condition, but VA will assume that you did not incur it in service.

If it is going to take you some time to assemble the evidence for the application, do an "Intent to File" using the following form:

VA Form 21-0966 INTENT TO FILE

Forms That Might Be Used:
VA Form 10-5345 – Request for and Authorization to Release VHA Medical Records
VA Form 10-5345a – Individual's Request for a Copy of His or Her Own VA Medical Records
VA Form 21-526EZ – Application for Disability Compensation and Related Compensation Benefits
VA Form 21-4142 – Authorization and Consent to Release information to the Department of Veterans Affairs
VA Form 21-0847 – Request for Substitution of Claimant upon Death of Claimant

Forms for Representation for Assistance if Desired
VA Form 21-22A – Appointment of Individual a Claimant's Representative
VA Form 21-0845 – Authorization to Disclose Personal Information to a Third Party

Checklist Steps in the Fully Developed Claim Process to Follow:

Go to Page 214 for more detail on these steps

1. Determine Entitlement Based on Service and the Merit of Your Claim
2. Submit an Intent to File, VA Form 21-0966, but Don't File a Claim at This Point
3. Obtain a Copy of Your Discharge
4. Obtain Copies of Your Military Personnel File
5. Obtain of Copies of VA Medical Center Records
6. Obtain Copies of Your Own Private Medical Records
7. Obtain Your Own DBQs from Private Clinicians
8. Follow Our Instructions in Chapter 4 for Submitting the Claim

2. Prisoner of War – Chronic Conditions, Service-Connected with No Time Limit

Details:
The veteran must have 90 continuous days or more of service. There are 20 diseases or disorders considered service-connected for a prisoner of war depending on the length of imprisonment and manifested any time after separation to a disabling degree of 10% or more. Manifesting does not necessarily mean medical diagnosis, only that evidence shows the existence. Because service connection is presumed, it is not required to produce evidence for service connection – only evidence of the manifestation of the disorder or disease. Evidence must be provided that shows the claimant was a prisoner of war for the prescribed amount of imprisonment. Here is the list.

- psychosis,
- any of the anxiety states,
- dysthymic disorder,
- organic residuals of frostbite,
- post-traumatic osteoarthritis,
- atherosclerotic heart disease or hypertensive vascular disease and their complications,
- stroke and its complications,
- residuals of stroke and
- effective October 10, 2008, osteoporosis if the veteran has post-traumatic stress disorder (PTSD).

For former POWs who were imprisoned for at least 30 days, the following conditions are also presumed to be service-connected:

- avitaminosis,
- beriberi,
- chronic dysentery,
- helminthiasis,
- malnutrition (including optic atrophy associated with malnutrition),
- pellagra and/or other nutritional deficiencies,
- irritable boil syndrome,
- peptic ulcer disease,
- peripheral neuropathy except where related to infectious causes,
- cirrhosis of the liver,
- and effective September 28, 2009, osteoporosis.

Where Disability Compensation is claimed by a former prisoner of war, omission of history or findings from clinical records made upon repatriation is not determinative of service connection, particularly if evidence of comrades in support of the incurrence of the disability during confinement is available. Special attention will be given to any disability first reported after discharge, especially if poorly defined and not obviously of intercurrent origin. The circumstances attendant upon the individual veteran's confinement and the duration thereof will be associated with pertinent medical principles in determining whether disability manifested subsequent to service is etiologically related to the prisoner of war experience.

If it is going to take you some time to assemble the evidence for the application, submit an "Intent to File" using the following form:

VA Form 21-0966 INTENT TO FILE

Forms That Might Be Used:
VA Form 10-5345 – Request for and Authorization to Release VHA Medical Records
VA Form 10-5345a – Individual's Request for a Copy of His or Her Own VA Medical Records
VA Form 21-526EZ – Application for Disability Compensation and Related Compensation Benefits
VA Form 21-4142 – Authorization and Consent to Release Information to the Department of Veterans Affairs

Forms for Representation for Assistance if Desired
VA Form 21-22A – Appointment of Individual a Claimant's Representative
VA Form 21-0845 – Authorization to Disclose Personal Information to a Third Party

Checklist Steps in the Fully Developed Claim Process to Follow:

Go to Page 214 for more detail on these steps

1. Determine Entitlement Based on Service and the Merit of Your Claim
2. Submit an Intent to File, VA Form 21-0966, but Don't File a Claim at This Point
3. Obtain a Copy of Your Discharge
4. Obtain Copies of Your Military Personnel File
5. Obtain of Copies of VA Medical Center Records
6. Obtain Copies of Your Own Private Medical Records
7. Obtain Your Own DBQs from Private Clinicians
8. Follow Our Instructions in Chapter 4 for Submitting the Claim

3. Ionizing Radiation – Chronic Conditions Presumed Service-Connected

Details:
Careful attention is paid to whether the veteran was actually exposed to radiation to a degree to cause a number of conditions which are mostly cancers. Exposure is generally assumed to be related to nuclear detonations or experiments of which there is a specific list and the veteran must prove he was involved at the time. Manifestation of these diseases or disorders can occur generally any time after a certain prescribed period of time, depending on the condition. Manifesting does not mean medical diagnosis, only that evidence shows the existence.

Because service connection is presumed, it is not required to produce evidence for service connection – only evidence of the manifestation of the disorder or disease. That said, the claimant must provide evidence of being in the defined locations where the claimant was presumably exposed to ionizing radiation and in sufficient doses to result in one of the chronic conditions on the list. This might prove a difficult task. Here is the list.

- All forms of leukemia (except for chronic lymphocytic leukemia);
- cancer of the thyroid, breast, pharynx, esophagus, stomach, small intestine, pancreas, bile ducts, gall bladder, salivary gland, urinary tract (renal pelvis, ureter, urinary bladder and urethra), brain, bone, lung, colon, and ovary;
- bronchiolo-alveolar carcinoma;
- multiple myeloma;
- lymphomas (other than Hodgkin's disease), and
- primary liver cancer (except if cirrhosis or hepatitis B is indicated).

If it is going to take you some time to assemble the evidence for the application, do an "Intent to File" using the following form: VA Form 21-0966 INTENT TO FILE

Forms That Might Be Used:
VA Form 10-5345 – Request for and Authorization to Release VHA Medical Records
VA Form 10-5345a – Individual's Request for a Copy of His or Her Own VA Medical Records
VA Form 21-526E – Application for Disability Compensation and Related Compensation Benefits
VA Form 21-4142 – Authorization and Consent to Release information to the Department of Veterans Affairs

Forms for Representation for Assistance if Desired
VA Form 21-22A – Appointment of Individual a Claimant's Representative
VA Form 21-0845 – Authorization to Disclose Personal Information to a Third Party

Checklist Steps in the Fully Developed Claim Process to Follow:

Go to Page 214 for more detail on these steps

1. Determine Entitlement Based on Service and the Merit of Your Claim
2. Submit an Intent to File, VA Form 21-0966, but Don't File a Claim at This Point
3. Obtain a Copy of Your Discharge
4. Obtain Copies of Your Military Personnel File
5. Obtain of Copies of VA Medical Center Records
6. Obtain Copies of Your Own Private Medical Records
7. Obtain Your Own DBQs from Private Clinicians
8. Follow Our Instructions in Chapter 4 for Submitting the Claim

4. Agent Orange – Chronic Conditions, Service-Connected with No Time Limit

Details:

The veteran must have 90 continuous days or more of service. Herbicides were used in Vietnam to defoliate trees in order to remove cover for the enemy. During the manufacturing process, significance amounts of harmful contaminants called dioxins were produced. Different blends of herbicides were used but the most common was one called "Agent Orange." Being on the ground in Vietnam, during the war or on the inland waterways is sufficient for presumption for service connection. Harmful exposure other than the automatic "boots on the ground" for Vietnam is generally considered to be inhalation and not topical.

Exposure also occurred in Thailand for perimeter duties on Air Force bases, the demilitarized zone in Korea and on all ships anchored within the 12 mile territorial limit of Vietnam. In addition, numerous storage, spraying operations, testing and loading sites – outside the country and inside the US – could have resulted in exposure. The claimant must prove that he or she was exposed to Agent Orange. Proving that the claimant was in Vietnam or in any other locations where VA recognizes there was exposure to Agent Orange is relatively easy, based on service records. You can refer to the Claim Support Disc that has extensive information on agent orange exposure. Being exposed to Agent Orange under other circumstances might be a difficult task. They following illnesses are presumed to be service-connected for Agent Orange veterans:

- AL amyloidosis,
- chloracne or other acne Form disease similar to chloracne,
- porphyria cutanea tarda,
- soft-tissue sarcoma (other than osteosarcoma, chondrosarcoma,
- Kaposi's sarcoma or mesothelioma),
- Hodgkin's disease,
- multiple myeloma,
- respiratory cancers (lung, bronchus, larynx, trachea),
- non-Hodgkin's lymphoma,
- prostate cancer,
- acute and subacute peripheral neuropathy,
- diabetes mellitus (Type 2),
- all chronic B-cell leukemias (including, but not limited to, hairy-cell leukemia and chronic lymphocytic leukemia),
- Parkinson's disease, and
- ischemic heart disease.

You will note that some of these disorders such as type II diabetes, ischemic heart disease (insufficient blood supply to the heart likely due to cardiovascular disease) and Parkinson's disease are fairly common among the elderly. We expect the number of claims for Agent Orange to go up considerably because of the aging population of Vietnam Era veterans.

Here is how VA defines ischemic heart disease.

"***Arteriosclerotic heart disease***, also diagnosed as ischemic heart disease and coronary heart disease, is a disease of the heart caused by the diminution of blood supply to the heart muscle due to narrowing of the cavity of one or both coronary arteries due to the accumulation of fatty material on the inner lining of the arterial wall."

Here is the rating table for ischemic heart disease.

7005 Arteriosclerotic heart disease (Coronary artery disease):	
With documented coronary artery disease resulting in:	
Chronic congestive heart failure, or; workload of 3 METs or less results in dyspnea, fatigue, angina, dizziness, or syncope, or; left ventricular dysfunction with an ejection fraction of less than 30 percent	100
More than one episode of acute congestive heart failure in the past year, or; workload of greater than 3 METs but not greater than 5 METs results in dyspnea, fatigue, angina, dizziness, or syncope, or; left ventricular dysfunction with an ejection fraction of 30 to 50 percent	60
Workload of greater than 5 METs but not greater than 7 METs results in dyspnea, fatigue, angina, dizziness, or syncope, or; evidence of cardiac hypertrophy or dilatation on electrocardiogram, echocardiogram, or X-ray	30
Workload of greater than 7 METs but not greater than 10 METs results in dyspnea, fatigue, angina, dizziness, or syncope, or; continuous medication required	10
Note: If nonservice-connected arteriosclerotic heart disease is superimposed on service-connected valvular or other non-arteriosclerotic heart disease, request a medical opinion as to which condition is causing the current signs and symptoms.	

Please note that approximately 2,000 flight crewmembers of the National Guard who flew C123 aircraft that were used to disperse herbicide in Vietnam, although not considered veterans for benefits, are eligible under law to file claims for Disability Compensation for Agent Orange exposure. The rationale is that the planes were so saturated with the herbicide, that they still posed a risk to the National Guard crews who flew in them 30 or 40 years later after the planes were donated to the guard..
Here is the rating table for diabetes.

Here is the rating chart for type II diabetes

7913 Diabetes mellitus	
Requiring more than one daily injection of insulin, restricted diet, and regulation of activities (avoidance of strenuous occupational and recreational activities) with episodes of ketoacidosis or hypoglycemic reactions requiring at least three hospitalizations per year or iekly visits to a diabetic care provider, plus either progressive loss of weight and strength or complications that would be compensable if separately evaluated	100
Requiring insulin, restricted diet, and regulation of activities with episodes of ketoacidosis or hypoglycemic reactions requiring one or two hospitalizations per year or twice a month visits to a diabetic care provider, plus complications that would not be compensable if separately evaluated	60
Requiring insulin, restricted diet, and regulation of activities	40
Requiring insulin and restricted diet, or; oral hypoglycemic agent and restricted diet	20
Manageable by restricted diet only	10
Note (1): Evaluate compensable complications of diabetes separately unless they are part of the criteria used to support a 100 percent evaluation. Noncompensable complications are considered part of the diabetic process under diagnostic code 7913.	
Note (2): When diabetes mellitus has been conclusively diagnosed, do not request a glucose tolerance test solely for rating purposes.	

Remember, the key issue here is you must prove you were in Vietnam or other exposure locations during the war. Your service and personnel records from the National Records Center should prove this, but if your records were lost in the fire, you will need to look for an alternative source. Generally, your discharge does not reflect that you were in Vietnam – but it could. If you are trying to prove exposure in some location other than Vietnam, your job is definitely cut out for you, but we understand some people have won awards based on exposure outside of Vietnam or its territorial waters.

On the Claim Support Disc, we have a list of all of the storage and testing sites known for Agent Orange in the United States and internationally. If you want to pursue a claim for exposure beyond Vietnam, this will give you a head start. In addition this topic the Claim Support Disc includes several newsletters from the VA and some additional information on the subject.

If it is going to take you some time to assemble the evidence for the application, submit an "Intent to File" using the following form:

VA Form 21-0966 INTENT TO FILE

Forms That Might Be Used:
VA Form 10-5345 – Request for and Authorization to Release VHA Medical Records
VA Form 10-5345a – Individual's Request for a Copy of His or Her Own VA Medical Records

VA Form 21-526EZ – Application for Disability Compensation and Related Compensation Benefits

VA Form 21-4142 – Authorization and Consent to Release information to the Department of Veterans Affairs

Forms for Representation for Assistance if Desired

VA Form 21-22A – Appointment of Individual a Claimant's Representative

VA Form 21-0845 – Authorization to Disclose Personal information to a Third Party

Checklist Steps in the Fully Developed Claim Process to Follow:

Go to Page 214 for more detail on these steps

1. Determine Entitlement Based on Service and the Merit of Your Claim
2. Submit an Intent to File, VA Form 21-0966, but Don't File a Claim at This Point
3. Obtain a Copy of Your Discharge
4. Obtain Copies of Your Military Personnel File
5. Obtain of Copies of VA Medical Center Records
6. Obtain Copies of Your Own Private Medical Records
7. Obtain Your Own DBQs from Private Clinicians
8. Follow Our Instructions in Chapter 4 for Submitting the Claim

5. Disability Caused by Illness, Combat or Other Injury Incurred in the Service

Details:

This type of disability is not presumed to be service-connected. These claims are known by the title "Direct Service-Connected Claims." Evidence must be produced to show that the incurrence in service is service-connected. Proving service connection adds an additional degree of difficulty over those conditions that are presumed. Generally, evidence of the illness or injury in service should be contained in service medical records of the claimant. If no medical evidence is available, service connection may still be established through other means such as lay testimony or historical reports from individuals who observed the injury or illness of the claimant. Lay testimony alone is not considered sufficient evidence. On the other hand, lay testimony alone may be sufficient evidence for injuries or illnesses that occurred because of combat duty. There is no time frame for making a claim.

The first part of this chapter covers these types of claims in great detail. Use all of the information in Parts 2 and 3 if you want a successful service-connected claim.

Sometimes, the injury or illness does not manifest as chronically disabling for many years after separation. Medical evidence soon after separation of the existence of the illness or injury and prior to manifestation of disability is often necessary in establishing service connection and what VA calls continuity of the disabling condition. These types of claims are very common for any age of veteran, be it a young veteran or a veteran who is aged. For some other types of claims involving direct service connection, continuity of symptoms must be established but not necessarily manifestation early on. Some disabling conditions may not show up for years. For claims where evidence is lacking of manifestation of a continuity of chronic conditions resulting from incurrence in service but show up many years after discharge, a medical opinion from a licensed health care practitioner must be provided to establish a link between the incurrence in service and the current condition.

Here's an interesting ruling from the Board of the Veterans Appeals concerning these kinds of claims. We think it is an interesting study in detail as to how decisions for direct service-connected claims are made.

> Service connection may be granted for disability resulting from a disease or injury incurred in or aggravated by military service. 38 U.S.C.A. § 1110; 38 C.F.R. § 3.303. In addition, service connection may be presumed for certain chronic diseases, including arthritis, that are manifested to a compensable degree within one year after service. 38 U.S.C.A. §§ 1101, 1112; 38 C.F.R. §§ 3.307, 3.309(a). For the showing of chronic disease in service, there must be a combination of manifestations sufficient to identify the disease entity and sufficient observation to establish chronicity at the time. If chronicity in service is not established, evidence of continuity of symptoms after discharge is required to support the claim. 38 C.F.R. § 3.303(b). Service connection may also be granted for a disease diagnosed after discharge when all the evidence, including that pertinent to service, establishes that the disease was incurred in service. 38 C.F.R. § 3.303(d).
>
> To establish service connection, there must be (1) medical evidence of current disability; (2) medical, or in certain circumstances, lay evidence of in-service incurrence or aggravation of a disease or injury; and (3) medical evidence of a nexus between the claimed in-service disease or injury and the current disability. Hickson v. Ist, 12 Vet. App. 247 (1999); see also Degmetich v. Brown, 104 F.3d 1328 (Fed. Cir. 1997); Brammer v. Derwinski, 3 Vet. App. 223 (1992). This determination is based on an analysis of all the evidence of record and evaluation of its credibility and probative value. Baldwin v. Ist, 13 Vet. App. 1 (1999).
>
> There is no reference to back problems, symptoms, or diagnoses in any of the veteran's service medical records. Nor is there any mention of the veteran's use of any back support, as he testified.
>
> Moreover, there is no record of any complaint of or treatment for any back disorder for many years after service. Indeed, on a September 1951 reserve service examination, the veteran's spine was clinically normal. On an accompanying medical history report, the veteran denied any back injury or back problems.
>
> The first mention of any back symptoms was in non-VA treatment in December 2001, that is, over 50 years after service. The diagnosis at that time was backache.
>
> None of the available competent VA or non-VA records attributes any current back problems to the veteran's service.

The Board is mindful of an August 2004 VA examination that concluded that degenerative joint disease of the lumbar spine was "at least as likely as not related to an inservice back injury." The examiner noted having revieid the claims folder. The examiner specifically described a history of an in-service fall (in 1944); the use of a back brace throughout the remainder of the veteran's active service; treatment for back problems at a VA facility in Memphis, Tennessee, in 1962; and constant back pain ever since the in-service incident. However, that history cannot be based on a review of the claims folder and relevant medical history, since there is no documentation of the specified treatment at those particular times. Indeed, the VA facility in Memphis has replied that it does not have records of any treatment for the veteran. Moreover, the service medical records do not document any treatment for a 1944 or other in-service back injury or the use of a back brace in service. Thus, it appears that the August 2004 VA examination is premised on the veteran's recitations.

A bare conclusion (even from a medical professional) is not probative without a factual predicate in the record. Miller v. Ist, 11 Vet. App. 345 (1998). A medical opinion premised on an unsubstantiated account is of no probative value and does not verify the occurrences described. Swann v. Brown, 5 Vet. App. 229 (1993); cf. Howell v. Nicholson, No. 04-0624, __ Vet. App. __, 2006 WL 760181 (Vet. App. Mar. 23, 2006). The Board is not bound to accept a doctor's opinion based exclusively on a claimant's recitations. Reonal v. Brown, 5 Vet. App. 458, 461 (1993). As a result, the August 2004 VA examination is not probative as to any relationship between the veteran's service and any current back disorder.

Thus, the Board finds that the weight of the credible, competent evidence demonstrates that the veteran did not develop a back disorder during his service or because of any incident therein. As the preponderance of the evidence is against this claim, the "benefit-of-the-doubt" rule does not apply, and the Board must deny the claim. 38 U.S.C.A. § 5107(b) (Ist 2002).

In this particular case, the doctor's opinion was evidently biased. If enough evidence is produced to show that there is a reasonable assumption or inference that the current disability exhibits a continuity of symptoms as well as some sort of evidence of injury in the service, then an appropriately prepared opinion from a physician allows VA to make a favorable decision.

Also remember that for these types of claims, especially where there is scanty evidence of the incurrence of an illness or injury in the service, current disabling conditions that could be attributed to combat or being a prisoner of war are usually accepted based on the testimony of the claimant alone with no other corroborating evidence. For peacetime service or noncombatant service, testimony of the claimant or other witnesses is not enough without other supporting physical evidence such as service treatment records or personnel records or credible buddy statements where inference can be drawn that the in-service incurrence took place.

If it is going to take you some time to assemble the evidence for the application, do an "Intent to File" using the following form: VA Form 21-0966 INTENT TO FILE

Forms That Might Be Used:
VA Form 10-5345 – Request for and Authorization to Release VHA Medical Records
VA Form 10-5345a – Individual's Request for a Copy of His or Her Own VA Medical Records
VA Form 21-526EZ – Application for Disability Compensation and Related Compensation Benefits
VA Form 21-4176 – Report of Accidental Injury in Support of Claim for Compensation or Pension Statement of Witness to Accident
VA Form 21-4142 – Authorization and Consent to Release information to the Department of Veterans Affairs
Forms for Representation for Assistance if Desired
VA Form 21-22A – Appointment of Individual a Claimant's Representative
VA Form 21-0845 – Authorization to Disclose Personal information to a Third Party

Checklist Steps in the Fully Developed Claim Process to Follow:

Go to Page 214 for more detail on these steps

1. Determine Entitlement Based on Service and the Merit of Your Claim
2. Submit an Intent to File, VA Form 21-0966, but Don't File a Claim at This Point
3. Obtain a Copy of Your Discharge
4. Obtain Copies of Service Treatment Records
5. Obtain Copies of Your Military Personnel File
6. Obtain of Copies of VA Medical Center Records
7. Obtain Copies of Your Own Private Medical Records
8. Obtain Your Own DBQs from Private Clinicians
9. Obtain Your Own Private Medical Opinions
10. Write a Detailed and Credible Lay Statement to Describe Your Claim
11. Follow Our Instructions in Chapter 4 for Submitting the Claim

6. Secondary Service Connection or Aggravation of a Preservice Condition

Details:
Here are the rules for this type of claim from 38 CFR § 3.310 and § 3.322

(Section 3.310)
(a) General. Except as provided in §3.300(c), disability which is proximately due to or the result of a service-connected disease or injury shall be service connected. When service connection is thus established for a secondary condition, the secondary condition shall be considered a part of the original condition.

(b) Aggravation of nonservice-connected disabilities. Any increase in severity of a nonservice-connected disease or injury that is proximately due to or the result of a service-connected disease or injury, and not due to the natural progress of the nonservice-connected disease, will be service connected. However, VA will not concede that a nonservice-connected disease or injury was aggravated by a service-connected disease or injury unless the baseline level of severity of the nonservice-connected disease or injury is established by medical evidence created before the onset of aggravation or by the earliest medical evidence created at any time between the onset of aggravation and the receipt of medical evidence establishing the current level of severity of the nonservice-connected disease or injury. The rating activity will determine the baseline and current levels of severity under the Schedule for Rating Disabilities (38 CFR part 4) and determine the extent of aggravation by deducting the baseline level of severity, as well as any increase in severity due to the natural progress of the disease, from the current level.

(c) Cardiovascular disease. Ischemic heart disease or other cardiovascular disease developing in a veteran who has a service-connected amputation of one lower extremity at or above the knee or service-connected amputations of both lower extremities at or above the ankles, shall be held to be the proximate result of the service-connected amputation or amputations.

(Section 3.322)
(a) Aggravation of preservice disability. In cases involving aggravation by active service, the rating will reflect only the degree of disability over and above the degree of disability existing at the time of entrance into active service, whether the particular condition was noted at the time of entrance into active service, or whether it is determined upon the evidence of record to have existed at that time. It is necessary to deduct from the present evaluation the degree, if ascertainable, of the disability existing at the time of entrance into active service, in terms of the rating schedule except that if the disability is total (100 percent) no deduction will be made. If the degree of disability at the time of entrance into service is not ascertainable in terms of the schedule, no deduction will be made.

(b) Aggravation of service-connected disability. Where a disease or injury incurred in peacetime service is aggravated during service in a period of war, or conversely, where a disease or injury incurred in service during a period of war is aggravated during peacetime service, the entwere disability flowing from the disease or injury will be service connected based on the war service.

Here is a summary of these rules.
Service connection can be granted under 38 CFR 3.310 above when disabilities are proximately due to or the result of a service-connected condition or the increase in severity of a non-service-connected disability. This increase in severity of a non-service-connected disability has to be attributable to aggravation by a service-connected disability and not due to the natural progress of that non-service-connected disability.

The baseline of the non-service connected disability which was aggravated by a service-connected disability must be established by medical evidence created before the onset of aggravation. Or if this is not possible, the earliest medical evidence that can be created between the onset of aggravation and receipt of medical evidence establishing the current level of severity of the non-service connected disability. If it is impossible to establish a baseline to determine the severity of aggravation, it is unlikely that there will be an award. Medical records are critical to this type of claim. The veteran must furnish medical evidence of the current level of severity of the non-service connected disability and medical evidence of its level of severity prior to the point at which it was being aggravated by the service-connected disability.

Once the rating authority has this information, a medical examination will be requested directing an opinion by the examiner to establish whether the examiner feels that the severity of the non-service connected disability is proximately due to the service-connected disability. The examiner must have all of the private records of the veteran establishing the baseline for review when providing an opinion on the issue of aggravation. The examiner's report must separately address all of the following medical issues in order to be considered adequate for rating a claim for secondary service connection based on aggravation:

- the current level of severity of the non-service connected disease or injury
- an opinion as to whether a service-connected disability proximately caused the non-service connected disability to increase in severity, and
- the medical considerations supporting this opinion.

The rating activity will use this information as the primary source of evidence for making a decision whether there was aggravation or not and whether it is ratable or not.

If enough evidence is produced to show that there is a reasonable assumption or inference that the non-service connected secondary disability is due to the service-connected disability, then a strong opinion letter from a physician might sway VA to make a favorable decision. With these particular kinds of claims you may also want to provide your own private doctor's opinion.

If it is going to take you some time to assemble the evidence for the application, do an "Intent to File" using the following form:

VA Form 21-0966 INTENT TO FILE

Forms That Might Be Used:
VA Form 10-5345 – Request for and Authorization to Release VHA Medical Records
VA Form 10-5345a – Individual's Request for a Copy of His or Her Own VA Medical Records
VA Form 21-4142 – Authorization and Consent to Release information to the Department of Veterans Affairs
VA Form 21-526EZ – Application for Disability Compensation and Related Compensation Benefits

Forms for Representation for Assistance if Desired
VA Form 21-22A – Appointment of Individual a Claimant's Representative
VA Form 21-0845 – Authorization to Disclose Personal information to a Third Party

Steps in the Claim Process to Follow:
This is a new application unless there has been a previous decision relating to the same set of conditions within one year. You will use form 21-526EZ for this application if it is been longer than a year. You will use VA Form 20-0995, supplemental claim, if it has been less than a year since a decision notice. VA already has your pertinent information for service connection in

VBMS and as such you will not have to resubmit your discharge documents or documents relating to your dependents. You should furnish your VA file number on the particular form you are using.

Application for Secondary Disability

For secondary disability, you simply need to furnish the appropriate medical records and in most cases you will need a medical opinion to establish the relationship between the underlying primary service-connected disability and the disability that is proximately due to it. If you have never made a claim for secondary disability, but you are entitled to a claim for direct service connection or presumptive service connection, we have found that due to incompetency in the Regional Office in understanding the difference between direct service connection and secondary service connection, that it is best to establish the service-connected disability first and then go back with submission of VA Form 20-0995 with the appropriate evidence to establish secondary service connection. As long as you do this within one year of the decision notice, VA will go back at least one year to the point at which the secondary disability was manifested as evidenced by medical records.

Application for Aggravation

The key to this application is support from your private medical records by establishing a level of disability from the non-service connected condition prior to aggravation. Later records must show a worsening of the non-service-connected disability and the presumption that it is connected to the service-connected disability. The better these records can show a contrast from the so-called "baseline," the better your chance of getting a favorable opinion, if indeed the service-connected disability is the cause.

Also, have your physicians or specialists prepare a "Disability Benefit Questionnawere" pertaining to the particular condition or illness for which you are requesting an evaluation. These DBQ's are found on the claim support Claim Support Disc.

Make sure that you submit all of your private medical records as well as the DBQ pertaining to the new condition along with the change request Form. This will allow your application to be treated as fully developed and should result in a medical examination fairly quickly. Otherwise, without all of the additional information, the development team may take a long time to get around to getting more evidence in order to have the rating activity order an exam.

This is an initial application for disability. You will use VA Form 21-526 EZ along with the other documents and evidence recommended in this section.

7. Exposure to Hazards, Chemicals and Harmful Environmental Conditions

Camp Lejeune

From the 1950s through the 1980s, people living or working at the U.S. Marine Corps Base Camp Lejeune, North Carolina, were potentially exposed to drinking water contaminated with industrial solvents, benzene, and other chemicals.

VA has established a presumptive service connection for Veterans, Reservists, and National Guard members exposed to contaminants in the water supply at Camp Lejeune from August 1, 1953 through December 31, 1987 who later developed one of the following eight diseases:

- Adult leukemia
- Aplastic anemia and other myelodysplastic syndromes
- Bladder cancer
- Kidney cancer
- Liver cancer
- Multiple myeloma
- Non-Hodgkin's lymphoma
- Parkinson's disease

Presently, these conditions are the only ones for which there is sufficient scientific and medical evidence to support the creation of presumptions; however, VA will continue to review relevant information as it becomes available.

Veterans who are experiencing other health conditions that they think may be related to contaminated water at Camp Lejeune are encouraged to contact their primary care provider and to file a claim. VA reviews and decides Disability Compensation claims on a case-by-case basis.

In accordance with the 2012 Camp Lejeune health care law, VA provides cost-free health care for certain conditions to Veterans who served at least 30 days of active duty at Camp Lejeune from January 1, 1957 and December 31, 1987.

Qualifying health conditions include:

- Esophageal cancer
- Breast cancer
- Kidney cancer
- Multiple myeloma
- Renal toxicity
- Female infertility
- Scleroderma
- Non-Hodgkin's lymphoma
- Lung cancer
- Bladder cancer
- Leukemia

- Myelodysplastic syndromes
- Hepatic steatosis
- Miscarriage
- Neurobehavioral effects

Veterans eligible for health care under the 2012 Camp Lejeune health care law may enroll in VA health care and receive medical services for the 15 covered health conditions at no cost (including copayments).

Not yet enrolled in VA health care? Apply online or call 1-877-222-8387 for help. In Form VA staff that you served on active duty at Camp Lejeune for at least 30 days during the time period.

Family members of Veterans who also resided at Camp Lejeune during the qualifying period are eligible for reimbursement of out-of-pocket medical expenses related to the 15 covered health conditions. VA can pay treatment costs that remain after payment from your other health plans.

Apply online for reimbursement or call 1-866-372-1144 for help.

What type of evidence can I submit with my application?

- Documentation showing dependent relationship to a Veteran who served at Camp Lejeune, such as marriage license or birth certificate
- Documentation showing you lived on the base for 30 days or more between Aug. 1, 1953 and Dec. 31, 1987 such as copies of orders or base housing records
- You paid health care expenses for a covered condition respective to the following date ranges.
- If you lived on Camp Lejeune between January 1, 1957 and December 31, 1987, then you can be reimbursed for care that you received on or after August 6, 2012
- If you lived on Camp Lejeune between August 1, 1953 and December 31, 1956, then you can be reimbursed for care that you received on or after December 16, 2014

When evidence is not submitted, VA will use all relevant evidence from internal sources and the Department of Defense (DoD) to support your application. Please be aware it may take longer to review your application.

OTHER HAZARD APPLICATIONS

Details:
The veteran may have been exposed to any one or more of the following during active duty:

- Harmful sounds from guns, equipment and machinery used during military service
- Vietnam Era veterans who are at risk for hepatitis C
- Depleted uranium used in military tank armor and some bullets
- (Qarmat Ali) Hexavalent chromium in contaminated sodium dichromate dust; water treatment plant in 2003
- Camp Lejeune Water Supplies

- Burn Pits – Open-air pit waste disposal at military sites
- (Gulf War) Substances used to repel or destroy pests such as insects and pathogens
- PCBs – Polychlorinated biphenyls used as coolant and insulating fluid
- Industrial Solvents – Usually a liquid used to dissolve, degrease, clean, strip paint, etc.
- Exposure during military service to the airborne hazards listed below could potentially cause certain health problems in Veterans, depending on a number of other factors.
  - Atsugi Waste Incinerator Atsugi, Japan: Combustion waste disposal that burned industrial and medical waste
  - Oil Well Fire, Smoke (Gulf War)
  - Oil or gas wells that caught on fire and burned during the 1990-1991 Gulf War
  - Sand, Dust and Particulates Tiny airborne matter that can cause respiratory and other health problems
  - Sulfur Fire (Al Mishraq, Iraq)
  - Responding to concerns of many returning Veterans, VA will continue to study the health risks of pollution in Iraq and Afghanistan, including burn pit smoke, and establish a burn pit registry for eligible
- Asbestos Mineral – fiber used in older buildings and an older ships; if inhaled deeply into the lungs can cause health problems
- Vibration – Periodic back and forth movement that if severe, can cause health conditions
- Lead Metal that can be toxic for certain uses
- Noise – Harmful sounds from guns, equipment, airplanes, combat vehicles and machinery that is often experienced during military service
- Exposure to extreme heat or extreme cold
- Heavy equipment including armored vests that may cause deterioration of bodily joints
- Herbicide Tests and Storage
- Radiation – Dental technicians, nuclear iapons technicians, and others with routine and usually safe exposure
- CARC Paint – Chemical Agent Resistant Coating (CARC) used on military vehicles to resist corrosion and chemical agents
- Fuels (Petroleum, Oils, Lubricants) – Fuels such as diesel and JP-8 used to operate vehicles in the military
- Use of biological toxins or infectious agents with intent to kwell or incapacitate
- Nerve Agents – Toxic chemicals that attack the body's nervous system
- Mustard Gas – Odorless, poisonous gas used during World War I, II, and military tests in the 1940s
- Project 112/Project SHAD – Military tests of chemical/biological warfare materials conducted in the 1960s to early 1970s
- Edgewood/Aberdeen Experiments – Classified medical studies of low-dose chemical agents conducted from 1955-1975
- Agent Orange and other herbicides used in Vietnam. Agent Orange and other herbicides used in Vietnam were tested or stored elsewhere, including some military bases in the United States.
  - Exposure to Agent Orange in Vietnam Exposure on land in Vietnam or on a ship operating on the inland waterways of Vietnam between January 9, 1962 and May 7, 1975

- Blue Water Veterans Possible exposure on open sea ships off the shore of Vietnam during the Vietnam War
- U.S. Navy and Coast Guard Ships in Vietnam List of ships and boats with operations in Vietnam between January 9, 1962 and May 7, 1975
- Korean Demilitarized Zone Exposure along the demilitarized zone in Korea between April 1, 1968 and August 31, 1971
- Thailand Military Bases Possible exposure on or near the perimeters of military bases between February 28, 1961 and May 7, 1975
- Herbicide Tests and Storage Outside Vietnam Possible exposure due to herbicide tests and storage at military bases in the United States and locations in other countries
- Agent Orange Residue on Airplanes Used in the Vietnam War Possible exposure of crew members to herbicide residue in C-123 planes flown after Vietnam War

On the Claim Support Disc, we provide a list of all of the storage and testing sites known for Agent Orange in the United States and internationally. If you want to pursue a claim for exposure beyond Vietnam, this will give you a head start.

Almost without exception, these types of claims typically do not involve treatment in service and as such there is no service medical record. In addition, the conditions which show up, such as cancer many years later, do not manifest the continuity of symptoms from discharge. These are the most difficult claims to receive an award for service connection.

The key to this type of application is demonstrating that "you were in the right place at the right time" so to speak. The more likely the nexus between your current condition and the exposure, the more likely the inference that it occurred in service. Conditions caused by these types of exposure may not manifest until many years after getting out of the service. Trying to show evidence of the continuity of symptoms, as in other claims, is more difficult with one of these claims. The crucial issue in establishing service connection is that the chronic condition that you currently have is known to be caused by the particular exposure that you incurred in service. You most definitely must have an opinion letter from your treating physicians as to the probability of this link to service connection. And you will most definitely require additional medical literature evidence that substantiates a link between the type of exposure and the current condition. The exception here is hearing loss, which is generally accepted by VA if there is proof of exposure to loud noises or sudden pressure changes in service.

This is likely going to be one of those claims based on reasonable doubt. VA will not be able to prove beyond a 50-50 probability that you did not incur the current disability because of an exposure in service, and must use the principle of reasonable doubt to award you the benefit.

Proving you were at an assignment where you were exposed to the hazard, the chemicals or the environment is crucial. There also has to be some sort of evidence that the level of exposure was sufficient enough to cause injury, disease or disorder. Or this must be self-evident because of the assignment. In addition you may have to provide medical literature that corroborates whatever is wrong with you now, could have been caused by the exposure. For example, certain cancers are known to be caused to by exposure to CARC Paint or to solvents and so forth.

If enough evidence is produced to show that there is a reasonable assumption or inference that the current disability is service-connected, then a strong opinion letter from a private physician is needed to sway VA to make a favorable decision. Relying on a VA scheduled opinion exam will likely not get you the benefit. Contract examiners providing opinions for VA for these types of claims are almost without exception going to provide an opinion that there is no service connection. Careful medical literature research and collaboration with a medical specialist is typically the best way to win one of these claims.

If it is going to take you some time to assemble the evidence for the application, do an "Intent to File" using the following form:

VA Form 21-0966 INTENT TO FILE

Forms That Might Be Used:
VA Form 10-5345 – Request for and Authorization to Release VHA Medical Records
VA Form 10-5345a – Individual's Request for a Copy of His or Her Own VA Medical Records
VA Form 21-526EZ – Application for Disability Compensation and Related Compensation Benefits
VA Form 21-4192 – Request for Employment information in Connection With Claim for Disability Benefits
VA Form 21-8951-2 -1 – Notice of Waiver of VA Compensation to Receive Military Pay and Allowances

Forms for Representation for Assistance if Desired
VA Form 21-22A – Appointment of Individual a Claimant's Representative
VA Form 21-0845 – Authorization to Disclose Personal information to a Third Party

Checklist Steps in the Fully Developed Claim Process to Follow:

Go to Page 214 for more detail on these steps

1. Determine Entitlement Based on Service and the Merit of Your Claim
2. Submit an Intent to File, VA Form 21-0966, but Don't File a Claim at This Point
3. Obtain a Copy of Your Discharge
4. Obtain Copies of Service Treatment Records
5. Obtain Copies of Your Military Personnel File
6. Obtain of Copies of VA Medical Center Records
7. Obtain Copies of Your Own Private Medical Records
8. Obtain Your Own DBQs from Private Clinicians
9. Obtain Your Own Private Medical Opinions
10. Write a Detailed and Credible Lay Statement to Describe Your Claim
11. Follow Our Instructions in Chapter 4 for Submitting the Claim

8. PTSD – Posttraumatic Stress Disorder

Details:

Posttraumatic Stress Disorder is a mental disorder classified as an "anxiety" by VA. It is a mental health problem that can occur after someone goes through a traumatic event like war, assault, or disaster. Most people have some stress reactions after a trauma. If the reactions don't go away over time or disrupt your life, you may have PTSD. Because PTSD can affect a person's ability to make an income, it is considered a disabling condition subject to Compensation, if it is severe enough to be rated. Oftentimes, these are difficult claims to establish service connection and a rating, because PTSD cannot be quantifiably measured like other conditions. It requires special evaluations from psychiatrists or other assessment specialists. And if the claimant has been employed, statements from previous employers are usually required in order to establish a rating.

In addition, the service connection is sometimes difficult to establish when PTSD is not caused by engaging in combat. For many sufferers this is the case. <u>If you or the claimant believes you are suffering from PTSD as a result of service and it is causing chronic disability use the research information we have provided for you under "Reference Material" on the Claim Support Disc.</u>

PTSD is becoming a very common claim for disability with applications soaring in the last 10 or so years. In addition, PTSD is often caused by Military Sexual Trauma (MST) which has become an important issue in recent years due to cover up of this atrocious crime with military commanders not reporting incidents or suppressing such complaints. PTSD also leads to the inability to work and many PTSD claims are combined with individual unemployability claims.

38 CFR § 3.304

(f) Posttraumatic stress disorder. Service connection for posttraumatic stress disorder requires medical evidence diagnosing the condition in accordance with §4.125(a) of this chapter; a link, established by medical evidence, between current symptoms and an in-service stressor; and credible supporting evidence that the claimed in-service stressor occurred. The following provisions apply to claims for service connection of posttraumatic stress disorder diagnosed during service or based on specified in-service stressors:

> (1) If the evidence establishes a diagnosis of posttraumatic stress disorder during service and the claimed stressor is related to that service, in the absence of clear and convincing evidence to the contrary, and provided that the claimed stressor is consistent with the circumstances, conditions, or hardships of the veteran's service, the veteran's lay testimony alone may establish the occurrence of the claimed in-service stressor.

> (2) If the evidence establishes that the veteran engaged in combat with the enemy and the claimed stressor is related to that combat, in the absence of clear and convincing evidence to the contrary, and provided that the claimed stressor is consistent with the circumstances, conditions, or hardships of the veteran's service, the veteran's lay testimony alone may establish the occurrence of the claimed in-service stressor.

(3) If the evidence establishes that the veteran was a prisoner-of-war under the provisions of §3.1(y) of this part and the claimed stressor is related to that prisoner-of-war experience, in the absence of clear and convincing evidence to the contrary, and provided that the claimed stressor is consistent with the circumstances, conditions, or hardships of the veteran's service, the veteran's lay testimony alone may establish the occurrence of the claimed in-service stressor.

(4) If a posttraumatic stress disorder claim is based on in-service personal assault, evidence from sources other than the veteran's service records may corroborate the veteran's account of the stressor incident. Examples of such evidence include, but are not limited to: records from law enforcement authorities, rape crisis centers, mental health counseling centers, hospitals, or physicians; pregnancy tests or tests for sexually transmitted diseases; and statements from family members, roommates, fellow service members, or clergy. Evidence of behavior changes following the claimed assault is one type of relevant evidence that may be found in these sources. Examples of behavior changes that may constitute credible evidence of the stressor include, but are not limited to: a request for a transfer to another military duty assignment; deterioration in work per Formance; substance abuse; episodes of depression, panic attacks, or anxiety without an identifiable cause; or unexplained economic or social behavior changes. VA will not deny a posttraumatic stress disorder claim that is based on in-service personal assault without first advising the claimant that evidence from sources other than the veteran's service records or evidence of behavior changes may constitute credible supporting evidence of the stressor and allowing him or her the opportunity to furnish this type of evidence or advise VA of potential sources of such evidence. VA may submit any evidence that it receives to an appropriate medical or mental health professional for an opinion as to whether it indicates that a personal assault occurred.

In order to provide your own private evaluations, you should always seek treatment with a psychiatrist or a PhD psychologist for the evaluation, treatment and an opinion letter. Any other expert would not be considered comparable to the examiners that VA uses. Here are the examiners that VA will use when ordering an examination, which is required for this claim.

- Board-certified psychiatrists.
- Psychiatrists who have successfully completed an accredited psychiatry residency and who are appropriately credentialed and privileged.
- Licensed doctoral-level psychologist.
- Non-licensed doctoral-level psychologists working toward licensure under close supervision by a board-certified, or board-eligible, psychiatrist or a licensed doctoral-level psychologist.
- Psychiatry residents under close supervision by a board-certified, or board-eligible,

If enough evidence is produced to show that there is a reasonable assumption or inference that the PTSD is service-connected, then a strong opinion letter from a psychiatrist or PhD psychologist will be needed to sway VA to make a favorable decision.

The VASRD code for PTSD is 9411 which is included among a large number of mental disorders that are rated or lumped together under the following table.

General Rating Formula for Mental Disorders

	Rating
Total occupational and social impairment, due to such symptoms as: gross impairment in thought processes or communication; persistent delusions or hallucinations; grossly inappropriate behavior; persistent danger of hurting self or others; intermittent inability to per Form activities of daily living (including maintenance of minimal personal hygiene); disorientation to time or place; memory loss for names of close relatives, own occupation, or own name.	100
Occupational and social impairment, with deficiencies in most areas, such as work, school, family relations, judgment, thinking, or mood, due to such symptoms as: suicidal ideation; obsessional rituals which interfere with routine activities; speech intermittently wellogical, obscure, or irrelevant; near-continuous panic or depression affecting the ability to function independently, appropriately and effectively; impawered impulse control (such as unprovoked irritability with periods of violence); spatial disorientation; neglect of personal appearance and hygiene; difficulty in adapting to stressful circumstances (including work or a worklike setting); inability to establish and maintain effective relationships.	70
Occupational and social impairment with reduced reliability and productivity due to such symptoms as: flattened affect; circumstantial, circumlocutory, or stereotyped speech; panic attacks more than once a iek; difficulty in understanding complex commands; impairment of short- and long-term memory (e.g., retention of only highly learned material, forgetting to complete tasks); impawered judgment; impawered abstract thinking; disturbances of motivation and mood; difficulty in establishing and maintaining effective work and social relationships.	50
Occupational and social impairment with occasional decrease in work efficiency and intermittent periods of inability to per Form occupational tasks (although generally functioning satisfactorily, with routine behavior, self-care, and conversation normal), due to such symptoms as: depressed mood, anxiety, suspiciousness, panic attacks (iekly or less often), chronic sleep impairment, mild memory loss (such as forgetting names, directions, recent events).	30
Occupational and social impairment due to mild or transient symptoms which decrease work efficiency and ability to per Form occupational tasks only during periods of significant stress, or symptoms controlled by continuous medication.	10
A mental condition has been Formally diagnosed, but symptoms are not severe enough either to interfere with occupational and social functioning or to require continuous medication.	0

Instructions for PTSD Claims from the Adjudication Manual M 21-1

Establishing Stressors for In-Service Connection for PTSD
Under 38 CFR 3.304(f), service connection (SC) for posttraumatic stress disorder (PTSD) associated with an in-service stressor requires

- credible supporting evidence that the claimed in-service stressor actually occurred

- medical evidence diagnosing the condition in accordance with 38 CFR 4.125, and
- a link, established by medical evidence, between current symptomatology and the claimed in-service stressor.

When a Veteran's Lay Testimony Alone May Establish an In-Service Stressor
A Veteran's lay testimony alone may, under specified circumstances, establish an in-service stressor for purposes of establishing SC for PTSD if

- PTSD is diagnosed in service, and the stressor is related to that service, or
- the stressor is related to the Veteran's
  - engagement in combat with the enemy
  - experience as a former prisoner of war (FPOW) as defined by 38 CFR 3.1(y), or
  - the stressor is related to fear of hostile military or terrorist activity or duties as a drone aircraft crew member, if a Department of Veterans Affairs (VA) psychiatrist or psychologist, or contract equivalent, confirms
  - the claimed stressor is adequate to support a diagnosis of PTSD, and
  - the Veteran's symptoms are related to the claimed stressor.

For the Veteran's lay testimony alone to establish the occurrence of a claimed stressor the stressor must be consistent with the

- circumstances, conditions, or hardships of service for claims based on an in-service PTSD diagnosis or FPOW or combat service, or
- places, types, and circumstances of service for claims based on a fear of hostile military or terrorist activity or duties as a drone aircraft crew member, and
- there must be no clear and convincing evidence to the contrary.

For claims decided prior to July 13, 2010, a Veteran's testimony alone could not establish the occurrence of a stressor that was related to the Veteran's fear of hostile military or terrorist activity. The July 13, 2010, amendment of 38 CFR 3.304(f) is not considered a liberalizing rule under 38 CFR 3.114(a).

Engaging in Combat with the Enemy
Engaging in combat with the enemy means personal participation in events constituting an actual fight or encounter with a military foe or hostile unit or instrumentality. It includes presence during such events either as a

- combatant, or
- service member performing duty in support of combatants, such as providing medical care to the wounded.

Fear of Hostile Military or Terrorist Activity
Fear of hostile military or terrorist activity means
- the Veteran experienced, witnessed, or was confronted with an event or circumstance that involved
  - actual or threatened death or serious injury, or

- - a threat to the physical integrity of the Veteran or others, and
  - the Veteran's response to the event or circumstances involved a psychological or psycho-physiological state of fear, helplessness, or horror.
- Examples of exposure to hostile military or terrorist activity include presence at events involving
  - actual or potential improvised explosive devices (IEDs)
  - vehicle-embedded explosive devices
  - incoming artwellery, rocket, or mortar fire
  - small arms fire, including suspected sniper fire, or
  - attacks upon friendly aircraft.

Individual Decorations as Evidence of Combat Participation

When a Veteran has received any of the combat decorations listed below, VA will presume that the Veteran engaged in combat with the enemy, unless there is clear and convincing evidence to the contrary

- Air Force Achievement Medal with "V" Device
- Air Force Combat Action Medal
- Air Force Commendation Medal with "V" Device
- Air Force Cross
- Air Medal with "V" Device
- Army Commendation Medal with "V" Device
- Bronze Star Medal with "V" Device
- Combat Action Badge (CAB)
- Combat Action Ribbon (CAR) (*Note*: Prior to February 1969, the Navy Achievement Medal with "V" Device was awarded.)
- Combat Aircrew Insignia
- Combat Infantry/Infantryman Badge (CIB)
- Combat Medical Badge
- Distinguished Flying Cross
- Distinguished Service Cross
- Fleet Marine Force (FMF) Combat Operations Insignia
- Joint Service Commendation Medal with "V" Device
- Medal of Honor
- Navy Commendation Medal with "V" Device
- Navy Cross
- Purple Heart, and/or
- Silver Star.

Receipt of one of the decorations cited above is not the only acceptable evidence of engagement in combat.

Establishing a Stressor Related to Fear of Hostile Military or Terrorist Activity and When to Schedule an Examination

Schedule an examination if there is evidence of a PTSD diagnosis or symptoms, and the Veteran's DD 214, Certificate of Release or Discharge From Active Duty, or other service records, shows service in an area of potential hostile military or terrorist activity.

Notes:
- Service personnel records must be requested prior to or concurrently with any necessary examination being ordered so as to avoid unnecessary delays in claims processing.
- The receipt of military awards such as, but not limited to, the Vietnam Service or Campaign Medal, Kuwait Liberation Medal, Iraq Campaign Medal, and Afghanistan Campaign Medal is generally considered evidence of service in an area of potential hostile military or terrorist activity.
- The receipt of military awards such as the National Defense Service Medal, Armed Forces Service Medal, and Global War on Terrorism (GWOT) Service Medal generally does not indicate service in locations that involve exposure to hostile military or terrorist activity because these are general medals that do not denote service in a particular area or campaign. If the Veteran served in an area of potential hostile military or terrorist activity, he/she would have received a more specific medal for such service.

Establishing a Stressor Related to Drone Aircraft Crew Member Duties and When to Schedule an Examination

The GWOT has seen expansive use of armed drone aircraft, including, but not limited to, the Predator and Reaper. Schedule an examination if there is evidence of a PTSD diagnosis or symptoms, and the Veteran's DD 214 or other service records shows service as an armed drone aircraft crew member. Service personnel records must be requested prior to or concurrently with any necessary examination being ordered so as to avoid unnecessary delays in claims processing.

When In-Service Stressor Corroboration Is Required

Develop to corroborate the details of a claimed in-service stressor only when the claimed stressor does not meet one of the criteria in M21-1, Part III, Subpart iv, 4.H.3.a. Examples of claimed stressors that must be corroborated are

- a plane crash caused by severe iather
- a severe motor vehicle accident
- witnessing the death, injury, or threat to the physical being of another person caused by something other than hostile military or terrorist activity, and
- actual or threatened death or serious injury, or other threat to one's physical being, caused by something other than hostile military or terrorist activity.

Primary Evidence to Corroborate a Claimed In-Service Stressor

Primary evidence is generally considered the most reliable source for corroborating in-service stressors and should be carefully revieid when corroboration is required. It is typically obtained from the National Archives and Records Administration (NARA) or Department of Defense (DoD) entities, such as service departments, the U.S. Army and Joint Services Records Research Center (JSRRC), and the Marine Corps University Archives (MCUA).

Primary evidence includes

- service personnel records and pay records
- military occupation evidence
- hazard pay records
- military performance reports
- verification that the Veteran received Combat/Imminent Danger/Hostile Fire Pay
- unit and organizational histories
- daily staff journals
- operational reports-lessons learned (ORLLs)
- after action reports (AARs)
- radio logs, deck logs, and ship histories
- muster rolls
- command chronologies and war diaries, and
- monthly summaries and morning reports.

Notes:

- Many of the unit documents listed above are available on the Compensation Service Intranet site, Stressor Verification.
- A Veteran's military occupation may be specified on his/her DD 214 or in service personnel records.
- This information may be requested from the Department of Defense Finance and Accounting Service (DFAS).
- Military performance reports may be requested via the Personnel Information Exchange System (PIES).
- Combat/Imminent Danger/Hostile Fire Pay may be requested through the Veterans Information Solution (VIS).
- While confirmation of receipt of Combat/Imminent Danger/Hostile Fire Pay through VIS alone does not constitute verification of a combat-related stressor, it may, in combination with other evidence, "tip the scales" in favor of the Veteran's assertion of his/her involvement in combat.

Secondary Sources of Evidence That May Corroborate a Claimed In-Service Stressor
Review the following secondary sources of evidence critically and carefully for information confirming participation in combat or to otherwise corroborate a claimed in-service stressor when corroboration is required

- buddy statements
- contemporaneous letters and diaries
- newspaper archives, and
- information from Veterans Benefits Administration (VBA)-sanctioned ib sites, which may be accessed through the PTSD Rating Job Aid ib site.

Important: It may not be necessary to corroborate the claimed stressor if it is related to the Veteran's fear of hostile military or terrorist activity or drone aircraft crew member duties, and consistent with the places, types, and circumstances of the Veteran's service.

Accepting Buddy Statements of a Fellow Veteran as Corroboration of a Claimed In-Service Stressor

Accept a buddy statement from a fellow Veteran as corroboration of a claimed in-service stressor if the statement is consistent with the time, place, and circumstances of the service of both the Veteran and the fellow Veteran making the buddy statement. If the evidence available calls into question the qualifications of the fellow Veteran to make the statement, ask the person to submit his/her DD 214 or other evidence of service with the claimant.

Notes:

Upon receipt of a DD 214 (or other document containing personally identifiable information (PII)) from a fellow Veteran in support of a paper-based claim

- place the document in a separate envelope in the claims folder, and
- annotate on the envelope that the contents must not be
- reproduced, or
- revieid by the Veteran to whom the claims folder pertains or his/her representative.
- In paperless claims processing, individual documents bearing the PII of a Veteran other than the claimant should be designated with a VBMS bookmark or SUBJECT value that clearly identifies the restricted nature of the content.

When to Request Evidence from the Veteran to Establish an In-Service Stressor

Request the Veteran provide credible supporting evidence to establish that an in-service stressor occurred unless the evidence of record shows that

- PTSD was diagnosed in service, and the claimed stressor is related to that service, or
- the claimed stressor is related to the Veteran's
- verified combat or FPOW service and consistent with the circumstances, conditions, or hardships of such service, or
- fear of hostile military or terrorist activity, or the Veteran served as a drone aircraft crew member, and exposure to such activity is consistent with the places, types, and circumstances of the Veteran's service.

Minimum Information Required From the Veteran Related to an In-Service Stressor

At a minimum, the Veteran must provide the following

- a stressor that can be documented
- the location where the incident took place
- the approximate date (within a two-month period) of the incident, and
- the unit of assignment at the time the stressful event occurred.

Inform the Veteran that

- the information is necessary to obtain supportive evidence of each of the stressful events, and
- failure to respond or an incomplete response may result in denial of the claim.

Exception: There is no regulatory requirement for credible supporting evidence of a pre-service stressor resulting in delayed onset of PTSD in service. If a Veteran is sound on enlistment and develops delayed or late-onset PTSD in service related to a pre-service stressor, SC may be established under 38 U.S.C. 1110, which contains the general criteria for establishing SC for a chronic disability.

Notes:
- Specific details of claimed stressful events may also be gathered from such sources as VA or private medical treatment reports and examination reports.
- Veterans Service Representatives (VSRs) may obtain the date and location of well-documented events, such as the Tet Offensive, from VBA-sanctioned ib sites (available through the PTSD Rating Job Aid ib site) and supply this information on the Veteran's behalf.

When to Request Corroboration of an In-Service Stressor Unrelated to Personal Trauma or MST *(Military sexual trauma, or MST, is the term used by the Department of Veterans Affairs (VA) to refer to experiences of sexual assault or repeated, threatening sexual harassment that a Veteran experienced during his or her military service.)*

Submit a request for corroboration of an in-service stressor unrelated to personal trauma or MST if

- the evidence does not corroborate the Veteran's claim that he/she engaged in combat, served as an FPOW, was exposed to hostile military or terrorist activity, served as a drone aircraft crew member, or experienced other in-service stressor(s)
- the in-service stressor claimed is capable of being documented
- the Veteran's records contain
- evidence of a diagnosis of PTSD, such as outpatient treatment records showing treatment for PTSD,

OR
- competent lay evidence of persistent or recurrent symptoms of PTSD, such as the Veteran's description of symptoms indicative of PTSD, and
- development is complete in every respect except for
- corroboration of the in-service stressor, and
- a confirmed diagnosis of PTSD.

Important:
- Do not schedule a VA examination before receiving corroboration of the claimed in-service stressor.
- A diagnosis of PTSD is not a prerequisite for initiating the stressor verification process.

- Some stressors are clearly impossible to document and should not be referred to the JSRRC (formerly the U.S. Armed Services Center for Unit Records Research (CURR)), NARA, or the Marine Corps. If, after requesting/obtaining pertinent facts from the Veteran it is obvious that corroboration simply is not feasible, the claim should be decided based on the evidence of record.

General Information on Personal Trauma

Personal trauma for the purpose of VA Disability Compensation claims based on PTSD refers broadly to stressor events involving harm perpetrated by a person who is not considered part of an enemy force.

Examples: Assault, battery, robbery, mugging, stalking, harassment.
Military sexual trauma is a subset of personal trauma and refers to sexual harassment, sexual assault, or rape that occurs in a military setting.

Evidence Required to Establish Service Connection Based on In-Service Personal Trauma

To establish SC for PTSD based on in-service personal trauma, there must be credible evidence to support the Veteran's assertion that the stressful event occurred. This does not mean that the evidence actually proves that the incident occurred, but that there is at least an approximate balance of positive and negative evidence that the event did occur.

Note: Veterans whose stressor occurred during inactive duty for training (INACDUTRA) are eligible for SC in the same manner as those whose stressor occurred during active duty or active duty for training. VA Office of General Counsel concluded in VAOPGCPREC 08-2001 that "PTSD resulting from sexual assault may be considered a disability resulting from an injury."

Process for Obtaining Information From the Veteran in Claims Based on In-Service Personal Trauma

Identifying possible sources of evidence to support the claim may require asking the Veteran for information concerning the traumatic incident. Make this request as compassionately as possible in order to avoid causing further trauma. Although personal trauma is most often thought of as involving female Veterans, male Veterans may also be involved. Be sure requests for evidence/ information reflect the appropriate gender of the Veteran.

DoD's Reporting Procedures Following MST Incidents

DoD offers two reporting options for MST, restricted and unrestricted. Restricted reporting allows a service member to file a report confidentially without initiating the investigative process. Following an MST incident, a service member may elect one of these reporting options by completing DD Form 2910, Victim Reporting Preference Statement. The service member may also elect an optional sexual assault forensic examination (SAFE), which is performed by a health care provider and is documented on DD Form 2911, Forensic Medical Report: Sexual Assault Examination.
Notes:
- DoD may have used other forms prior to the issuance of DD Form 2910. For example, the Department of the Navy used the form NAVPERS 1752/1, Sexual Assault Incident Data Collection Report.

- In restricted reporting cases, DoD stores the evidence, including results from the SAFE, for one year following the date of the victim's report of sexual assault. If the victim does not claim the evidence or elect an unrestricted report within one year, DoD destroys it.

Problems Associated With Development in Claims Based on Personal Trauma

Because a personal trauma is an extremely personal and sensitive issue

- many incidents of personal trauma are not officially reported, and
- the victims of this type of in-service trauma may find it difficult to produce evidence to support the occurrence of the stressor.

It is often necessary to seek alternative evidence that may demonstrate the presence of markers. The term marker refers to evidentiary signs, events, or circumstances indicating a possibilitythat the claimed stressor occurred, such as reports, lay statements, or behavioral changes that may be associated with the approximate timeframe of the claimed stressor.

Alternative Sources for Information in Claims Based on Personal Trauma

Service records not normally requested may be needed to develop claims for SC for PTSD based on personal trauma, including MST. Responses to a request for information may identify alternative sources for information, such as

- a rape crisis center or center for domestic abuse
- a counseling facility or health clinic
- family members or roommates
- a faculty member
- civilian police reports
- medical reports from civilian physicians or caregivers who treated the Veteran immediately following the incident or sometime later
- a chaplain or clergy
- fellow service members, and
- personal diaries or journals.

We have more information on PTSD on the Claim Support Disc. You may want to read this information to learn more about it before you make a claim.

VA Form 21-0966 INTENT TO FILE

Forms That Might Be Used:

VA Form 10-5345 – Request for and Authorization to Release VHA Medical Records
VA Form 10-5345a – Individual's Request for a Copy of His or Her Own VA Medical Records
VA Form 21-526EZ – Application for Disability Compensation and Related Compensation Benefits
VA Form 21-0781a – Statement in Support of Claim for Service Connection for PTSD Secondary to Personal Assault
VA Form 21-0781 – Statement in Support of Claim for Service Connection for PTSD

VA Form 21-4142 – Authorization and Consent to Release Information to the Department of Veterans Affairs

Forms for Representation for Assistance if Desired
VA Form 21-22A – Appointment of Individual a Claimant's Representative
VA Form 21-0845 – Authorization to Disclose Personal Information to a Third Party

9. Hearing Loss with or without Tinnitus

Details:
Tinnitus and hearing loss are the #1 and #2 most common awarded conditions for Compensation. Tinnitus, by itself, connected to service is ratable at 10% disability. Tinnitus is a ringing or rushing or other sound only perceived by the individual and not by anyone else. Most people describe it as extremely high-pitched. Depending on the degree, it can be very disconcerting and interfere with normal functioning. Generally, service-connected tinnitus should be persistent – meaning it is present most of the time. This establishes it as chronic. Establishing service connection for tinnitus by itself is generally not that difficult. This is because there is no definitive test for this condition and VA must accept the word of the person that it exists.

Tinnitus at 10% – as a combined rating – is often awarded in combination with noise induced hearing loss which is typically rated at 0%. This is because tinnitus is a common symptom of noise induced hearing loss. The hearing loss is much easier to establish as a service connection because the condition can be recognized through testing and because it is well-known that certain noise exposure conditions will cause it. For most cases of hearing loss, you must have the tinnitus or you will only get a 0% rating. With the tinnitus you get 10% as a combined rating.

As long as duty can be established where the claimant was exposed sufficiently to loud noise or sudden air pressure changes resulting in hearing loss, these types of claims are not that difficult to generate an award. If the hearing loss by itself is severe enough, it could result in a combined or single rating of 20%, 30% or even 100%.

Establishing a duty assignment in the service that is consistent with producing noise induced hearing loss and enough exposure over time is often important to winning one of these claims. Your personnel records or other evidence should show that you had such assignments in the service. Listed on the next pages are duty assignments from the Army that VA considers most likely to result in hearing loss. The probability is assigned to each MOS as "highly probable" "moderate probable" and "low probable." This gives you an idea for your own duty assignment.

MOS	JOB TITLE	HIGHLY PROBABLE	MODERATE	LOW
35T	MILITARY INTELLIGENCE SYSTEMS MAINTAINER/INTEGRATOR			X
35X	INTELLIGENCE SENIOR SERGEANT/CHIEF INTELLIGENCE SERGEANT			X
35Y	CHIEF COUNTER INTELLIGENCE/HUMAN INTELLIGENCE SERGEANT			X
35Z	SIGNALS INTELLIGENCE (ELECTRONIC WARFARE) / SENIOR SERGEANT / CHIEF		X	
36B	FINANCIAL MANAGEMENT TECHNICIAN			X
37F	PSYCHOLOGICAL OPERATIONS SPECIALIST			X
38B	CIVIL AFFAIRS SPECIALIST			X
42A	HUMAN RESOURCES SPECIALIST			X
42F	HUMAN RESOURCES INFORMATION SYSTEMS MANAGEMENT SPECIALIST			
42R	ARMY BANDPERSON	X		
42S	SPECIAL BAND MEMBER	X		
43F	HUMAN RESOURCES INFORMATION SYSTEMS MANAGEMENT SPEC			X
46Q	PUBLIC AFFAIRS SPECIALIST			X
46R	PUBLIC AFFAIRS BROADCAST SPECIALIST		X	
46Z	CHIEF PUBLIC AFFAIRS NCO			X
51C	AQUISITION, LOGISTICS & TECHNOLOGY (AL&t) CONTRACTING NCO			X
56M	CHAPLAIN ASSISTANT			X
68A	BIOMEDICAL EQUIPMENT SPECIALIST			X
68D	OPERATING ROOM SPECIALIST			X
68E	DENTAL SPECIALIST		X	
68G	PATIENT ADMINISTRATION SPECIALIST			X
68H	OPTICAL LABORATORY SPECIALIST			X
68J	MEDICAL LOGISTICS SPECIALIST			X
68K	MEDICAL LABORATORY SPECIALIST			X
68M	NUTRITION CARE SPECIALIST			X
68P	RADIOLOGY SPECIALIST			X
68Q	PHARMACY SPECIALIST			X
68R	VETERINARY FOOD INSPECTION SPECIALIST			X
68S	PREVENTIVE MEDICINE SPECIALIST			X
68T	ANIMAL CARE SPECIALIST			X
68V	RESPIRATORY SPECIALIST			X
68W	HEALTH CARE SPECIALIST			X
68X	BEHAVIORAL HEALTH SPECIALIST			X
68Z	CHIEF MEDICAL NCO			X
74D	CHEMICAL, BIOLOGICAL, RADIOLOGICAL AND NUCLEAR (CBRN) SPECIALIST		X	
79R	RECRUITER NCO			X
79S	CAREER COUNSELOR			X
79T	RECRUITING & RETENTION NCO (ARMY NATIONAL GUARD OF THE UNITED STATES)			X
79V	RETENTION & TRANSITION NCO, USAR			X

MOS	JOB TITLE	HIGHLY PROBABLE	MODERATE	LOW
14Z	AIR DEFENSE ARTILLERY SENIOR SERGEANT	X		
15B	AIRCRAFT POWERPLANT REPAIRER	X		
15D	AIRCRAFT POWERTRAIN REPAIRER	X		
15F	AIRCRAFT ELECTRICIAN	X		
15G	AIRCRAFT STRUCTURAL REPAIRER	X		
15H	AIRCRAFT PNEUDRAULICS REPAIRER	X		
15J	OH-58D/ARH ARMAMENT/ELECTRICAL/AVIONICS SYSTEMS REPAIRER	X		
15K	AIRCRAFT COMPONENTS REPAIR SUPERVISOR	X		
15M	UH-1 HELICOPTER REPAIRER (RC)	X		
15N	AVIONICS MECHANIC	X		
15P	AVIATION OPERATIONS SPECIALIST	X		
15Q	AIR TRAFFIC CONTROL OPERATOR	X		
15R	AH-64 ATTACK HELICOPTER REPAIRER	X		
15S	OH-58D/ARH HELICOPTER REPAIRER	X		
15T	UH-60 HELICOPTER REPAIRER	X		
15U	CH-47 HELICOPTER REPAIRER	X		
15V	OBSERVATION/SCOUT HELICOPTER REPAIRER (RC)	X		
15W	UNMANNED AERIAL VEHICLE OPERATOR		X	
15X	AH-64A ARMAMENT/ELECTRICAL/AVIONICS SYSTEMS REPAIRER	X		
15Y	AH-64D ARMAMENT/ELECTRICAL/AVIONICS SYSTEMS REPAIRER	X		
15Z	AIRCRAFT MAINTENANCE SENIOR SERGEANT	X		
18B	SPECIAL FORCES WEAPONS SERGEANT	X		
18C	SPECIAL FORCES ENGINEER SERGEANT	X		
18D	SPECIAL FORCES MEDICAL SERGEANT	X		
18E	SPECIAL FORCES COMMUNICATIONS SERGEANT	X		
18F	SPECIAL FORCES ASSISTANT OPERATIONS & INTELLIGENCE SERGEANT	X		
18Z	SPECIAL FORCES SENIOR SERGEANT	X		
19D	CAVALRY SCOUT	X		
19K	M1 ARMOR CREWMAN	X		
19Z	ARMOR SENIOR SERGEANT	X		
21B	COMBAT ENGINEER (conversion to 12B 1 Oct 10)	X		
21C	BRIDGE CREWMEMBER (conversion to 12C 1 Oct 10)	X		
21D	DIVER (conversion to 12D 1 Oct 10)		X	
21E	CONSTRUCTION EQUIPMENT OPERATOR (conversion to 12N 1 Oct 10)	X		
21G	QUARRYING SPECIALIST (RC) (conversion to 12G 1 Oct 10)	X		
21H	CONSTRUCTION ENGINEERING SUPERVISOR (conversion to 12H 1 Oct 10)	X		
21K	PLUMBER (conversion to 12K 1 Oct 10)		X	
21M	FIREFIGHTER (conversion to 12M 1 Oct 10)	X		
21N	HORIZONTAL CONSTRUCTION ENGINEER (conversion to 12N 1 Oct 10)	X		

MOS	JOB TITLE	HIGHLY PROBABLE	MODERATE	LOW
88H	CARGO SPECIALIST		X	
88K	WATERCRAFT OPERATOR		X	
88L	WATERCRAFT ENGINEER		X	
88M	MOTOR TRANSPORT OPERATOR		X	
88N	TRANSPORTATION MANAGEMENT COORDINATOR			X
88P	RAILWAY EQUIPMENT REPAIRER (RC)	X		
88T	RAILWAY SECTION REPAIRER (RC)	X		
88U	RAILWAY OPERATIONS CREWMEMBER (RC)	X		
88Z	TRANSPORTATION SENIOR SERGEANT	X		
89A	AMMUNITION STOCK CONTROL & ACCOUNTING SPECIALIST			X
89B	AMMUNITION SPECIALIST			X
89D	EXPLOSIVE ORDNANCE DISPOSAL SPECIALIST	X		
91A	M1 ABRAHMS TANK SYSTEM MAINTAINER (FORMERLY 63A)	X		
91B	WHEELED VEHICLE MECHANIC (FORMERLY 63B)	X		
91C	UTILITIES EQUIPMENT REPAIRER (FORMERLY 52C)	X		
91D	POWER-GENERATION EQUIPMENT REPAIRER (FORMERLY 52D)	X		
91E	ALLIED TRADES SPECIALIST (FORMERLY 44E)	X		
91F	SMALL ARMS/ARTILLERY REPAIRER (FORMERLY 45B)		X	
91G	FIRE CONTROL REPAIRER (FORMERLY 45G)	X		
91H	TRACK VEHICLE REPAIRER (FORMERLY 63H)	X		
91J	QUARTERMASTER & CHEMICAL EQUIPMENT REPAIRER (FORMERLY 63J)		X	
91K	ARMAMENT REPAIRER (FORMERLY 45K)		X	
91L	CONSTRUCTION EQUIPMENT REPAIRER (FORMERLY 62B)	X		
91M	BRADLEY FIGHTING VEHICLE SYSTEM MAINTAINER (FORMERLY 63M)	X		
91P	ARTILLERY MECHANIC (FORMERLY 63D)	X		
91W	METAL WORKER (FORMERLY 44B)	X		
91X	MAINTENANCE SUPERVISOR (FORMERLY 63X)	X		
91Z	MECHANICAL MAINTENANCE SUPERVISOR (FORMERLY 63Z)	X		
92A	AUTOMATED LOGISTICAL SPECIALIST			X
92F	PETROLEUM SUPPLY SPECIALIST			X
92G	FOOD SERVICE SPECIALIST (FORMERLY 94B)			X
92L	PETROLEUM LABORATORY SPECIALIST			X
92M	MORTUARY AFFAIRS SPECIALIST			X
92R	PARACHUTE RIGGER			X
92S	SHOWER/LAUNDRY & CLOTHING REPAIR SPECIALIST			X
92W	WATER TREATMENT SPECIALIST		X	
92Y	UNIT SUPPLY SPECIALIST			X
92Z	SENIOR NONCOMISSIONED LOGISTICIAN			X
94A	LAND COMBAT ELECTRONIC MISSILE SYSTEM REPAIRER		X	

When initiating one of these claims, you should always go to a private ear nose and throat doctor (otolaryngologist) who has a hearing lab and a state certified audiologist on staff. This will tell you whether you have noise induced hearing loss or not. Without your own lab test, you cannot do a fully developed claim and it could take a long time before VA will order its own hearing test. In your consultation with the doctor, you must establish – as a matter of record and based on your own testimony – that the hearing loss or the tinnitus or both manifested within a reasonable time of leaving the service. If it has been 50 years, and you just developed tinnitus, VA is going to question whether it was service-connected even though it takes that many years to catch up to you. Make sure that the Doctor puts in your record that he or she believes they hearing loss is service-connected and most importantly if you have tinnitus, that the doctor states that you have persistent tinnitus that you believe has been present since discharge.

You may be convinced the hearing loss or tinnitus or both are due to service, but you can't prove that you were exposed to any conditions that may have caused the hearing loss and/or tinnitus. If enough evidence is produced to show there is a reasonable assumption or inference that the current disability is service-connected, then a strong opinion letter from a physician might sway VA to make a favorable decision even with the absence of any evidence of exposure.

Make sure you include your hearing test along with the doctor consultation – establishing that you have had persistent tinnitus for a long time – with your initial claim. VA will always order a hearing examination at a VA hearing clinic for this kind of claim. Because you have paved the way with fully developed information, the exam will likely be scheduled within a matter of months of filing. Otherwise, who knows how long you would have to wait if you did not pave the way with fully developed information. When you show up for the VA hearing exam, you must also establish as a matter of record, with your own testimony, that the tinnitus is persistent and that it first manifested sometime close to getting out of service.

This is another one of those claims that rely on inference and probability. VA cannot provide evidence that your hearing loss and accompanying tinnitus was not incurred in service. Again it's a 50-50 probability that it was service-connected or was not. Just as it is with the exposure claims above – which noise is – VA will have to use the principle of reasonable doubt and award you the claim. This is why there are so many veterans on hearing loss claims or hearing loss with tinnitus or tinnitus alone.

If it is going to take you some time to assemble the evidence for the application, do an "Intent to File" using the following form:

VA Form 21-0966 INTENT TO FILE

Forms That Might Be Used:
VA Form 10-5345 – Request for and Authorization to Release VHA Medical Records
VA Form 10-5345a – Individual's Request for a Copy of His or Her Own VA Medical Records
VA Form 21-526EZ – Application for Disability Compensation and Related Compensation Benefits
VA Form 21-4142 – Authorization and Consent to Release information to the Department of Veterans Affairs
VA Form 21-526EZ – Application for Disability Compensation and Related Compensation Benefits

Forms for Representation for Assistance if Desired
VA Form 21-22A – Appointment of Individual a Claimant's Representative
VA Form 21-0845 – Authorization to Disclose Personal Information to a Third Party

Checklist Steps in the Fully Developed Claim Process to Follow:

> Go to Page 214 for more detail on these steps

1. Determine Entitlement Based on Service and the Merit of Your Claim
2. Submit an Intent to File, VA Form 21-0966, but Don't File a Claim at This Point
3. Obtain a Copy of Your Discharge
4. Obtain Copies of Your Military Personnel File
5. Obtain of Copies of VA Medical Center Records
6. Follow Our Instructions in Chapter 4 for Submitting the Claim

10. PTIU – Permanent and Total Disability Due to Individual Unemployability

Details:

we have provided detailed information on unemployability on the Claim Support Disc. You may want to read this information in order to understand this claim before applying.

This is a rating increase for someone already on claim to produce the equivalent of 100% disabled, even though the existing underlying rating remains the same. However, Individual Unemployability pays out at the 100% rate. The veteran must currently be service connected for a single disability evaluated at least 60 percent disabling or service connected for multiple disabilities evaluated at least 70 percent disabling, with one of the multiple disabilities rated at least 40 percent disabling. There are circumstances where the requirement for a single 60 or 40 percent disability may be met by a combination of disabilities that can be considered a single disability. There is no age test for this rating. This means a returned 85-year-old who meets the criteria could just as well be considered unemployable as a younger person.

Unemployability means the inability of a veteran to secure or follow a substantially gainful occupation. A finding of unemployability cannot be made if the evidence shows that the veteran is engaged in, or is capable of being engaged in, a substantially gainful occupation. However, a finding could be made if the evidence shows marginal employment. Marginal employment is defined in terms of a veteran's earned annual income.

For a retired individual, not producing earned income, this alternative test for marginal employment would not be appropriate and the test of "capable of being engaged in a substantially gainful occupation" would have to be the test. This marginal employment income should generally not exceed the government's established poverty threshold for one person. Exceeding this threshold may indicate a substantially gainful occupation, as noted by the Court of Appeals for Veteran's Claims (CAVC) in Faust v. Ist, 13 Vet.App. 342 (2000), where a substantially gainful occupation was defined as "one that provides annual income that exceeds the poverty threshold for one person."

In addition to the income criteria, evidence showing that employment is marginal rather than substantially gainful may also exist on a "facts found" basis. Examples of this marginal status include employment in the protected environment of a family business or sheltered workshop. Such fact-based marginal employment is consistent with a finding of unemployability.

Just filling out the appropriate form and submitting it to the Regional Office is an ineffective way to get an award. This approach will most likely result in requests for substantial documentation from various sources and slow down the claim. These claims are difficult and require a great deal of effort and evidence in order to pull them off. On the other hand, the difference in income between 60% or 70% and 100% is significant and often warrants the effort. In addition, anyone deemed housebound and wanting SMC schedule S, must be 100% disabled or individually unemployable (IU) in order to receive the additional monetary allowances for SMC schedule S.

We suggest that you receive expert opinion letters on unemployability due to your service connected disability, not only from your private physician, but also engage the services of a qualified employment counseling specialist who makes determinations of this sort for Social Security disability. You can generally find these people by calling a law office that deals in Social Security and explaining to them what you are doing. They will cooperate with you because they are not interested in this type of representation but they do want to help veterans.

§4.16 Total disability ratings for Compensation based on unemployability of the individual.
(a) Total disability ratings for Compensation may be assigned, where the schedular rating is less than total, when the disabled person is, in the judgment of the rating agency, unable to secure or follow a substantially gainful occupation as a result of service-connected disabilities: *Provided* That, if there is only one such disability, this disability shall be ratable at 60 percent or more, and that, if there are two or more disabilities, there shall be at least one disability ratable at 40 percent or more, and sufficient additional disability to bring the combined rating to 70 percent or more. For the above purpose of one 60 percent disability, or one 40 percent disability in combination, the following will be considered as one disability: (1) Disabilities of one or both upper extremities, or of one or both lower extremities, including the bilateral factor, if applicable, (2) disabilities resulting from common etiology or a single accident, (3) disabilities affecting a single body system, e.g. orthopedic, digestive, respiratory, cardiovascular-renal, neuropsychiatric, (4) multiple injuries incurred in action, or (5) multiple disabilities incurred as a prisoner of war. It is provided further that the existence or degree of nonservice-connected disabilities or previous unemployability status will be disregarded where the percentages referred to in this paragraph for the service-connected disability or disabilities are met and in the judgment of the rating agency such service-connected disabilities render the veteran unemployable. Marginal employment shall not be considered substantially gainful employment. For purposes of this section, marginal employment generally shall be deemed to exist when a veteran's earned annual income does not exceed the amount established by the U.S. Department of Commerce, Bureau of the Census, as the poverty threshold for one person. Marginal employment may also be held to exist, on a facts found basis (includes but is not limited to employment in a protected environment such as a family business or sheltered workshop), when earned annual income exceeds the poverty threshold. Consideration shall be given in all claims to the nature of the employment and the reason for termination.

(Authority: 38 U.S.C. 501)

(b) It is the established policy of the Department of Veterans Affairs that all veterans who are unable to secure and follow a substantially gainful occupation by reason of service-connected disabilities shall be rated totally disabled. Therefore, rating boards should submit to the Director, Compensation Service, for extra-schedular consideration all cases of veterans who are unemployable by reason of service-connected disabilities, but who fail to meet the percentage standards set forth in paragraph (a) of this section. The rating board will include a full statement as to the veteran's service-connected disabilities, employment history, educational and vocational attainment and all other factors having a bearing on the issue.

[40 FR 42535, Sept. 15, 1975, as amended at 54 FR 4281, Jan. 30, 1989; 55 FR 31580, Aug. 3, 1990; 58 FR 39664, July 26, 1993; 61 FR 52700, Oct. 8, 1996; 79 FR 2100, Jan. 13, 2014]

No Age Limit on Individual Unemployability (IU)
Taken from Tuckerdisability.com website

Veterans often ask if they can file a claim for Individual Unemployability after their normal retirement age. The answer is YES! VA is prohibited from considering a veteran's age in service-connected disability claims. A disabled veteran whose disabilities prevent them from working may file a claim for Individual Unemployability at any age. VA's regulations clearly state:

> 38 C.F.R. § 4.19 Age in service-connected claims.
> Age may not be considered as a factor in evaluating service-connected disability; and unemployability, in service-connected claims, associated with advancing age or intercurrent disability, may not be used as a basis for a total disability rating. Age, as such, is a factor only in evaluations of disability not resulting from service, i.e., for the purposes of pension.

Despite the law which requires VA to ignore age in claims for Total Disability Based on Individual Unemployability (TDIU), it is not uncommon for age to factor into VA's analysis about the reasons why a veteran cannot work. Cases have even worked their way up to the Court of Appeals for Veterans Claims, where the Board of Veterans Appeals improperly considered age. For example, in Pratt v. Derwinski, 3 Vet.App. 269 (Vet. App. 1992), the Veterans Court had to specifically call out the Board for doing exactly that. The Court held that "a determination concerning unemployability indeed must be made on the basis of service-connected disabilities alone." As recently as last year, the Veterans Court again had to overturn a Board of Veterans Appeals for considering age in a TDIU case in Vanosdall v. McDonald, No. 14–3766, 2015 WL 7254207 (Vet. App. November 17, 2015).

TAKEAWAY: You can file a claim for Individual Unemployability at any age if your VA service-connected disabilities keep you from working. If you already filed your claim for TDIU and VA used your age as part of the reason why VA denied the claim, you have grounds for an appeal, and you should consult an attorney immediately.

Not Granting Unemployability for Veterans Older Than Age 65
Over the years, Congress has repeatedly made efforts to impose an age limit on unemployability. This proposed legislation has decidedly led to opposition from Veteran Service Organizations. Even currently, as of this publication, there is a pending bill. On its face, it is only reasonable that someone who is retired and no longer working should not deserve reimbursement for being retired and not working. We take no stand on this issue at this time.

Taken from Stars & Stripes website at www.stripes.com

Vet groups warn lawmakers not to impose age factor on unemployability benefit
By TOM PHILPOTT | Special to Stars and Stripes | Published: July 16, 2015

Representatives of The American Legion and Disabled American Veterans have warned lawmakers to reject calls to impose an age ceiling or other new cost control on VA Compensation payments to veterans whose service-connected disabilities leave them unemployable.

An age ceiling is perhaps the most tempting cost-control option discussed in a new Government Accountability Office report that examines iaknesses and inefficiencies in the way the Department of Veterans Affairs administers Individual Unemployability (IU) benefits for 318,000 recipients.

Bradley Flohr, a senior advisor on VA Compensation for the Veterans Benefits Administration, told the House Veterans Affairs Committee on Wednesday that VA is adopting more measured GAO recommendations to improve its process of monitoring IU pay and deciding future IU recipients.

These steps include fielding improved guidance for VA claim revieirs on determining IU eligibility, and better quality assurance screens so that IU claim decisions are more consistent across VA regions.

VA also promises to launch by January long-delayed software that will allow electronic verification of income reported by IU recipients, by matching it with earnings on file at IRS and the Social Security Administration. The department also promises to study whether it should use age or vocational assessments to tighten eligibility for new IU claimants.

More than 316,000 veterans see their monthly VA Disability Compensation enhanced by IU eligibility. These are veterans with service-connected disabilities rated below 100 percent by the VA rating schedule. But the department verifies that the same disabilities prevent these veterans from working, at least in jobs that pay wages above federal poverty guidelines.

Given IU status, veterans draw Compensation at the 100 percent level despite having lower-rated disabilities. To qualify, they must have at least one service-connected disability rated at least 60 percent, or two or more disabilities with a combined rating of 70 percent with at least one disability rated 40 percent. They also must be "unable to maintain substantially gainful employment" as a result of their disabilities.

The raise in Compensation from IU status is significant. A 60-percent disabled veteran with no dependents draws monthly Compensation under IU of $2,907 instead of $1,059, a difference of more than $22,000 a year. A 70-percent disabled vet with a spouse and a child and IU status will receive $3,188 per month instead of $1,531 for their rated disability alone.
The GAO reports concludes that in recent years lax VA procedures have resulted in IU benefit decisions that are not "well supported." The report notes that IU payments increased 30 percent from 2009 to 2013. The Compensation gain for veterans from IU status totaled $5.2 billion in 2013.

Rep. Jeff Miller, R-Fla., chaired the hearing only long enough to make an opening statement, but he turned a spotlight on concerns raised in the GAO report that, he said, "question of whether VA should consider age as a factor when deciding that a veteran is eligible to receive IU benefits."

Miller noted that 180,000 veterans, more than half of those receiving IU benefits, are at least 65 years old. And at ages when many Americans have left the workforce, many vets are filing first claims for IU Compensation due to disabilities that prevent them from holding down decent jobs.

Even "more surprising," Miller said, "408 veterans age 90 and older began receiving IU benefits for the first time in fiscal year 2013."

The rising number of IU claims and age of claimants are not the result of "a failure or fault in the administration of this benefit," said Paul R. Varela, assistant national legislative director of Disabled American Veterans.

Factors truly responsible, Varela said, include increases in the number of VA claims being processed, due in part to an intense outreach to veterans with disabilities; a 2009 easing of rules on rating post-traumatic stress disorders, and a 2010 expansion of the list of diseases presumed caused by Agent Orange exposure during the Vietnam War.

Ian de Planque, legislative director for The American Legion, joined Varela in cautioning the committee against reducing or eliminating IU benefits based on age. First, he said, current law is clear that a veteran's age shouldn't be considered in eligibility for any VA Compensation.

Second, the rising age of veterans who find they want to work and can't is "reflective of the modern workforce" with the number of Americans over age 65 who are still working having doubled over the past 30 years.

Third, de Planque said, most U.S. workers can build a retirement nest egg over the course of their working lives to support them in old age. That isn't true for many veterans with service-connected disabilities.

Flohr, testifying for VA, agreed with the veteran service organizations that the notion of using an age threshold, whether set at 65, 75 or 90, as a cutoff for IU benefits is not supported by VA regulation or recent case law involving VA Compensation claims.

Daniel Bertoni, director of income security audits at GAO, said when veterans "at the outer reaches of these ages" are found eligible for IU, it "strains the credibility" of the program. He suggested that an intent-to-work factor could be built to require new elderly IU claimant to show they "at least tried and fell out of the work force periodically" in, say, the past decade.

Rep. Phil Roe, R-Tenn., agreed that boosting VA Compensation of veterans 90 and older due to "unemployability" seems to fail a "straight face test." Roe said he also is sympathetic to arguments that these disabled vets deserve and, most likely, depends today on IU. But because "probably no one is working at that age, i may wish to label it something else."

Intervieid after the hearing, Flohr said that no veterans currently eligible for IU benefits need to worry that the ideas floated by the GAO or debated in Congress will result in their own Compensation being cut.
"They should have no concern," Flohr said. "The rating schedule specifically states that any time there is a change in the schedule, people are grandfathered at their current evaluation, regardless of whether it would be lowered under the new schedule."

Establishing Entitlement to Individual Unemployability
Excerpts taken from adjudication manual M21-1

To establish entitlement to a total disability rating for Compensation based on individual unemployability, the Veteran must be unemployable in fact (unable to secure or follow substantially gainful employment) by reason of service-connected (SC) disability and either

- meet the schedular requirements of 38 CFR 4.16(a), or
- have an extra-schedular individual uemployability (IU) evaluation, under the provisions of 38 CFR 4.16(b), approved by Compensation Service (211B).

Note: IU is also referred to as total disability based on individual unemployability (TDIU).

Unemployable Vs. Unemployed
Being unemployable and being unemployedare not synonymous for the purpose of determining entitlement to an IU rating under 38 CFR 4.16.
A Veteran may be unemployed and even have a history of unemployment from several jobs, but not be incapable of substantially gainful employment (unemployable). Unemployment can be due to economic factors, work performance issues, or other reasons and not necessarily related to being unable to secure or follow substantially gainful employment due to SC disability.
A Veteran might also be unemployed from one job due to an SC disability, but still be capable of securing or following another substantially gainful occupation.

Definition: Substantially Gainful Employment:
Substantially gainful employment is defined as employment at which non-disabled individuals earn their livelihood with earnings comparable to the particular occupation in the community where the Veteran resides. It suggests a living wage.

Substantially gainful employment is

- competitive (not protected) employment, and with
- earnings exceeding the amount established by the U.S. Department of Commerce, U.S. Census Bureau, as the poverty threshold for one person.

Definition: Marginal Employment

Marginal employment exists

- when a Veteran's earned annual income does not exceed the amount established by the U.S. Department of Commerce, U.S. Census Bureau, as the poverty threshold for one person, or
- on a facts-found basis, and includes, but is not limited to, employment in a protected environment, such as a family business or sheltered workshop, when earned annual income exceeds the poverty threshold.

Important:
- Marginal employment is by definition not substantially gainful employment.
- Do not consider amounts received from participation in the Veterans Health Administration's (VHA's) Compensated Work Therapy (CWT) Program as income for IU purposes.

General Evidence Requirements in IU Claims

A decision concerning entitlement to an IU evaluation is based on a review of all available evidence, which should be sufficient to evaluate the

- current severity of the SC disability(ies) that the Veteran states and/or the evidence indicates prevent(s) substantially gainful employment
- the impact of SC disability(ies) upon employability, and
- employment status.

Forward a VA Form 21-8940, Veteran's Application for Increased Compensation based on Unemployability, to the Veteran if a request for IU is

- expressly raised by the Veteran, or
- reasonably raised by the evidence of record.

Important:
- Any written communication indicating a Veteran is unable to work because of SC disability(ies) may establish the inference of IU, such that the Department of Veterans Affairs (VA) will solicit a claim.
- A Veteran's statement of having been terminated from his or her employment may only reasonably raise a claim for IU if the Veteran indicates that termination was due to a SC disability.

VA Form 21-8940

A substantially complete VA Form 21-8940 is required to establish entitlement to IU because it gathers relevant and indispensable information regarding a claimant's disabilities and employment and educational histories. The form concludes with a series of sworn certification statements, and in endorsing it, a Veteran

- attests to his/her employment status, and

251

- signals understanding of the IU benefit's incompatibility with substantially gainful work.

A properly signed and executed VA Form 21-8940 enables VA to gather the information necessary to determine the Veteran's entitlement to IU and recover IU Compensation that is later discovered to have been awarded on fraudulent terms. While a substantially complete VA Form 21-8940 is necessary to provide VA with information needed to substantiate entitlement to IU, it is not necessary to raise the issue of IU. VA must make a decision on IU when the issue is

- explicitly raised by the Veteran, or
- reasonably raised by the evidence of record.
- If IU is raised and the Veteran fails to complete and return VA Form 21-8940, VA must make a decision on the issue of IU based on the available evidence of record and may deny entitlement as described in M21-1, Part IV, Subpart ii, 2.F.4.j.

Important:
- If the issue of IU is raised by the Veteran or reasonably raised by the evidence of record and the only VA Form 21-8940 of record was received as part of a finally adjudicated claim, a new VA Form 21-8940 must be provided to the Veteran.
- A VA Form 21-8940 must be signed by the Veteran and not a third party source such as a power of attorney (POA).

Medical Evidence and Examination Requirements in IU Claims
A claim for IU must contain sufficient medical evidence to support a current evaluation of the SC disabilities alleged by the claimant to be causing unemployability. The evidence should reflect the Veteran's condition within the past 12 months and include, but need not be limited to

- the results of VA examination(s)
- hospital reports, and/or
- outpatient treatment records.

Important: A medical examination is notautomatically required in every IU claim. An examination is required if the information and evidence of record do not contain sufficient competent medical evidence to decide the claim.

Requesting an Examination in IU Claims
When an examination is indicated, it is normally sufficient to request condition-specific disability benefits questionnaire (DBQs) for the conditions alleged to cause unemployability on the VA Form 21-8940 (for example, Joints, Mental, and Peripheral Nerves DBQs).

Schedule a General Medical Examination only if the rating activity determines that it is needed to fairly and fully adjudicate the IU claim, such as when the claim is made in connection with original claims for Disability Compensation or where it is alleged that multiple SC and/or non-service-connected (NSC) disabilities may have an impact on employability. However, do not order examinations for disabilities not alleged to cause or contribute to unemployability, even if the Veteran has received a previous award of service connection (SC) for the disabilities.

Do not ask the examiner to opine as to whether or not the Veteran is "unemployable" due to his or her SC disabilities. A determination that a Veteran is unemployable is a legal determination that rests solely with the rating activity. Instead, request that the examiner

- comment on the Veteran's ability to function in an occupational environment, and
- describe functional impairment caused solely by the SC disabilities.

It is acceptable for an examiner to comment regarding what kind of work tasks or work environments (if any), to include employment that is sedentary in nature and employment requiring physical labor, the Veteran could perform despite his/her SC disability(ies). Note: The language generated upon selection of the IU block in the Exam Request Builder (ERB)tool is legally sufficient to elicit the necessary information.

Employment History Requirements in IU Claims

VA Form 21-8940 requires the Veteran to furnish an employment history for the last five years that he or she worked. In determining whether the Veteran provided work history information for the required time period, review the entries in Blocks 14 and 15 on the VA Form 21-8940. Note: The minimum required work history, for the purpose of requesting employment information from the Veteran's employer(s), must include the last year of employment.

Important: If the Veteran fails to provide employment history, the underlying claim(s) for increased evaluation must still be adjudicated even though the claim for IU may result in denial. A claim for IU may not be freestanding, but must be part of a claim for increased evaluation or original service connection.

Veteran's Responsibility to Specify a Disability or Disabilities That Cause Unemployability

VA will no longer presume a claim for IU is a claim for increase in all SC disabilities. As part of a substantially complete application for IU, VA will require that the claimant with multiple SC disabilities specify at least one disability that he or she believes causes the unemployability.

Identifying Reasonably Raised Claims of IU

Reasonably raised claims of IU may arise in a Veteran's original claim or in a claim for an increased rating. VA must consider a claim for IU if

- the Veteran's SC rating meets the minimum schedular criteria found in 38 CFR 4.16(a), and
- there is current evidence of unemployability due to SC disability(ies) in the Veteran's claims folder or under VA control.

Considering IU Claims for National Guard and Reservists

If a Veteran is currently serving in the National Guard or Reserves, the revieir should

- determine if a medical examiner has indicated that a Veteran is unable to perform his/her military duties due to SC disability, and

- make sure that the latest service treatment records (STRs) are of record, as such records may aid in determining if the disability is preventing the Veteran from performing his/her current Guard or Reserve duties.

If the evidence of record is not sufficient to award increased Compensation based on IU, request that the unit commander complete and return VA Form 21-4192.

Self-Employment Development
Development to produce the evidence necessary to establish the degree to which SC disability has impawered the Veteran's ability to engage in self-employment must generally be more extensive than development in cases in which the Veteran worked for others. Request that the Veteran furnish a statement regarding the

- types of work performed
- number of hours worked per iek, and
- amount of time lost in the previous 12 months due to SC disabilities.

Deciding Whether Self-Employed Individuals Are Unemployable Due to an SC Disability
When determining entitlement of self-employed individuals to increased Compensation based on IU, consider the relationship between the frequency and the type of service performed by the Veteran for his/her business and the Veteran's net and gross earnings for the past 12 months. Consider facts of the case, such as

- low gross earnings that support a finding of marginal employment, especially when the amount of time lost from work due to SC disability is taken into account, or
- high gross earnings that indicate the Veteran is capable of engaging in a substantially gainful occupation.

Notes:
- Consider low net earnings in conjunction with gross income.
- The inability to make a profit is not always indicative of the inability to engage in substantially gainful employment.

Definition: Tightly Held Corporation
A tightly held corporation (or closely held corporation) is usually a family corporation. A corporation bearing the Veteran's name is usually indicative of a tightly held corporation.

Evaluating Evidence Showing Income from a Tightly Held Corporation
Since the Veteran may control the amount of wages paid to himself/herself, do not make a finding of marginal employment solely on the basis of low wages. Keep in mind that the issue for consideration is whether the frequency and type of service performed by the Veteran equates to substantially gainful employment. Therefore, consider evidence that the Veteran received, or was entitled to receive, other remuneration from the corporation, such as stock dividends or loans, in lieu of wages.

Note: If the reported wages appear low for the work performed, request a field examination per M21-1, Part III, Subpart vi, 8.8 to determine the Veteran's entitlement to the corporation and corporate earnings.

Considerations When Deciding an IU Claim

When deciding an IU claim, the rating activity must take into account

- the Veteran's current physical and mental condition
- the Veteran's employment status, including
- the nature of employment, and
- the reason employment was terminated, and whether

  - the disability requirements set forth in 38 CFR 4.16 are met, or
  - extra-schedular consideration under 38 CFR 4.16(b) is warranted.

Important: Do not defer a decision as to the schedular degree of disability pending receipt of evidence sufficient to adjudicate the issue of IU.

Applicability of the Concept of Average Impairment in Earning Capacity to IU Claims

Do not apply the concept of average impairment in earning capacity set forth in 38 CFR 4.1 to determinations regarding IU. This concept applies only to determinations of the percentage of disability for schedular evaluations.

IU for Incarcerated Veterans

An IU rating that would first become effective while a Veteran is incarcerated in a Federal, State, or local penal institution for conviction of a felony shall not be assigned during such period of incarceration. If an IU evaluation is in effect prior to incarceration in excess of 60 days for conviction of a felony, the IU evaluation will be reduced to 10 percent in accordance with 38 CFR 3.665.

Considering IU on a Temporary Basis

38 CFR 4.16 authorizes the VA to assign an IU rating due to a Veteran's temporary inability to follow a substantially gainful occupation.

Notes:
Not every period of inability to work will establish an inability to follow a substantially gainful occupation warranting an IU rating, because it may be possible to secure and retain employment and to earn significant income despite occasional periods of incapacity.
VA must make determinations regarding ability or inability to secure or follow a substantially gainful occupation on a case-by-case basis, taking into account such factors as
- the frequency and duration of periods of incapacity or time lost from work due to disability
- the Veteran's employment history and current employment status, and
- the Veteran's annual income from employment, if any.

Considering Multiple Disabilities in IU Claims

Under certain circumstances, multiple disabilities may be considered one disability for the purpose of meeting the requirements of 38 CFR 4.16(a). As stated in 38 CFR 4.16(a), for the purpose of meeting the requirement of having one 60-percent or one 40-percent disability, the following will be considered as one disability

- disabilities of one or both upper extremities, or of one or both lower extremities, including the bilateral factor, if applicable
- disabilities resulting from common etiology or a single accident
- disabilities affecting a single body system
- multiple disabilities incurred in combat, or
- multiple disabilities incurred as a former prisoner of war (FPOW).

Example:
Consider multiple disabilities of the musculoskeletal system as one disability because the multiple disabilities affect a single body system or multiple gunshot wounds as the result of combat service as one disability because the multiple disabilities were incurred in combat.

Important:
In determining whether the Veteran's SC disabilities meet the schedular requirement as stated in 38 CFR 4.16(a), all SC disabilities will be considered. This determination is not restricted to only those SC disabilities that cause or contribute to unemployability.

Example:
A Veteran is SC for diabetes mellitus at 40 percent, right shoulder arthritis at 30 percent, ulcerative colitis at 30 percent, and posttraumatic stress disorder (PTSD) at 30 percent. The combined disability evaluation is 80 percent. The evidence demonstrates that all SC disabilities, except for diabetes mellitus, cause or contribute to rendering the Veteran unable to secure or maintain substantially gainful employment.

Result:
TDIU would be awarded under 38 CFR 4.16(a), as the Veteran meets the schedular requirements of the regulation (combined disability evaluation of at least 70 percent and one disability, diabetes mellitus, rated at least 40 percent).

Rationale:
The regulation does not require that the 40-percent disability specifically cause or contribute to the unemployability when multiple SC disabilities are present and collectively render the Veteran unemployable.

Entitlement to SMC at the Housebound Rate if IU Rating Is Based on a Single Disability

A Veteran in receipt of IU benefits may be entitled to special monthly Compensation (SMC) at the housebound rate under 38 U.S.C. 1114(s) if the evidence shows that

- the unemployability is the result of one SC disability, and
- the Veteran has

- additional SC disability(ies) independently rated at least 60-percent disabling, or
- been determined to be permanently housebound, in fact, as a result of the SC disability that rendered the Veteran unemployable.

Example: A Veteran would be entitled to SMC at the housebound rate if

- his/her total IU evaluation is based on a 70-percent SC rating for posttraumatic stress disorder, and
- he/she has additional SC evaluations for headaches and a back condition that combine to 60 percent.

Notes:
- Entitlement to housebound benefits under 38 U.S.C. 1114(s) cannot be established if the IU rating is based on multiple disabilities considered as one disability under 38 CFR 4.16.
- Do not put entitlement to SMC at issue, unless benefits will be awarded or the issue has been explicitly claimed by the Veteran.

Determining Whether to Substitute a Single 100 Percent Schedular Evaluation for IU in Housebound Cases

VA is obligated to maximize the benefits awarded. In determining whether to substitute a 100-percent schedular evaluation for IU, consider whether substitution would result in the Veteran no longer being entitled to SMC at the Housebound rate. VA decision makers are to assess whether the Veteran still meets the criteria for IU based on a single disability before substituting a combined total schedular rating for the IU as indicated in Bradley v. Peake, 22 Vet. App. 280 (2008). As a result, in cases where a single SC condition supports an IU rating and the Veteran has other SC conditions entitling him or her to statutory Housebound, the IU evaluation should be retained if the Veteran would otherwise lose the SMC rate if the IU were to be discontinued.

When an IU Evaluation is Considered Moot

A single SC disability rated 100-percent disabling generally renders an IU evaluation moot, as no additional benefit would typically flow to the Veteran by substituting an IU evaluation for a single SC disability rated 100-percent disabling.

Exception: The IU evaluation is not moot if the effective date of the single schedular 100-percent evaluation is from a later date than that which can be assigned based on entitlement to IU (such as when an effective date for IU may be assigned from the day following discontinuation of last employment).

Determining the Effect of SC Disabilities on Employability

Determine whether the severity of the SC disabilities precludes the Veteran from securing or following substantially gainful employment.

The following factors **have no bearing** on a determination of whether SC disability renders a Veteran unemployable:

- AGE
- NSC disabilities
- injuries occurring after military service
- availability of work, or
- voluntary withdrawal from the labor market.

Reasons for Denying IU Claims

Deny entitlement to IU only if the facts demonstrate that the Veteran

- is not precluded from securing or following substantially gainful employment by reason of SC disability
- is gainfully employed, or
- has failed to cooperate with development, such as failing to return a completed VA Form 21-8940 when requested.

Notes:

- The fact that a Veteran is participating in a program of rehabilitation does not preclude a finding of IU.
- The fact that a Veteran has completed a program of rehabilitation does not mandate discontinuance of IU unless sustained employment is also demonstrated.
- When IU is claimed following a completed program of rehabilitation, pay special attention to evidence of program results that indicate the Veteran's ability and willingness to engage in a substantially gainful occupation.

Handling Claims Requiring Compensation Service Approval

Submit any claim to Compensation Service (211B) for extra-schedular IU consideration if the schedular requirements of 38 CFR 4.16(a) are not met but the evidence of record supports a finding that the Veteran is unemployable by reason of SC disability.

Editor's note: This option is often overlooked by claim representatives helping veterans with individual unemployability. The assumption is if the schedular requirements as outlined in the regulation are not met, individual unemployability is not awarded. Many claims are awarded using extra-schedular consideration. The claim representative should always be prepared to request such consideration in the event of a denial. Evidence must indicate that despite not meeting the requirements of 38 CFR 4.16(a), the claimant is indeed disabled to the point where gainful employment cannot be maintained.

Monitoring Changes in Employability Status

Changes in the employability of Veterans for whom IU is established is monitored through the

- annual release of VA Form 21-4140, Employment Questionnawere, via the Hines Information Technology Center (ITC), and
- Income Verification Match (IVM).

When Monitoring Changes in Employability Status Is Not Required

Monitoring changes in employability status is not required when the Veteran

- <u>is 69 years of age or older</u>
- <u>has an IU rating that has been in effect for 20 or more continuous years, or</u>
- <u>has had an IU rating replaced with a 100-percent schedular evaluation.</u>

Marginal Employment Based on Income below the Poverty Threshold

38 CFR 4.16(a) provides that marginal employment is generally deemed to exist when a Veteran's earned income does not exceed the amount established by the U.S. Census Bureau as the average poverty threshold for one person. For more information on the U.S. Census Bureau's poverty thresholds, see http://www.census.gov/hhes/www/poverty/data/historical/people.html.

Poverty Threshold for One Person

The table below lists the poverty threshold for one person by year.

Year	Amount
1998	$8,316
1999	$8,501
2000	$8,794
2001	$9,039
2002	$9,183
2003	$9,393
2004	$9,645
2005	$9,973
2006	$10,294
2007	$10,590
2008	$10,991
2009	$10,956
2010	$11,137
2011	$11,484
2012	$11,720
2013	$11,888
2014	$12,316
2015	$12,331
2016	$12,228
2017	$12,060
2018	$12,784

Filing for Individual Unemployability

If it is going to take you some time to assemble the evidence for the application, submit an "Intent to File" using the following form:

VA Form 21-0966 INTENT TO FILE

Forms That Might Be Used:

VA Form 10-5345 – Request for and Authorization to Release VHA Medical Records
VA Form 10-5345a – Individual's Request for a Copy of His or Her Own VA Medical Records
VA Form 21-4142 – Authorization and Consent to Release information to the Department of Veterans Affairs
VA Form 21-8940 – Veteran's Application for Increased Compensation Based on Unemployability

You will use VA Form 21-8940 for this application.

Forms for Representation for Assistance if Desired
VA Form 21-22A – Appointment of Individual a Claimant's Representative
VA Form 21-0845 – Authorization to Disclose Personal Information to a Third Party

Steps in the Claim Process to Follow:

This is not an original claim but a request for a change in your current disability rating. You will fill out the appropriate form above and provide the following information below with your claim.

Checklist Steps in the Fully Developed Claim Process to Follow:

Go to Page 214 for more detail on these steps

1. Determine Entitlement Based on Service and the Merit of Your Claim
2. Submit an Intent to File, VA Form 21-0966, but Don't File a Claim at This Point
3. Obtain of Copies of VA Medical Center Records
4. Obtain Copies of Your Own Private Medical Records
5. Obtain Your Own Private Medical Opinions
6. Write a Detailed and Credible Lay Statement to Describe Your Claim
7. Follow Our Instructions in Chapter 4 for Submitting the Claim

11. Sleep Apnea

Details:

<u>This type of disability is not presumed to be service-connected.</u> Evidence must be produced to show that it was service-connected. Proving service connection adds an additional degree of difficulty over those conditions that are presumed. Generally, evidence of the illness or injury should be contained in service medical records of the claimant. If no medical evidence is available, service connection can still be established through other means such as lay testimony or historical reports from individuals who observed the injury or illness of the claimant. There is no time frame for making a claim.

Sometimes, the injury or illness does not manifest as chronically disabling for many years after separation. Medical evidence soon after separation of the existence of the illness or injury and prior to manifestation of disability is often necessary in establishing service connection and what VA calls continuity of the chronic condition. These types of claims are very common for any age of veteran, be it a young veteran or a veteran who is aged. For some other types of claims involving direct service connection, chronicity must be established but not necessarily manifestation early on. Some disabling conditions may not show up for years.

Sleep apnea claims have become more prevalent in the last few the years. This is probably due to the fact that sleep apnea is often a secondary service connected condition to PTSD. If this is your case, go to the claim category for secondary service connection and follow those instructions. Secondary service connection for sleep apnea doesn't just have to be PTSD. It could be any number of conditions that are already service-connected for which the veteran is on claim and that would also aggravate or directly cause the difficulty breathing asleep.

If this is a claim for direct service connection, it may be difficult to establish. Sleep apnea by itself is not a disease, but it is a cluster of symptoms that revolve around several underlying causes which prevent a person from breathing properly, particularly at night. Sleep apnea in service may be just simply a condition that is developed and that has been reported and treated in service and contained in service treatment records.

Lacking any medical records from service, the applicant can possibly use lay statements to establish incurrence in service, however VA will typically not accept lay statements for sleep apnea from the veteran who is the claimant. This is because VA thinks, and perhaps rightly so, that because sleep apnea occurs while one is asleep, the veteran cannot possibly describe his or her symptoms that are supposed to be observable, because the veteran is asleep. Lay statements must be from other individuals who witnessed veteran's sleep apnea episodes in service. But this is not all, there must be some sort of corroborating evidence – lacking medical evidence – that can back up the lay statements. These might be personnel records of some kind that show reassignment due to lack of sleep or inattention or something like that.

On the next page is how VA handles the claim and what the Regional Office is looking for.

VA Development of a Sleep Apnea Claim

The diagnosis of sleep apnea must be confirmed by sleep study for Compensation rating purposes. Receipt of medical evidence disclosing a diagnosis of sleep apnea without confirmation by a sleep study is sufficient to trigger the duty to assist for scheduling an examination if the other provisions of 38 CFR 3.159(c)(4) have been satisfied. However, such evidence is not sufficient to award SC for sleep apnea. A home sleep study is only accepted if it has been clinically determined that the Veteran can be appropriately evaluated by a home sleep study, and a competent medical provider has evaluated the results.

Evaluate sleep apnea using the criteria in 38 CFR 4.97, DC 6847 (sleep apnea syndromes (obstructive, central, mixed). When determining whether the 50-percent criteria are met, the key consideration is whether use of a qualifying breathing assistance device is required by the severity of the sleep apnea. There are two related considerations

- what devices qualify, and
- whether use of a qualifying device is necessary.

On the question of what qualifies as a breathing assistance device, the DC lists a CPAP machine as an example. Other qualifying breathing assistance devices include:

- other positive airway pressure machines (automatic positive airway pressure device (APAP); bilevel positive airway pressure device (BiPAP))
- nasopharyngeal appliances (nasal dilators; nasopharyngeal stents)
- oral appliances (mandibular advancement devices (MAD); tongue-retaining mouthpieces), and
- implanted genioglossal nerve stimulation devices.

Positive airway pressure machines may also be called non-invasive positive pressure ventilation (NIPPV) or non-invasive ventilation (NIV).

On the question of whether sleep apnea requires use of a breathing device, there are two important and related points

- Use absent a medical determination that the device is necessary does not qualify. The regulation requires that the device be necessary and this is a medical question.
- If the competent medical evidence of record shows that use of a qualifying breathing assistance device is medically required, the fact that the claimant is not actually using it as prescribed is not relevant.

6847 Sleep Apnea Syndromes (Obstructive, Central, Mixed):	
Chronic respiratory failure with carbon dioxide retention or cor pulmonale, or; requires tracheostomy	100
Requires use of breathing assistance device such as continuous airway pressure (CPAP) machine	50
Persistent day-time hypersomnolence	30
Asymptomatic but with documented sleep disorder breathing	0

More Discussion

Here's an interesting ruling from the Board of the Veterans Appeals concerning these kinds of claims. I think it is an interesting study in detail as to how decisions for these types of claims are made.

Service connection may be granted for disability resulting from a disease or injury incurred in or aggravated by military service. 38 U.S.C.A. § 1110; 38 C.F.R. § 3.303. In addition, service connection may be presumed for certain chronic diseases, including arthritis, that are manifested to a compensable degree within one year after service. 38 U.S.C.A. §§ 1101, 1112; 38 C.F.R. §§ 3.307, 3.309(a). For the showing of chronic disease in service, there must be a combination of manifestations sufficient to identify the disease entity and sufficient observation to establish chronicity at the time. If chronicity in service is not established, evidence of continuity of symptoms after discharge is required to support the claim. 38 C.F.R. § 3.303(b). Service connection may also be granted for a disease diagnosed after discharge when all the evidence, including that pertinent to service, establishes that the disease was incurred in service. 38 C.F.R. § 3.303(d).

To establish service connection, there must be (1) medical evidence of current disability; (2) medical, or in certain circumstances, lay evidence of in-service incurrence or aggravation of a disease or injury; and (3) medical evidence of a nexus between the claimed in-service disease or injury and the current disability. Hickson v. Ist, 12 Vet. App. 247 (1999); see also Degmetich v. Brown, 104 F.3d 1328 (Fed. Cir. 1997); Brammer v. Derwinski, 3 Vet. App. 223 (1992). This determination is based on an analysis of all the evidence of record and evaluation of its credibility and probative value. Baldwin v. Ist, 13 Vet. App. 1 (1999).

There is no reference to back problems, symptoms, or diagnoses in any of the veteran's service medical records. Nor is there any mention of the veteran's use of any back support, as he testified.

Moreover, there is no record of any complaint of or treatment for any back disorder for many years after service. Indeed, on a September 1951 reserve service examination, the veteran's spine was clinically normal. On an accompanying medical history report, the veteran denied any back injury or back problems.

The first mention of any back symptoms was in non-VA treatment in December 2001, that is, over 50 years after service. The diagnosis at that time was backache.

None of the available competent VA or non-VA records attributes any current back problems to the veteran's service.

The Board is mindful of an August 2004 VA examination that concluded that degenerative joint disease of the lumbar spine was "at least as likely as not related to an *inservice back injury." The examiner noted having revieid the claims folder. The examiner specifically described a history of an in-service fall (in 1944); the use of a back brace throughout the remainder of the veteran's active service; treatment for back problems at a VA facility in Memphis, Tennessee, in 1962; and constant back pain ever since the in-service incident. <u>However, that history cannot be based on a review of the claims folder and relevant medical history, since there is no documentation of the specified treatment at those particular times. Indeed, the VA facility in Memphis has replied that it does not have records of any treatment for the veteran. Moreover, the service medical records do not document any treatment for a 1944 or other in-service back injury or the use of a back brace in service. Thus, it appears that the August 2004 VA examination is premised on the veteran's recitations.</u>*

A bare conclusion (even from a medical professional) is not probative without a factual predicate in the record. Miller v. lst, 11 Vet. App. 345 (1998). A medical opinion premised on an unsubstantiated account is of no probative value and does not verify the occurrences described. Swann v. Brown, 5 Vet. App. 229 (1993); cf. Howell v. Nicholson, No. 04-0624, __ Vet. App. __, 2006 WL 760181 (Vet. App. Mar. 23, 2006). The Board is not bound to accept a doctor's opinion based exclusively on a claimant's recitations. Reonal v. Brown, 5 Vet. App. 458, 461 (1993). As a result, the August 2004 VA examination is not probative as to any relationship between the veteran's service and any current back disorder.

<u>Thus, the Board finds that the weight of the credible, competent evidence demonstrates that the veteran did not develop a back disorder during his service or because of any incident therein. As the preponderance of the evidence is against this claim, the "benefit-of-the-doubt" rule does not apply, and the Board must deny the claim.</u> 38 U.S.C.A. § 5107(b) (lst 2002).

In this particular case, the doctor's opinion was evidently biased. If enough evidence is produced to show that there is a reasonable assumption or inference that the current disability exhibits a continuity of symptoms as well as some sort of evidence of injury in the service, then an appropriately prepared opinion from a physician allows VA to make a favorable decision.

Also remember that for these types of claims, especially where there is scanty evidence of the incurrence of an illness or injury in the service, current disabling conditions that could be attributed to combat or being a prisoner of war are usually accepted based on the testimony of the claimant alone with no other corroborating evidence. For peacetime service or noncombatant service, testimony of the claimant or other witnesses is not enough without other supporting physical evidence such as service treatment records or personnel records or credible buddy statements where inference can be drawn that the in-service incurrence took place.

If it is going to take you some time to assemble the evidence for the application, submit an "Intent to File" using the following form:

VA Form 21-0966 INTENT TO FILE

Forms That Might Be Used:
VA Form 10-5345 – Request for and Authorization to Release VHA Medical Records
VA Form 10-5345a – Individual's Request for a Copy of His or Her Own VA Medical Records
VA Form 21-526EZ – Application for Disability Compensation and Related Compensation Benefits
VA Form 21-4176 – Report of Accidental Injury in Support of Claim for Compensation or Pension Statement of Witness to Accident
VA Form 21-4142 – Authorization and Consent to Release information to the Department of Veterans Affairs

Forms for Representation for Assistance if Desired
VA Form 21-22A – Appointment of Individual a Claimant's Representative
VA Form 21-0845 – Authorization to Disclose Personal Information to a Third Party

Checklist Steps in the Fully Developed Claim Process to Follow:

Go to Page 214 for more detail on these steps

1. Determine Entitlement Based on Service and the Merit of Your Claim
2. Submit an Intent to File, VA Form 21-0966, but Don't File a Claim at This Point
3. Obtain a Copy of Your Discharge
4. Obtain Copies of Service Treatment Records
5. Obtain Copies of Your Military Personnel File
6. Obtain of Copies of VA Medical Center Records
7. Obtain Copies of Your Own Private Medical Records
8. Obtain Your Own DBQs from Private Clinicians
9. Obtain Your Own Private Medical Opinions
10. Write a Detailed and Credible Lay Statement to Describe Your Claim
11. Follow Our Instructions in Chapter 4 for Submitting the Claim

12. Gulf War Disorders – Service Connection Is Presumed with a Time Limit

By NIKKI INTLING | STARS AND STRIPES Published: October 17, 2016

WASHINGTON – For the next five years, veterans will have an easier time seeking benefits for illnesses linked to service in the Gulf War because of an extension issued Monday by the Department of Veterans Affairs.

Since 1994, the VA has automatically presumed a connection from Gulf War service, which included a toxic environment of oil fires and chemical iapons, to an increased risk for several illnesses. The connection enables veterans to receive a disability rating and benefits more quickly.

But the presumed connection and the ability to seek benefits was set to expwere at the end of this year, after being extended four times previously. Effective Monday, the VA extended it a fifth time, to Dec. 31, 2021.

"This end date creates such an anxiety among the Gulf War veterans that gets so high as that deadline approaches," said James Bunker, the executive director of the National Gulf War Resource Center in Topeka, Kansas. "[Secretary Bob] McDonald promised us the beginning of this year that this extension would happen."

As justification for the extension, the VA cited a report from the National Academies of Sciences, Engineering, and Medicine in February that found veterans deployed to the Gulf War have an increased risk for chronic fatigue syndrome, functional gastrointestinal conditions and mental health disorders, as well as a myriad of symptoms including headaches, joint pain, insomnia and respiratory issues that make up Gulf War illness.

In the extension filed with the Federal Register on Monday, the VA wrote symptoms could manifest in Gulf War veterans at any point, and there was "no medical or scientific basis" for stopping veterans from seeking benefits at the end of year. The rule applies to veterans who served in Southist Asia from 1990 to now, including ones from Operation Iraqi Freedom and Operation New Dawn.

"Currently, military operations in the Southist Asia theater continue," the extension read. "No end date for the Gulf War has been established by Congress or the President. If extension of the current presumptive period is not implemented, servicemembers whose conditions manifest after Dec. 31, 2016 would be substantially disadvantaged."

Bunker has a 100 percent service-connected disability rating from his time in the Gulf War, he said. He deployed with the First Infantry Division out of Fort Riley in Kansas and was medically evacuated in 1991 after struggling with respiratory and muscle problems. The VA granted Bunker service connection in 1992 for symptoms included in Gulf War illness.

Through the National Gulf War Resource Center, Bunker has appealed to Congress to eliminate the deadline permanently. The VA secretary is the only one with the authority to extend it.

"I know veterans wish the end date would be removed," he said. "I wish i could get rid of it. Congress is the only body that can get rid of the end date, and they should do that to ease the anxiety of veterans."

Of the 700,000 servicemembers deployed to the Gulf War in 1990 and 1991, 36.5 percent were experiencing some symptoms of Gulf War illness in 2005, according to a previous NAS study. The federal government spent more than $500 million on research related to Gulf War veterans from 1994 to 2014, but there have been few findings about Gulf War illness and specific chemical agents that could be causing it, according to the NAS study from February.

Besides fighting to allow veterans to continue to seek benefits for Gulf War illness, advocates are tackling high rejection rates for Gulf War claims.

In March, the group Veterans for Common Sense issued a report stating the VA denied about 80 percent of claims filed by Gulf War veterans in the first half of 2015.

At a hearing before the House Committee on Veterans' Affairs that month, the Veterans of Foreign Wars charged the VA was denying claims to try to rule out Gulf War illness intentionally, Stars and Stripes reported. VA officials at the hearing said its accuracy rate on Gulf War claims was about 90 percent.

"VA still has a hard time properly rating these claims," Bunker said. "They seem to be in a constant Form of denial when they do make mistakes on the benefits side."

Details:

Veterans may receive Disability Compensation for chronic disabilities resulting from undiagnosed illnesses and/or medically unexplained chronic multi-symptom illnesses defined by a cluster of signs or symptoms. A disability is chronic if it has existed at least 6 months.

The undiagnosed illnesses must have appeared either during active service in the Southist Asia Theater of Operations during the Gulf War period of Aug. 2, 1990, to July 31, 1991, or to a degree of at least 10 percent at any time since then through Dec. 31, 2016. **(Please note that the manifestation date has been pushed up to 2021.)**

This theater of operations includes Iraq, Kuwait, Saudi Arabia, the neutral zone between Iraq and Saudi Arabia, Bahrain, Qatar, the United Arab Emirates, Oman, the Gulf of Aden, the Gulf of Oman, the Persian Gulf, the Arabian Sea, the Red Sea, and the airspace above these locations.

Because service connection is presumed, it is not required to produce evidence for service connection – only evidence of the manifestation of the disorder or disease. That said, the claimant must provide evidence of being in the service in the particular theater of operation. Disability has to become manifest to 10% or more from the time of active duty and no later than December 31, 2011. Examples of symptoms of an undiagnosed illness and medically unexplained chronic multi-symptom illness defined by a cluster of signs and symptoms include:

- chronic fatigue syndrome,
- fibromyalgia,
- irritable boil syndrome,
- fatigue,
- signs or symptoms involving the skin,
- skin disorders,
- headache,
- muscle pain,
- joint pain,
- neurological signs or symptoms,
- neuropsychological signs or symptoms,
- signs or symptoms involving the respiratory system (upper or lower),
- sleep disturbances,
- gastrointestinal signs or symptoms,
- cardiovascular signs or symptoms,
- abnormal weight loss, and
- menstrual disorders.

If no previous claim has been made or if a previous claim was made but there was no chronic disability for an award, it may be possible to submit a new claim or reopen the previous claim as long as this is done within one year of any correspondence with VA. It is important to note that the condition had to have manifest itself at 10% or more prior to December 31, 2016. You would have to provide concrete medical evidence of the manifestation of symptoms prior to December 31, 2016 to even proceed. Otherwise, don't bother to make a claim.

If it is going to take you some time to assemble the evidence for the application, submit an "Intent to File" using the following form:

VA Form 21-0966 INTENT TO FILE

Forms That Might Be Used:
VA Form 10-5345 – Request for and Authorization to Release VHA Medical Records
VA Form 10-5345a – Individual's Request for a Copy of His or Her Own VA Medical Records
VA Form 21-526EZ – Application for Disability Compensation and Related Compensation Benefits
VA Form 21-4142 – Authorization and Consent to Release information to the Department of Veterans Affairs

Forms for Representation for Assistance if Desired
VA Form 21-22A – Appointment of Individual a Claimant's Representative
VA Form 21-0845 – Authorization to Disclose Personal information to a Third Party

The VA has extended the deadline to receive disability benefits for Persian Gulf War Veterans with certain presumptive conditions. The deadline was previously set to expwere on December 31, 2016, but has been extended to December 31, 2021.

This means that Gulf War Veterans who have qualifying medically unexplained illnesses will receive presumptive service-connection if their symptoms began anytime between the beginning of their active duty service in the Southist Asia Theater of military operations and December 31, 2021. Veterans who have not yet experienced symptoms and veterans who have experienced symptoms, but have not yet documented their symptoms with a medical provider, will both benefit from this extension.

Conditions that Qualify For Presumptive Status

The VA has previously granted presumptive service-connection for medically unexplained illnesses among Gulf War Veterans. These conditions have been collectively referred to as "Gulf War Syndrome", but they are actually not a single condition because symptoms can vary widely.

Two groups of conditions qualify as medically unexplained illnesses among Gulf War Veterans. The first category includes undiagnosed illnesses, which are indicated by a cluster of chronic symptoms, but do not fit into any known medical diagnosis. Common symptoms are fatigue, muscle and joint pain, headaches, memory problems, and sleep disorders. Other symptoms may be present as well.

The second category of conditions involves a known diagnosis, but an unknown cause of the condition. Conditions that fit into this category include Chronic Fatigue Syndrome, Fibromyalgia, and functional gastrointestinal disorders such as irritable boil syndrome, functional dyspepsia, and functional abdominal pain syndrome.

To receive Compensation, a Gulf War Veteran must have experienced symptoms for at least six months, and the symptoms must be at least 10 percent disabling.

Benefits should be awarded for these conditions without regard to their cause. The VA sometimes mistakenly denies these claims because evidence of a specific event or injury causing the disability has not been provided. If your claim for a medically unexplained illness has been denied for this reason, you should consider appealing your claim denial.

A wide variety of symptoms can qualify a Gulf War Veteran for presumptive service-connection, so veterans who are experiencing unexplained medical issues shouldfile a claim for benefits or consult with a veterans attorney.

Checklist Steps in the Fully Developed Claim Process to Follow:

Go to Page 214 for more detail on these steps

1. Determine Entitlement Based on Service and the Merit of Your Claim
2. Submit an Intent to File, VA Form 21-0966, but Don't File a Claim at This Point
3. Obtain a Copy of Your Discharge
4. Obtain Copies of Service Treatment Records
5. Obtain Copies of Your Military Personnel File
6. Obtain of Copies of VA Medical Center Records
7. Obtain Copies of Your Own Private Medical Records
8. Obtain Your Own DBQs from Private Clinicians
9. Obtain Your Own Private Medical Opinions
10. Write a Detailed and Credible Lay Statement to Describe Your Claim
11. Follow Our Instructions in Chapter 4 for Submitting the Claim

13. Request for Reevaluation or Change for an Existing Benefit

Taken from the 2019 VA Budget Proposal
Reopened workload projections aid in forecasting changes to a Veteran's degree of disability rating. These claims result when Veterans file amended claims because their disabilities worsen, new evidence of service-connection becomes available, and/or new legislation or regulation allows for additional Compensation. In 2017, 291,139 Veterans, or 6.5 percent of Veterans on the Compensation rolls, received an increase to their disability benefits, as shown on the following chart. The average increased rating level in 2017 was to 73.3 percent. This is an increase over 2016 levels, when 252,157 Veterans received an increased rating and the average increased rating level was to 72.0 percent. The higher increased rating levels in 2017 compared to 2016 is consistent with recent trends, and has contributed to the increases to the overall average degree of disability.

Veterans Compensation 2017 Increased Disability Rating Levels											
	Disability Level Increase										
Current	10%	20%	30%	40%	50%	60%	70%	80%	90%	100%	**Total**
0%	65	66	52	46	29	27	28	20	11	82	**426**
10%	-	9,729	5,842	6,699	2,550	5,490	3,412	1,894	831	3,398	**39,845**
20%	-	-	6,948	6,915	2,993	4,406	2,397	2,844	985	2,828	**30,316**
30%	-	-	-	8,227	6,261	4,882	4,842	3,463	1,343	3,399	**32,417**
40%	-	-	-	-	7,309	10,10	6,880	5,750	2,407	4,257	**36,705**
50%	-	-	-	-	-	8,295	7,693	5,408	2,826	3,955	**28,177**
60%	-	-	-	-	-	-	12,74	11,58	5,939	6,670	**36,940**
70%	-	-	-	-	-	-	-	15,07	9,080	9,036	**33,190**
80%	-	-	-	-	-	-	-	-	19,83	11,58	**31,424**
90%	-	-	-	-	-	-	-	-	-	21,69	**21,699**
Total	65	9,795	12,84	21,88	19,14	33,20	37,99	46,03	43,26	66,90	**291,139**

Details:

Veterans already on claim are getting older and in many cases their disabilities are increasing in severity. If they have legitimate medical or work-related evidence of an increase in disability, there is a possibility for an increased rating and more monthly income.

It can also work in the opposite direction. Sometimes, a request for reevaluation of a rating can result in downgrading that rating or even reevaluating whether a service connection exists. I have heard of veterans not only losing the rating but losing the service connection and the entwere award. You should always be careful in requesting a change that you have a legitimate increase in disability and that a reevaluation won't reduce your existing award. If you have been service-connected for at least 10 years, that service connection is protected and VA cannot take it away from you. If you have had the same rating for at least 20 years, that rating is protected and VA can only increase it but not decrease it.

Some veterans have developed secondary conditions, meaning that their primary disability has resulted in conditions that are caused by the primary disability. For example, service-connected diabetes can result in cardiovascular disease which would be a new condition but would be considered secondary to the diabetes and therefore service-connected. If the cardiovascular disease results in disability with a rating, VA will combine those ratings to produce a new larger rating. Combined ratings are not additive. For example a 40% rating for diabetes and a 20% rating for cardiovascular disease results in a 50% combined rating not a 60% additive rating.

If you have developed a disability that has been aggravated or caused by a service-connected disability, do not continue in this section. Instead, go to the section above that is devoted to this type of claim "#6 Secondary Service Connection or Aggravation of an Existing Condition."

Also please note that if your disability has worsened or you have developed new disabilities to the point that you are severely disabled and could qualify under "Special Monthly Compensation," (SMC) go ahead and go to that section below for this type of application instead of going to claim for secondary disability.

If enough evidence is produced to show that there is a reasonable assumption or inference that the current disability is worsened, then a strong opinion letter from a physician might sway VA to make a favorable decision.

You should not submit a request for a change or increase in rating unless you are sure that your disability has worsened or you have developed a new service-connected disability. I suspect many veterans submit a request not really understanding what they are doing and simply hope that they will somehow get a larger check. For example, a veteran with diabetes has developed numbness in his feet – a possible new service-connected disability associated with diabetes for Agent Orange exposure – but it has not affected his ability to ambulate, to dress, to bathe or in any other way to function over what he had experienced in the past. An increase or change may not be justified. The claimant has to justify any increase or change with medical evidence that the service-connected disability has worsened, a new ratable service-connected disability has appeared or a new secondary disability has developed. Without this, you are wasting the time of the veteran service representatives and adding to the backlog – preventing other veterans from getting benefits.

If it is going to take you some time to assemble the evidence for the application, do an "Intent to File" using the following form:

VA Form 21-0966 INTENT TO FILE

Forms That Might Be Used:
VA Form 10-5345 – Request for and Authorization to Release VHA Medical Records
VA Form 10-5345a – Individual's Request for a Copy of His or Her Own VA Medical Records
VA Form 21-4192 – Request for Employment information in Connection With Claim for Disability Benefits
VA Form 21-526EZ – Application for Disability Compensation and Related Compensation Benefits

Forms for Representation for Assistance if Desired
VA Form 21-22A – Appointment of Individual a Claimant's Representative
VA Form 21-0845 – Authorization to Disclose Personal information to a Third Party

Steps to Follow:

Follow our instructions in Chapter 4 for submitting this type of claim.

Checklist Steps in the Fully Developed Claim Process to Follow:

Go to Page 214 for more detail on these steps

1. Obtain of Copies of VA Medical Center Records
2. Obtain Copies of Your Own Private Medical Records
3. Obtain Your Own DBQs from Private Clinicians
4. Obtain Your Own Private Medical Opinions
5. Write a Detailed and Credible Lay Statement to Describe Your Claim
6. Follow Our Instructions in Chapter 4 for Submitting the Claim

14. Section 1151 Claim

Details:

This non-service-connected disability benefit is named after the section in Title 38 United States Code where it is found. If a non-service-connected disabling condition is caused by or aggravated by VA examination, hospital care, medical or surgical treatment, Vocational Rehabilitation, or (beginning November 1, 2000) a program of Compensated Work Therapy under 38 USC 1718, then Compensation is payable for that condition as though the condition was service-connected.

Remember, however, that even though Compensation will be paid, the condition is in fact NOT service-connected, and should not be called such. Because of this, ancillary benefits beyond Compensation are limited in Section 1151 cases: in general, they are restricted to the applicable priority medical care; a clothing allowance (where applicable); and, where the qualifying level of compensable disability is present, an automobile and appropriate special adaptive equipment under 38 USC, Chapter 39 and special adapted housing under 38 USC, Chapter 21.

Compensation for disabilities under Section 1151 may be combined with Compensation for any service-connected conditions the veteran may also have. If the veteran is awarded any amount from a judicial award, settlement, or compromise for the same condition(s) for which Compensation under Section 1151 has been (or will be) authorized, the Compensation otherwise payable for such condition(s) must be withheld until the full amount of the award, settlement, or compromise has been recovered. [38 USC 1151; 38 CFR §§ 3.358, 3.361–3.363, 3.800] Such recovery does not affect entitlement to any Compensation payable for service-connected disabilities, however.

These types of claims are not common because the burden of proof is so high. In order to meet qualifications of 38 U.S.C. 1151, the proximate cause of additional disability or death must be

- carelessness, negligence, lack of proper skwell, error in judgment, or similar instance of fault on the part of VA in furnishing the hospital care, medical or surgical treatment, or examination
- an event not reasonably foreseeable, or
- the provision of

- training and rehabilitation by VA or one of its service providers as part of an approved rehabilitation program under 38 U.S.C. Chapter 31, or
- a CWT program.

Even if you succeed in getting one division of VA to blame the other division of VA for doing wrong, you still have to demonstrate the exact nature of your disability before and after the treatment. Evidence for this claim must be some sort of hardcopy evidence from hospital or clinical or organizational records. You would have a difficult time establishing an award based on personal testimony or testimony of witnesses. This is not to say it can't be done.

For example, if you had a knee operation for joint replacement and they did it on your good knee instead of your bad knee, this is pretty easy to establish. Or if you have a mastectomy and they removed the wrong breast, that's pretty simple to prove. Or if they operated on you and left a surgical instrument inside – pretty straightforward. It's the errors or negligence involving treatment protocols or surgical procedures and what was right and what was wrong for the particular condition that might be difficult to prove.

VA will consider as an informal claim for benefits under 38 U.S.C. 1151, any statement showing an intent to file a claim for benefits resulting from

- hospital, medical or surgical treatment by VA
- examination by VA, or
- pursuit of a course of vocational rehabilitation.

Note: If an individual or his or her representative files an in formal claim, VA send him or her the appropriate application form.

You should seek help with representation for such a claim. Likely it will require an attorney who specializes in these types of medical malpractice claims for veterans. Perhaps a service organization has experience with these claims as well.

15. Tropical Diseases – Service Connection Is Presumed with a Time Limit

(These claims also include certain presumptive conditions for Afghanistan veterans)

Details:
The veteran must have 90 continuous days or more of service. The disorder or disease must manifest disability to a degree of 10% or more within one year from date of separation or at the end of the standard incubation period. Disorders or diseases caused by treatment may also be considered service-connected. Because service connection is presumed, it is not required to produce evidence for service connection – only evidence of the manifestation of the disorder or disease. Manifesting does not mean medical diagnosis, only that evidence shows the existence.

- Amebiasis.
- Blackwater fever.

- Cholera.
- Dracontiasis.
- Dysentery.
- Filariasis.
- Leishmaniasis, including kala-azar.
- Loiasis.
- Malaria.
- Onchocerciasis.
- Oroya fever.
- Pinta.
- Plague.
- Schistosomiasis.
- Yaws.
- Yellow fever.

Qualifying periods of service for the following infectious diseases include active military, naval, or air service in the Southist Asia theater of operations during the Gulf War period of August 2, 1990, to July 30, 1991, or active military, naval, or air service on or after September 19, 2001, in Afghanistan.

- Brucellosis,
- Campylobacter jejuni,
- Coxiella burnetti (Q fever),
- Malaria,
- Mycobacterium tuberculosis,
- Nontyphoid Salmonella,
- Shigella,
- Visceral leishmaniasis, and
- Ist Nile virus.

If it is going to take you some time to assemble the evidence for the application, submit an "Intent to File" using the following form:

VA Form 21-0966 INTENT TO FILE

Forms That Might Be Used:
VA Form 10-5345 – Request for and Authorization to Release VHA Medical Records
VA Form 10-5345a – Individual's Request for a Copy of His or Her Own VA Medical Records
VA Form 21-526EZ – Application for Disability Compensation and Related Compensation Benefits
VA Form 21-4142 – Authorization and Consent to Release information to the Department of Veterans Affairs

Forms for Representation for Assistance if Desired
VA Form 21-22A – Appointment of Individual a Claimant's Representative
VA Form 21-0845 – Authorization to Disclose Personal information to a Third Party

16. Special Monthly Compensation (SMC)

Details:

The majority of service-connected disabilities are defined by a percentage ranging from 0 to 100 percent to reflect the severity of the condition(s) and the disabling effects they have on the veteran. These percentages are explicitly defined by Federal Regulations under the Schedule for Rating Disabilities (there is a copy of this on the Claim Support Disc) and are assigned a monetary Compensation award based on the vocational limitations that these injuries or disorders cause and subsequently the effect they may have on monetary earnings.

Some injuries and disorders are more severe in nature and result in several additional debilitating residual conditions that can have additional adverse affects on an individual's socioeconomic state. To better assist with meeting the specialized needs of these individuals, additional benefits are available under Special Monthly Compensation (SMC) ratings provided under Title 38 of U.S.C. 1114. These ratings are in addition to the numerical ratings established under the standard rating schedule and are identified by letters such as SMC (k), SMC (l), SMC (m), SMC (n), SMC (o), SMC(p), SMC (r), SMC (s) and the recently added SMC (t). These rates are simply named after the subsections of the Code of Federal Regulations that outline the required eligibility requirements for each level of SMC. SMC provides additional monetary Compensation awards and where applicable can establish entitlement to additional ancillary benefits such as the VA's Specially Adapted Housing Grant and the Automobile and Adaptive Equipment Grants.

The basic elements of Special Monthly Compensation Ratings include anatomical (or physical) loss or the loss of use of limbs, hands, feet and/or reproductive organs; aphonia; deafness; blindness; loss of boil and bladder control; being permanently housebound; and a need for regular aid and attendance with activities of daily living or a higher level of care—all of which must be a result of the veteran's service-connected disabilities.

Most veterans suffering these disabilities are fully aware of the possibility of receiving SMC where it is appropriate and have long since applied. One never knows, however, if someone fell through the cracks and never bothered to apply.

If it is going to take you some time to assemble the evidence for the application, submit an "Intent to File" using the following form:

VA Form 21-0966 INTENT TO FILE

Forms That Might Be Used:
VA Form 10-5345 – Request for and Authorization to Release VHA Medical Records
VA Form 10-5345a – Individual's Request for a Copy of His or Her Own VA Medical Records
VA Form 21-526EZ – Application for Disability Compensation and Related Compensation Benefits
VA Form 21-4142 – Authorization and Consent to Release information to the Department of Veterans Affairs

17. Specific Ancillary Benefits, Allowances and Grants

Even though many disabled veterans are aware of these special allowances and grants, it doesn't hurt to reiterate what is available. Perhaps the veteran is in need at this point and never bothered to apply previously. This is a reminder of these benefits. We provide no further instructions here. Here is a list of these special allowances.

Housing Grants for 2020 and their amounts are discussed in greater detail in Chapter 8

- SAH Grant
- SHA Grant
- *Temporary Residence Adaptation (TRA)*
- Supplemental Financing

Automobile Allowance
Clothing Allowance
Medal of Honor Pension
HISA Grants

We discuss these grants in Chapter 1 this book and in Chapter 3 and Chapter 8. For more information on Medal of Honor Pension go to the VA website at www.VA.gov

The clothing allowance is available through the Veterans Health Administration. You need to be enrolled in health care to get this. The other benefits require special application due to certain severe disabilities. Contact a service organization if you need help getting these special allowances.

Here are the forms that are appropriate to some of these benefits.

VA Form 10-0103 – Assistance in Acquiring Home Improvement and Structural Alterations (HISA Grant)
VA Form 21-4502 – Application for Automobile or Other Conveyance and Adaptive Equipment
VA Form 26-4555 – Application in Acquiring Special Housing Adaptations

CHAPTER 6
Applying for Pension and Survivors Pension with Aid and Attendance

IN THIS CHAPTER:

Eligibility for VA Pension and Survivor Pension Benefits

Veterans Pension and Survivor's (Death) Pension are disability income programs available to veterans or to the single surviving spouses or dependent children of deceased veterans. Pension is often referred to as "**The Aid and Attendance Benefit.**" **This is a misnomer, but the title still lives on.** These programs provide <u>tax-free income</u> ranging from about $768 a month to about $3,032 a month. For a younger totally disabled veteran, the benefit can also include payments for his or her dependent children.

Eligibility requirements for Veterans Pension – a living veteran – require active duty service for at least consecutive 90 days, with at least one of those days during a period of war AND an honorable discharge or a discharged classified as other than dishonorable. Service in combat is not required. Had the veteran been discharged before 90 days of service because of a disability incurred or aggravated in service or had a service-connected disability at the time of discharge that would have justified a discharge for disability, he or she is still eligible. For veterans of the Gulf War, the service requirement is 24 months or completion of the requirement for active

duty service, whichever comes first. Eligibility for Survivors Pension – certain survivors of a veteran – requires the same wartime service for the deceased veteran.

Here is a condensed Period of War chart for Pension benefit purposes from 38 CFR § 3.2:

Period of War	Beginning and Ending Dates
World War 2	December 7, 1941 through December 31, 1946
Korean Conflict	June 27, 1950 through January 31, 1955
Vietnam Era	August 5, 1964 through May 7, 1975; for veterans who served "in country" before August 5, 1964, February 28, 1961 through May 7, 1975
Gulf War	August 2, 1990 through a date to be set by law or Presidential Proclamation

Veterans Pension is the companion benefit to Disability Compensation. Compensation – a much more common benefit covered in Chapter 5 – is for veterans who are disabled because of injuries or illnesses incurred or aggravated while on active duty. <u>A veteran household cannot receive Pension and Compensation at the same time. Likewise, a surviving spouse cannot receive both Survivors Pension and DIC at the same time</u>. A decision must be made as to which benefit is a better fit. Fortunately, the claimant may switch back and forth between the two benefits.

<u>Please note, VA defines a "claimant" as any person who intends on making application for veterans benefits or has made application for benefits</u>. Those receiving benefits are generally called "beneficiaries".

Here are some recent figures for those on claim for benefits.

Beneficiaries	2018	2019	2020 Estimate
Compensation & DIC	5,070,505	*5,281,013	5,476,521
Pension & Survivor Pension	462,849	447,805	443,832
Education Program Trainees	893,656	883,625	876,743
New Housing Loans	581,767	556,280	562,178

Source: DVA 2020 Budget Proposal

Pension and Survivors Pension will pay the difference between the claimant's gross household income (less exclusions), and the applicable Pension rate in either of the 2 tables provided below. There is a special provision, which we will explain later, which allows the claimant to deduct long term care expenses, like assisted living, from income. In many cases, claimants must be "medically rated" in order to allow for these deductions and qualify for a larger benefit amount.

Aid and Attendance Is a Misnomer

Veterans Pension and Survivors Pension are sometimes nicknamed the "Aid and Attendance Benefit." This misnomer is used due to a common need for an aid and attendance rating to qualify. "Aid and attendance" or "housebound" labels pertain to medical ratings associated with 18 different monetary allowances available with Veterans Pension, Survivors Pension, Disability Compensation, Dependency and Indemnity Compensation (DIC) and certain forms of Special Monthly Compensation (SMC). See Chapter 3 for more information on these allowances and how to apply for the allowances unique to those other benefits.

In regard to Pension and Survivors Pension, there is no such benefit called the "Aid and Attendance Benefit." The benefit is either called Veterans (VA) Pension, Survivors Pension, or Special Monthly Pension if you are seeking a medical rating for "aid and attendance" to qualify.

A full checklist of forms and supporting evidence required to file a Fully Developed Claim can be found below, on the Claim Support Disc that comes with this book or online at SupportDisc.com.

2020 Maximum Annual Veterans Pension Rates (MAPR) Effective December 1, 2019 – 1.6% COLA Increase		
If you are a veteran...	**Annual**	**Monthly**
Without Spouse or Child	$13,752	$1,146
No dependents, medical expenses must exceed 5% of MAPR	$687	$57
With One Dependent	$18,008	$1,500
With dependents, medical expenses must exceed 5% of MAPR	$900	$75
Housebound Without Dependents	$16,805	$1,400
Housebound With One Dependent	$21,063	$1,755
A&A Without Dependents	$22,939	$1,911
A&A With One Dependent	$27,195	$2,266
Two Vets Married to Each Other	$18,008	$1,500
Two Vets Married to Each Other One H/B	$21,063	$1,755
Two Vets Married to Each Other Both H/B	$24,114	$2,009
Two Vets Married to Each Other One A/A	$27,195	$2,266
Two Vets Married to Each Other One A/A One H/B	$30,241	$2,520
Two Vets Married to Each Other Both A/A	$36,387	$3,032
Add for Each Additional Child to any category above	$2,351	$195
Add for Each Additional Child	$2,351	$195
MAPR FOR CHILD ALONE	$2,351	$195
Child Earned Income Exclusion effective 1/1/2000	$7,200	$600

Disability Requirements for a Veteran Claimant

If a veteran is younger than age 65, he or she must be permanently and totally disabled (can be a non-service connected disability). This means he or she cannot maintain any gainful employment. Evidence of disability must be submitted with the claim. If the veteran is receiving Social Security Disability, this will qualify as being totally disabled and VA will accept evidence of Social Security Disability to qualify the veteran for Pension (make sure, before applying, that VA Pension will not offset the claimant's Social Security Disability). Being on group or personal disability insurance benefits may or may not qualify the veteran for Pension prior to age 65. If the veteran claimant is age 65 and older, there is no requirement for permanent and total disability.

A full checklist of VA forms and supporting evidence required to submit a Fully Developed Claim for Survivors Pension can be found below as well as on the Claim Support Disc that comes with this book or online at www.SupportDisc.com.

2020 Maximum Annual Survivors Pension Rates (MAPR) Effective December 1, 2019 – 1.6% COLA Increase		
If you are a surviving spouse...	Annual	Monthly
MAPR Without Dependent Child	$9,224	$768
No dependents, medical expenses must exceed 5% of MAPR	$461	$38
MAPR With One Dependent Child	$12,072	$1,006
With dependents, medical expenses must exceed 5% of MAPR	$603	$50
Housebound Without Dependents	$11,273	$939
Housebound With One Dependent	$14,116	$1,176
A&A Without Dependents	$14,742	$1,228
A&A Without Dependents (SAW Veteran's Surviving Spouse)	$15,339	$1,278
A&A With One Dependent	$17,586	$1,465
A&A With One Dependent (SAW Veteran's Surviving Spouse)	$18,119	$1,509
SBP/MIW Annuity Limitation	$9,224	$768
Add for Each Additional Child	$2,351	$195
MAPR FOR CHILD ALONE	$2,351	$195
Child Earned Income Exclusion effective 1/1/2000	$7,200	$600

The entitlement issues for aid and attendance or housebound ratings as well as the application of income and asset and net worth test requirements are the same for Veterans Pension and Survivors Pension. There are some minor entitlement differences between the two benefits which we will discuss below.

No Disability Requirements for a Surviving Spouse Claimant

The single surviving spouse can be any age and does not have to be permanently and totally disabled prior to age 65. The veteran, who died, did not have to be totally disabled if death occurred before age 65. The veteran who died does have to qualify based on at least 90 days active duty service as well as serving during a period of war. Since 1980, the requirement for active duty service is at least 24 months or fulfillment of an active duty call up if less than 24 months.

Marriage Requirements for a Surviving Spouse Claimant

Application should <u>not</u> be made unless it is certain that the surviving spouse meets the rules as a surviving spouse. <u>All of these following conditions must apply,</u> or the surviving spouse is not eligible. Also see 38 CFR § 3.50 and 38 CFR § 3.205

1. The surviving spouse must have met the conditions to be married under VA rules. Generally, this means a marriage lasting at least one year or a child was born as a result of the marriage regardless of the length of time married. Under certain conditions, VA will also accept common-law marriages or marriages where the couple held themselves out to be married and can prove that was their intent. See information on marriage in in the Appendix.

2. The surviving spouse must have lived continuously with the veteran while they were married unless they were separated due to the fault of the veteran. Evidence regarding such a separation will be required.

3. The surviving spouse must have been married to the veteran when the veteran died.

4. The surviving spouse cannot have remarried after the veteran's death even if the surviving spouse is currently single. <u>There is one exception to this rule.</u> If the surviving spouse remarried after the veteran's death and that marriage was terminated either through death or divorce prior to November 1 of 1990 and the surviving spouse has since remained single, that person is eligible. See 38 CFR § 3.55

5. If the surviving spouse was married more than once and the most recent marriage was to a veteran who served during a period of war and that marriage ended in the death of the veteran, and the surviving spouse did not remarry, the surviving spouse is eligible for Survivors Pension based on this second marriage.

Effective Date for a Survivor Claimant

In Chapter 2, we discussed in detail effective dates for back-pay purposes. Understanding various effective dates can be confusing. <u>For a survivor claimant who makes an original claim within one year of the veteran's death, the effective date is the first day of the month in which the veteran died.</u>

<u>If an original claim is filed one year after the veteran's death, the effective date is the date VA received either the claim (VA Form 21p-527EZ or 534EZ) or an Intent to File (generally made via VA Form 21-0966).</u>

The Income Test for Pension and Survivor Pension

Pension is based on a maximum yearly income amount called the "Maximum Annual Pension Rate" (MAPR), shown in the previous tables above. A claimant's household income – the combined income of husband, wife and dependent residents where applicable – must be less than the applicable

MAPR for that particular type of claim in order to qualify for a benefit. The actual benefit paid to the claimant is the difference between the applicable MAPR and the combined gross household income reduced for medical costs and adjusted by a 5% deductible. This adjusted income is called "Income for VA Purposes" or IVAP by VA. If the veteran or spouse has a need for the aid and attendance of another person the MAPR is increased to adjust for care costs of the household.

If a claimant's calculation for IVAP is a negative amount, the IVAP is considered to be zero dollars. This is important because this concept of a negative calculation for IVAP being zero income applies to the new net worth limit, which for 2020 is $129,094.

The medical deductible is calculated by multiplying .05 (5%) times the basic MAPR for the application category. The basic MAPR is that amount that does not include any allowances for aid and attendance or housebound. For example, for a single veteran applicant, the basic annual MAPR in 2020 is $13,752 and the deductible is $687. For a veteran applicant with one dependent the basic MAPR in 2020 is $18,008 and the deductible is $900. For a single surviving spouse, the basic MAPR in 2020 is $9,224 and the deductible is $461.

Claimants, qualifying on income alone without a rating for aid and attendance or housebound, typically need to make such little money they are likely below the poverty level. You should make application for low income veterans even when the benefit might only be a few hundred dollars.

For example, if a single veteran is healthy and his gross household income is $700/month ($8,400/year), he would qualify for the difference between the Basic Pension Rate of $13,752/month less the $8,400 and the 5% deductible. The monthly benefit for him in this situation would be (($1,146 - $700) - $57) = $389/month.

Another example, using rates for 2020, a husband and spouse (the dependent) with no medical rating will not qualify if their income exceeds $18,008/year or $1,500/month from all sources. Fortunately, their gross household income can be reduced by ongoing care and medical costs to qualify (under certain conditions) which we will discuss below. Households earning as much as $5,000 a month or more may still qualify even though income is far greater than the MAPR.

VA considers income to be anything that comes through the door as cash or the equivalent of cash in a given year. Withdrawals from IRAs, 401(k)s and other retirement accounts are considered income. The cash left in the IRA is considered an asset. Gross Social Security income and monthly retirement from employer pensions are considered income. Long Term Care Insurance, gifts, winnings from gambling, and inheritances are also considered income in a given year.

See how a claimant's IVAP and benefit is calculated on the following page:

IVAP for Initial Application

	Estimated Annual Income
Minus	Estimated Recurring Medical Expenses
Plus	Medical Deductible
Equals	IVAP

Benefit for Initial Application

	Applicable MAPR
Minus	IVAP for Initial Application
Equals	Annual Benefit Amount
Divided by	12
Rounded down	Monthly Benefit Amount

IVAP for Claimant Receiving Benefits

	Actual Annual Income
Minus	All Allowable Medical Expenses
Plus	Medical Deductible
Equals	IVAP

Benefit for Claimant Receiving Benefits

	Applicable MAPR
Minus	IVAP for Claimant Receiving Benefits
Equals	Annual Benefit Amount
Divided by	12
Rounded down	Monthly Benefit Amount

Some Important Examples of What Is Included as Income

The following are some important examples of countable income from a larger list found in the Adjudication Manual M21-1, Part V, Subpart iii, Chapter 1, Section I and 38 CFR § 3.271

> ➤ **REMEMBER, income is the combined household GROSS income – before deductions – to include a spouse and a dependent child under certain circumstances.**

➢ **Income from VA Disability Compensation is considered income when applying for Pension and should be reported on the application**. A veteran must ultimately elect to receive either VA Pension or Compensation. He or she cannot collect both.

➢ The following types of income are all countable income for Pension purposes:
  ➢ earnings
  ➢ retirement or survivors' programs
  ➢ interest
  ➢ dividends
  ➢ unemployment Compensation
  ➢ operation of a business, and
  ➢ life insurance proceeds received before December 10, 2004, because of the death of a Veteran

➢ If a claimant's benefits, such as Social Security, are subject to involuntary withholding due to legal action initiated by a third party, count the entire amount even though the claimant does not receive it all.

➢ When an individual retirement account (IRA) or similar instrument (401(k), 403(b), etc.) starts paying benefits, count the entire amount even though it represents a partial return of principal.

➢ Count, on an annual basis, only the amount of interest received from a non-retirement annuity or similar instrument if the beneficiary purchased the annuity using funds the Department of Veterans Affairs (VA) already considered as a part of net worth, or conversion of assets from a property sale. In all other situations, count the entire amount received as income.

➢ If a claimant receives a distribution of retirement benefits, count the entire amount received. This is the case, even though all or part of the distribution might represent a return of withheld wages which were previously counted as IVAP as part of the claimant's gross wages.

➢ Regular cash contributions for the purpose of paying for the claimant's maintenance are not considered countable gifts. If a third party pays for medical expenses, those same medical expenses cannot be allowed as deductions from the claimant's or beneficiary's income.

➢ If a beneficiary is entitled to receive income, such as a retirement benefit, but waives the income, the amount that would be received if not for the waiver still counts as income as described in 38 CFR 3.276(b). The intent of this provision is to prevent a person from creating a need for Pension.

➢ Count net winnings from gambling as income. Gambling losses may be deducted from gross winnings during the same year to arrive at net gambling income.

➢ Count the following as income

- United States Government Life Insurance (USGLI) proceeds
- National Service Life Insurance (NSLI) proceeds, and
- Total Disability Insurance Payments (TDIP).

➤ Count child support payments as income of the custodial parent if they are payable to the custodial parent.

➤ Count VA education or <u>Disability Compensation</u> benefits, including <u>Dependency and Indemnity Compensation (DIC)</u>, and benefits paid to a claimant as accrued amounts based on the entitlement and death of another beneficiary.

➤ There is some confusion as to how to account for insurance payments that reimburse for medical expenses that would ordinarily qualify for a deduction to calculate IVAP. It is important to note that medical expenses are called "Unreimbursed Medical Expenses" or UMEs. Thus, any expenses that are paid by insurance are obviously not deductible as they have been reimbursed. On the other hand, for purposes of application, the Pension Management will often compensate for the confusion between reimbursed medical expenses and unreimbursed medical expenses by counting recurring insurance reimbursements such as monthly reimbursement from long-term care insurance as income.

Some Important Examples of What Is Excluded as Income as Well As Other Income Issues

Following are some important examples of exclusions from income from a larger list found in the Adjudication Manual M21-1, Part V, Subpart iii, Chapter 1, Section I and 38 CFR § 3.272

➤ VA will not count payments if federal law requires they be excluded from income and/or net worth for purposes of VA benefit calculations, regardless of whether the payment or program is specified in M21-1, Part V, Subpart iii, 1.I.3, or M21-1, Part V, Subpart iii, 1.I.11.

➤ Social Security Administration (SSA) subsequently determines he individual was actually entitled to regular Social Security benefits. SSA converts the SSI payments to regular Social Security payments, and lists the income as SSI Windfall.

➤ Do not count income tax refunds, including the Federal Earned Income Credit.

➤ Do not count Social Security or similar benefits withheld to recoup a prior overpayment from SSA or other non-VA organization. Count the check amount received, if any, plus any Medicare deduction. If the withholding is due to legal action by a third party, such as a garnishment order, count the entire gross income benefit and not the net amount left after garnishment.

➤ Chore Services Payments. Do not count amounts paid by a governmental entity to an individual to care for a disabled VA claimant in the claimant's home, provided eligibility for the payments is based on the disabled VA claimant's financial need. Payments are not countable if they are paid to a dependent of the disabled VA claimant where counting the payments would reduce the disabled VA beneficiary's rate of Pension, and eligibility for the payments is based on the VA beneficiary's financial need.

Example 1: A spouse of a veteran beneficiary is paid by the State to take care of the Veteran in their home under a chore services program. The income is not countable. It makes no difference whether the State pays the spouse directly or pays the Veteran.

Example 2: A surviving spouse beneficiary is paid by the State to take care of a neighbor in the neighbor's home under a chore services program. The chore services payments are countable earned income since eligibility for the payments derives from the neighbor's financial need and not the financial need of the VA beneficiary.

➢ In general, do not count interest on IRAs if it cannot be withdrawn without incurring a substantial penalty. However, when the claimant starts drawing down his/her IRA, all payments, including interest and principal, are countable income.

➢ Loans, including Reverse Mortgages. Do not count loans to a claimant as long as the claimant incurs a legally binding obligation to repay the loan. Do not count funds received from a reverse mortgage. A reverse mortgage is considered a home equity loan that must be repaid when the homeowner no longer lives in the home. Loans must be distinguished from gifts. A gift disguised as a loan is countable.

➢ Do not count VA Pension that is paid as an accrued benefit.

➢ Do not count insurance dividends, as they are considered to be a return of excess premium payments. However, if insurance dividends are left on deposit, count any interest earned. Count TDIP (cash payments to totally disabled policyholders) as income.

➢ Do not count withdrawals from regular bank accounts and certificates of deposit, as they do not constitute income events because the interest is counted as it accrues, and withdrawal is merely a conversion of assets. However, if the assets are in an IRA or other retirement account, apply the provisions as outlined above.

➢ Do not count the proceeds of cashed-in life insurance policies as income. Such proceeds are considered profit realized from the disposition of real or personal property, which is excluded under 38 CFR 3.272(e).

➢ Under Public Law 108-454, do not count the lump sum proceeds of a life insurance policy on a Veteran who dies after December 9, 2004.

➢ Exclude up to $5,000 per year of income from a State or municipality that is paid to the Veteran as a Veterans' benefit due to injury or disease when determining annual income for Veterans Pension benefits. This applies to determinations of annual income for calendar years beginning January 1, 2012.

➤ Do not count the amount received from an insurance policy when a claimant loses property due to fire, flood, theft, or other casualty loss as long as it does not exceed the value of the lost property.

➤ In general, do not count any reimbursement income received from an insurance company, other than for personal injury. This exclusion applies only to loss or damage to property and does not apply to personal injury. See the treatment for long-term care insurance.

➤ Exclude proceeds of casualty insurance from net worth unless evidence of record shows that the beneficiary has no intention of using the money received as reimbursement for property loss to repair or replace that property. Request documentation showing the beneficiary's commitment to replace or repair the property if needed.

➤ Do not count VA burial benefits. If a beneficiary claims a final expense deduction and subsequently receives VA burial benefits as reimbursement for paying those same expenses, adjust the award.

➤ Proceeds received from the sale of property are generally viewed as a conversion of assets and are not countable income for Pension purposes. VA does, however, include the net proceeds from the sale of property as new assets when determining the net worth of a claimant.

➤ If a beneficiary who operates a business sells property or merchandise in connection with the business, add any profit received from the sale of the property to the other income of the business. For information on deductions from gross business income, see M21-1, Part V, Subpart iii, 1.G.11.a.

➤ Counting Income from Installment Sales. If a claimant or dependent sells property and receives payment in installments, count as income any amounts received over and above the sales price, but not until an amount equal to the sales price has been received by the seller. This principle applies regardless of whether the sale occurred before or after the date of entitlement to Pension. It is not necessary to distinguish between payment of principal and interest in the installment sale context. As soon as the down payment and installment payments received by the beneficiary equal the sales price, all subsequent installment payments count as income.

The Ratings for Aid and Attendance or Housebound

A Rating Allows for Special Deductions and Additional Income Allowances
If a veteran is younger than age 65, he or she must be totally disabled to receive Pension. Disability does not have to be service connected but can be due to any cause. Medical evidence must be submitted for these types of applications to prove total disability. Being on Social Security Disability is generally adequate proof of total disability prior to age 65 (ensure VA Pension will not adversely affect Social Security Disability before applying). At age 65 and older there is no requirement for total disability.

VA will provide additional income in the form of an allowance on top of the basic Pension benefit of $13,752/year or $1,146/month if the veteran has a regular medical (care) need for assistance or a need for supervision due to disability. This is sometimes called "Special Monthly Pension."

A medical need for assistance or supervision due to disability is, in many cases, crucial to getting the Pension or Survivors Pension benefit. A "rating" from VA recognizes either the regular need for aid and attendance from a caregiver or the condition of being housebound. This rating, determined by a doctor's examination, on *VA Form 21-2680*, allows certain medical and care expenses and ancillary non-medical expenses to be subtracted or deducted from income.

A "rating" also increases the allowable Veterans Pension or Survivor Pension rate in the MAPR rate tables. For example, a single veteran with no rating is only eligible for basic Pension, up to $1,146 a month. If the same veteran becomes disabled (or health deteriorates due to age, for example) and shows a need for the ongoing aid and attendance of another individual, that veteran would be eligible for up to $1,911 a month.

A married veteran, who is rated for "aid and attendance," could be paid up to $2,266 a month.

If a non-veteran spouse of a healthy-living veteran has a regular need for assistance or supervision, a lesser benefit without the additional income allowance is also available. This rate is for Pension with One Dependent and currently pays up to $1,500 a month.

Except for very poor veteran households, most veteran households could not get the Pension benefit without this special rating provision for the deduction of personal care and medical-related expenses, simply because their income is too high.

The high cost of medical and medical-related expenses associated with long term care such as home care, assisted living or nursing home care are usually the main deductible expenses VA counts when calculating the benefit. A single veteran, for example, who is paying $3,000/month for care at assisted living and has income of $2,800/month would qualify for full Special Monthly Pension (which includes the aid and attendance allowance of $1,911 a month) IF the veteran was "medically rated" for the need of aid and attendance of another person.

Unfortunately, not all eligible claimants – especially aging claimants – are receiving Pension or Survivor Pension. Most do not know about the benefit or this special medical deduction to reduce income. Often, these unknowing claimants will call VA or go to a local service office for assistance and they will be asked what their income is. In many cases, the people who provide this assistance are not aware of or do not discuss the special rules allowing for reduction of income due to medical costs. If potential claimants have an income greater than the MAPR for their rating category, they often will be told INCORRECTLY that they do not qualify.

Criteria for Determining a Need for "Aid and Attendance"

VA's criteria for evaluating the claimant's need for "Aid and Attendance" or being "Housebound" are outlined in 38 CFR Part 3. Below is an excerpt of the criteria for aid and attendance.

38 CFR § 3.351-352   Criteria for determining need for aid and attendance and "permanently bedridden."

Basic criteria for regular aid and attendance and permanently bedridden. The following will be accorded consideration in determining the need for regular aid and attendance:

- inability of claimant to dress or undress himself (herself), or to keep himself (herself) ordinarily clean and presentable;
- frequent need of adjustment of any special prosthetic or orthopedic appliances which by reason of the particular disability cannot be done without aid (this will not include the adjustment of appliances which normal persons would be unable to adjust without aid, such as supports, belts, lacing at the back, etc.);
- inability of claimant to feed himself (herself) through loss of coordination of upper extremities or through extreme weakness;
- inability to attend to the wants of nature;
- or incapacity, physical or mental, which requires care or assistance on a regular basis to protect the claimant from hazards or dangers incident to his or her daily environment.
- "bedridden" will be a proper basis for the determination (need for aid and attendance). For the purpose of this paragraph "bedridden" will be that condition which, through its essential character, actually requires that the claimant remain in bed. The fact that claimant has voluntarily taken to bed or that a physician has prescribed rest in bed for the greater or lesser part of the day to promote convalescence or cure will not suffice.

It is not required that all of the disabling conditions above be found to exist before a rating may be issued. The particular personal functions which the veteran is unable to perform should be considered in connection with his or her condition as a whole. It is only necessary the evidence establish the veteran or surviving spouse is so helpless as to need regular aid and attendance, not that there be a constant need.

Determinations that the veteran or surviving spouse is so helpless, as to be in need of regular aid and attendance will not be based solely upon an opinion that the claimant's condition is such as would require him or her to be in bed. They must be based on the actual requirement of personal assistance.

Our Interpretation of 38 CFR 3.351-352

We have taken rules from 38 CFR §3.351-352 and applied them to a more modern terminology of what the rating officer in the Regional Office is looking for in order to make determination for a rating. Here is our list based on our experience with the Regional Offices.

1. Assistance with bathing or showering
2. Assistance with toileting and incontinence
3. Assistance with feeding (having a need to be fed by someone else)

4. Assistance with dressing or undressing
5. Assistance with transferring in or out of a bed or chair, ambulating, and/or walking
6. Assistance with frequent need of adjustment of special prosthetic or orthopedic devices which cannot be done without the aid of another person
7. Having an incapacity (physical or mental) requiring care or assistance on a regular basis to protect the patient from hazards or dangers incident to his or her daily environment
8. Is blind or so nearly blind as to have corrected visual acuity of 5/200 or less, in both eyes, or concentric contraction of the visual field to 5 degrees or less in both eyes
9. Is a patient in a nursing home because of mental or physical incapacity
10. Meets the criteria of being totally bedridden as defined in the regulation

As mentioned in the regulation, there does not need to be a certain number of these incapacities in order to determine a rating for aid and attendance. The rating service representative simply must determine from the evidence whether the claimant is so helpless as to require the regular aid and attendance of another person based on one or more of these conditions.

From our experience with the rating activity, the individual applying should exhibit the need for and be receiving at least two or more of the services from #1 through #6 above. If #7 through #11 are more relevant, only one of these need apply.

The Housebound Rating
This will be the only instance in this chapter where we discuss the relevance of having a "housebound rating." Essentially, being housebound means the claimant is substantially confined to his or her residence. The living arrangement can be a personal residence, assisted living, a nursing home or any other similar institution. This does not mean applicants need to be imprisoned in their living arrangement. They can be allowed to leave the residence for purposes of doctors' visits or other necessary services, if accompanied.

We hardly ever see a rating for housebound. This is because people who are housebound are just as likely to need the aid and attendance of another person and there would be no need for the housebound rating as the MAPR for housebound is a lesser amount.

This does not mean that a housebound rating is of no use. If a claimant is applying for Pension based on a very low income and indeed has few medical deductions to offset income, and the claimant could qualify for a housebound rating, then the MAPR for this rating is a larger amount than the basic MAPR and would result in a larger partial benefit.

Examples of the Importance of a "Rating" when Deducting Expenses
A medical or disability rating for "Aid and Attendance" or "Housebound" is not only important in producing a larger possible Pension income – due to the larger rating allowance MAPR – but also in receiving credit for unreimbursed medical expenses (UMEs). A list of allowable medical expenses is provided further on.

If, for example, a veteran in assisted living who is there primarily for retirement and social interaction and not because of the need for assistance could not apply his or her room and board costs towards reduction of his or her income. VA would not allow these expenses without a rating.

On the other hand, with a rating for "Aid and Attendance", the cost of food and lodging is deductible from income, so long as the care involves 2 or more activities of daily living.

Here is another example for someone receiving care at home. Without the additional disability ratings, the only recurring medical costs the veteran may count as unreimbursed medical expenses (UMEs) are those paid to licensed health professionals providing care in the home. With a rating for "Aid and Attendance," the veteran's payments to unlicensed caregiver attendants such as children, friends, church members or neighbors would be considered UMEs by VA. Payments to a spouse for care are not recognized even though they reduce income, because the payments also represent income so it's just a matter of shifting money from one pocket to another within the same household. Unfortunately, the deduction doesn't work for paying a spouse.

If the disabled veteran has been rated "Housebound" or in the need of "Aid and Attendance," VA will allow deduction of all fees paid to a non-licensed in-home attendant as long as the attendant provides what VA calls "custodial services" for the disabled person. In this case this means assistance with 2 or more Activities of Daily Living (ADLs). As an example, helping the care recipient shower and dress would be considered counted as two ADLs and allow for the medical deduction. The overall deduction for care may include payments for Instrumental Activities of Daily Living (IADLs) – services such as cooking, laundry, and housecleaning so long as two ADLs are part of the care. The next section will provide you a larger list of IADLs.

Certain medical expense deductions require distinguishing persons who are and who are not eligible to be rated for aid and attendance or housebound. For Pension, veterans and surviving spouses may be rated for aid and attendance or housebound. Spouses of living veterans or children or any other relative who is a member or constructive member of the household may not be rated for aid and attendance or housebound. This same rule applies to dependents of surviving spouses as well.

Unreimbursed Medical Expenses

M21-1, Part V, Subpart iii, Chapter 1, Section G - Pension - Deductible Expenses and 38 CFR §3.278 - Deductible medical expenses.

Unreimbursed medical expenses can be used to reduce combined gross household income to meet the income test. This is an extremely important provision in the Pension rules that allows claimant households with large incomes to receive entitlement to the benefit where they otherwise would not qualify due to incomes above the MAPR. In some cases, claimants with household incomes of $5,000 a month or more could still qualify for Pension if their out-of-pocket medical expenses were large enough.

If Pension is to be awarded for a veteran with a dependent or a surviving spouse with a dependent, it is important to note the veteran or the surviving spouse claimant does not have to generate the unreimbursed medical expenses. Those expenses can be generated by the dependent. If the dependent is a non-veteran spouse of a veteran claimant and the veteran is healthy, but the spouse is disabled and needs to pay for health care services or custodial care, those expenses can be deducted from the combined household income. The same would be true for a surviving spouse claimant who might have a disabled dependent child. This is an important distinction to remember. Medical expenses are determined by the rules contained in 38 CFR §3.278 – Deductible medical expenses. Here are excerpts from 38 CFR and clarification from M21-1 for those rules.

Medical expenses for VA purposes.

Generally, medical expenses for VA needs-based benefit purposes are payments for items or services are medically necessary; that improve a disabled individual's functioning; or that prevent, slow, or ease an individual's functional decline. Medical expenses may include, but are not limited to, the payments specified in the paragraphs below.

Care by a health care provider. Payments to a health care provider for services performed within the scope of the provider's professional capacity are medical expenses.

Medications, medical supplies, medical equipment, and medical food, vitamins, and supplements. Payments for prescription and non-prescription medication procured lawfully under Federal law, as well as payments for medical supplies or medical equipment, are medical expenses. Medically necessary food, vitamins, and supplements as prescribed or directed by a health care provider authorized to write prescriptions are medical expenses.

Adaptive equipment. Payments for adaptive devices or service animals, including veterinary care, used to assist a person with an ongoing disability are medical expenses. Medical expenses do not include non-prescription food, boarding, grooming, or other routine expenses of owning an animal.

Transportation expenses. Payments for transportation for medical purposes, such as the cost of transportation to and from a health care provider's office by taxi, bus, or other form of public transportation are medical expenses. The cost of transportation for medical purposes by privately owned vehicle (POV), including mileage, parking, and tolls, is a medical expense.

Health insurance premiums. Payments for health, medical, hospitalization, and long-term care insurance premiums are medical expenses. Premiums for Medicare Parts A, B, and D and for long-term care insurance are medical expenses.

Institutional forms of care and in-home care. Unreimbursed medical expenses (UMEs) paid by a claimant (or by a claimant's dependent(s) for VA purposes) may be used to reduce the claimant's countable income. This would include:

- Hospitals, nursing homes, medical foster homes, and inpatient treatment centers
- Care from a home health provider or private in-home care. Payments for assistance with ADLs and IADLs by an in-home attendant are medical expenses as long as the attendant provides the disabled individual with health care or custodial care
- Other Care Facilities providing custodial care and/or 2+ activities of daily living (ADLs)

Health care provider means:

An individual licensed by a State or country to provide health care in the State or country in which the individual provides the health care is considered a healthcare provider. The term includes, but is not limited to,

- ❖ a physician
- ❖ physician assistants (PAs)
- ❖ psychologist
- ❖ chiropractor
- ❖ registered nurse
- ❖ licensed vocational nurse
- ❖ licensed practical nurse, and
- ❖ physical or occupational therapist

A nursing assistant or home health aide who is supervised by a licensed health care provider is also considered a healthcare provider. For the purposes of the medical expense deduction, a licensed health care provider refers to a person licensed to furnish health services by the state or country in which the services are provided. Licensed health care providers may include, but are not limited to,

- ❖ a physician
- ❖ physician assistants (PAs)
- ❖ psychologist
- ❖ chiropractor
- ❖ registered nurse
- ❖ licensed vocational nurse
- ❖ licensed practical nurse, and
- ❖ physical or occupational therapist

Instrumental activities of daily living (IADLs) mean independent living activities, such as

- shopping,
- medical alert equipment,
- socializing activities
- food preparation,
- housekeeping,
- laundering,
- managing finances,
- handling medications, and
- transportation for non-medical purposes.

Custodial care means regular:

- Assistance with two or more ADLs; or
- Supervision because an individual with a physical, mental, developmental, or cognitive disorder requires care or assistance on a regular basis to protect the individual from hazards or dangers incident to his or her daily environment.

Custodial care differs from skilled nursing care. Skilled nursing care is the provision of services and supplies that can only be given by or under the supervision of a skilled or licensed health care provider. Mental, developmental, or cognitive disorders encompass a wide range of mental health conditions that affect thinking and behavior. Examples include schizophrenia, Alzheimer's disease, and significant dementia.

Medical Deduction Rules for In-Home Care and Care Facilities

Residing at Home with Care Provided by an In-Home Attendant

Payments for assistance with ADLs and IADLs by an in-home attendant are medical expenses so long as the attendant provides the disabled individual with health care or custodial care. Payments must be commensurate with the number of hours that the provider offers to the disabled person. This means payments must be based on hourly rates and not on arbitrary payment schedules. There are few guidelines for what those hourly rates should be. We must assume that the rates should be reasonable compared with similar rates in the community for similar services.

It is important to note that deductible medical expenses are applicable to all members of the household. If there is a healthy veteran claimant who has an unhealthy spouse who is generating medical expenses, these are deductible from the combined household gross income. If there is a healthy veteran claimant who has another dependent family member living in the household, who is generating medical expenses, these are also deductible from the combined household gross income. Likewise, a healthy surviving spouse claimant with an unhealthy dependent family member such as a dependent child or adult child who is dependent on the family income, can still deduct medical expenses for that dependent family member. **REMEMBER, income is the combined household GROSS income to include a spouse and a dependent child under certain circumstances.**

Care Provided by Licensed Health Care Providers

Payments to a health care provider for services performed within the scope of the provider's professional capacity are medical expenses. Health care in the home might include such services as skilled nursing care, physical therapy, taking of vital signs, providing injections, changing IVs, inserting catheters, treating pressure wounds or changing dressings. For health care to be deductible medical services the attendant must be a licensed health care provider. (See definition in previous section) This licensed health care provider may also provide custodial care such as assistance with ADLs or supervision because of dementia or other mental limitations.

All reasonable fees paid to the in-home attendant for personal care of the disabled person and maintenance of the disabled person's immediate environment may be allowed. This includes such services as cooking for the disabled person, housecleaning for the disabled person, and other IADLs. It is not necessary to distinguish between medical and non-medical services. However, services that are beyond the scope of personal care of the disabled person and maintenance of the disabled person's immediate environment, may not be allowed.

Home health agencies that are Medicare or Medicaid certified can offer health care services which are termed by these agencies "skilled care" and these agencies will also offer custodial care by home health aides who may or may not be licensed. Home health aides or nursing assistants working for home health agencies are supervised by licensed home health agency care providers and as such their services are considered deductible as well.

Likewise, non-medical home care companies that do not provide skilled care can offer paid custodial care services which is also deductible. In most states, these providers must be licensed and as such they would be considered health care providers and their services would be deductible. In those states where licensing is not required, VA will still allow for services paid to these providers to be deductible. This is likely because VA considers them to be health care providers as they are offering professional custodial services.

Examples of custodial care include assisting a person with ADLs and **may include assisting a person with IADLs ALONE when the person has a serious mental, developmental, or cognitive disorder**. This special provision allowing for IADLs is a new and more liberal rule then was previously in place.

Custodial Care Provided by Non-Licensed Providers
Custodial care can also be provided by non-licensed in-home attendants such as family members, friends or non-licensed individuals hired to provide custodial care. Payments made for services to these non-licensed providers are also deductible **if the disabled claimant is rated for aid and attendance or is rated for housebound.**

Custodial care provided in the home means regular assistance with two or more ADLs; or supervision because an individual with a physical, mental, developmental, or cognitive disorder requires care or assistance on a regular basis to protect the individual from hazards or dangers incident to his or her daily environment. Custodial care **may include assisting a person with IADLs ALONE when the person has a serious mental, developmental, or cognitive disorder**. This special provision allowing for IADLs is a new and more liberal rule.

If the disabled individual needing custodial care is not eligible for a rating such as the unhealthy, non-veteran spouse of a veteran claimant, there is an alternative way to create a deduction for this non-eligible person as well. The alternative way to create a deduction is where a physician, physician assistant, certified nurse practitioner, or clinical nurse specialist states in writing that, due to a physical, mental, developmental, or cognitive disorder, the individual requires the health care or custodial care that the non-licensed in-home attendant provides.

It should be noted, if the non-ratable individual is generating medical deductions, the additional allowance for aid and attendance or housebound is not available. In this case, the basic MAPR either for a veteran with a dependent or a surviving spouse with a dependent is applicable. The resulting benefit is much smaller than a benefit with a rating for aid and attendance or housebound.

All reasonable fees paid to the attendant for personal care of the disabled person and maintenance of the disabled person's immediate environment may be allowed. This includes such services as cooking for the disabled person, housecleaning for the disabled person, and other IADLs. It is not necessary to distinguish between medical and non-medical services. However, services that are beyond the scope of personal care of the disabled person and maintenance of the disabled person's immediate environment, may not be allowed.

For an example suppose a veteran claimant receives an aid and attendance rating by VA. The veteran pays an attendant to administer medication and provide for his or her personal needs such as bathing and dressing. The attendant also cooks the veteran's meals and cleans house. The entire amount paid for all of these services is a deductible medical expense. The attendant does not have to be a licensed health care provider as well.

When the fees for an in-home attendant are an allowable expense, receipts or other proof of payment documentation of this expense are required. Documentation could include any of the following

- a receipt or paid invoice
- statement on the provider's letterhead
- computer summary
- an Internal Revenue Service (IRS) Form W-2
- ledger, or
- bank statement.

The evidence submitted must include all of the following

- amount paid
- date payment was made
- purpose of the payment (the nature of the product or service provided)
- name of the person to or for whom the product or service was provided, and
- identification of the provider to whom payment was made.

<u>No annual verification of in-home attendant annual fees paid is required</u>. The claimant is only required to submit documentation of expenses when in-home attendant fees are first claimed, or when the person or company providing the service changes. **Maintaining records of payments for care is extremely important in case of an audit**.

Using the Pension Benefit to Remain in the Home

About 70% of all people in this country, who are receiving long term care services – such as assistance with ADLs or IADLs or skilled care – are in their homes. Care is typically provided by family members, but there is a growing trend for private companies to provide this care as well. This is because family members are often employed full-time or live long distances away and cannot provide assistance. The vast majority of those people receiving homecare wish to stay in their homes and not have to move to a care facility.

The Pension benefit is particularly useful to pay private companies or family members to provide home care. But it is not always a suitable solution where household incomes are larger than $2,500 a month or the Pension benefit does not cover the full cost of care. It also works best for married couples where the claimant is the veteran because this provides the most amount of money. We will discuss below how the Pension benefit fits to allow Pension claimants to remain in their homes.

Using a Private Home Care Services Company for In-Home Care

There are two types of home care companies – home health agencies and non-medical home care or personal home care companies. Home health agencies are licensed by the state and typically certified by Medicare and Medicaid to provide services under these government programs. The person receiving care at home typically does not have to pay out-of-pocket for home health agency services. It is typically covered by Medicare or Medicaid. However, these services are limited to providing rehabilitation from an injury or disease or rehabilitation from a hospital stay or nursing rehabilitation home stay. They offer both skilled care and home health aides to help with ADLs and IADLs. For individuals who have chronic conditions and require long-term custodial care, home health agencies are not the solution. In addition, government programs will only pay for this care for a limited period of time based on how well the care recipient is recovering.

Home health agencies also may provide hospice services which are paid for by Medicare. This is skilled care and custodial care for individuals who are considered terminally ill. Hospice care is usually provided in a home setting.

Non-medical or personal care home companies typically are not paid by government programs with the exception that Medicaid will sometimes provide home care services by contracting with these companies. The services of non-medical home care companies are predominantly paid out-of-pocket by the care recipient. The Pension benefit fits in with non-medical home care companies and not with home health agencies, unless home health agencies also provide non-medical home care services as a side business.

A non-medical home care company is not allowed to provide skilled care and can only provide custodial care. These companies may or may not be licensed by their state health department. Only about two thirds of the states require licensing for these companies. They typically charge by the hour with rates ranging from $15 an hour up to $40 an hour. The more hours that the care recipient utilizes per month, typically the lower the hourly rate. The services of these companies fit in with the Pension benefit. Let's look at 3 examples to see how it works.

In the first example, we have a couple where the veteran is the claimant. The combined gross household income is $4,000 a month. For purposes of this example let's suppose that the Pension benefit for this couple with the aid and attendance allowance is $2,266 a month and the 5% deductible is $75 a month. From previous sections, we know that this couple needs to pay at least $4,075 a month to generate the full Pension benefit of $2,266 a month. This creates a dilemma. If this couple relies on the majority of their income to pay for maintenance costs such as food, lodging, utilities, loans and other costs, they are going to experience a deficit until benefits are granted – the reimbursement of $2,266 a month from VA will hopefully cover those costs.

This arrangement only works if they absolutely need the home care in the first place and have no choice but to pay for it out-of-pocket. They either have to live on less money or they have to have savings to help subsidize their maintenance costs. They may also consider taking out a reverse mortgage to generate some cash to cover the home care costs especially if they were going to pay for those costs anyway were the VA benefit not to exist. If they would have been stuck with the costs without the VA benefit, the benefit actually is a blessing because it produces an extra $2,266 a month that is tax-free

The second example is a single veteran who makes $2,000 a month. For purposes of this example, let's assume that the Pension benefit with the aid and attendance allowance for a single veteran is

$1,911 a month. This example works because the veteran can pay out a little over $2,000 a month for home care services and receive back from VA $1,911 a month as reimbursement for that. Hopefully the $2,000 a month for services provides for enough care to allow the veteran to remain in his home.

The third example is a single surviving spouse who makes $1,600 a month. For purposes of this example, let's assume that the Pension benefit with the aid and attendance allowance for the surviving spouse is $1,228 a month. She would have to pay out a little over $1,600 a month for home care services and would receive back from VA a reimbursement of $1,228 a month. She comes up short about $400 a month to pay her bills. Single surviving spouses, using Survivor's Pension benefit to pay for private home care services from a company that provides this care does not work perfectly. First of all, she may not receive enough Survivor's Pension money to provide for the actual care that she needs on a monthly basis and second, the Survivor's Pension benefit may be inadequate for her to survive at home without having some extra savings.

Using a Personal Care Arrangement for In-Home Care
The personal care arrangement using a member of the family, or a friend or a private live in caregiver solves a lot of the challenges discussed in the section above. This arrangement works due to a provision in the Pension income rules that allows the paid caregiver to turn around and use the money she is receiving for her services to pay the household maintenance costs. If you remember from a section above, if someone furnishes a claimant free room and board, or pays the claimant's bills, the value of room and board or the amount paid for bills is not countable as income to the claimant. Or under another provision of that rule, regular cash contributions to the claimant are considered maintenance, and are not counted as income, if evidence shows that the donor has assumed all or part of the burden of regular maintenance of the claimant, and cash contributions are used by the claimant to pay for basic necessities, such as food or housing. In other words, a person can pay the claimant for maintenance costs and does not necessarily have to pay the claimant's bills as long as the claimant uses the money for that purpose.

With a personal care arrangement, a member of the family such as a child or grandchild or other relative or even a caring friend draws up an agreement with the claimant to provide custodial care based on a reasonable hourly rate. The caregiver providing the custodial services may live in the claimant's home or the claimant receiving the care may live in the household of the caregiver. Or sometimes the caregiver lives nearby and can drop in every day to provide the services.

Let's use one of the examples in a previous section to show how a personal care arrangement works. In our example previously, we have a couple where the veteran is in need of care. The combined gross household income is $3,000 a month. For purposes of this example, let's suppose the Pension benefit for this couple with the aid and attendance allowance is $2,266 a month and the 5% deductible is $75 a month. From previous sections, we know that this couple needs to pay at least $3,075 a month to generate the full Pension benefit of $2,266 a month. The couple sets up a personal care arrangement with their daughter. They agree to pay her $2,875 a month for custodial services based on a reasonable hourly rate. They also report $200/month in health insurance premiums on the application. This creates a benefit of $2,266 a month from VA. The total household income with the Pension benefit is now $5,266 a month.

The daughter can use a portion of the entire household income of $5,266 a month to pay her parent's monthly maintenance costs and herself as the ongoing care giver. As we will discuss below, she needs to retain enough of this money to pay for the income taxes that she will incur by being paid for her services.

Issues with the Personal Care Arrangement

VA continues to audit a small percentage of Pension claims, especially if there is an issue of incompetency. Meaning VA has determined the beneficiary cannot handle their own finances. The audit will require additional documentation to verify the actual costs and services provided. In the event of an audit, in order to protect the individuals providing care, there should be an appropriate care contract in place. In addition, members of the family or other informal caregivers being paid for care fall under the IRS domestic employee rules -- the so-called "nanny tax." Taxes need to be withheld and paid and a W-2 needs to be issued. Even though a burden, this has a benefit as it will also create a paper trail to verify that money is exchanging hands on a month-to-month basis and legitimate services are being provided.

Establishing a formal paper trail has another advantage. Often, after these personal care arrangements are set up, the claimant fails to pay the caregiver after a few months because money is coming in from the US Treasury. Why continue to pay for care when money flows in every month without any follow-up? <u>This failure to pay eventually would lead to a retroactive denial of benefits and a demand from VA to repay all of the benefits for those months where the beneficiary did not pay the caregiver any money</u>. By setting up a formal arrangement with the taxes being accounted for, the money must be paid every month. A formal arrangement creates the continuity of month-to-month payments that ensures the deduction for medical care can be claimed consistently. Without a proper paper trail, it may be difficult to prove that services were paid for.

If the contract also meets Medicaid rules in those states that allow personal care contracts in anticipation of Medicaid, this is an additional benefit to setting up these personal care arrangements. In fact, if the arrangement set up for receiving the Pension benefit does not meet the contract requirements under the Medicaid rules in a particular state and an application for Medicaid is made at some future date, Medicaid may declare the money paid to the children a transfer for less than value. This will create a penalty for Medicaid because Medicaid will argue that the parents transferred the money to the children in a deliberate attempt to get rid of their assets to qualify for Medicaid.

This transfer for less than value problem would only present itself if excess income were being held over to future months. Money received and spent in the same month is not an asset for Medicaid purposes and the transfer for less than value rule would not apply. In the event money is being held over to the next month, it is necessary for the proper contract if there is an application for Medicaid.

If VA assigns a fiduciary for the benefit award – which is sometimes the case – the fiduciary service representative will require the caregiver to set up accounts according to the way Fiduciary Services requires it. This may be in contradiction to what we are relating here. The requirements from Fiduciary Services may also create a problem under Medicaid.

As far as a personal care attendant being a contractor and receiving a 1099 as opposed to being a domestic employee and requiring a W-2, caregivers are considered domestic employees. On the other hand, if the caregiver is indeed in the personal-care business and has other clients that the caregiver is servicing with care services, then he or she can receive a 1099 for contract services. Otherwise, if the caregiver only has the parent or relative as a client, he or she is considered a domestic employee under IRS rules and social security and unemployment taxes need to be withheld and a W-2 issued.

Residing in Independent Living

Many individuals, for various reasons, can no longer live in their homes and must find alternative living arrangements. Perhaps the person living at home no longer desires to maintain a house and yard, or is lonely and desires social interaction, or for various reasons can no longer cook meals, do the laundry or maintain other household tasks. Perhaps this person may also need limited assistance with instrumental activities of daily living but can still manage without the need for custodial care which is assistance with activities of daily living. Perhaps the person lives in a neighborhood that is not safe, or he or she can no longer drive and as a result is prevented from shopping, visiting family or getting to see the doctor.

Independent living facilities offer an opportunity for those persons who can no longer live at home by renting these persons an apartment in a complex that has many residents who have the same needs. Independent living typically provides 3 meals a day, laundry services, cleaning services and limited assistance with getting to the private dining room. There is also opportunity to interact socially with other people as there are all kinds of activity programs provided by these facilities. Transportation is sometimes offered for those who can no longer drive.

Independent living facilities are not licensed to provide custodial care or health care. On the other hand, they are often much less expensive than residing in assisted living where custodial care and oftentimes health care are available. It is becoming more common for individuals, who actually need custodial care, to move into independent living because they can receive a limited amount of assistance without paying the higher cost of assisted living. In many instances, these individuals are disabled to the point where they should be residing in assisted living, but in order to fill up beds, the independent living facility will accommodate them. This creates a dilemma. Prior to the year 2014, VA reluctantly allowed for expenses in independent living to qualify as medical expense deductions for Pension. All of this changed with VA imposing more strict rules for health care and custodial care expense deductions for independent living after 2014.

It is important to remember under the new rules for medical deductions for independent living and assisted living the following is true.

1. Unreimbursed health care expenses are always deductible for Pension and Survivor Pension purposes.
2. Unreimbursed expenses for custodial care are deductible under certain conditions.
3. Unreimbursed expenses for food and lodging in independent living and assisted living are only deductible under certain conditions.

Private Home Care Company Services in Independent Living as Deductible Expenses

- The independent living itself may contract for outside private home care company services in which case the resident paying for this can deduct this cost from income for Veterans Pension and Survivors Pension purposes as this is considered medical expenses.

- The resident in independent living may also contract directly for private home care company services and the cost is deductible for Pension purposes as this is considered medical expenses.

Care Services Provided by Family or Friends in Independent Living as Deductible Expenses
The disabled resident in independent living may pay family or friends for assistance with ADLs and IADLs – who are not licensed health care providers – and these services are considered deductible medical expenses under the following conditions:

The disabled individual is receiving health care or custodial care in the facility and

1. The disabled individual is rated for aid and attendance or housebound

OR

2. A physician, physician assistant, certified nurse practitioner, or clinical nurse specialist states in writing that, due to a physical, mental, developmental, or cognitive disorder, the individual needs to be in a protected environment.

Expenses for Food and Lodging and Other Expenses in Independent Living as Deductible
Payments for meals and lodging, and other facility expenses not directly related to health care or custodial care, are medical expenses if:

1. The facility **provides or contracts for health care or custodial care** for the disabled individual;

OR

2. A physician, physician assistant, certified nurse practitioner, or clinical nurse specialist states in writing that the individual must reside in the facility to separately contract with a third-party provider to receive health care or custodial care or to receive **paid or unpaid** health care or custodial care from family or friends.

When Both Health Care or Custodial Care and Food and Lodging Are Deductible Together
Health care and or custodial care and lodging and other charges incidental to being in independent living are all medical deductions:

1. When the disabled individual pays out-of-pocket for medical or custodial care services **contracted directly** by the independent living

OR

2. A physician, physician assistant, certified nurse practitioner, or clinical nurse specialist states in writing that the individual must reside in the facility to separately contract with a third-party provider to receive health care or custodial care or to receive **paid or unpaid** health care or custodial care from family or friends.

Here are our suggestions for meeting the requirements outlined on the previous page:

1. Physician certifies, in writing, the veteran or unhealthy spouse must reside at the Independent Living community to contract for the 3rd party care. <u>Physician must specifically name and prescribe the Independent Living and the 3rd party care services for the claimant's well-being</u>. This statement must be written somewhere on the VBA Form 21-2680 or on the doctor's letter head:

   "I, the signing medical practitioner, certify that _____ (claimant) must reside in _____ (the Independent Living Community) to contract and receive _____'s (the Contracted 3rd Party Care Provider) assistance with their Activities of Daily Living (ADLs). I prescribe the custodial care outlined in the application the 3rd Party Care Provider will offer the claimant in that facility."

2. Independent Living completes *Form FV22 – Independent Living Certification of Services*

3. 3rd Party Care Provider completes *Form FV13 – Care Provider Certification of Services*

If ALL the above criteria are met, VA will deduct the ongoing independent living food, lodging and other ancillary costs AND the 3rd party care costs. If not, VA will only deduct the 3rd party care. Use the Claim Support Disc and the checklist further on to help you file this type of claim.

Residing in Assisted Living

Assisted living is exactly as it says. Living in an apartment or facility where you receive assistance with daily personal needs. Residents remain independent while receiving assistance as needed with personal care, medications, transportation, housekeeping, meals, and other daily living needs.

Assisted living facilities offer a less expensive and often more desirable arrangement to a nursing home. They are designed for those people who have some care needs, but don't have the physical, medical, or mental impairments that require a nursing home.

Assisted living definitions vary from state to state. Each state has its own licensing requirements and regulations for these types of facilities. Most states do not refer to these facilities as "assisted living." They may call them residential care home, assisted care living facilities, congregate living facilities, personal care homes and a raft of other titles. Each state licensing agency has its own definition of the term it uses to describe assisted living. Because the term assisted living is not defined in many states, it is often more a marketing term used by a variety of senior living communities to identify a commonly recognized source of assistance. Thus, these facilities may be titled differently and offer varying degrees and types of services depending on state law.

The physical structure of assisted living facilities can range from a dwelling that looks like a home in a residential area where the caregiver is the owner and operator, to a large, apartment-style building staffed with many employees. The care style is different in these two examples.

A board-and-care in a residential area, with three to eight beds provides a homelike environment and closer association with the other residents. Each resident has his or her own room and bathroom.

Living room and dining areas are commonly shared with other residents. With little support staff, the resident needs to be mobile enough to get himself around, and other services may be limited.

In contrast, large assisted living facilities may be staffed with numerous health aides, 24-hour nursing care, a help desk, entertainment, and educational programs and provide large private apartments. Arrangements are sometimes made for home health agencies, therapists, or visiting doctors for residents' needs. Transportation, excursions and field trips are also available.

Assisted living facilities or residential home care facilities are licensed to provide custodial care and, in some cases, can provide licensed health care as well. As such, the portion of the monthly fee that pertains to these services is deductible as a medical expense.

In addition, the payments for meals and lodging, and other facility expenses not directly related to health care or custodial care are medical expenses if the facility provides or contracts for health care or custodial care for the disabled individual. It is not necessary for the disabled individual to be rated for aid and attendance or housebound for this deduction. On the other hand, most individuals who are in assisted living generally have a need for aid and attendance. Also, the benefit in assisted living is much larger when the MAPR also includes an allowance for aid and attendance.

Residing in a Nursing Home, Hospital or Inpatient Treatment Center
Payments to hospitals, nursing homes, medical foster homes, and inpatient treatment centers – including inpatient treatment centers for drug or alcohol addiction and including the cost of meals and lodging charged by such facilities – are medical expenses.

If it is established that a claimant or relative in a governmental institution is participating in a program of therapy or rehabilitation supervised by a physician, or a physician, physician assistant, certified nurse practitioner, or clinical nurse specialist states in writing that the claimant or relative has a medical condition that makes such a level of care necessary, the entire amount paid is deductible expense.

A physician, physician assistant, certified nurse practitioner, or clinical nurse specialist's statement specifically addressing the issue of whether an individual who is not entitled to aid and attendance or housebound needs to be in a protected environment must be of record, even if the individual's diagnosis is known.

A medical expense deduction for nursing home fees is allowed if a responsible official of the nursing home certifies that the claimant or relative is a patient – as opposed to only being a resident – of the nursing home.

VA will also verify nursing home fees if or when one of the following situations exists:

- nursing home fees are first claimed
- the claimant or relative transfers to a new facility, or
- the nursing home-related expenses increase substantially more than the cost-of-living increase compared to the expenses allowed during the prior reporting period.

Examples of verification include

- VA Form 21-0779, Request for Nursing Home Information in Connection with Claim for Aid and Attendance, and
- an official statement provided by the nursing home, and
- financial statements showing proof of monthly payment.

It should be noted VA Form 21-0779 is for a veteran claimant only. If the claimant is a spouse of a living veteran or a single surviving spouse of a veteran, other means of verification must be used to substantiate patient status and payments. This would include:

- VA Form 21-2680, Examination for a Rating, and
- a Care Provider Statement from the Nursing Home, and
- financial statements showing proof of monthly payment.

The Net Worth Limit

The net worth limit for Pension or Survivor Pension entitlement is $129,094 as of December 1, 2019. This limit is increased by the same percentage as the COLA in Social Security benefits each year on December 1 of each year and will parallel Medicaid's Community Spousal Resource Allowance (CSRA). The divisor for calculating a penalty period, which we will describe below, is now $2,266.

Definition of Net Worth and the Bright Line Test

Effective October 18, 2018, the Department of Veterans Affairs (VA), changed the net worth criteria for Pension claims. Net Worth on or after October 18, 2018 is the sum of a claimant's:

- Assets

PLUS

- Income for VA purposes (IVAP), including the income of a spouse and dependent children under certain circumstances

Please note when IVAP is a negative number, it is to be considered zero dollars. As a result, assets cannot be further reduced by negative income. Net worth can only be reduced to the extent that there is no income to add to the assets and thus if IVAP is zero, the net worth is the value of the assets alone. Also, the IVAP calculation is based on an initial application for Pension. This means that only reasonably predictable medical expenses can be subtracted from household gross income such as recurring health insurance premiums, the recurring cost of paying caregivers or care facilities and possibility the recurring cost of renting medical devices.

Income for net worth purposes includes the income of the claimant and spouse or the income of a single surviving spouse.

VA calculates net worth when eligibility has been met and then only under the following conditions:

- with an original Pension or Survivor Pension claim;
- with a new claim after a period of non-entitlement;
- with a request to establish a new dependent; or
- with information that a veteran's, surviving spouse's, or child's net worth has increased or decreased

If the evidence shows that net worth exceeds the net worth limit, VA may decide the claim before determining if the claimant meets other entitlement factors. VA will notify the claimant of the entitlement factors that have not been established.

VA will deny or discontinue Pension if a claimant's or beneficiary's net worth exceeds the net worth limit. This is referred to as the Bright Line net worth test.

If the claimant does not meet other factors necessary for Pension entitlement, such as military service requirements, VA will deny the claim without calculating net worth.

Here are some eligibility examples involving net worth:

Example 1 – The net worth limit is $129,094. A claimant has assets of $116,000, annual retirement income of $8,000, and annual predictable nursing home expenses of $29,000. Apply the nursing home expenditure to income, which decreases annual income to $0. Because income is $0, the claimant's net worth is $116,000; therefore, his/her net worth is not excessive for VA Pension.

Example 2 – The net worth limit is $129,094 and the maximum annual Pension rate (MAPR) is $13,752. A claimant has assets of $129,000 and annual retirement income of $10,000. The claimant pays reasonably predictable annual medical expenses of $9,000. In this case, medical expenses that exceed $687 (5% of the MAPR) are deductible from income. After applying the expenditures, annual income decreases to $1,000. Adding income to assets produces net worth of $130,000, which is over the bright line limit, just barely. VA must deny the claim for excessive net worth. The claimant may re-apply as soon as their net-worth is spent down below VA's limit.

Defining Assets

Assets are the fair market value of all property that an individual owns, including all real and personal property, unless excluded under 38 CFR 3.275. If the total value of an annuity or similar financial instrument is used when calculating the asset amount, VA does not include the monthly income derived from the same annuity or similar financial instrument when calculating income for net worth. This would result in double counting for calculating net worth.

Fair market value is the price at which an asset would change hands between a willing buyer and seller. VA will use the best available information to determine fair market value, such as inspections, appraisals, public records, and the market value of similar property. Fair market value is determined based on valuations at the time of application.

The following are rules for asset inclusion for net worth.

➢ If the claimant is a veteran then the veteran's assets include the assets of the veteran as well as the assets of his or her spouse.

➢ If the claimant is a surviving spouse, the assets include only the assets of the surviving spouse.

➢ If the claimant is a surviving child and he or she has no custodian or is in the custody of an institution, the child's assets include only the assets of the child.

➢ If a surviving child has a custodian other than an institution, the child's assets include the assets of the child as well as the assets of the custodian. If the child is in the joint custody of his or her natural or adoptive parent and a stepparent, the child's assets also include the assets of the stepparent.

Annuities, Trusts, and Similar Financial Instruments

The total value of an annuity, trust or other similar financial instrument is counted as an asset if the claimant has the ability to liquidate the entire balance. For example, if an asset is locked up in an irrevocable trust and unavailable for the claimant's maintenance, it is not considered an asset (so long as the trust was created prior to October 2018 and is not being used for the claimant's household maintenance). Likewise, if an income annuity is income only and has no feature to retrieve original purchase amount, it is not an asset (so long as the annuity was created prior to October 2018 and the monies used to purchase the trust are not retrievable). Other such arrangements such as limited partnerships, private stock or an installment sale would likely not have an option to sell or liquidate and as a result would also not be counted as assets.

If the claimant can liquidate the value of the annuity, trust or other similar financial instrument or information about the liquidity of an annuity is unavailable, VA will likely count the monthly income received as income for net worth purposes and include the financial instrument value as part of the claimant's net worth.

Primary Residence and other Exclusions from Assets

The value of a claimant's primary residence (single-family unit) – including 2 acres of residential lot area – in which the claimant has an ownership interest is excluded as an asset. VA recognizes one primary residence per claimant. If the residence is sold after an Intent and/or claim is filed, or if entitlement is established, any net proceeds from the sale is an asset except to the extent the proceeds are used to purchase another residence within the same calendar year as the year in which the sale occurred.

This rule concerning reinvesting proceeds from the sale of a house prior to the end of the calendar year is not reasonable. For example, suppose the house sold in December. A new house would have to be purchased with the proceeds prior to the end of that month. When it initiated the rules changes, VA pointed out this was an inevitable requirement. It has to do with not what is reasonable but what is already in the rules pertaining to counting assets during a calendar year. The asset from a sale must be counted by the end of the calendar year. VA argues this rule is not as onerous as it seems. If a new house is purchased in February of the following year, the claimant only loses one-month worth of benefit – the month of January.

VA will not include a claimant's primary residence as an asset even if the claimant resides in:

- a nursing home, medical foster home, other care facility, or
- the home of a family member for health care or custodial care.

It is not spelled out if the claimant resides somewhere other than the primary residence and that place of residence is not a living arrangement associated with health care or custodial care, whether the primary residence is still exempt.

Rental income on a primary residence not occupied by the claimant or a dependent is countable income and sale of the property is a conversion of assets.

If the primary residence is sold, this creates additional assets (called a conversion of assets) and may disqualify the claimant for receiving future benefits if VA's net worth limit is exceeded.

The size of the residential lot area that can be excluded from net worth consideration is determined by the degree to which the property is connected to the dwelling and the typical size of lots in the immediate area. For claims received on or after October 18, 2018, residential lot area means the lot on which a residence sits that does not exceed 2 acres, unless the additional acreage is not marketable.

In some instances, a claimant's place of residence and place of business are the same. As an example, a farmer may live in a house on the farm or a grocer may live in an apartment over the store. In such cases, the value of the residence area must be considered separately from the value of the business area. The value of the residence area may be excluded. The value of the business area is considered an asset the same as any other business asset.

If the claimant lives on a farm which is not used for business purposes, VA will exclude the value of the residence area, including the lot allowance, and consider the rest of the farm as an asset. This rule can create a problem. Many individuals who live in rural areas have lots larger than 2 acres – sometimes up to 10 or 15 acres. In many cases, they do not use their acreage for farming. VA has recognized this dilemma for rural residents and generally proving a statement that the extra acreage cannot be sold is sufficient to allow an exception for the larger lot size.

State laws may provide that certain property is part of the claimant's homestead or exempt from the claims of creditors. Such homestead and exemption statutes are of no consequence in determining if the value of the property is to be considered part of a claimant's estate for VA purposes.

VA will not adjust countable assets other than the exempt primary residence by subtracting any mortgages or encumbrances from those countable assets that are attached to the primary residence.

The value of personal effects suitable to and consistent with a reasonable mode of life, such as appliances and family transportation vehicles are also exempt from counting as assets. VA will also exclude from assets any amount designated by statute as not countable as a resource, regardless of whether or not it is listed in 38 CFR §3.279 – the source of the rules above.

Determining the Value of Property and its Effect on Net Worth

When a claimant makes application, it may be necessary to determine the value of property for declaring net worth. Claimants who have held parcels of real estate for long periods of time may be unaware of current real estate prices, and greatly underestimate the value of their holdings. If it appears to an adjudicator that a claimant is underestimating the value of real property, the claimant will be asked to furnish evidence of the current market value of the real estate.

Acceptable sources of information about property value include a

- formal appraisal of the value of the property
- statement from a real estate broker in the area as to the value of comparable real estate in the vicinity
- statement from a county farm agent as to the value of the land or other real estate

- statement from a local bank loan officer as to the value of comparable real estate in the vicinity, and
- statement from the local taxing authority as to the value of the real estate. Any statement from a taxing authority should show the relationship between assessed value and market value.

For claims received on or after October 18, 2018, residential lot area means the lot on which a residence sits that does not exceed 2 acres, unless the additional acreage is not marketable. If the size of the residential lot area is not listed on the application, the adjudicator will request more information. As a general rule a claimant's statement that additional acreage is not marketable will be accepted as fact, unless there is contradictory evidence in the record.

The New VA Form 21-0969 Income and Assets Statement

The new application for Veterans Pension on VA Form 21-527EZ and Survivors Pension on VA Form 21-534EZ includes the new questions concerning assets (see below). Any questions that are answered "yes" on this portion of the 527EZ from question 29A through question 29E requires filling out the new VA Form 21-0969. Likewise, any questions that are answered "yes" on this portion of the 534EZ from question 43A through question 43D also requires a 21-0969.

IMPORTANT: VA matches income information reported with Federal tax information. Report ALL income you and your dependents receive on the appropriate sections of this form and VA Form 21P-0969, Income and Asset Statement, if appropriate.

43A. OTHER THAN SOCIAL SECURITY, DO YOU OR YOUR DEPENDENTS RECEIVE ANY INCOME?
☐ YES ☐ NO

43B. OTHER THAN SOCIAL SECURITY, DID YOU OR YOUR DEPENDENTS RECEIVE ANY INCOME LAST YEAR?
☐ YES ☐ NO

43C. DO YOU OR YOUR DEPENDENTS HAVE MORE THAN $10,000 IN ASSETS? (NOTE: Assets are all the money and property you or your dependents own. Assets *do not* include your primary residence or personal effects such as appliances and vehicles you or your dependents need for transportation)
☐ YES ☐ NO

43D. IN THE THREE CALENDAR YEARS BEFORE THIS YEAR, DID YOU OR YOUR DEPENDENTS TRANSFER ANY ASSETS? (Examples of asset transfers include giving them away, selling them, purchasing an annuity, or using them to establish a trust)
☐ YES ☐ NO

43E. DID YOU ANSWER "YES," TO ANY OF THE QUESTIONS IN ITEMS 43A THRU 43D?
☐ YES ☐ NO   (If "Yes," you *must* also complete VA Form 21P-0969, *Income and Asset Statement*)

Here are the questions which will trigger filling out Form 21-0969:

- Other than Social Security, do you or your dependents receive any income?
- Other than Social Security, did you or your dependents receive any income last year?
- Do you or your dependents have more than $10,000 in assets? (Excluding primary residence or personal effects)
- In the three calendar years before this year, did you or your dependents transfer any assets?
- Did you answer yes to any of the questions above? (If "yes," you must complete VA Form 21P-0969, Income and Asset Statement)

In the past, VA used an honor system for reporting income and assets. No documentation was required. All of that has changed.

Form 21-0969 requires reporting and documentation of all current income, previous income, anticipated income, self-employment business records, current assets, previous assets and any previously unreported assets. In addition, documentation of encumbrances, mortgages or liens on any property is also required. Finally, detailed documentation and description of any assets that were transferred during the 3 prior tax years is required which includes a report with documentation of any annuities purchased or trusts established during the prior three tax years. There is also a section devoted to any intent to waive income during the coming 12 months.

Adjustments in Excessive Net Worth

If a claimant was denied benefits as a result of excessive net worth, the claimant may reapply for benefits when the net worth is spent-down below the bright line limit. If this is done within one year of the denial, entitlement is granted as of the date net worth is no longer excessive. This would be done on the appropriate claim form and under the new rules for denials and claim review this would be called a supplemental claim. If one year has passed since the denial of entitlement, the beneficiary must complete a new application and payment will be made from the date of claim.

Here are some eligibility examples involving excessive net worth:

Example 1 – A veteran with no income and $164,000 in cash assets applies for Pension on February 5, 2020. The claim is denied on June 10, 2020 because assets exceed the bright line limit. By September, 2020, the veteran spends $15,000 on home improvements to his primary residence and $20,000 for home care. The veteran submits a supplemental claim in October, 2020 showing assets decreased to $129,000 by September, 2020.

Because the veteran submitted a supplemental claim within one year of the decision notice, VA can grant benefits from the date net worth is no longer excessive. The Veteran's assets decreased by purchasing goods and services at fair market value. VA may require receipts or other documentation if there is reason to question an asset reduction.

If more than one year has passed from the denial due to excessive net worth, a new application must be filed and if granted, the benefit will start on the date of application, not the date on which net worth was excessive.

Example 2 – A surviving spouse with $40,000 in annual income and no prospective medical expenses and cash assets of $100,000 applies for Pension on February 10, 2020. The claim is denied on May 15, 2020 because net worth (assets + IVAP) exceeds the bright line limit. On June 25, 2020, the surviving spouse enters a health care facility and prospective medical expenses increase to $45,000 annually. The surviving spouse submits a supplemental claim on June 25, 2020 showing that IVAP is $0 as of July 1, 2020 and assets remain $100,000.

Because the surviving spouse submitted a supplemental claim within one year of the decision notice, VA can grant benefits from the date net worth is no longer excessive. The surviving spouse's assets decreased in July 2020 because IVAP reduced to $0.

Asset Transfers and Penalties

VA Pension is a needs-based benefit and is not intended to preserve the estates of individuals who have the means to support themselves. Accordingly, a claimant may not create entitlement by transferring 'covered' assets. VA will review the terms and conditions of asset transfers made during a 3-look-back period to determine whether the transfer constituted transfer of a 'covered' asset. However, VA will disregard asset transfers made before October 18, 2018.

Before we began our discussion of asset transfers and related penalties, it is necessary to understand certain terms VA uses to describe these issues. Here are some important definitions relating to the look back, transfers and calculation of a penalty period.

Look Back Period - 38 CFR § 3.276
The look back period is 36 months immediately preceding the date on which VA receives either an Intent to File, an original Pension or Survivor Pension claim, or a new claim after a period of non-entitlement. For a claim submitted after a period of non-entitlement, the look back starts from the date of that claim. <u>This definition does not include any date before October 18, 2018, although, VA can question transfers made before October 2018 to ensure irrevocability and no use for maintenance.</u>

Transfer for Less Than Fair Market Value
Transfer for less than fair market value means selling, conveying, gifting or exchanging an asset for an amount less than fair market value. It also means a voluntary asset transfer to, or purchase of any financial instrument that reduces net worth unless the entire balance of the asset can be liquidated for the claimant's benefit. In other words, if the claimant can recapture the value of the asset that was transferred – whether he or she wants to or not – then that value is considered not transferred and instead counts towards the net estate limit.

VA presumes an asset transfer made during the look back period was for the purpose of decreasing net worth to establish Pension entitlement. VA does not recognize such a transfer could have been done without knowledge of the Pension benefit or for reasons entirely unrelated to an application for Pension. Adjudicators will, however, consider clear and convincing evidence that the transfer can be disregarded if the assets were moved as a result of fraud, misrepresentation or unfair business practice related to the sale or marketing of financial products or services for purposes of establishing entitlement to Pension. Evidence for the purpose of substantiating this exemption may include a complaint filed with state local or federal authorities reporting the incident. Nevertheless, the assets in question will still count toward the net estate limit.

Here's an example of a transfer for less than value. A veteran reported that he voluntarily purchased an irrevocable annuity on November 1, 2018. The purchase price of the annuity was $200,000. The annuity pays $1,000 per month to the veteran for the life of the contract. On March 25, 2020, the veteran applies for Pension. As a result of this transaction the veteran cannot receive a return of his $200,000 annuity purchase because the annuity is irrevocable. The purchase of the annuity is STILL a transfer for less than fair market value and will be used to calculate a penalty period.

Here is another example. A surviving spouse voluntarily purchased a trust for her grandson on December 5, 2018. The purchase price of the trust was $200,000. She did not purchase this trust with any knowledge of the Pension benefit. She has total control of the trust and can liquidate the trust at any time for her own benefit. On April 10, 2020, she applies for Pension. Since the applicant can liquidate the trust for her own benefit, this is not a transfer for less than fair market value. The value of the trust on April 10, 2020 is $197,000. This value must be included in the claimant's net worth.

Covered Asset Amount
A covered asset is an asset that was part of a claimant's net worth and was transferred for less than fair market value during the 3 year look-back period, and if not transferred, would have caused or partially caused the claimant's net worth to exceed the net worth limit. In other words, it is the amount of assets transferred in excess of the net worth limit. A trust established on behalf of a child of a veteran that VA rated incapable of self- support should not be included as a covered asset if distributions of the trust cannot benefit the veteran, veteran's spouse or veteran's surviving spouse.

The covered asset amount is the monetary value by which a claimant's net worth would have exceeded the limit due to covered asset(s) alone if the uncompensated value of the covered asset(s) had been included in net worth.

Here is an example. The net worth limit is $129,094. Today, the claimant's assets total $116,600 and his annual IVAP income is $0. Last year, the claimant gave $30,000 his friend. This transfer was within the lookback period. As a result, had claimant not transferred the $30,000, his net worth would have been $146,600, which exceeds the net worth limit. The claimant's covered asset amount is $17,506, because this is the amount by which the claimant's net worth would have exceeded the limit due to the covered asset. It is this $17,506 that will be subject to a penalty.

Calculating the Penalty Period
The penalty period constitutes the following:

- It is a period of non-entitlement due to the transfer of a covered asset(s) during the look-back period, and cannot exceed 5 years
- It begins on the first day of the month following the date of the last transfer, and it is calculated by dividing the total covered asset amount by the monthly penalty rate and rounding down. The resulting whole number is the number of months VA will not pay Pension.
- If a penalty period covers any portion of a liberalized legislation period, the claimant is not entitled to benefits for the entire liberalized legislation period. (See liberalization law at the end of this chapter)
- Penalty periods end the last day of the last month of the penalty period so in accordance with 38 CFR 3.31, the payment date becomes the first day of the following month.

The divisor for the monthly penalty rate is ALWAYS the MAPR for a veteran with a dependent and with the aid and attendance allowance. It is the current annual rate in force on the effective date of the claim. This annual rate is divided by 12 and rounded down to the nearest whole dollar. This becomes the monthly penalty rate divisor. This divisor is the same for all claimants whether a single veteran, a veteran with a spouse or a single surviving spouse. **The divisor for claims with an effective date on or after of December 1, 2019 is $2,266.**

Claimants must apply during the last month of the penalty period to receive benefits with a payment date as of the first day of the month following the penalty period. If benefits are paid from the first of the month following a penalty period, the initial year also starts on the first of the month following the penalty period. Claims made after the expiration of the penalty period will be paid based on the date of claim. However, if the penalty period expires before the claim is processed, benefits can be awarded from the first of the month after the penalty period expired. There is no need for the claimant to resubmit a claim.

Here's an example of calculating the monthly penalty period.

A surviving spouse applies for Survivors Pension on April 2, 2020. Her current net worth is equal to the net worth limit. In October and November of 2019, she transferred assets totaling $10,000. VA deems these $10,000 transfers 'covered assets' and penalizes her using the $2,266 divisor. The penalty period will begin on December 1, 2019, the month following the last transfer. The penalty period is $10,000 divided by $2,266 per month which results in 4.41 months. This is rounded down to 4 months which becomes the penalty period. If the result would have been greater than 4.5 months but less than 5 months, you would still round down to 4 months. The penalty period expires on March 31, 2020. Since the 4-month penalty period expired before the date of her claim, benefits can still be paid from the original date of the claim in April.

In this example, the surviving spouse was really not penalized by having to wait to make her claim, because the penalty period expired before she actually filed her claim.

Potential Ways to Meet the Net Worth Limit

OUR DISCLAIMER – This book and this chapter specifically address how to apply for veterans benefits. It is not our purpose or intent to recommend or be involved in financial planning to move assets in order to meet the bright line net worth test. In this section, we are passing on arrangements that practitioners in the field may be applying or thinking about applying. Since the new rules pertaining to asset transfers for less than value have only been in effect since October 18, 2018, we do not know which of these concepts meet the rules and which do not. The planning ideas that very likely pass muster are those that fit in with what is allowed under the current rules. The planning ideas that are questionable are those not directly addressed by the current rules, but seem to fit under interpretation of the regulations as a whole. **WE TAKE NO RESPONSIBILITY AND WE ARE NOT LIABLE FOR YOUR LOSS IF YOU CHOOSE TO ADOPT ANY OF THESE CONCEPTS AND AS A RESULT ARE DENIED ENTITLEMENT TO BENEFITS. WE ARE SIMPLY LISTING IN THIS SECTION WHAT OTHER PEOPLE ARE DOING. WE DO NOT DO ANY OF THIS PLANNING OURSELVES. PROCEED AT YOUR OWN RISK.**

Understanding How Net Worth Decreases
Net worth can decrease in three ways:

- The veteran, surviving spouse, child, or someone acting on their behalf, may decrease assets by spending them on any items or services for which fair market value is received. Purchases cannot add to the assets that determine net worth. The expenses must be those of the veteran, surviving spouse, or child, or a relative of the veteran, surviving spouse, or child. The relative must be a member or constructive member of the veteran's, surviving spouse's, or child's household,

OR
- The IVAP decreases due to a decrease in income

OR
- The IVAP decreases due to an increase in medical expenses.

A transfer of assets such as a purchase of an annuity, trust, or similar financial instrument does not decrease assets.

It is important to understand what a member of the household or constructive member of the household means. Purchases on behalf of these people also count towards the reduction of net worth. For planning purposes, expenditures on behalf of other family members could be a significant way to reduce assets. A member of the household is defined by state and federal laws, which vary by jurisdiction. The Internal Revenue Service (IRS) defines a member of household as a person who is related to you or lives with you for the entire year as a member of your household.

The IRS further explains a member of household for tax purposes as follows:

"If the person is not related to you, he or she must have lived in your home as a member of your household for the entire year (except for temporary absences, such as for vacation or school). A person is not a member of your household if at any time during your tax year the relationship between you and that person violates local law."

Based on this definition, a member of the household does not have to be a relative except that under the rules above, purchases cannot be made for someone who is not a relative.

But what is a constructive member of the household? There is no specific legal definition for a constructive member of the household. However, the word "constructive" is often used legally in relation to possession of something or an inherent right to something where presumption of that legal right is treated as fact. Perhaps in this context a constructive member of the household would be one where the person might not be residing in the home, but is treated for all practical purposes as if he or she were a member of the household. Perhaps it could be a child who is away at school, or a daughter or son or a friend or neighbor who are not living in the household but who interact with the household by providing care services, monetary support or maintenance services as well as looking out for the welfare and safety of the other members of the household. For all practical purposes these people might be presumed to be members of the household. <u>Please note that our interpretation of a constructive member of the household has not been tested with applications for Pension, so we do not know how VA actually interprets what a constructive member of the household is.</u>

The VA Income Verification Match (IVM) Program through Federal Tax Information (FTI)

VA has direct encrypted intranet connections to records from the Department of Social Security and the Internal Revenue Service (IRS). A dedicated data processing center in the Department routinely requests income information from both of these agencies. Social Security provides information on earned income – current wage earners – and Social Security retirement beneficiaries to include both the claimant and dependents such as a spouse. The data VA receives pertains to any records either of these agencies may have regarding income. VA cannot obtain W-2s themselves nor are 1040 tax returns available. VA refers to the data from Social Security and the IRS as Federal Tax Information (FTI).

The income information from the IRS consists mainly of excerpts from 1040s and information contained on IRS 1099 forms. There are a multitude of 1099 forms that report on different types of income but here are the most common ones that VA would be interested in.

1099-MISC, the most common 1099 form, the 1099-MISC is used to report payments received of at least $600 or more for any income such as service fees, contract fees, gambling income, insurance payments, rentals, prizes and awards and so forth

1099-B, A 1099-B is used to report brokerage transactions such as bonds, commodities, certain contracts, mutual funds and stocks

1099-C, cancellation of debts is viewed as income by the debtor being relieved of the debt and, as such, needs to be reported

1099-DIV, banks, company owned stocks and other financial institutions such as mutual fund companies are required to file the 1099-DIV to report dividends and similar distributions of at least $10 or more

1099-INT, savings and loans, banks and other qualifying financial institutions must file a 1099-INT to report income from interest paid on checking or savings account, savings bonds or treasury bills if the accumulation of interest equals or exceeds $10

1099-R, distributions of $10 or more to include: annuities, disability payments, IRAs and other tax deferred accounts, insurance payments, Pensions and profit sharing

1099-S, real estate brokers, trust companies and similar professionals are required to report the proceeds from a sale or transaction of any property

When receiving an application for Pension, the Pension Management Center will initiate an initial Income Verification Match (IVM) with Social Security and the IRS to include not only income for the year of application but also income for the previous 2 years. <u>Any discrepancies that are detected require adequate explanation from the claimant or the application is denied</u>. The adjudication manual calls either for sending a written request for handling discrepancies or allowing for a phone call to settle questions.

In addition, interest income from net worth will also be compared for the Income Verification Match. Here is what will trigger further inquiry into undisclosed assets for net worth purposes.

- assets which may be earning interest, but it is not clear whether or not they are,
- when FTI is not available and interest bearing net worth is $5,000 or more with no interest income reported
- interest or dividend income of over $20, but claimant does not report the source of the dividends or interest as net worth, or
- the same amount of interest and net worth, as the claimant most likely confused the two fields.

Failure to respond to a request for information based on the net worth determination criteria above, will result in a denial of benefits.

Previous to the new rules changes for net worth on October 18, 2018, all discrepancies were handled individually without the use of a standard form. If a claimant admitted that assets had been transferred prior to application, to meet the net worth limit, VA would request additional information. Even though previous rules did allow, under certain circumstances, for gifting assets to qualify, the department did not like this. If the adjudicator could find a reason for denying the claim based on gifting of assets, that would likely happen.

For example, if cash assets had been given to a child or children, the adjudicator would typically interpret that to mean the children would use the cash to support their parents. In this case, VA would not consider the gift to be legitimate. Another example would be the use of a trust to transfer assets. VA would always request a copy of the trust and trust schedule to see if the transfer met validity requirements outlined by precedent opinions from the Office of General Counsel. In addition, annuities were frowned upon and often disallowed.

The Regional Office will also conduct what are called "Post Award Audits," for individuals who are already on claim. These requests for audits are not based on specific dates but on the workload of the data center that processes the income matching. Thus, an inquiry for discrepancies could come at any time during the year or even in future years depending on a priority list of whether discrepancies are egregious or more likely mistakes or other minor errors.

How the New VA Form 21-0969 Might Affect Planning Options

In a previous section we discussed the requirement for VA form 21-0969. Again, here is the list of questions both on the VA Form 21-527EZ and VA Form 21-534 EZ that will trigger a requirement to fill out this new form.

- Other than Social Security, do you or your dependents receive any income?
- Other than Social Security, did you or your dependents receive any income last year?
- Do you or your dependents have more than $10,000 in assets? (Excluding primary residence or personal effects)
- In the three calendar years before this year, did you or your dependents transfer any assets?
- Did you answer yes to any of the questions above? (If "yes," you must complete VA Form 21P-0969, Income and Asset Statement)

The 21-0969 form is very detailed and initiates inquiries on all types of income and assets and trusts for the purpose of detecting asset transfers and assessing accurate net worth. Corroborating documents must also be submitted with this form. If an attorney or someone else has assisted a potential claimant in reducing net worth within the three year look back period and this advisor believes the strategy is legitimate, the claimant may not be required to submit a 21-0969. But that is unlikely. Anyone with enough assets to want to rearrange those assets to meet the net worth limit is going to have income other than Social Security – either in the year of application or in the previous year. Even if assets are less than $10,000, it is almost certain that the applicant who is attempting to transfer assets is going to have to fill out the form.

One of the first things the Regional Office will do is initiate an Income Verification Match on this claimant. With much more detail on income and assets that are available to the adjudicator with the new form 21-0969, that was not available previously, any discrepancies will be easier to identify. Even if the claimant did not fill out a 21-0969, the IVM could likely uncover income that was not disclosed. An explanation for discrepancies will be demanded from the claimant – not from the advisor who used the strategy to reduce net worth. It has been our experience that when claimants have been assisted with methods to meet the net worth test by third parties in the past, they often have not understood that process. Because of this, the claimant will readily give up information to the adjudicator about what happened to reduce net worth. If the adjudicator feels the strategy was legitimate, then we have evidence with the new rules of what is likely acceptable. If the adjudicator rejects the strategy, then we have a problem.

WAYS TO REDUCE NET WORTH THAT APPEAR TO FIT IN WITH CURRENT RULES

The ideas presented in this section appear to fit within the current rules from VA concerning net worth. Because these rules have only been in effect since October 18, 2018, we don't entirely know how VA would accept the concepts below. Therefore, proceed with caution at your own risk. We are not providing any legal opinions here for you to rely on nor are we asking you to rely on these ideas as planning that will be accepted by the Regional Office.

Purchases for Personal Products and Services

38 CFR §3.274   Net worth and VA Pension.
(f) (1) *How assets decrease.* A veteran, surviving spouse, or child, or someone acting on their behalf, may decrease assets by spending them on any item or service for which fair market value is received unless the item or items purchased are themselves part of net worth. *See* §3.276(a)(4) for the definition of "fair market value." The expenses must be those of the veteran, surviving spouse, or child, or a relative of the veteran, surviving spouse, or child. The relative must be a member or constructive member of the veteran's, surviving spouse's, or child's household.

We have discussed in a previous section, this rule for allowing a reduction in net worth. We also discussed what we think a constructive member of the household might be. Here are some ideas on how money could be spent to reduce net worth.

- cost of repairs, maintenance or <u>remodeling to the personal residence</u> or any other property
- <u>purchase of a preneed funeral plan</u> (a Medicaid funeral trust or final needs policy would likely qualify if a list of goods and services was produced with the establishment of the trust. It would likely be considered a transfer for less than value if no evidence could be provided that tangible value was received for the money set aside.)
- cost of <u>medical insurance</u> for the claimant or other members of the household
- cost of <u>vacations</u> or tours for members of the household
- payment of <u>education costs</u> for members of the household
- <u>paying off debt</u> for members of the household (remember that proceeds from personal loans including reverse mortgages are neither assets nor income for determining net worth)

Please don't take this as a legal opinion because, at this point, we don't know what is allowable and what is not. It should also be noted any purchases that would add to the assets for determination of net worth would simply be shifting money from one pocket to another and is not allowed in the regulation. For example, purchasing a second home or a business or some other asset under this rule would not decrease net worth.

Increase Deductible Medical Costs

> **§3.274   Net worth and VA Pension.**
> (f) *How net worth decreases.* Net worth may decrease in three ways: Assets can decrease, annual income can decrease, or both assets and annual income can decrease.

The net worth calculation is the sum of the market value of all assets plus IVAP. IVAP – "Income for VA Purposes" – is annual gross income of the household adjusted for deductible medical expenses. IVAP can never be less than zero dollars. But based on this calculation, there should be an attempt to reduce the IVAP to zero dollars if that is feasible. With personal care arrangements that we have discussed previously, this adjustment would not be that hard, because the care that is provided at home is probably not fully reimbursed under a personal care arrangement and thus there is latitude to increase the charge for that care based on a legitimate need.

If care services are being provided in independent living or assisted living or perhaps even a nursing home under certain conditions, a personal care arrangement could be considered in addition to the care being provided to increase the medical deduction costs. Finally, once someone is on claim, an attempt should be made to apply all deductible medical costs which were not available with the initial application.

Purchases of Personal Effects

> **38 CFR §3.275   How VA determines the asset amount for Pension net worth determinations.**
> (b) *Exclusions from assets.* Assets do not include the following:
> (2) *Personal effects.* Value of personal effects suitable to and consistent with a reasonable mode of life, such as appliances and family transportation vehicles.

Under 38 CFR §3.274 for purchases in return for fair market value, purchases that trade one form of net worth for another are not allowed. Under this rule in 38 CFR 3.275 any purchases for personal effects would not be trading one form of net worth for another, because the value of personal effects are not considered part of net worth – they are excluded. VA does not elaborate on what it considers to be personal effects. Under the previous rule in effect before October 18, 2018, VA was a little more specific and included this description in adjudication manual M21-1 – V.iii.1.J.1.e.

> "Normal household objects and possessions are not included in a net worth determination. Likewise, motor vehicles used for family transportation are not included in determining net worth, nor is the claimant's primary residence. However, personal property that is owned primarily as an investment, for example, an antique automobile or a coin collection, is included in determining net worth. The term personal property includes all tangible property that is not land (real property) or fixtures on land."

The current description in M21-1 for "personal effects" after October 18 is the exact language in the regulation above. We have no idea whether VA will consider the more detailed description of personal property which was part of the prior rules. We have to assume that they would likely take the same approach to what they now call "personal effects" and what they used to call "personal property." In lieu of any other interpretation, we would have to assume that personal effects include all household objects and possessions as well as motor vehicles and appliances. There is, however, no ban in the current rules on buying personal effects that could be considered an investment. We will simply have to see how VA interprets the new regulation. Here are some suggestions on what might allowably be purchased under this rule.

- a new car or perhaps more than one new car for other members of the household
- new furniture and new appliances
- possibly personal collectibles that have value as this has not been singled out as disallowed
- other vehicular toys for other members of the household

Please don't take this as a legal opinion as we don't know at this point what is allowable and what is not. You must be very careful here because if there is an application for Medicaid in the future, Medicaid is very strict on what can be purchased for personal use including a car. Perhaps all of the purchases listed above could create disqualifying problems with Medicaid.

Let the Penalty Period Run Out before Applying for the Benefit
This idea works if net worth is only slightly above the net worth limit. In fact, we will show how it works with an actual example that was taken from the Adjudication Manual M21-1. Here is the example from VA.

EXAMPLE: A surviving spouse applies for Survivors Pension on April 2, 2020. Her current net worth is equal to the net worth limit. In October and November of 2019, she transferred assets totaling $10,000. VA deems these $10,000 transfers 'covered assets' and penalizes her using the $2,266 divisor. The penalty period will begin on December 1, 2019, the month following the last transfer. The penalty period is $10,000 divided by $2,266 per month which results in 4.41 months. This is rounded down to 4 months which becomes the penalty period. If the result would have been greater than 4.5 months but less than 5 months, you would still round down to 4 months. The penalty period expires on March 31, 2020. Since the 4-month penalty period expired before the date of her claim, benefits can still be paid from the original date of the claim in April. In this example, the claimant was really not penalized by having to wait to make her claim, because the penalty period expired before she actually submitted her claim.

The important issue here is to trigger the look back penalty by transferring covered assets. If no assets had been transferred in this example and the net worth would have exceeded the net worth limit by $10,000, the claimant would have triggered the penalty at the point of application and would have been denied benefits even though otherwise entitled. The claimant would then have to wait 4 months before reapplying.

This idea should be a last resort to reduce net worth after applying all of the spending and medical deduction strategies we have outlined earlier in this section.

Start the Clock Ticking with the Penalty before Actually Being Entitled to Benefits

The goal of this idea is to start the clock ticking on the penalty period. This concept works where the potential claimant would not currently be entitled to benefits as there is no current need for health care or custodial care. As such there would be no rating for aid and attendance. The question may be asked here, without a need for care, what would motivate someone to preplan at this stage to be ready for a claim? Typically, when a potential claimant starts losing his or her independence and needs some limited assistance with IADLs, inquiries are made for veterans benefits – often online – or perhaps a member of the family attends a presentation about Pension. This is often the way people find out about the Pension benefit. This early inquiry can lead to the type of pre-planning we address here.

Here is how it works. Covered assets above the net worth limit will be gifted to a member of the family or someone else. Without this step, assets that are over the net worth limit would likely still be over the net worth limit when the need for care would arise in the future. If the claim were made when the need for care arises, the penalty period would be triggered at that point not earlier as with this strategy. Generally, this strategy would be a last attempt effort to reduce net worth after the other strategies have been employed, and there is still net worth remaining above the limit.

Let's look at an example of how this works. Mary is an 85-year-old surviving spouse claimant. She has $187,000 in a CD in her bank from the sale of her home. She is living in her daughter's home and her daughter Andrea is helping Mary with meals, shopping, laundry and assistance with paying her bills. Mary cannot yet qualify for a rating for aid and attendance.

Mary's gross income is $1,400 a month from Social Security and a survivor's retirement benefit from her deceased husband's retirement plan of $700 a month – a total of $2,100 a month. If she has a future need for care and can get a rating, she plans to submit a claim using a personal care arrangement with her daughter providing the care. Net worth is the sum of income plus assets minus adjustments for medical costs. That's why this strategy works best with the personal care arrangement, because Mary will utilize her entire income to pay Andrea and for VA purposes make her income zero. This strategy works well for home care situations where there is a family caregiver because the family caregiver will turn around and use the money she is receiving to pay for monthly maintenance costs and end up with an additional monthly amount from VA to increase the overall household income.

The net worth limit in effect on the date of her claim is $129,094 and the divisor for calculating the penalty period is $2,266 a month. Mary transfers $60,000 of her savings into an account owned by her daughter. This transfer now puts Mary's assets below the net worth limit. The covered amount subject to penalty is $57,906. When Mary makes her application in the future, the first thing that VA will do is to calculate the penalty by dividing $57,906 by the penalty divisor of $2,266 a month which results in a penalty of 25.55 months which is rounded down to 25 months. (Please note here that this is only an example and the net worth limit in the future will likely be larger as well as the divisor due to inflation.) VA will not process the claim whether Mary is entitled otherwise until the penalty period has been met.

Mary will now be eligible to reapply for Pension within the 25th month after gifting the assets, assuming that her IVAP is zero dollars at that time. If she needs to apply sooner, perhaps within 15 months after making the transfer, she only has to wait 11 months to apply. Had she not used this strategy and had her savings likely remained around $187,000 and had she applied at 15 months from now without making a transfer, she would be facing roughly a 25 month penalty for having assets above the net worth limit – not the remaining 11 months from the transfer. By starting the clock ticking now, through gifting, when she is ready to apply, her remaining penalty period will be much less than 25 months.

Mary could also transfer more of her savings to her daughter to preserve assets in anticipation of applying for Medicaid. On the other hand, there is a 5 year look back on transfers for less than value for Medicaid and the penalty does not start on the date of transfer but on the date of application for Medicaid. If Mary wants to incorporate Medicaid planning with the approach we are discussing here for VA benefits, it is important that she works with someone who understands VA rules and Medicaid rules. Such an experienced person will make sure that Mary doesn't create a problem for herself if she ever applies for Medicaid.

Here is another note of caution for this strategy. Suppose that instead of $187,000 in assets, Mary had $280,000 in assets. And suppose that she transferred as a gift, $153,000 to her daughter reducing her assets below the net worth limit for assets only. Assume her IVAP is again zero dollars. The penalty would now be over 60 months. Fortunately, the maximum penalty that can be imposed is 60 months. However, this is still an unwise move. She should not trigger the penalty if the penalty period exceeds the 3 year look back period. She can certainly gift the assets now, but she should not apply for benefits and trigger the penalty. Instead of triggering a 60 month penalty by applying, she would simply wait more than 36 months for the look back and then apply and there would be no penalty.

This idea should be a last resort to reduce net worth after applying all of the spending and medical deduction strategies we have outlined earlier in this section.

Private Pay through the Penalty Period
Unlike the strategy to trigger the clock on the look back period where there is currently no need for health care or custodial care, this idea is used to allow transfer of assets above the net worth limit to someone else while maximizing the amount of those assets and minimizing the penalty that is created. This idea works best for someone who is already in independent living or assisted living and paying out-of-pocket for that cost. It might also work for out-of-pocket costs for home care which involves a personal home care company that is paid for these services.

Consider this example. Martha, a widow, is 83 years of age, and is a resident of an assisted living facility. With countable assets of $250,000, she exceeds the current net worth asset limit by having covered assets of $120,906. This amount was determined by subtracting the current asset limit of $129,094 from Martha's countable assets of $250,000. The assisted living charges $4,000 per month for her care, and with her income being $2,200 a month from social security and a school district pension, she has a monthly income shortfall of $1,800. However, Martha would like to qualify for pension benefits as soon as possible. In this example, her IVAP is zero and the net worth calculation represents only the value of her assets.

The first step is to add Martha's monthly income shortfall of $1,800 a month to VA's penalty divisor of $2,266 a month. This amount is $4,066 a month and is called the monthly burn rate. The next step is to divide the covered amount of assets of $120,906 by the burn rate which results in 29.7 months. This is called the 'term of the plan' which will also be the penalty period calculation that VA will impose and rounded down. The amount she can gift is determined by multiplying the term of the plan times the VA penalty divisor which results in an amount of $67,381.45. This gift of $67,381.45 will result in a penalty period of 29 months which is the same as the burn rate calculated above. She will use the $53,524.55 (the amount that she retained and did not gift) to pay for her shortfall of $1,800 a month for 29 months. After the 29 months, her net worth will be below the net worth limit of $129,094 assuming her IVAP is still zero. This will then allow her to apply for Pension with aid and attendance and without penalty.

Let's assume that with inflation, the Pension rate is $1,300 a month at the time of her application and that her assisted living cost has not increased. With the extra Pension income, she now has a shortfall of $500 a month instead of $1,800 a month. This is $6,000 a year. She will have to use part of her allowable assets of $129,094 (this will be more at that time due to inflation) to pay for this shortfall. Had the case involved a single veteran, he would have received about $1,900 a month after the 30 month penalty and he would have no shortfall at all.

It should be noted, if an application for Medicaid is anticipated, this planning idea must absolutely be integrated with Medicaid planning using someone who understands how to do this. Any gifting prior to application for Medicaid will likely result in a Medicaid penalty as well.

This particular idea should be a last resort to reduce net worth after applying all of the spending and medical deduction strategies we have outlined earlier in this section.

Involuntary Transfers from Retirement Plans
The idea here hinges on the portion of the regulation below and whether a so-called transfer for less than fair market value is VOLUNTARY or as the definition implies but does not state – NOT VOLUNTARY. Clearly a transfer that is NOT VOLUNTARY is exempt from this rule. This is based on input from the comment period when VA first proposed this rules change in January 2015. The final rules' proposal in September 2018 in the Federal Register discussed why the word Voluntary was used. We include that discussion from VA below to show that certain asset transfers are allowable under this rule.

§3.276 Asset transfers and penalty periods.
(a) (5) *Transfer for less than fair market value* means—
(i) Selling, conveying, gifting, or exchanging an asset for an amount less than the fair market value of the asset; or
(ii) A voluntary asset transfer to, or purchase of, any financial instrument or investment that reduces net worth by transferring the asset to, or purchasing, the instrument or investment unless the claimant establishes that he or she has the ability to liquidate the entire balance of the asset for the claimant's own benefit. If the claimant establishes that the asset can be liquidated, the asset is included as net worth.

Here is VA's discussion of this particular rule from the September 18, 2018 edition of the Federal Register –83 FR 47246

> "Multiple commenters expressed that certain types of trusts and annuities should not be included in the definition of "transfer for less than fair market value." We agree that certain annuities and trusts should not be included as a transfer for less than fair market value. Thus, based on a number of comments discussed below, we are revising § 3.276(a)(5)(ii) to provide that a transfer for less than fair market value means a <u>voluntary</u> asset transfer to, or purchase of, any financial instrument or investment that reduces net worth by transferring the asset to, or purchasing, the instrument or investment unless the claimant establishes that he or she has the ability to liquidate the entire balance of the asset for the claimant's own benefit. We also provide that, if the claimant establishes that the asset can be liquidated, the asset is included as net worth.
>
> Second, several commenters noted that some transfers to annuities are mandated upon retirement. The conversion of deferred accounts to an immediate annuity is required under some retirement plans. We concur with these comments and final § 3.276(a)(5)(ii) excludes mandatory conversions. This means that we will not count, as a covered asset, the amount transferred to such an annuity, although distributions from the annuity will continue to count as income."

There is no question that VA has given license to transfers from certain types of trusts and annuities that are exempt as being transfers for less than value. In addition, certain retirement plans also requiring conversion to an immediate annuity – when the retirement option is selected – are allowed. The question is, what are the criteria for determining these involuntary transfers and what types of plans fall under this exception.

We are aware of certain deferred annuities that by contract provision only allow withdrawal of assets through some sort of immediate annuity plan furnished by that insurance company. We are also aware of tax-sheltered annuities that are available to education organizations and nonprofit hospitals that have similar provisions. Whether other such deferred annuities or trust arrangements meet the definition of "not voluntary," we don't know the answer yet.

We also question whether required minimum distributions (RMD's) for IRAs and other tax qualified retirement plans might also fall under this exception. At age 70 ½, these tax qualified plans require minimum yearly distributions based on a calculation of life expectancy. But, the IRS also allows RMD's to be taken out of tax qualified plans as income annuities. The question is whether the requirement for an RMD is the non-voluntary part of the plan which results in a voluntary selection of either recalculating the withdrawal every year based on life expectancy or rolling the entire amount or a portion of the amount into an immediate income annuity.

WAYS TO REDUCE NET WORTH THAT ARE NOT DIRECTLY ADDRESSED IN THE CURRENT RULES

The ideas presented under this section do not come from us. In this section, we are simply passing on some ideas that have been presented from others on the Internet or as a result of enclaves from attorneys and others. We take absolutely no responsibility for any of these arrangements whether they will work or not. We are not providing any legal opinions here for you to rely on nor are we asking you to rely on these approaches as planning strategies that will actually be accepted by the Pension Management Centers. We have however, endeavored to describe these ideas with enough detail so that they can be understood

Pay Medical Costs in Advance

> **38 CFR §3.274   Net worth and VA Pension.**
> (f) (1) *How assets decrease.* A veteran, surviving spouse, or child, or someone acting on their behalf, may decrease assets by spending them on any item or service for which fair market value is received unless the item or items purchased are themselves part of net worth. *See* §3.276(a)(4) for the definition of "fair market value." The expenses must be those of the veteran, surviving spouse, or child, or a relative of the veteran, surviving spouse, or child. The relative must be a member or constructive member of the veteran's, surviving spouse's, or child's household.

Under the regulation above, net worth can be reduced by purchasing services for fair market value. Certainly, services for healthcare or custodial care can also be purchased under these rules. Additionally, these purchases also represent deductible medical expenses under certain circumstances pertaining to when these expenses are deductible are not. The question is whether services can be paid in advance – perhaps even many years in advance. Below are two potential approaches from numerous planners who hope that prepaid care expenses are allowed. We definitely don't know the details of how these are to be set up, but we do have some comments on what might not make them acceptable to VA

Prepay Custodial and Medical Care in Advance

The idea here would be to pay a care facility in advance for services provided. It might include a year's worth of payments or 2 years or payments for the life expectancy of the care beneficiary. This appears to be a legitimate purchase and possibly changes assets to an obligation where the potential claimant gives up access to this money. And this is probably the key as to whether VA would accept this or not. The claimant would have to give up the right to a refund. Otherwise, whether the money is set aside for care or not, if it can be converted back into an asset, then it was not a legitimate purchase.

Special Escrow Account for Pre-Funding Personal Care Arrangements

The State of Florida Medicaid Department allows money to be set aside in a special account to pay for personal care of an individual for the life expectancy of that individual. As long as the account is set up properly, this money is not considered a resource for Medicaid purposes. Many Medicaid planners in Florida use this strategy. Prior to the rules changes for Pension, the strategy also fit in well with application for Pension benefits. The question here is whether the particular trust or other escrow account that is set up would be acceptable to VA as a legitimate purchase of future care costs. We won't know until the issue comes up with new applications after October 18, 2018.

Gifting Exempt Assets

§3.275 How VA determines the asset amount for Pension net worth determinations.
(b) *Exclusions from assets.* Assets do not include the following:
(1) *Primary residence.* The value of a claimant's primary residence (single-family unit), including the residential lot area, in which the claimant has an ownership interest. VA recognizes one primary residence per claimant. If the residence is sold after Pension entitlement is established, any net proceeds from the sale is an asset except to the extent the proceeds are used to purchase another residence within the same calendar year as the year in which the sale occurred.
(i) *Personal mortgage not deductible.* VA will not subtract from a claimant's assets the amount of any mortgages or encumbrances on a claimant's primary residence.
(ii) *Claimant not residing in primary residence.* Although rental income counts as annual income as provided in §3.271(d), VA will not include a claimant's primary residence as an asset even if the claimant resides in any of the following as defined in §3.278(b):
(A) A nursing home or medical foster home;
(B) A care facility other than a nursing home; or
(C) The home of a family member for health care or custodial care.
(2) *Personal effects.* Value of personal effects suitable to and consistent with a reasonable mode of life, such as appliances and family transportation vehicles.

Gifting the Principal Residence

Many attorneys and other planners interpret the rules above to mean that the home that is owned and occupied by the claimant or other members of the household is – under all circumstances – exempt as an asset for VA purposes. Interpretation is that there are no exceptions to this. Based on this interpretation, ownership in the home can be gifted at any time prior to application or while on claim and not affect the net estate of the claimant.

Under this interpretation, the house as an exemption is never conditional. Did VA really intend for this exemption to be unconditional? Evidence that this might not be the case is when on claim – under the new rules – if the house is sold, the proceeds become an asset. Would not a gift of the house while on claim also be considered a conversion of that asset? Under Medicaid rules the principal residence is only exempt as an asset as a conditional rule. Transfer for less than value of the home prior to application for Medicaid results in a penalty. Likewise transfer for less than value of the home while receiving Medicaid benefits also results in a penalty.

This type of planning has been going on for years and as far as the planners who are doing this nothing has changed. They have been transferring the principal residence in special trusts either prior to application or while the claimant is receiving benefits.

Here's the problem. These transfers were hidden from view previously so that VA never really knew about them. They can still be hidden from view as they don't show up anywhere in the Federal Tax Information that VA receives. On the other hand, if an adjudicator makes an inquiry for some other issue based on assets, and VA form 21-0969 was not sent in originally, the Pension

Management Office may send that form for further clarification. The claimant will receive the form – not the attorney who set up the trust. Our guess is that claimants will not understand that they do not have to disclose the trust and they will include a copy of the trust as is required by this new form. Once VA finds out what is going on, then we will know whether they will allow these transfers are not.

Gifting Personal Effects

Some planners will suggest that claimants purchase expensive personal items such as luxury cars for $80,000 or expensive collectibles such as antique furniture, rare ceramics, statues, paintings, stamp collections and then gift this personal property to members of the family who are not a part of the household. Gifts to members of the family who are part of a household might have a different interpretation as they were not allowed under the old rules for transfers of assets.

The purpose is to convert a high net worth estate into exempt property under the regulation and then gift that property to members of the family. This would transfer that estate and reduce the net worth for purposes of VA's net worth limit. As is the case with gifting the principal residence, we would find it hard to believe that VA would condone this practice.

Installment Sales

Installment sales are recognized as legitimate transactions in the regulations and in M21-1, Part V, Subpart iii, Chapter 1, Section I - Improved Pension - Counting Specific Types of Income

V.iii.1.I.9.b. Definition: Installment Sale	An *installment sale*, for Pension purposes, is any sale in which the seller receives more than the sales price over the course of the transaction. The actual number of installments is irrelevant.
V.iii.1.I.9.d. Counting Income From Installment Sales	If a claimant or dependent sells property and receives payment in installments, count as income any amounts received over and above the sales price, but not until an amount equal to the sales price has been received by the seller. *Note*: This principle applies regardless of whether the sale occurred before or after the date of entitlement to Pension. *Reference*: For information on the impact of installment sales on Section 306 or Old Law Pension, see M21-1, Part V, Subpart iii, 1.C.7.
V.iii.1.I.9.f. Ensuring Proper Documentation Prior to Computation of Income	Ensure that the following information is of record before attempting to compute countable income from the sale of property: • sales price • amount of the down payment • date the first installment payment is received • frequency of installment payments • amount of each installment payment, and • date the last installment payment will be received.
V.iii.1.I.9.g. Not Distinguishing	It is not necessary to distinguish between payment of principal and interest in the installment sale context. As soon as the down payment and installment payments

Between Principal and Interest in Installment Sales

received by the beneficiary equal the sales price, all subsequent installment payments count as income.

Example: A Veteran reports the sale of a house for $60,000 on December 1, 1997. The Veteran received $20,000 down and will receive installment payments of $400 per month for the next 10 years. The first payment was received January 1, 1998. The Veteran's return from the sale of property will exceed $60,000 during May 2006. Charge recurring income of $400 per month effective June 1, 2006.

With an installment sale, the owner of the property transfers ownership to another person in exchange for receiving a series of payments equal to the selling price. The seller also receives interest from the purchaser with each payment for the purchaser's use of the property during the period of the sale. A typical installment sale will include the seller maintaining a security interest in the property in case of default. The security interest would typically be a lien against the property. Installment sales are private transactions.

Sales involving commercial mortgages are not installment sales as the commercial mortgage company pays the seller a lump sum amount for the property and then assumes the risk of making sure that the buyer makes the appropriate payments to the commercial mortgage company for the purchase of the property.

Let's look at an example of how an installment sale works. Suppose the claimant has a personal residence with no liens against it and a market value of $200,000. For Pension purposes a principal residence is exempt under the net estate determination. However, let's suppose the claimant's family decides to sell the property using a commercial mortgage company. However, this is after the claimant has been receiving monthly benefits. This sale of the personal residence transforms an exempt asset into a countable asset for the net estate determination. When VA finds out about the sale, it will discontinue the benefit and demand repayment from the point at which the net asset test was exceeded unless the proceeds from the sale are reinvested in a new principal residence.

Instead of using a commercial real estate loan and receiving a lump sum amount, the family decides to sell the home to another member of the family using an installment contract. The contract requires 200 monthly payments of $1,200 which represents $1,000 of principal and $200 of interest (for simplicity we are using simple interest instead of compound interest). VA considers the full $1,200 each month to be a conversion of the asset that accrues to the seller who is the claimant receiving benefits. As long as these small piecemeal conversions of asset are spent and not allowed to accumulate, the claimant will never exceed the net estate limit.

Even though the $1,200 a month includes interest of $200, VA does not consider this to be the case. The entire $1,200 is considered a conversion of the asset until 167 of the 200 payments have been made. The 167 payments represent $200,000 or the original selling price. VA considers the remaining 23 payments totaling $27,600 to be income. So, the claimant will not have to reckon with an increase in income for Pension purposes until 14 years have elapsed.

In essence, this planning idea to deal with the net estate test could be used to sell any property or asset such as a farm, a business, a duplex or possibly even a savings or investment account. It is interesting to note that due to the ability of the installment sale to break up an asset into very small pieces and the rule that allows payments to avoid income for a number of years, this makes an installment sale a potential planning tool with Pension.

However, VA could well consider installment sales to be financial instruments that transfer property for less than value.

It should be noted, if an installment sale is used for Pension planning purposes, the contract should include provisions to be non-assignable and irrevocable. Otherwise, if VA reviews the contract and determines that it could have market value, the installment sale may be disallowed.

An installment sale is considered by VA to be a conversion of an asset. Instead of receiving the full value of the asset up front, the seller receives the asset piecemeal over a period of time until the entire value of the asset has been returned to the seller plus interest. For Pension application purposes, the payment received in the month of application would be considered an asset, but it could be lumped in with other assets as long as the net worth limit was not exceeded.

As long as payments from an installment sale are not allowed to accumulate and are used for maintenance costs or other purchases such as care costs each month, the claimant receiving an award would not have to report these payments to VA as a change in assets. For Pension application purposes, payments from an installment sale are not income until the total of all payments equal the selling price and payments after that represent interest and our income for VA purposes.

If a claimant uses an installment sale to transfer ownership of an asset to some other person, income from that sale does not need to be reported to VA until the entire principal has been repaid, but for IRS purposes, interest income must be reported with each payment when filing taxes. If an installment sale is used, the claimant should include 12 months of interest income on the Pension application even though it is not required. VA will do an Income Verification Match and find that interest income and want to know what it is. By disclosing it up front, there would be no challenge. Also, by disclosing income from an installment sale, the claimant has let VA know that an installment sale is in effect. If VA is going to allow installment sales, everyone will know pretty soon whether they are allowable or not.

If one were to compare a single premium purchased income annuity for a period certain, with an installment sale, they appear to be the same thing with different names. And as we know, VA considers the annuity to be a transfer for less than value. During the comment period for the new rules change proposal in January 2015, one commenter wanted to know why VA did not include installment sales as transfers for less than value when they did include annuities as transfers for less than value. Here is VA's discussion of this particular issue from the September 18, 2018 edition of the Federal Register –83 FR 47246

> "One commenter stated that the purchase of an immediate annuity meets the definition of an installment sale. VA's current procedure manual defines an installment sale for Pension purposes as any sale in which the seller receives more than the sales price over the course of the transaction. However, there are different types of annuity plans, and the seller (annuitant) might not receive more than the sales price over the course of the transaction,

for example, if the plan terminates payments upon the seller's death. Although the commenter draws this comparison to an installment sale in furtherance of his argument that annuity payments should not be treated as income, Congress has spoken explicitly on the question of whether annuity payments are income, as further discussed below. See 38 U.S.C. 1503(a) ("all payments of any kind or from any source (including . . . retirement or annuity payments . . .)," shall be considered income unless expressly excluded by statute). We make no change based on the comment."

This means that they do not consider annuities to be equivalent to installment sales. Does this then mean that they would recognize installment sales as a means to transfer property to someone else?

Understanding an Initial Claim for Pension or Survivor Pension

Understanding how VA applies income and medical expenses and assets in estimating and paying benefits for the first year is perhaps one of the most confusing aspects of applying for Pension.

An initial or original application (claim) for Pension is generally based on income estimates, asset estimates and medical expense estimates beginning the month of application and extending 12 months into the future. There may be some exceptions to this, but let's keep it simple at this point. Income and medical expenses prior to application are not pertinent and are disregarded by VA. Many people make the mistake of listing medical expenses for previous months. Or they may list some sort of extraordinary income receipt prior to application. Providing this information just confuses the Pension Management Center and could result in a denial.

The application is an estimate of the three factors above for the future 12 months starting from the month of application or filed Intent. Finally, personal care expenses and health insurance premiums that can be applied to offset income are only those that can be certified by the applicant to recur each month for the future 12-month period from the date of the application going forward.

General Medical Costs Eligible for the 12 Month Look Ahead Deduction
Only certain recurring, out-of-pocket – UNREIMBURSED – medical expenses will be considered by VA for the initial application. Here are the most common. Combined household medical expenses are used, not just those of the claimant.

1. The monthly recurring out-of-pocket cost of long-term care services for home care provided by professionals or family, Independent Living with 3rd Party care (certified by a physician), assisted living, adult day services and nursing home services when VA determines the services are deductible.

2. The recurring out-of-pocket cost for health insurance premiums such as Medicare Part B, Medicare supplements, Medicare advantage plans, supplemental health insurance plans and long-term care insurance but not to include reimbursement policies such as AFLAC.

3. The out-of-pocket cost for possible visits for medical treatment that can be proven that need to be performed on a regular basis. An example might be dialysis. Another example might be ongoing chiropractic treatments.

4. The out-of-pocket cost for renting medical equipment on a monthly basis such as health monitoring equipment, hospital beds and so on.

If you can come up with any other recurring costs that are not reimbursed and are out-of-pocket – as long as you can prove that they will exist month to month – VA will probably accept them.

Prescription drug costs, although ongoing and which can be reasonably estimated, are not counted as a deductible expense by VA.

Medical Costs Eligible for Ongoing Receipt of Pension after Initial Application
After receiving the initial benefit, you may choose to submit evidence of medical expenses that are not recurring as well as actual evidence of all of the expenses that were used to estimate the benefit initially. This is important for several reasons.

1. Often the recurring medical expenses that you estimated for the initial application were actually less than those you estimated. Unless you can come up with additional expenses that are allowable after the initial award, you may have a reduction in future benefits.

2. Often the income that you estimate for the initial application may be less than your actual income for the period. Again, without offsetting medical expenses, you may see a reduction in future benefits.

3. If your initial award is less than the maximum that was available, evidence of additional medical expenses will allow VA to give you a catch-up payment for those benefits that you missed.

4. You apply for past benefits under the Liberalization Law. See below.

You should use VA Form *21P-8416 Medical Expense Report* to provide VA a full accounting of your one-time and ongoing medical expenses after you are on claim. The 8416 form should be accompanied by *VA Form 21-4138 - Statement in Support of Claim*, which is the standard communication form used by all claimants, mainly as a cover letter. All of these forms are available on the Claim Support Disc included with this book. Details on how to do this reporting are outlined in a section below.

The list on the next page shows many of the common allowable medical expenses, but this list is not all-inclusive. Any expenses are allowable that are directly related to medical care. These must be unreimbursed expenses paid out-of-pocket by the beneficiary and/or spouse. Remember, claims based on long term care expenses like home care, assisted living, and nursing home care are the most likely to succeed as these expenses are ongoing and significantly drain income and assets.

- Abdominal supports
- Acupuncture service
- Ambulance hire
- Anesthetist
- Arch supports
- Artificial limbs and teeth
- Back supports
- Braces
- Cardiographs
- Chiropodist
- Chiropractor
- Convalescent home (for medical treatment only)
- Crutches
- Dental service, for example, cleaning, x-ray, filling teeth
- Dentures
- Dermatologist
- Drugs, prescription and nonprescription
- Gynecologist
- Hearing aids and batteries
- Home health care services
- Hospital expenses
- Insulin treatment
- Insurance premiums, for medical insurance only
- Invalid chair
- Lab tests
- Lip reading lessons designed to overcome a disability
- Lodging incurred in conjunction with out-of-town travel for treatment (to be determined on a facts-found basis)
- Medicare Part B premiums
- Neurologist
- Nursing services for medical care, including nurse's board paid by claimant
- Occupational therapist
- Ophthalmologist
- Optician
- Optometrist
- Oral surgery
- Osteopath, licensed
- Pediatrician
- Physical examinations
- Physician
- Physical therapy
- Podiatrist
- Psychiatrist
- Psychoanalyst
- Psychologist
- Psychotherapy
- Radium therapy
- Sacroiliac belt
- Seeing-Eye dog and maintenance
- Speech therapist
- Splints
- Surgeon
- Telephone/teletype special communications equipment for the deaf
- Transportation expenses for medical purposes (54 cents per mile effective January 1, 2016)
- Vaccines
- Wheelchairs
- Whirlpool baths for medical purpose

Sample Pension and Survivor Pension Cases

Sample Case #1   Veteran and Spouse - Veteran Receiving Paid Long-Term Care at Home

This case illustrates a partial VA Pension Benefit with the Aid and Attendance Allowance. It shows how Pension can be used to help pay for home care aides. The case also illustrates how being rated for Aid and Attendance qualifies the veteran for free VA Health Care and possibly a grant of up to $2,266 to help him renovate his home to accommodate his disability. These are additional and valuable benefits available because he is receiving Pension and has a medical rating for Aid and Attendance.

John is an 87-year-old veteran of the Korea Conflict. Although he did not serve in a combat zone, he served for several years during the war and was honorably discharged. Mary, his wife, is 86 years old. John is frail and requires assistance with transfers, bathing, dressing, and maintaining good hygiene. Mary is concerned about leaving him alone and struggles to take care of him given her age and his needs.

John and Mary have a combined gross income of $3,125 a month which consists of Social Security for both, a small employer-based Pension and interest income. They have $66,000 in retirement savings and own a house and a car.

Mary has found it necessary to hire a non-medical home care agency which costs them $2,000 each month. The agency helps John with his physical needs which also allows Mary to leave the home and still have John supervised. She uses their income and savings to pay the agency. Their other recurring unreimbursed medical expenses amount to $300 a month.

John applies and is granted Veterans Pension with the "Aid and Attendance" allowance. Based on his continuing need for care, VA will allow him to count 12 months of future recurring care costs towards the calculation of his benefit. He may also be eligible now for a VA home renovation grant of $2,000 to help cover the cost of needed home modifications.

Estimates from the table below show that John and Mary now have an additional $1,366 per month with the Pension benefit to apply to their medical costs each month.

Due to his medical rating, John is now also eligible for benefits from VA Health Care. John applies and is accepted. All of his health care costs are now free, and his medications costs will also be capped. This is a huge advantage over his old drug plan.

Veteran and Spouse – Veteran Receiving Paid Long Term Care at Home

Total 12-month, future family income from all sources	$37,500
Less 12 months-worth, prospective, unreimbursed medical expenses	$27,600
Subtract 5% of basic MAPR for this category	$900
Medical Expenses Adjusted for Deduction	$28,500
IVAP (Income for VA Purposes) (Future income less future medical costs)	$10,800
Couples Pension MAPR with Aid and Attendance	$27,195
Less IVAP	$10,800
Calculated Yearly Pension Amount	$16,395
Monthly Pension Award (yearly divided by 12 and rounded down)	$1,366

Sample Case #2   Single Veteran – Veteran Receiving Care in Assisted Living
This case illustrates a maximum Veterans Pension benefit available with the Aid and Attendance Allowance.

Jim is 85 years old, single, and is an Army veteran of the Korean Conflict. Although he did not serve in a combat zone, he served for several years during the war and was honorably discharged. Jim is a large man with several medical problems. He has difficulty attending to his own needs without help. Christine, John's daughter, has difficulty helping him get out of bed, dress, bathe and move about.

She is also limited on time. Jim suffers from dementia and is often confused, even with simple things. It is becoming increasingly difficult for him to stay in his apartment.

Jim's gross income of $2,100 a month consists of Social Security, a small Pension and interest income. He also has $25,000 in retirement savings and a car. Christine and Jim decide he needs to live in an assisted living facility which will cost $3,200 a month.

Jim completes and files *VA Form 21P-527EZ, VA Form 21-2680*, his discharge papers from the Army, and a detailed statement from the assisted living facility. He subsequently qualifies for Pension with the "Aid and Attendance" Allowance.   An estimate of his benefit is below. Also due to his medical rating, John is now also eligible for healthcare from VA Health Care. John applies and is accepted.

Single Veteran – Veteran Receiving Care in Assisted Living

Total 12-month, future family income from all sources	$25,200
Less 12 months-worth, prospective, unreimbursed medical expenses	$38,400

Subtract 5% of basic MAPR for this category	$687
Medical Expenses Adjusted for Deduction	$37,713
IVAP (Income for VA Purposes) (Future income less future medical costs)	$0
Single Veteran Pension MAPR with Aid and Attendance	$22,939
Less IVAP	$0
Calculated Yearly Pension Amount	$22,939
Monthly Pension Award (yearly divided by 12 and rounded down)	$1,911

Sample Case #3   Veteran and Spouse – Veteran in a Nursing Home
This case illustrates a Veterans Pension Benefit with the Aid and Attendance Allowance. Residency in a skilled care nursing home automatically includes the aid and attendance allowance for a veteran. The case was specifically designed to illustrate how Medicaid and Veterans Pension could dovetail in providing more income. As a general rule, Veterans Pension does not work well with Medicaid unless there is a spend down of assets (as in this case) or if the nursing home has no Medicaid beds.

William is 84 years old and is a veteran of the Korean Conflict. His duration of service and discharge qualify for him for Veterans Pension. Shannon, his wife, is 85 years old. William has many medical problems. He takes a variety of expensive prescription drugs and has extreme difficulty attending to his own needs without help. Shannon is a moderately frail woman and has difficulty helping him get out of bed, dress, bathe and move about. William also suffers from dementia and is often confused. Shannon is overwhelmed and cannot leave him alone. It is difficult for him to leave his home without using a walker and an aide to help him transfer.

Shannon decides she cannot care for him at home and, after being told by several assisted living facilities they cannot take him, she finds she must place William in a nursing home. William and Shannon have a combined income of $3,175 a month which consists of Social Security for both, a small annuity income and interest income. They have $66,000 in retirement savings, a house and a car.

Because of the differential in cost between the nursing home and their income, William will qualify for Pension with the aid and attendance allowance and he will also qualify for Medicaid.

Based on the previous analysis (example #1) we know VA will not pay more than $2,266 a month in Pension that could be applied to William's nursing home cost. On the other hand, Medicaid will pay the much higher cost between the nursing home and his income in lieu of the Veterans Pension benefit. Should Shannon worry about applying for the Pension benefit knowing Medicaid may cover the entire cost of the nursing home and allow a guaranteed spousal income?

In this particular example, Shannon could come away with more money for her personal needs by using both the VA benefit and Medicaid. To understand why the combination of the two benefits is better we need to understand how Medicaid works.

Suppose William and Shannon do not have the VA benefit. Medicaid will not start paying for William's nursing home costs until he has spent his portion of the family assets down to less than $2,000. In the state in which he resides, William is responsible for spending $33,000 of their $66,000 in retirement savings. He can spend this on anything he wants but in this case the money needs to go towards the nursing home or he won't have a place to live (assume no Medicaid planning is done).

William's income is $2,375 a month and Shannon's is $800 a month. The cost of his skilled nursing home care is $6,000 a month. William must pay $3,625 a month out of his spend down savings allowance money to the nursing home. After 10 months he will be below $2,000 and Medicaid will take over paying the $3,625 a month. After Medicaid takes over, because William's income must go towards the nursing home, Shannon could be impoverished.

In addition to $800 a month, Shannon has her own $33,000 of the remaining assets. Medicaid will not impoverish her completely and Medicaid will give her back $1,600 a month from William's income to bring her income to $2,400 a month. This is called the minimum monthly needs allowance. But this is only after William has spent down his $33,000 and qualifies for Medicaid. Shannon has to live on something else in the meantime.

Now let's suppose that Shannon and William apply for the Veterans Pension with aid and attendance and Medicaid at the same time. William must go through his spend down but VA will also provide additional money for this period of time. The benefit estimate is on the next page.

Veteran and Spouse – Veteran in a Nursing Home

Total 12-month, future family income from all sources	$38,100
Less 12 months-worth, prospective, unreimbursed medical expenses	$72,000
Subtract 5% of basic MAPR for this category	$900
Medical Expenses Adjusted for Deduction	$71,100
IVAP (Income for VA Purposes) (Future income less future medical costs)	$0
Couples Pension MAPR with Aid and Attendance	$27,195
Less IVAP	$0
Calculated Yearly Pension Amount	$27,195
Monthly Pension Award (yearly divided by 12 and rounded down)	$2,266

They now have an additional $2,266 a month to use for income and to apply to the nursing home while William is going through his spend down. Over the period of months where William is applying his spend down money, this is an additional money they have wouldn't be there without the VA benefit. If nothing else, this simply sustains their standard of living for an additional number of months.

VA will continue to pay $2266 a month when William becomes eligible for Medicaid as long as Shannon is alive. If she dies, his Veterans Pension will be reduced to $90 a month. William's other income must go towards his nursing home cost and Medicaid will cover the balance.

Sample Case #4   Healthy Veteran with Non-Veteran Spouse Generating the Medical Costs
This case illustrates a maximum Veterans Pension Benefit with one dependent (his wife). It shows how Pension can be used to help pay for home care aides for the unhealthy spouse of a veteran.

A non-veteran spouse of a healthy-living veteran is receiving paid home care. Under VA rules, and older disabled woman does not technically qualify for a rating but does meet the special medical needs test because her medical costs are deductible and count toward the household medical expenses. Her doctor completes a *VA Form 21-2680* Exam for her and produces a letter outlining her ongoing personal care needs and explains why she needs to be in a "protected environment." The home care providers are not licensed, but the exam from the doctor –*VA Form 21-2680* – is completed and signed by the veteran. This is necessary even though the form is for his wife as he is the claimant. Their household income and her care costs are listed below. The family meets the net worth test and qualifies.

Healthy Veteran with Non-Veteran Spouse Generating the Medical Costs

Total 12-month, future family income from all sources	$20,000
Less 12 months-worth, prospective, unreimbursed medical expenses	$22,000
Subtract 5% of basic MAPR for this category	$900
Medical Expenses Adjusted for Deduction	$21,100
IVAP (Income for VA Purposes) (Future income less future medical costs)	$0
Couples Pension MAPR with No Rating	$18,008
Less IVAP	$0
Calculated Yearly Pension Amount	$18,008
Monthly Pension Award (yearly divided by 12 and rounded down)	$1,500

Sample Survivor's Pension Case

This case was designed to illustrate Survivor's Pension is totally dependent upon income and whether or not there are large offsetting and recurring medical costs such as home care or assisted living. It is precisely these types of cases that represent the majority of widow's receiving Survivor's Pension. In other words, most of those receiving Survivor's Pension qualify because of low income or because of substantial long-term care expenses.

You will see below even though Beverly has a low income, it is still above the basic Survivor Pension threshold and without offsetting recurring medical costs and a medical rating, she will not receive Survivor's Pension. The case goes on to illustrate the power of using recurring medical costs that eventually allow Beverly to qualify

Beverly is the surviving spouse of a Korean veteran who died three years ago. Because she is the surviving spouse of a qualifying veteran, Beverly believes she is eligible for Survivor's Pension. Beverly has not remarried and was married to her husband and living with him when he died. She is reasonably healthy, her gross income is $1,300/month and her unreimbursed, annualized medical expenses are a mere $1,000 each year. These expenses consist mainly of health insurance premiums. She files a claim for Survivor's Pension. Her claim includes a marriage certificate, her husband's death certificate and military records, and *VA Form 21P-534EZ*. The Pension Management Center uses the information and calculates her possible benefit as follows:

Surviving Spouse of a Veteran – No Large Offsetting Medical Costs	
Total 12-month, future family income from all sources	$15,600
Less 12 months-worth, prospective, unreimbursed medical expenses	$1,000
Subtract 5% of basic MAPR for this category	$461
Medical Expenses Adjusted for Deduction	$539
IVAP (Income for VA Purposes) (Future income less future medical costs)	$15,041
Single Survivor Death Pension MAPR with Aid and Attendance	$14,742
Less IVAP	$15,041
Calculated Yearly Pension Amount	$0
Monthly Pension Award (yearly divided by 12 and rounded down)	$0

Based on her total income and IVAP, her application for Survivor's Pension is denied.

A year and a half passes after the denial was received. Beverly's health has declined and she decides to move into a residential care home that provides assisted living. She needs help with dressing, transfers, maintaining proper hygiene, and supervision with her medications. She also desires the social stimulation of being around other people her own age. She finds a care home in a residential neighborhood that will charge her $1,850 a month. Beverly's unreimbursed, annualized medical expenses with the additional cost of residential care now amount to a total of $24,000 a year. She files a new claim for Survivor's Pension with an aid and attendance allowance. Her claim includes a new *VA Form 21-534EZ* to give the adjudicator an updated look at her income, assets, medical expenses, and surviving spouse status. She also files *VA Form 21-2680* completed by her doctor, a *Care Provider Statement* from her facility, and a paid invoice provided by the facility. Beverly does not re-submit her marriage certificate nor her husband's death certificate and military records. VA has these items already in her folder. The Pension Management Center uses the information and calculates her claim as follows:

Surviving Spouse of a Veteran - With Large Offsetting Medical Costs

Total 12-month, future family income from all sources	$15,600
Less 12 months-worth, prospective, unreimbursed medical expenses	$24,000
Subtract 5% of basic MAPR for this category	$461
Medical Expenses Adjusted for Deduction	$23,539
IVAP (Income for VA Purposes) (Future income less future medical costs)	$0
Single Survivor Death Pension MAPR with Aid and Attendance	$14,742
Less IVAP	$0
Calculated Yearly Survivor Pension Amount	$14,742
Monthly Pension Award (yearly divided by 12 and rounded down)	$1,228

This time, Beverly is granted benefits which pays her an additional $1,128 a month (tax free) and brings her total income to $2,528 a month. She now has enough money to cover the cost of her new living and care arrangement.

The Claim Support Disc

This disc is a valuable asset. All the forms necessary to file a claim for Veterans Pension or Survivors (Death) Pension can be found on the Disc. The disc also contains checklists and instructions on how to prepare a Fully Developed Claim and gather supporting evidence to strengthen a claim. Some of these documents are standard VA forms; however, there are a great number of valuable forms that we have designed to produce more efficient and timely results.

One unique advantage of the disc is that you can print any mix of forms and documents you need at your leisure. Or if you choose not to print and fill them out by hand, most of these PDF forms are fillable (you can complete them on your computer or email them across the country for someone else to complete on their computer, print, then sign with a pen). Whichever you prefer, remember VA likes wet signatures and clean-readable faxes. Copies of copies mixed with bad hand writing can ruin a claim.

When you examine the Claim Support Disc you will see 5 major folders. These folders are devoted to applications for Veterans Pension and Survivor's Pension, Compensation and DIC, Health Care Benefits and Burial benefits and reference material. Centralized Mail Processing info, the adjudication manual M21-1, and benefit rates are also included on the disc.

Here is a screenshot of the folder called "1 Application for Pension and Survivor's (Death) Pension"

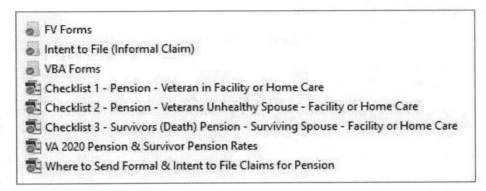

- FV Forms
- Intent to File (Informal Claim)
- VBA Forms
- Checklist 1 - Pension - Veteran in Facility or Home Care
- Checklist 2 - Pension - Veterans Unhealthy Spouse - Facility or Home Care
- Checklist 3 - Survivors (Death) Pension - Surviving Spouse - Facility or Home Care
- VA 2020 Pension & Survivor Pension Rates
- Where to Send Formal & Intent to File Claims for Pension

Note Checklist 2, the veteran is alive and reasonably healthy. In this case, the veteran would not earn any type of medical rating. Rather, it is the unhealthy spouse who requires the aid and attendance of another person or is housebound. The veteran in this case is still the claimant but the couple is seeking Pension based off the spouse's needs and costs. The veteran signs the application.

Under the "VBA Forms" folder, you will find several different VA forms. You will never use all of these forms for an initial application. Many are support or ancillary documents that might be used but seldom come into play during an initial application. Here is a list of each form in this folder:

Form Used to Obtain DD 214*
SF 180 – Request Pertaining to Military Records. We recommend you fax this to (314) 801-9195
* order military records online (archives.gov/veterans/military-service-records/) or (aardvarkresearchgroup.com)

Initial Application Forms
VBA-21P-534EZ – Application for DIC, Survivors (Death) Pension, and/or Accrued Benefits
VBA-21P-527EZ – Application for Pension

Forms Used for Additional Representation
VBA-21-22A – Appointment of Individual as Claimant's Representative
VBA-21-0845 – Authorization to Disclose Personal Information to a Third Party

Form Used for Ratings
VBA-21-2680 – Exam for Housebound Status or Permanent Need for Regular Aid and Attendance

Form Used by Nursing Homes
VBA-21-0779 – Request for Nursing Home Information in Connection with Claim for Aid and Attendance

General-Purpose Communication Forms
VBA-21-4138 – Statement in Support of Claim

Forms used for Fiduciary Appointments
VBA-21-4138 – Response to an Incompetency Proposal
Incompetency Notice Response

Forms Used if Claimant Dies before the Claim Is Approved or is money is owed the deceased
VBA-21P-0847 – Request for Substitution of Claimant upon Death of Claimant
VBA-21P-534EZ – Application for DIC, Survivors (Death) Pension, and/or Accrued Benefits
VBA-21P-601 – Application for Accrued Amounts due a Deceased Beneficiary

Forms Used to Verify Relationships Such As Marriage or Death
VBA-21-686c – Declaration of Status of Dependents

Forms Used to Verify or Notify VA of Any Change in Income, Assets or Medical Expenses
VBA-21P-8049 – Request for Details of Expenses
VBA-21P-8416 – Medical Expense Report
VBA-21P-0969 – Income and Asset Statement

Under the folder titled "FV Forms" you will find several helpful forms. You will never use all of these forms for an initial application. Many are support or ancillary documents that will be called on depending on the situation. Here is a list of each form in this folder:

Attendant Affidavit
FV 11 – Cover Letter for Submission
FV 12 – Doctor's Report Addendum
FV 13 – Care Provider Certification of Services
FV 18 – Certification of Provided Information & Acknowledgment of Understanding
FV 22 – Independent Living Community Certification of Services
FV106 – Sample Care Invoice

The Fully Developed Pension or Survivor Pension Claim

In this section, we will discuss the forms above and how they can be used to produce a successful claim for Pension with the Aid and Attendance Allowance (Special Monthly Pension). You want to give VA every possible document the adjudicators might need to make a decision. Any missing or incomplete documents may result in an inquiry called a development letter. Inquiries can slow claim processing down by 30 days or more. This is required by law in order to allow you enough time to respond. You want to avoid any inquiries by submitting a perfect claim the first time.

A Word about Development and Denial Letters
If a development or denial letter is sent to you or a claimant you are assisting, it is generally not necessary to initiate an appeal. We warn you to use the words "appeal" and "disagree" cautiously and only as a last resort. Generally, a supplemental application with new and relevant evidence will satisfy an inquiry and give VA enough reason to continue processing the claim without having to appeal. We have done this ourselves many times and have never had to initiate an appeal. Appeals are unpleasant and can take years. In the past, we took care of this informally and it was not a problem submitting Form 20-0995 along with other relevant evidence.

Fully Developed Claim
All of the forms we use for the initial application are part of a process VA calls a "Fully Developed Claim." VA describes the Fully Developed Claim program as such:

> "The Fully Developed Claim (FDC) Program is the fastest way to get your claim processed, and there is no risk to participate! Participation in the FDC Program is optional and will not affect the quality of care you receive or the benefits to which you are entitled. If you file a claim in the FDC Program and it is determined that other records exist and VA needs the records to decide your claim, then VA will simply remove the claim from the FDC Program

(Optional Expedited Process) and process it in the Standard Claim Process. See [*VA Form 21P-527EZ of Form 21P-534EZ*] for more information.

Using the Fully Developed Claim process, you can often cut your decision time from 8+ months down to 5 months or less. You also have a greater probability of a favorable decision for benefits.

Unfortunately, we cannot promise any specific processing timeframe or guarantee a successful decision. Pension centers are known to make mistakes. Sometimes the very best prepared claims will not require any inquiry from the veteran service representatives but still take 6 months or more to complete. We have no idea why this happens. We have sent almost identical claims to the same Pension center and observed one is processed in a matter of weeks and the other in 6 months.

Below are descriptions of the most important forms used in the Fully Developed Claim process.

Military Records

You must submit the original or a certified copy of veteran's discharge (DD 214 or equivalent). You can often get a county recorder to certify a copy of an original for you. If you submit a black and white photocopy of the discharge with the initial application there is a high probability you are going to slow things down. VA will generally not proceed until they have a certified or original copy. Some adjudicators will let it slide if the veteran already has a file.

If you can't locate an original, you can submit *Standard Form 180* to the records center in St. Louis to get a new certified copy. This can take up to 3 months with the current backlog at the records center. Getting your hands on the discharge is the very first action you must initiate. Even if you are viewing a copy VA will not accept, still you should take time to verify the veteran's service (branch, dates, and character of discharge). Take note of whether or not the veteran was a reservist. This can be a deal breaker. <u>There are private services like aardvarkresearchgroup.com that can get discharge records in 5 business days</u>. Your state may also have an archive of military records.

WARNING!!!! VA will not return military records. We highly recommend submitting a certified copy and retain the original.

VBA-21P-527EZ – Application for Pension

This is the application a married or single veteran will use to apply for Veterans Pension – with or without the aid and attendance or housebound allowance. The veteran is always the claimant if he or she is alive even if the veteran is claiming expenses from the spouse's care. You must fill out every portion of the 527EZ. Don't leave any box blank. If a box isn't applicable write "n/a." If an amount box isn't applicable write "0" or "none." If you leave questions unanswered, VA will send a development letter asking for explanations.

It is especially important to remember the marriage and income sections must be filled out completely. Complete marriage information includes month and year dates, city state and county locations, full names, and the type of marriage. Basically, no information can be missing and partial answers are not tolerated. If you are not absolutely thorough with this form, VA will return it to you to be completed accurately and you will have lost 30 - 60 days in processing time.

Make sure everything is signed by the veteran, even if the veteran can only mark an "X." When an "X" mark is given, two witnesses must sign near the "X" and list their mailing addresses and print their names. The veteran's Power of Attorney may not sign VA Forms on behalf of the veteran. Court appointed guardians or fiduciaries are the only individuals who may sign for the veteran.

If the veteran's application is based on low income and assets only – without significant medical deductions or a medical rating – the veteran's claim simply requires having a certified copy or the original discharge (DD 214 or equivalent) and a completed *VA Form 21-527EZ* and possibly VA Form 21-0969. That is it. The form and mailing information for submitting the application to the Pension Management Center is included on the Claim Support Disc. Generally, healthy veterans who are making less than the basic Pension rate of $1,146 per month are the only veterans who can qualify in this scenario.

VBA-21-534EZ – Application for DIC, Death Pension, and/or Accrued Benefits

This is the application a surviving spouse will use to apply for Survivor's (Death) Pension with or without the aid and attendance or housebound allowance. You must fill out every portion of the 534EZ. Don't leave any box blank. If a box isn't applicable write "n/a." If an amount box isn't applicable write "0" or "none." If you leave questions unanswered, VA will send a development letter asking for explanations. It is especially important to remember the marriage and income sections must be filled out completely. Complete marriage information includes month and year dates, city and county's and state locations, full names, and the type of marriage. Basically, no information can be missing and partial answers are not tolerated. If you are not absolutely thorough with this form, Pension management will return it to you to be completed accurately and you will have lost 30 - 60 days in processing time.

Make sure everything is signed by the surviving spouse, even if he or she can only mark an "X." When an "X" mark is given, two witnesses must sign near the "X" and list their mailing addresses and print their names. The surviving spouses' Power of Attorney may not sign VA Forms on behalf of the surviving spouse. Court appointed guardians or fiduciaries are the only individuals who may sign for him or her.

If the surviving spouse's application is based on low income and assets only – without significant medical deductions or a medical rating – the surviving spouse's claim simply requires having a certified copy or the veteran's original discharge (DD 214 of equivalent), a marriage certificate, the veteran's death certificate with the cause of death shown and a completed *VA Form 21-534PEZ* and possibly VA Form 21-0969. That is it. The form and mailing information for submitting the application to Pension management is included on the Claim Support Disc. Generally, surviving spouses who are making less than the basic Survivor's Pension rate of $768 per month are the only widows who can qualify in this scenario.

VBA-21-22a-ARE – Appointment of Individual as Claimant's Representative

This authorization allows an individual to act as a claimant's representative. Generally, the best practice is to use VA Accredited individuals or service claim representatives to act as the representative. Check the box titled "INDIVIDUAL PROVIDING REPRESENTATION UNDER SECTION 14.630" if the representative is not accredited. Avoid all of the restrictive options on the form.

VBA-21-0845-ARE – Authorization to Disclose Personal Information to a Third Party

Pension Management will disclose information pertaining to the claim to the individual named on *VA Form 21-22a* or this form. ONLY ONE NAME AND ADDRESS may be listed under #13a-b. This individual may call VA's National Hotline for claims status at (800) 827-1000.

VBA-21-2680-ARE – Exam for Housebound Status or Permanent Need for Regular Aid and Attendance

This form is essential for earning a rating for aid and attendance or housebound. With a rating, a claimant can qualify for Special Monthly Pension rather than basic Pension. For example, basic Pension will pay up to only $1,146 per month for a single veteran. If that same veteran can earn a rating for aid and attendance, the veteran is eligible for up to $1,911 a month.

Help the signing physician make sure he or she understands the form is for a medical rating for personal care, particularly directed towards activities of daily living. In short, VA is looking for language which justifies custodial care needs and highlights specific activities of daily living (ADLs) like bathing, walking, dressing, toileting, feeding, protected environment, etc… Statements like "patient requires assistance to bathe and dress" are far more convincing then vague statements like "poor motor skills and general weakness due to age."

The basic criteria VA follows to determine if a claimant requires the regular aid and attendance of another person or is permanently bedridden can be found above or in 38 CFR § 3.352.

Note: If the veteran's doctor indicates he or she has dementia or Alzheimer's or cannot manage his or her financial affairs, VA will "propose to rate the claimant incompetent to handle financial affairs." This proposal will be given after an award is determined. This action will hinder any back (retro) payments due and will likely lead the beneficiary down the path of fiduciary appointment. We will discuss this in more detail below.

VBA-21-0779-ARE – Request for Nursing Home Information in Connection with Claim for Aid and Attendance

If the veteran is a permanent patient in a skilled nursing home, a rating for aid and attendance is automatic. As long as #13 is marked "Skilled Nursing Care" there is no need for the doctor's exam, made on *Form 21-2680*, nor for any caregiver to certify that the caregiver is providing custodial care. This form takes the place of that evidence. VA may ask for additional evidence if #13 is marked "Intermediate Nursing Care." This form is not applicable for the spouse of a veteran.

VA Form 21-0969 Income and Asset Statement

The new application for Veterans Pension on VA Form 21-527EZ includes the new questions concerning assets. The new application for Survivors Pension on VA Form 21-534EZ also contains the same questions although they are numbered differently. Any questions that are answered "yes" on this portion of the 527EZ from question 29A through question 29E requires filling out the new VA Form 21-0969. Likewise, any questions that are answered "yes" on this portion of the 534EZ from question 43A through question 43D also requires a 21-0969.

Please note, VA considers interest earnings from savings/checking accounts to be income.

FV 12 – Doctor Report Addendum

We designed this form to a supplement to *VA Form 21-2680*. It is especially useful to help certify a claimant must live in a "protected environment" because of a cognitive condition.

FV13 – Care Provider Certification of Services

We designed this form. It is not a VA form but is very important. Even though the doctor is required to produce medical evidence for the claimant to meet the criteria for aid and attendance or housebound outlined above, <u>without evidence the claimant is receiving and paying for these services, there likely will be no benefit</u>. This general-purpose form covers all types of care services from facilities to family members providing care. Make sure the form is completed accurately, the proper sections are filled out, and it is signed by the provider. VA will likely reach out to the care provider to verify what is reported here.

<u>The care provider must also complete a WORKSHEET</u>, found on the final pages of VA Form 21p-527ez and VA Form 21p-534ez.

Consider backing up the care provider's statement with a recently paid invoice (proof of payment). If a care provider is part of the equation, you are seeking to deduct unreimbursed medical expenses (UMEs) from the claimant's household income. Proof of payment will provide further evidence of these expenses. After you submit the application, if the costs you report on this form change or if the claimant moves, notify VA immediately.

FV 22 – Independent Living Community Certification of Services

This form must be completed by an administrator of the community if the veteran or spouse resides in independent living. Remember, independent living room and board costs alone are not considered to be unreimbursed medical expenses (UMEs). Housing, meals, room maintenance, emergency pull cords, 24-hour staffing, and locked exterior doors are not medical or nursing services (custodial care) by themselves.

VA will deduct independent living room and board when, due to poor health, the veteran or unhealthy spouse hires additional 3rd party care to meet their care needs AND the doctor certifies this arrangement.

For all claims involving independent living, include an *FV13* Form completed by the contracted 3rd party care and a letter from the doctor, signed, with this specific language:

> "I, the signing medical practitioner, certify _____ (claimant) must reside in _____ (the Independent Living Community) to receive _____'s (the Contracted 3rd Party Care Provider) assistance with their Activities of Daily Living (ADLs) and custodial care needs. I prescribe the care outlined in the application the 3rd Party Care Provider will offer the claimant in that facility."

If ALL of the above criteria are met, VA will deduct the room and board costs and the 3rd party care costs. If not, VA will only deduct the 3rd party care costs. If there is no apparent need for a 3rd party care, do not bother making application.

FV 11 – Cover Letter for Submission

It is a good idea to create a cover letter to organize all of the claim's forms and supporting evidence and to identify the claim as fully developed for the veteran service representatives who will adjudicate the claim. We believe it helps move the claim along more quickly. The cover letter is provided in Word format so that you can edit at your leisure.

Make sure you are mailing and faxing claims to the correct Pension Management Center. There is one intake center but each of the three Pension centers has their own PO Box. Please see below or check the Claim Support Disc.

Other Necessary Forms

Other possible necessary documentation might include supporting items like:

- a marriage certificate,
- a death certificate <u>with a cause of death shown</u> (VA must be able to clearly read the cause of death. Adjudicators are required to look for instances of suspicious death, homicide, and whether the death was service connected). Adjudicators will also check to see if the veteran was married at the time of death,
- name change records,
- recently paid receipts/invoices from care providers (proof of payment),
- a current bank statement, social security statement, insurance statement, asset statement(s), or supplemental insurance statement(s).

Submitting an "Intent to File" - VBA Form 21-0966

Before applying for benefits, a veteran or surviving spouse claimant may wish to establish an effective date by submitting an "Intent to File." An "Intent to File" can be submitted in three different ways (see 38 CFR 3.155). The most common and most convenient way is to fax *VA Form 21-0966* to VA's Intake Center at (844) 655-1604. Make sure to address it to the attention of the appropriate Pension Management Center and <u>include a copy of the veteran's discharge or evidence of discharge</u>. This will help VA identify the veteran and create his or her file. The "Intent to File," formerly known as an Informal Claim, can be sent to VA even though a claimant is not yet prepared to apply. This is done to 'lock-in a date' for back-pay purposes while the claimant is gathering supporting evidence to include in their application.

Using an "Intent to File" to establish an effective date before the claimant has sufficiently prepared his or her application will allow the claimant to receive a larger lump sum retroactive payment than he or she otherwise would have.

<u>For Pension and Survivor Pension claims with the aid and attendance allowance, if the applicant meets the medical requirement for a rating, is receiving aid and attendance services and can demonstrate having paid at least one month's worth of those services and in addition meets the war service test, and meets the Net Worth limit (asset test) and the income test, you should submit an "Intent to File" as soon as possible.</u> This will establish an effective date.

If you do not meet all of the criteria for an "Intent to File" above, ABSOLUTELY DO NOT FILE. It will mess up the process and create delays and confusion on the part of the service representatives or worse, cause ineligibility.

If a Power of Attorney (POA) signs on behalf of the claimant, you must include *VA Form 21-22a* signed by both the claimant and POA. Save yourself a step and just have the claimant sign everything.

Save your fax transmission reports so you can prove facsimile at a later time if necessary. On the Claim Support Disc, we provide the addresses and fax number of the Intake Centers and Pension Management Center for your geographic area. You can also go to your local Regional Office and have the form date-stamped before the end of the month and then send it on to the appropriate Pension Management Center.

Making Application Using Our Checklists

If you are filing a claim for those who are low income and are too healthy to earn a medical rating then simply follow the instructions we have given you above. You will not need a checklist. The checklists contained in the Claim Support Disc are meant for those:

- who seek a housebound or aid and attendance rating to qualify for maximum rates,
- who wish to deduct long-term care costs like home care or assisted living, and
- who want to submit a Fully Developed Claim.

The checklists cover the necessary documents to prepare a Fully Developed Claim for a veteran or unhealthy spouse of a living veteran receiving long term care under the following circumstances:

- Home care from professional aides or home care from a private company or individual care giver
- Assisted living or other residential care
- Independent Living with 3rd party care
- Adult day services
- Nursing home – skilled or intermediate

As of January 2020 – according to workload reports found on www.va.gov, there were 34,550 initial claims for pension and survivors pension pending review with VA – 36.5% of these claims were pending longer than 125 days. Ever since VA lumped pension claim into the national work queue with compensation claims, processing time has increased, drastically. We are certain if a claimant follows our checklists closely their claims will be developed as quickly as possible.

Even though you can bring these checklists up on your computer in PDF or print them, we will show them below so that you can get an appreciation of how they work.

Checklist 1 - Pension – Unhealthy Veteran - Facility or Home Care (2 pages)
Checklist 2 - Veteran - Unhealthy Spouse - Facility or Home Care (2 pages)
Checklist 3 – Death Pension – Surviving Spouse in Facility or Home Care (2 pages)

Checklist 2 covers the necessary documents to prepare a Fully Developed Claim when the living and married veteran is reasonably healthy and not generating any significant recurring medical costs, but the non-veteran spouse is. The medical and care costs of the spouse can be used to offset the household income for the claim. <u>This type of application must go through the veteran and the veteran is the claimant.</u> Since the veteran has no need for aid and attendance and is not housebound, there will be no rating allowance. This means that the couple's potential benefit will be cut down to the basic MAPR of $1,500/month which is about $766 less than the benefit would be if the veteran was rated for aid and attendance.

If the veteran has significant health problems but is not receiving care, it is advisable to submit *VA Form 21-2680* on the veteran and request a rating for the veteran. VA has been known to issue a rating which then would result in VA paying the full couples benefit with the aid and attendance allowance. In some cases, it is worth a shot.

Checklist 1 - Pension
Unhealthy Veteran - Facility or Home Care

Please complete the forms and supply the documents below as part of the application process. This checklist will help you prepare a fully developed claim for faster processing. You, the veteran, are the claimant. Instructions on how to fill out each form are included with each form.

Name _____ Contact Information: _____

Application for Pension with the Aid and Attendance Allowance

☐ **VBA Form 21P-527EZ – APPLICATION FOR PENSION**
Use the attached instructions to complete this form in its entirety. The veteran must sign page 9.
If there are mistakes or questions, a VA Accredited individual can help correct them prior to submitting.
To substantiate costs shown in Section VIII, you may include Bank, Income, Financial Statements, etc…

☐ **VBA Form 21P-0969 – INCOME AND ASSET STATEMENT**
Use the attached instructions to complete this form in its entirety. The veteran should only complete this form if she/he answers YES to #29E of the 21P-527EZ Application. To substantiate assets, income, interest/dividends, you may be required to supply bank and/or financial statements

The Veteran Completes or Provides the Following Documentation

☐ **Original Discharge or Certified Copy of Original Discharge (DD 214 or equivalent)**

☐ **VBA 21-22a – APPOINTMENT OF IDIVIDUAL AS CLAIMANT'S REPRESENTATIVE**
OPTIONAL - The veteran should fill out this form as directed and sign it. A VA Accredited individual will sign the form to serve as the claimant's representative

☐ **VBA 21-0845 - PERSONAL INFORMATION TO A THIRD PARTY**
OPTIONAL - The veteran should fill out this form as directed and sign it. You may list one individual to act as the authorized 3rd party under #13a & #13b

☐ **Marriage Certificate for current marriage (copy) – if applicable**

☐ **FV18 - CERTIFICATION OF PROVIDED INFORMATION & ACKNOWLEDGEMENT…**
OPTIONAL - The veteran must read this form in its entirety and sign it. An Accredited VA individual will sign the document if VBA Form 21-22a was completed

Documents to Be Completed by the Veteran's Physician - M.D or D.O

☐ **VBA 21-2680 - DOCTOR'S EXAMINATION FOR A RATING**
This form is filled out and signed by the veteran's doctor. If you are also claiming expenses for your spouse, please complete a separate 21-2680 Exam for him or her

☐ **FV12 - DOCTOR'S REPORT ADDENDUM** (OPTIONAL)
This optional form is filled out and signed by the veteran's physician.

Continue to the next page….

Documents to Be Completed by the Veteran's Care Provider(s)

Complete the following if the veteran lives in a *nursing home*

- ☐ **VBA Form 21P-527EZ – APPLICATION FOR PENSION, Section III, #17a-17d**

- ☐ **VBA Form 21-0779 – Request for Nursing Home Information**
  A Nursing Home Official must complete/sign this form

Complete *if using assisted living, adult day services or similar facility*

- ☐ **VBA Form 21P-527EZ – APPLICATION FOR PENSION, Page 11 WORKSHEET**

- ☐ **FV13 - CARE PROVIDER CERTIFICATION OF SERVICES**
  The Care Provider must complete/sign this document. The veteran must also sign.

Complete the following *if using in-home care or a private in-home attendant*

- ☐ **VBA Form 21P-527EZ – APPLICATION FOR PENSION, Page 12 WORKSHEET**
  The Care Provider must complete/sign this WORKSHEET FOR IN-HOME ATTENDANT EXPENSES

- ☐ **FV13 - CARE PROVIDER CERTIFICATION OF SERVICES**
  The Care Provider must complete/sign this document. The veteran must also sign.

Complete *if living in independent living & contracting for 3rd party care*

- ☐ **FV22 - CARE PROVIDER CERTIFICATION OF SERVICE**
  A Community Administrator from the Independent Living Facility must complete/sign this document.

- ☐ **VBA Form 21P-527EZ – APPLICATION FOR PENSION, Page 12 WORKSHEET**
  The Care Provider must complete/sign this WORKSHEET FOR IN-HOME ATTENDANT EXPENSES

- ☐ **FV13 - CARE PROVIDER CERTIFICATION OF SERVICES**
  The 3rd Party Care Provider must complete/sign this document. The veteran must also sign.

- ☐ **DOCTOR'S STATEMENT - This statement must be written on the physician's letterhead**

  "I, the signing medical practitioner, certify that _____ (claimant) must reside in _____ (the Independent Living Community) to receive _____'s (the Contracted 3rd Party Care Provider) assistance with their Activities of Daily Living (ADLs) and custodial care. I prescribe the care outlined in the claimant's application that the 3rd Party Care Provider will offer the claimant in that facility."

Checklist 2 - Pension
Healthy Veteran - Unhealthy Non-Veteran Spouse in a Facility or Home Care

Please complete the forms and supply the documents below as part of the application process. This checklist will help you prepare a fully developed claim for faster processing. Although your spouse is unhealthy and you will be making a claim for benefits based on your spouse's needs, you, the veteran, are still the claimant.

Name _____ Contact Information: _____

Application for Pension with the Aid and Attendance Allowance

☐ **VBA Form 21P-527EZ – APPLICATION FOR PENSION**
Use the attached instructions to complete this form in its entirety. The veteran must sign page 8.
If there are mistakes, a VA Accredited Individual can help correct them prior to submitting the application.

☐ **VBA Form 21P-0969 – INCOME AND ASSET STATEMENT**
Use the attached instructions to complete this form in its entirety. The veteran should only complete this form if she/he answers YES to #29E of the 21P-527EZ Application. To substantiate assets, income, interest/dividends, you may be required to supply bank or financial statements.

The Veteran Completes or Provides the Following Documentation

☐ **Original Discharge or Certified Copy of Original Discharge (DD 214 or equivalent)**

☐ **VBA 21-22a – APPOINTMENT OF IDIVIDUAL AS CLAIMANT'S REPRESENTATIVE**
OPTIONAL - The veteran should fill out this form as directed and sign it. A VA Accredited individual will sign the form to serve as the claimant's representative.

☐ **VBA 21-0845 - PERSONAL INFORMATION TO A THIRD PARTY**
OPTIONAL - The veteran should fill out this form as directed and sign it. You may list one individual to act as the authorized 3rd party under #13a & #13b

☐ **Marriage Certificate for current marriage** (photo copy)

☐ **FV18 - CERTIFICATION OF PROVIDED INFORMATION & ACKNOWLEDGEMENT...**
OPTIONAL - The veteran must read this form in its entirety and sign it. An Accredited VA individual will sign the document if VBA Form 21-22a was completed.

Documents to Be Completed by the Spouse's Physician - M.D or D.O

☐ **VBA 21-2680 - DOCTOR'S EXAMINATION FOR A RATING**
This form is filled out and signed by the spouse's doctor. The spouse will appear as the claimant.

☐ **FV12 - DOCTOR'S REPORT ADDENDUM**
This form is filled out and signed by the spouse's doctor.

Continue to the next page...

Documents to Be Completed by the Spouse's Care Provider(s)

Complete the following _if_ the spouse is in a _nursing home_

☐ **VBA Form 21P-527EZ – APPLICATION FOR PENSION, Section III, #17a-17d**

☐ **FV13 - CARE PROVIDER CERTIFICATION OF SERVICES**
A Nursing Home Official must complete/sign this document. The veteran must also sign.

Complete _if_ spouse is using _assisted living_, _adult day services_, or _similar facility_

☐ **VBA Form 21P-527EZ – APPLICATION FOR PENSION, Page 11 WORKSHEET**
A Supervisor or Facility Administrator must complete/sign this WORKSHEET FOR AN ASSISTED LIVING, ADULT DAY CARE, OR A SIMILAR FACILITY.

☐ **FV13 - CARE PROVIDER CERTIFICATION OF SERVICES**
The Supervisor or Facility Administrator must complete/sign this document. The veteran must also sign.

Complete _if_ spouse is using _in-home care_ or _private in-home attendant_

☐ **VBA Form 21P-527EZ – APPLICATION FOR PENSION, Page 12 WORKSHEET**
The Care Provider must complete/sign this WORKSHEET FOR IN-HOME ATTENDANT EXPENSES.

☐ **FV13 - CARE PROVIDER CERTIFICATION OF SERVICES**
The Care Provider must complete/sign this document. The veteran must also sign.

Complete _if_ spouse is in _independent living & contracting for 3rd party care_

☐ **VBA Form 21P-527EZ – APPLICATION FOR PENSION, Page 12 WORKSHEET**
The Care Provider must complete/sign this WORKSHEET FOR IN-HOME ATTENDANT EXPENSES.

☐ **FV22 - INDEPENDENT LIVING COMMUNITY CERTIFICATION OF SERVICES**
A Community Administrator from the Independent Living Facility must complete/sign this document.

☐ **FV13 - CARE PROVIDER CERTIFICATION OF SERVICES**
The 3rd Party Care Provider must complete/sign this document. The veteran must also sign.

☐ **DOCTOR'S STATEMENT – This statement must be written on the physician's letterhead**

_"I, the signing medical practitioner, certify that _____ (unhealthy spouse) must reside in _____ (the Independent Living Community) to receive _____'s (the Contracted 3rd Party Care Provider) assistance with their Activities of Daily Living (ADLs) and custodial care. I prescribe the care outlined in the claimant's application that the 3rd Party Care Provider will offer the in that facility."_

Checklist 3 – Survivors (Death) Pension Application
Surviving Spouse - Facility or Home Care

Please complete the forms and supply the documents below as part of the application process. This checklist will help you prepare a fully developed claim for faster processing. The surviving spouse of the veteran is the claimant (no exceptions). Instructions on how to fill out each form below are included with each form.

Name _____ Contact Information: _____

Application for Death Pension with the Aid & Attendance Allowance

☐ **VBA Form 21P-534EZ – APPLICATION FOR DIC, DEATH PENSION, &/OR ACCRUED BENEFIT**
Use the attached instructions to complete this form in its entirety. The surviving spouse must sign pg 11.
If there are mistakes or questions, a VA Accredited individual can help correct them prior to submitting.
To substantiate costs shown in Section IX, you may include Bank, Income, Financial Statements, etc...

☐ **VBA Form 21P-0969 – INCOME AND ASSET STATEMENT**
Use the attached instructions to complete this form in its entirety. The surviving spouse should only complete this form if she/he answers YES to #43E of the 21P-534EZ Application.
To substantiate assets, interest/dividends, you may be required to supply bank or financial statements

The Spouse Completes or Provides the Following Documentation

☐ **Original Discharge or Certified Copy of Original Discharge (DD 214 or equivalent)**

☐ **VBA 21-22a – APPOINTMENT OF IDIVIDUAL AS CLAIMANT'S REPRESENTATIVE**
OPTIONAL - The surviving spouse should fill out this form as directed and sign it. An Accredited
VA Individual will sign the form to serve as the claimant's representative.

☐ **VBA 21-0845 - PERSONAL INFORMATION TO A THIRD PARTY**
OPTIONAL - The surviving spouse should fill out this form as directed in the instructions and sign it.
You may list one individual to act as the authorized 3rd party under #13a & #13b.

☐ **Marriage Certificate for marriage to veteran** (photo copy)

☐ **Death Certificate of the Veteran** (photo copy)
This certificate must show the veteran's cause of death and marital status at the time of death.

☐ **FV18 - CERTIFICATION OF PROVIDED INFORMATION & ACKNOWLEDGEMENT...**
OPTIONAL - The spouse must read this form in its entirety and sign it. An Accredited VA individual will sign
the document if VBA Form 21-22a was completed.

Documents to Be Completed by the Spouse's Physician

☐ **VBA 21-2680 - DOCTOR'S EXAMINATION FOR A RATING**
This form is filled out and signed by the surviving spouse's doctor (a nurse may not sign this form).

☐ **FV12 - DOCTOR'S REPORT ADDENDUM**
This form is filled out and signed by the surviving spouse's physician.

Continue to the next page....

Documents to Be Completed by the Surviving Spouse's Care Provider(s)

Complete the following *if* the surviving spouse lives in a *nursing home*

☐ **VBA Form 21P-534EZ – APPLICATION FOR SURVIVORS PENSION, Section VII, #37-38b**

☐ **FV13 - CARE PROVIDER CERTIFICATION OF SERVICES**
A Nursing Home Official must complete/sign this document. The spouse must also sign

Complete *if using* *assisted living*, *adult day services* or a *similar facility*

☐ **VBA Form 21P-534EZ – APPLICATION FOR SURVIVORS PENSION, Page 12 WORKSHEET**
A Supervisor or Facility Administrator must complete/sign this WORKSHEET FOR AN ASSISTED LIVING, ADULT DAY CARE, OR A SIMILAR FACILITY

☐ **FV13 - CARE PROVIDER CERTIFICATION OF SERVICES**
The Supervisor or Facility Administrator must complete/sign this document. The spouse must also sign

Complete the following *if using* *in-home care* or a *private in-home attendant*

☐ **VBA Form 21P-534EZ – APPLICATION FOR SURVIVORS PENSION, Page 13 WORKSHEET**
The Care Provider must complete/sign this WORKSHEET FOR IN-HOME ATTENDANT EXPENSES

☐ **FV13 - CARE PROVIDER CERTIFICATION OF SERVICES**
The Care Provider must complete/sign this document. The spouse must also sign

Complete *if living in* *independent living & contracting for 3rd party care*

☐ **FV22 - INDEPENDENT LIVING COMMUNITY CERTIFICATION OF SERVICES**
A Community Administrator from the Independent Living Facility must complete/sign this document.

☐ **VBA Form 21P-534EZ – APPLICATION FOR SURVIVORS PENSION, Page 12 WORKSHEET**
A Supervisor or Facility Administrator must complete/sign this WORKSHEET FOR AN ASSISTED LIVING, ADULT DAY CARE, OR A SIMILAR FACILITY

☐ **FV13 - CARE PROVIDER CERTIFICATION OF SERVICES**
The 3rd Party Care Provider must complete/sign this document. The spouse must also sign.

☐ **DOCTOR'S STATEMENT** – This statement must be written on the physician's letterhead:

"I, the signing medical practitioner, certify that _____ (claimant) must reside in _____ (the Independent Living Community) to receive _____'s (the Contracted 3rd Party Care Provider) assistance with their Activities of Daily Living (ADLs) and custodial care. I prescribe the care outlined in the claimant's application that the 3rd Party Care Provider will offer the claimant in that facility."

How to Submit the Claim

We enjoy working with the Veterans Service Representatives (VSRs) employed by VA's Pension Management Centers and the Regional Offices of St Paul, MN; Milwaukee, WI; and Philadelphia, PA. The VSRs who manage the application processing and call centers are skilled, friendly, and reasonable people.

Although we have not provided the call center phone numbers to you in this book, if you are accredited by VA and need the phone number of a certain call center, please get in touch with us. We will give you the number(s). The call center phone lines are generally not busy and the VSRs can give you updates on claims you represent and answer eligibility questions.

	Pension & Survivors Pension							
	Non-Rating		Entitlement			Award Adjustment		
	Claims Pending	Avg. Days Pending	Claims Pending	Pending over 125 days	Percent Pending over 125 days	Claims Pending	Pending over 125 days	Percent Pending over 125 days
USA Pension	27,295	215.5	34,550	12,612	36.5%	31,659	22,454	70.9%
Philadelphia PMC	9,598	214.1	13,823	5,233	37.9%	11,597	8,250	71.1%
Milwaukee PMC	8,272	214.8	9,514	3,447	36.2%	9,821	6,952	70.8%
St. Paul PMC	7,886	202.0	10,394	3,609	34.7%	8,702	5,921	68.0%
Pension Other	1,539	297.7	819	323	39.4%	1,539	1,331	86.5%

Source: benefits.va.gov/REPORTS/detailed_claims_data.asp

As of January 4, 2020, there were 34,550 Pension and Survivors Entitlement Claims pending at VA, an increase of over 7,000 claims from 2019. 36.5% of the 34,550 claims have remained in development after 125 days. Last year, before VA lumped pension applications into the national work queue to be processed alongside compensation claims, only 9% of pension claims were still being processed after 125 days. This has been a major let down to claimants from years past. VA's plan was to increase the speed of compensation claim processing by utilizing VSRs from Pension Management, which they have. Unfortunately, pension claimants have suffered.

Formal Claim Submission
See the next page for Pension Management's PO Boxes and the intake center's fax and mailing.

Fax and mail the claimant's entire claim for Pension – all forms and supporting evidence in one packet - to VA's Intake Center in Jainesville, Wisconsin. Make sure to use the correct Pension Management Center PO Box. This will depend on the state in which the claimant lives. Make a copy of everything you send before mailing anything. VA is known to lose paperwork. Some people, in order to ensure receipt by the center, choose to fax and mail their claims.

WARNING!!!! VA Intake Centers will not return military records. We highly recommend submitting a certified copy and retain the original for keep-sake.

Intake Center
The Intake Center in Jainsville, Wisconsin will scan and upload digital images of the claim into Virtual VA. These images will be used to create a new VA File or added to the veteran's existing file. The claim will then be routed to one of the Pension Management Centers for processing.

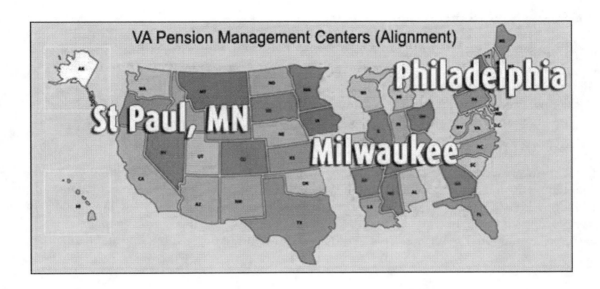

St. Paul Pension Management
Fax: (844) 655-1604
States: AK, HI, WA, OR, CA, NV, ID, MT, UT, AZ, WY, CO, NM, ND, SD, NE, KS, OK, TX, MN & IA
Mailing:
Claims Intake Center
Attention: **St Paul** *Pension Management*
PO BOX 5365
Janesville, WI 53547-5365

Milwaukee Pension Management
Fax: (844) 655-1604
States: WI, MI, IL, IN, OH, MO, KY, TN, AR, LA, MS, & AL
Mailing:
Claims Intake Center
Attention: **Milwaukee** *Pension Management*
PO BOX 5192
Janesville, WI 53547-5192

Philadelphia Pension Management
Fax: (844) 655-1604
States: ME, VT, RI, CT, NJ, NH, DE, DC, MD, MA, NY, PA, VA, NC, SC, GA, & FL
Mailing:
Claims Intake Center
Attention: **Philadelphia** *Pension Management*
PO BOX 5206
Janesville, WI 53547-520

What Documents Not to Submit with the Claim

Certain Financial Statements and Paid Invoices
Generally, the most recent month's paid care invoice or financial statement will suffice when substantiating income, assets, and ongoing medical expenses. VA does not need pages and pages of financial statements and invoices dating back months and months. There is no reason to overload them with too much information.

Prescription Costs
VA will not allow prescription costs as deductible medical expenses for initial applications. Don't bother including any prescription information in a claim. Remember, once a veteran is on claim for Special Monthly Pension and is medically rated – recognized to be in need of the aid and attendance of another person – the veteran qualifies for VA Healthcare. Prescription costs are capped at very low prices for those in VA Healthcare. It is worth the extra effort to apply for VA Healthcare. See Chapter 10.

Black and White Non-Certified Copies of DD 214s
Uncertified black and white photo copies of military records might not be considered as evidence of service by Pension Management. Always attempt to submit original DD 214s, the equivalent to a DD 214, or certified copies of an original.

REMEMBER!!!! VA will not return military records. We highly recommend submitting a certified copy and retain the original.

Power of Attorney (POA) Forms
We are not talking about VA Form 21-22a here.

VA does not need POA documents nor does they recognize the claimant's power of attorney as a signor or one who can speak on behalf of the claimant. If the claimant's POA wants to represent him or her, that person may complete VA Form 21-22a and mark the box called INDIVIDUAL PROVIDING REPRESENTATION UNDER SECTION 14.630. We recommend that family, and others wishing to receive follow up letters on a claim, be listed on VA Form 21-0845 (under #13a-b) and leave the 21-22a form for accredited individuals to sign along with the claimant.

POAs may not sign VA Forms on behalf of claimants under any circumstance, even when they are listed on VA Form 21-22a. Only court appointed guardians and fiduciaries may sign and speak on behalf of claimants. Please turn in all pertinent guardian/fiduciary forms along with the claimant's original application.

What Happens When the Claimant Dies before a Decision Letter is Issued

Substitution for the Claimant

If a claimant dies on or after October 10, 2008 and VA has their fully developed claim on hand, an eligible dependent may request to substitute for the deceased claimant in a claim for periodic monetary benefits (other than insurance and servicemembers' indemnity) under laws administered by the Secretary, or an appeal of a decision with respect to such a claim, that was pending before the agency of original jurisdiction or the Board of Veterans' Appeals when the claimant died. Upon VA's grant of a request to substitute, the substitute may continue the claim or appeal on behalf of the deceased claimant for purposes of processing the claim or appeal to completion. Any benefits ultimately awarded are payable to the substitute and other members of a joint class in equal shares.

The most common type of claim substitution is when a married veteran dies before his or her application is approved. VA has all the information they need to make a decision but the veteran unexpectedly passes away. The surviving spouse can send the following to VA and is entitled to the veteran's back-pay and month of death check.

1. VA Form 21P-0847 - Request for Substitution of Claimant
2. Veteran's Death Certificate

At a later date, if eligible, the surviving spouse should be encouraged to file their own claim for Survivor's Pension or Dependency and Indemnity Compensation. See Chapter 7 for more detail.

Accrued Benefits

Sometimes, a single claimant – unmarried veteran or surviving spouse with no dependents – dies before the adjudication process is complete (before a decision has been issued). There is usually a number of months between the effective date of the claim and the date of death of the claimant. Because of the difference between the claim date and date of decision there is likely retroactive payments due under a pending claim. VA calls these benefits "accrued benefits."

If the unmarried claimant has passed away, any person not in the hierarchy for receiving accrued benefits such as an adult child, a relative, or a friend may be eligible for what is called reimbursement accrued benefits. These people can be reimbursed if they personally paid for any of the claimant's final expenses such as hospital, hospice, funeral or burial costs of the claimant AND there was money due or likely due the claimant. Money is generally only owed if the claimant passed away before benefits were granted or if VA was withholding back-pay due to an incompetency proposal. Note, that final expenses do not include facility and home care expenses.

Fax and mail the following in one envelope to Pension Management to apply for accrued benefits:

- VA Form 21-4138s – This will act as a cover letter, signed by the child, relative, etc...
- VA Form 21P-601 - Application for Accrued Benefits - signed by the child, relative, etc...
- Copy of Claimant's Death Certificate
- Other applicable evidence (e.g. paid invoices of final expenses individual paid which can include hospice, hospital, funeral and/or burial).

Incompetency Proposals and Appointment of a Fiduciary

If the claimant's doctor indicates, on *VA Form 21-2680*, that the veteran or spouse has memory issues such as dementia or Alzheimer's and/or cannot manage his or her own financial affairs, the medical rating team at VA will "propose to rate the beneficiary incompetent to handle personal financial affairs" at the time Special Monthly Pension is granted. <u>This action will hinder any back payments owed to the beneficiary (the former claimant)</u>.

The beneficiary may (1) argue the incompetency proposal through a hearing, (2) remain silent and wait for VA to appoint a fiduciary to handle the his or her finances, (3) respond and agree to the proposal of incompetency and simultaneously request a fiduciary of their choosing, or (4) disagree with the proposal and request that VA withdraw the proposal and release the owed back pay.

1. If the award beneficiary wants a hearing, follow the instructions VA has provided in the correspondence letter proposing incompetency. Our recommendation is to NEVER DO THIS. We recommend either #3 or #4

2. If the award beneficiary remains silent, after 60 days VA will begin to look for the most logical fiduciary (like a family member or VA fiduciary) through their own procedures.

3. If the Beneficiary is truly incompetent to handle finances up and wishes to appoint their own fiduciary (like a responsible family member), use the attached form in the VA Award Letter, "Incompetency Notice Response." Make sure to mail the attached form to the Fiduciary Hub address in the VA letter AND also fax to (844) 655-1604. Follow all the instructions in the VA letter sent to the beneficiary as VA may want other forms or documents returned as well.

4. If the beneficiary believes he or she can handle their own finances, and there was no or very little indication of memory issues on the 21-2680 doctor's exam, but the beneficiary still needs a caregiver for ADLs, the beneficiary may "DISAGREE with the proposal of incompetency" on the "Incompetency Notice Response." He or she must also state on VA Form 21-4138 something like "although I need help with several ADLs and personal care, I am still well enough to handle my finances". The beneficiary must also request "VA no longer seek to appoint a fiduciary and withdraw the incompetency proposal." Finally, the beneficiary must provide VA a new letter from a physician stating something like "my patient [beneficiary's name] can independently handle their own finances." If they do this, VA will withdraw the incompetency proposal and release the back pay. <u>Be careful if you choose this approach. Doing this runs the risk of VA believing the beneficiary is too healthy to need ongoing care because they can handle their own finances.</u>

The Fiduciary Hubs
The fiduciary hubs work on their own timeline (usually 4-5 months) as to the scheduling, interviewing, and eventual appointment of fiduciaries. Here is a direct link and contact information to VA's Fiduciary Program: http://www.benefits.va.gov/fiduciary/contact-us.asp

Potential Issues That May Cause Problems

All information provided in an application should be true and as accurate as possible. Once application is made, VA will seek to verify the veteran's service, household's financial information, stated care services, and marital status with the Internal Revenue Service (IRS), Social Security Administration (SSA), and other government entities. If there appears to be a discrepancy, an inquiry will be initiated.

Keep VA Fully Informed

If the claimant's marital status, address, ongoing medical expenses, care services, income, or assets change in any way, it is the claimant's responsibility to immediately notify VA. Being forthright and responsive to status changes can save the beneficiary from losing benefits or owing overpaid monies. Accredited individuals should continually assist the veteran's household with these issues.

IRS Crosschecks

The Regional Office that has jurisdiction over the claim will continue to monitor claimants from year-to-year to make sure they qualify and meet the income and asset requirements. The department receives yearly 1099's and other information from the IRS as well as reports from the Social Security Administration concerning marital status, assets, and income, including things like property sales, interest, dividends, and distributions from IRA's.

Generally, anything which caused or will cause a tax event will be seen by VA at the time of application, using past IRS records, or the following year on upcoming IRS records. VA has been known to check back as far as 3 years of IRS records to verify information provided in an initial application for Pension.

Following are instances where VA found items that were unreported on the claimant's application.

We need additional evidence from you. **Please use the enclosed envelope (labeled FTI), put your VA file number on any correspondence or evidence you provide.**

- On your application, you reported that you received in $ 1,664.28 in projected interest income for 2014 for $43,150.00 in Stock, bonds or mutual fund assets. VA received from the Internal Revenue Service information that in 2013 you received income of $11,460.00 in interest or pension distributions. The IRS also showed you reported $229,250.00 in real estate sales in 2013. The amount you reported on your application for this payment, $1,664.28, is $9,795.72 less than IRS reported to VA for the 2013 tax year. The $229,250.00 in real estate sales may be considered a conversion of assets if the proceeds are from the sale of your home.

On your application, you reported that you received in 2014 1323.90 for Social Security, Retirement of 368.28 a month and 808.38 a month from Genworth. VA received from the Internal Revenue Service information that in 2013 you received the following amounts and sources of income in 2013 that you did not report on your application:

$49,138.00 Distributions, from pensions, annuities, IRA's, Etc.... account #▓▓▓▓▓▓

$1,617.00 Distributions, from pensions, annuities, IRA's, Etc.... account ▓▓▓▓▓

$171.00 Distributions, from pensions, annuities, IRA's, Etc.... account #▓▓▓▓▓

$1366.00 Distributions, from pensions, annuities, IRA's, Etc.... account ▓▓▓▓▓▓▓

To help us decide your claim, please provide information explaining the difference between the amount of income you reported on your application and the amount the IRS VA for 2013. If you believe the payment information reported by IRS or SSA is incorrect, please tell us in a written statement and provide any information you have to support the statement. Acceptable information to

What Do We Still Need from You?

We need additional evidence from you. *Please use the enclosed envelope (labeled FTI), put your VA file number on any correspondence or evidence you provide.*

- On your application, you reported that you receive $430.69 in pension income and $1,242.90 in Social Security benfits. VA received from the Internal Revenue Service information that in 2013 you received gross distributions as follows; $108,195.00 from account I▓▓▓▓▓▓, $1,219.00 from account 9▓▓▓00000▓▓▓▓▓▓▓, and $1,159.00 from account GA▓▓▓ C▓▓. These amounts or income sources were not reported on your application.

To help us decide your claim, please provide information explaining why these incomes were not reported on your application. If you believe the payment information reported by the IRS is incorrect, please tell us in a written statement and provide any information you have to support the statement. Acceptable information to support a statement would include a statement from the person or entity that paid you showing the amount, type, frequency and date last paid. If you no longer receive the income reported by the IRS, please provide a statement from the person or entity that paid you showing the date this income stopped.

Financial Issues to Be Aware of

Here's a brief description of several financial and other application issues you must be aware of:

1. **The Home** – If you sell your primary residence or other property after you make application or file Intent, VA will eventually find out about the sale from the IRS. The sale is usually discovered through a 1099s issued the property is sold. This document shows the owner's name(s) at the time of sale. VA considers this a conversion of assets. If the proceeds from the sale are significant – anything that may cause net-worth to exceed $120,000 – VA will likely halt benefits and may even deny benefits retroactively. The beneficiary will have to make amends with any overpayments and will not be able to get back on claim until the new assets are naturally spent down to allowable limits.

2. **Reporting Interest Income** – You are required to report interest and dividend income on VA Form 21P-0969. If there are not enough assets to support the amount of interest and dividends income you report, the VSR is required to ask if non-reported assets exist which are supporting the income. The same holds if VA sees unreported interest or dividends from IRS Crosschecks. If you can't provide a reasonable answer about ALL interest and dividends, VA's manual allows the VSR to count un-reported interest and dividends from the IRS which could increase income and cause a denial.

3. **Sourcing Annuities** – VA will likely follow up with claimants if they report income streams from annuities. Some claimants are using annuities to dilute assets by creating income streams prior to application. In some cases, VA will seek to count income annuities, for example, as an income and an asset. You may need to be prepared to argue your case with VA if this is a situation you are in. Your argument will carry more weight if the annuity purchase was made before October 2018 and the principal amount used to buy the annuity is truly "non-transferable, non-assignable, non-commutable, non-surrenderable, totally and permanently irrevocable, and has no cash value."

4. **Cashing out Tax Deferred Savings Accounts Prior to Application** – Any withdrawals or surrenders from retirement accounts such as IRAs, annuities, 401(k)s and so forth that occur in the year of your application will show up as income in that year. VA will scrutinize these transfers heavily. They will receive 1099's from the IRS concerning these surrenders. The service representatives will have no idea whether this occurred before or after your application was made. Be aware you may have to answer some sort of inquiry about any sort of a withdrawal or surrender in the year of application – possibly even a year or two after your award is approved.

5. **Selling Property Prior to the Application** – Even though it may have been a legitimate sale prior to application, be prepared to provide an answer why this happened. Inquiry may come a year or two after the award has been approved. Remember, other property – property that is not the primary residence and a reasonable amount of land on which it resides – must be reported as an asset on the veteran's application.

6. **Incompetent to Handle Finances** - If the doctor indicates on *VA Form 21-2680,* or on any other piece of medical evidence, the veteran has dementia or Alzheimer's and/or cannot manage his or her own financial affairs VA will 'propose to rate the beneficiary incompetent to handle their financial affairs.' This proposal will be issued after an award is made. This

action will hinder any retroactive payments due and will likely lead the veteran down the path of fiduciary appointment.

7. **Long Term Care Insurance** (LTCi) – LTCi, when actively paying for services for the veteran or spouse, is a countable income. You must report LTCi on the application and take the monthly amount into account as you calculate a potential benefit. If the LTCi will not kick in until after a claimant has filed, you must notify VA when the LTCi will begin payments and take into account the effects that new income will have.

8. **Life Insurance** – The cash value of the policy is the amount VA considers as an asset.

9. **Reporting Costs Separately** – Never combine the costs for care or any other ongoing medical expense for a husband and wife into a single entry on an application. Report each ongoing medical expense for the Veteran in separates rows distinguishable from the spouse's. If you are seeking to deduct care costs such as home care or assisted living, for both individuals, you must submit two *21-2680* forms. One for the veteran and one for the spouse.

10. **Trusts and Gifts** – *38 CFR 3.274-276* and adjudication manual *M21-1* govern net worth and gifting rules. Annuity purchases and transferring assets to trusts (even if the trusts and contracts are irrevocable) are subject to a penalty if done within the 36 month look back ONLY if the "asset cap" would have exceeded the $129,094.00 net-worth limit.

    Understand, even if the asset transfer occurred 37 months ago, VA may still ask for documentation to verify a proper transfer. VA will also ask if any portion of the transfer is being used or will be used to pay for, no matter how small, the maintenance of the veteran and/or spouse. If the answer is YES to that question, VA can count the transferred asset as part of the claimant's net worth. VA will likely ask other questions like "why did you transfer the asset?" and "do you have any type of control over this asset?" If the claimant cannot provide VA with good reasons and evidence, things will go south quickly.

11. **Evidence of Ongoing Care Expenses** - You must provide proof of payment for ongoing care and show at least one month's worth of payments.

12. **Dovetailing with Medicaid** – If any financial planning has occurred and assets have been moved or retitled, you need to consider the effect of this on Medicaid eligibility if for some reason you need to apply for Medicaid within the next 5 years. It is extremely important that you work with someone who understands both Medicaid eligibility and VA eligibility as well as failure to do this could result in substantial penalties if you ever apply for Medicaid.

13. **Welfare Programs** – If you or someone you are helping is in receipt of government assistance, speak directly with the agency in charge of the program before you apply for VA benefits. Although VA benefits are tax-free, other programs may count the benefits as income. This could potentially disqualify the individual from continuing to receive certain welfare assistance. This may include programs like Housing Assistance, Supplemental Security Income (SSI), and Social Security Disability Insurance (SSDI).

The Liberalization Law

This liberalization law can amount to a lot of back-pay money for a veteran.

Under Public Law 107-103 subject to *38 CFR 3.114*, Pension may be awarded to a veteran retroactive for one year prior to the date of receipt of the claim (effective date) if any of the following criteria are continuously met from September 17, 2001 until the date of claim:

- Age 65; or
- Found disabled by Social Security Administration (SSA) for the purpose of Social Security disability benefits; or
- a patient in a nursing home for long-term care because of disability

38 CFR §3.114
…(1) If a claim is reviewed on the initiative of VA within 1 year from the effective date of the law or VA issue, or at the request of a claimant received within 1 year from that date, benefits may be authorized from the effective date of the law or VA issue.

For those under age 65, there are special provisions which may allow for one year of retroactive payments. Please see *38 CFR 3.400(b)(1)*.

Unfortunately, surviving spouses are not eligible to file for this retroactive pay under the Liberalization Law.

These 12 months of retroactive payments are not automatically given. The veteran must be able to prove financial, expense, and possibly medical eligibility exactly one year prior to the effective date. After entitlement to Veterans Pension has been granted, VA (along with the award letter) should send a notifying the veteran of the opportunity to apply for an earlier effective date through this law.

If the veteran's net-worth was greater than VA's limits just prior to making application, do not attempt to apply for retroactive payments under this law.

If the veteran and those assisting him or her think there is a good chance for eligibility for this 12 months of retro-payments available under this regulation, the veteran should submit the following to Pension management:

- *VA Form 21-4138 – Statement in Support of Claim* requesting the retro-payments under the Liberalization Law and outlining the veteran's reasons why he or she believes they qualify,
- *VA Form 21P-8416* showing all medical expenses for the 12 months preceding the veteran's effective date,
- Proof of care from care provider(s) if applicable
- Paid medical expenses if applicable. Invoice, receipts, paid checks, etc…,
- If applicable, medical evidence of poor health. This could include physician's statements and a back dated *VA Form 21-2680* exam, and
- *VA Form 21-0516-1 Improved Pension Eligibility Verification Report* showing all income for the 12 months preceding the veteran's effective date

Chapter 7
Survivor Benefits and Burial Benefits

IN THIS CHAPTER:

Overview of Survivor and Burial Benefit Issues Discussed in This Chapter

Dependency and Indemnity Compensation (DIC)
Dependency and Indemnity Compensation (DIC) is a tax free monetary benefit generally payable to a surviving spouse, child, or parent of a service member who died while on active duty, active duty for training, or inactive duty training. It is also available to survivors of veterans who died from their service-connected disabilities. DIC for parents is an income based benefit.

Survivor's Pension
Survivor's Pension is a disability income program available to the single surviving spouse or dependent child(ren) of a deceased veteran. Survivor's Pension is often referred to as "The Aid and Attendance Benefit." This is a misnomer, but the title still lives on. This program can provide tax-free income ranging from $768 a month to about $1,465 a month. Since a claim for Survivor's Pension is so similar to VA Pension, we explain the application process for both benefits in Chapter 6.

Burial Benefits
For veterans who died from service connection, $2,000 is available for burial and funeral and certain other costs are provided for free. Veterans who died and were on claim for Disability Compensation or Pension, but did not die from service connection causes, can receive $300 for funeral and $796 a month by to be used towards a burial plot. All other veterans who die can receive a marker for the grave, a casket flag, an honor ceremony and a letter from the President.

Survivors and Dependents Education Eligibility

Surviving spouses and eligible children can receive certain education benefits for veterans who died on active duty or who died after active duty and did not use all of their education benefits which can then be transferred to surviving spouses or children. The Survivors' and Dependents' Educational Assistance (DEA) program offers education and training opportunities to eligible dependents of Veterans who are permanently and totally disabled due to a service-related condition or of Veterans who died while on active duty or as a result of service connection.

Survivors and Dependents Employment Services

Veterans dependents who are eligible for educational assistance may also receive career choice counseling, coaching and personalized support for job training and for finding employment.

Survivors and Caregivers Health Care

CHAMPVA is available to survivors of living or deceased veterans who were or are totally disabled or died on active duty. Benefits are also available to children of Vietnam veterans and caregivers of veterans

Survivors Home Loans

The unmarried surviving spouse of a veteran who died on active duty or as the result of a service-connected disability is eligible for the VA home loan benefit. In addition, a surviving spouse who obtained a VA home loan with the veteran prior to his or her death (regardless of the cause of death), may obtain a VA guaranteed interest rate reduction refinance loan.

Death of the Claimant before a Decision Is Made

Sometimes, the claimant will die before a decision is made on the application. This happens more frequently with Pension claims, because many Pension claimants are older and in need of eldercare and are already unhealthy. But the rules apply to any applicant. There are 2 options for receiving benefits when this happens: accrued benefits and substitution for the claimant.

Definition of a Surviving Spouse and Child

This chapter is focused on benefits for survivors of deceased veterans. In order to understand eligibility, it is useful to understand VA terminology for the words "surviving spouse," "dependents" and "child." This is very important as the definitions are quite specific and don't necessarily mean the same as used outside of the world of VA. We provide below the definition of "surviving spouse" and "child." When the Department literature refers to "dependents" in the context of survivor benefits this generally means

- a surviving spouse was married to the veteran when he or she died and has not remarried
- a child is a minor 18 years or younger or attending school up through age 23 or a totally dependent adult who became so before the age of 18
- parents are defined as entirely dependent on the veteran

In this book, we don't address benefits for dependent parents. We don't run across it that often in practice and we decided not to broach the subject in order to save space.

Providing Evidence of Death for Burial and Survivor Benefits

The regulation below is quite complete and we do not need to add additional comment on the various ways to provide evidence of death.

Title 38 CFR § 3.211 Death.
Death should be established by one of the following types of evidence:
(a)
(1) A copy of the public record of the State or community where death occurred.
(2) A copy of a coroner's report of death or a verdict of a coroner's jury of the State or community where death occurred, provided such report or verdict properly identified the deceased.
(b) Where death occurs in a hospital or institution under the control of the United States Government:
(1) A death certificate signed by a medical officer; or
(2) A clinical summary or other report showing fact and date of death signed by a medical officer.
(c) An official report of death of a member of a uniformed service from the Secretary of the department concerned where death occurs while deceased was on the retired list, in an inactive duty status, or in the active service.
(d) Where death occurs abroad:
(1) A United States consular report of death bearing the signature and seal of the United States consul; or
(2) A copy of the public record of death authenticated (see § 3.202(b)(4) for exception) by the United States consul or other agency of the State Department; or
(3) An official report of death from the head of the department concerned, where the deceased person was, at the time of death, a civilian employee of such department.
(e) If the foregoing evidence cannot be furnished, the reason must be stated. The fact of death may then be established by the affidavits of persons who have personal knowledge of the fact of death, have viewed the body of the deceased, know it to be the body of the person whose death is being established, setting forth all the facts and circumstances concerning the death, place, date, time, and cause thereof.
(f) If proof of death, as defined in paragraphs (a) through (e) of this section cannot be furnished, a finding of fact of death, where death is otherwise shown by competent evidence, may be made by an official authorized to approve such findings. Where it is indicated that the veteran died under circumstances which precluded recovery or identification of the body, the fact of death should be established by the best evidence, which from the nature of the case must be supposed to exist.
(g) In the absence of evidence to the contrary, a finding of fact of death made by another Federal agency will be accepted for the purposes of paragraph (f) of this section.

Dependency and Indemnity Compensation (DIC)

Dependency and Indemnity Compensation (DIC) is a tax free monetary benefit generally payable to a surviving spouse, child, or parent of a service member who died while on active duty, active duty for training, or inactive duty training. It is also available to survivors of veterans who died from their service-connected disabilities. DIC for parents is an income based benefit.

Dependency and Indemnity Compensation (D1C) is paid to surviving spouses and dependent children when the service member dies while on active duty; or, when death occurs after military service AND if a service-connected disability either directly caused or contributed substantially and materially to the death of the veteran. DIC can also be granted if the veteran dies from medical treatment received through the VA medical system or from Vocational Rehabilitation training. DIC for spouses and dependent children is not means tested. The recipient of DIC can have any amount of income or assets. It is really a life insurance benefit.

DIC Granted Automatically

DIC will be granted automatically when the veteran was rated 100% service-connected or paid at the rate of 100% for 10 or more years at the time of death and died from non-service-connected causes other than willful misconduct. DIC is also payable when the veteran was rated 100% service-connected for at least 5 years immediately after discharge. With this rule, there is no need to prove service connection death.

Flat Rate DIC Payments

For veterans dying after January 1, 1993, a flat rate of D1C is payable. Prior to this date, DIC was paid based on the military rank of the veteran. Under the flat rate plan, an additional allowance is payable for those veterans rated totally disabled due to service connected condition(s) for 8 or more years at the time of their death with the surviving spouse having been married to the veteran for 8 or more years immediately preceding the death. Surviving spouses can also qualify for Housebound or Aid & Attendance allowances under 38 CFR§ 3.351.

Remarriage of a Surviving Spouse Receiving DIC

If a surviving spouse remarries, DIC is terminated. However, if the subsequent marriage is dissolved by death, divorce, annulment, or voided, the now single spouse is eligible to reapply for DIC benefits.

On December 16, 2003, the President signed the Veterans Benefits Act of 2003. This Act amended Title 38 of the United States Code in several ways. Previously, 38 U.S.C. § 103(d) prohibited a surviving spouse who remarries from receiving DIC and also from receiving related housing and education benefits during the length of the remarriage. The Act now allows a surviving spouse who remarries on or after his or her 57th birthday to remain eligible for DIC, home loan, and education benefits. It also allows for reinstatement after turning age 57.

The surviving spouse must have been married to the veteran for at least one year prior to the death of the veteran or for any length of time if a child was born of the marriage, or was born to them before the marriage. The spouse must also have been married to the veteran when the veteran died. An exception is 38 CFR § 3.54 (c)(1), which covers marriages within fifteen years of leaving military service on or after January 1, 1957

Concurrent Receipt of SBP and DIC

SBP is the survivor annuity provided under military retirement if the veteran receiving military retirement died. If the surviving spouse is awarded DIC by the VA based on the death of the same member who provided the SBP coverage, the Department of Defense reduces the spouse's SBP annuity by the amount of the DIC award.

1. If the DIC payment offsets the entire SBP annuity, no annuity is paid and the SBP premiums for spouse coverage paid by the member are refunded to the surviving spouse.
2. If the DIC payment is less than the SBP annuity, the spouse is paid an SBP annuity equal to the difference between the full annuity and the DIC. A refund of SBP premiums is made based on the difference between the costs actually incurred and the costs that would have been incurred in order to provide the annuity payable after the DIC reduction.

For example if the SBP is $2,500, and DIC is $1,250, the surviving spouse would get $1,250 DIC and $1,250 SBP.

Special Survivor Indemnity Allowance (SSIA)

Since October 2008 surviving spouses whose Survivor Benefit Plan (SBP) payments have been offset (partially or totally) as a result of receiving Dependency and Indemnity Compensation (DIC), including surviving spouses of members who died while serving on active duty, are eligible for the SSIA. Monthly payments are taxable and are $323 a month for the year beginning January 1, 2020. SSIA was made permanent in The National Defense Authorization Act (NDAA) for FY2018. The NDAA contained a provision to amend section 1450 of USC Title 10 to permanently extend the authority to pay SSIA with an annual cost-of-living adjustment..

Examples:

Example 1

In the following example, the base amount selected for SBP coverage is $2,500 which would provide an annuity of $1,375 (55 percent of the base amount) and the 2014-2015 SSIA rate. It assumes that a claim for DIC was filed by the surviving spouse within one year after the member's death and DIC was approved by the VA.

SBP entitlement	$1,375
Minus DIC entitlement	$1,254
Net SBP payable	$ 121
SSIA payable (FY2015)	$ 200
Total payable after DIC	$ 321

Note:
The total of SBP and DIC is still equal to what SBP would have paid alone ($121 + $1,254 = $1,375); however, the DIC portion of the payment is not taxable as income. The spouse received a refund of SBP premiums deducted from retired pay except the cost that would have been paid to provide an SBP benefit of $121, unless the member died on active duty.

Example 2

In the following example, the base amount selected for SBP coverage is $1,500 which would provide an annuity of $825 (55 percent of the base amount) and the 2009-2010 SSIA rate. It assumes that a claim for DIC was filed by the surviving spouse within one year after the member's death and DIC was approved by the VA.

SBP entitlement	$ 825
Minus DIC entitlement	$ 1,254
Net SBP payable	$ 0
SSIA payable (FY2010)	$ 200
Total payable after DIC	$ 200

Note:

The DIC entitlement is greater than the SBP payment. In this case, all spouse costs deducted from retired pay for SBP would be refunded to the surviving spouse, unless the member died on active duty.

Offsets to DIC

DIC will not be paid if the survivor receives an award for damages due to the veteran's death of any of the following:

- judicial or administrative proceeding
- settlement
- administrative award,
- tort award,
- compromise, or
- Radiation Exposure Compensation Act (RECA) settlement payment.

Any such awards will be deducted from DIC or demanded back for overpayment. Attorney's fees, court costs, and other expenses incident to the civil claim are not deductible from the total amount awarded or accepted.

Other Benefits Available with a DIC Claim

A DIC claim is also a claim for Survivors Pension and accrued benefits. The same form – *VA Form 21-534EZ* – is used to apply for any of the three benefits. The applicant must designate on the form which benefit or benefits are being applied for. VA will consider all of them if appropriate to the situation. If VA considers all three applications for an award, either VA or the beneficiary can determine which award would be the best. An individual can receive only one of these three benefits at a time.

We will discuss at the end of this chapter the other death benefit from VA form 21-534EZ which is accrued benefits. We already discussed Survivors Pension in Chapter 6 on Pension.

A surviving spouse receiving DIC is also eligible for The Civilian Health and Medical Program of the Department of Veterans Affairs (CHAMPVA). This program provides reimbursement for most medical expenses for the surviving spouse through a health insurance plan sponsored by the Department of Veterans Affairs and administered through the Denver Regional Office. There are no premiums for this health insurance, however there are co-pays of 25% of the allowable billing amount up to a maximum out-of-pocket of $3,000 per calendar year. Benefits include:

- inpatient
- outpatient
- mental health
- prescription medication
- skilled nursing care, and
- durable medical equipment.

Dependency and Indemnity Compensation (DIC) for 2020

Basic Monthly Rate = $1,340.14, with 1 Child $1,672.14, with 2 Children $2,004.14, etc.

Allowances: with A&A $1,672.14, with Housebound $1,495.67, with 8 Yrs Continuous Disabled $1,624.71

1. Add **$284.57** for veteran's death, if veteran was in receipt of or entitled to receive compensation for a service-connected disability rated totally disabling (including a rating based on individual unemployability) for a continuous period of at least 8 years immediately preceding death AND the surviving spouse was married to the veteran for those same 8 years. (38 U.S.C. 1311(a)(2))
2. Add the following allowance for each dependent child under age 18: Effective 12/1/14 **$332.00** per child (38 U.S.C. 1311(b))
3. If the surviving spouse is entitled to Aid and Attendance, add **$332.00.** (38 U.S.C. 1311(c))
4. If the surviving spouse is entitled to Housebound, add **$155.53** (38 U.S.C. 1311(d))
5. If the surviving spouse has one or more children under the age 18 on the award, add the 2-year transitional benefit of **$286.00** effective, December 1, 2014 (38 U.S.C. 1311(f))

Understanding a Claim for DIC

There are a number of ways to create entitlement to DIC.

1. The veteran died while on active service

2. The veteran had a <u>service-connected disability or disabilities</u> that were either the principal or contributory cause of the veteran's death

3. The veteran died from <u>non service-connected injury or disease</u> AND was receiving, or entitled to receive VA Compensation for a service-connected disability rated totally disabling (rated 100% or TDIU) for at least 10 years immediately before death;

4. The veteran died from <u>non service-connected injury or disease</u> AND was receiving, or entitled to receive VA Compensation for a service-connected disability rated totally disabling (rated 100% or TDIU) for at least 5 years after the veteran's release from active duty preceding death;

5. The veteran died from <u>non service-connected injury or disease</u> AND was receiving, or entitled to receive VA Compensation for a service-connected disability rated totally disabling (rated 100% or TDIU) for at least 1 year before death, if the veteran was a former prisoner of war who died after September 30, 1999

<u>It is important to note that total disability for purposes of DIC means either a rating of 100% or being totally disabled due to individual unemployability (TDIU). This alternative allows a veteran rated 60% or more for a single disability or 70% or more for combined disabilities (with at least one at 40%) to qualify due to unemployability for the 100% rating. For more information on unemployability please go to the Claim Support Disc.</u>

Further Information on Understanding the Different Types of Claims
The different benefit triggers for receiving DIC result in 4 different options for filing applications
for the benefit. Although all claims for DIC have certain elements that are common, each of
these options has a different approach to making application that is beyond these common
elements. Here are the 4 types of claims.

1. **Automatic Benefit**
    The veteran was on claim for Disability Compensation and was married to a surviving spouse when
    the veteran died. The veteran <u>did</u> meet one of the three <u>non-service-connected death</u> requirements
    at 100% disability or TDIU above and as such the benefit should be automatically awarded based on
    filing VA Form 21-534EZ for DIC.

2. **The Veteran Was on Claim for Compensation and the Death Was Service Connected**
    The veteran was on claim for Disability Compensation and was married to a surviving spouse when
    the veteran died. The veteran <u>did not</u> meet any of the requirements for non-service-connected
    death for the automatic benefit of total disability, but the death certificate shows that the service-
    connected disability was the primary or contributory cause to the death.

3. **The Veteran Was Receiving Compensation but the Death Certificate Was Deficient**
    The veteran was on claim for Disability Compensation and was married to a surviving spouse when
    the veteran died. The veteran did not meet any of the requirements for non-service-connected
    death for the automatic benefit of total disability. The service-connected disability was the primary
    or contributory cause to the death. However the death certificate fails to identify the service-
    connected disability as a primary or contributory cause of death.

4. **The Veteran was not on Claim for Compensation but Death Was Service-Connected**
    The veteran <u>was not</u> on claim for Disability Compensation and was married to a surviving spouse
    when the veteran died. A claim for Disability Compensation was never made while the veteran was
    alive, but the surviving spouse believes that the death was caused by an injury, exposure or illness
    incurred during service that is <u>presumed to be service-connected</u>. This type of claim could be very
    feasible if the veteran was in Vietnam and exposed to Agent Orange and died as a result of one of
    the presumptive conditions for Agent Orange such as type II diabetes or arteriosclerotic heart
    disease. However, the veteran never made claim while the veteran was alive. Also note that
    element #3 above can also apply to this type of service-connected death where the veteran never
    made claim and the death certificate is also deficient. We have seen a number of these types.

Elements Common to All Four Claims for DIC

1. You must submit a death certificate for the deceased veteran for a claim for DIC. If the
    veteran died under circumstances where there is no death certificate or has been missing and
    presumed dead, there are equivalent ways to establish death. There is VA Form 21-1775 –
    Statement of Disappearance, on the Claim Support Disc if the veteran has been missing and
    presumed dead for seven years or longer. VA will accept that as evidence of death if the
    absence is of this length or longer. For alternative evidence of death, refer to the section
    above. See regulation above for alternative proof of death.

2. A copy of the marriage license is required for application for DIC. It may not be required for
    other applications for other benefits, but it is in this case. If a marriage license is not
    available there are alternative ways to establish a marriage relationship. Please read the
    section on evidence for death and marriage in the Appendix on the claim support disc.

3. Entitlement to DIC will be from the first day of the month in which the veteran died if a claim is made within one year of the date of the veteran's death.

4. If a claim is made beyond one year of the date of the veteran's death, entitlement will from the date on which the claim was received.

Obtaining Evidence of the Death

We discussed in a section above how under Title 38 CFR 3.211 evidence of death is determined. In almost all cases, evidence will be provided through a civil record death certificate. The following is a description from Wikipedia concerning a death certificate

Nature of a certificate

Each governmental jurisdiction prescribes the form of the document for use in its preview and the procedures necessary to legally produce it. One purpose of the certificate is to review the cause of death to determine if foul-play occurred as it can rule out an accidental death or a murder going by the findings and ruling of the medical examiner. It may also be required in order to arrange a burial or cremation to provide prima facie evidence of the fact of death, which can be used to prove a person's will or to claim on a person's life insurance. Lastly, death certificates are used in public health to compile data on leading causes of death among other statistics (See: Descriptive statistics)

Before issuing a death certificate, the authorities usually require a certificate from a physician or coroner to validate the cause of death and the identity of the deceased. In cases where it is not completely clear that a person is dead (usually because their body is being sustained by life support), a neurologist is often called in to verify brain death and to fill out the appropriate documentation. The failure of a physician to immediately submit the required form to the government (to trigger issuance of the death certificate) is often both a crime and cause for loss of one's license to practice. This is because of past scandals in which dead people continued to receive public benefits or voted in elections.[1] Death certificates may also be issued pursuant to a court order or an executive order in the case of individuals who have been declared dead in absentia. Missing persons and victims of mass disasters (such as the sinking of the RMS Lusitania) may be issued death certificates in one of these manners.

In some jurisdictions, a police officer or a paramedic may be allowed to sign a death certificate under specific circumstances. This is usually when the cause of death seems obvious and no foul play is suspected, such as in extreme old age. In such cases, an autopsy is rarely performed. This varies from jurisdiction to jurisdiction; in some areas police officers may sign death certificates for victims of SIDS,[citation needed] but in others all deaths of individuals under 18 must be certified by a physician. Accident deaths where there is no chance of survival (decapitations, for instance) may be certified by police or paramedics, but autopsies are still commonly performed if there is any chance that alcohol or other drugs played a role in the accident.

A full explanation of the cause of death includes four items:

- the immediate cause of death, such as the heart stopping,
- the intermediate causes, which triggered the immediate cause, such as a myocardial infarction,
- the underlying causes, which triggered the chain of events leading to death, such as atherosclerosis, and
- any other diseases and disorders the person had at the time of death, even though they did not directly cause the death.[2]

Here is the top portion of the standard form design, a variation of which, should be used by all jurisdictions. This is issued by the Center for Disease Control (CDC). We provide this sample in order to show that not only the primary cause of death should be listed, but any contributing conditions to the death should also be listed. This form – as should be the case with most state death certificates – has spaces for at least 3 causes of death. Having a complete cause of death with contributing conditions is extremely important for a claim for DIC which is not automatic.

U.S. STANDARD CERTIFICATE OF DEATH

LOCAL FILE NO.   STATE FILE NO.

NAME OF DECEDENT — For use by physician or institution

To Be Completed/Verified By: FUNERAL DIRECTOR:

1. DECEDENT'S LEGAL NAME (Include AKA's if any) (First, Middle, Last)	2. SEX	3. SOCIAL SECURITY NUMBER

4a. AGE-Last Birthday (Years)	4b. UNDER 1 YEAR		4c. UNDER 1 DAY		5. DATE OF BIRTH (Mo/Day/Yr)	6. BIRTHPLACE (City and State or Foreign Country)
	Months	Days	Hours	Minutes		

7a. RESIDENCE-STATE	7b. COUNTY	7c. CITY OR TOWN

7d. STREET AND NUMBER	7e. APT. NO.	7f. ZIP CODE	7g. INSIDE CITY LIMITS? ☐ Yes ☐ No

8. EVER IN US ARMED FORCES? ☐ Yes ☐ No	9. MARITAL STATUS AT TIME OF DEATH ☐ Married ☐ Married, but separated ☐ Widowed ☐ Divorced ☐ Never Married ☐ Unknown	10. SURVIVING SPOUSE'S NAME (If wife, give name prior to first marriage)

11. FATHER'S NAME (First, Middle, Last)	12. MOTHER'S NAME PRIOR TO FIRST MARRIAGE (First, Middle, Last)

13a. INFORMANT'S NAME	13b. RELATIONSHIP TO DECEDENT	13c. MAILING ADDRESS (Street and Number, City, State, Zip Code)

14. PLACE OF DEATH (Check only one: see instructions)

IF DEATH OCCURRED IN A HOSPITAL: ☐ Inpatient ☐ Emergency Room/Outpatient ☐ Dead on Arrival	IF DEATH OCCURRED SOMEWHERE OTHER THAN A HOSPITAL: ☐ Hospice facility ☐ Nursing home/Long term care facility ☐ Decedent's home ☐ Other (Specify):

15. FACILITY NAME (If not institution, give street & number)	16. CITY OR TOWN., STATE, AND ZIP CODE	17. COUNTY OF DEATH

18. METHOD OF DISPOSITION: ☐ Burial ☐ Cremation ☐ Donation ☐ Entombment ☐ Removal from State ☐ Other (Specify):	19. PLACE OF DISPOSITION (Name of cemetery, crematory, other place)

20. LOCATION-CITY, TOWN, AND STATE	21. NAME AND COMPLETE ADDRESS OF FUNERAL FACILITY

22. SIGNATURE OF FUNERAL SERVICE LICENSEE OR OTHER AGENT	23. LICENSE NUMBER (Of Licensee)

ITEMS 24-28 MUST BE COMPLETED BY PERSON WHO PRONOUNCES OR CERTIFIES DEATH	24. DATE PRONOUNCED DEAD (Mo/Day/Yr)	25. TIME PRONOUNCED DEAD

26. SIGNATURE OF PERSON PRONOUNCING DEATH (Only when applicable)	27. LICENSE NUMBER	28. DATE SIGNED (Mo/Day/Yr)

29. ACTUAL OR PRESUMED DATE OF DEATH (Mo/Day/Yr) (Spell Month)	30. ACTUAL OR PRESUMED TIME OF DEATH	31. WAS MEDICAL EXAMINER OR CORONER CONTACTED? ☐ Yes ☐ No

CAUSE OF DEATH (See instructions and examples)

32. PART I. Enter the chain of events--diseases, injuries, or complications--that directly caused the death. DO NOT enter terminal events such as cardiac arrest, respiratory arrest, or ventricular fibrillation without showing the etiology. DO NOT ABBREVIATE. Enter only one cause on a line. Add additional lines if necessary.

Approximate interval: Onset to death

IMMEDIATE CAUSE (Final disease or condition ——→ resulting in death) a. _____
Due to (or as a consequence of): _____

Sequentially list conditions, if any, leading to the cause listed on line a. Enter the **UNDERLYING CAUSE** (disease or injury that initiated the events resulting in death) **LAST**
b. _____
Due to (or as a consequence of): _____

c. _____
Due to (or as a consequence of): _____

d. _____

PART II. Enter other significant conditions contributing to death but not resulting in the underlying cause given in PART I

33. WAS AN AUTOPSY PERFORMED? ☐ Yes ☐ No
34. WERE AUTOPSY FINDINGS AVAILABLE TO COMPLETE THE CAUSE OF DEATH? ☐ Yes ☐ No

374

List of Forms That Could Be Needed for DIC Claims

These forms are found on the Claim Support Disc under the folder entitled "2 Application for Compensation and DIC." These are the forms that might be used for the 3 application types discussed above. Not every application type will require all of these forms.

VA Form 21-0966 – INTENT TO FILE
VA Form 21P-534EZ – Application for DIC, Death Pension, and or Accrued Benefits
VA Form 21-4170 – Statement of Marital Relationship
VA Form 21-4171 – Supporting Statement Regarding Marriage
VA Form 21-4103 – Information from Remarried Widow
VA Form 21-1775 – Statement of Disappearance
VA Form 21-8416b – Report of Medical, Legal, and Other Expenses Incident to Recovery for Injury or Death
VA Form 21-4142 – Authorization and Consent to Release Information to the Department of Veterans Affairs

Forms for Representation for Assistance if Desired
VA Form 21-22A – Appointment of Individual as a Claimant's Representative
VA Form 21-0845 – Authorization to Disclose Personal Information to a Third Party
DIC Explanation of My Claim Template Blank
DIC VA 21-4138 Page 1 Explanation of My Claim
DIC VA 21-4138 Pages 2 through 20 Explanation of My Claim

The Case Where the Death Certificate Is Deficient

This problem arises where the primary cause of death was not service-connected, but underlying causes or contributing causes were service-connected. For example, type II diabetes from exposure to herbicide is a presumptive service connected condition and the veteran may have been on claim or even not have been on claim for diabetes. If not on claim for diabetes and the record shows the veteran was stationed in Vietnam, the Regional Office will infer service connection for the purpose of granting DIC but not necessarily grant an award. This is because diabetes by itself is not often a cause for death. The death could be due to heart failure or any number of organ failures brought on by the diabetes. In this example, if the death certificate were complete and the relationship between the diabetes and the actual cause of death were certified to be connected, there would likely be an award for DIC. On the other hand, in this example, if the death certificate were deficient, there would be no award.

In the case where the government issuing authority uses an incomplete death certificate which does not list all of the contributing causes, or the contributing causes are not filled in for some reason, we have provided instructions further on for you to submit a claim where the primary cause of death would not be considered service-connected by VA, but the death is actually service-connected and VA, with proper evidence, would award DIC.

You may have to provide alternate evidence of death as outlined in Title 38 CFR 3.211. For this you will either need an amended death certificate that shows the alternate cause of death or you will need a medical opinion from the treating physician or attending physician of the deceased veteran that supports a contributing cause of death not listed on the death certificate. Getting an amended death certificate with alternate cause of death may be an impossible task due to the demanding requirements for this option from various states. Getting a medical opinion is generally the easiest way to go about providing the evidence.

Death Caused by Treatment at a VA Medical Facility

VA will also help you develop a claim for DIC that is not automatic if the veteran was treated at a VA medical center prior to his or her death and the treatment record could be tied to the death. In this case make sure you fill out this portion of the VA Form 21P-534EZ shown below.

SECTION VI: DIC *(COMPLETE ONLY IF CLAIMING DEPENDENCY AND INDEMNITY COMPENSATION (DIC))*	
(Skip to Section VII if you are NOT claiming DIC)	
35. WHAT BENEFIT ARE YOU CLAIMING? ☐ DIC ☐ DIC under 38 U.S.C. 1151 (RARE)	
36. LIST ANY VA MEDICAL CENTERS WHERE THE VETERAN RECEIVED TREATMENT PERTAINING TO YOUR CLAIM AND PROVIDE TREATMENT DATES:	
A. NAME AND LOCATION OF VA MEDICAL CENTER	B. DATE(S) OF TREATMENT

Death Suspected to Be Direct Service-Connected and Not Presumed Service-Connected

A direct service-connected Compensation claim has to be proved through evidence such as medical evidence from service treatment records or combat related injuries or illnesses that later resulted in disability or disease after discharge. In order to be entitled to Compensation from direct service connection, the veteran would need to be alive to submit a VA Form 21-526EZ. Direct service connection presumably cannot be established in any other way. It is likely, a deceased veteran cannot establish direct service connection. On the other hand, presumed service connection does not require submitting evidence for service connection. It is presumed and therefore there would be no need to submit a VA Form 21-526EZ.

Even though regulations require that the proper form be used to establish direct service connection, it might be possible to bypass those rules by establishing direct service connection through submitting a VA Form 21-534EZ if the link between the in-service incident and death from direct service connection is pretty clear. For example, asbestos exposure is known to produce certain types of cancer and if the veteran was exposed in service and died from one of these cancers, it would take certain records and a medical opinion to establish that. That direct service connection theoretically could be established through filing a VA Form 21-534EZ. We have never done a claim where the deceased veteran could have been direct service-connected.

The only definitive possibility that we know of for establishing direct service connection for a deceased veteran is when the veteran died while awaiting a decision for direct service connection. This can certainly happen and one of our case studies on the Claim Support Disc is based on a real claim where this happened. It took several years to get the claim adjudicated and the veteran died along the way. His wife took over as a substitute claimant and eventually received an award with all of the back payment due. In addition, she received the $2,000 burial benefit for a service-connected death and she received entitlement to DIC for the rest of her life.

Submitting An application for DIC

1. Application for the Automatic DIC Benefit

The veteran was on claim for Disability Compensation and was married to the surviving spouse when the veteran died. The veteran <u>did</u> meet one of the three <u>non-service-connected death</u> requirements at 100% disability and as such the benefit should be automatically awarded based on a formal claim for DIC. Here are the triggers for this automatic benefit award.

1. The veteran died from a <u>non service-connected injury or disease</u> AND was receiving, or entitled to receive VA Compensation for a service-connected disability rated totally disabling (rated 100% or TDIU) for at least 10 years immediately before death; OR

2. The veteran died from a <u>non service-connected injury or disease</u> AND was receiving, or entitled to receive VA Compensation for a service-connected disability rated totally disabling (rated 100% or TDIU) for at least 5 years after the veteran's release from active duty preceding death; OR

3. The veteran died from a <u>non service-connected injury or disease</u> AND was receiving, or entitled to receive VA Compensation for a service-connected disability rated totally disabling (rated 100% or TDIU) for at least 1 year before death, AND the veteran was a former prisoner of war who died after September 30, 1999

The surviving spouse will notify VA of the death as required by law. VA will respond by requesting the death certificate. The VBMS record will be examined and it will be noted that the veteran met one of the criteria above. A VA Form 21-534EZ will be sent to the surviving spouse to be filled out as a claim for DIC. If you file a claim within a year of the veteran's death, you will be paid from the first day of the month following the month of the veteran's death.

2. Veteran Was on Claim for Compensation and the Death Was Service-Connected

The veteran was on claim for Disability Compensation and was married to the surviving spouse when the veteran died. The veteran <u>did not</u> meet any of the requirements for non-service-connected death for the <u>automatic benefit</u> at total disability, but the service-connected disability <u>was the cause of or contributory cause</u> to the death.

The key issue here is that the death certificate must reflect a primary or contributing cause of death that is the same condition from which the veteran was receiving a Disability Compensation. For example, the veteran was on claim for bladder cancer that was due to exposure to hazardous chemicals while in the service. The death certificate listed heart failure as the primary cause of death, but a contributory cause of death was listed on the death certificate as bladder cancer.

After the death of the veteran, the surviving spouse notifies VA of the death and is instructed to submit the death certificate.

Submitting a claim for DIC is fairly straightforward as the Regional Office recognized from the death certificate and from the ongoing award that there was a match and sent out to the survivor claimant the VA Form 21-534EZ.

If you file a claim within a year of the veteran's death, you will be paid from the first day of the month following the month of the veteran's death. Otherwise, if it takes more than a year for some reason to file a claim, you will be paid from the first day of the month following the date of claim. That's the reason for the intent to file.

3. Veteran Was Receiving Compensation but the Death Certificate Was Deficient

The veteran was on claim for Disability Compensation and was married to the surviving spouse when the veteran died. The veteran <u>did not</u> meet any of the requirements for non-service-connected death for the <u>automatic benefit</u> at total disability, but the service-connected disability <u>was the cause of or contributory cause</u> to the death.

After the death of the veteran, the surviving spouse notifies VA of the death and is instructed to submit the death certificate. Unfortunately, the death certificate does not list any primary or contributing cause of death that matches the disability or disease for which the veteran was on claim. On the other hand, that disability or disease really was a contributing factor, but the physician who signed the death certificate was not aware of that contributing factor or dismissed it as relevant to the death.

A deficient death certificate is more common than most people know. In this case, VA will not notify the surviving spouse that he or she can file for DIC and basically the case is closed. We run across these types of claims more often than not. The surviving spouse is not aware of entitlement and unless we question him or her about the death of the veteran, we would not be aware of a possible DIC claim either.

This particular claim requires a full filing for DIC based on a strategy that we will share with you further on. The key here is matching the service connection claim with the cause of death. We have developed some forms for you to use as well as instructions on how to get a proper determination of death.

4. Veteran Was Not on Claim for Compensation but Death Was Service-Connected

This claim is treated as an original claim for benefits and requires evidence of duty assignments and assignment locations in service as well as evidence of a disease, disability or condition that is presumed to be service-connected. This type of claim has one major advantage over a typical service-connected claim and that is service connection does not have to be established – it is presumed. <u>There are well over 120 different diseases or conditions that are considered presumed service-connected. You need to refer to Chapter 5 for the lists.</u>

Even though many of these conditions need to manifest to a degree of 10% or more within one year of discharge, it is important to understand that application for these conditions could be made many years after discharge and does not require an application within the one-year period. In fact, many veterans may not be aware that they could make application for one of these presumptive conditions and never bothered to make application. Yet, if the death was due to one of these presumptive conditions, the surviving spouse could be entitled to DIC.

There are exceptions to the one year rule. For former prisoners of war there is a long list of conditions that can manifest at any time after discharge. There are also presumptive conditions for Camp Lejeune water consumption that can manifest at any time. ALS or Lou Gehrig's disease is automatically presumptive even if the veteran only went through basic training and never served active duty but was a member of the guard or reserve. Certain tropical diseases for Afghanistan veterans also are presumptive but can show up at any time. Likewise with exposure to ionizing radiation and Gulf War disorders. Manifestation does not have to be diagnosed, only that there is a record of the symptoms that could be interpreted to be that particular disease.

The most common presumptive conditions that can manifest at any time are those associated with Agent Orange exposure. These presumptive conditions apply to over 3 million veterans who served "boots on the ground" in Vietnam , on ships anchored inside the territorial waters of Vietnam or other areas where this herbicide was sprayed or stored. These are called agent orange presumptive conditions. These conditions are the most likely to crop up for DIC applications resulting in death where the veteran never made claim. Here is the list of agent orange presumptive conditions.

- AL amyloidosis,
- chloracne or other acne Form disease similar to chloracne,
- porphyria cutanea tarda,
- soft-tissue sarcoma (other than osteosarcoma, chondrosarcoma,
- Kaposi's sarcoma or mesothelioma),
- Hodgkin's disease,
- multiple myeloma,
- respiratory cancers (lung, bronchus, larynx, trachea),
- non-Hodgkin's lymphoma,
- prostate cancer,
- acute and subacute peripheral neuropathy,
- diabetes mellitus (Type 2),
- all chronic B-cell leukemias (including, but not limited to, hairy-cell leukemia and chronic lymphocytic leukemia),
- Parkinson's disease, and
- ischemic heart disease. (Blockage of the arteries in the heart)

Some of these conditions such as prostate cancer, type II diabetes, Parkinson's disease, cancer of the respiratory system and blockage of the heart arteries are fairly common in older veterans. Most of these Vietnam veterans are in their late sixties and seventies. Many are at an age where there is a higher risk of death. And in many of these deaths, these common conditions such as prostate cancer, diabetes, Parkinson's disease, blocked arteries and the rest of the agent orange presumptive conditions could directly cause or contribute to a death. In many of these death cases, the veteran was never on claim for Disability Compensation because of the exposure.

This particular claim requires a full filing for DIC based on the information below. The key here is matching the presumed service connection claim with the cause of death.

If you are reasonably certain that the death was primarily due or secondarily due to the disabilities for which the veteran was presumed service-connected but not on claim, then proceed with the process for this type of claim.

If the death was due to a presumptive service connection disease or disorder or disability, but the death certificate fails to prove that, follow our instructions in the section titled **"Our Process for Submitting an Application Where the Death Certificate Is Deficient"** below.

If it is going to take you some time to assemble the evidence for DIC, do an "Intent to File" using the following form:

VA Form 21-0966 – INTENT TO FILE

If you file a claim within a year of the veteran's death, you will be paid from the first day of the month following the month of the veteran's death. Otherwise, if it takes more than a year for some reason to file a claim, you will be paid from the first day of the month following the date of claim. That's the reason for the intent to file.

Reference: For more information on the types of evidence required to confirm the cause of death, see 38 CFR 3.211 above.

Forms to Use:
A copy of the death certificate or equivalent evidence
A copy of the marriage certificate or equivalent evidence
VA Form 21-534EZ – Application for DIC, Death Pension, and or Accrued Benefits
VA Form 21-4138 – Statement in Support of Claim

Potential Alternative Forms
FV30 – Determining Cause of Death for Awarding Income Benefit
VA Form 21-4142 – Authorization and Consent to Release Information to the Department of Veterans Affairs
VA Form 21-4170 – Statement of Marital Relationship (if needed)
VA Form 21-4171 – Supporting Statement Regarding Marriage (if needed)
VA Form 21-4103 – Information from Remarried Widow (if needed)
VA Form 21-1775 – Statement of Disappearance (if needed)

Forms for Representation for Assistance if Desired
VA Form 21-22A – Appointment of Individual as a Claimant's Representative
VA Form 21-0845 – Authorization to Disclose Personal Information to a Third Party

Steps in the Claim Process by Providing:

- The completed DIC section of VA Form 21P-534 EZ
- A certified copy of the veterans DD 214
- Evidence that the deceased veteran served in a location considered to be an exposure hazard for a presumptive condition OR
- Evidence that the deceased veteran has one of the presumed conditions that are not tied to a location or exposure
- A copy of the death certificate that lists the cause of or contributory causes of death OR
- Evidence from some other source that documents the cause of or contributory causes of death

- A copy of the marriage certificate
- A copy of the private medical records of the deceased veteran OR
- Evidence showing VA that the deceased veteran was treated at a VA medical center if applicable
- Other forms as needed and listed above including forms for representation for assistance
- Filling out VA Form 21-4138 with a narrative that the veteran's death was due to or significantly contributed to by a presumptive service condition (name the condition) and you are requesting DIC as a result of that. Make sure that the form uses the veteran's name and not the surviving claimant's name.
- Follow instructions in previous chapters for Disability Compensation claims for gathering the evidence needed above and submitting the claim to the Janesville scanning facility.

Incorporating the steps above, you may also choose to use the application process that we have designed in the next section that provides the evidence in a logical and consistent manner in order to make it easier for the adjudicator to make a decision.

Claims for DIC are submitted to one of the 3 regional Pension Management Centers that serve your area. Please refer to Chapter 6 on Pension for information pertaining to how to submit claims to one of the management centers.

Our Process for Submitting an Application Where the Death Certificate Is Deficient
You can use this strategy for applications where the death was service connected and the veteran was on claim, but the death certificate lacks evidence of matching the service connection with the death. You will also use this strategy for a presumptive service connected death where the veteran was not on claim, and the death was due to a presumptive service connection, but the death certificate does not list the right cause of death for whatever reason.

This process is also designed to be more convincing to the Regional Office and you can also use it for a presumptive service connected death that IS supported by the death certificate.

This process is based on a method where you need to be convincing in your approach so that the Veteran Service Representative in the Pension Management Center can see your logic and put all the pieces together by your providing a pathway for the decision.

Follow All of the Instructions in Chapter 5 for Obtaining Records
Read the instructions in Chapter 5 for obtaining records. This same information applies to DIC claims as it does to Compensation claims. Also follow the instructions for filling out the document submission table found in a special VA 21-4138 that we have furnished for this purpose for DIC. The 21-4138 that is used in Chapter 5 is similar to the one that we have developed for DIC claims. We have also developed a 21-4138 Page 1 for DIC claims that is similar to the the 21-4138 Page 1 that we have developed for Compensation claims. We will provide you further on an example of the special 4138 that we have developed for DIC. Make sure that you organize and label all of your documents using the same principles found in Chapter 5. Obviously, you will use a different VA form for submitting your claim.

Here is a list of the special documents that we have designed you to use our process for filing a DIC claim under the provisions of this section. They are found on the Claim Support Disc.

- DIC Explanation of My Claim Template
- DIC VA 21-4138 Page 1 Explanation of My Claim
- DIC VA 21-4138 Pages 2 through 7 Explanation of My Claim

An Example of Using Our Process

In the subsections following we will show you a case example of how our process works. This example is based on a real claim. Names, dates and some of the circumstances have been changed so as not to parallel the actual claim itself although the basis is still much the same.

In the next subsection we will use this example to show you how to fill out the document submission table. The following subsection will provide a somewhat different version of the actual claimant's lay statement. Finally we will show you a somewhat different version of the actual Doctor's opinion including the cover page for that opinion. All documents that are submitted should have a cover page which includes the title of the document and the VBMS document type.

Filling out the Submitted Documents Table

We highly recommend that you provide a list of the document evidence that you are submitting, rather than relying on VA to organize that list for you. We have designed a table for you shown on the next page which you can use for that purpose and is contained in your VA Form 21-4138 which will be entitled "Explanation of My Claim," or any other title that you choose in case you have more than one event with your claim.

On the following pages are a sample table filled out. The 4138 forms for this application table are found on the Claim Support Disc in a folder called **"Special 21-4138 Forms for Our Application System." Here are all those forms.**

- DIC – VA 21-4138 Page 1 Standard
- DIC – VA 21-4138 Pages 2 through 6
- Other forms with prefix DIC – VA 21-4138 to show you samples of how to do it

List of Documents Submitted with This Claim

TITLE OF DOCUMENT

List of Documents Submitted with This Claim

TITLE OF DOCUMENT
DD-214
VA 21-526EZ Fully Developed Claim
VA 21-686c Declaration of Status of Dependents
VA 21-4138 Explanation of My Claim
Military records from Fort Benning, Georgia
Most Recent Personal Medical Records
Opinion for Service Connection, John Crew, M.D.
DBQ 21-0960M-8 Hip and Thigh Conditions
VA Form 21-22 POA Appointment
VA Form 21-0845 Third-Party Information Release
Medical Literature Evidence for My Claim

Sample Medi cal Opinion with Cover Page

Roger P Moore MD
524 Britton Rd. Suite 200
Liverpool, Iowa
555-636-1234

November 31, 2018

Medical Opinion for Cause of Death

I had been the attending physician for James Smith for the 10 years prior to his death. I am a general practitioner internist and not a specialist for treating cancer. On the other hand, I had received all of his hospital and oncologist records and had been up-to-date on all of his cancer treatment. In January 2010 Mister Smith was diagnosed with bladder cancer from a biopsy and a pathology report. In March 2010 he was also diagnosed with advanced prostate cancer through biopsy and pathology report. In December 2011 he was diagnosed with metastastic lung cancer through biopsy either through spread from the prostate or the bladder.

Bladder cancer can spread to lymph nodes or through the bloodstream to other parts of the body. If bladder cancer does spread it is more likely to spread to lymph nodes, lungs, liver or bones. Bladder cancer can also invade the outer wall of the bladder into the interstitial fat and spread into tissue that is adjacent to the bladder such as seminal vesicles, proximal lymph nodes, the urethra and the prostate. In the case of Mr. Smith, this had not occurred and the cancer was localized to the bladder. Metastasis to the lungs likely occurred through the bloodstream and was likely from the prostate and not the bladder.

It is highly unlikely that without direct invasion, the bladder cancer would have spread to the prostate. It is much more likely that he developed prostate cancer initially and that the prostate cancer metastasized to the bladder. This happens more frequently and is the logical cancer progression in Mr. Smith's case. Therefore, it is my opinion that it is at least as likely as not that Mr. Smith developed prostate cancer before developing bladder cancer and the bladder cancer was a result of metastasis from the prostate.

It is also my opinion that the prostate cancer was the initial culprit leading to Mister Smith's death by metastasizing to other parts of the body and that the death certificate for James Smith dated May 11, 2012 should have included prostate cancer as one of the contributory causes of death.

Roger Moore MD
Iowa License 6346

Sample Medical Opinion

Roger P Moore MD
524 Britton Rd. Suite 200
Liverpool, Iowa
555-636-1234

November 31, 2018

Medical Opinion for Cause of Death

I had been the attending physician for James Smith for the 10 years prior to his death. I am a general practitioner internist and not a specialist for treating cancer. On the other hand, I had received all of his hospital and oncologist records and had been up-to-date on all of his cancer treatment. In January 2010 Mister Smith was diagnosed with bladder cancer from a biopsy and a pathology report. In March 2010 he was also diagnosed with advanced prostate cancer through biopsy and pathology report. In December 2011 he was diagnosed with metastastic lung cancer through biopsy either through spread from the prostate or the bladder.

Bladder cancer can spread to lymph nodes or through the bloodstream to other parts of the body. If bladder cancer does spread it is more likely to spread to lymph nodes, lungs, liver or bones. Bladder cancer can also invade the outer wall of the bladder into the interstitial fat and spread into tissue that is adjacent to the bladder such as seminal vesicles, proximal lymph nodes, the urethra and the prostate. In the case of Mr. Smith, this had not occurred and the cancer was localized to the bladder. Metastasis to the lungs likely occurred through the bloodstream and was likely from the prostate and not the bladder.

It is highly unlikely that without direct invasion, the bladder cancer would have spread to the prostate. It is much more likely that he developed prostate cancer initially and that the prostate cancer metastasized to the bladder. This happens more frequently and is the logical cancer progression in Mr. Smith's case. Therefore, it is my opinion that it is at least as likely as not that Mr. Smith developed prostate cancer before developing bladder cancer and the bladder cancer was a result of metastasis from the prostate.

It is also my opinion that the prostate cancer was the initial culprit leading to Mister Smith's death by metastasizing to other parts of the body and that the death certificate for James Smith dated May 11, 2012 should have included prostate cancer as one of the contributory causes of death.

Roger Moore MD
Iowa License 6346

My Statement Detailing Events Leading to Death

My husband, James Smith, was a veteran who served in country in the Republic of Vietnam from 1968 to 1969. He remained in the service for one more year and then was discharged with an Honorable discharge in 1970. As far as I know, he never made any application for any veterans benefits, nor did he use any medical benefits provided for veterans. He did make ample use of the G.I. bill to complete his college education. We met and were married in 1972 and were married and lived continuously together for another 40 years until his death in 2012. I have remained single since his death.

In 2005, he was diagnosed with type II diabetes which was managed initially through diet and then in his later years required medication. As far as I know, I have never been told that his death was due to diabetes. In January of 2010 James was diagnosed with bladder cancer. I have included the pathology report for this diagnosis with the evidence for this claim. In March 2010 James was also diagnosed with prostate cancer from a biopsy. I also include the pathology report for this diagnosis. Over the next 2 years, despite aggressive treatment, his cancer spread to his lungs. I include the pertinent medical records for his cancer treatment.

My husband James died on May 10, 2012. The death certificate listed bladder cancer as his cause of death and lung cancer as a contributory cause. No other causes of death were listed on the death certificate.

I recently talked with a representative who helps people like me with claims for veterans benefits and he suggested that I might have a claim for DIC based on my husband's prostate cancer and the fact that he was stationed in Vietnam. He calls this an Agent Orange claim. He also told me that in order to get this benefit, I would have to show that the prostate cancer contributed to my husband's death and that it could not be a result of the bladder cancer spreading to the prostate but just the reverse. He suggested that I consult with Doctor Roger Moore who was my husband's attending physician for 10 years up through my husband's death. Doctor Moore did not sign the death certificate.

After consulting with Doctor Moore and explaining to him what I needed, he agreed to help me. He explained that it was very possible that the prostate cancer showed up first and then spread to the bladder as he says that is what usually happens with prostate cancer and the reverse of going from the bladder to the prostate does not happen very often. He explained that just because the bladder cancer was diagnosed before the prostate cancer, it does not mean that the prostate cancer didn't occur first. In fact, he said that was the more likely scenario.

Doctor Moore agreed to write a letter for me that would add prostate cancer as one of the contributing causes of my husband's death and also he agreed to provide an opinion that the prostate cancer as least as likely as not preceded the bladder cancer and that the bladder cancer was a result of the prostate cancer metastasizing to the bladder. I have enclosed this letter as part of my evidence.

I have also included all of the medical records that pertain to my husband's medical conditions prior to his death.

Finished Sample DIC VA 21-4138

OMB Control No. 2900-0075
Respondent Burden: 15 minutes
Expiration Date: 12/31/2020

VA Department of Veterans Affairs

VA DATE STAMP
(DO NOT WRITE IN THIS SPACE)

STATEMENT IN SUPPORT OF CLAIM

INSTRUCTIONS: Read the Privacy Act and Respondent Burden on Page 2 before completing the form. Complete as much of Section I as possible. The information requested will help process your claim for benefits. If you need any additional room, use the second page.

SECTION I: VETERAN/BENEFICIARY'S IDENTIFICATION INFORMATION

NOTE: You will *either* complete the form online or by hand. Please print the information request in ink, neatly, and legibly to help process the form.

1. VETERAN/BENEFICIARY'S NAME *(First, Middle Initial, Last)*

JAMES   W SMITH

2. VETERAN'S SOCIAL SECURITY NUMBER

922 - 00 - 1921

3. VA FILE NUMBER *(If applicable)*

4. VETERAN'S DATE OF BIRTH *(MM/DD/YYYY)*

Month 06 — Day 31 — Year 1947

5. VETERAN'S SERVICE NUMBER *(If applicable)*

6. TELEPHONE NUMBER *(Include Area Code)*

555-66-7777

7. E-MAIL ADDRESS *(Optional)*

Eleanor@email.com

8. MAILING ADDRESS *(Number and street or rural route, P.O. Box, City, State, ZIP Code and Country)*

No. & Street: 55 EAST RIVER ST

Apt./Unit Number:

City: RIVER CITY

State/Province: IA   Country: US   ZIP Code/Postal Code: 01023 -

SECTION II: REMARKS
(The following statement is made in connection with a claim for benefits in the case of the above-named veteran/beneficiary.)

Explanation of My Claim for DIC

My spouse was a veteran. We were legally married when my spouse died. My spouse was not on claim for Disability Compensation at death. However, I believe that the death was service-connected even though I have never made a claim based on the death. I now have evidence that the death of my spouse was service-connected and I am submitting that evidence with this claim for DIC. I provide with this "Statement in Support of Claim" the following:

- List of Documents Submitted with This Claim; see Page 2

- My Statement Detailing Events Leading to Death; see Page 3

VA FORM
DEC 2017 **21-4138**

EXISTING STOCKS OF VA FORM 21-4138, JAN 2015, WILL BE USED.

Page 1

VETERAN'S SOCIAL SECURITY NO. ☐☐☐ – ☐☐ – ☐☐☐☐

List of Documents Submitted with This Claim

TITLE OF DOCUMENT
DD-214 for James Smith
VA Form 21-22a
VA Form 21-534EZ
Evidence of Service in Vietnam
Death Certificate for James Smith
Marriage Certificate for James and Eleanor Smith
Medical Opinion for Cause of Death, Roger Moore MD
Medical Records for James Smith

Continued on Page 3

SECTION III: DECLARATION OF INTENT

I CERTIFY THAT the statements on this form are true and correct to the best of my knowledge and belief.

9. SIGNATURE *(Sign in ink)*	10. DATE SIGNED *(MM/DD/YYYY)*

PENALTY: The law provides severe penalties which include fine or imprisonment, or both, for the willful submission of any statement or evidence of a material fact, knowing it to be false.

PRIVACY ACT INFORMATION: The VA will not disclose information collected on this form to any source other than what has been authorized under the Privacy Act of 1974 or Title 38, Code of Federal Regulations 1.576 for routine uses (i.e., civil or criminal law enforcement, congressional communications, epidemiological or research studies, the collection of money owed to the United States, litigation in which the United States is a party or has an interest, the administration of VA Programs and delivery of VA benefits, verification of identity and status, and personnel administration) as identified in the VA system of records, 58VA21/22/28, Compensation, Pension, Education, and Vocational Rehabilitation and Employment Records - VA, published in the Federal Register. Your obligation to respond is required to obtain or retain benefits. VA uses your SSN to identify your claim file. Providing your SSN will help ensure that your records are properly associated with your claim file. Giving us your SSN account information is voluntary. Refusal to provide your SSN by itself will not result in the denial of benefits. The VA will not deny an individual benefits for refusing to provide his or her SSN unless the disclosure of the SSN is required by Federal Statute of law in effect prior to January 1, 1975, and still in effect. The requested information is considered relevant and necessary to determine maximum benefits under the law. The responses you submit are considered confidential (38 U.S.C. 5701). Information submitted is subject to verification through computer matching programs with other agencies.

RESPONDENT BURDEN: We need this information to obtain evidence in support of your claim for benefits (38 U.S.C. 501(a) and (b)). Title 38, United States Code, allows us to ask for this information. We estimate that you will need an average of 15 minutes to review the instructions, find the information, and complete this form. VA cannot conduct or sponsor a collection of information unless a valid OMB control number is displayed. You are not required to respond to a collection of information if this number is not displayed. Valid OMB control numbers can be located on the OMB Internet Page at www.reginfo.gov/public/do/PRAMain. If desired, you can call 1-800-827-1000 to get information on where to send comments or suggestions about this form.

SECTION II: REMARKS *(Continued)*
(The following statement is made in connection with a claim for benefits in the case of the above-named veteran/beneficiary.)

My Statement Detailing Events Leading to Death

My husband, James Smith, was a veteran who served in country in the Republic of Vietnam from 1968 to 1969. He remained in the service for one more year and then was discharged with an Honorable discharge in 1970. As far as I know, he never made any application for any veterans benefits, nor did he use any medical benefits provided for veterans. He did make ample use of the G.I. bill to complete his college education. We met and were married in 1972 and were married and lived continuously together for another 40 years until his death in 2012. I have remained single since his death.

In 2005, he was diagnosed with type II diabetes which was managed initially through diet and then in his later years required medication. As far as I know, I have never been told that his death was due to diabetes. In January of 2010 James was diagnosed with bladder cancer. I have included the pathology report for this diagnosis with the evidence for this claim. In March 2010 James was also diagnosed with prostate cancer from a biopsy. I also include the pathology report for this diagnosis. Over the next 2 years, despite aggressive treatment, his cancer spread to his lungs. I include the pertinent medical records for his cancer treatment.

My husband James died on May 10, 2012. The death certificate listed bladder cancer as his cause of death and lung cancer as a contributory cause. No other causes of death were listed on the death certificate.

I recently talked with a representative who helps people like me with claims for veterans benefits and he suggested that I might have a claim for DIC based on my husband's prostate cancer and the fact that he was stationed in Vietnam. He calls this an Agent Orange claim. He also told me that in order to get this benefit, I would have to show that the prostate cancer contributed to my husband's death and that it could not be a result of the bladder cancer spreading to the prostate but just the reverse. He suggested that I consult with Doctor Roger Moore who was my husband's attending physician for 10 years up through my husband's death. Doctor Moore did not sign the death certificate.

Continued on Page 4

SECTION III: DECLARATION OF INTENT

I CERTIFY THAT the statements on this form are true and correct to the best of my knowledge and belief.

9. SIGNATURE *(Sign in ink)*	10. DATE SIGNED *(MM/DD/YYYY)*

PENALTY: The law provides severe penalties which include fine or imprisonment, or both, for the willful submission of any statement or evidence of a material fact, knowing it to be false.

PRIVACY ACT INFORMATION: The VA will not disclose information collected on this form to any source other than what has been authorized under the Privacy Act of 1974 or Title 38, Code of Federal Regulations 1.576 for routine uses (i.e., civil or criminal law enforcement, congressional communications, epidemiological or research studies, the collection of money owed to the United States, litigation in which the United States is a party or has an interest, the administration of VA Programs and delivery of VA benefits, verification of identity and status, and personnel administration) as identified in the VA system of records, 58VA21/22/28, Compensation, Pension, Education, and Vocational Rehabilitation and Employment Records - VA, published in the Federal Register. Your obligation to respond is required to obtain or retain benefits. VA uses your SSN to identify your claim file. Providing your SSN will help ensure that your records are properly associated with your claim file. Giving us your SSN account information is voluntary. Refusal to provide your SSN by itself will not result in the denial of benefits. The VA will not deny an individual benefits for refusing to provide his or her SSN unless the disclosure of the SSN is required by Federal Statute of law in effect prior to January 1, 1975, and still in effect. The requested information is considered relevant and necessary to determine maximum benefits under the law. The responses you submit are considered confidential (38 U.S.C. 5701). Information submitted is subject to verification through computer matching programs with other agencies.

RESPONDENT BURDEN: We need this information to obtain evidence in support of your claim for benefits (38 U.S.C. 501(a) and (b)). Title 38, United States Code, allows us to ask for this information. We estimate that you will need an average of 15 minutes to review the instructions, find the information, and complete this form. VA cannot conduct or sponsor a collection of information unless a valid OMB control number is displayed. You are not required to respond to a collection of information if this number is not displayed. Valid OMB control numbers can be located on the OMB Internet Page at www.reginfo.gov/public/do/PRAMain. If desired, you can call 1-800-827-1000 to get information on where to send comments or suggestions about this form.

VETERAN'S SOCIAL SECURITY NO. ☐☐☐ – ☐☐ – ☐☐☐☐

I recently talked with a representative who helps people like me with claims for veterans benefits and he suggested that I might have a claim for DIC based on my husband's prostate cancer and the fact that he was stationed in Vietnam. He calls this an Agent Orange claim. He also told me that in order to get this benefit, I would have to show that the prostate cancer contributed to my husband's death and that it could not be a result of the bladder cancer spreading to the prostate but just the reverse. He suggested that I consult with Doctor Roger Moore who was my husband's attending physician for 10 years up through my husband's death. Doctor Moore did not sign the death certificate.

After consulting with Doctor Moore and explaining to him what I needed, he agreed to help me. He explained that it was very possible that the prostate cancer showed up first and then spread to the bladder as he says that is what usually happens with prostate cancer and the reverse of going from the bladder to the prostate does not happen very often. He explained that just because the bladder cancer was diagnosed before the prostate cancer, it does not mean that the prostate cancer didn't occur first. In fact, he said that was the more likely scenario.

Doctor Moore agreed to write a letter for me that would add prostate cancer as one of the contributing causes of my husband's death and also he agreed to provide an opinion that the prostate cancer as least as likely as not preceded the bladder cancer and that the bladder cancer was a result of the prostate cancer metastasizing to the bladder. I have enclosed this letter as part of my evidence.

I have also included all of the medical records that pertain to my husband's medical conditions prior to his death.

Eleanor Smith
December 25, 2018

SECTION III: DECLARATION OF INTENT

I CERTIFY THAT the statements on this form are true and correct to the best of my knowledge and belief.

9. SIGNATURE *(Sign in ink)*	10. DATE SIGNED *(MM/DD/YYYY)*

PENALTY: The law provides severe penalties which include fine or imprisonment, or both, for the willful submission of any statement or evidence of a material fact, knowing it to be false.

VA FORM 21-4138, DEC 2017

Page 4

Submitting a Claim for Burial Benefits

Information from the VA 2020 Budget Request
In 2018, NCA (National Cemetery Administration) interred 135,306 veterans and eligible family members. Annual veteran deaths are projected to be over 584,000 in 2019, and are projected to slowly decline. The number of interments is expected to peak at about 137,140 in 2021, after which interments will decline gradually. The total number of gravesites is expected to increase from nearly 3.75 million in 2018 to more than 3.92 million in 2020. The number of gravesites maintained is expected to reach over 4 million in 2021. In addition, the number of developed acres to maintain is expected to increase to over 9,500 acres systemwide with the opening of new cemeteries and gravesite expansion projects underway.

NCA's Memorial Programs Service (MPS) is responsible for administering the Headstone and Marker and the Presidential Memorial Certificate (PMC) programs. MPS provides the following

- receives and processes applications for headstones and markers;
- determines eligibility of the decedent;
- assists Veterans, next-of-kin, Veterans Service Organizations, funeral homes, and other customers with status, replacements, and general information concerning government headstones and markers to be installed on graves in private cemeteries; and
- administers the PMC program by providing certificates to families of deceased Veterans.

In 2020, NCA expects to process 383,570 headstones and marker applications, an increase of 9.1 percent over the 351,556 headstone and marker applications processed in 2018. In addition, NCA will expand its initiative to provide same-day (i.e. on the day of interment) Presidential Memorial Certificates (PMC) at National Cemeteries. NCA issued nearly 518,000 PMCs in 2018; and in the period 2018 to 2022, NCA will deliver nearly 3.5 million PMCs.

Applying for Burial Benefits
Claimants should send all burial and survivor benefit application directly to VA's Intake Center in Jainesville, Wisconsin. The intake center will scan and upload the digital images of the burial or survivor benefit application for processing. Please refer to the Claim Support Disc for the appropriate PO Box in Jainesville, WI.

Folder #4 *Application for Burial Benefits*, found in the Claim Support Disc, contains the following forms to help you apply:

> SF 180 – Request Pertaining to Military Records
> VA40-4970 – Request for Disinterment
> VBA-21-8834-ARE – Application for Reimbursement of Headstone or Marker Expense
> VBA-27-2008-ARE – Application for United States Flag for Burial Purposes

Effective July 7, 2014: VA changed its monetary burial benefits regulations to simplify the program and pay eligible survivors more quickly and efficiently. These regulations authorized VA to pay, without a written application, most eligible surviving spouses basic monetary burial benefits at the maximum amount authorized in law through automated systems rather than reimbursing them for actual costs incurred.

- Under the previous regulations, VA paid for burial and funeral expenses on a reimbursement basis, which required survivors to submit receipts for relatively small one-time payments that VA generally pays at the maximum amount permitted by law.
- The new burial regulations permit VA to pay, at a flat rate, burial and plot or interment allowances thereby enabling VA to automate payment of burial benefits to most eligible surviving spouses and more efficiently process other burial benefit claims.
- The burial allowance for a non-service-connected death is $300, and $2,000 for a death connected to military service.

Burial Allowances
The information below was taken from the US department of Veterans Affairs web site

Burial and Plot Rate Table 2020 – Effective October 1, 2019

SERVICE CONNECTED DEATH	$2,000
NON-SERVICE CONNECTED DEATH (Reimbursement; veteran dies while hospitalized by VA)	$796
NON-SERVICE CONNECTED DEATH (Reimbursement for Veterans not hospitalized by VA)	$300
NSC DEATH STATE CEMETERY (Paid to a state veterans cemetery for the plot/burial)	$796
NSC DEATH PLOT ALLOWANCE (This amount will be paid to reimburse for a private-paid plot)	$796
NSC HEADSTONE OR MARKER ALLOWANCE (If not provided by the Department)	$195

A service-connected death is one where the veteran was receiving monthly payments for Disability Compensation and the death was due to the disability or condition for which the veteran was receiving pay. It is also possible to receive a service-connected death if the disability or condition was not the direct cause but the disability or condition contributed substantially to the death.

A non-service-connected death is one where the veteran was receiving monthly payments for Disability Compensation or Veterans Pension but the death was due to some other cause not related to the disabilities or conditions for which the veteran was receiving pay.

It should be noted that generally a non-service-connected death can produce $1,096 a month if the survivors have to pay for a funeral plot. Note that if the veteran died while hospitalized by VA and the survivor has to pay for a funeral plot the total amount available is $1,872.

Burial Benefits for Service-Related Death
An annual increase in burial and plot allowances for deaths occurring after October 1, 2011 began in 2013 based on the Consumer Price Index for the preceding 12-month period. Eligibility Requirements

- You paid for a Veteran's burial or funeral, AND
- You have not been reimbursed by another government agency or some other source, such as the deceased Veteran's employer, AND
- The Veteran was discharged under conditions other than dishonorable, AND
- The Veteran died because of a service-related disability, OR
- The Veteran was receiving VA Pension or Compensation at the time of death, OR
- The Veteran was entitled to receive VA Pension or Compensation, but decided not to reduce his/her military retirement or disability pay, OR

- The Veteran died while hospitalized by VA, or while receiving care under VA contract at a non-VA facility, OR
- The Veteran died while traveling under proper authorization and at VA expense to or from a specified place for the purpose of examination, treatment, or care, OR
- The Veteran had an original or reopened claim pending at the time of death and has been found entitled to Compensation or Pension from a date prior to the date or death, OR
- The Veteran died on or after October 9, 1996, while a patient at a VA-approved state nursing home. NOTE: VA does not pay burial benefits if the deceased:
    - Died during active military service, OR
    - Was a member of Congress who died while holding office, OR
    - Was a Federal prisoner

Evidence Requirements:

- Acceptable proof of death as specified in 38 CFR 3.211., AND
- Receipted bills that show that you made payment in whole or part, OR
- A statement of account, preferably on the printed billhead of the funeral director or cemetery owner. The statement of account must show:
- The name of the deceased Veteran for whom the services and merchandise were furnished, AND
- The nature and cost of the services and merchandise, AND
- All credits, AND
- The amount of the unpaid balance, if any

How to Apply

- Complete and submit a VA Form 21-530, Application for Burial Allowance. You can find an office on our Facility Locator page, OR
- Apply online using eBenefits, OR
- Work with an accredited representative or agent, OR
- Go to a VA Regional Office and have a VA employee assist you. You can find your Regional Office on our Facility Locator page.

For more information on how to apply and for tips on making sure your claim is ready to be processed by VA, visit our How to Apply page.

Burial and Memorial benefits

Eligibility

1. Veterans discharged from active duty under conditions other than dishonorable and
2. service members who die while on active duty, active duty for training, or inactive duty training, as well as
3. spouses and dependent children of Veterans and active duty service-members, may be eligible for VA burial and memorial benefits. The Veteran does not have to die before a spouse or dependent child for them to be eligible.

With certain exceptions, active duty service beginning after Sept. 7, 1980, as an enlisted person, and after Oct. 16, 1981, as an officer, must be for a minimum of 24 consecutive months or the full period of active duty (as in the case of reservists or National Guard members called to active duty for a limited duration). Active duty for training, by itself, while serving in the reserves or National Guard, is not sufficient to confer eligibility. Reservists and National Guard members, as well as their spouses and dependent children, are eligible if they were entitled to retired pay at the time of death, or would have been upon reaching requisite age. See Chapter 8 for more information.

VA's National Cemetery Scheduling Office or local national cemetery directors verify eligibility for burial. A copy of the Veteran's discharge document that specifies the period(s) of active duty and character of discharge is usually sufficient to determine eligibility. In some instances, a copy of the deceased's death certificate and proof of relationship to the Veteran (for eligible family members) may be required.

Burial in VA National Cemeteries
Burial in a VA national cemetery is available for eligible Veterans, their spouses and dependents at no cost to the family and includes the gravesite, grave-liner, opening and closing of the grave, a headstone or marker, and perpetual care as part of a national shrine. For Veterans, benefits also include a burial flag (with case for active duty) and military funeral honors. Family members and other loved ones of deceased Veterans may request Presidential Memorial Certificates.

VA operates 131 national cemeteries, of which 72 are open for new casketed interments and 18 are open to accept only cremated remains. Burial options are limited to those available at a specific cemetery but may include in-ground casket, or interment of cremated remains in a columbarium, in ground or in a scatter garden. Contact the national cemetery directly, or visit our Web site at: www.cem.va.gov to determine if a particular cemetery is open for new burials, and which other options are available.

The funeral director or the next of kin makes interment arrangements by contacting the National Cemetery Scheduling Office or, in some cases, the national cemetery in which burial is desired. VA normally does not conduct burials on weekends. Gravesites cannot be reserved; however, VA will honor reservations made under previous programs.

Surviving spouses of Veterans who died on or after Jan. 1, 2000, do not lose eligibility for burial in a national cemetery if they remarry. Burial of dependent children is limited to unmarried children under 21 years of age, or under 23 years of age if a full-time student at an approved educational institution. Unmarried adult children who become physically or mentally disabled and incapable of self-support before age 21, or age 23 if a full-time student, also are eligible for burial.

Burial in Arlington National Cemetery
Arlington National Cemetery is a national cemetery administered by the Department of the Army. The primary mission of Arlington National Cemetery is to serve as the final resting place

for the men and women who honorably served in the Armed Forces and their immediate family members. The cemetery routinely performs 20 to 30 funeral services each day.

Burial in State Veterans Cemeteries

You should contact your State veterans department for more information on state veterans cemeteries which are maintained by each state.

Certain Eligible Parents for VA Burial

A new federal law passed in 2010 (Public Law 111-275) extends burial benefits to certain parents of service-members who die as a result of hostile activity or from training-related injuries who are buried in a national cemetery in a gravesite with available space. The biological or adopted parents of a service-member who died in combat or while performing training in preparation for a combat mission, who leaves no surviving spouse or dependent child, may be buried with the deceased service-member if the Secretary of Veterans Affairs determines that there is available space. The law applies to service-members who died on or after Oct. 7, 2001 and to parents who died on or after Oct. 13, 2010.

Headstones, Markers and Medallions

Veterans, active duty service members, and retired Reservists and National Guard service members, are eligible for an inscribed headstone or marker for their grave at any cemetery – national, State Veterans, or private. VA will deliver a headstone or marker at no cost, anywhere in the world. For eligible Veterans whose deaths occurred on or after Nov. 1, 1990, VA may provide a government headstone or marker even if the grave is already marked with a private one, or VA may provide a medallion instead of a headstone or marker for Veterans' graves in private cemeteries when the grave is already marked with a privately-purchased headstone or marker. Spouses and dependent children are eligible for a government headstone or marker only if they are buried in a national or State Veterans cemetery.

Flat markers are available in bronze, granite or marble. Upright headstones come in granite or marble. In national cemeteries, the style provided will be consistent with existing monuments at the place of burial. Niche markers are available to mark columbaria used for inurnment of cremated remains. Medallions are made of bronze and are available in three sizes: 5-inch, 3-inch, and 1 ½-inches.

Headstones, markers and medallions previously provided by the government may be replaced at the government's expense if badly deteriorated, illegible, vandalized or stolen. To check the status of a claim for a headstone or marker for placement in a national or State Veterans cemetery, call the cemetery. To check the status of one being placed in a private cemetery, call 1-800-697-6947.

Inscription

Headstones and markers must be inscribed with the name of the deceased, branch of service, and year of birth and death. They also may be inscribed with other optional information, including an authorized emblem of belief and, space permitting, additional text including military rank; war service such as "World War 2;" complete dates of birth and death; military awards; military organizations; civilian or Veteran affiliations; and personalized words of endearment.

Private Cemeteries

To submit a claim for a headstone, marker or medallion for a private cemetery, mail a completed VA Form 40-1330 (available at www4.va.gov/vaforms/va/pdf/VA40-1330.pdf), Application for Standard Government Headstone or Marker, and a copy of the Veteran's military discharge document to Memorial Programs Service (41A1), Department of Veterans Affairs, 5109 Russell Rd., Quantico, VA 22134-3903. The form and supporting documents may also be faxed toll free to 1-800-455-7143. Before ordering, check with the cemetery to ensure that the Government-furnished headstone or marker will be accepted. All installation fees are the responsibility of the applicant.

"In Memory Of" Markers

VA provides memorial headstones and markers with "In Memory Of" as the first line of inscription, to memorialize those whose remains have not been recovered or identified, were buried at sea, donated to science or cremated and scattered. Eligibility is the same as for regular headstones and markers. There is no fee when the "In Memory Of" marker is placed in a national cemetery. All installation fees at private cemeteries are the responsibility of the applicant.

Medallions in Lieu of Government Headstone/Marker

Public Law 110-157 enacted December 26, 2007, expanded VA authority to provide a medallion instead of a headstone or marker for Veterans' graves in private cemeteries when the grave is already marked with a privately-purchased headstone or marker. Claimants will have the option to apply for either a traditional headstone or marker to place on the grave, or a medallion to affix to a privately-purchased headstone or marker. VA anticipates the medallion will be available during 2010. Current information regarding medallion availability is located at www.cem.va.gov.

Presidential Memorial Certificates

These are issued upon request to recognize the United States military service of honorably discharged deceased Veterans. Next of kin, relatives and other loved ones may apply for a certificate by mailing, e-mailing, or faxing a completed and signed VA Form 40-0247 along with a copy of the Veteran's military discharge documents or proof of honorable military service. The form and eligibility requirements can be found at www.cem.va.gov. All requests must be sent with supporting military documents or proof of honorable military service.

Burial Flag

A United States flag is provided, at no cost, to drape the casket or accompany the urn of a deceased veteran who served honorably in the U. S. Armed Forces. It is furnished to honor the memory of a veteran's military service to his or her country. VA will furnish a burial flag for memorialization for each other than dishonorable discharged

- veteran who served during wartime
- veteran who died on active duty after May 27, 1941
- veteran who served after January 31, 1955
- peacetime veteran who was discharged or released before June 27, 1950

- certain persons who served in the organized military forces of the Commonwealth of the Philippines while in service of the U.S Armed forces and who died on or after April 25, 1951
- certain former members of the Selected Reserves

Generally, the flag is given to the next-of-kin, as a keepsake, after its use during the funeral service. When there is no next-of-kin, VA furnishes the flag to a friend making request for it. For VA national cemeteries with an Avenue of Flags, families of veterans buried in national cemeteries may donate the burial flags of their loved ones to be flown on patriotic holidays.

You may apply for the flag by completing VA Form 21-2008, Application for United States Flag for Burial Purposes. You may get a flag at any VA Regional Office or U.S. Post Office. Generally, the funeral director will help you obtain the flag.

The law allows us to issue one flag for a veteran's funeral. We cannot replace it if it is lost, destroyed, or stolen. However, some veterans' organizations or other community groups may be able to help you get another flag.

The proper way to display the flag depends upon whether the casket is open or closed. VA Form 21-2008 does provide the correct method for displaying and folding the flag. The burial flag is not suitable for outside display because of its size and fabric. It is made of cotton and can easily be damaged by weather.

Military Funeral Honors

Upon request, DoD will provide military funeral honors consisting of folding and presentation of the United States flag and the playing of "Taps." A funeral honors detail consists of 2 or more uniformed members of the armed forces, with at least one from the deceased's branch of service.

Family members should inform their funeral director if they want military funeral honors. DoD maintains a toll-free number (1-877-MIL-HONR) for use by funeral directors only to request honors. VA can help arrange honors for burials at VA national cemeteries. Veterans service organizations or volunteer groups may help provide honors. For more information, visit www.militaryfuneralhonors.osd.mil.

Veterans Cemeteries Administered by Other Agencies

Arlington National Cemetery

Administered by the Department of the Army. Eligibility is more restrictive than at VA national cemeteries. For information, call (703) 607-8000, write Superintendent, Arlington National Cemetery, Arlington, VA 22211, or visit www.arlingtoncemetery.mil.

Department of the Interior

Administers two active national cemeteries – Andersonville National Cemetery in Georgia and Andrew Johnson National Cemetery in Tennessee. Eligibility is similar to VA national cemeteries.

State Veterans Cemeteries

Seventy-nine State veterans cemeteries offer burial options for veterans and their families. These cemeteries have similar eligibility requirements but many require state residency. Some services, particularly for family members, may require a fee. Contact the State cemetery or State Veterans affairs office for information.

Survivors and Dependents Education Eligibility

Overview of Veterans' Spouses, Dependents, and Survivors Education Eligibility

VA provides education and training opportunities for certain Veterans' spouses, dependents, and survivors through various programs to help cover the cost of tuition, housing, books, and supplies. Education benefits may be used toward a traditional degree, non-college degree, on-the-job training, apprenticeships, and more. Explore the following programs online:

- Marine Gunnery Sergeant John David Fry Scholarship
- Survivors' and Dependents' Educational Assistance

The Marine Gunnery Sergeant John David Fry Scholarship

The Marine Gunnery Sergeant John David Fry Scholarship provides Post-9-11 GI Bill® benefits to the children and surviving spouses of service members who died in the line of duty while on active duty after September 10, 2001. Eligible beneficiaries attending school may receive up to 36 months of benefits at the 100% level.

Full tuition and fees paid directly to the school for all public school in-state students. For those attending private or foreign schools, tuition and fees are capped at a statutory maximum amount per academic year.

- A monthly housing allowance.
- A books and supplies stipend.

Children of active duty members of the Armed Forces who died in the line of duty after September 10, 2001, are eligible for this benefit.
- A child may begin an approved program of education before the age of 18.
- Eligibility ends on the child's 33rd birthday.
- A child's marital status has no effect on eligibility.

Surviving spouses of active duty members of the Armed Forces who died in the line of duty after September 10, 2001, are also eligible for this benefit.
- A surviving spouse can receive benefits for terms beginning on or after January 1, 2015.
- A surviving spouse's eligibility generally ends 15 years after the Servicemember's death.
- A spouse will lose eligibility to this benefit upon remarriage if this occurs during the 15 year period.

If the child or surviving spouse is eligible under the Montgomery GI Bill Active Duty, Montgomery GI Bill Selected Reserve, and/or the Reserve Educational Assistance Program

(REAP), then he or she must relinquish eligibility under one of those programs to receive benefits under Post-9-11 GI Bill.

- A child's character of discharge from his or her own service does not impact eligibility resulting from the line of duty death of a parent or spouse.
- A child or surviving spouse on active duty will receive benefits at the active duty benefit rate.
- A child or surviving spouse eligible for benefits under the Fry Scholarship Program can also be eligible for Post-9-11 GI Bill benefits based on his/her won service, and may also eligible to use transferred entitlement.

Children eligible for the Fry Scholarship may also be eligible for DEA. Effective August 1, 2011, children are not able to establish eligibility for both Fry Scholarship and DEA benefits based on a parent's death in the line of duty.

A child whose parent died after July 31, 2011, must make an irrevocable election between the Fry Scholarship and DEA (Dependents Educational Assistance) when applying for benefits. A child whose parent died before August 1, 2011, may still be eligible for both benefits, but he/she may only use one program at a time, and combined benefits are capped at a total of 81 months of full-time training.

Surviving spouses eligible for the Fry Scholarship may also be eligible for DEA (see section below). Surviving spouses are not able to establish eligibility for both Fry Scholarship and DEA benefits based on a parent's death in the line of duty. Surviving spouses must make an irrevocable election of which benefit he or she wishes to receive for any and all school enrollments beginning on or after January 1, 2015..

The Survivors' and Dependents' Educational Assistance (DEA) Program
The Survivors' and Dependents' Educational Assistance (DEA) program offers education and training opportunities to eligible surviving spouses and dependent children of

- Veterans who are permanently and totally disabled due to a service-related condition (rated 100% or being paid at 100%) or

- Veterans who died while on active duty or

- Veterans who died as a result of a service-related condition.

Type of Assistance
Benefits may be used for degree and certificate programs, apprenticeship, and on-the-job training. If you are a spouse, you may take a correspondence course. Remedial, deficiency, and refresher courses may be approved under certain circumstances.

Available Benefits and Eligibility
You may receive up to 45 months of education benefits. Effective Oct. 1, 2013, some DEA beneficiaries may be eligible for up to 81 months of GI Bill benefits if they use the Survivors and Dependents Educational Assistance program in conjunction with an entitlement from other VA education programs. Currently the monthly stipend is about $1,200 a month.

If you are eligible for both Fry Scholarship and DEA, you will be required to make an irrevocable election between the two programs when you apply. Dependents are not eligible to receive both DEA and Fry Scholarship based on the same event (like a Servicemember dying in the line of duty) unless he or she is a child whose parent died prior to August 1, 2011. A child whose parent died before August 1, 2011, may be eligible for both benefits but he/she may only use one program at a time and combined benefits are capped at a total of 81 months of full-time training. In this situation, the two benefit programs cannot be used concurrently.

Eligibility
You must be the eligible son, eligible daughter, or spouse of:

- A Veteran who died or is permanently and totally disabled as the result of a service-connected disability. The disability must arise out of active service in the armed forces.
- A Veteran who died from any cause while such permanent and total service-connected disability was in existence.
- A Servicemember missing in action or captured in line of duty by a hostile force.
- A Servicemember forcibly detained or interned in line of duty by a foreign government or power.
- A Servicemember who is hospitalized or receiving outpatient treatment for a service connected permanent and total disability and is likely to be discharged for that disability. This change is effective Dec. 23, 2006.

Other Factors to Consider
If you are a son or daughter and wish to receive benefits for attending school or job training, you must be between the ages of 18 and 26. In certain instances, it is possible to begin before age 18 and to continue after age 26. Marriage is not a bar to this benefit. If you are in the armed forces, you may not receive this benefit while on active duty. To pursue training after military service, your discharge must not be under dishonorable conditions. VA can extend your period of eligibility by the number of months and days equal to the time spent on active duty. This extension cannot generally go beyond your 31st birthday, but there are some exceptions.

Please note that a child over 18 years old using DEA will not be eligible to receive Dependency Indemnity Compensation (DIC) payments from VA. Receiving DEA payments bars a child from receiving DIC payments.

If you are a spouse, benefits end 10 years from the date VA finds you eligible or from the date of death of the Veteran. If VA rated the veteran permanently and totally disabled with an effective date of three years from discharge, a spouse will remain eligible for 20 years from the effective date of the rating. This change is effective Oct. 10, 2008, and no benefits may be paid for any training taken prior to that date. A spouse using DEA (of the Fry Scholarship) remains eligible to receive DIC payments from VA.

For surviving spouses of Servicemembers who died on active duty, benefits end 20 years from the date of death.

Apply
To apply, obtain and complete VA Form 22-5490, Dependents Application for VA Education Benefits. Send it to the VA Regional Office with jurisdiction over the state where you will advance your education and training. If you are a son or daughter, under legal age, a parent or guardian must sign the application. If you are eligible for both DEA and Fry, you will be

required to make an irrevocable election *unless* you are a child of a Servicemember who died in the line-of-duty prior to August 1, 2011.

Additional Assistance

Those eligible for DEA benefits may also be eligible for this additional assistance:

> **Special Restorative Training** *VA may prescribe special restorative training where needed to overcome or lessen the effects of a physical or mental disability for the purpose of enabling an eligible person to pursue a program of education, special vocational program, or other appropriate goal. Medical care and treatment or psychiatric treatments are not included.*

> **Special Vocational Training** *VA may also approve these benefits for an eligible person who is not in need of special restorative training, but who requires such a program because of a mental or physical disability.*

> *Section 301 of Public Law 109-461 adds a new category to the definition of eligible person for DEA benefits. The new category covers the spouse or child of a person who VA determined has a service-connected permanent and total disability; and is at the time of VAs determination is a member of the armed forces who is hospitalized or receiving outpatient medical care, services, or treatment; and is likely to be discharged or released from service for this service-connected disability. Persons eligible under this new provision may be eligible for DEA benefits effective Dec. 23, 2006, the effective date of the law.*

> *You may be eligible for more than one of these programs. In most situations, you will be required to make an irrevocable election between the DEA program and Fry Scholarship when you apply. Beneficiaries cannot use the same qualifying event for more than one benefit unless you are a child of a Servicemember that died in the line of duty prior to August 1, 2011.*

Survivors and Dependents Employment Services

If you are a family member caring for a service-disabled veteran, you may be eligible for counseling to determine your career goals and training to increase your skills.

Veterans' dependents who are eligible for the VA Survivors' and Dependents' Educational Assistance program may also receive the following assistance from the Vocational Rehabilitation and Employment program:

- Career choice – Understand the best career options based on your interests and capabilities.
- Benefits coaching – Make effective use of your VA benefits and/or other resources to achieve education and career goals.
- Personalized support – Receive academic or adjustment counseling and personalized support to remove barriers to your success.

Survivors and Dependents Health Care

CHAMPVA

A health care benefits program that provides coverage to the spouse or widow(er) and to the dependent children of a qualifying sponsor who:

- is rated permanently and totally disabled due to a service-connected disability, or
- was rated permanently and totally disabled due to a service-connected condition at the time of death, or
- died of a service-connected disability, or
- died on active duty, and
- the dependents are not otherwise eligible for Department of Defense TRICARE benefits.

Under CHAMPVA, VA shares the cost of covered health care services and supplies with eligible beneficiaries.

On the Claim Support Disc, we provide a 96 page outline of the champ VA program entitled "A Complete Guide to CHAMP VA Services."

Children of Women Vietnam Veterans (CWVV) Program

The CWVV Health Care Program is a Federal health benefits program administered by the Department of Veterans Affairs, for children with certain birth defects born to women Vietnam Veterans. The CWVV Program is a Fee for Service (indemnity plan) program. The CWVV Program provides reimbursement for medical care-related conditions associated with certain birth defects except spina bifida, which is covered under the VA's Spina Bifida Program.

Children whose biological mother is a Vietnam Veteran, who were conceived after the date on which the Veteran entered the Republic of Vietnam, during the period beginning on February 28, 1961, and ending May 7, 1975, and who have one of the covered birth defects, as determined by the Veterans Benefits Administration (VBA) are eligible for the program.

Spina Bifida Healthcare Program

The Spina Bifida Health Care Program is a health benefit program administered by the Department of Veterans Affairs for Vietnam and certain Korean Veterans' birth children who have been diagnosed with spina bifida (except spina bifida occulta). The program provides reimbursement for medical services and supplies.

Caregiver Program

Primary caregivers of OEF/OIF Veterans may be eligible to receive a stipend and access to healthcare coverage if they are not already entitled to care or services under a health plan contract, including Medicare, Medicaid or worker's Compensation. Mental health counseling, including marriage and family counseling, will also be provided. Caregivers may also be eligible for travel, lodging and per diem when they accompany the Veteran for care or attend training.

Survivors Home Loans

VA Home Loans for Surviving Spouses
VA offers three home loan guaranty programs to eligible surviving spouses of veterans and service members. These programs may be used to refinance a mortgage or help purchase, construct, or improve a home. Certain surviving spouses may be eligible for the following

- Purchase Loans
- Cash-Out Refinance Home Loans
- Interest Rate Reduction Refinance Loans

Eligible Surviving Spouse
VA home loan eligibility for surviving spouses includes widows who have not remarried and:

- Survived a spouse who died in service or from a service-related disability
- Survived a spouse who was missing in action (MIA) or a prisoner of war (POW) for at least 90 days (limited to one-time use of benefit)
- Survived a spouse who was rated continuously totally disabled for the specified period of time, and was eligible for disability compensation at the time of death by any cause

Purchase Loan
With a Purchase Loan, VA can help you purchase a home at a competitive interest rate, and if you have found it difficult to find other financing.

Cash-Out Refinance Home Loans
VA's Cash-Out Refinance Loan is for homeowners who want to take cash out of your home equity to take care of concerns like paying off debt, funding school, or making home improvements. The Cash-Out Refinance Loan can also be used to refinance a non-VA loan into a VA loan. VA will guaranty loans up to 100% of the value of your home.

About the VA Home Loan Guaranty
Most VA Home Loans are handled entirely by private lenders and VA rarely gets involved in the loan approval process. VA "stands behind" the loan by guaranteeing a portion of it. If something goes wrong and you can't make the payments anymore, the lending institution can come to us to cover any losses they might incur. The VA loan guaranty is the "insurance" that we provide the lender.

VA Home Loan Advantages
The guarantee VA provides to lenders allows them to provide you with more favorable terms, including:

- No down payment as long as the sales price doesn't exceed the appraised value.
- No private mortgage insurance premium requirement.
- VA rules limit the amount you can be charged for closing costs.
- Closing costs may be paid by the seller.
- The lender can't charge you a penalty fee if you pay the loan off early.
- VA may be able to provide you some assistance if you run into difficulty making payments.

You should also know that:

- You don't have to be a first-time homebuyer.
- You can reuse the benefit.
- VA-backed loans are assumable, as long as the person assuming the loan qualifies

If the Claimant Dies While the Application Is Pending

Sometimes the claimant will die before the adjudication process is complete and before a decision has been made on the claim. There is almost always a number of weeks or months between the effective date of the claim and the date of death of the claimant. Because of the difference between the claim date and date of decision there could be retroactive payments due under a pending claim to a survivor of the claimant under certain conditions. VA calls these benefits "accrued benefits."

We have already discussed in a previous chapter, that if a veteran was already receiving Disability Compensation benefits and the new claim was for a reevaluation or secondary service condition, a surviving spouse or dependent child will receive one month's worth of disability income for the month of death of the veteran. But this is not an accrued benefit, it is a benefit guaranteed under the regulation.

If the claimant is a single veteran or a surviving spouse of a veteran or a dependent child of a veteran there is generally no "accrued benefit" that would be made for a pending claim unless there is one or more remaining dependent children of the veteran. This is not always the case.

In this chapter we will discuss the rules pertaining to what happens if a claim is pending and a decision has not been made when the claimant dies. The regulation on the next page is applicable when un-paid monies are owed the deceased. This is found in Title 38 CFR §3.1000.

38 CFR §3.1000   Entitlement under 38 U.S.C. 5121 to benefits due and unpaid upon death of a beneficiary.

(a) Basic entitlement. Except as provided in §§3.1001 and 3.1008, where death occurred on or after December 1, 1962, periodic monetary benefits (other than insurance and servicemembers' indemnity) authorized under laws administered by the Department of Veterans Affairs, to which a payee was entitled at his or her death under existing ratings or decisions or those based on evidence in the file at date of death, and due and unpaid will, upon the death of such person, be paid as follows:

(Authority: 38 U.S.C. 5121(a)

(1) Upon the death of a veteran to the living person first listed as follows:

> *(i) His or her spouse;*

> *(ii) His or her children (in equal shares);*

> *(iii) His or her dependent parents (in equal shares) or the surviving parent.*

(2) Upon the death of a surviving spouse or remarried surviving spouse, to the veteran's children.

(3) Upon the death of a child, to the surviving children of the veteran entitled to death Pension, Compensation, or dependency and indemnity Compensation.

(4) Upon the death of a child claiming benefits under chapter 18 of this title, to the surviving parents.

(5) In all other cases, only so much of the accrued benefit may be paid as may be necessary to reimburse the person who bore the expense of last sickness or burial. (See §3.1002.)

(b) *we removed these rules as they are not pertinent to our discussion here*

(c) Claims and evidence. Application for accrued benefits must be filed within 1 year after the date of death. A claim for death Pension, Compensation, or dependency and indemnity Compensation, by an apportionee, surviving spouse, child or parent is deemed to include claim for any accrued benefits. (See §3.152(b)).

(1) If an application for accrued benefits is incomplete because the claimant has not furnished information necessary to establish that he or she is within the category of eligible persons under the provisions of paragraphs (a)(1) through (a)(5) or paragraph (b) of this section and that circumstances exist which make the claimant the specific person entitled to payment of all or part of any benefits which may have accrued, VA shall notify the claimant:

(i) Of the type of information required to complete the application;

(ii) That VA will take no further action on the claim unless VA receives the required information; and

(iii) That if VA does not receive the required information within 1 year of the date of the original VA notification of information required, no benefits will be awarded on the basis of that application.

(2) Failure to file timely claim, or a waiver of rights, by a preferred dependent will not serve to vest title in a person in a lower class or a claimant for reimbursement; neither will such failure or waiver by a person or persons in a joint class serve to increase the amount payable to another or others in the class.

The Scope of 38 CFR §3.1000
This regulation covers several different issues.

1. The first issue is if the death occurred and there was no evidence in the file at the date of death that would have entitled the claimant to any ratings or decisions based on the information in the file, there would be no benefit. (Exception: See information for substitute claimant)

2. The second issue is if at the death of the claimant there was evidence in the file to award a decision and entitlement under existing rules, an "accrued benefit" would be paid to any one of a hierarchy of survivors.

3. The hierarchy or priority – as VA calls it – of survivors who would be paid or possibly apportioned the "accrued benefit" would be in this order

   a. the veteran's spouse
      or
   b. if the veteran's spouse is deceased or dies, the veteran's children in equal shares
      or
   c. if the veteran's spouse is deceased and there are no dependent children, the veteran's dependent parents in equal shares

In a previous section we discussed VA's definition of "child" and "parent." Be aware that these are individuals who are either minor children or children in school up to age 23 or children who became totally dependent prior to age 18 or parents who are totally dependent on the deceased veteran. It is important to remember that the "accrued benefit" to survivors can only be paid under the specific conditions outlined in this regulation and no other.

There is no provision under the rules to pay the estate of the claimant if there are no survivors in the hierarchy above. There is still potential for payment from a portion of the accrued benefits or all of the accrued benefits which is called a "reimbursement accrued benefit." This amount, which could be a part of or up to the total amount of accrued benefit, is paid to other persons not in the hierarchy. This payment could be made for reimbursement for final expenses incurred on behalf of the claimant. Reimbursement could include out-of-pocket costs for final expenses of the deceased, out-of-pocket repayment for just debts and so forth. Final expenses include hospital, hospice, funeral, and burial. They do not include expenses like unpaid homecare or nursing home bills. Reimbursement will not be paid for any out-of-pocket costs that are reimbursed by insurance or other means.

The regulation also specifies that certain education benefits, certain back payments and allowances will be paid regardless. Evidence on file with VA is also further defined in the adjudication manual. We will discuss all of these issues in a subsequent section in detail below.

Claims for Accrued Benefits can be made using *VA Form 21-601*. We have provided this form on the Claim Support Disc. It is advisable to include the deceased veteran's death certificate and all receipts and paid invoices that the person paid on behalf of the deceased claimant.

A Cure for VA Avoiding Payment of a Retroactive Amount
Because of the requirement that at the death, sufficient evidence had to be in the file in the Regional Office or at the Board of Veterans Appeals in order to approve a claim, very few claims involving death of a claimant in the past were actually approved. The suspicion was that VA had the information but because the claimant was dead, none of the survivors knew the true nature of the case – only the Regional Office had the details. In this case of a pending claim, reasons for not awarding a benefit could easily be explained away by the Regional Office. This injustice commonly resulted in the phrase "the claim dies with the claimant."

We don't really believe VA would act in this manner as federal law requires the Regional Office to always be an advocate for the claimant. There are specific rules pertaining to pending claims at the death of the claimant and we will discuss them further on in this chapter.

Nevertheless, a surviving spouse or dependent child or dependent parent should have a right to continue the claim or an appeal before the BVA on behalf of the claimant.

Congress recognized the inequity of this situation and passed legislation in 2008 to correct it. On the next page is what Congress provided for relief of a pending claim at the death of a claimant.

38 CFR §3.1010 Substitution under 38 U.S.C. 5121A following death of a claimant
(a) Eligibility. If a claimant dies on or after October 10, 2008, a person eligible for accrued benefits under §3.1000(a) listed in 38 CFR 3.1000(a)(1) through (5) may, in priority order, request to substitute for the deceased claimant in a claim for periodic monetary benefits (other than insurance and servicemembers' indemnity) under

laws administered by the Secretary, or an appeal of a decision with respect to such a claim, that was pending before the agency of original jurisdiction or the Board of Veterans' Appeals when the claimant died. Upon VA's grant of a request to substitute, the substitute may continue the claim or appeal on behalf of the deceased claimant for purposes of processing the claim or appeal to completion. Any benefits ultimately awarded are payable to the substitute and other members of a joint class, if any, in equal shares.

(b) Time and place for filing a request. A person may not substitute for a deceased claimant under this section unless the person files a request to substitute with the agency of original jurisdiction no later than one year after the claimant's death.

(c) Request format.

(1) A request to substitute must be submitted in writing. At a minimum, a request to substitute must indicate intent to substitute; include the deceased claimant's claim number, Social Security number, or appeal number; and include the names of the deceased claimant and the person requesting to substitute.

(2) In lieu of a specific request to substitute, a claim for accrued benefits, survivor's Pension, or dependency and indemnity Compensation by an eligible person listed in §3.1000(a)(1) through (5) is deemed to include a request to substitute if a claim for periodic monetary benefits (other than insurance and servicemembers' indemnity) under laws administered by the Secretary, or an appeal of a decision with respect to such a claim, was pending before the agency of original jurisdiction or the Board of Veterans' Appeals when the claimant died. A claimant for accrued benefits, survivor's Pension, or dependency and indemnity Compensation may waive the right to substitute in writing over the claimant's signature.

(d) Evidence of eligibility. A person filing a request to substitute must provide evidence of eligibility to substitute. Evidence of eligibility to substitute means evidence demonstrating that the person is among those listed in the categories of eligible persons in §3.1000(a)(1) through (5) and first in priority order. If a person's request to substitute does not include evidence of eligibility when it is originally submitted and the person may be an eligible person, the Secretary will notify the person—

(1) Of the evidence of eligibility required to complete the request to substitute;

(2) That VA will take no further action on the request to substitute unless VA receives the evidence of eligibility; and

(3) That VA must receive the evidence of eligibility no later than 60 days after the date of notification or one year after the claimant's death, whichever is later, or VA will deny the request to substitute.

(e) Decisions on substitution requests. Subject to the provisions of §20.1302 of this chapter, the agency of original jurisdiction will decide in the first instance all requests to substitute, including any request to substitute in an appeal pending before the Board of Veterans' Appeals.

(1) Notification. The agency of original jurisdiction will provide written notification of the granting or denial of a request to substitute to the person who filed the request, together with notice in accordance with § 3.103(b)(1).

(2) Appeals. The denial of a request to substitute may be appealed to the Board of Veterans' Appeals pursuant to 38 U.S.C. 7104(a) and 7105.

(3) Joint class representative.

(i) A joint class means a group of two or more persons eligible to substitute under the same priority group under §3.1000(a)(1) through (a)(5), e.g., two or more surviving children.

(ii) In the case of a joint class of potential substitutes, only one person of the joint class may be a substitute at any one time. The first eligible person in the joint class to file a request to substitute will be the substitute representing the joint class.

(f) Adjudications involving a substitute. The following provisions apply with respect to a claim or appeal in which a survivor has been substituted for the deceased claimant:

(1) Notice under §3.159. VA will send notice under §3.159(b), "Department of Veterans Affairs assistance in developing claims," to the substitute only if the required notice was not sent to the deceased claimant or if the notice sent to the deceased claimant was inadequate.

(2) Expansion of the claim not permitted. A substitute may not add an issue to or expand the claim. However, a substitute may raise new theories of entitlement in support of the claim.

(3) Submission of evidence and other rights. A substitute has the same rights regarding hearings, representation, appeals, and the submission of evidence as would have applied to the claimant had the claimant not died. However, rights that may have applied to the claimant prior to death but which cannot practically apply to a substitute, such as the right to a medical examination, are not available to the substitute. The substitute must complete any action required by law or regulation within the time period remaining for the claimant to take such action on the date of his or her death. The time remaining to take such action will start to run on the date of the mailing of the decision granting the substitution request.
(4) Board of Veterans' Appeals procedures. The rules and procedures governing appeals involving substitutes before the Board of Veterans' Appeals are found in parts 19 and 20 of this chapter.

(g) Limitations on substitution. The following limitations apply with respect to substitution:

(1) A claim or appeal must be pending.

(i) A claim is considered to be pending if the claimant had filed the claim with an agency of original jurisdiction but dies before the agency of original jurisdiction makes a decision on the claim. A claim is also considered to be pending if, at the time of the claimant's death, the agency of original jurisdiction has made a decision on the claim, but the claimant has not filed a notice of disagreement, and the period allowed by law for filing a notice of disagreement has not expired.

(ii) An appeal is considered to be pending if a claimant filed a notice of disagreement in response to a notification from an agency of original jurisdiction of its decision on a claim, but dies before the Board of Veterans' Appeals issues a final decision on the appeal. If the Board issued a final decision on an appeal prior to the claimant's death, the appeal is not pending before VA for purposes of this section, even if the 120-day period for appealing the Board's decision to the Court of Appeals for Veterans Claims has not yet expired.

(2) Benefits awarded. Any benefits ultimately awarded are limited to any past-due benefits for the time period between the effective date of the award and what would have been the effective date of discontinuance of the award as a result of the claimant's death.

(3) Benefits for last sickness and burial only. When substitution cannot be established under any of the categories listed in §3.1000(a)(1) through (a)(4), only so much of any benefits ultimately awarded may be paid as may be necessary to reimburse the person who bore the expense of last sickness and burial. No part of any benefits ultimately awarded shall be used to reimburse any political subdivision of the United States for expenses incurred in the last sickness or burial of any claimant.

(4) Substitution by subordinate members prohibited. Failure to timely file a request to substitute, or a waiver of the right to request substitution, by a person of a preferred category of eligible person will not serve to vest the right to request substitution in a person in a lower category or a person who bore the

expense of last sickness and burial; neither will such failure or waiver by a person or persons in a joint class serve to increase the amount payable to other persons in the class.

(5) Death of a substitute. If a substitute dies while a claim or appeal is pending before an agency of original jurisdiction, or an appeal of a decision on a claim is pending before the Board, another member of the same joint class or a member of the next preferred subordinate category listed in §3.1000(a)(1) through (5) may substitute for the deceased substitute but only if the person requesting the successive substitution files a request to substitute no later than one year after the date of the substitute's death (not the date of the claimant's death).

(Authority: 38 U.S.C. 5121, 5121A) [79 FR 52982, Sep. 5, 2014]

Further Discussion of the Substitution Option

VA Form 21-0847 is usually required to initiate the substitution covered in the regulation above. Substitution can also be initiated through written request.

If an accrued benefit appears to exist, VA will <u>not notify</u> a survivor of the possibility of substituting for the claim. Instead, the Regional Office will send the appropriate forms for an accrued benefit, but this is not always the appropriate response. In a way, this is a disfavor to following through on a claim where perhaps substitution might be a better strategy. In other words, a survivor may never know about the opportunity for substitution, because of the way VA handles accrued benefits.

Consider this example. The Regional Office has enough information to make a decision when the veteran dies, but the evidence has not been fully weighed for a final award or denial. The Regional Office would not notify the surviving spouse of substitution because there is an accrued benefit. In this example, substitution would be important because the deceased claimant had additional evidence to submit and then died. This new evidence would have resulted in a more favorable decision. These types of situations where more evidence is pending at death but not submitted, occur quite frequently.

Unfortunately, if VA has enough evidence on file to make a decision the Regional Office will send out the forms pertaining to accrued benefits and not the form for substitution. But what if the decision for accrued benefits is not favorable such as a lower disability rating or no disability rating at all. Or as in the case we discuss below, a denial was issued, but the veteran was in the process of reopening the claim with new and relevant evidence when he died. The surviving spouse in this case had no idea that she could step in and continue the claim on his behalf. The claim was closed as far as VA was concerned. There are numerous cases like these where the survivors may never know about the option for substitution and they lose the potentially better benefit or they lose the benefit entirely.

If there is a pending claim and the claimant dies and there is no evidence in the Regional Office to create an accrued benefit, VA will send out the substitution claim form VA Form 21-0847. <u>Having the right of substitution is an extremely important option. We demonstrate the power of this option in Case #1 that is found in the Claim Support Disc. In that particular case, the veteran died after receiving a denial letter and before the Regional Office had adequate information to reopen the claim. The surviving spouse, as a substitute, submitted new and material evidence to reopen the claim along with a strong opinion letter from the veteran's treating physician. This new evidence did allow the Regional Office to award a benefit.</u>

Had we not taken the initiative to assist the surviving spouse to become a substitute, using *VA Form 21-0847*, the entire award of $32,500 for back payment, $2,000 for funeral and burial and an award of DIC for $1,254 a month (subject to annual increases) to the surviving spouse for the rest of her life would have been lost. There would have been no benefit at all. Without our assistance, the surviving spouse had no idea she could step in and take over for her deceased husband.

We have provided *VA Form 21-0847* for you on the Claim Support Disc.

Forms to Use If the Claimant Dies before the Claim Is Approved or Denied

Forms Used if the Claimant Dies before the Claim Is Approved or Denied

> VA Form 21-4138– Statement in Support of Claim (if needed for clarification)
> VA Form 21-0847 – Request for Substitution of Claimant upon Death of Claimant
> VA form 21-534EZ– Application for DIC, Death Pension, and/or Accrued Benefits

> ***See the Claim Support Disc for submitting to VA's Claims Intake Center in Janesville Wisconsin

Where there is no surviving spouse, surviving child or surviving parent, application for the reimbursement accrued benefit is made using the following

> VA Form 21-601-ARE – Application for Accrued Amounts Due A Deceased Beneficiary
> Paid Invoices of Final Expenses made on behalf of the deceased (hospice, hospital, funeral, and/or burial)
> Death Certificate of the Deceased Claimant

Chapter 8
Unfavorable Decisions and the New Review Process

IN THIS CHAPTER:

The New Modernized Review System for Unfavorable Decisions

The Meaning of Unfavorable Decision

The use of the term "unfavorable decision" is a term that we have developed for this book. This term refers to outcomes from any claims process where the decision notice has not been acceptable to the claimant. This unacceptable decision could mean a denial or a disability rating that was less than expected or for Pension a monthly income that is less than the maximum allowable. VA calls a reduced award a partial denial. As we discussed in the previous chapter, the VA claims processing model is nowhere near perfect. In fact, we believe this model is flawed to the point where claims that should have resulted in more favorable decisions, based on the evidence submitted, instead are more frequently less than favorable or downright denials.

We discuss in this chapter the Modernized Review System that was effective February 19, 2019 for challenging unfavorable decisions from the adjudication process. The previous process for challenging decisions included various actions that could be taken within the Regional Office and if those didn't work, the claimant could follow a complex process of appealing the decision that by 2018 was taking up to 7 years for a final decision from the Board of Veterans Appeals (BVA). The new process puts more emphasis on solving a challenge in the Regional Office and avoiding the BVA, but if an appeal is necessary, the appeal process has been greatly simplified.

The Need for the New Review System

The following quote from the Federal Register of August 10, 2018 expresses the Department of Veterans Affairs desire for changing the laws relating to the appeals process

"Modernizing the appeals process is a top priority for VA. In fiscal year (FY) 2017, claimants generally waited less than 125 days for an initial decision on VA disability compensation claims; however, they waited an average of 3 years for a final decision if they chose to appeal. Moreover, in FY2017 those claimants who chose to continue their appeal to the Board waited an average of 7 years for a decision from the date that they initiated their appeal, and the Board decision may not have resolved the appeal.

Public Law (Pub. L.) 115-55, the Veterans Appeals Improvement and Modernization Act of 2017 (hereinafter "Pub. L. 115-55") provides much-needed comprehensive reform for the legacy

appeals process, to help ensure that claimants receive a timely decision on review where they disagree with a VA claims adjudication. It replaces the current VA appeals process with a new review process that makes sense for veterans, their advocates, VA, and stakeholders.

In the current (previous) VA appeal process, which is set in law, appeals are non-linear and may require VA staff to engage in gathering and receiving evidence and re-adjudicating appeals based on new evidence. This process of gathering evidence and readjudication can add years to the appeals process, as appeals churn between the Board and the agency of original jurisdiction. Additionally, jurisdiction of appeals processing is shared between the Board and the agency of original jurisdiction, which, for purposes of the changes made by this proposed rule, is typically the Veterans Benefits Administration (VBA).

The new statutory appeals framework features three differentiated lanes from which a claimant may choose in seeking review of a VA denial (or partial denial) of a claim.

1. **One lane is for review of the same evidence by a higher-level claims adjudicator in the agency of original jurisdiction (higher-level review);**

2. **One lane is for submitting new and relevant evidence with a supplemental claim to the agency of original jurisdiction (supplemental claim); and**

3. **One lane is the appeals lane for seeking review by a Veterans Law Judge at the Board by filing a Notice of Disagreement (appeal to the Board).**

In an appeal to the Board, Public Law 115-55 eliminates intermediate and duplicative steps previously required, such as the Statement of the Case (SOC) and the substantive appeal. Furthermore, the new law will allow the Board to maintain three separate dockets for handling the following categories of appeals: (1) Appeals where the claimant has requested a hearing, (2) appeals with no request for a hearing but where the claimant elects to submit other forms of evidence, and (3) appeals where the claimant requests Board review on the same evidence that was before the agency of original jurisdiction. These separate dockets will allow the Board to more efficiently and effectively manage distinctly different types of work. As a result of the new lane options, claimants will have increased choice for resolving disagreements with a VA decision on a claim."

In addition, the differentiated lanes will allow the agency of original jurisdiction to be the claim development entity within VA and the Board to be the appeals entity. This design is intended to reduce the uncertainty caused by the current process, in which a claimant initiates an appeal in the agency of original jurisdiction and the appeal is often a years-long continuation of the claim development process. It ensures that all claim development by the agency of original jurisdiction occurs in the context of either an initial or supplemental claim filed with the agency of original jurisdiction, rather than in an appeal...."

Here is a graphic of how the new system works

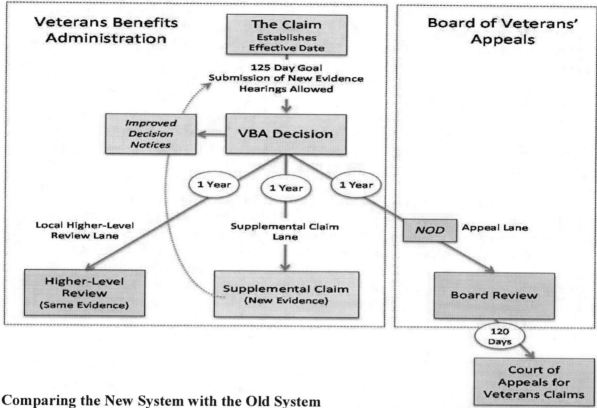

Comparing the New System with the Old System

VA asserts under the old system there was really only one lane and that was to file a notice of disagreement and eventually find oneself before the Board of Veterans Appeals. However this is not entirely true. The old system did allow for filing new and material evidence in order to reconsider the decision. This is similar to the Supplemental Claim Lane. The old system also allowed for a denovo review with a Decision Review Officer (DRO). In addition the old system allowed for any number of Regional Office hearings with a hearing officer – not necessarily a DRO – at any time during the process although the new system does allow this as well but only with a pending decision for a supplemental claim or with an appeal with the Board. The old system hearing options and denovo reviews correspond to the new higher-level review lane. But by offering hearings at any time, the old was definitely superior to the new higher-level review <u>because it does not allow for any hearings</u>. Finally, the old system did allow for moving the appeal to the appeal track and eventually on to the Board, with at least one review by a DRO.

<u>The new system is much more restrictive with two exceptions</u>. Under the new system, a claimant can theoretically recycle the claim continuously between the Regional Office and Board through new evidence with supplemental claims. It allows for more "bites at the apple" so to speak. Using this new process, theoretically, any number of higher-level reviews could be conducted with the same claim as long as new evidence was submitted using the Supplemental Claim Lane. A recycling could follow this theoretical path: *An unfavorable higher-level review decision could lead to a new supplemental claim with new evidence resulting in*

another unfavorable decision and resulting in a request for a new higher-level review being initiated resulting in another unfavorable decision but perhaps this time leading to an appeal to the Board with an unfavorable decision which can lead to a new supplemental claim and so forth. An endless cycle is possible. This cycle applies to all 3 lanes and a Board decision is never final until a final adjudication when the one year period for holding open the effective date expires.

The process above could go on indefinitely if "new and relevant" evidence could be continually uncovered. And the original effective date is guaranteed throughout this process as long as more than one year does not elapse from any NEW decisions along the way. <u>Note however that if VA reaffirms a previous decision that reaffirmation is not a final decision and it does not hold open the effective date by allowing 1 year from that reaffirmation</u>.

In theory, the claim could remain in the Regional Office for years and years and still have the same effective date. <u>In practice, this endless cycle will not happen</u>. The key to keeping a claim alive under the new system is coming up with new and relevant evidence. This is then submitted to the original office of jurisdiction and most likely to the same adjudication team that made the original decision. That team can determine whether the evidence is new and relevant or not. In addition, if the original team was prejudiced against the claim, which happens from time to time, that team is unlikely to accept any new evidence at all. This becomes a chokepoint if a determination is made that the evidence is not acceptable. At that point, the adjudicators have no obligation to reopen the file and the claim is dead unless an appeal is made.

Relevant evidence is a lesser burden than material evidence under the old system and theoretically uncovering a buddy statement or a new medical record, even though these might be redundant and not material under the old system, could theoretically be accepted under the lesser burden of relevant evidence. Relevant evidence is any evidence that could be used to prove the claim. Evidence is relevant if it indicates a relationship between facts that increases the probability of the existence of the other. New evidence is defined as *"existing evidence not previously submitted to agency decision-makers. Material evidence means existing evidence that, by itself or when considered with previous evidence of record, relates to an unestablished fact necessary to substantiate the claim. <u>New and material evidence can be neither cumulative nor redundant of the evidence of record at the time of the last prior final denial of the claim sought to be reopened, and must raise a reasonable possibility of substantiating the claim</u>." Isaac v. Shinseki, 2009 U.S. App. Vet. Claims LEXIS 2021, 7-8 (U.S. App. Vet. Cl. Nov. 18, 2009)*

One advantage of the old system is that when seeking a denovo review with a DRO, new evidence could be submitted along with a Regional Office hearing. Under the new system, new evidence is not allowed with a higher-level review and there is no Regional Office hearing other than a phone interview with the adjudicator.

The Advantages of the New System
The differentiated lanes will allow the agency of original jurisdiction to be the claim development entity within VA and the Board to be the appeals entity. This design is intended to reduce the uncertainty caused by the current process, in which a claimant initiates an appeal in the agency of original jurisdiction and the appeal is often a years-long continuation of the claim

development process. It ensures that all claim development by the agency of original jurisdiction occurs in the context of either an initial or supplemental claim filed with the agency of original jurisdiction, rather than in an appeal.

The agency of original jurisdiction's duty to assist in developing evidence will continue to apply when a claimant initiates a new or supplemental claim. However, where a claimant seeks review of an agency of original jurisdiction decision, the duty to assist generally no longer applies, unless and until the claimant elects to file a supplemental claim, at which point the duty to assist applies to the supplemental claim.

The new regulations also contain a mechanism to correct any duty to assist errors occurring before the agency of original jurisdiction, if such errors are discovered on review or appeal, by requiring that the claim be returned to the agency of original jurisdiction for correction of the error, unless the maximum benefit is granted. The new regulations require claim decision notices to be clearer and more detailed. The improved notices will help claimants and their advocates make informed choices as to which review option makes the most sense. What this means is that unlike current notices which only offer a notice of disagreement leading to an appeal, these new notices will offer other options.

New Concepts and Discontinued Concepts with the New System

The new system comes with a whole new set of terminology and revises some previous definitions. New concepts have been introduced and several old concepts eliminated. In order to better understand how the system works, we will define some of these new concepts and terminology and talk about discontinued concepts on the following pages.

Legacy Claim
A legacy claim is any claim for benefits filed before the inception date of the new system. Legacy claims will be processed under the old rules. Likewise, claims already in the system prior to the effective date, which was February 19, 2009, will also be processed under the old rules. Since, a number of claims can stay in the system for years in some cases, hundreds of thousands of Legacy claims will continue to be processed after the inception date.

A legacy claim can be moved to the new system when an unfavorable decision is made. This has been occurring since 2018 where invitations have been sent out with unfavorable decisions offering opt in to the RAMP program. This program was the pilot test for the new system since passage of the new law in the summer of 2017. As of the summer of 2018, about 12% of veterans receiving notices had opted into the program. <u>After February 19, 2019 RAMP is no longer be available</u>. <u>Claimants with a legacy claim can opt into the new system after a notice of disagreement and Statement of the Case has been issued</u>.

Legacy Appeal
Legacy appeals are those appeals still in the system after February 19, 2019. No one is certain how many of these appeals are still in the system; however, the VA plans to have all legacy appeals adjudicated by the year 2022. Legacy appeals are processed under the old rules.

415

The Forms to Use for Application
Here are the 3 forms to use under the New Review System

VA Form 20-0995 – Decision Review Request: Supplemental Claim
VA Form 20-0996 – Decision Review Request: Higher-Level Review
VA Form 10182 – Decision Review Request: Board Appeal (Notice of Disagreement)

Filing a Claim and Duty to Assist
Under current rules VA has a right to require applications for benefits to be submitted on prescribed forms designated by the Department. Currently, applications for Compensation are to be filed with VA Form 21-526EZ. As of this writing, earlier versions of the 526 are no longer being accepted. Applications for Pension are to be filed with VA Form 21-527EZ and for Survivors Pension, DIC and accrued benefits on VA Form 21-534EZ, with earlier versions not accepted. These forms will continue to be used for what VA now calls "initial claims."

By filing an initial claim, the applicant has one year to complete any missing information. Submitting an Intent to File allows for the same one year extension, except that a "Substantially Complete Application" must be submitted prior to the end of that year if an Intent to File has been submitted. Failure to meet the foregoing requirements loses the effective date and requires a new application. A substantially complete claim also triggers VA's duty to assist. Under the new rules, a substantially complete claim is defined as following: 1) the claimant's name, 2) his or her relationship to the veteran if applicable, 3) sufficient service information for VA to verify the claimed service if applicable, 4) the benefit sought and any medical conditions on which it is based, 5) the claimant's signature, OR 5) with claims for nonservice connected disability or death Pension and parents dependency and indemnity Compensation, a statement of income, OR 6) with supplemental claims, inclusion of potentially new evidence, OR 7) for a higher level review, identification of the date of decision for which review is sought.

A substantially complete application triggers VA's duty to assist with some additional requirements under the new rules. Duty to assist is also triggered with a supplemental claim and ends with a decision on that claim. In order for duty to assist to apply to a supplemental claim, there is an additional requirement to identify potentially new evidence. Duty to assist with a supplemental claim will not happen if the office of original jurisdiction decides the evidence is not new or not relevant. Providing an incomplete supplemental claim will result in no further assistance from VA until the claim is complete.

With existing rules, a "Complete Application" is an application that will move through for a decision. If the claimant fails to provide information required for a complete application, and if one year has elapsed since the initial filing or the Intent to File, and the application still remains incomplete, the effective date will be lost. A new application must be filed.

§ 3.1 Definitions.
(p) Claim means a written or electronic communication requesting a determination of entitlement or evidencing a belief in entitlement, to a specific benefit under the laws administered by the Department of Veterans Affairs submitted on an application form

prescribed by the Secretary. (See scope of claim, § 3.155(d)(2); complete claim, § 3.160(a); issues within a claim, § 3.151(c)).

> (1) Initial claim. An initial claim is any complete claim, other than a supplemental claim, for a benefit on a form prescribed by the Secretary. The first initial claim for one or more benefits received by VA is further defined as an original claim. (See original claim, § 3.160(b)). Initial claims include:
>> (i) A new claim requesting service connection for a disability or grant of a new benefit, and
>> (ii) A claim for increase in a disability evaluation rating or rate of a benefit paid based on a change or worsening in condition or circumstance since the last decision issued by VA for the benefit.

> (2) Supplemental claim. A supplemental claim is any complete claim for a VA benefit on an application form prescribed by the Secretary where an initial or supplemental claim for the same or similar benefit on the same or similar basis was previously decided. (See supplemental claim; § 3.2501.)

Under the new rules, a "supplemental claim" is any claim for benefits under laws administered by the Secretary filed by a claimant who had previously filed a claim for the same or similar benefits on the same or similar basis. A supplemental claim pertains to an initial claim that needs to be reevaluated, re-adjudicated or otherwise looked at again. A supplemental claim can also be filed after a finally adjudicated decision, which is a decision made where one year has elapsed and no action has been taken on a previous decision. A claim for secondary disability or for a request for increase is a new claim for benefits and is not a supplemental claim.

Issues within a Claim

38 CFR § 3.151(c) defines an issue for this purpose as an adjudication of a specific entitlement. For example, with respect to service-connected Disability Compensation, an issue would be entitlement to Compensation for a particular disability (and any ancillary benefits). This definition of "issue" is consistent with the definition of issue in § 20.1401(a), as interpreted by the U.S. Court of Appeals for Veterans Claims. See Hillyard v. Shinseki, 24 Vet. App. at 353 (equating the term issue with a "claim" and "not a theory or an element of a claim," citing Disabled American Veterans, 234 F.3d at 693).

The option to pursue any concurrent issues with one or more of the 3 different review lanes would not extend to specific components of the same entitlement claim. Allowing a claim to be splintered into several pieces for review, each potentially subject to different evidentiary rules and timelines, would render the new review system unworkable and pose a risk of self-contradictory decision-making by VA. Allowing this would defeat Congressional intent to streamline the review process and reduce processing times.

A simple hypothetical serves to illustrate this intent. Suppose a claimant seeks Disability Compensation for a knee disability, and for a mental disorder. The claimant must receive an initial decision on both issues before the claimant can elect to place the knee issue and the mental disorder issue in separate lanes under the new appeals system for further review.

Or, the claimant may be satisfied with the decision on the knee but not with the decision on the mental disorder and can pursue a review of the mental disorder as a separate issue. The claimant had to wait for a decision on both issues so as not to splinter up the claim initially into different issues. After the decision, the claimant may not challenge the effective date assigned for the knee in one lane, and simultaneously challenge the assigned degree of disability for the knee in another lane. These effective dates were determined by the original decision.

In addition, VA includes a new paragraph, § 3.151(d), providing that the evidentiary record for a claim closes upon issuance of notice of a decision on the claim.

§ 3.151(c) Issues within a claim.
(1) To the extent that a complete claim application encompasses a request for more than one determination of entitlement, each specific entitlement will be adjudicated and is considered a separate issue for purposes of the review options prescribed in § 3.2500. A single decision by an agency of original jurisdiction may adjudicate multiple issues in this respect, whether expressly claimed or determined by VA to be reasonably within the scope of the application as prescribed in § 3.155(d)(2). VA will issue a decision that addresses each such identified issue within a claim. Upon receipt of notice of a decision, a claimant may elect any of the applicable review options prescribed in § 3.2500 for each issue adjudicated.

(2) With respect to service-connected Disability Compensation, an issue for purposes of paragraph (c)(1) of this section is defined as entitlement to Compensation for a particular disability. For example, if a decision adjudicates service-connected Disability Compensation for both a knee condition and an ankle condition, Compensation for each condition is a separate entitlement or issue for which a different review option may be elected. However, different review options may not be selected for specific components of the knee disability claim, such as ancillary benefits, whether a knee injury occurred in service, or whether a current knee condition resulted from a service-connected injury or condition.

(d) Evidentiary record. The evidentiary record before the agency of original jurisdiction for an initial or supplemental claim includes all evidence received by VA before VA issues notice of a decision on the claim. Once the agency of original jurisdiction issues notice of a decision on a claim, the evidentiary record closes as described in § 3.103(c)(2) and VA no longer has a duty to assist in gathering evidence under § 3.159. (See § 3.155(b), submission of evidence).

Decision Notice
The new rules do away with the various terminologies used to describe decisions issued in Section 5103 Notices as discussed in Chapter 4. All such decisions are now called either "Notice of Decision" or "Decision Notice" in compliance with the regulation listed below that requires more detailed notification. The idea behind this more detailed notification is to allow the claimant to receive assistance from VA in developing new evidence or understanding why the evidence did not result in a favorable decision.

VA will still use the old terminology of "Finally Adjudicated Decision" or "Final Decision" to refer to decisions that have become final because the one year period for responding to any adverse action has expired. A final decision requires reapplication as a supplemental claim unless a claim for a new disability is filed. Also under the old rules, one could "reopen" a claim after a final decision with new and material evidence. This did not require a new application but did result in loss of the original effective date. The concept of reopening a claim has been eliminated under the new rules and replaced by the filing of a supplemental claim. Also, new and material evidence under the old rules could be submitted at any time requiring VA to consider that evidence and reconsider the original decision and still maintain the effective date as long as the new and material evidence was filed at least one year from the latest adverse decision. This is no longer the case.

The rules for revising final decisions due to clear and unmistakable error have also been changed. These new rules are found in the revised section – *§ 3.105 Revision of decisions.*

§ 3.103 (f) Notification of decisions.

The claimant or beneficiary and his or her representative will be notified in writing of decisions affecting the payment of benefits or granting of relief. Written notification must include in the notice letter or enclosures or a combination thereof, all of the following elements:

(1) Identification of the issues adjudicated;

(2) A summary of the evidence considered;

(3) A summary of the laws and regulations applicable to the claim;

(4) A listing of any findings made by the adjudicator that are favorable to the claimant under § 3.104(c);

(5) For denied claims, identification of the element(s) required to grant the claim(s) that were not met;

(6) If applicable, identification of the criteria required to grant service Start Printed Page 39843connection or the next higher-level of Compensation;

(7) An explanation of how to obtain or access evidence used in making the decision; and

(8) A summary of the applicable review options under § 3.2500 available for the claimant to seek further review of the decision.

Closing the Evidentiary Record after a Decision

From VA's perspective, the closing of the evidentiary record after a decision is one of the important features of the Appeals Modernization Act, and one of its most valuable provisions. This new rule allows processing of claims and appeals more efficiently. Under the old rules, requiring VA to notify claimants each time evidence was submitted during the decision process or list or summarize such evidence individually in review decisions was time-consuming.

Providing these notices required VA personnel to review and identify or summarize late-flowing evidence when preparing the decision notice. Such procedures required "by hand" review and processing of evidence by VBA adjudicators, similar to the review required for simply considering the evidence for decisional purposes. Previously, Veteran Service Representatives used up limited adjudicative resources reading and processing documents that were not part of the record and eventually would not be the basis for a decision.

Allowing this previous process under the new rules would dilute much of the administrative value of having a closed record following the initial decision.

§ 3.103 Procedural due process and other rights.

(b) * * *

(1) General. Claimants and their representatives are entitled to notice of any decision made by VA affecting the payment of benefits or the granting of relief. Such notice will clearly set forth the elements described under paragraph (f) of this section, the right to a hearing on any issue involved in the claim as provided in paragraph (d) of this section, the right of representation, and the right, as well as the necessary procedures and time limits to initiate a higher-level review, supplemental claim, or appeal to the Board of Veterans' Appeals.

* * * * *

(c) Submission of evidence—

(1) General rule. VA will include in the record, any evidence whether documentary, testimonial, or in other form, submitted by the claimant in support of a pending claim and any issue, contention, or argument a claimant may offer with respect to a claim, except as prescribed in paragraph (c)(2) of this section and § 3.2601(f).

(2) Treatment of evidence received after notice of a decision. The evidentiary record for a claim before the agency of original jurisdiction closes when VA issues notice of a decision on the claim. The agency of original jurisdiction will not consider, or take any other action on evidence that is submitted by a claimant, associated with the claims file, or constructively received by VA as described in paragraph (c)(2)(iii) of this section, after notice of decision on a claim, and such evidence will not be considered part of the record at the time of any decision by the agency of original jurisdiction, except as described in § 3.156(c) and under the following circumstances:

> (i) Receipt of a complete claim. The agency of original jurisdiction subsequently receives a complete application for a supplemental claim or initial claim; or
>
> (ii) Board and higher-level review returns. A claim is pending readjudication after identification of a duty to assist error (which includes an error resulting from constructive receipt of evidence prior to the notice of decision), during a higher-level review or appeal to the Board of Veterans' Appeals. Those events reopen the record and any evidence previously submitted to the agency of original jurisdiction or associated with the Start Printed Page 167claims file while the record was closed will become part of the evidentiary record to be considered upon readjudication.
>
> (iii) Constructive receipt of VA treatment records. Records within the actual custody of the Veterans Health Administration are deemed constructively received by the Veterans Benefits Administration at the time when the Veterans Benefits Administration had knowledge of the existence of said records through information furnished by the claimant sufficient to locate those records (see 38 U.S.C. 5103A(c)).

Understanding the Effective Date

VA has long maintained the practice of allowing claimants to maintain effective dates through the submission of new evidence. As a result of this practice, the effective date of an original claim could be retained as long as new evidence was submitted and resulted in a new decision within one year of the previous decision. In other words, as long as new evidence could be submitted and accepted for readjudication, resulting in a new decision, the claim could be kept alive long after the one year allowance for filing an appeal after the initial decision was made.

The new system provides the same rights, as claimants are entitled to a readjudication based on new and relevant evidence submitted within the one-year appeal period, while their effective date is protected. Rather than providing for an automatic readjudication, however, claimants must submit the new evidence in connection with a choice of review options. The claimant may file either a supplemental claim pursuant to § 3.2501 or a Notice of Disagreement with the Board indicating selection of a docket allowing for the submission of additional evidence.

If either filing is completed within the one-year period under the new rules on new evidence, the original effective date can be retained as long as the new evidence is indeed "new and relevant" and results in a new decision. If the Regional Office determines that the evidence is not new and relevant, readjudication will not happen and the original effective date will be determined by the most recent previous decision. If the one-year period runs out from the most recent previous decision, then that decision becomes a final decision and the effective date is lost. A notice of reaffirmation of a previous decision is not a new decision.

Supplemental Claim As a Means to Keep the Claim Alive

When a "decision notice" is issued the claimant can keep his or her application alive by submitting new and relevant evidence and triggering a reconsideration of the decision. This is done through submitting a supplemental claim. Likewise, an initial ruling from the Board of Veterans Appeals also allows the claimant to go back to the Regional Office, submit a supplemental claim with new and relevant evidence and receive a new adjudication decision. Board rulings are now no longer final as long as there is new and relevant evidence. As long as the claimant can uncover new and relevant evidence that is proven to be "new and relevant," the claimant could keep his or her application alive forever in the

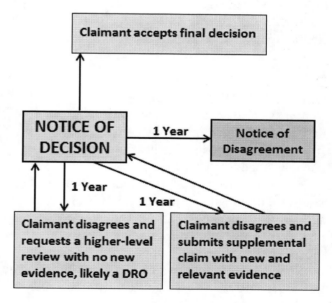

Regional Office or and never have to go to an appeal. Or even go to an appeal receive a ruling and then find new and relevant evidence and come back and receive reconsideration of the claim from the Regional Office.

The "Intent to File" provisions do not apply to supplemental claims. You cannot submit an Intent to File in anticipation of filing a supplemental claim. This is because the new rules provide that a claimant can maintain the effective date of a potential benefits award by submitting a request for review under any of the three new lanes within one year of the date of the decision denying benefits. Consistent with this requirement, the Intent to File provisions would not apply to supplemental claims as this provision would allow for the submission of a supplemental claim beyond the one-year period provided by statute for protection of effective dates. In other words, if a supplemental claim were submitted after the 1 year protection period from a notice of decision, the supplemental claim would be treated as an initial claim and the original effective date would be lost.

If the effective date is lost in the process of adjudicating a claim, the claimant can file a new application with the a new effective date. This would NOT be done as an initial application with a new 21-526 EZ as the initial claim is retained in VBMS. The new filing would be done as a supplemental claim.

Higher-Level Review

Under 38 U.S.C. 5104B, a claimant in the new system may request a higher-level review of a decision on a claim by the agency of original jurisdiction. This review is allowable during the one year period to seek review following issuance of the notice of decision. The higher-level review option gives claimants a second look at their claims, but that review is based solely on the same evidence that was before the initial adjudicator.

Under the old rules you could request a Regional Office hearing at any time with new evidence and with a new adjudicator. If it was determined at this hearing that the new evidence was probative, you would receive a new decision. In addition under the old rules, when you filed a Notice of Disagreement you were optionally entitled to a Decision Review Officer (DRO) hearing with the opportunity to submit new evidence. This hearing required a complete review of your record and required a new decision whether new evidence was submitted or not. Decision Review Officers are the most experienced adjudicators in any Regional Office. Under the old rules, their expertise could be tapped into in order to ensure a more informed and fairer decision on any claim. Under the new rules DRO's play a significantly lesser role in reviewing challenges to a decision. You can no longer request a DRO review.

Under the new rules, the Higher-Level Review does not allow for submitting any new evidence. The Higher-Level Review does require a new decision. Even though new evidence is not allowed, the review does allow for submitting arguments as to why the previous decision was not properly adjudicated and this could include identifying an improper theory of service connection or the failure to examine certain evidence.

This Higher-Level Review does allow for a phone conversation with the higher-level adjudicator. We would assume that everyone would take advantage of scheduling this phone conversation to present any arguments relating to the previous decision. To not request the phone interview would be a significant mistake. The intent is for the Higher-Level Review to use an adjudicator who has more experience and can render a more reasoned, thorough and reliable decision. There is no requirementfor the Higher-Level Review to be conducted by a DRO which was an option under the old rules.

VA has established 3 locations where these reviews will be conducted. They are called Decision Review Operations Centers or DROCs. One of them is in the Seattle Regional Office and the other one is in the St. Petersburg Regional Office and the third is Appeals Resource Center in the Washington DC Regional Office. For 2019, in Seattle they will have a staff of 227 employees for St. Petersburg 485 employees and four Washington DC 183 employees. Each DROC is staffed with decision review officers DRO's, journey-level and non-journey-level rating Veterans Service Representatives, Veterans Service Representatives, and claims assistants.

Certain restricted claims such as those from VA employees or accredited representatives, are currently assigned to the Milwaukee regional office and any higher-level reviews for those particular claims will be retained in the Milwaukee regional office and not sent out to one of the higher-level review Regional Offices.

To comply with the statutory requirement of a closed evidentiary record, claimants or representatives are not allowed to supplement the evidentiary record during the informal conference through the submission of new evidence or introduction of facts not present at the time of the prior decision. These efforts to speak with a claimant or his or her representative, when requested, will be done telephonically. This is the method to honor all requests for informal conferences unless determined not feasible in an individual case, such as when the Regional Office, after reasonable efforts, is unable to make contact with the claimant or his or her representative.

Under 38 U.S.C. 5103A(f), if the higher-level adjudicator discovers a duty to assist error, the claim returns to the original adjudication activity for correction unless the higher-level adjudicator determines that it would be appropriate to grant the maximum benefit for the claim. In accordance with 38 U.S.C. 5109B, Regulations have been changed requiring expedited processing to correct these types of errors and to define "maximum benefit" for Disability Compensation as the maximum scheduler evaluation for the issue, and for other types of benefits, the granting of the benefit sought.

Because the filing date of a request for higher-level review is relevant to maintaining the effective date of any award, provisions for determining the filing date that are similar to the provisions currently in § 3.155 will apply to applications for benefits.

VA has added § 3.2502 to 38 CFR Part 3, subpart D, to implement the requirement in new 38 U.S.C. 5109B for expedited processing of claims returned from a higher-level adjudicator and remands from the Board. Upon receipt of a returned claim or remand by the Board, the agency of original jurisdiction will take immediate action to expedite readjudication of the claim in accordance with new 38 U.S.C. 5109B. The agency of original jurisdiction will retain jurisdiction of the claim.

In readjudicating the claim, the rating activity will correct all identified duty to assist errors, complete a new decision and issue notice to the claimant and or his or her legal representative in accordance with § 3.103(f). For issues readjudicated, the effective date of an evaluation and award of Pension, Compensation, or DIC will be determined in accordance with the date of receipt of the initial claim as prescribed under § 3.2500(g).

Board of Veterans Appeals
The huge advantage under the new system is that the formal preparation of an appeal for certification to the Board of Appeals has been eliminated. No more requirement for a Statement of the Case or a Supplemental Statement of the Case or a certification through Form 9. The appeal will simply go directly to the Board with three different docket options.

Here are the three different docket options.

1. appeals where the claimant has requested a hearing,

2. appeals with no request for a hearing but where the claimant elects to submit other forms of evidence, and

3. appeals where the claimant requests Board review on the same evidence that was before the agency of original jurisdiction.

These separate dockets will allow the Board to more efficiently and effectively manage distinctly different types of work. As a result of the new docket lane options, claimants will have increased choice for resolving disagreements with a VA decision on a claim. Also, the docket with the review of the original evidence with no hearing and no new evidence will be an expedited appeal and could result in a decision more quickly than with the other options. VA promises that this expedited option will take no longer than a year for a decision.

Under the old rules, Board decisions were final, pending an appeal to the CAVC, but under the new rules, Board decisions, the CAVC and even the Circuit Court can be challenged with a supplemental claim back to the office of original jurisdiction.

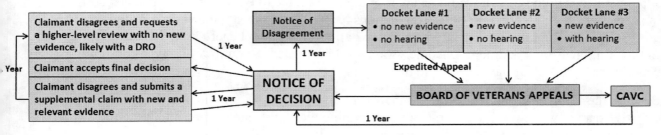

New and Relevant Evidence
As noted in the House of Representatives Committee Report (H. Rept.115-135, May 19, 2017, page 3), Congress's intent "behind the change from material to relevant evidence is is to lower the current burden" to have a claim readjudicated based on new evidence. Public Law 115-55 defines "relevant evidence" under 38 U.S.C. 101(35) as "evidence that tends to prove or disprove

a matter in issue." This new standard purportedly reduces a claimant's threshold in identifying or submitting evidence as part of a supplemental claim. Title 38 CFR § 3.156(d), regarding supplemental claims, includes a reference to new § 3.2501 which provides further details regarding the filing and adjudication of supplemental claims and the "new and relevant" evidence standard.

Claims to reopen that were filed, but not initially adjudicated, prior to the effective date of the new rules will be adjudicated under the more favorable "new and relevant" standard applicable to supplemental claims. In addition, a supplemental claim subject to the more favorable standard may be filed after the effective date of the modernized review system, even with respect to legacy claims finally adjudicated prior to the effective date of the new system.

Under the new framework, the agency of original jurisdiction will take action on new evidence that is received with an application for a supplemental claim, or received or obtained prior to issuance of a decision on the supplemental claim. As indicated in § 3.103, the record closes upon issuance of a notice of decision on the claim, subject to reopening upon certain later events. This limits the applicability of the current rule under paragraph (b), allowing for the submission of new and material evidence during the appeal period, to pending legacy claims that are not subject to the modernized review system.

The new lesser burden of using relevant evidence instead of material evidence under the old rules could have an impact if we can grasp an understanding of how evidence that is disallowed as not material under the old rules may have affected that claim while evidence allowed as relevant may have affected the same claim.

One of the questions that will eventually come up, is given certain evidence, would that same evidence have NOT been considered material under the old rules but now be considered relevant under the new rules? In the M21-1 are examples of material evidence and examples of evidence that is not material. Here are those examples of material evidence

- VA allows a new opinion for Nexus as material, or
- a medical report showing the current disability where service connection was denied because the disability did not exist, or
- a denial for service connection as no back injury was incurred in service but the veteran submits a buddy statement with the buddy certifying he witnessed the veteran injured his back.
- A photograph showing evidence of the injury in service

Here are the examples where the evidence is not new or material

- a record photocopied from the claims folder that was considered in the previously denied claim
- a new medical nexus opinion incorporating an inaccurate history. See *Reonal v. Brown*, 5 Vet.App. 458 (1993) for more information.
- written testimony from an eyewitness that is substantially identical to a statement already on file

- a layperson's assertion about the cause (but not the onset) of a disability, or
- medical evidence that reveals the existence of a disability when previous evidence already revealed that the disability existed.

Unfortunately, these examples pertain more to the test for new evidence as opposed to being material to the claim with the exception of the layperson's statement. This exception might be considered relevant where VA would not have considered it material.

If new evidence is relevant to the case, then VA must accept a supplemental claim with this new evidence and execute its duty to assist to develop for this new evidence. It should be noted however that just because the new relevant evidence forces the Regional Office to reconsider a previous notice of decision by re-examining the claim, it does not mean that new and relevant evidence would have any effect on a new decision.

Don't confuse submission of new and relevant evidence as necessarily affecting the outcome of a previous decision. Under the rules, the new and relevant evidence pertains only to reconsideration of that decision by accepting a supplemental claim with that evidence and developing under duty to assist. If the new evidence does not change the decision then the original decision remains. Additionally, if the new evidence were not relevant, VA would reject the supplemental claim and not consider the new evidence at all.

§ 3.156 New evidence
New evidence means evidence not previously submitted to agency adjudicators.

(a) New and material evidence. (Under the old rules for legacy claims)
For claims to reopen decided prior to the effective date provided in § 19.2(a), the following standards apply. A claimant may reopen a finally adjudicated legacy claim by submitting new and material evidence. Material evidence means existing evidence that, by itself or when considered with previous evidence of record, relates to an unestablished fact necessary to substantiate the claim. New and material evidence can be neither cumulative nor redundant of the evidence of record at the time of the last prior final denial of the claim sought to be reopened, and must raise a reasonable possibility of substantiating the claim. (Authority: 38 U.S.C. 501, 5103A(h), 5108)

(d) New and relevant evidence. (Under the new rules)
On or after the effective date provided in § 19.2(a), a claimant may file a supplemental claim as prescribed in § 3.2501. If new and relevant evidence is presented or secured with respect to the supplemental claim, the agency of original jurisdiction will readjudicate the claim taking into consideration all of the evidence of record.

One Final Note on the Test for Relevancy
We provide a decision table below from a previous version of Adjudication Manual M21-1. It is interesting to note that Step #2 incorporates a test for materiality and Step #3 incorporates a test for relevancy. When the adjudication manual is revised due to the new rules, will VA simply

eliminate Step #2? If this is the case, then the apparent lesser standard for relevant evidence versus material evidence may simply be a moot point.

Follow the steps in the table below when evaluating evidence.

Step	Action
1	Determine what facts are required and what standard of proof applies based on the criteria for entitlement to the specific benefit sought and the procedural issue (original, new, increase, reopen, presumption, proposed adverse action, and stabilization).
2	Discount any admitted evidence that is not *material* to (that does not relate to) the components of the entitlement standard or procedural issue at issue in the case.
3	Determine the probative value of evidence that bears on the entitlement standard or procedural issue. This means deciding to which extent those items of evidence are *relevant* in tending to make the matter more probable or less probable. Discuss and apply VA guidance (including court precedents) on competency to determine whether the evidence from a particular source can establish a particular fact that requires the application of special expertise or first-hand knowledge of facts based on recollection or perception. *Evidence from a source not having the requisite competency to offer a particular type of evidence has no probative value.* Discuss and apply VA guidance on credibility where there is a reasonable factual basis (for example, demonstrable bias or inconsistency) for questioning believability. *Evidence that is not believable does not have probative value.*
4	Resolve questions of relative weight or persuasiveness when there are various items of evidence that have been determined to have probative value in order to find facts (to determine what facts the evidence proves). *Note*: It is important to explain why certain evidence was accepted as more probative than other evidence, especially when giving less value to evidence tending to support the benefit sought by the claimant/beneficiary.
5	Apply the found facts to draw corresponding conclusions of law necessary to support the decision outcome for the benefit sought and procedural issue. Clearly explain in the rating decision why the evidence is found to be persuasive or unpersuasive.

Regional Office Hearing
Previous rules allowed the right to a hearing at any time during the adjudication process. The new rules still allow hearings but restrict the hearing to introducing new evidence prior to a notice of decision on an initial or supplemental claim.

§ 3.103 (d) The right to a hearing.
(1) Upon request, a claimant is entitled to a hearing on any issue involved in a claim within the purview of part 3 of this chapter before VA issues notice of a decision on an initial or supplemental claim. A hearing is not available in connection with a request for higher level review under § 3.2601. VA will provide the place of hearing in the VA field office having original jurisdiction over the claim, or at the VA office nearest the claimant's home having adjudicative functions, or videoconference capabilities, or, subject to available resources and solely at the

427

option of VA, at any other VA facility or federal building at which suitable hearing facilities are available. VA will provide one or more employees who have original determinative authority of such issues to conduct the hearing and be responsible for establishment and preservation of the hearing record. Upon request, a claimant is entitled to a hearing in connection with proposed adverse actions before one or more VA employees having original determinative authority who did not participate in the proposed action. All expenses incurred by the claimant in connection with the hearing are the responsibility of the claimant.

(2) <u>The purpose of a hearing is to permit the claimant to introduce into the record, in person, any available evidence which he or she considers relevant and any arguments or contentions with respect to the facts and applicable law which he or she may consider pertinent. All testimony will be under oath or affirmation.</u> The claimant is entitled to produce witnesses, but the claimant and witnesses must be present. The agency of original jurisdiction will not normally schedule a hearing for the sole purpose of receiving argument from a representative. It is the responsibility of the VA employees conducting the hearings to explain fully the issues and suggest the submission of evidence which the claimant may have overlooked and which would be of advantage to the claimant's position. To assure clarity and completeness of the hearing record, questions which are directed to the claimant and to witnesses are to be framed to explore fully the basis for claimed entitlement rather than with an intent to refute evidence or to discredit testimony.

New or Revised Regulations Pertaining to the Modernized Review System

Review of Decisions, Concurrent Multiple Review Lanes and Effective Dates
In the legacy appeals process, claimants who were dissatisfied with the initial decision on their claim were given only one avenue to seek review of that decision. Public Law 115-55 created a new claims and appeals process with several different review options for pursuing VA benefits. Congress added 38 U.S.C. 5104C to provide claimants with streamlined choices within the agency of original jurisdiction and through an appeal to the Board.

VA has added § 3.2500 to part 3, subpart D, to implement the new review options and set forth the rules that apply to those options under new 38 U.S.C. 5104C. In line with the statutory requirements, a claimant can file for one of the three review options upon receipt of a decision by the agency of original jurisdiction on an initial claim. Under proposed § 3.2500(b), a claimant would be able to elect a different review option for each different issue adjudicated in the decision. The term "issue" is defined in § 3.151(c) as a distinct determination of entitlement to a benefit, such as a determination of entitlement to service-connected Disability Compensation for a particular disability. We discussed how issues are treated in a previous section

A claimant or the claimant's duly appointed representative may withdraw a request for higher-level review or a supplemental claim at any time prior to the Regional Office issuing notice of decision. If the withdrawal takes place within the one year period following notice of the decision being reviewed, a claimant may timely elect another review option to continuously pursue the claim and preserve potential entitlement to benefits effective as of the date of the initial claim.

Under new 38 U.S.C. 5104C, after receiving notice of a decision on an issue, claimants generally have up to one year to submit new and relevant evidence with a supplemental claim, request a higher-level review, or file an appeal to the Board to preserve the effective date associated with their initial claim. If a claimant remains dissatisfied with the decision on review, depending on the type of review requested, he or she would still have the option to file another review request.

The review options available to a claimant after a decision on each type of review are set forth in § 3.2500(c). Paragraph (g) contains effective date protections for continuously pursued claims and the effective date rule for supplemental claims filed more than one year after notice of a decision (i.e., where the underlying claim is finally adjudicated). For example, a claimant who receives an unfavorable decision on a higher-level review request may submit a supplemental claim with new and relevant evidence or appeal to the Board within one year of the decision notice date to protect the effective date.

If, following a further denial, the claimant elects to file a supplemental claim with new and relevant evidence within one year of the decision notice date and VA grants the benefit sought, VA will consider this to be a continuously pursued claim **and continue to base the effective date of an award on the filing date of the initial claim.**

Changes to Title 38 CFR Part 3

The appeals modernization act resulted in numerous changes to Title 38 CFR Part 3. We have discussed the more important of those changes in the section previous to this one. The other major change to Part 3 is a revision of the existing *§3.2600 Review of benefit claims decisions* and the addition of the instructions for the new rules. The existing section 3.2600 has been retained for legacy claims only. New sections based on the new rules effective February 2019 have been added. Here are the pertinent sections.

- § 3.2400 Applicability of modernized review system.
- § 3.2500 Review of decisions.
- § 3.2501 Supplemental claims.
- § 3.2502   Return by higher-level adjudicator or remand by the Board of Veterans' Appeals.
- § 3.2600 Legacy review of benefit claims decisions
- § 3.2601 Higher-level review.

The rules covered here have been well written and well laid out and provide a blueprint for the new Modernized Review System. You will be able to go to these new sections in Part 3 and follow all of the requirements for using the new system. We have provided these rules for you at the in the section after this one.
.

Changes to Title 38 CFR Part 14

The new act also made changes to 38 CFR Part 14 which pertains to representation for benefits. Changes include the following.

- Allowing a denial for accreditation to be appealed directly to the Board of Veterans Appeals
- Gifts from a VA claimant to a VA accredited individual are not permitted in any situation where a fee could also not be charged
- Clarifying administrative handling of susPension or removal of accreditation
- <u>Allowing accredited agents and accredited attorneys to charge a fee for assistance with claims after VA's issuance of notice of an initial decision on a claim</u>
- Clarifying that an initial decision on a claim includes a decision adjudicating a supplemental claim unless the claimant is continuously pursuing the claim by choosing any of the other three procedural options for review (This was discussed previously that once a decision has been made, a claim can be broken up into separate review lanes for each issue involved.)
- Clarifying issues on contested fees

The change to allow for charging of fees at an earlier stage of the claims process is a HUGE opportunity for accredited agents and accredited attorneys. We discuss the charging of fees in general, including this new change, in the "Appendix" that comes with the Claim Support Disc.

Changes to Title 38 CFR Parts 19 and 20

VA has decided to retain title 38 CFR Part 19 to preserve and consolidate regulations concerning legacy appeals. Part 19 has been revised as needed and is now only applicable to legacy appeals and this section has no authority over the new review process. The new review system is now covered by the 2000 series of sections found in 38 CFR Part 3 which can be found.

VA has restructured subparts A and B of Part 20 by adding applicable procedures from Part 19 that apply to the new process and revising the existing rules in Part 20 to apply to the new review system. Subparts C through O of Part 20 have also been modified to accommodate the new rules. In other words, Part 19 will be used for existing legacy appeals and Part 20 will incorporate all of the new changes for the Modernized Review System.

Chapter 9
Loan Guaranty, Housing and Education Benefits

IN THIS CHAPTER:

- Loan Guaranty Program; pg. 431
- Housing Support for Disabled Veterans; pg. 435
- Education Benefits; pg. 437

The information in this chapter was taken directly from the VA website at
www.VA.gov

Loan Guaranty Program

VA helps service members, veterans, and eligible surviving spouses become homeowners. As part of our mission to serve you, we provide a home loan Guaranty benefit and other housing-related programs to help you buy, build, repair, retain, or adapt a home for your own personal occupancy. VA Home Loans are provided by private lenders, such as banks and mortgage companies. VA Guarantys a portion of the loan, enabling the lender to provide you with more favorable terms.

Purchase Loans and Cash out Refinance Loans
A Purchase Loan helps you purchase a home at a competitive interest rate often without requiring a down payment or private mortgage insurance. With a Purchase Loan, VA can help you purchase a home at a competitive interest rate, and if you have found it difficult to find other financing.

VA's Cash-Out Refinance Loan is for homeowners who want to take cash out of your home equity to take care of concerns like paying off debt, funding school, or making home improvements. The Cash-Out Refinance Loan can also be used to refinance a non-VA loan into a VA loan. VA will Guaranty loans up to 100% of the value of your home.

Interest Rate Reduction Refinance Loan (IRRRL)
The VA Interest Rate Reduction Refinance Loan (IRRRL) lowers your interest rate by refinancing your existing VA home loan. By obtaining a lower interest rate, your monthly mortgage payment should decrease. You can also refinance an adjustable rate mortgage (ARM) into a fixed rate mortgage.

IRRRL Facts
- No appraisal or credit underwriting package is required when applying for an IRRRL.
- An IRRRL may be done with "no money out of pocket" by including all costs in the new loan or by making the new loan at an interest rate high enough to enable the lender to pay the costs.
- When refinancing from an existing VA ARM loan to a fixed rate loan, the interest rate may increase.
- No lender is required to give you an IRRRL, however, any VA lender of your choosing may process your application for an IRRRL.
- Veterans are strongly urged to contact several lenders because terms may vary.
- You may NOT receive any cash from the loan proceeds.

Eligibility
An IRRRL can only be made to refinance a property on which you have already used your VA loan eligibility. It must be a VA to VA refinance, and it will reuse your original entitlement.

Additionally:
- A Certificate of Eligibility (COE) is not required. If you have your Certificate of Eligibility, take it to the lender to show the prior use of your entitlement.
- No loan other than the existing VA loan may be paid from the proceeds of an IRRRL. If you have a second mortgage, the holder must agree to subordinate that lien so that your new VA loan will be a first mortgage.
- You may have used your entitlement by obtaining a VA loan when you bought your house, or by substituting your eligibility for that of the seller, if you assumed the loan.
- The occupancy requirement for an IRRRL is different from other VA loans. For an IRRRL you need only certify that you previously occupied the home.

Application Process
A new Certificate of Eligibility (COE) is not required. You may take your Certificate of Eligibility to show the prior use of your entitlement or your lender may use our e-mail confirmation procedure in lieu of a certificate of eligibility.
Loan Limits

VA does not set a cap on how much you can borrow to finance your home. However, there are limits on the amount of liability VA can assume, which usually affects the amount of money an institution will lend you. The loan limits are the amount a qualified Veteran with full entitlement may be able to borrow without making a down payment. These loan limits vary by county, since the value of a house depends in part on its location.

The basic entitlement available to each eligible Veteran is $36,000. Lenders will generally loan up to four times a Veteran's available entitlement without a down payment, provided the Veteran is income and credit qualified and the property appraises for the asking price.

VA Funding Fee
Generally, all Veterans using the VA Home Loan Guaranty benefit must pay a funding fee. This reduces the loan's cost to taxpayers considering that a VA loan requires no down payment and

has no monthly mortgage insurance. The funding fee is a percentage of the loan amount which varies based on the type of loan and your military category, if you are a first-time or subsequent loan user, and whether you make a down payment. You have the option to finance the VA funding fee or pay it in cash, but the funding fee must be paid at closing time. You do not have to pay the fee if you are a:

- Veteran receiving VA Compensation for a service-connected disability, OR
- Veteran who would be entitled to receive Compensation for a service-connected disability if you did not receive retirement or active duty pay, OR
- Surviving spouse of a Veteran who died in service or from a service-connected disability.

The funding fee for second time users who do not make a down payment is slightly higher. Also, National Guard and Reserve Veterans pay a slightly higher funding fee percentage. See Loan Fees for more information about loan costs. Some lenders offer IRRRLs as an opportunity to reduce the term of your loan from 30 years to 15 years. While this can save you money in interest over the life of the loan, you may see a very large increase in your monthly payment if the reduction in the interest rate is not at least one percent (two percent is better). Beware: It could be a bigger increase than you can afford.

Native American Direct Loan (NADL) Program
Since 1992, the Native American Veteran Direct Loan (NADL) program has provided eligible Native American Veterans and their spouses the opportunity to use their Department of Veterans Affairs (VA) home loan Guaranty benefit on Federal trust land.

What is a NADL?
VA provides direct home loans to eligible Native American Veterans to finance the purchase, construction, or improvement of homes on Federal Trust Land, or to refinance a prior NADL to reduce the interest rate.

Why Use the NADL Program?
- The lender is the Department of Veterans Affairs
- Dedicated VA staff to assist you
- No down payment
- Easy to qualify
- No Private Mortgage Insurance cost
- 4.25% interest rate. Interest rates are subject to change due to market fluctuations. VA evaluates these market trends and determines if interest rate reductions or increases are warranted.
- Low closing costs
- $424,100 loan maximum limit in most areas; some high-cost counties have higher loan limits
- Fixed-rate 30-year mortgage
- Re-usable benefit

How to Use the NADL Program

To obtain a NADL, the law requires that the tribal government must have signed a Memorandum of Understanding (MOU) with the Secretary of Veterans Affairs. The MOU spells out the conditions under which the program will operate on its trust lands.

Am I Eligible to Use the NADL Program?

- You must have a valid Certificate of Eligibility to be eligible for the VA home loan benefit and have available entitlement. Please visit this page for information on how to get a Certificate of Eligibility.
- The loan must be to purchase, construct, or improve a home on Federally-recognized trust, allotted lands, Alaska Native corporations and Pacific Island territories.
- You must occupy the property as your home.
- You must be a satisfactory credit risk.
- Your income and that of your spouses, if any, must be shown to be stable and sufficient to meet the mortgage payments, cover the other costs of owning a home, take care of other obligations and expenses, and have enough left over for family support.

Housing Support for Disabled Veterans

What Is a Specially Adapted Housing (SAH) Grant?
The SAH grant is designed to help disabled Veterans by providing a barrier-free living environment, such as a wheelchair accessible home, that affords Veterans a level of independent living they may not otherwise enjoy. Veterans and service members with specific service-connected disabilities may be entitled to a grant for the purpose of constructing or modifying a home to meet their adaptive needs, up to the **current maximum of $90,364 for 2020.**

SAH grants help Veterans with certain service-connected disabilities live independently in a barrier-free environment. SAH grants can be used in one of the following ways:

- Construct a specially adapted home on land to be acquired
- Build a home on land already owned if it is suitable for specially adapted housing
- Remodel an existing home if it can be made suitable for specially adapted housing
- Apply the grant against the unpaid principal mortgage balance of an adapted home already acquired without the assistance of a VA grant

Specially Adapted Housing (SAH) Grant Eligibility

Eligibility	Living Situation	Ownership	Number of Grants You Can Use
<ul><li>Loss of or loss of use of both legs, **OR**</li><li>Loss of or loss of use of both arms, **OR**</li><li>Blindness in both eyes having only light perception, plus loss of or loss of use of one leg, **OR**</li><li>The loss of or loss of use of one lower leg together with residuals of organic disease or injury, **OR**</li><li>The loss of or loss of use of one leg together with the loss of or loss of use of one arm, **OR**</li><li>Certain severe burns, **OR**</li><li>The loss, or loss of use of one or more lower extremeties due to service on or after September 11, 2001, which so affects the functions of balance or propulsion as to preclude ambulating without the aid of braces, crutches, canes, or a wheelchair</li></ul>	Permanent	Home is owned by an eligible individual	Maximum of 3 grants, up to the maximum dollar amount allowable

What Is a Special Housing Adaptation (SHA) Grant?

The SHA grant can be used to increase the mobility of eligible Veteran and service members throughout their residences. Veterans and service members with specific service-connected disabilities may be entitled to this type of grant, up to the **maximum of $18,074 for 2020.**

SHA grants help Veterans with certain service-connected disabilities adapt or purchase a home to accommodate the disability. You can use SHA grants in one of the following ways:

- Adapt an existing home the Veteran or a family member already owns in which the Veteran lives
- Adapt a home the Veteran or family member intends to purchase in which the Veteran will live
- Help a Veteran purchase a home already adapted in which the Veteran will live

Special Housing Adaptation (SHA) Grant Eligibility

Eligibility	Living Situation	Ownership	Number of Grants You Can Use
• Blindness in both eyes with 20/200 visual acuity or less, **OR** • Loss of or loss of use of both hands, **OR** • Certain severe burn injuries, **OR** • Certain severe respiratory injuries	Permanent	Home is owned by an eligible individual or family member	Maximum of 3 grants, up to the maximum dollar amount allowable

What Is a Temporary Residence Assistance (TRA) Grant?

A temporary grant may be available to SAH/SHA eligible Veterans and service members who are or will be temporarily residing in a home owned by a family member. **The maximum amount available to adapt a family member's home for the SAH grant is $39,669 and for the SHA grant is $7,083 for 2020.**

How to Apply

To apply for a grant, fill out and submit the *Application in Acquiring Specially Adapted Housing or Special Home Adaptation Grant* (VA Form 26-4555). You can access this form by:

- Applying online via www.ebenefits.va.gov
- Downloading the form at www.va.gov/vaforms and sending to a Regional Loan Center
- Calling VA toll free at 1-800-827-1000 to have a claim form mailed to you
- Visiting the nearest VA Regional Office. To find the VA Regional Office nearest you, go to our website or call VA toll-free at **1-800-827-1000**

Education Benefits

Post 9-11 GI Bill (Chapter 33)

Chapter 33 was enacted in the "Post 9-11 Veterans Educational Assistance Act of 2008" (P.L. 110-252), and greatly expanded education benefits on August 1, 2009. The Veterans Educational Assistance Improvement Act of 2010 (P.L. 111-377), signed into law on January 4, 2011, amended the Post 9-11 GI Bill by expanding eligibility for certain individuals, and modifying the amount of assistance and the types of approved programs. The Choice Act extended the Fry scholarship to spouses, and allows VA to disapprove courses of education in which the state charges Veterans or service members higher rates than that of in-state residents.

Eligibility to use chapter 33 benefits lasts for 15 years from last period of active duty service based on at least 90 consecutive days of active duty service. Students generally have up to 36 months of entitlement. Based on length of active duty service and training rate, students are entitled to a percentage of the following:

- Full cost of tuition and fees for all public school in-state students, or up to $21,084.89 (as of August 1, 2015) for those attending out-of-state, private or foreign schools;
- Monthly housing allowance equal to the basic allowance for housing payable to a military E-5 with dependents, in the same zip code as the school (paid to student);
- Yearly books and supplies stipend of up to $1,000 per year (paid to student);
- A one-time payment of $500 to certain individuals relocating from highly rural areas (paid to student);
- Payments for those pursuing a non-IHL program such as a non-college degree (NCD), on the job training (OJT), apprenticeship training, flight programs, or a correspondence program; and
- Other benefits such as the Yellow Ribbon program, kickers, and refund of chapter 30 payroll deductions will also be available to certain students.

The Yellow Ribbon G.I. Education Enhancement Program was enacted to potentially assist eligible Chapter 33 individuals with payment of their tuition and fees in instances where costs exceed the most expensive in-state undergraduate tuition at a public institution of higher education. To be eligible, the student must be: a Veteran receiving benefits at the 100 percent benefit rate payable; a transfer-of-entitlement-eligible dependent child; or a transfer-of-entitlement eligible spouse of a Veteran. The school of attendance must have accepted VA's invitation to participate in the program, state how much student tuition will be waived (up to 50 percent) and how many participants will be accepted into the program during the current academic year. VA will match the school's percentage (up to 50 percent) to reduce or eliminate out-of-pocket costs for eligible participants.

The Marine Gunnery Sergeant John David Fry Scholarship entitles children and spouses (with the enactment of the Veterans Choice Act) of those who die in the line of duty on or after September 11, 2001, to use Post-9-11 GI Bill benefits. Eligible children are entitled to 36 months of benefits at the 100 percent level and have 15 years to use the benefit beginning on their 18th birthday. These beneficiaries are not eligible for the Yellow Ribbon Program. In addition to the Fry Scholarships, certain members of the Armed Forces who are still on active duty may be eligible to transfer benefits to a spouse or dependent children based on DoD policy.

All-Volunteer Force Educational Assistance Program/Montgomery GI Bill (Chapter 30)

The predecessor of Chapter 33 program, and still in wide use, the Chapter 30 VA educational benefits may be used while the service member is on active duty or after the service member's separation from active duty with a fully honorable military discharge. Discharges "under honorable conditions" and "general" discharges do not establish eligibility. Eligibility generally expires 10 years after the service member's discharge. However, there are exceptions for disability, re-entering active duty, and upgraded discharges.

Effective October 1, 2015, the rate for full-time training in college, technical or vocational school will be $1,789 a month for those who served three years or more or two years plus four years in the Selected Reserve. For those who served less than three years, the monthly rate is $1,454. Benefits are reduced for part-time training. Payments for other types of training follow different rules. VA will pay an additional amount, called a "kicker" or "college fund," if directed by DoD. The maximum number of months Veterans can receive payments is 36 months at the full-time rate or the part-time equivalent.

The following types of education and training are available under Chapter 30:

- Courses at colleges and universities leading to associate, bachelor or graduate degrees, including accredited independent study offered through distance education;
- Courses leading to a certificate or diploma from business, technical or vocational schools;
- Apprenticeship or on-the-job training for those not on active duty, including self-employment training begun on or after June 16, 2004, for ownership or operation of a franchise;
- Correspondence courses, under certain conditions;
- Flight training, if the Veteran holds a private pilot's license upon beginning the training and meets the medical requirements;
- State-approved teacher certification programs;
- Preparatory courses necessary for admission to a college or graduate school;
- License and certification tests approved for Veterans; and
- Entrepreneurship training courses to create or expand small businesses.

Survivors' and Dependents' Educational Assistance (Chapter 35)

Chapter 35 provides education and training opportunities to eligible dependents of certain Veterans. The program offers up to 45 months of education benefits. These benefits may be used for degree and certificate programs, apprenticeship, and on-the-job training. A spouse may take a correspondence course. Remedial, deficiency, and refresher courses may be approved under certain circumstances.

To be eligible, one must be the son, daughter, or spouse of:

- A Veteran who died or is permanently and totally disabled as the result of a service-connected disability. The disability must arise out of active service in the Armed Forces;
- A Veteran who died from any cause while such permanent and total service-connected disability was in existence;
- A service member missing in action or captured in line of duty by a hostile force;
- A service member forcibly detained or interned in line of duty by a foreign government or power; or

- A service member who is hospitalized or receiving outpatient treatment for a service connected permanent and total disability and is likely to be discharged for that disability. (This change was effective December 23, 2006.)

A son or daughter must be between the ages of 18 and 26 to receive benefits for attending school or job training. If you are in the Armed Forces, you may not receive this benefit while on active duty. For spouses, benefits end 10 years from the date VA finds you eligible or from the date of death of the Veteran, unless the VA rated the Veteran permanently and totally disabled, in which case a spouse may remain eligible for 20 years from the effective date of the rating. For surviving spouses (spouses of service members who died on active duty) benefits end 20 years from the date of death.

Educational Assistance for Members of the Selected Reserve (MGIB-SR) (Chapter 1606)
Chapter 1606 may be available to a member of the Selected Reserve if they meet the eligibility requirements established by their respective components. The Selected Reserve includes the Army Reserve, Navy Reserve, Air Force Reserve, Marine Corps Reserve and Coast Guard Reserve, and the Army National Guard and the Air National Guard. The program may be used for degree programs, certificate or correspondence courses, cooperative training, independent study programs, apprenticeship/on-the-job training, and vocational flight training programs. Remedial, refresher and deficiency training are available under certain circumstances. Up to 36 months of education benefits may be available.

Specific eligibility requirements include:

- Have a six-year obligation to serve in the Selected Reserve signed after June 30, 1985. For some types of training, it is necessary to have a six-year commitment that begins after September 30, 1990;
- Complete initial active duty for training (IADT);
- Meet the requirement to receive a high school diploma or equivalency certificate before completing IADT; and
- Remain in good standing while serving in an active Selected Reserve unit.

In addition, a discharge from Selected Reserve service due to a disability or being ordered to active duty may extend eligibility for the program beyond service in a Selected Reserve unit.

Reserve Educational Assistance Program (REAP) (Chapter 1607)
Chapter 1607 was established as a part of the Ronald W. Reagan National Defense Authorization Act for Fiscal Year 2005. It is a DoD education benefit program designed to provide educational assistance to members of the Reserve components called or ordered to active duty in response to a war or national emergency (contingency operation) as declared by the President or Congress. This program makes certain reservists who were activated for at least 90 days after September 11, 2001 either eligible for education benefits or eligible for increased benefits.

Some reservists may contribute up to an additional $600 to the GI Bill to receive increased monthly benefits. For an additional $600 contribution, they may receive up to $5,400 in additional GI Bill benefits. One must be a member of a Ready Reserve component (Selected Reserve, Individual Ready Reserve, or Inactive National Guard) to pay into the "buy-up" program.

Reserve Educational Assistance Program (REAP)

REAP provides educational assistance to members of the Reserve components called or ordered to active duty in response to a war or national emergency declared by the president or Congress.

Change in REAP Eligibility

The National Defense Authorization Act of 2016 ended REAP on November 25, 2015. Some individuals will remain eligible for REAP benefits until November 25, 2019; while others are no longer eligible for REAP benefits.

The Post-9-11 GI Bill in many ways has replaced REAP because it also provides educational assistance benefits for Reserve and National Guard members called to active duty on or after September 11, 2001, and in many cases provides a greater benefit than REAP.

We are committed to ensuring that Reservists, National Guard members, and Veterans understand this change, and we are working to identify individuals who no longer have eligibility for REAP and inform them of potential eligibility to other benefit programs.
This change affects beneficiaries differently:

Current Reap Beneficiaries

Veterans who were attending an educational institution on November 24, 2015, or during the last semester, quarter, or term ending prior to that date, are eligible to continue to receive REAP benefits until November 25, 2019.

Reap Beneficiaries Not Attending School

Veterans who applied for REAP but were not
attending an educational institution on November 24, 2015, or during the last semester, quarter, or term ending prior to that date, are no longer eligible to receive REAP benefits. You may be eligible to receive benefits under the Post-9-11 GI Bill.

New Reap Applicants

Veterans who have not enrolled in school and applied for REAP benefits prior to November 25, 2015, are no longer eligible for REAP benefits. However, in most cases, you will be eligible for the Post-9-11 GI Bill.

You may be eligible for Post-9-11 GI Bill benefits depending on the dates of your periods of service. If we receive a new application for REAP on or after November 25, 2015, we will evaluate your eligibility for all programs, including Post-9-11 GI Bill, and may award you benefits under a different program.

If you're using REAP but would like to learn how to make an irrevocable election to use the Post-9-11 GI Bill instead, please call us at 1-888-GIBILL-1 (7 a.m. – 6 p.m. CST Monday – Friday) to speak with an Education Call Center Agent.

Veterans Educational Assistance Program (VEAP)

VEAP is available if you elected to make contributions from your military pay to participate in this education benefit program. The government matches your contributions on a 2-for-1 basis.

Types of Training

Assistance may be used for <u>college degree and certificate programs</u>, <u>technical or vocational</u> courses, <u>flight training</u>, <u>apprenticeships or on-the-job training</u>, <u>high-tech training</u>, <u>licensing and certification tests</u>, <u>entrepreneurship training</u>, certain <u>entrance</u> examinations, and <u>correspondence</u> courses. In certain circumstances, remedial, deficiency, and refresher training may also be available. Get the <u>VEAP pamphlet.</u>

You may use these benefits for degree, certificate, correspondence, apprenticeship/on-the-job training programs, and vocational flight training programs.

Available Benefits and Eligibility

Benefit entitlement is for one to 36 months depending on the number of monthly contributions. You have 10 years from your release from active duty to use VEAP benefits. If the entitlement is not used after the 10-year period, your portion remaining in the fund will be automatically refunded.

Eligibility

You must meet the following requirements to qualify:

- Entered service for the first time between Jan. 1, 1977, and June 30, 1985
- Opened a contribution account before April 1, 1987
- Voluntarily contributed from $25 to $2,700;
- Completed your first period of service and were discharged or released from service under conditions other than dishonorable.
- If you are currently on active duty and wish to receive VEAP benefits, you must have at least three months of contributions available.

Other Factors to Consider

Contributions may be withdrawn if you do not meet the basic eligibility requirements or if you formally request a refund of the contributions withheld.

Apply

To apply, take these steps depending on your situation:

- Make sure that your selected program is approved for VA training. VA can inform you and the school or company about the requirements.
- Obtain and complete <u>VA Form 22-1990</u>, Application for Education Benefits. Send it to the VA Regional Office with jurisdiction over the state where you will pursue education and training. If you are not on active duty, send copy 4 (Member Copy) of your DD 214, Certificate of Release or Discharge From Active Duty.
- If you are on active duty, you must have your enrollment approved by your base Education Services Officer, and you must have your service verified by your Commanding Officer.
- If you have started training, take your application and Member Copy of DD 214 to your school or employer. Ask them to complete VA Form 22-1999, Enrollment Certification, and send all the forms to VA.
- If you wish to withdraw your contributions from VEAP, obtain and complete <u>VA Form 22-5281</u>, Application for Refund of Educational Contributions, and send it to your nearest VA Regional Office.

Educational Assistance Pilot Program

The Educational Assistance Pilot Program, created by the Department of Defense Authorization Act of 1981 (Public Law 96-342), allows for the payment of monthly education benefits to encourage enlistment and reenlistment in the U.S. Armed Forces. Benefits may be available to individuals who entered on active duty after Sept. 30, 1980, and before Oct. 1, 1981 (or before Oct. 1, 1982, if entry was under a delayed enlistment contract signed between Sept. 30, 1980, and Oct. 1, 1981). (Note: Although this law established a start date for the test program as Oct. 1, 1980, the military service departments did not start offering the test program to new enlistees until Dec. 1, 1980.)

Air Force Eligibility Requirements

service members must meet all three of the following criteria to be eligible for this benefit :
Must have enlisted between Dec. 1, 1980, and Sept. 30, 1981
Enlistment was in one of the following Air Force Specialties: 20723, 20731, 20830, 46130, 46230A, B, C, D, E, F, G, H, J, or Z, 46430, 81130
Enlistment must have taken place at one of the following locations: Beckley, W.V.; Buffalo, N.Y.; Dallas ; Fargo, N.D.; Houston ; Jackson, Miss. ; Louisville, K y.; Memphis, T enn.; Omaha, Neb .; Philadelphia ; Seattle ; Sioux Falls, S.D.; Syracuse, N.Y.

National Testing Program

Advancing your education often requires you to take costly national tests. Students can be reimbursed all required (mandatory) fees charged for national admission tests and national tests for college credit.

Type of Assistance

The following tests are approved for reimbursement:

- SAT (Scholastic Assessment Test)
- LSAT (Law School Admission Test)
- GRE (Graduate Record Exam)
- GMAT (Graduate Management Admission Test)
- AP (Advanced Placement Exam)
- CLEP (College-Level Examination Program)
- ACT (American College Testing Program)
- DAT (Dental Admissions Test)
- MAT (Miller Analogies Test)
- MCAT (Medical College Admissions Test)
- OAT (Optometry Admissions Testing)
- PCAT (Pharmacy College Admissions Test)
- TOEFL (Test of English as a Foreign Language)
- DSST (DANTES Subject Standardized Tests)
- ECE (Excelsior College Examinations)
- PLA (Prior Learning Assessment) testing through Learningcounts.org
- TECEP (Thomas Edison College Examination Program)

Available Benefits

Although VA will reimburse a Veteran for required test fees, some fees connected to the testing process are not covered. The following test fees may be covered:

- Registration fees
- Fees for specialized tests
- Administrative fees
- The following fees are not covered by VA:
- Fees to take pre-tests (such as Kaplan tests)
- Fees to receive scores quickly
- Other costs or fees for optional items which are not required to take an approved test
- You do not normally have to submit a receipt or proof of payment for the test. However, in these situations, proof of payment is necessary: DSST tests and in certain situations related to CLEP, MAT, and PCAT tests. Mail the documentation to the Regional Office that handles your claim or use the Ask a Question section of our website to send us the information required and attach copies of any required documents.

Apply
Follow these steps to apply:
First apply for GI Bill benefits.
Complete a VA Form 22-0810 (Application for Reimbursement of National Exam Fee).

National Call to Service Program
This National Call to Service Incentive program is a benefit provided to those who perform a period of national service. It is a Department of Defense program that is administered by VA.

Type of Assistance
Participants who elect to receive an educational assistance incentive are not entitled to additional assistance under Chapter 1606 or Chapter 30 benefits unless the participant completes the service requirements necessary to establish eligibility. An individual who receives benefits under this program who also establishes eligibility under Chapter 1606 or Chapter 30 will have those entitlements reduced accordingly. Get more information in the pamphlet.

Available Benefit and Eligibility
Participants can choose from the following incentives:

- Cash bonus of $5,000
- Repayment of a qualifying student loan not to exceed $18,000
- Entitlement to allowance equal to the three-year monthly Montgomery GI Bill Active-Duty rate for 12 months
- Entitlement to allowance equal to 50 percent of the less than three-year monthly Montgomery GI Bill Active-Duty rate for 36 months
- Coordination with Montgomery GI Bill Benefits

Eligibility
There is a three-tiered service requirement to qualify for incentives

- First, after completion of initial entry training, individuals must serve on active duty in a military occupational specialty designated by the Secretary of Defense for a period of 15 months.

- After this, and without a break in service, these individuals must serve either an additional period of active duty as determined by the Secretary of Defense, or a period of 24 months in an active status in the Selected Reserve.
- After completion of this period of service, and without a break in service, the remaining period of obligated service specified in the agreement will be served as follows:
- On active duty in the armed forces
- In the Selected Reserve
- In the Individual Ready Reserve
- In AmeriCorps, or another domestic national service program jointly designated by the Secretary of Defense and the head of such a program
- Any combination of the service referred to above may also be approved by the Secretary of the military department concerned pursuant to regulations prescribed by the Secretary of Defense and specified in the agreement.

Chapter 10
Veterans Health Care

IN THIS CHAPTER:

Brief Description of VA Healthcare

- Only available to certain qualifying veterans and in some cases surviving spouses or designated family caregivers under CHAMPVA
- The Veterans Health Administration is America's largest integrated health care system
- 1,700 sites of care, serving 8.76 million Veterans each year.
- 152 medical centers
- Most VA medical centers are teaching hospitals providing access to state-of-the-art care from medical school health professionals
- VA healthcare is rated as high quality care by independent ratings organizations
- VA also offers extensive long-term care services to qualifying aging veterans
- VA offers hearing loss services to include free hearing aids and batteries as well as vision and dental services to certain veterans in the health care system

The VA healthcare system seems to be in the news quite a bit lately with service problems at local hospitals being sensationalized by various media and by complaints of individual veterans online. It is not that the system is staffed with poor quality people. On the contrary, VA healthcare consistently receives positive ratings from the veterans who use the system. Let's examine the problem.

The Veterans Health Administration is a very large and diverse operation with locations in every state – over 1,700 sites of care serving almost 9,000,000 veterans per year. The medical centers are up-to-date and offer all of the services of the private sector healthcare system. In addition, most medical centers are teaching hospitals, and as a result, the staff is augmented by professors from a local medical school. Even though medical students, interns and residents offer much of the healthcare services, they are backed up by primary care physicians who are experienced in the leading edge of their specialties by being part of a University medical school.

The biggest problem recently with the VA system is that it is entrusted with serving so many patients for free. Even though VA healthcare receives a great deal of funding from the federal government, this funding does not keep up with the increased number of patients being served. This overcrowding has led to some problems of service in some areas, but Congress and VA are on top of trying to correct the deficiencies and improve.

Another important aspect of VA healthcare is that it is primarily serving a geriatric community. Most of the veterans in the system are seniors, and their healthcare needs are much greater than the cross-sectional needs of Americans being served in private sector healthcare. Because of its focus on geriatric care, VA offers a large range of long-term care services to qualifying veterans. In addition, the needs of senior veterans are served through hearing and eyesight clinics associated with each regional hospital. Most veterans are eligible for free hearing aids and batteries, as well as free vision services and eyeglasses. Dental services are available to certain veterans as well.

Eligibility for VA Health Care

- Most Veterans who enlisted after September 7, 1980, or entered active duty after October 16, 1981, must have served 24 continuous months or the full period for which they were called to active duty in order to be eligible for VA health care, but they must also meet the other criteria below in order to get in.
- Current and former members of the Reserves or National Guard who were called to active duty by a federal order and completed the full period for which they were called or ordered to active duty may be eligible for VA health benefits but they must meet the criteria below
- Qualifications for VA health care for those who meet the qualifying period and duty of service or have an alternative qualifying reason to get into the system are the following

➢ Are a Former Prisoner of War (POW)
➢ In receipt of the Purple Heart Medal.
➢ In receipt of the Medal of Honor.
➢ Have a compensable VA awarded service-connected disability of 10% or more.
➢ In receipt of a VA Pension benefit.
➢ Were discharged from the military because of a disability (not preexisting), early out, or hardship.
➢ Served in a Theater of Operations – OEF/OIF/OND Veterans – and will receive benefits for 5 years post discharge.
➢ Served in the Republic of Vietnam from January 9, 1962 to May 7, 1975 and U.S. Navy and Coast Guard ships associated with military service in Vietnam
➢ Served in the Persian Gulf from August 2, 1990 to November 11, 1998.
➢ Were stationed or resided at Camp Lejeune for 30 days or more between August 1, 1953 and December 31, 1987.
➢ Are found by VA to be Catastrophically Disabled.
➢ Previous years' household income is below VA's National Income or Geographical-Adjusted Thresholds.

It is difficult to find a complete list of qualification criteria anywhere. We did a lot of research into compiling this information that you see above. We recently attended a Veterans Commission planning meeting for our state where all of the movers and shakers associated with veterans issues were in attendance, as well as numerous legislators. In particular, the head of the State Veterans Department was there, along with the state directors of the American Legion, VFW and the DAV. One of the legislators posed a question to the commission members in attendance asking how a veteran could qualify for VA health care. No one in the room had an adequate answer, and the directors of the Veterans Service Organizations actually gave erroneous information. You actually have to refer to a list, or you would not be able to remember all of the ways to get into the system.

Medical and Medical Support Services Provided

- Comprehensive Medical services both inpatient and outpatient
- Surgery
- Mental Health Care
- Dialysis
- Intensive Care Units (medical, surgical, mental health, cardiac)
- Transplant Services
- Spinal Cord Injury Centers
- Traumatic Brain Injury
- PolyTrauma Centers
- Audiology (hearing)
- Blind and Vision Rehabilitation
- Chiropractic Services
- Dental
- Psychological, psychiatric and counseling services
- Diagnostic Laboratory
- Nutrition and Food Service
- Occupational Therapy
- Pharmacy
- Physical Therapy
- Prosthetics (artificial limbs, equipment, devices)
- Radiology (x-rays and imaging)
- Radiation Oncology (cancer care)
- Recreation and Creative Arts Therapies (music, art, dance and drama)
- Respiratory Therapy
- Social Work (housing, discharge planning, family support)
- Speech/Language Pathology (speech, language, voice, fluency, cognition, and swallowing)
- Traumatic Brain Injury

This is a comprehensive list, and we are not going to go through a description all of these services that are available through the VA healthcare system. It is important to note that not all VA medical centers offer all of these services in one place. Certain specialized services such as organ transplants, rehabilitation, and surgery for missing limbs, specialized treatment for combat casualties, and other specialized counseling and treatment unique to veterans, is done in medical centers specifically designated for these needs. Each medical center will arrange to send qualifying veterans to these other facilities for treatment. The whole system is integrated together.

Pharmacy Services

- VA will provide medications that are prescribed by VA healthcare providers in conjunction with VA medical care
- For priority groups 2 through 8, preferred generic medications are $5.00 per prescription for 30 days, non-preferred generic meds , $8.00 for 30 days and brand-name meds are $11.00 for 30 days
- Medications are prescribed from an approved formulary which may not include all of the newest available medications
- VA will fill prescriptions prescribed by a non-VA provider only if all of the following criteria are met:
  - o Patient is enrolled in VA health benefits
  - o Patient has an assigned Primary Care Provider
  - o Patient has provided the VA health care provider with medical records from the non-VA provider
  - o The VA health care provider agrees with the medication prescribed by the non-VA provider.
- A VA health care provider is under no obligation to prescribe a medication recommended by a non-VA provider

Understanding that a great majority of individuals in the system are seniors, and that many are taking multiple medications, some of them very costly, VA Healthcare can save these people a great deal of money. On the other hand, VA healthcare does not always include newer medications that may or may not be more effective than older medications in its formulary. VA doctors are not subject to the same pressure from pharmaceutical companies to push the newest and greatest if there is something available that will do the same job at a lesser cost. Also, unlike Medicare which is prohibited from negotiating with the drug companies for better prices, the VA is not under that same constraint and because of the huge size of the VA health care system, it typically negotiates much better prices for popular medications.

Many senior veterans express a motivation to get into healthcare in order to receive the pharmaceutical benefits. We don't have the heart to tell these people that not just anyone can get into the system just because that person is a veteran. It doesn't work that way. Also, the word has gotten out that if one can get into VA Healthcare, one does not have to use VA doctors but can use a personal family physician and have VA fill the prescriptions. As you can see from the rules above, that is not such an easy process. The VA doctor wants to be involved in the treatment and may or may not approve the medication.

Services for Family Caregivers of Post-9/11 Veterans

- Veterans eligible for this program are those who sustained a serious injury – including traumatic brain injury, psychological trauma or other mental disorder – incurred or aggravated in the line of duty, on or after September 11, 2001.
- Veterans eligible for this program must also be in need of personal care services because of an inability to perform one or more activities of daily living and/or need supervision or protection based on symptoms or residuals of neurological impairment or injury.
- To be eligible for the Program of Comprehensive Assistance for Family Caregivers, Veterans must first be enrolled for VA health services, if not enrolled previously
- Services Available to Family Caregivers through this Program
  - Monthly payment to reimburse family caregivers for their time
  - Travel expenses (including lodging and per diem while accompanying Veterans undergoing care)
  - Access to health care insurance (if the Caregiver is not already entitled to care or services under a health care plan)
  - Mental health services and counseling
  - Comprehensive VA Caregiver training provided by Easter Seals
  - Respite care for the caregiver (not less than 30 days per year)

The services listed here are self-explanatory. As a general rule, this is a program unique to the VA healthcare system. The private care system under Medicaid or Medicare does not allow for paying family caregivers to take care of loved ones. Some states through their Medicaid services have self-directed programs where the care recipient is given a budget to hire his or her own caregivers, but the amount of funds available to the care recipient are minimal and the oversight from the program managers makes it difficult to manage.

Co-Pays and Priority Groups for VA Health Care

- VA has 8 categories of veterans – called priority groups – to which co-pays and eligibility for healthcare and other services apply
- Priorities 2 through 6 generally have no co-pays except for prescriptions and long term care services
- Priority 7 veterans are eligible because of low income and have co-pays
- Priority 8 is for any other veteran who was accepted in the system prior to 2003, but other than combat service since 1998, VA no longer accepts such veterans and priority 8 veterans are subject to large inpatient co-pays
- Priority group 8 and priority group 7 who are in the system based on income only, pay primary care services of $15 per visit and specialty care services of $50 per visit and pay the Co-Pays listed below
- Most veterans pay $5.00/$8.00/$11.00 for each 30 day supply of prescription medication but for certain priority groups, prescriptions are free
- Veterans receiving 10% Compensation or more generally have no co-pays for long-term care services, but for other veterans there are daily co-pays depending on the service

Priority Group 7 and certain other Veterans are responsible for paying 20 percent of VA's inpatient copay rate for 2020.

- Inpatient Copay for the first 90 days of care during a 365-day period – $281.60
- Inpatient Copay for each additional 90 days of care during a 365-day period – $140.80
- Daily Charge – $2/day

Priority Group 8 and certain other Veterans are responsible for VA's full inpatient copay rate.

- Inpatient Copay for the first 90 days of care during a 365-day period – $1,408
- Inpatient Copay for each additional 90 days of care during a 365-day period – $704
- Daily Charge – $10/day

Priority groups under VA healthcare are somewhat complicated, and understanding how a priority group dovetails with services provided through health care gets a little confusing. The primary message here is that priority groups with a higher number end up paying more of the cost of care, especially veterans in priority groups 7 and 8. Because of demands on the system, VA healthcare no longer accepts priority group 8 veterans. However, those who are already in the system can remain in the system as long as they follow the rules and don't give VA an excuse to kick them out.

Hearing, Vision and Dental

- Hearing and vision medical services are available for certain veterans in healthcare as well as free eyeglasses and free hearing aids and hearing aid batteries
- Eligible veterans for hearing and vision include 10% or more service-connected Compensation, prisoner of war, Purple Heart, receiving housebound or aid and attendance allowances and other veterans severely disabled with hearing or eyesight problems.
- Veterans who are 10% or more service-connected disabled and have a dental condition due to service or to their disability as well as veterans 100% service-connected disabled due to injury or illness or unemployability as well as homeless veterans can receive free dental care

For some veterans, these benefits are the only reason they are in the system. We don't believe the private sector - except for very good insurance plans - offers these types of benefits for free.

HISA Grants – Home Improvements and Structural Alterations

- Available through the prosthetics department of the veteran's local regional medical center
- Veteran must be enrolled in VA health care
- Requires a prescription from a VA physician for a medical condition to justify the alterations
- Will provide improvements and structural alterations to the primary residence such as ramps, walk-in tubs, widening doorways, providing railings, lowering countertops,

improving entrances and modifying plumbing and electrical systems for the installation of home medical equipment
- Provides a one-time payment of $6,800 for veterans who are service-connected
- Provides a one-time payment of $2,000 for veterans who are disabled due to a non-service-connected condition such as Pension with aid and attendance or who are on Medicaid

These grants are another benefit exclusive to the healthcare system. The one-time payments can be a valuable resource to help pay for modifications to the home to allow for disability. In the past, getting one of these grants was difficult as three bids from contractors had to be submitted and the contract work had to be completed prior to VA paying out the stipend. Most contractors would have to wait up to 90 days to receive payment. Just recently, the program has changed making it easier to get one of these grants through only one bid and advance monies are provided to start the project.

Applying for a HISA Grant
The veteran must be registered with VA health care. In order to receive a HISA grant, the Veteran must first have a prescription from a VA or fee-basis physician. This must include:

- The diagnosis with medical justification
- The Veteran's name, address, SSN, and phone number(s)

To apply, the Veteran must first provide:

- A completed VA Form 10-0103, <u>VETERANS APPLICATION FOR ASSISTANCE In Acquiring Home Improvement and Structural Alterations</u>

- If a leased or rented property, written permission from the owner
- Quotes from at least 1 licensed contractor (if required by state law), to include:
- The contractors name, address, telephone, and Federal tax ID number or social security number
- The Veteran's name, address, and telephone number
- Plans and drawings
- An itemized list of estimated materials, cost, and labor cost
- All permits required (it is the contractors responsibility to obtain these)
- A picture of the work site prior to construction

Following are the types of projects that HISA grants will pay for. This is not all inclusive and other appropriate projects may be approved.

(1) Roll-in showers
(2) Construction of wooden or concrete, permanent ramping to provide access to the home
(3) Widening doorways to bedroom, bathroom, etc., to achieve wheelchair access
(4) Lowering of kitchen or bathroom counters and sinks
(5) Improving entrance paths and driveways in immediate area of home to facilitate access to the home
(6) Construction of concrete pads and installation of exterior types of wheelchair lift mechanisms if the installation cost exceeds $500.00

(7) Interior and exterior railing deemed necessary for patients with ambulatory capability or for veterans rated legally blind if the installation cost is over $500.00

(8) Improvements to plumbing or electrical systems made necessary due to the installation of dialysis equipment in the home

(9) Any cost associated with permits, inspection fees, etc., that are required by local ordinances.

HISA will not pay for:

- Walkways to exterior buildings
- Widening of driveways (in excess of a 7ft x 6ft area)
- Spa, hot tub, or Jacuzzi
- Exterior decking (in excess of 8ft x 8ft)

VA Nursing Home and Other Facility Care

The Department of Veterans Affairs (VA) provides both short-term and long-term care in nursing homes to veterans who aren't sick enough to be in the hospital but are too disabled or elderly to take care of themselves. Priority is given to veterans with service-connected disabilities. VA is required to provide nursing home care to any veteran who:

- needs nursing home care because of a service-connected disability
- has a combined disability rating of 70% or more, or
- has a disability rating of at least 60% and is:
    o deemed unemployable, or
    o has been rated permanently and totally disabled.
- Other veterans in need of nursing care will be provided services if resources are available after the above groups are taken care of.

Community Living Centers

Some VA Medical Centers have Community Living Centers (these used to be called Nursing Home Care Units or VA Nursing Homes). These centers are typically located within the VA Medical Center itself or in a separate building. To receive care in a Community Living Center/VA nursing home, a veteran must:

- be enrolled in the VA Health Care System
- be psychiatrically and medically stable
- provide documentation specifying whether short or long-term care is needed, an estimation of how long the stay will be, and when discharge will occur, and
- show priority for a stay in a Community Living Center.

However, meeting the above criteria does not automatically ensure admission. CLCs make decisions about whether to admit a veteran based on the following factors:

- availability of services in the CLC
- what sort of care the veteran needs, and
- whether the CLC can competently provide the type of care the veteran needs.

Co-pays are required for the following veteran patients:

- without a service-connected disability rated at least 10%, and
- whose income is higher than the VA's maximum annual Pension rate.

Community Nursing Home

VA contracting services with public or private nursing homes is also available to some veterans. Stays in these nursing homes can be limited, however, for veterans with ratings less than 70% and for veterans who do not need care due to a service-connected disability.

Any veteran who needs this contract nursing home care for a service-connected disability or is receiving VA home health care after discharge from a VA hospital is eligible for direct admission. To be admitted, all that is required is for a VA physician or authorized private physician to determine that nursing home care is needed. Veterans rated 70% or more service-connected are also be eligible.

Other veterans are eligible to be transferred into community nursing home care if the VA determines the care is needed and:

- the veteran is in a VA hospital, nursing home, domiciliary, or has been receiving VA outpatient care, or
- an active member of the Armed Forces who was in a DOD hospital, needs nursing care, and will be an eligible veteran upon discharge.

Veterans who are not in the priority groups for community living centers are technically limited to six months of care, but this may be reduced to 30 to 60 days if resources are limited. Veterans in the priority groups are technically entitled to unlimited free care, but again may receive shorter stays due to a lack of funding and resources to accommodate them.

State Veterans Homes

Chapter 10 in this book covers state veterans homes.

Geriatric Care Services

Adult Day Health Care

Adult Day Health Care is a program Veterans can go to during the day for social activities, peer support, companionship, and recreation.

The program is for Veterans who need skilled services, case management and help with activities of daily living. Examples include help with bathing, dressing, fixing meals or taking medicines. This program is also for Veterans who are isolated or their caregiver is experiencing burden. Adult Day Health Care can combined with other Home and Community Based Services.

Health services such as care from nurses, therapists, social workers, and others may also be available. Adult Day Health Care can provide respite care for a family caregiver and can also help Veterans and their caregiver gain skills to manage the Veteran's care at home.

The program may be provided at VA medical centers, State Veterans Homes, or community organizations. For a list of State Veterans Homes locations, visit the National Association of

State Veterans Homes. You can also use the Locate Services page, found on the left navigation menu, to help you find Adult Day Health Care programs.

Since Adult Day Health Care is part of the VHA Standard Medical Benefits Package, all enrolled Veterans are eligible IF they meet the clinical need for the service and it is available.

A copay for Adult Day Health Care may be charged based on VA service-connected disability status and financial information. Contact a VA social worker/case manager to complete the Application for Extended Care Benefits (VA Form 10-10EC) to learn the amount of your copay.

Adult Day Health Care can be a half-day or full-day program. Usually, you would go to an Adult Day Health Care center 2 to 3 times per week, but you may be able to go up to 5 times a week.

Based on availability and need, you can create a regular schedule that works for you and your family caregiver. You may be able to get assistance with transportation to and from an Adult Day Health Care center.

Home-Based Primary Care

Home Based Primary Care is health care services provided to Veterans in their home. A VA physician supervises the health care team who provides the services. Home Based Primary Care is for Veterans who have complex health care needs for whom routine clinic-based care is not effective.

The program is for Veterans who need skilled services, case management and help with activities of daily living. Examples include help with bathing, dressing, fixing meals or taking medicines. This program is also for Veterans who are isolated or their caregiver is experiencing burden. Home Based Primary Care can be used in combination with other Home and Community Based Services.

Since Home Based Primary Care is part of the VHA Standard Medical Benefits Package, all enrolled Veterans are eligible IF they meet the clinical need for the service and it is available.

A copay for Home Based Primary Care may be charged based on your VA service-connected disability status and financial information. You may have a basic copay each time a VA staff team member comes to your home for a medical visit (the same as if you went to a VA clinic). Contact your VA social worker/case manager to complete the Application for Extended Care Benefits (VA Form 10-10EC) to learn the amount of your copay. If you qualify for Home Based Primary Care, your care plan includes:

- Primary care visits at home by a physician, nurse practitioner or physician's assistant
- Care management through a nurse practitioner, physician's assistant, or nurse
- Coordination of your services by a social worker
- Therapy visits from a physical, occupational, or speech therapist
- Mental health services
- Nutrition counseling from a dietitian
- Help managing your medicines

Homemaker and Home Health Aide Care

A Homemaker or Home Health Aide is a trained person who can come to a Veteran's home and help the Veteran take care of himself and his daily activities.

Homemakers and Home Health Aides are not nurses, but they are supervised by a registered nurse who will help assess the Veteran's daily living needs.

This program is for Veterans who need skilled services, case management and help with activities of daily living. Examples include help with bathing, dressing, fixing meals or taking medicines. This program is also for Veterans who are isolated or their caregiver is experiencing burden. Homemaker and Home Health Aide services can be used in combination with other Home and Community Based Services.

Homemaker Home Health Aides work for an organization that has a contract with VA. A Homemaker or Home Health Aide can be used as a part of an alternative to nursing home care, and as a way to get Respite Care at home for Veterans and their family caregiver. The services of a Homemaker or Home Health Aide can help Veterans remain living in their own home and can serve Veterans of any age.

Since Homemaker Home Health Aide services are part of a service within the VHA Standard Medical Benefits Package, all enrolled Veterans are eligible if they meet the clinical need for the service. A copay for Homemaker and Home Health Aide services may be charged based on your VA service-connected disability status. Homemaker Home Health Aide services can be used in combination with other Home and Community Based Services.

Services are based on your assessed needs. Talk with a VA social worker to find out what specific help you may be able to receive. For example, an aide may be able to come to your house several times a week or just once in a while. Examples of daily activities you may be able to receive help with include:

- Eating
- Getting dressed
- Bathing
- Using the bathroom
- Moving from one place to another
- Shopping for food
- Cooking
- Cleaning
- Doing laundry
- Paying bills or managing money
- Taking medication
- Getting to appointments
- Using the telephone

Hospice and Palliative Care

Hospice is a comfort based form of care for Veterans who have a terminal condition with 6 months or less to live. Palliative care is a form of treatment that emphasizes comfort care but does not require the Veteran have a terminal condition. Since Hospice and Palliative Care are part of the VHA Standard Medical Benefits Package, all enrolled Veterans are eligible IF they meet the clinical need for the service. Copays may be charged for palliative care, but there are NO COPAYS for HOSPICE care whether it is provided by the VA or an organization with a VA contract.

Hospice and Palliative Care provides treatment that relieves suffering and helps to control symptoms in a way that respects your personal, cultural, and religious beliefs and practices. Hospice also provides bereavement support to your family.

You and your family are assessed by a care team and a plan of care is developed to meet your medical, social, spiritual and psychological needs. This care is available to Veterans in their home, community, outpatient or inpatient settings.

Respite Care

Respite Care is a service that pays for a person to come to a Veteran's home or for a Veteran to go to a program while their family caregiver takes a break. While a Veteran gets Respite Care, the family caregiver can run errands or go out of town for a few days without worrying about leaving the Veteran alone at home. Respite Care can be helpful to Veterans of all ages, and their caregiver. Veterans can receive Respite Care in an inpatient, outpatient or home setting.

The program is for Veterans who need skilled services, case management and help with activities of daily living. Examples include help with bathing, dressing, fixing meals or taking medicines. This program is also for Veterans who are isolated or their caregiver is experiencing burden. Respite Care can be used in combination with other Home and Community Based Services. Respite Care can help lower the stress the Veterans and their family caregiver may feel when managing a Veteran's long term care needs at home.

Since Respite Care is part of the VHA Standard Medical Benefits Package, all enrolled Veterans are eligible IF they meet the clinical need for the service and it is available. A copay for Respite Care may be charged based on your VA service-connected disability status and financial information. Contact your VA social worker/case manager to complete the Application for Extended Care Benefits (VA Form 10-10EC) to learn the amount of your copay. You may be able to get Respite Care in a number of ways:

- A paid Home Health Aide could come to your home
- You could attend an Adult Day Health Care center
- You could go to a Community Living Center (VA Nursing Home) or a VA medical center for a short inpatient stay

Depending on the Respite Care services in your area, you can choose which options are best for you and your family caregiver. For example: If your caregiver has lots of errands to run or appointments, you could have a Home Health Aide come to your home while your caregiver is out of the house. If your caregiver needs time at your home alone, you could attend an Adult Day Health Care center for the day. Or, if your caregiver is out of town for a few days, you could stay at a Community Living Center (VA Nursing Home) during the time they are away. No matter which option you use, trained staff will help you with your care needs.

Respite Care services may be available up to 30 days each calendar year. These 30 days may be used in different ways. For example:

- You might stay in a Community Living Center (VA Nursing Home) for 1 visit of 30 days, or have 10 short stays of 3 days each during the year.
- You might have a Home Health Aide come to your home to stay with you for up to 6 hours in a row, day or night. Each visit (even if it is less than the 6-hour maximum) counts as 1 day of Respite Care.

Skilled Home Health Care

Skilled Home Health is short-term health care services that can be provided to Veterans if they are homebound or live far away from VA. The care is delivered by a community-based home health agency that has a contract with VA.

The program is for Veterans who need skilled services, case management and help with activities of daily living. Examples include help with bathing, dressing, fixing meals or taking medicines. This program is also for Veterans who are isolated or their caregiver burdened. Skilled Home Health Care can be used in combination with other Home and Community Based Services.

Since Skilled Home Health Care is part of the VHA Standard Medical Benefits Package, all enrolled Veterans are eligible IF they meet the clinical need for the service and it is available.

A copay for Skilled Home Health Care may be charged based on your VA service-connected disability status and financial information. Contact your VA social worker/case manager to complete the Application for Extended Care Benefits (VA Form 10-10EC) to learn the amount of your copay. If you are eligible for Skilled Home Health, based on your needs you may receive:

- Nursing care (such as wound care or catheter care)
- Therapy visits for physical, occupational or speech therapy
- Patient education (about managing your medicines or illness)
- A home safety evaluation
- Social work support

Home Telehealth

Home Telehealth, also known as Care Coordination/Home Telehealth, is a service that allows the Veteran's physician or nurse to monitor the Veteran's medical condition remotely using home monitoring equipment. Veterans can be referred to a care coordinator for enrollment in Home Telehealth services by any member of their care team.

A care coordinator gets health information that each Veteran provides through personalized questions answered on special equipment, and then checks in with the Veteran by phone, if needed. If any of the Veteran's health measurements do not seem normal, the care coordinator talks with their physician or nurse and then gets back to the Veteran with next steps.

Since Telehealth Care is part of the VHA Standard Medical Benefits Package, all enrolled Veterans are eligible IF they meet the clinical need for the service and it is available. Home Telehealth can be used in combination with other Home and Community Based Services.

There is no copay for Home Telehealth services. However, there may be a copay charge when in-home video visits are provided in addition to standard Home Telehealth services. Home Telehealth services are based on your care needs. Home Telehealth may be used to track your:

- Blood pressure
- Blood sugar level
- Pulse
- Weight
- Blood oxygen level
- Heart and lung sounds

You may need a phone line to transfer your health information to VA, however technologies are also available for mobile/cell phone connections. A video screen and camera, or video phone, may also be given to you so that the care coordinator can see you when you talk together. You would be able to turn the video camera off when you are not using it to talk with your care coordinator.

Veteran Directed Care

Veteran-Directed Home and Community Based Services gives Veterans of all ages the opportunity to receive the Home and Community Based Services they need in a consumer-directed way.

Veteran-Directed Care is for Veterans who need skilled services, case management, and assistance with activities of daily living (e.g., bathing and getting dressed) or instrumental activities of daily living (e.g., fixing meals and taking medicines); are isolated or their caregiver is experiencing burden.

Veterans in this program are given a flexible budget for services that can be managed by the Veteran or the family caregiver. Veteran-Directed Care can be used to help Veterans continue to live at home or in their community. As part of this program, Veterans and their caregiver have more access, choice and control over their long term care services. For example, Veterans can:

- Decide what mix of services will best meet their needs
- Hire their own personal care aides (which might include their own family member or neighbor)
- Buy items and services that will help them live independently in the community

Since Veteran-Directed Care is part of the VHA Standard Medical Benefits Package, all enrolled Veterans are eligible IF they meet the clinical need for the service and it is available. NOTE: This is a new VA program and is only available in certain locations. There is no copay with this program. However, you may still have a copay if you use Home and Community Based Services

If you are enrolled in this program, you can decide what mix of Home and Community Based services will best meet your needs.

Chapter 11
State Veterans Benefits

IN THIS CHAPTER:

- Introduction to State Veterans Benefits; pg. 459
- About State Veterans homes; pg. 460
- Other State Veterans Benefits; pg. for 67
- National Care Planning Council List of State Veterans homes; pg. 468

Introduction to State Veterans Benefits

All states offer veterans special services, tax breaks and fee waivers. Many available benefits are unique to each state. But in general, all states offer at least the following programs.

- State Veterans homes
- burial in state veterans cemeteries
- specialty license plates
- free license plates for disabled veterans
- hiring preference
- credit for state retirement plans

These are the most current links to state Departments of Veterans Affairs. State benefits are always changing and a check on the state website will indicate what benefits are available currently.

Alaska http://www.dmva.alaska.gov/
Alabama http://www.va.state.al.us/
Arkansas http://www.veterans.arkansas.gov/
Arizona http://www.azdvs.gov/
California http://www.calvet.ca.gov/
Colorado http://www.colorado.gov/dmva/
Connecticut
http://www.ct.gov/ctva/site/default.asp
Delaware http://veteransaffairs.delaware.gov/
District of Columbia http://ova.dc.gov/
Florida http://www.floridavets.org/
Georgia http://veterans.georgia.gov/
Hawaii http://dod.hawaii.gov/
Idaho http://www.veterans.idaho.gov/
Illinois http://www.illinois.gov/veterans
Indiana http://www.in.gov/dva/index.htm
Iowa http://va.iowa.gov/

Kansas http://kcva.ks.gov/
Kentucky http://veterans.ky.gov
Louisiana http://vetaffairs.la.gov/
Maine http://www.maine.gov/dvem/bvs/
Maryland http://veterans.maryland.gov/
Massachusetts http://www.mass.gov/veterans/
Michigan http://www.michigan.gov/dmva
Minnesota http://mn.gov/mdva/
Mississippi http://www.vab.ms.gov/
Missouri http://mvc.dps.mo.gov/
Montana http://dma.mt.gov/
Nebraska http://www.vets.state.ne.us/
Nevada http://www.veterans.nv.gov/
New Hampshire http://www.nh.gov/nhveterans/
New Jersey http://www.state.nj.us/military/
New Mexico http://www.dvs.state.nm.us/
New York http://veterans.ny.gov/

North Carolina http://www.milvets.nc.gov/
North Dakota http://www.nd.gov/veterans/
Ohio http://ohio.gov/
Oklahoma https://www.ok.gov/odva/
Oregon http://www.oregon.gov/ODVA/
Pennsylvania http://www.dmva.pa.gov
Rhode Island
http://www.va.gov/directory/guide/state.asp?STATE
=RI&dnum=ALL
South Carolina
http://www.va.gov/directory/guide/state.asp?State
=SC&dnum=ALL

South Dakota http://military.sd.gov/
Tennessee http://www.tn.gov/
Texas http://www.tvc.state.tx.us/
Utah http://veterans.utah.gov/
Vermont http://veterans.vermont.gov/ova
Virginia http://www.dvs.virginia.gov/
Washington http://www.dva.wa.gov/
West Virginia http://www.veterans.wv.gov
Wisconsin http://dva.state.wi.us/
Wyoming
http://www.va.gov/directory/guide/state.asp?dnum
=ALL&STATE=WY

About State Veterans homes

Every state now has at least one veterans home. Some states have eight or more veterans homes.
There are still a number of states that only have one home. There is great demand for this type
of housing and it appears from news releases and Internet articles that a number of states are in
the process of considering for construction or actually building more Veterans homes.

Veterans homes are generally available to former active duty veterans but some states have beds
for people who served with the reserves or National Guard and for the spouses of veterans. The
majority of these homes offer nursing care but some may offer assisted living or domiciliary
care. Generally there is no income or asset test. Most veterans in most states would qualify.
Many states have waiting lists of weeks to months for available beds. Each facility has different
eligibility rules and there is an application process.

You cannot simply walk in the door and arrange for nursing care on the spot. You must contact
the veterans home you are interested in to find out the availability of beds and the application
process. For veterans who are on Disability Compensation or are currently in the VA healthcare
system, there are significant subsidies available from the Department of Veterans Affairs. For
veterans who are not on claim, there may be co-pays for the services of a State Veterans Home
depending on the income of the veteran or the spouse who might also be eligible for a bed.

Available to Most Veterans but Not Always Free of Cost
State veterans homes fill an important need for veterans with low income and veterans who
desire to spend their last years with "comrades" from former active-duty. The predominant
service offered is nursing home care. VA nursing homes must be licensed for their particular
state and conform with skilled or intermediate nursing services offered in private sector nursing
homes in that state. State Homes may also offer assisted living or domiciliary care which is a
form of supported independent living.

Every state has at least one veterans home and some states like Florida and Texas have eight of
them. There is great demand for the services of these homes, but lack of federal and state
funding has created a backlog of projects waiting construction over the years.

Unlike private sector nursing homes where the family can walk in the front door and possibly that same day make arrangements for a bed for their loved one; State Veterans homes have an application process that could take a number of weeks or months. Many State Homes have waiting lists especially for their Alzheimer's long term care units.

No facilities are entirely free to any veteran with an income unless the veteran is also receiving Disability Compensation at a certain disability rating. The veteran must pay his or her share of the cost. In some states the veterans contribution rates are set and if there's not enough income the family may have to make up the difference. Federal legislation, effective 2007, also allows the federal government to substantially subsidize the cost of veterans with service-connected disabilities in State Veterans homes. For veterans who are 70% or more disabled, the per diem contribution from the federal government, in most areas, is more than enough to cover the nursing home cost and for these veterans, there is no out-of-pocket cost.

The Appeal of Living in a State Veterans Home

We believe most veterans or their families seek out residency in a state veterans nursing home because they believe this service is one more VA entitlement that should be available to them.

But there is also a similar entitlement available to anyone in most private sector nursing homes -- facilities that may be geographically closer to the family than the nearest veterans home. This is Medicaid. Veterans seeking long term care from VA programs generally don't have the funds for private pay in a nursing home; however, Medicaid will also cover these same people in a private sector Medicaid certified facility. Most families who are seeking help for their loved ones, who are veterans, generally look to VA first before considering Medicaid. Or they are simply not aware of Medicaid. In many cases, Medicaid may be the better choice.

Aside from seeking long term care because of an expectation of entitlement are there any other reasons that veterans would prefer a State home? We asked this question of ourselves because we have noticed that in some states veterans homes are in distant rural areas. The fact that some of these homes are hundreds of miles from urban areas where the most veterans would tend to live, made us wonder why some veterans would move long distances to reside in these facilities.

To answer this question we contacted a number of rural State Veterans Homes on the phone and asked them why a veteran or his or her family would seek out their services as opposed to seeking services in a closer non-veterans facility under Medicaid. Almost unanimously the answer we got was that some veterans like the idea of sharing their living arrangement with other veterans. The facilities almost always referred to this as "camaraderie" – a band of brotherhood.

Statistically, private sector nursing homes are mostly populated by older women who are generally in poor health. Some men may not feel comfortable in an environment where the activities and the social atmosphere are centered around women. In contrast, veterans homes are almost exclusively populated by men. In addition, based on our observation, we suspect the population of State Homes is younger and healthier than that of private sector facilities.

These demographics would suggest that activities and the social atmosphere revolve around the needs of men not women. A younger, healthier population would also suggest veterans homes would offer more opportunity in the form of transportation or scheduled outings for the residents to be out in the community. One veterans home reported to us that they regularly scheduled fishing trips and outings to sporting events for their residents. These would be unheard-of activities for the typical private nursing home.

The second most common reason reported to us why veterans seek out State Homes is for financial reasons. In many states the cost of the home is subsidized for veterans who meet an income test. The vet's income is considered sufficient to cover the cost. These veterans may own a home or other assets that they wish to protect from Medicaid and leave to their family. Many State Veterans Homes will allow them to give these assets to the family without penalty. Medicaid would require a spend down of those assets or impose a penalty for gifting.

Another reason related to finances may be there are no available Medicaid beds in the veteran's area. The veteran may be paying out of pocket for a nursing facility but have his name on a waiting list for a State Home where the out-of-pocket cost would be much less. When his name comes up he will move to the State home.

A financial incentive for the veteran is that all State Veterans homes will apply for the Pension benefit for those residents who are eligible. Federal law prohibits VA from paying any more than $90 a month to single veterans who are eligible for Medicaid in a non-veteran nursing home. State Veterans homes are exempt from this rule and the single veteran can keep the entire Pension amount although most of it will have to apply to the cost of care. For those State Veterans Homes that also accept Medicaid, Pension represents additional disposable income.

History of State Veterans homes
Our nation was faced with a staggering number of soldiers and sailors in critical need of medical care following the Civil War, and although national care provider homes were in operation at the time, their capacity was inadequate to meet the demand. At that time, several states established veterans homes, at their own expense, to provide for those residents who had served so honorably in the military.

In 1888, the U.S. Congress authorized federal cost-sharing for State Veterans Homes --about 30 cents per resident per day. Since the creation of the Veterans Administration in 1930, the program's per diem payments have increased every year with inflation.

Challenges Facing the Construction of New Homes
The State Veterans Home Program is a partnership between the U.S. Department of Veterans Affairs and the States to construct or acquire nursing home, domiciliary or adult day health care facilities. A State nursing home, domiciliary or adult day care is owned and operated by the State.

Under the State Home Construction Grant program, States are required to provide at least 35 percent of the total cost and federal grants can provide no more than 65 percent of the total cost.

Only projects that already have State matching funds qualify as Priority List Group 1 projects.

- For FY 2014, the federal share for proposed State Home Construction Grants was $928 million, of which $489 million were Priority Group List 1 projects. NASVH had recommended $250 million to cover half of the Priority 1 projects, but only $85 million was appropriated by Congress.
- For FY 2015, total estimated share of State Home Construction Grant requests rose to $976 million, of which $409 are Priority Group 1. For FY 2015, Congress appropriated $90 million, a small increase over VA's request, but not enough to seriously address the backlog of requests.
- For FY 2016, NASVH requests $200 million for the State Home Construction Grant program, to cover approximately half of the expected Priority Group 1 list. Unfortunately, VA's new FY 2016 budget submission actually decreased the request to just $80 million.

For Fiscal Year 2015 Project Funding VA received $90 million for the Fiscal Year 2015 program funding plus Fiscal Year 2014 carryover amounts by completing the final award of all fiscal year 2014 conditional grants.

For Fiscal Year 2015 VA will provide 18 new state home grants of $107 million which includes carryover funds. These funds are used for new facilities and repair and replacement on existing facilities for

- Little Rock Arkansas,
- Minneapolis Minnesota,
- Walla Walla Washington,
- Kearney Nebraska,
- Truth or Consequences New Mexico

VA received 36 initial grant applications for Fiscal Year 2016 for a total cost with matching funds from states of $385 million. This includes new construction and bed replacements for projects in TX, LA, NC, KY and SC.

Daily Per Diem Rates

Basic Per Diem Program
The Veterans Administration pays the State Veterans homes an annually adjusted rate per day for each veteran in the home. This is called the per diem and applies to veterans who are paying the out-of-pocket deductible and who don't qualify for the special per diem rate by being on claim for Disability Compensation.

The State Home basic per diem rates are listed in the table below by fiscal year (FY):

Fiscal Year	Adult Day Health Care Per Diem Rate	Domiciliary Per Diem Rate	Nursing Home Per Diem Rate
FY 2020	$89.52 per day	$48.50 per day	$112.36 per resident per day
FY 2019	$87.42 per day	$47.36 per day	$109.73 per resident per day

Fiscal Year	Adult Day Health Care Per Diem Rate	Domiciliary Per Diem Rate	Nursing Home Per Diem Rate
FY 2018	$85.37 per day	$46.25 per day	$107.16 per resident per day
FY 2017	$84.52 per day	$45.79 per day	$106.10 per resident per day
FY 2016	$82.54 per day	$44.72 per day	$103.61 per resident per day
FY 2015	$81.56 per day	$44.19 per day	$102.38 per resident per day
FY 2014	$79.96 per day	$43.32 per day	$100.37 per resident per day
FY 2013	$77.33 per day	$41.90 per day	$97.07 per veteran per day

The per diem program and construction subsidies mean that State Veterans Homes can charge less money for their services than private facilities. Some states have a set rate, as an example $1,600 a month, and they may be relying on the Pension benefit with aid and attendance plus the per diem to cover their actual costs. These states also may be relying on other in-state subsidies other than VA to help cover the costs. Other states may charge a percentage of the veterans income but be relying on other subsidies to cover the balance. Still, in other states, the rate may simply be the difference between all of the subsidies and the actual monthly cost of operation.

Most of the states with income-determined rates are selective about the veterans they accept. These states may rely on a variety of private and public sources to help fund the cost of care.

Example of Subsidy from the VA and the State.

Actual per Veteran Monthly Cost of Operation	$7,000
Per Diem Monthly to Subsidize the Veteran's Cost	$3,071
Possible State or Other Subsidies	$1,000
Possible VA Aid and Attendance Benefit	$1,789
Available to Pay for Care from All Sources above	$5,860
Veterans Out-of-Pocket Cost	$1,140

States without set rate subsidies may charge 50% to 70% of the rate of private facilities based on private or semi-private room occupancy and if the veteran does not have enough income, these homes accept Medicaid or Medicare to make up the difference. In these states the Veterans homes are Medicaid and possibly Medicare certified. Approximately 30% of all State Veterans homes are CMS certified.

Prevailing Rate Per Diem Program
VA processes two different nursing home per diem rates:

- The prevailing rate (higher rate)
- The basic rate which we have discussed above

There are three ways a Veteran may qualify for the prevailing or higher rate:
- The Veteran has a service-connected disability of 70% or greater and is in need of nursing home care
- The Veteran has a rating of total disability based on individual unemployability (TDIU or IU). Veterans rated for P&T are not eligible for higher per diem. To validate eligibility of TDIU or IU, verify with your local Regional Office.
- The Veteran is seeking care for a specific, rated service-connected disability that is less than 70% (0-60%)

Payment for care under this second option constitutes payment in full for all routine nursing home care provided to the veteran in the state nursing home. As a condition for receiving this per diem, the veteran must receive medications through the state nursing home rather than from VA. The veteran must also utilize the VA for any services not provided by the nursing home, such as hospital care, hearing aids, and eyeglasses. If the veteran chooses to utilize other service providers, the veteran will be responsible for payment for those services.

Medication Subsidy
In addition to the per diem payments discussed above, VA will also furnish drugs and medicines to a facility recognized as a State Veterans Home that are ordered by a duly licensed physician as specific therapy in the treatment of illness of injury for a veteran receiving care in a state home if the veteran:

1. has a singular or combined rating of less than 50 percent based on one or more service-connected disabilities and is in need of such drugs and medicines for a service-connected disability and is in need of nursing home care for reasons that do not include care for a VA adjudicated service-connected disability; or

2. has a singular or combined rating of 50 or 60 percent based on one or more service-connected disabilities and is in need of such drugs and medicines and is in need of nursing home care for reasons that do not include care for a VA adjudicated service-connected disability.

The drug or medicine must be included in VA's national formulary unless VA determines a non-formulary drug or medicine is medically necessary.

Type of Care Provided
Some state facilities offer assisted living or domiciliary care in addition to nursing care. Some states even build facilities devoted entirely for domiciliary. According to the Veterans Administration the definition of domiciliary care is as follows: "To provide the least intensive level of VA inpatient care for ambulatory veterans disabled by age or illness who are not in need

of more acute hospitalization and who do not need the skilled nursing services provided in nursing homes. To rehabilitate the veteran in anticipation of his/her return to the community in a self-sustaining and independent or semi-independent living situation, or to assist the veteran to reach his/her optimal level of functioning in a protective environment."

A domiciliary is a living arrangement similar to assisted living without substantial assistance but is not intended as a permanent residence. Domiciliary rooms in veterans medical centers are designed around this concept and are used for rehabilitation recovery from surgery or accident, alcohol abuse, drug abuse, mental illness or depression.

The domiciliary concept does not work well in a State Veterans Home setting and in that context domiciliary is simply another name for assisted living without the assistance. This represents a form of independent retirement living with a little more support where the veteran can stay as long as he or she needs to. As far as State Veterans homes go you should think of domiciliary as a substitute for supported independent retirement living.

Many state veterans facilities have set aside a wing for Alzheimer's patients. In some states this is the most popular service sought by veterans or their families and waiting lists could require a number of years before a bed opens up. A small number of facilities offer adult day care.

It appears that in most of the states, facilities are run by state employees through their State departments. Some states may contract with third-party administrators to run their programs.

Eligibility and Application Requirements for State Veterans homes
From state to state, facilities vary in their rules for eligible veterans. And even in the same state it is common, where there is more than one state home, for some homes to have very stringent eligibility rules and others to be more lenient. These differing rules are probably based on the demand for care and the available beds in that particular geographic area.

Some homes require the veteran to be totally disabled and unable to earn an income. Some evaluate on the basis of medical need or age. Some evaluate entirely on income – meaning applicants above a certain level will not be accepted. Some accept only former active-duty veterans, while others accept all who were in the military whether active duty or reserve. Still others accept only veterans who served during a period of war. Some homes accept the spouses or surviving spouses of veterans and some will accept the parents of veterans but restrict that to the parents of veterans who died while in service (Goldstar parents).

Federal regulations allow that 25% of the bed occupants at any one time may be veteran-related family members, i.e., spouses, surviving spouses, and/or gold star parents who are not entitled to payment of VA aid. When a State Home accepts grant assistance for a construction project, 75% of the bed occupants at the facility must be veterans.

Domicile residency requirements vary from state to state. The most stringent seems to be a three-year prior residency in the state whereas other homes may only require 90 days of residency. All states require an application process to get into a home. Typically a committee or board will approve or disapprove each application. Many states have waiting lists for beds.

State Veterans Home admission is only for eligible Veterans and certain categories of Veteran-related family members. The homes are not open to the general public. The categories of family members (non-Veteran residents) are:

- The spouses of Veterans; or
- The surviving spouses of Veterans; or
- Gold Star Parents
- The parents of children who have died while serving in the U.S. Armed Forces

The State Veterans homes Per Diem Program provides per diem payments to State Veterans Homes for the care of eligible Veterans only. Per diem is provided for the care of Veterans irrespective of whether the Veteran has wartime or peacetime service. VA does not have authority to control the management or operation of State Homes, including their admission practices. VA per diem may be paid for a Veteran who is eligible for care in a VA facility, but it is very important to know that not all veterans, on whose behalf VA pays per diem, are eligible for enrollment in VHA health care.

Application for the per diem program is made through using VA Form 10-10SH and VA Form 10-10EZ within 10 calendar days of admission.

Other State Veterans Benefits

Burial in State Veterans Cemeteries
At least 43 states have established state veterans cemeteries. Some states only have one cemetery while other states such as Hawaii offer as many as 8 different cemeteries. Eligibility is similar to Department of Veterans Affairs (VA) national cemeteries, but may include residency requirements. Even though state cemeteries may have been established or improved with government funds through VA's State Cemetery Grants Program, state veterans cemeteries are run solely by the states.

Motor vehicles and License Plates
Motor vehicle registration, sales tax on a vehicle and license plates are generally free in those states where veterans are receiving disability grants from VA towards purchase or modification of a motor vehicle. In most states special design license plates identifying status, discharge or other service status of a veteran are available at no charge or additional charge. In most states, veterans who are disabled can receive license plates and registration for free.

Other Available Benefits

- free hunting or fishing licenses for disabled veterans
- free admission to state parks sometimes for all veterans but typically only for disabled veterans
- free copies of vital records for veterans making application for benefits
- free drivers licenses for disabled veterans

- free recording of discharge papers by county recorders
- free copies of certified discharge papers by county recorders
- tuition assistance for veterans, National Guard and dependents
- property tax exemptions for certain disabled veterans as well as for their widows
- partial property tax exemptions sometimes for any veteran but generally for those who are disabled
- one time grants and stipends for certain veterans or any veteran up to $3,000 in one state
- archiving of discharge records
- state income tax exemption for certain veterans or veterans recently discharged
- disability parking placards for disabled veterans
- honorary high school diplomas for World War 2 or Korean veterans
- in some states disabled veterans are exempt from payment of occupational taxes, administration fees, and regulatory fees imposed by local governments for peddling, conducting a business, or practicing a profession or semi profession.

The National Care Planning Council maintains a current list of state veterans homes.

This list can be found at the following URL:

https://www.longtermcarelink.net/ref_state_veterans_va_nursing_homes.htm

Chapter 12
Vocational Rehabilitation and Homeless Veterans Support

IN THIS CHAPTER:

The majority of information in this chapter was taken from the Department of veterans Affairs website at www.VA.gov.

Vocational Rehabilitation

Veterans and service members may receive Vocational Rehabilitation and Employment (VR&E) services to help with job training, employment accommodations, resume development, and job seeking skills coaching. Other services may be provided to assist veterans in starting their own businesses or independent living services for those who are severely disabled and unable to work in traditional employment.

Vocational Rehabilitation and Employment (VR&E) (Chapter 31)
The Chapter 31 program assists veterans who have service-connected disabilities obtain and maintain suitable employment. Independent living services are also available for severely disabled veterans who are not currently ready to seek employment.

To be eligible, a veteran must have a VA service-connected disability rated at least 20 percent with an employment handicap, or rated 10 percent with a serious employment handicap, and be discharged or released from military service under other than dishonorable conditions.

Service members pending medical separation from active duty may also apply if their disabilities are reasonably expected to be rated at least 20 percent following their discharge. A VA counselor must decide if the individual has an employment handicap based upon the results of a comprehensive evaluation. After an entitlement decision is made, the individual and counselor will work together to develop a rehabilitation plan. The rehabilitation plan will specify the rehabilitation services to be provided. The majority of program participants enter education or training programs. All program costs, including tuition, books, and fees, if appropriate, are borne by VA, and the veteran is provided with a monthly subsistence allowance.

Rehabilitation services provided to participants in the VR&E program are under one of five tracks. VA pays the cost of approved training that is included in an individual's rehabilitation plan. The tracks are:

Reemployment with Previous Employer: For individuals who are separating from active duty or in the National Guard or Reserves and are returning to work for their previous employer.

Rapid Access to Employment: For individuals who either wish to obtain employment soon after separation or who already have the necessary skills to be competitive in the job market in an appropriate occupation.

Self-Employment: For individuals who have limited access to traditional employment, need flexible work schedules, or who require more accommodation in the work environment due to their disabling conditions or other life circumstances.

Employment Through Long-Term Services: For individuals who need specialized training and/or education to obtain and maintain suitable employment.

Independent Living Services: For veterans who are not currently able to work and need rehabilitation services to live more independently.

Generally, veterans must complete a program within 12 years from their separation from military service or within 12 years from the date VA notifies them that they have a compensable service-connected disability. Depending on the length of program needed, veterans may be provided up to 48 months of full-time services or their part-time equivalent. These limitations may be extended in certain circumstances.

In some cases, a veteran requires additional education or training to become employable. A subsistence allowance is paid each month during training and is based on the rate of attendance (full- or part-time), the type of education or training, the number of dependents, and the type of training. The example below demonstrates one of the many rate structures possible.

On the next page are the subsistence allowances that will be paid through October 2020

Chapter 31 Subsistence Allowance Rate Increase As of October 1, 2019
Based Upon 2.04% Consumer Price Index (CPI) Increase

Type of Training	Training Time	No Dependents	One Dependent	Two Dependents	Each Additional Dependent
Institutional; Nonpay or nominal pay work experience in a facility of a Federal, State, local, or federally recognized Indian tribe agency; Improvement of Rehabilitation Potential:	Full-Time	$644.74	$799.74	$942.44	$68.68
	¾ Time	$484.45	$600.68	$704.61	$52.83
	½ Time	$324.14	$401.62	$472.08	$35.24
	¼ Time[1]	$162.05	$200.84	$236.04	$17.58
Nonpay or nominal pay on-job training in a facility of a Federal, State, local, or federally recognized Indian tribe agency; Training in the home; Vocational course in a rehabilitation facility or sheltered workshop; Independent instructor:	Full-Time Only	$644.74	$799.74	$942.44	$68.68
Farm Cooperative, Apprenticeship or other On-Job Training[2]:	Full-Time Only	$563.71	$681.70	$785.65	$51.09
Combination of Institutional and On-Job Training (Institutional Greater than One Half); Non-farm Cooperative Institutional Training and Non-farm Cooperative On-Job Training (FT Non-Farm Coop/Institutional):	Full-Time Only	$644.74	$799.74	$942.44	$68.68
Combination of Institutional and On-Job Training (On-the-Job Greater than ½); Non-farm Cooperative Institutional Training and Non-farm Cooperative On-Job Training (FT Non-Farm Coop/On-the-Job):	Full-Time Only	$563.71	$681.70	$785.65	$51.09

Effective 10-01-2019, the maximum monthly rate for Chapter 31 Subsistence Allowance is **$2,728[3]**.

Take the next step into civilian life

VA Benefits I and II Briefings are part of VA's portion of Transition Goals, Plans, Success (GPS), which is designed to help transitioning service members, to include Guard and Reserve members demobilizing after 180 days or more of active service, adjust to life after the military. All transitioning service members are required to attend Transition GPS.

The briefings consist of two classroom modules: a four-hour VA Benefits I Briefing and a two-hour VA Benefits II Briefing.

- VA Benefits I Briefing provides you with information on education, health care, compensation, life insurance, and home loans, as well as vocational rehabilitation and employment benefits information and counseling.
- VA Benefits II Briefing helps you understand some of the services and programs related to your VA health care and understand the VA disability compensation process. Additionally, you will learn how to navigate through eBenefits.

Spouses and family members are encouraged to attend both briefings.

Optional Two-Day Technical Training Track
VA is leading an optional two-day technical training track. This workshop assists transitioning Service members in identifying civilian occupations, establishing career goals, and beginning applications for credentialing and vocational training.

Additional optional tracks focusing on education and entrepreneurship are also available, and are led by the military services and Small Business Administration.

Vocational Rehabilitation and Employment (VR&E)

Veteran Employment Tracks
Vocational Rehabilitation Counselors (VRC) and Employment Coordinators (EC) are ready to help veterans and Service members who have service-connected disabilities and an employment barrier/handicap find suitable careers. Your VRC will provide vocational counseling, refer you to appropriate opportunities and services specific to your needs, and help you reach your employment goals. If you are entitled to Vocational Rehabilitation and Employment (VR&E) benefits and services, you will work with a VRC to develop a personalized rehabilitation plan following one of five tracks:

Reemployment
When possible, VR&E helps veterans and Service members return to work with a former employer by supporting the employer's efforts to provide accommodations that enable the Veteran to continue along the same or similar career path.
Rapid Access to Employment

VR&E helps veterans and Service members who are ready to enter the workforce, find, apply for, and secure suitable jobs. VA may provide professional job placement assistance, job accommodations, and other specialized support.

Self-Employment
Self-employment can be fulfilling and may offer the flexibility a Veteran with service-connected disabilities needs. VR&E may aid veterans, who have limited access to traditional employment and have the skill and interest to start a business, by helping to analyze the proposed business plan and providing training on how to market and operate a small business.

Employment through Long-Term Services

For veterans and service members who require additional skills or training to find competitive, suitable employment, VR&E will provide assistance, which may include education benefits, on-the-job training, work study, apprenticeships, or other job preparation programs to help them to obtain appropriate employment.
Independent Living

Some veterans and service members may be unable to currently return to work, but with assistance from VR&E, they can lead a more independent life. VA helps them with access to community-based support services, the use of assistive technologies and accommodations, and independent living skills training.

Veteran Employment Resources

The tools below can help you get prepared for the transition to your civilian career. Learn what to expect when you enter the job market and how to reflect your military skills on your résumé, and then search for positions at VA's veterans Employment Center jobs portal.

Veterans Employment Center at https://www.vets.gov/employment/

If you have a service-connected disability that makes it difficult for you to work in your previous profession, VA offers counseling, training, education, job placement, and other services to help you launch a new career. Find out if you are eligible. apply online at www.eBenefits.VA.gov.

VetSuccess on Campus

The Department of veterans Affairs (VA) is developing innovative ways to help veterans make the transition to college life. The VetSuccess on Campus (VSOC) program aims to help veterans, service members, and their qualified dependents succeed and thrive through a coordinated delivery of on-campus benefits assistance and counseling, leading to completion of their education and preparing them to enter the labor market in viable careers.

The VSOC program provides a VA Vocational Rehabilitation Counselor (VRC) to each VSOC school. These VRCs are called VetSuccess on Campus (VSOC) Counselors. A VA Vet Center Outreach Coordinator is also provided, and co-located on many campuses, to provide peer-to-peer counseling and referral services.

Through the VSOC program, VA is strengthening partnerships with institutions of higher learning and creating opportunities to help veterans achieve success by providing outreach and transition services during their transition from military to college life. VSOC Counselors ensure that veterans receive the support and assistance needed to pursue their educational and employment goals. Because VSOC Counselors are easily accessible on campus they help resolve any problems that could potentially interfere with a Veteran's educational program, to include assisting with disability accommodations. If needed, are referrals for health services through VA Medical Centers, Community-Based Outpatient Clinics, or Vet Centers.

The VSOC program began as a pilot program in 2009 at the University of South Florida. The VSOC program expanded to 32 schools by the end of Fiscal Year 2012. In Fiscal Year 2013, the VSOC program expanded again to an additional 62 campuses, bringing the total number of VSOC sites to 94. See the Claims Support Disc for list of campuses and counselors.

Independent Living

Independent Living services may be provided to individuals who are not currently able to work because of the effects of service-connected disabilities. Provided services are limited to those required to improve independence at home and in the community.

Each Individualized Independent Living Plan is personalized to meet the individual's specific needs. In general, independent living services cannot last more than 24 months. Services may be extended if certain criteria are met.

Individuals who are pursuing employment goals may also receive independent living services if these services are required to support the achievement of their vocational objective. Independent living services may include:

- Evaluation and counseling services to help determine independent living needs and identify goals
- Coordination of consultations with specialists such as physicians, physical and/or occupational therapists, and rehabilitation engineers
- Information about and referral to resources which may provide health care services, special technology and equipment, community living support, disability support and family counseling
- Information and assistance with exploring eligibility for VA home modification benefits including the Specially Adapted Housing (SAH) grant and the Home Improvements and Structural Alterations (HISA) grant
- Ongoing case support to help individuals achieve the independent living goals included in the Individualized Independent Living Plan

Eligibility and Entitlement to Vocational Rehabilitation

Services that may be provided by the VR&E Program include:

- Comprehensive evaluation to determine abilities, skills, and interests for employment
- Vocational counseling and rehabilitation planning for employment services
- Employment services such as job-training, job-seeking skills, resume development, and other work readiness assistance
- Assistance finding and keeping a job, including the use of special employer incentives and job accommodations
- On the Job Training (OJT), apprenticeships, and non-paid work experiences
- Post-secondary training at a college, vocational, technical or business school
- Supportive rehabilitation services including case management, counseling, and medical referrals
- Independent living services for veterans unable to work due to the severity of their disabilities

Who is Eligible for VR&E Services?
Active Duty Service Members are eligible if they:

- Expect to receive an honorable or other than dishonorable discharge upon separation from active duty
- Obtain a memorandum rating of 20% or more from the Department of veterans Affairs (VA), and
- Apply for VR&E services Or (until December 31, 2017)

  - Are participating in the Integrated Disability Evaluation System (IDES) or are certified by the military as having a severe injury or illness that may prevent them from performing their military duties
  - Apply for VR&E services, and
  - Report for an evaluation with a VR&E counselor before separating from active duty

Veterans are eligible if they:

- Have received a discharge that is other than dishonorable
- Have a service-connected disability rating of at least 10% from VA
- Apply for VR&E services

Basic period of Eligibility
The basic period of eligibility ends 12 years from the date of notification of one of the following:

- Date of separation from active military service, or
- Date the veteran was first notified by VA of a service-connected disability rating.

The basic period of eligibility may be extended if a Vocational Rehabilitation Counselor (VRC) determines that a Veteran has a Serious Employment Handicap.

What Happens after Eligibility is established?
The veteran is scheduled to meet with a VRC for a comprehensive evaluation to determine if he/she is entitled for services. A comprehensive evaluation includes:

- An assessment of the veteran's interests, aptitudes, and abilities
- An assessment of whether service connected disabilities impair the microphone off ability to find and/or hold a job using the occupational skills he or she has already developed
- Vocational exploration and goal development leading to employment and/or maximum independence in the Veteran's daily living at home and in the community

What is an Entitlement Determination?
A VRC works with the Veteran to complete a determination if an employment handicap exists. An employment handicap exists if the Veteran's service connected disability impairs his/her ability to obtain and maintain a job. Entitlement to services is established if the veteran has an

employment handicap and is within his or her 12-year basic period of eligibility and has a 20% or greater service-connected disability rating.

If the service connected disability rating is less than 20%, or if the veteran is beyond the 12-year basic period of eligibility, then a serious employment handicap must be found to establish entitlement to VR&E services. A serious employment handicap is based on the extent and complexity of services required to help a said to overcome the significant restrictions caused by his or her service and non-service connected disabilities, permitting the return to suitable employment.

What Happens after the Entitlement Determination is made?
The veteran and VRC work together to:

- Determine transferable skills, aptitudes, and interests
- Identify viable employment and/or independent living services options
- Explore labor market and wage information
- Identify physical demands and other job characteristics
- Explore vocational options to identify a suitable employment goal
- Select a VR&E program track leading to an employment or independent living goal
- Investigate training requirements
- Identify resources needed to achieve rehabilitation
- Develop an individualized rehabilitation plan to achieve the identified employment or independent living goals

What is a Rehabilitation Plan?
A rehabilitation plan is an individualized, written plan of services, which outlines the resources and criteria that will be used to achieve employment or independent living goals. The plan is an agreement that is signed by the veteran and the VRC and is updated as needed to assist the veteran to achieve his/her goals.

Depending on their circumstances, veterans will work with their VRC to select one of the following five tracks of services (see definitions for more detail):

- Reemployment (with a former employer)
- Direct job placement services for new employment
- Self-employment
- Employment through long term services including OJT, college, and other training
- Independent living services

What Happens after the Rehabilitation Plan is developed?
After a plan is developed and signed, a VRC or case manager will continue to work with the Veteran to implement the plan to achieve suitable employment and/or independent living. The VRC or case manager will provide ongoing counseling, assistance, and coordinate services such as tutorial assistance, training in job-seeking skills, medical and dental referrals, adjustment counseling, payment of training allowance, if applicable, and other services as required to help the veteran achieve rehabilitation.

How can I get paid the Post-9-11 GI Bill rate for my Vocational Rehabilitation program?

A veteran participating in the VR&E Program who qualifies for Post-9-11 GI Bill benefits can elect to receive the GI Bill rate of pay instead of the regular Chapter 31 subsistence allowance. In most cases, the GI Bill rate is higher than the regular Chapter 31 rate of pay. To elect the GI Bill rate, the Veteran must have remaining eligibility for the Post-9-11 GI Bill, and must formally choose (or "elect") the GI Bill rate. Your VRC can help you with election. Veterans participating in the VR&E Program who elect the Post-9-11 rate are paid at the 100% rate level for their school and training time, even if their Post-9-11 GI Bill eligibility is less than 100%. Additional benefits are also available through the VR&E Program, such as payment of all required books, fees and supplies as well as other supportive services.

Subsistence Allowance Rates

In some cases, veterans participating in the VR&E program may receive a subsistence allowance while they pursue an educational or training program in preparation for a future career. The subsistence allowance is paid each month, and is based on the rate of attendance in a training program (full time, three quarter time, or half time), the number of dependents, and the type of training. If a veteran qualifies for the Post-9-11 GI Bill he/she may be eligible to receive the Basic Allowance for Housing (BAH) rate for subsistence..

Homeless veterans Statistics

The information in this section is taken from the website of the
National Alliance to End Homelessness
http://www.endhomelessness.org/
Updated April 2015

47,725, or about 8% of the homeless population, are veterans. This represents a 35% decrease since 2009. Homeless veterans have served in several different conflicts from WWII to the recent wars in Afghanistan and Iraq. Washington, D.C., has the highest rate of veteran homelessness in the nation (145.8 homeless veterans per 10,000). 45% of homeless veterans are black or Hispanic. While less than 10% of homeless veterans are women, that number is rising.

1.4 million veterans are at risk of homelessness. This may be due to poverty, overcrowding in government housing, and lack of support networks. Research indicates that those who served in the late Vietnam and post-Vietnam era are at greatest risk of homelessness. War-related disabilities or disorders often contribute to veteran homelessness, including physical disabilities, Post Traumatic Stress Disorder (PTSD), traumatic brain injury, depression and anxiety, and addiction.

How many homeless veterans are in America?

In January 2014, communities across America identified 49,933 homeless veterans during point-in-time counts, which represents 8.6 percent of the total homeless population. This represents a substantial decrease (67.4 percent) in the number of homeless veterans counted only five years previously in 2009.i Though veterans continue to remain overrepresented in the homeless population in America, these recent decreases demonstrate the marked progress that has been made in ending veteran homelessness.

What are the typical demographics of homeless veterans?
Homeless veterans tend to be male (91 percent), single (98 percent), live in a city (76 percent), and have a mental and/or physical disability (54 percent). Black veterans are substantially overrepresented among homeless veterans, comprising 39 percent of the total homeless veteran population but only 11 percent of the total veteran population.

As troops return from operations in Iraq and Afghanistan, the face of veteran homelessness has changed: homeless veterans are increasingly younger, female, and heads of households. Despite this, homeless veterans are still most likely to be males between the ages of 51 and 61 (43 percent)iii and to have served in the Vietnam War. And, in the next 10 to 15 years, it is projected that the number of homeless veterans over the age of 55 could increase drastically.

Why do veterans experience homelessness?
Veterans are more likely than civilians to experience homelessness. Like the general homeless population, veterans are at a significantly increased risk of homelessness if they have low socioeconomic status, a mental health disorder, and/or a history of substance abuse. Yet, because of veterans' military service, this population is at higher risk of experiencing traumatic brain injuries and Post-Traumatic Stress Disorder (PTSD), both of which have been found to be among the most substantial risk factors for homelessness. Among the recent Iraq and Afghanistan cohort of veterans—who are more frequently female than their older counterparts—an experience of sexual trauma while serving in the military greatly increases the risk of homelessness. Additionally, veterans often experience difficulty returning to civilian life, particularly those without strong social support networks, and may not have skills that can be easily transferred to employment outside of the military. Veterans face the same shortage of affordable housing options and living wage jobs as all Americans, and these factors—combined with the likelihood that veterans will exhibit symptoms of PTSD, substance abuse, or mental illness—put veterans at a greater risk of homelessness than the general population.

What federal programs serve homeless veterans?
Homeless veterans can receive assistance both from the U.S. Department of veterans Affairs (VA), provided they have an eligible discharge status, and the U.S. Department of Housing and Urban Development (HUD), regardless of discharge status. In a joint supportive housing program between the two departments (HUD-VASH), Section 8 Housing Choice Vouchers housing vouchers are combined with case management and supportive services at VA medical centers. Since 2008, nearly 70,000 VASH vouchers have been awarded to Public Housing Authorities across the US. Evaluation of the HUD-VASH program has found a number of positive outcomes for participants, including an increase in employment and income, the number of days housed, and social networks. Additionally, the HUD-VASH program has been found to have a one-year cost savings of approximately on $6,000 per participant on health services.

In 2012, VA introduced the Supportive Services for Veteran Families (SSVF) program, with the parallel goals of both preventing veteran homelessness and rapidly re-housing veterans and veteran families who do fall into homelessness. The program provides a variety of time-limited services and financial assistance. In its first two years, the SSVF program aided almost 100,000 individuals in over 61,000 households, spending $2,480 per household; after being housed, only 9.4 percent of veteran families returned to homelessness one year after exiting the program, and only 15.5 percent returned to homelessness two years after exit.

SSVF and HUD-VASH are the main response to veteran homelessness in many communities; however, there are numerous other resources for assisting veterans in a housing crisis. The Grant and Per Diem transitional housing program and Domiciliary Care programs funded through the veterans Health Administration offer temporary assistance to veterans as bridge or crisis housing. The Homeless Veteran Reintegration Program under the Department of Labor assists homeless veterans with employment skills and job searches.

Are we ending veteran homelessness?

In 2009, then-VA Secretary Eric Shinseki, in tandem with President Barack Obama, set forth the audacious goal of ending veteran homelessness by 2015. Current VA Secretary Robert MacDonald also supports this goal. To help secure commitments to this goal, in June 2014 First Lady Michelle Obama announced the Mayors Challenge to End Veteran Homelessness. The First Lady has received pledges from 355 mayors, 7 governors, and 112 county and city officials to end veteran homelessness in their communities by the end of 2015.xii

In January 2015, New Orleans became the first major city to announce that it had ended veteran homelessness. Throughout 2015, other communities are sure to follow. The success of the HUD-VASH, SSVF, and other programs targeted to veterans, combined with the dedication and commitment of America's communities prove that ending veteran homelessness is possible.

Department of veterans Affairs Homeless veterans Support

Many veterans face challenges throughout their lives that may lead them to lose their home, eventually becoming homeless. VA recognizes that every homeless veteran's story is different, including their specific needs to help them get back into permanent and stable housing. There are many VA benefits that may support homeless veterans

Homeless veterans may be eligible for a wide-variety of benefits available to all U.S. military veterans. VA benefits include disability compensation, pension, education and training, health care, home loans, insurance, vocational rehabilitation and employment, and burial. See our veterans page for an overview of the benefits available to all veterans.

In 2015, over 64,902 homeless or at-risk veterans (including formerly homeless veterans) accessed services and nearly 36,000 veterans and their family members were prevented from becoming homeless. In 2017, VA will continue to focus on prevention and treatment services. This involves providing a comprehensive continuum of care that addresses the psychosocial factors surrounding homelessness while building the capacity of available residential, rehabilitative, transitional, and permanent housing supply.

VHA continues to work closely with the Department of Housing and Urban Development and other Federal and State agencies, VSOs, national advocacy groups, and community-based providers. The request for 2017 of $1.6 billion is based on a comprehensive analysis that provided VA with the information on what type of resources is most needed and where they are needed across the country.

Get a Veteran to Call for Help

VA is the only federal agency that provides substantial hands-on assistance directly to homeless veterans—but we can't do it without you. VA relies on partners, community organizations, and families and friends of homeless veterans to connect veterans with the health care services they deserve. Providing health care for the homeless is key to advancing VA's goal to end veteran homelessness by 2015. No matter who you are, if you know a Veteran who is homeless or at risk of homelessness and in need of help, contact VA's toll-free hotline.

VA's National Call Center for Homeless veterans provides 24/7 access to trained responders for federal, state, and local partners and community agencies. To reach trained VA staff members, call 1-877-4AID-VET (1-877-424-3838).

The Health Care for Re-Entry veterans Program helps incarcerated veterans successfully rejoin the community through supports, including addressing their mental health and substance use needs. To learn more, call VA's toll-free hotline, 1-877-4AID-VET, or visit the Health Care for Re-Entry veterans Program web page.

Health Care Benefits for veterans

Direct Health Care Services

The VA Health Care Network provides care to veterans across the nation at VA Medical Centers, Community-Based Outpatient Clinics, and Vet Centers. Many of these facilities offer health care programs for homeless veterans, including mental health services.

The Veterans Health Administration continues to work with its interagency partners to end Veteran homelessness. This multi-year program has seen great success – reducing veterans' homeless from 74,770 in 2010 to less than 48,000 as of the last official "Point in Time" Count in January 2015. This is over a 36 percent decline in five years.

VA's Health Care for Homeless veterans (HCHV) Program offers outreach, exams, treatment, referrals, and case management to homeless veterans at more than 135 sites where trained, caring VA specialists provide tools and support necessary to get your life on a better track. Call VA's toll-free hotline, 1-877-4AID-VET, or visit the Health Care for Homeless veterans (HCHV) Program page.

VA's Homeless Veterans Dental Program provides dental treatment for eligible veterans in a number of programs: Domiciliary Residential Rehabilitation Treatment, VA Grant and Per Diem, Compensated Work Therapy/Transitional Residence, Healthcare for Homeless Veterans (contract bed), and Community Residential Care. VA is working to expand dental care to all eligible veterans within this program.

Homeless Veterans Dental Program

The Homeless Veterans Dental Program was established by the Veterans Administration in 1992. The program is funded through the Office of Dentistry and located at the James A. Haley Veterans' Hospital.

The dental needs of homeless veterans are well documented. In surveys listing and ranking the 10 highest unmet needs for homeless veterans, dental care was consistently ranked by homeless veterans as one of their top 3 unmet needs, along with long-term permanent housing and childcare. Dental problems, such as pain and/or missing teeth can be tremendous barriers in seeking and obtaining employment. Studies have shown that after dental care, veterans report significant improvement in perceived oral health, general health and overall self-esteem, thus, supporting the notion that dental care is an important aspect of the overall concept of homeless rehabilitation.

There is some limited dental eligibility for veterans who are in certain VA-sponsored rehabilitation programs. VHA Handbook 1130.01 (page 13) outlines eligibility for these groups in detail. Our goal is to facilitate a process in which the intent of this Initiative is carried out and to assist veterans in these programs in re-entering society as productive, self-sufficient people.

Persons wishing to obtain information regarding the homeless dental program in their area should contact their nearest VA's homeless coordinator.

Domiciliary Care Program

VA's Domiciliary Care for Homeless Veterans (DCHV) Program has been providing medical services to disadvantaged veterans since the Civil War. Today's DCHV program uses modern, advanced medical techniques in a residential setting for 24/7 support that enables veterans to live independent, fulfilling, and healthy lives. Domiciliary Care for Homeless Veterans (DCHV) Program

The Domiciliary Care Program is the Department of Veterans Affairs (VA) oldest health care program. Established through legislation passed in the late 1860's, the Domiciliary's purpose was to provide a home for disabled volunteer soldiers of the Civil War. Domiciliary care was initially established to provide services to economically-disadvantaged veterans, and it remains committed to serving that group. The Domiciliary has evolved from a "Soldiers' Home" to become an active clinical rehabilitation and treatment program for male and female veterans and domiciliary programs are is now integrated with the Mental Health Residential Rehabilitation and Treatment Programs (MH RRTPs).

Health Care for Homeless Veterans (HCHV) Program

Initially serving as a mechanism to contract with providers for community-based residential treatment for homeless veterans, many HCHV programs now serve as the hub for a myriad of housing and other services that provide VA with a way to reach and assist homeless veterans by offering them entry to VA care.

Outreach is the core of the HCHV program. The central goal is to reduce homelessness among veterans by conducting outreach to those who are the most vulnerable and not currently receiving services and engaging them in treatment and rehabilitative programs.

Another aspect of HCHV is the Contract Residential Treatment program, which places veterans with serious mental health diagnoses into quality, community-based, supportive housing.

Mental Health Residential Rehabilitation and Treatment Programs (MH RRTPs).

The MH RRTPs are designed to provide state-of-the-art, high-quality residential rehabilitation and treatment services for veterans with multiple and severe medical conditions, mental illness, addiction, or psychosocial deficits. The MH RRTP identifies and addresses goals of rehabilitation, recovery, health maintenance, improved quality of life, and community integration in addition to specific treatment of medical conditions, mental illnesses, addictive disorders, and homelessness. The residential component emphasizes incorporation of clinical treatment gains into a lifestyle of self-care and personal responsibility. Treatment intensity, environmental structures, milieu, and type of supervision vary based on population served, and need to be relevant to the diversity of the population, e.g., age, ethnicity, and culture.

Housing Assistance

HUD-VASH

This collaborative program between HUD and VA combines HUD housing vouchers with VA supportive services to help veterans who are homeless and their families find and sustain permanent housing. As of Sept. 30, 2015, HUD had allocated more than 78,000 vouchers to help house veterans across the country.

Through public housing authorities, HUD provides rental assistance vouchers for privately owned housing to veterans who are eligible for VA health care services and are experiencing homelessness. VA case managers may connect these veterans with support services such as health care, mental health treatment and substance use counseling to help them in their recovery process and with maintaining housing in the community. Among VA homeless continuum of care programs, HUD-VASH enrolls the largest number and largest percentage of veterans who have experienced long-term or repeated homelessness.

Homeless Providers Grant and Per Diem (GPD) Program

State, local and tribal governments and nonprofits receive capital grants and per diem payments to develop and operate transitional housing—including short-stay bridge housing—and/or service centers for veterans who are homeless.

VA funds an estimated 600 agencies that provide over 14,500 beds for eligible veterans. Grantees work closely with an assigned liaison from the local VAMC. The VA GPD liaison monitors the services the grantees offer to veterans and provides direct assistance to them. Grantees also collaborate with community-based organizations to connect veterans with employment, housing and additional social services to promote housing stability. The maximum stay in this housing is up to 24 months, with the goal of moving veterans into permanent housing.

Enhanced-Use Lease (EUL) Program

Too many veterans are without safe, affordable housing. At the same time, some VA campuses have real estate that is underused. That's where VA's Enhanced-Use Lease program comes in.

EUL is a VA portfolio management tool that allows certain land and buildings to be leased to eligible private entities for approved supportive housing and related projects for homeless and at-risk veterans. In addition to supportive housing, VA's EUL partners often provide veterans with job training, financial management, haircuts, computer and laundry facilities, fitness centers and other services. veterans and their families are prioritized for EUL developments, which are also convenient to VA health care facilities.

Acquired Property Sales for Homeless Providers Program

This program sells VA-foreclosed properties to homeless provider organizations at a discount for use as transitional housing for homeless veterans.

Project CHALENG

Project CHALENG (Community Homelessness Assessment, Local Education and Networking Groups) brings together providers, advocates, and other concerned citizens to identify the needs of homeless veterans and work to meet those needs through planning and cooperative action. This process has helped build thousands of relationships between VA and community agencies so that together they can better serve homeless veterans.

Since 1994, CHALENG has built thousands of partnerships—involving community and veterans' groups, law enforcement agencies and federal, state and local government—that are improving services for homeless veterans. Project CHALENG has two main components:

- CHALENG surveys that assess local challenges faced by homeless veterans, identify unmet needs and encourage partnership action to meet those needs

- CHALENG meetings fostering collaboration between VA and community service providers to address CHALENG-identified barriers to housing veterans who are homeless and preventing homelessness among veterans

Data from CHALENG has assisted VA in developing new services for veterans, including the Homeless Veteran Dental Program, the expansion of the Department of Housing and Urban Development-VA Supportive Housing program, the veterans Justice Outreach programs and the Supportive Services for Veteran Families program. Community organizations also use CHALENG data in applications for grants that assemble VA, other government and foundation dollars to address the local needs of veterans who are homeless or at risk of homelessness.

Employment Assistance

VA has many employment and training programs that provide homeless veterans and veterans at-risk of homelessness the opportunity to return to healthy, productive lifestyles within their communities.

The Homeless Veteran Supported Employment Program (HVSEP) provides vocational assistance, job development and placement, and ongoing supports to improve employment outcomes among homeless veterans and veterans at-risk of homelessness. Formerly homeless veterans who have been trained as Vocational Rehabilitation Specialists (VRSs) provide these services.

VA's Compensated Work Therapy (CWT) Program is a national vocational program comprised of three unique programs which assist homeless veterans in returning to competitive employment: Sheltered Workshop, Transitional Work, and Supported Employment. Veterans in CWT are paid at least the federal or state minimum wage, whichever is higher.

VA's National Cemetery Administration and Veterans Health Administration have also formed partnerships at national cemeteries, where formerly homeless veterans from the CWT program have received work opportunities.

The Vocational Rehabilitation and Employment (VR&E) Program assists veterans with service-connected disabilities to prepare for, find, and keep suitable jobs. Services that may be provided include: comprehensive rehabilitation evaluation to determine abilities, skills, and interests for employment; employment services; assistance finding and keeping a job; and On the Job Training (OJT), apprenticeship, and non-paid work experiences.

For information about possible employment services in their area, veterans can call the National Call Center for Homeless Veterans hotline at 1-877-4AID-VET.

Foreclosure Assistance
If you have a VA loan but are having trouble making your mortgage payments, it is very important that you take steps to avoid a foreclosure. VA may be able to help.

The Department of Veterans Affairs' (VA) mission is to provide eligible veterans every opportunity to retain their home or avoid foreclosure. VA urges all veterans who are encountering problems making their mortgage payments to speak with their loan servicer as soon as possible to explore options to avoid foreclosure or contact the nearest Regional Loan Center at (877) 827-3702.

OPTIONS TO AVOID FORECLOSURE
The following options are generally available to all borrowers to avoid foreclosure:

- Repayment Plan – The borrower makes their regular installment each month plus part of the missed installments.
- Special Forbearance – The servicer agrees not to initiate foreclosure to allow time for borrowers to repay the missed installments.
- Loan Modification – Provides the borrower a fresh start by adding the delinquency to the loan balance and establishing a new payment schedule.
- Additional time to arrange a private sale – The servicer agrees to delay foreclosure to allow a sale to close if the loan will be paid off.

- Short Sale – When the servicer agrees to allow a borrower to sell his/her home for a lesser amount than what is currently required to pay off the loan.
- Deed-in-Lieu of Foreclosure - The borrower voluntarily agrees to deed the property to the servicer instead of going through the foreclosure process.

SERVICE MEMBERS CIVIL RELIEF ACT

Veteran borrowers may be able to request relief pursuant to the Service members Civil Relief Act (SCRA). SCRA is intended to ease the economic and legal burdens on military personnel during their active service. In order to qualify for certain protections available under the Act, the borrower must request protection under the Act, and the loan must have originated prior to the current period of active military service. SCRA may provide for a lower interest rate, or prevent foreclosure, or eviction. Please contact your nearest VA Loan Technician at (877) 827-3702 if you have any questions.

VETERANS WITH VA-GUARANTEED HOME LOANS

Loan servicers have the primary responsibility of resolving loan defaults, so it is imperative borrowers contact their loan servicer as quickly as possible. However, in cases where the servicer is unable to help the Veteran borrower, Loan Guaranty has Loan Technicians in nine Regional Offices who take an active role in interceding with the servicer to explore all options to avoid foreclosure. Service members or veterans with VA-guaranteed home loans can call (877) 827-3702 to reach the nearest Loan Guaranty office where Loan Technicians are prepared to discuss potential ways to help save the home.

VETERANS WITH NON-VA GUARANTEED HOME LOANS

For a veteran or service member with a conventional or sub-prime loan, VA does not have the legal authority to intervene on the borrower's behalf. It is imperative that the borrower contacts his/her servicer as quickly as possible. Visit VA's home loans website or call toll-free (877) 827-3702 to speak with a VA Loan Technician for advice on approaches to take with your servicer.

NATIONAL CALL CENTER FOR HOMELESS VETERANS

veterans who believe they may be facing homelessness can call (877) 4AID VET (877-424-3838) or go to our homeless veterans website to receive immediate assistance from VA.

OTHER ASSISTANCE

In addition to the resources offered by VA, the Department of Housing and Urban Development (HUD) offers assistance to homeowners by sponsoring local housing counseling agencies. To find an approved agency in your area, please search the HUD Office of Housing Counseling website, or call HUD's interactive voice system at (800) 569-4287.

Nonprofit Organizations Working under VA Grants for Disadvantaged veterans

VA provides grants for nonprofit organizations to help disadvantaged veterans, particularly those who are homeless. Here is information from one of these organizations from their website.

Veterans Resource Center
vrc@vetsresource.org

We offer a wide range of programs to address the unique needs of veterans.

- Homeless Prevention & Re-Housing
- Employment & Training Program
- Transitional Housing
- Behavioral Health Treatment
- Permanent Supportive Housing
- Nutrition Services
- Case Management
- Resource Centers
- Humanitarian Efforts

Homeless Prevention & Rapid Re-Housing

VRC provides supportive services to very low-income veteran families living in or transitioning to permanent housing through the Supportive Services for Veteran Families (SSVF) grant. VRC provides eligible Veteran families with outreach, case management, and assistance in obtaining VA and other mainstream benefits that promote housing stability and community integration.

Employment & Training Program

The unemployment rate for post-9-11 veterans has been steadily declining. But those who are still out of work say that they face discrimination, and are often only offered jobs that are beneath their expertise level.

According to the Bureau for Labor Statistics, the unemployment rate for vets who served at any time since September 2001 dropped to 9 percent last year, down from 9.9 percent in 2012. While the improved rates are heartening, vets who are struggling to find work don't yet see a light at the end of the tunnel.

One of the agency's most successful employment training programs is "Winning the Employment Game" (WEG). This program focuses on helping individuals achieve results by providing a personalized career exploration and job-search program. With a 90% success rate, "WEG" graduates attain jobs they want.

In our efforts to strengthen our employment training programs, VRC also offers comprehensive placement services by providing clients with job leads, resume preparation, informational resources and interview preparation.

Transitional Housing

VRC provides transitional housing for homeless veterans through the VA's Homeless Providers Grant and Per Diem Program. The purpose is to promote the development and provision of supportive housing and/or supportive services with the goal of helping homeless veterans achieve residential stability, increase their skill levels and/or income, and obtain greater self-determination.

VRC currently operates 104 beds of housing where homeless veterans may stay for up to two years serving both male and female veterans in Northern California. As part of our goal to carry on the legacy of support and hope for those less fortunate, VRC has constructed transitional housing projects which offer a safe environment where veterans are supported in their efforts to overcome a variety of obstacles. By providing an effective network of services, veterans are connected to employment and training programs, counseling and legal services. These programs were developed by veterans to help veterans build better lives for themselves, their families and our communities.

Behavioral Health Treatment
The long wars are winding down and the troops are coming home, but thousands of military service members, veterans and their families must tend to the psychological wounds of battle for years to come. Mental health disorders, signature injuries of the wars in Iraq and Afghanistan, affect one in five active duty service members and are the most common cause of hospitalization. Too often, once a war is over, the mental health needs of those who have served are forgotten.

VRC provides dual diagnosis mental health services including 57 beds for behavioral health, social recovery services at three sites in Northern California and anticipates opening another facility in Reno, Nevada in the late summer or fall of 2014.

Permanent Supportive Housing
Permanent supportive housing gives our most vulnerable military veterans—even those who have spent years bouncing from street to shelter and back again—the chance to reclaim their health and their independence. For many, it offers a future in which they long ago lost hope.

Veterans Resource Centers of America has 52 units of permanent supportive housing under construction and 200 units planned to assist veterans returning from service transition successfully to civilian life. Linked to case management and supportive services, permanent supportive housing is a proven solution to veterans' homelessness, a problem that affects men and women who have been recently discharged as well as those who served decades ago.

VRC operates case management services for 50 chronically homeless veterans in permanent supportive housing in Eureka California through the HUD-VASH program.

Nutrition Services
"And just as our troops need your leadership and support, their families do as well. Because they sacrifice and serve this nation right alongside anyone who wears our uniform." -First Lady Michelle Obama

Veterans served our country proudly and honorably. Through the CalFresh program and local food drives, all of our residential clients and many low income veterans throughout California benefit from improved access to nutritious meals and information presented to improve the health and well-being of qualified veteran households and individuals.

Case Management

We understand how difficult it can be for veterans to access the benefits and services they have earned. With so many different resources and the red tape of bureaucracy, it's easy to get confused and feel lost. Veterans Resource Centers of America case managers help connect veterans with the right resources to help them live healthy lives and achieve their goals.

All veterans meet with a VRC case manager upon arrival to perform an initial assessment. Based on this assessment, the case manager works in collaboration with the veteran to devise a service plan addressing identified needs and objectives. Each veteran has a personalized service plan outlining barriers and goals related to substance abuse, mental health, medical needs, finances, education, employment and housing. The case manager meets with the veteran on a regular basis to monitor progress. In addition to scheduled meetings, case managers are always available to provide additional support or assistance.

Case management is an interactive process that provides veterans with support and services that are essential to treatment. The goal of case management is to help veterans develop the skills necessary to achieve and maintain independence.

Resource Centers

"Honor to the soldier and sailor everywhere, who bravely bears his country's cause. Honor, also, to the citizen who cares for his brother in the field and serves, as he best can, the same cause." — Abraham Lincoln

Veterans Resource Centers of America operates thirteen Centers across Northern California, Northern Arizona and Northern Nevada and provides critical service and support for our veterans; their spouses and dependents. Our service centers are staffed by a diverse, professional and talented staff in order to serve all veterans in a respectful and positive way, including case managers, business consultants, drug and alcohol counselors, program support staff, teachers and mental health therapists.

Humanitarian Efforts

After emerging from years of war and political isolation, Vietnam endured years of economic stagnation. With economic liberalization, the country has enjoyed relative economic stability in recent years. But the challenges to the health sector remain at the forefront, particularly in rural and impoverished communities. High rates of maternal mortality, pediatric malnutrition and childhood disease are still critical issues.

Veterans Resource Centers of America commitment to service has enabled us to take our humanitarian efforts to other parts of the world. In 1997 VRC opened a health clinic in Luong Son to serve the impoverished people of Vietnam. In 2002, partnering with the East Meets West Foundation, VRC was able to build a school. Principle liaisons to the works in Vietnam have been Ahn and Jim Larson, Dr. Le Thi Ngoc and her staff. The new facility replaced a dilapidated and substandard school building and now provides safe and sanitary classrooms for nearly 100 children

Chapter 13
Using the Claim Support Disc

The Claim Support Disc contains 10 folders which in turn contain hundreds of worksheets and claim forms. You will never use anywhere near this number of pieces of paper to prepare a claim. These are most of the forms available from VA for benefits in this book. We also include thousands of pages of reference material which we we hope will help you with your claims.

1. Application for Pension and Survivors Pension
2. Application for Disability Compensation and DIC
3. Application for Health Care Benefits
4. Application for Burial Benefits
5. Reference Material
6. Rules Changes for Pension
7. Appendix – Additional Information for Accredited Representatives
8. Sources for Claims Support Services
9. Disability Claims Case Studies
10. Forms for Decision Reviews

In addition, we have provided for you at the root level of this disc, a PDF file where to send claims and appeals titled **"CENTRALIZED MAIL PROCESSING - Where to Send Claims"**

1. Application for Pension and Survivors Pension

FV Forms
Intent to File – VA Form 21-0966
VA Forms including Pension and Death Pension Applications Checklists, 2020 Rates, Proposed Rule Changes, and Pension Center Info

2. Application for Compensation and DIC

Special 21-4138 Forms for Our Application System Compensation and DIC Application Forms Disability Benefits Questionnaires

3. Application for Health Care Benefits

Forms needed for health care applications

4. Application for Burial Benefits

Forms needed for burial benefits applications

5. Reference Material

Thousands of pages of reference material to include Title 38 CFR Part 3, Title 38 CFR Part 4, Adjudication Manual M21-1, VA budget proposals and reports and other useful tables, studies and addenda. (Continued on next page)

6. Rules Changes for Pension

Final Rules Changes in the Federal Register of September 18, 2018 and Pertinent Adjudication Manual procedures for the new rules changes

7. Appendix – Additional Information for Accredited Representatives

This is information that could be important to accredited representatives who are using this book. We will update this information from time to time but currently it contains the following:

- Legally Charging Fees for Assistance with Claims
- Adjudication Manual Rules for DIC, Accrued Benefits and Substitution for Claimant
- Adjudication Manual Marriage Rules
- Adjudication Manual Rules for Evaluating Evidence and Decision-Making
- Adjudication Manual Rules for Determining Service Connection
- Further Discussion of Flaws in the Current Claims Processing Model

8. Sources for Claim Support Services

This folder currently contains a PDF document which is updated on a regular basis and contains lists of specialists across the country who provide all of the services listed in the title of this document. We will add new documents and new sources as time goes on

9. Disability Claims Case Studies

10. Forms for Decision reviews

Updates of the Claim Support Disc

Benefits rules, forms and sources of information are constantly changing. We update the claim support disc when changes occur. You can request a physical copy of the most recent update of this DVD by calling us at 800-989-8137 and we will send you the newest disc for a reasonable cost.

Claim Support Disc Online

We also maintain the Claim Support Disc online and as new elements come out, we update on a regular basis. If you want to access this information go to **www.supportdisc.com**